Implementing New Business Models in For-Profit and Non-Profit Organizations:

Technologies and Applications

Te Fu Chen
Lunghwa University of Science and Technology, Taiwan

BUSINESS SCIENCE REFERENCE
Hershey · New York

Senior Editorial Director: Kristin Klinger
Director of Book Publications: Julia Mosemann
Editorial Director: Lindsay Johnston
Acquisitions Editor: Erika Carter
Development Editor: Joel Gamon
Production Coordinator: Jamie Snavely
Typesetters: Keith Glazewski & Natalie Pronio
Cover Design: Nick Newcomer

Published in the United States of America by
Business Science Reference (an imprint of IGI Global)
701 E. Chocolate Avenue
Hershey PA 17033
Tel: 717-533-8845
Fax: 717-533-8661
E-mail: cust@igi-global.com
Web site: http://www.igi-global.com/reference

Library of Congress Cataloging-in-Publication Data

Implementing new business models in for-profit and non-profit organizations : technologies and applications / Te Fu Chen, editor.
p. cm.
Includes bibliographical references and index.
Summary: "This book provides relevant theoretical frameworks and the latest empirical research findings on a new platform of business models and explores the relationship between the new Business 2.0 alliance and Web 2.0"--Provided by publisher.
ISBN 978-1-60960-129-4 (hbk.) -- ISBN 978-1-60960-131-7 (ebook) 1. Information technology--Management. 2. Web 2.0. 3. Online social networks--Economic aspects. 4. Management--Social aspects. 5. Business planning. I. Chen, Te Fu
HD30.2.I485 2011
658.4'012--dc22

2010051773

British Cataloguing in Publication Data
A Cataloguing in Publication record for this book is available from the British Library.

Table of Contents

Detailed Table of Contents

This chapter adopted modified data envelopment analysis (DEA) to measure the relative operational efficiency of international tourist hotels in Taiwan. After using DEA to evaluate hotel's operational efficiency this research used a qualitative approach to further explore the critical success factors that contribute to hotels having good performance in Taiwan. Through determination of these factors, this research provides hotel managers with a list of advice and recommendations to develop effective strategies and a new business model to meet a highly competitive environment.

This chapter intended to bring forward various KM strategies specially framed for the service industries looking forward for the global market and need to create advantage in providing customer satisfaction and enhancing the growth prospects, applications in organizations, indicate how to improve knowledge based performance and act a base for the service industry for developing innovation, creating global opportunities for better service. The case study highlighting knowledge strategies is designed to achieve the required knowledge sharing and output. Open ended and closed ended strategies plays a significant role in collaborative learning, development, building the potential and providing the knowledge-creation and sharing capacities needed for strategic formulation and decision-making to create competitiveness.

This chapter studies the role that small and medium-sized enterprises (SMEs) play in the e-supply chain management. It has two objectives: (1) it explores how a SME embraces and implements electronic supply chain management (e-SCM) and the challenges facing it, and (2) it develops strategy to deal with the challenges. The chapter draws upon a case study of IFC Global Logistics (IFC), a small-to-medium-sized third party logistics provider. The case study illustrates how the SME embraces enabling technologies, the Internet, and modern business practices to integrate its supply chain management processes and to create for itself differentiation and a competitive advantage in the tough logistics industry. Based upon a literature review and the case study, the chapter explores effective strategy for SMEs in e-supply chain management.

This chapter discusses the banking industry as a user of Internet and other modern information and communication technology (ICT). Author uses Germany and Finland as case examples and make comparisons between them. His research idea is that the banking industry has utilized several technologies of computer networking over several decades, and also got a "flying start" to the Internet technologies, that nowadays are a backbone of the banking industry. This chapter makes a comparison between the developments in Germany and in Finland.

This chapter reports a study on B2E portal use and employee attitudes from a large Australian university, and highlights that employees' attitudes towards portal use are only somewhat positive, and not overwhelmingly favourable. Although not statistically significant, attitudes of employee varied based on age and educational background. Senior management of organisations should thus formulate strategies to develop positive attitudes for portal use to accelerate its diffusion among employee community. Such strategies should take into consideration of the possible effect of employees' age and educational characteristics.

This chapter indicates the present study was designed to evaluate Web users' behaviors related to the music piracy empirically. In light of the newly ratified copyright law in Taiwan, the behavioral intentions of Web users towards the music downloading and/or P2P file sharing were studied using a sample of 317 of Taiwan's Internet users. Results indicated that Web users were likely to reduce or modify their behaviors in order not to be in conflict with the new law. Results also showed that methods of music piracy used by respondents had nothing to do with lifestyle, but were more correlated to Internet self-efficacy.

Foreword

I am delighted to write the foreword to this new book, *Implementing New Business Models in For-Profit and Non-Profit Organizations: Technologies and Applications*.

This is a very timely book as new business models of technologies and applications will increasingly impact almost all aspects of organizational profit.

This book examines the implications of new business models in For-Profit and Non-Profit Organizations from technologies and applications perspectives so that current and future managers could make better decisions regarding where, when and how to utilize these technologies and how to apply the new business model. It includes the theories and practices of leading experts and practitioners from global related disciplines regarding to technologies and applications of new business models.

The scope and content of this book provide For-Profit and Non-Profit Organizations with the essential ingredients for planning, constructing and implementing new business models, as well as ensuring the anticipated benefits are realized.

This book begins with "*Emerging Business Models: Value Drivers in e-Business 2.0 and towards Enterprise 2.0*," covering the foundations of business models, technology, and application from theoretical and practical perspectives. It introduces Forrester's perspective on Web 2.0. It allows this research to clearly define the enabler aspect of Web 2.0 technologies that influence companies in e-Business, and allows a development of the concept 'e-Business 2.0'. Many writers and researchers use the term Web 2.0 as the next stage of the Internet and of e-Business. These researchers do not make a clear distinction between the technological enabler aspect and the social aspect. Introducing and developing a concept of e-Business 2.0 and having it implemented in the outmost circle of the figure help provide a better overview and framework for this research.

This research also makes a distinction between an internal and external focus. This research looks at e-Business 2.0 and has an external focus. E-Business 2.0 pure players depend on Web 2.0 to create and appropriate value with a focus to external customers, instead of internal organisations. The latter focus is called 'Enterprise 2.0', where "there is a new wave of business communication tools including blogs, wikis and group messaging." There are new digital platforms for generating, sharing and refining information that are already popular on the Internet. These platforms are collectively labeled 'Web 2.0 technologies'.

The term 'Enterprise 2.0' focuses only on those platforms in which companies can buy or build in order to make the practices and outputs of their knowledgeable workers visible. Enterprise 2.0 looks at Web 2.0 technologies and practices within organisations and businesses and is therefore, referred to as internal focus. Enterprise 2.0 is the term used to describe how a Web 2.0 approach can be used to work more collaboratively together in business. Harvard professor Andrew McAfee coined the phrase 'Enterprise 2.0', defining it as "the use of emergent social software platforms within companies or between companies and their partner or customers." However Enterprise 2.0 is much more than just 'Web 2.0

for business'. It will provide the infrastructure for technologies and application of new business model, the infrastructure includes Section 1: Implementing New Business Models in For-Profit Organizations (*Emerging Business Models: Value Drivers in E-Business 2.0 and towards Enterprise 2.0*; *Management 2.0: Managing Knowledge Workers in the 21st Century*; *The CSFs Methodology and Modified DEA Approach to Construct a New Business Model to Evaluate Operational Performance of all International Tourist Hotels in Taiwan*; *Knowledge Management Approach as Business Model: Service Industry Prospective*; *The Role of Small and Medium Sized Enterprises in E-Supply Chain Management: A Case Study*; *Taiwan's Corporate Governance-Explorations from the Ethical Corporate Governance Model*).

Section 2: Implementing New Business Models in Non-Profit Organizations (*Adopting Web 2.0 in English Writing Course: A Collaborative Learning Approach in NPO Universities in Taiwan*; *A Case Study of Integrated Innovation Model in the Cultural Innovation Industry in Taiwan*; *An Innovative Business Model in NPOs: From Venture Philanthropy 1.0 to 2.0*).

Section 3: Implementing New Business Models: Technology and Applications (*Rethinking Business Process Reengineering: The Empirical Modelling Approach*; *Modeling Multi-Criteria Promotional Strategy Based on Fuzzy Goal Programming*; *Implementing an Electronic Infrastructure: Developments in Banking in Germany and Finland*; *Employee Attitudes towards Business-to-Employee (B2E) Portals Use: Analysing the Role of Demographic Characteristics*; *Assessing Empirical Relations of Music Piracy Behaviors with Lifestyle and Internet Self-Efficacy of Taiwan's Web Users*; *Validity and Reliability Evidence of a New Version of the Internet Self-Efficacy Scale*)

A chapter on "*Management 2.0: Managing Knowledge Workers in the 21st Century*" suggests a new management framework for managing today's knowledge workers. This framework is based on three perspectives: analyzing the manager's tasks, observing the knowledge worker's behaviors and expectations, and management recommendations via suggested underlying guiding principles. Together, these construct a framework for the new era's manager, defined here as the '2.0 manager'.

A case study on "*The CSFs Methodology and Modified DEA Approach to Construct a New Business Model to Evaluate Operational Performance of All International Tourist Hotels in Taiwan*" adopts modified data envelopment analysis (DEA) to measure the relative operational efficiency of international tourist hotels in Taiwan. After using DEA to evaluate hotels' operational efficiency, this research used a qualitative approach to further explore the critical success factors that contribute to hotels having good performance in Taiwan. Through determination of these factors, this research provides hotel managers with a list of advice and recommendations to develop effective strategies and new business model to meet a highly competitive environment.

A case study on "*Knowledge Management Approach as Business Model: Service Industry Prospective*" intends to bring forward various KM strategies specially framed for the service industries looking forward for the global market and need to create advantage in providing customer satisfaction and enhancing the growth prospects, applications in organizations, indicate how to improve knowledge based performance and act a base for the service industry for developing innovation, creating global opportunities for better service. The case study highlighting knowledge strategies is designed to achieve the required knowledge sharing and output. Open-ended and closed-ended strategies play a significant role in collaborative learning, development, building the potential and providing the knowledge-creation and sharing capacities needed for strategic formulation and decision making to create competitiveness.

The case study on "*Role of Small and Medium Sized Enterprises in E-Supply Chain Management: A Case Study*" studies the role that small and medium-sized enterprises (SMEs) play in the e-supply chain management. It has two objectives: (1) it explores how a SME embraces and implements electronic supply chain management (e-SCM) and the challenges facing it, and (2) it develops strategy to deal with the challenges. The chapter draws upon a case study of IFC Global Logistics (IFC), a small-to-medium-sized third party logistics provider. The case study illustrates how the SME embraces enabling technologies, the Internet, and modern business practices to integrate its supply chain management processes, and to create for itself differentiation and a competitive advantage in the tough logistics industry. Based upon a literature review and the case study, the chapter explores effective strategy for SMEs in e-supply chain management.

The chapter on "*Taiwan's Corporate Governance-Explorations from the Ethical Corporate Governance Model*" discusses the meaning and internal and external mechanisms of Taiwan's corporate governance, explains why this kind of mechanism cannot prevent the agency problem, and demonstrates the importance of business ethics by looking at the flaws in Taiwan's corporate governance. Other questions addressed in this study include what limitations are in the internal and external mechanisms of Taiwan's corporate governance, what makes the agency problem seem inevitable, and whether business ethics may compensate for the shortcomings in Taiwan's corporate governance. The findings of the new business model are discussed.

The chapter on "*Adopting Web 2.0 in English Writing Courses: A Collaborative Learning Approach in NPO Universities in Taiwan*" discusses how the emerging Web 2.0 collaborative approach is applied to English writing courses and their performance. This paper will introduce a collaborative learning approach based on Web 2.0 that facilitates the collaborative English learning for universities in Taiwan. Teaching English writing for universities in Taiwan focuses on traditional writing teaching methods. Usually, teachers try to explain the rules and use the textbooks, and students are just listeners during the writing class. The writing course may lack interactions between students and teachers. How teachers utilize the Internet in writing courses and encourage collaboration between students becomes an important issue in NPO's performance.

A case study on "*Integrated Innovation Model in the Cultural Innovation Industry in Taiwan*" indicates the development of the cultural innovation industry, and encompasses culture, art, technology, and local traditions. This paper describes the procedures of promotions formulated for the development of the cultural and creative industry, including definition, scope, development, strategies and government assistance. The chapter is intended to give the general public an idea of the chain effects expected to bring for the society by the development of the cultural and creative industry. This research was focused on case study based on qualitative analysis, literature review and depth interview, discussing inner management and external relations in Liuli Gongfang, in order to offer the concrete suggestion of development in the future.

The chapter on "*An Innovative Business Model in NPOs: From Venture Philanthropy 1.0 to 2.0*" indicates that there is a need for charities, NPOs, and organizations to look at new types of relationships with benefactors. The new philanthropist wants to be involved and emerge with self-gratification on a job well done. These relationships need to be cultivated and built into long-term partnerships, not just one-offs satisfying someone's individual desire to do well. In addition, to operationalize the concept of business model innovation, this paper proposes a new method that can be applied to assist innovation managers and entrepreneurs in identifying the unique attributes and designing an innovative business model in order to capture the full benefits of Venture Philanthropy. Moreover, this paper also proposes a new system that utilizes the concept of the web 2.0 and Venture Philanthropy to produce new knowledge, services or outlets for users to advance their needs.

The purpose of the chapter "*Rethinking Business Process Reengineering: The Empirical Modelling Approach*" is to introduce a new approach–Empirical Modelling–to computing and business modelling. Today, most business processes rely on informal knowledge and social behavior, but these are areas which have not, so far, been well suited for modelling with computer-based techniques. For this, the author introduces Empirical Modelling to modelling with computers which has natural application to business process modelling. We propose a way of applying this approach to integrated system development with BPR. A framework using this approach, SPORE (situated process of requirements engineering), is extended to encompass applications to participative BPR (i.e. supporting many users in a distributed environment). An outline of an application of our methods to a warehouse management system is also included.

A chapter on "*Modeling Multi-Criteria Promotional Strategy Based on Fuzzy Goal Programming*" indicates knowing how the target customer likes a thing can greatly influence the type of promotional item that they consider and how well the promotion performs in the marketing domain. Apart from designing advertising messages, the problem lies with selecting suitable advertising media vehicles to communicate the message to the right segment in right time. At the same time, it should have specific and measurable marketing objectives. This chapter presents a multi-criteria promotional model for a rural product of a co-operative society in TV channels through popular programmes. An interactive fuzzy goal programming model has been developed for the purpose of handling this problem for a selection of TV programmes in some networks to communicate the message of the product. A case study in Indian context has been considered for highlighting the promotion of handloom products by the bottom-of-pyramid producers of the Indian economy to be marketed in all segments through an optimal media selection process.

A case study on "*Implementing an Electronic Infrastructure: Developments in Banking in Germany and Finland*" indicates the Internet has already now revolutionized many industries. The biggest changes are perhaps yet to come in many industries, but the banking field can be seen as a pioneer in the application of modern Information Technology in general, and of the Internet in particular. For example, in banking, hardly anyone speaks about e-Banking; e-activity is banking as normal, no especial "e" is needed. This chapter discusses the banking industry as a user of Internet and other modern information and communication technology (ICT). We use Germany and Finland as case examples and make comparisons between them. Our research idea is that the banking industry has utilized several technologies of computer networking over several decades, and also got a "flying start" to the Internet technologies, that nowadays are a backbone of the banking industry. In the article we make a comparison of the developments in Germany and in Finland.

The chapter on "*Employee Attitudes towards Business-to-Employee (B2E) Portals Use: Analysing the Role of Demographic Characteristics*" points out that B2E portals represent a state of the art technology for organisations (businesses) to deal with employees using electronic communication, access and data management. B2E portals enable reduced operation costs for organisations and satisfied employees by offering them convenience, flexibility and agility. However, adoption, continued use, and eventual success of portals depend to a large extent on employees' attitudes towards portal use, and generally impinge on demographic characteristics of employees. To establish the influence of demographic characteristics on employee attitudes towards portal use, this chapter reports a study on B2E portal use and employee attitudes from a large Australian university. This chapter highlights that employees' attitudes towards portal use are only somewhat positive, and not overwhelmingly favorable. Although not statistically significant, attitudes of employees varied, based on age and educational background. Senior management of organisations should thus formulate strategies to develop positive attitudes for portal use to accelerate its diffusion among their employee community. Such strategies should take into consideration the possible effect of employees' age and educational characteristics. E-commerce researchers could undertake further research to find out whether demographic characteristics become more significant once the portals are in use for some time.

Unlike past research on online music piracy with a focus on the economic or the legal perspective, the chapter on "*Assessing Empirical Relations of Music Piracy Behaviors with Lifestyle and Internet Self-Efficacy of Taiwan's Web Users*" indicated the present study was designed to evaluate Web users' behaviors related to the music piracy empirically. In light of the newly ratified Copyright Law in Taiwan, the behavioral intentions of Web users towards music downloading and/or P2P file sharing were studied using a sample of 317 of Taiwan's Internet users. Results indicated that Web users were likely to reduce or modify their behaviors in order not to be in conflict with the new law. Results also showed that methods of music piracy used by respondents had nothing to do with lifestyle, but were more correlated to the Internet self-efficacy.

Applying the Internet self-efficacy scale, many studies have found significantly positive relationships between the Internet self-efficacy and behaviors under various settings. However, some late empirical researches have failed to support the strongly positive correlations involving the Internet self-efficacy (Mbengue & Hsu, 2006; Hsu, 2009). This might be attributed to two factors: self-efficacy is, as Bandura (2006) indicated, context-specific and/or domain specific, and the earlier Internet self-efficacy scales were out-of-date due to a drastic advancement of Internet technology. The purpose of the chapter on "*Validity and Reliability Evidence of a New Version of the Internet Self-Efficacy Scale*" was designed to bridge the gap and to update the Internet self-efficacy scale. Based on a sample of 1123 college students with 10 different majors in the northern, central, and southern portions of Taiwan, a new Internet self-efficacy scale based on 26 items was developed and validated statistically. The new version of the Internet self-efficacy scale was composed of five domains: including blogs, auction, video sharing, photo albums, and wiki.

This book cuts through a lot of the excitement and panache associated with marketing of technologies and applications of new business models. It provides a thorough examination of business contexts and provides a framework for requirements analysis, along with case studies to assist with analysis and specification. This book also integrates the academic rigour and the practical knowledge of the authors to assist professionals and organizations in gaining benefits from both perspectives.

I am pleased to be able to recommend this book to readers, be they those looking for substantive material on strategy, or those looking to understand an important aspect of new business model. I wish you the very best success with the implementations and realization of the many benefits of this technologies and applications.

Tsungting Chung

Tsungting Chung (鍾從定) *is a professor at the Department of Business Administration and Dean of International Affairs Office, National Yunlin University of Science and Technology, Yunlin, Taiwan, where he teaches International Management (MBA/EMBA, Ph.D. level), Cross-Culture Management, International Negotiation Theory and Practice (MBA/EMBA, Ph.D. level), and Cross Taiwan Strait Commercial Relations. He was the Chairman of Business Administration Department and Provost at Providence University, Taichung, Taiwan. Most of his research and publications are in the fields of negotiation and international management. Other than journal articles, he published two books, International Negotiation Theory and Practice and Research Methodology: Quantitative and Qualitative Approaches with co-author Chi-Shiun Lai. He is also a licensed mediator at Taichung District Court, and has served as Board member of Chamber of Commerce at Taichung City Government and Yunlin County Government, Taiwan, Republic of China. He received his Ph.D. from Graduate School of International Studies, University of Denver, USA and a certificate on Case Method and Participant-Centered Learning Program from Harvard Business School, Harvard University, USA.*

Preface

What is the difference between a business model and revenue model? E-Business Strategies, Inc. (2008) indicated that a Business Model is the umbrella term used to describe the method–position in the value chain, customer selection, products, pricing–of doing business. A Revenue Model lays-out the process by which a company actually makes money by specifying how it is going to charge for the services provided. The business model lays out the strategy-what should be done or how to create value? The revenue model spells out the execution-how to convert the value creation into cash-flow.

As Michael Rappa (2008) indicated, business models are perhaps the most discussed and least understood aspect of the Web; a business model is the method of doing business by which a company can sustain itself, that is, generate revenue. The business model spells out how a company makes money by specifying where it is positioned in the value chain (Porter, 1985).

Why new business models? Often the innovation rests not in the technology or product, but in the business model itself. The old principles no longer work in the new economy. Businesses have reached the old model's limits with respect to complexity and speed. Great shifts–genuine and radical transformation–have been shaping the economy and business environment in recent decades. Technology, especially information and communication technology, has radically altered the requirements for building and managing a successful business. Disruptive technologies require new business models.

The progress of Information Technology and the network tendency brings the commercial opportunity of industry of globalisation; this includes the enterprise to the enterprise, as well as the enterprise to individual, and moreover, includes satisfying of personalization demand. In the future 10 to 20 years, the enterprise with individual productive forces and the height of working efficiency will be decided by whether or not they can utilize the emerging technology and the auxiliary manpower. Given by the technology, the more convenient communication tool lets the people reduce the barrier of time difference, shortens life and the work custom difference between each other, and therefore will have more potential of the emerging commercial opportunity of industry.

The core value of next generation innovation industry will lie in satisfying the explicit and tacit demand from each person in different times and different life conditions. The industry must properly utilize emerging technology, and the right technology and wireless creativity content to provide individuals and the industry a simple start and fast use. Therefore, an appropriate fusion between the infrastructure of industry innovation and the business process will promote frequency and effectiveness. Developing each industry is necessary to have to be able to cover end-to-end process, and must be able to utilize the same principle at heart by clearly understanding industry object and demand, and thinking complete process and operation mechanism. The key successful factors of next generation innovation industries are: credible content, effective communication, and congenial experience.

Under the tendency of globalisation, technologicalization, and virtualization, the commercial opportunity for industrial business model innovation is extremely lucrative. Four great traits of the innovation industry are: professional, intimate, immediate and touching. If enterprises can provides these values at right time and right place, the customer's greatest needs, it is the successful key factor. Moreover, the ability to suitably utilize the web technology will pour into the new vigour for the innovation industries. Advanced countries gradually took the innovation industry as the core of their industrial structure, and observed global population structure change as well as the life condition transformation, developing the cross-regional innovation life support gradually to clarify situations of using the service. How well the industry grasps the new turning point of the innovation and urges the service content to trend to fine, high value-added and internationalisation development is actually the current, important topic. Therefore, under the life condition and the environmental variation, the study discusses the business model innovation, and might provide reference for innovative thought and developmental visions.

Google paved the way of a succession of "Peer production", they carried on the business model innovation, and their performance and profits are striking. Google obviously positively utilized the ICT tool to carry on the business model innovation of new generation web application, which has become the only way of industrial innovation for raising competitiveness.

Web 2.0 is the newest global network development; global hardware has quite high strength in the international market, but the question is how to unify the hardware superiority and coordination between the global software talent. Meanwhile, integrating hardware industry, existing network industry, as well as the newly created Web information service with resources integration, leveraging industry economy synergy is the key point which the future will develop. In the future, any organizations could become the best environment of empirical network innovation service in global area, developing so-called opening spirit of Web 2.0, recruiting more international talents, and, with some creativity, unifying global superiority of information hardware industry. All this will create positive, cooperative circulation among cross-industry. Finally, it will become concurrently "IT base" of both the "software and hardware" of the world.

There is a whole aspect of Web 2.0 that can drive genuine business value and significant competitive advantage in online software that encourages social collaboration, two-way use of the Web, services that are open and repurposable, Web-based applications, and more. But can we build and grow a real business with these ideas? To these concerns, the book points out that this is only one end of a spectrum. To illustrate this argument, the book has collected real-world Web 2.0 business success stories that demonstrate this point.

Although Web 2.0 is known as take the network as a platform, but O'Reilly actually thought this concept should not limit to moves on the homepage, but is extends the homepage activity to all kinds of installment, therefore, O'Reilly has also stressed, the Web 2.0 keys do not lie in it how newly, but lie in whether it has developed the true potential of network platform.

The book is aimed to explore how for-profit and non-profit organizations create and implement a platform of new business model; it is for making related industry join Business 2.0 platform to quickly response to global trend and large opportunity for emerging new business model.

Moreover, it is able to promote more commercial opportunities for other industries such as airline, traffic, transportation, hotel, restaurant and ICT industries etc. to form economic scale and even output to the world via this business 2.0 platform. In addition, it also can be used to facilitate commercial opportunities for high-tech industries, SMEs, Non-profit Organizations (such as education and cultural industry).

In brief, the importance of each of the chapter submissions is described as follows:

1. Enterprise 2.0 is an evolutionary step forward releasing employees from the constraints and limitations of the legacy communication and productivity tools. If people feel like they can make a difference, they will. The Enterprise 2.0 approach promotes open communications that encourage respect and participation, even across geographic and cultural boundaries. Access to knowledge empowers and motivates people to strive towards common goals together. Enterprise 2.0 addresses 'knowledge silos' by enabling a common space for knowledge capture and sharing. Enterprise 2.0 still suffers from a couple of myths coming from the "2.0" label. But, far from being a hype word applying Web 2.0 concepts to professional organisations, it refers to a tangible reality.
2. Management 2.0 is a management paradigm, based on the employee occupying the focal spot. Thus, the management 2.is a challenge, by definition, as management is defined serving organizations' needs. 2.0 Managers have to balance between these two polar aspects of organization and individual. The suggested framework includes specific techniques for handling the challenge, and these were emphasized in the chapter. In addition, supporting technologies were suggested, easing the 2.0 manager as s/he handles the management 2.0 challenge. The new "management 2.0" is employee-centric, yet retains responsibility of the manager for the employee, for the work and for external relations. To summarize all in one sentence, one might say: Management 2.0 has to do with transforming from a boss into a leader.
3. This chapter adopted the DEA to measure the operational efficiency of 57 international tourist hotels in Taiwan. By comparing relative efficiency, the benchmarking hotels and an individual hotel's competitiveness can be identified. Further analysis of the critical success factors contributing to hotels having good performance help managers understand the factors determining the good operational performance. In this chapter, the linkage between performance measurement and critical success factors were illustrated by Taiwanese international tourist hotels. It was expected that this thesis would provide useful information for future related research as well as identifying hotel management needs.
4. Knowledge is high-value resource that is integrated to apply for making organizational decisions and taking productive actions. It includes data, information, ideas, experience, insights and awareness. It is the combination of information or what we know or the state of knowing in-depth. The critical success factors for KM in a service organisation can be broadly classified as into four divisions- People, Processes, Technology & Sustainable development. Various principles, techniques, obstacles, strategies have been used for implementing KM. The case of KYC explains the effective knowledge use for development. This chapter highlights the implementation of KM in education providing KM strategies for organization change for effective implementation and achievement of organizational objectives.
5. By exploring the role that SMEs play in the e-supply chain management through a case study, this chapter contributes to a better understanding of the crucial issues in SME's adoption and implementation of e-SCM system and processes, and to effective strategy development to deal with the challenges. In spite of the contribution and significance stemming from this study, limitations need to be acknowledged in terms of being a single case study and relying largely on the information provided by the senior managers and the company. In view of the limitations, this study treated the data as illustrative rather than definitive. The author wishes to see more rigourous empirical studies on how to help SMEs, specifically and in practice, take on e-SCM to benefit their business in the literature.

6. This chapter indicated certain norms in business ethics and the values they reflect can help reduce the agency problem, thus ethical values such as trust, loyalty, honesty, consistency, and openness have all been emphasized. The idea of ethic climate is thus proposed when the above ethical values are treated as a part of the organizational culture. The chapter tries to use the concept and means of corporate governance under ethic climate to build a new business model.
7. This chapter combines Web 2.0 to English writing courses, and it may be a good method for the future writing course, particularly for college writing course. Because most writing course is two to four hours a week in Taiwan, the teacher can use the class blog to motivate students to write the article. In addition, from learning other classmates' writing, students can write better according to read more articles. Students also can imitate other classmates' writing to improve their own writing skills. In developing cooperative partnerships with cultural enterprises, governments must bear a heavy burden of responsibility for pressing forward systematization of their commercial operations. In this regard, they must bring together and organize their various administrative agencies in an effort to assure the effectiveness of cultural enterprise operations.
8. This chapter examines the case firm: Liuli Gongfang due to an integrated innovation model in the cultural innovation industry, explore how it grew from a small workshop into one of the world's leading glassware makers. Development of Liuli Gongfang: through sheer perseverance and constant willingness to learn, the Liuli Gongfang gradually found its feet. The company had played a leading role in the development of modern Chinese glassware making, and had succeeded in developing its own distinctive brand image.
9. This chapter indicates donors have always gathered in various communities, but today there are more and more people thinking about co-funding, funder collaborative and other ways that they can leverage their giving through interacting with other donors. In addition, as NPOs move from fundraising (philanthropy 1.0) to friend raising (philanthropy 2.0), they are recognizing the power of building a Web 2.0 community of supporters and donors are beginning to see the value of this community as well. Nonprofits and charities have a strong opportunity to engage in meaningful conversations (that may lead to contributions) with the social media savvy – especially those who are uncultivated. This indicates a growing market for distribution of information via social networks. Trust in social media is significant among social media savvy would-be donors. They trust social networks and blogs to provide important information. Social media use is also very high with users participating in social networks, participating in blogs, participating in message boards. Social Networking: It's about relationships and trust.
10. This chapter has introduced a novel approach to modelling that is based on a view of computation and programming that is significantly broader than conventional views. Empirical Modelling (EM) is a new and radically different approach to complex systems design and business modelling. The primary focus of EM is on the comprehension and on the use of computer-based interactive situation models (ISMs) that represent the way in which the aspects of systems behaviour are constructed in terms of agencies, observables and dependencies. On this EM view, computer-based models of business processes can be built in a way similar to that in which human beings make conceptual models of such processes. Author can then specialise and circumscribe our models to derive software systems. In this way EM can offer both cognitive and operational support to BPR from the very early, conceptual stages of modelling.
11. Several applications of this approach in the design of business models, viz., product planning, product design, marketing-mix, portfolio-selection, capital budgeting, resource allocation, etc. are

possible when such systems are modeled in MCDM format. When probability theory can handle imprecision due to randomness, fuzzy logic is an alternative to tackle problems with imprecision due to fuzziness. Business models for profit and non-profit sectors due to their socio-economic contexts can never be stated precisely and for that reason precise computational tools have limitations in handling them. However, some of these can be nicely captured and sorted out when the problems are viewed in a soft computing framework which can not only give a valid and reliable result but also with a meaning in socio-economic perspective. This empowers FGP with the ability for designing as well as solving complex business situations for meaningful decisions.

12. Electronic banking has a good soil to grow in both in Germany and Finland. Though differences can be found in many aspects through a detailed scanning of statistics, both countries are well off to prepare themselves for the electronic banking business. This analysis of the chapter on banking history should confirm the idea that the banking industry had prepared itself for the Internet era over decades. Innovations such as bank giro transfers and the SWIFT network paved the banks' way to the Internet world. However, much remains still to be done for example in the field of international harmonization, for example before we can really talk about a Single European Payment Area.
13. Drawing on the findings, this chapter however advises that management of organisations should formulate strategies to develop positive attitudes for portal use to accelerate its diffusion among employee community. Such strategies should take into consideration of the possible effect of employees' age and educational characteristics. E-commerce researchers should further examine ways to improve the attitudes of employees for portal use by addressing the requirements unique to various employee groups who may vary based on their age and academic orientations. This study even contributes to theory construction by developing an empirical foundation based on which operationalisation and analysis of employee attitudes towards B2E portal can be further extended.
14. The correlation between music downloading methods and the Internet self-efficacy is somewhat a different story. Three skills (factors) of the Internet self-efficacy were found statistically to be correlated to three methods of music downloading, thus upholding the second hypothesis regarding the Internet self-efficacy. The three skills were "video functions," "photo albums", and "video sharing." However, the three correlations, two positive and one negative, were all low, meaning while the correlations were statistically significant, their relationships were all weak. Since the P2P file sharing has a lot to do with the use of the instant messenger, the identification of the instant messenger skill in this case is justifiable and understandable. The existence of the correlation between the video sharing and the method of using Web forums to download and/or share music files does make sense. The skill of the file sharing is a necessary, though not a sufficient, skill to do the video sharing on the Web. Therefore, a person who is equipped with the skill of the video sharing online, he/she definitely will be able to carry out file sharing activities. Web privacy is the only variable that was found to carry a negative correlation with methods of downloading music. The negative sign between Web privacy and music downloading methods in theory may be interpreted as follows: The more concern a Web user has toward the privacy, the less likely he/she will be involved in the music downloading activities, whether they use the special downloading software or the Web forums to do the downloading.
15. This chapter presents a signal which is loud and clear. That signal is that the Internet self-efficacy instrument needs periodically update because self-efficacy is after all a context, and/or domain-specific, and because the Internet usage applications evolve so rapidly, so drastically, and so fundamentally. As such, it may be a good idea to revise the instrument once every few years. In

addition, mobile technology including 3G and 3.5G is gaining a lot attention lately. It may explain why on the development of a mobile computer self-efficacy scale is not a surprise at all and may be a new trend for future research as well.

In summary, the book may be the first book for introducing the whole aspects of business model 2.0 and for implementing new business models in for-profit organizations (Especially is in high-tech industries, SMEs, service industries and ICT industries), non-profit organizations (Especially is in education and cultural innovation industry), it will contribute scholarly value and potential contribution for practitioners. In addition, the book will focus on the implement of Web 2.0 and new business models in information science, technology and management fields. Definitely, it will make some contributions in these literatures.

The target audiences for this book are such as PhD and master students, scholars, managers, researchers, et cetera. The availability of such literature will aid this target audience to combine the theories and practices of business model 2.0. The potential uses for this book is that this book will be utilized by library reference, upper-level course supplement (such as Ph.D. and master courses), resource for instructors (academics and enterprises), research units, etc.

The potential benefits readers will gain from this book and benefits to enhance available literature are the book proposes to integrate the resources of innovative technology applications and innovative service to accelerate the growth of highly value-added Web-based industry. The platform will continuously play a critical role to drive global businesses to actively involve in business model innovation: technologies and applications with demonstrative, commonality, or integrative features with technological endowments. Such diversified development of novel operation model should stimulate new business opportunity for the industry. Successfully help companies from a variety of industries to develop new operating models and establish benchmarking for other companies to follow. Promote companies to invest self-raised funding and staffs in not only advanced technologies and applications but also management innovation. In addition, successfully plot the roadmap of global novel organizations in for-profit and non-profit. Other major contributions of the book include: collaboration innovation of Web 2.0 and innovation service models.

In summary, the book will explore business model, business model on the web, Web 2.0 business models, the technologies and applications of Web 2.0 and how these various business models can create real business value with Web 2.0 through building a platform of Business 2.0 to accelerate the growth of highly value-added industries whether they are for-profit or non-profit organizations.

Te Fu Chen
Lunghwa University of Science and Technology, Taiwan

Acknowledgment

First of all, many thanks for the submissions from global scholars including EU, UK, USA, Australia, NZ, West Asia, Middle East, India, China, HK, Singapore and Taiwan et cetera. Many of them are interdisciplinary experts and some of them are chief editors of international journals. I wish to establish a sustainable interpersonal network of academics via publishing this book, and as my motto is "Impossible = I am possible", finally, I made it come true! A cooperative book by global academics and practitioners was born.

Secondly, during the past one year, I deeply appreciated everyone who worked with me as a reviewer and contributed chapters to the success of this book. Though some scholars couldn't finish their chapters owing to personal factors, I still thank everyone for everything you have dedicated to this book.

Finally, I felt an immense gratitude to my family; if I haven't their care, attention, toleration and understanding, this book wouldn't be born.

Te Fu Chen
Lunghwa University of Science and Technology, Taiwan
June 2010

Section 1
Implementing New Business Models in For-Profit Organizations

Chapter 1
Emerging Business Models:
Value Drivers in E-Business 2.0 and towards Enterprise 2.0

Te Fu Chen
Lunghwa University of Science and Technology, Taiwan

ABSTRACT

Many writers and researchers do not make a clear distinction between the technological enabler aspect and the social aspect. Introducing and developing a concept of e-Business 2.0 and having it implemented in the outmost circle of the figure help provide a better overview and framework for this research. The objective of this research is to further develop Entrepreneurship and strategic management theory on value creation in e-Business, by providing first insights in value drivers in e-business companies that use Web 2.0. To reach this goal this research tries to give first answers to the central research question: are value drivers associated with Web 2.0 different from known value drivers in e-business? This research clearly defines the enabler aspect of Web 2.0 technologies that influence companies in e-Business, and allows a development of the concept 'e-Business 2.0'. Since the Internet bubble, Web 2.0 with its core applications and enabling technologies has become popular and successful influencing e-Business. Successful start-ups created a new area in e-Business where Web 2.0 was a key factor in creating value. The focus in this research is on these companies that embrace Web 2.0 enabling technologies and core applications that cause a behavioural shift.

This chapter, therefore, develops in scientific literature, the concept of e-Business 2.0 where e-Business companies are actively using Web 2.0 to create and appropriate value from, for, and with stakeholders. This research also makes a distinction between an internal and external focus. This research looks at

DOI: 10.4018/978-1-60960-129-4.ch001

e-Business 2.0 and has an external focus. E-Business 2.0 pure players depend on Web 2.0 to create and appropriate value with a focus to external customers, instead of internal organisations. There is a new wave of business communication tools including blogs, wikis and group messaging. There are new digital platforms for generating, sharing and refining information that are already popular on the Internet. These platforms are collectively labeled Web 2.0 technologies. The term 'Enterprise 2.0' focuses only on those platforms in which companies can buy or build in order to make the practices and outputs of their knowledgeable workers visible. Enterprise 2.0 looks at Web 2.0 technologies and practices within organisations and businesses and is therefore, referred to as internal focus. Enterprise 2.0 is the term used to describe how a Web 2.0 approach can be used to work more collaboratively together in business. Enterprise 2.0 is the use of emergent social software platforms within companies or between companies and their partner or customers. However Enterprise 2.0 is much more than just 'Web 2.0 for business'. Moreover, the study proposed a case study of Enterprise 2.0 to demonstrate by a detailed KPI analysis, how collaboration platforms (and related HR management) can drastically improve the global performance of an international group. Furthermore, the study was to further propose another case study of e-gov 2.0. Enterprise 2.0 is an evolutionary step forward releasing employees from the constraints and limitations of the legacy communication and productivity tools. The study concludes the challenges of the Enterprise 2.0: ten facts and Six Enterprise 2.0 - Myths. Enterprise 2.0, being more a philosophy than a technology, can truly create huge added value for organizations in any sector and it is often remarkable to see in what way the Enterprise 2.0 methods are used to solve specific problems.

INTRODUCTION

Market volatility makes understanding—let alone predicting strategic movements—very difficult. Practicing managers, consultants, investors, and students all face the problems associated with analyzing a dynamic market environment. As the environment changes, it becomes important to ask the following fundamental questions:

1. Do we understand the emerging business models?
2. Are we investing in the right business opportunities?
3. Are we attacking these opportunities using the right business model?
4. Are these opportunities ever going to be profitable?

In today's environment more than ever, managers of "old economy" companies need the right tools to support and improve their effectiveness when making major strategic moves, allocating scarce resources, and managing risk. Why? Because the large "old economy" companies from consumer products to industrial manufacturing have begun to see relatively small pieces of their markets taken away by new, Web-enabled firms. As a result, they're waking up to the e-business threat (and opportunity) and have started to push toward more efficient digital strategies based on optimizing customer experiences, integrating their value chains, and accelerating information flow. Clearly, we're in the early stages of a revolution that's changing the business landscape. As with any revolution, there will be moments of extreme optimism when the potential reveals itself; there will also be moments of extreme pessimism when skepticism rules. However, one thing is certain. E-business is creating new opportunities for companies willing to adapt. For other companies, this same revolution represents a destabilizing threat to the status quo of "business as usual."

Therefore, the general research question is "Are the value drivers associated with e-Business 2.0 different from the known value drivers in e-Business?", the research sub-questions are:

1. How is value created and how is value captured as a competitive advantage?
2. What are the value drivers in e-Business?
3. What are differences between e-Business and e-Business 2.0?

According to abovementioned, the objective of this research is to further develop Entrepreneurship and Strategic Management Theory on Value Creation in e-Business, by providing first insights in Value Drivers in e-Business 2.0.

LITERATURE REVIEW

New Web Mainstream Web 2.0

What is Web 2.0?

The concept of Web 2.0, it is just the summary of all common characters of the websites still survive in these few years. In other word, nowadays, the concept of E-business should also evolve from one-side Web1.0 to two-side Web 2.0. Website administration is evolving while the web users are evolving as well. Web is like a real body, and all the technologies and other web elements are flesh and blood. This newborn baby with infinite potential and infinite amazed now start to open his eye to see this world (Yin, 2009).

The definitions of relatively new concepts of Web 2.0 will be given in this Research: In the simplest terms Web 2.0 is the phrase being applied to 'the second coming' of the Internet. The 2.0 name is a clear allusion to the naming convention of software updates; this is the Internet version 2.0 (Sturgeon, 2006). Two or three years ago there was a feeling that innovation online had failed to emerge from the doldrums of the dot-com boom and bust cycle and had hit something of a dead end, but now innovation is arguably at its most frenetic level ever (Sturgeon, 2006). The bursting of the dot-com bubble in the Fall of 2001 marked a turning point for the web. Many people concluded that the web was over hyped, when in fact bubbles and consequent shakeouts appear to be a common feature of all technological revolutions (Perez, 2002). Shakeouts typically mark the point at which an ascendant technology is ready to take its place at Center stage. The pretenders are given the bum's rush, the real success stories show their strength, and there begins to be an understanding of what separates one from the other (O'Reilly, 2005). Looking back at the beginning of Web 2.0, a core of theories and aspects, are mentioned by O'Reilly, which he calls the seven principles of Web 2.0 (O'Reilly, 2005).

Does Traffic Equal Money?

Before start their E-business, many people just think about one thing: get traffic first. No matter which methods this website plan to adopt in the future to gain profit, if there is great traffic there will be the great chances. This thinking is not wrong, however, you can do much more and plan more precisely before simply consider about this. When we make the website, firstly we have to set the scheme of all the services your website will provide. For example, if the scheme of the website services is to provide shopping information and fashion news, then we can assume that the one visits this website suppose to be the consumer has great potential purchasing power. At the same time, if we highly categorize all the shopping information into different sections in order to bring convenient to the web users, then at the same time, web master will clearly define the shopping intention of the web users. If a web user were checking the information of facemask, the web master would not only knew that he want to buy something, but also clearly knew what he wants to buy is facemask. When you can clearly define your business target and service mode, your design concept of the whole website will be different. You won't strive to boost traffic just for having great traffic. Meaningless traffic will just waste your management resources, the same as meaningless members. The time when you start to charge users money is the time your business is on the decline. Successful website never actively asks web users to be their paid members. Although they provide different level services, only when the users need these specific services then they can choose to be members. All the information of the website is public, even you are not a member, but you still can read all the articles (Yin, 2009).

Many website starts to lock the articles or some basic functions when they develop into certain stage. In order to find a way to earn money, they ask users to pay for some basic services. In my opinion, this is not the way to run the website for long-term development. Website running cost supposes to be covered by advertisers or the sponsors. Just as we mentioned before, if we can define the need of the web users so clearly, definitely we can find the related supporters or sponsors. Therefore, we can see how important it is to have a clear plan to design the whole website. If you don't plan well in the first place, later on you will lose the direction. Because there are no sponsors, so the website has to sacrifice the benefit of the web users. When the websites start to do in this way, this is the time they start to be on the declines. Web 2.0 & social networking technologies are increasing enterprise profitability and changing the face of modern business more rapidly than ever. At E-Business 2.0, the study specializes in keeping business competitive with the latest tools & services to ensure that business remain relevant in today's uncertain marketplace. The study focuses on fundamental enabling technologies for e- business & web business (Yin, 2009).

Web as a Platform

Software as a Service (SaaS)

Web 2.0 services are a combination of software and data. Individual, the software and the databases are of limited value, but together they create a new type of service. In this context, the value of software lies in being able to manage the (vast amounts of) data. The better it can do, the more valuable the software becomes.

Harnessing the Long Tail

The Long Tail refers to the vast number of small sites that make up the Web as apposed to the few 'important' sites (Jaokar, 2006).

Harnessing Collective Intelligence

This principle deals with the metadata/content created by users that collectively adds value to the. To understand Collective Intelligence one should understand three aspects:

A. **Peer Production:** Is defined as a new model of economic production, different from both markets and firms, in which the creative energy of large numbers of people is coordinated (usually with the aid of the Internet) into large, meaningful projects, largely without traditional hierarchical organizational or financial compensation (Benkler, 2002). An Example are reviews on Amazon: Collectively, these small contributions lay the foundation for the 'Intelligence' of Web 2.0 also called the 'wisdom of crowds'
B. **The Wisdom of crowds:** Large groups of people are smarter than an elite few, now matter how brilliant the elite few may be. The wisdom of crowds is better at solving problems, fostering innovation, coming to wise decisions, and even predicting the future (Surowiecki, 2005).

C. **Network effects from user contributions:** The ability for users to add value (knowledge) easily and then the ability for their contributions to flow seamlessly across the whole community, thereby enriching the whole body of knowledge.

Data is the Next Intel Inside

Data is the key differentiator between a Web 2.0 service and non-Web 2.0 services. A Web 2.0 service always combines function (software) and data (which is managed by the software). Database management is a core competency of Web 2.0 companies. While data is valuable, the company needs not necessarily own the data. Although in most cases, the company serving the data also 'owns' the data (e.g., Google Maps, Google does not own the data, which are maps and information. Web 2.0 website are often a combination of data from two or more sources into one experience, this is called a mashup. According to O'Reilly (2005) the race is on to own certain classes of core data.

End of Software Release Cycle

A. Operations must become a core competency

The shift from software as artifact to software as service causes that the software will cease to perform unless it is maintained on a daily basis.

B. Users must be treated as co-developers

The open source dictum, "release early and release often" has morphed into an even more radical position, "the perpetual beta," in which the product is developed in the open, with new features slipstreamed in on a regular basis.

Lightweight Programming Models

Simpler technologies like RSS and Ajax are the driving force behind Web 2.0 services. Because lightweight programming models are oriented towards syndicating data, they are contrary to the traditional mindset of controlling access data. They are also designed for reuse. As a result of this architecture, innovation is given a boost because a new service can be created using existing services through mashups. This is one other important aspect of Web 2.0, called Innovation in assembly: When commodity components are abundant, you can create value simply by assembling them in novel or effective ways. Web 2.0 will provide opportunities for companies to beat the competition by getting better at harnessing and integrating services provided by others.

Software above the Level of a Single Device

One other feature of Web 2.0 is the fact that it is no longer limited to the PC platform. This principle is not new but rather a fuller realization of the true potential of the web platform, this phrase gives key insight into how to design applications and services for the new platform. iTunes is the best exemplar of this principle. This application seamlessly reaches from the handheld device to a massive web back-end (platform), with the PC acting as a control station. There have been many previous attempts to bring web content to portable devices, but the iPod/iTunes combination is one of the first such applications designed from the ground up to span multiple devices. O'Reilly (2005) expects to see some of the greatest change in this area of Web 2.0, as more and more devices are connected to the new platform. Real time traffic monitoring, flash mobs, and citizen journalism are only a few of the early warning signs of the capabilities of the new platform.

Rich User Experience

The competitive opportunity for new entrants is to fully embrace the potential of Web 2.0. Companies that succeed will create applications that learn from their users, using an architecture of participation to build a commanding advantage not just in the software interface, but also in the richness of the shared data. In exploring the seven principles, O'Reilly (2005) highlighted some of the principal features of Web 2.0: Services, not packaged software, with cost-effective scalability; Control over unique, hard-to-recreate data sources that get richer as more people use them; Trusting users as co-developers; Harnessing collective intelligence; Leveraging the long tail through customer self-service; Software above the level of a single device; Lightweight user interfaces, development models, and business models. In October 2005 one definition of Web 2.0 is given (O'Reilly, 2005): It is the network as platform, spanning all connected devices; Web 2.0 applications are those that make the most of the intrinsic advantages of that platform: delivering software as a continually-updated service that gets better the more people use it, consuming and remixing data from multiple sources, including individual users, while providing their own data and services in a form that allows remixing by others, creating network effects through an "architecture of participation," and going beyond the page metaphor of Web 1.0 to deliver rich user experiences.

Joakar and Fish (2006) state a 'unified view' of Web 2.0 based on the seven principles of Web 2.0 by O'Reilly (2005) by which the second principle (harnessing collective intelligence) encompasses the other six. Web 1.0 was hijacked by the marketers, advertisers and the people who wanted to push content into the market. The dot com bubble was the end of many who took this approach of the broadcast content. What is left is the Web as it was originally meant to be a global means of communication. The intelligence attributed to the Web (Web 2.0) arises from us (i.e. the collective/people) as we begin to communicate. This approach focuses on the 'Intelligent Web' or 'Harnessing Collective Intelligence' and deals with the principle of 'wisdom of crowds' (Surowiecki, 2005). A more simple definition from MacManus (2005) explains Web 2.0 as Platform. For corporate people, the Web is a platform for business. For marketers, the Web is a platform for communications. For journalists, the Web is a platform for new media. For geeks, the Web is a platform for software development.

According to Hinchcliffe (Hinchcliffe, 2006a) the Web itself has become a vast landscape of information services that can be wired together to reuse and take advantage of aggregated data and functionality. The hallmarks of these online applications are their pervasive availability, interactivity, social immersion, user-driven organization, community contribution, and particularly their reusable, remixable services. Web 2.0 also refers to the creation of far greater levels of interactivity, not just between users, or between users and the Internet but between complementary online services through mash-ups and web services (Sturgeon, 2006). Web 2.0 is either a collaborative web where the content is created by the users (this aspect is often called the social layer of Web 2.0), or a web where the network is the platform or web that uses funky technologies such as Ajax or ruby on Rails (this one is called the technical layer of Web 2.0) (van der Vlist & Vernet et al, 2007). The focus in this study is on the social layer of Web 2.0 and the technical layer can be seen as an enabler for the social side of Web 2.0.

Before the burst of new ideas that we call Web 2.0, the web seemed to have reached a stage where its growth would slowly start declining. The production of web content seemed deemed to be increasingly controlled by traditional media producers, and the alliance between AOL and Time Warner was showing that the web industry had started its consolidation phase. Socially, the Web had become a read-only medium where most of the content was published and broadcast pretty much like in conventional media. This hadn't always been the case: the Web was originally designed as a medium where scientist could easily share their documents. This was still the case in the early 1990's, when the Web was largely composed of home pages and link pages edited and published by web users from the benefit of other web users. This was possible because the technology was simple, and because the target audience was able and willing to edit web pages without much tool support. During the next iterations of web technologies more difficult tools where used and the audience expanded beyond the small circle of people willing to learn these technologies to publish their own content. As a result, the web became for most of its users a read only web, rather than the cooperative venture it had been originally.

The social layer of Web 2.0 is about making the Web a read/write web again. For some, this goal is motivated by philanthropic or political reasons: everyone should be able to express his or her ideas. For others, the motivation is financial: if the growth of the number of web readers is deemed to slow down, the growth of the web can only be fuelled by the growth of the number of people that create content on the web. The technical layer is a consequence of the social layer: the ability to write on the web that has been limited by the growing complexity of the web technology can only be given back to web users by using more technology. In other words, the flurry of Ajax, JavaScript, and XML technologies that characterize most of Web 2.0 applications are needed to lower the barrier to entry in the circle of web publisher that web 2.0 applications try to enlarge. It is important to note that content here is meant to be content at large. Many web 2.0 sites do not rely on their users for creating all their content but only to enrich their content. A significant example is amazon.com. Of course, the main content on the amazon.com web sites comes from the company's own database, however, what makes the difference between the amazon.com site and other similar sites is how it integrates content from amazon.com partners and users. Users are not only welcome to publish reviews, they contribute to the site each time they buy a new item and even by browsing the site: the simple actions are analyzed and they are used to publish tips such as the 'What do customers ultimately buy after viewing items like this?' that is currently displayed if you browse the description of this book on amazon.com. This is perhaps the most convincing example if a low entry barriers to contributing to a site's content! (van der Vlist & Vernet, et al., 2007)

Dion Hinchcliffe rather talks about social media: Social media describes the online tools and platforms that people use to share opinions, insights, experiences, and perspectives with each other. Social media can take many different forms, including text, images, audio, and video. Popular social mediums include blogs, message boards, podcasts, wikis, and vlogs (Hinchcliffe, 2007). Some ground rules of social media are (Hinchcliffe, 2007): Communication in the form of conversation, not monologue. This implies that social media must facilitate two-way discussion, discourse, and debate with little or no moderation or censorship. In other words, the increasingly ubiquitous comments section of your local blog or media-sharing site is NOT optional and must be open to everyone. Participants in social media are people, not organizations. Third-person voice is discouraged and the source of ideas and participation is clearly identified and associated with the individuals that contributed them. Anonymity is also discouraged but permissible in some very limited situations. Honesty and transparency are core values. Spin and attempting to control, manipulate, or even Spam the conversation are thoroughly discouraged. Social media is an often painfully candid forum and traditional organizations -- which aren't part of the conversation other than through their people -- will often have a hard time adjusting to this.

It's all about pull, not push. Like McKinsey & Company noted a year ago or so, push-based systems, of which one-way marketing and advertising and command-and-control management are typical examples are no where near as efficient as pull systems where people bring to them the content and relationships that they want, instead of having them forced on themselves. Far from being a management theory, much of what we see in Web 2.0 shows the power of pull-based systems with extremely large audiences. As you shape a social media community, understanding how to make embrace pull instead of push is one of the core techniques. In social media, people are in control of their conversations, not the pushers.

Distribution instead of centralization. One often overlooked aspect of social media is the fact that the interlocutors are so many and varied. Gone are the biases that inevitably creep into information when only a few organizations control the creation and distribution of information. Social media is highly distributed and made up of tens of millions of voices making it far more textured, rich, and heterogeneous than old media could ever be (or want to be). Encouraging conversations on the vast edges of our networks, rather than in the middle, is what this point is all about.

Value Drivers in Web 2.0

Vincent de la Mar (2007) indicated with Web 2.0 new features of the Internet transactions and participations are taking place. More and different stakeholders add value in e-business. This raises questions which (new) value drivers we can find in Web 2.0 and which ones are more important. By looking at these factors we are indirectly looking at the business models that are important in the New Internet. Providing more insight in value drivers and business models in Web 2.0 enables companies and entrepreneurs to adopt and prepare to take advantage of opportunities in this next stage of the Internet.

E-Business 2.0

The focus in this research is on the companies that embrace the web 2.0 enabling technologies and core applications that cause a behaviour shift (the outmost circle of Forrester's figure). This research therefore introduces the concept e-Business 2.0, by which the study means: e-Business companies that use Web 2.0 to create and appropriate value from, for and with stakeholders. This research will look at pure e-Business 2.0 companies with an external approach. The focus is on the customer, instead of an internal organisation (Enterprise 2.0) and the company is fully dependent on the web 2.0 technologies. Reason for this is that business-to-consumer developments occur often earlier than business-to-business developments. What is important to notice is that besides e-Business 2.0 pure players, also companies that acquire parts of e-Business 2.0 and regular e-Business (e.g. e-Commerce) companies are active? Companies can learn from these often-smaller e-Business 2.0 companies (start-ups) and use it to adopt to market changes and/or to enterprise 2.0 (de la Mar, 2007).

E-Business 2.0 Emerging Business Models

E-commerce experts Ravi Kalakota and Marcia Robinson highlight several emerging e-business models, including Net markets, collaborative click-and-brick, and mobile portals. Asking yourself which of these emerging business patterns your company is attempting to compete with. Answering this question will help you get started assessing technology enablers and what opportunities they may present. E-business is tricky business. In these turbulent times, how should management respond? They should begin by asking the right questions. By focusing on the right transition, companies can proactively alter the nature of competition. What are the transitions that are taking place? Traditional market channels are giving way to new channels, production-centric processes are yielding to customer-centric processes, old business models are morphing to new models, information is replacing inventory, and physical goods are being replaced by digital products. Before you jump into the deep end of e-business change and begin shifting your operation toward the future, it's important to stop and consider the emerging structural patterns that characterize the new economy, including e-channels, click-and-brick patterns, e-portals, e-market makers, and pure e and mobile portals. E-channels, or extension models of large companies, have evolved considerably. The first step was developing a stand-alone channel, or spin-off.com, independent of the parent company (for example, Proctor and Gamble spin-off venture Reflect.com); the second step was a stand-alone channel with some connection to the mother ship (for example, Wal-Mart.com). The new phase, channel synchronization, is a tightly integrated click-and-brick strategy, like CVS.com, that serves customers seamlessly no matter what the entry point is (Kalakota & Robinson, 2001).

At the same time, e-portals, or business-to-consumer models, have evolved in three phases in the last few years. The first was developing appropriate traffic (for example, Yahoo!); the second was fighting for transactions (for example, Amazon.com). Now in the third phase, companies are beginning to battle for margins with click-and-brick partnerships such as Amazon.com and Toys R Us. Expect to see more partnerships like this. It's interesting that both the e-channels and e-portals are converging on what appears to be the same business model: collaborative click-and-brick. The following sections discuss three e-business patterns that are fairly new—net markets, collaborative click-and-brick, and Pure E—to help you better understand the next set of e-wars (Kalakota & Robinson, 2001).

Collaborative Click-and-Brick (C&B)

Here's a formula for the electronic age: (brick-and-mortar) + (click-and-order) = click-and-brick (C&B). So-called brick-and-mortar (BAM) companies are looking increasingly like new economy companies as they harness technology to achieve greater productivity. An increasing number of BAM companies, such as Williams Sonoma, Circuit City, and Wal-Mart, are attempting to transform their operations to support a digital business model. At the same time, several Internet-based companies are looking to build a real-world physical channel in addition to their virtual channel. The hottest trends in e-tail going forward probably won't be pure-play companies selling strictly through the Net. The next trend is toward the click-and-brick pattern, a hybrid online/offline business model incorporating both physical and online business practices. The C&B model allows an existing offline business to profit from partnering with an emerging online presence. A great example of C&B is discount stockbroker Charles Schwab. Schwab's success has proven that storefronts can drive traffic to their Web sites. The firm continues to open new storefront offices every year, because that's where customers feel most comfortable signing up for their accounts. But once the relationship is established, the majority of the customers use Schwab's Web site to monitor and manage their accounts, where Schwab's customer-service costs are lower. This lesson has not been lost on other retailers, who are finally starting to see benefits of combining e-commerce with old-fashioned department store service. An established retailer's name has tangible advantages in cyberspace in a world where consumers are swamped with too many choices.

Business-to-Business (B2B) Net Markets

Business-to-business (B2B) business models are fairly young. But they're also evolving rather furiously. This section addresses some of the changes that are taking place in the area of net markets. However, a basic classification of the various types has already emerged. Broadly speaking, business-to-business applications can be further divided into the following categories:

A. Corporate Procurement Portals

Corporations with substantial "buying power" are racing to create private portals for the procurement of both production-related goods and non–production-related goods. Production goods include raw materials, components, assemblies, and other items needed to produce a finished good. Non-production goods are items that businesses need to run day-to-day business operations: capital equipment; MRO (maintenance, repair, and operations) products; office, computer, scientific, and industrial supplies; and travel and entertainment. However, for many companies, development of a truly effective integrated procurement strategy is still a long way off. For all but a relative few, there is no clear vision of what needs to be achieved through reengineering and integrating the procurement process, nor is there a good roadmap of how to get there—or even an idea of what "there" should look like.

B. Net Markets: Virtual Distributors, Auction Hubs

The first generation of Net markets (for example, VerticalNet) provided community features alone. However, in the second-generation, transaction revenue derived from buying and selling products is becoming crucial. An example of this genre of trading exchanges is virtual distributors. Virtual distributors offer one-stop shopping for a fragmented buyer and seller community by aggregating disparate product information, primarily associated with multiple catalogs, from multiple suppliers (that is, manufacturers) into one mega-catalog. Virtual distributors help streamline the systematic sourcing of direct goods and lower transaction costs by issuing a single purchase order and parsing the order to each relevant supplier that ships the product direct. Many are starting to add richer services, such as meshing with software that handles a company's back-end operation—from order-taking to tracking inventory. Virtual distributors generally don't carry inventory, nor do they directly supply products, but instead assist buyers in arranging for third-party carriers to transport the order goods. The jury is out on this model.

C. Industry Consortiums: Joint Venture Industry Procurement Hubs

In response to startups, large companies are using their clout to create industry consortiums, of two types: buyer consortiums and supplier consortiums. In a buyer consortium, a group of large companies aggregate their buying power, the premise being that more buying power drives down price. Traditional industry players have a big advantage over Net-born startups when it comes to starting exchanges for high-volume commodity goods: instant commercial activity and liquidity. An example is MetalSpectrum, which plans to be the online neutral marketplace for aluminum, stainless steel, and other specialty metals.

In response to exchanges and buyer consortiums, supplier consortiums have begun to emerge. Similar to their buyer-centric cousins, these consortiums are forming in industries where a few firms comprise a high concentration of market power. The big difference is that supplier consortiums must give sponsors the opportunity to promote and differentiate their products. They must provide the most compelling environment for buyers by aggregating the key industry suppliers, and offering a compelling amount of product depth, breadth, and selection and service. The future of industry consortiums is not clear. There are many issues to overcome around the areas of governance, technology, and antitrust. On the governance front, traditional competitors must form an independent company that promotes the interests of all the participants. The second big hurdle follows closely behind the first: technology selection. Again, with a cast of strong, powerful players, each with its own technology standards and systems, it will be difficult for the new entity to satisfy the requirements of all the members. The third hurdle is antitrust. In short, technology is no replacement for management or governance. And these issues have to be worked out.

D. Collaboration Hubs

Types of collaboration efforts can include product planning and design, demand forecasting, replenishment planning, and pricing and promotional strategies. Importantly, these platforms record historical trading data that can be analyzed in an effort to further improve future planning and forecasting, in turn enabling further compression of design and development cycles. These emerging exchanges go far beyond the transaction phase to help companies manage the supply chain end-to-end. Collaboration hubs seek to create one common Web platform that enables participants throughout an entire industry supply chain (for example, raw-material providers, manufacturers, importers/exporters, distributors, dealers) to share information, execute transactions, and collaborate on strategic and operational planning. Not only should this common platform facilitate new trading partnerships, but it should enable channel participants to better match production with demand (thereby reducing excess inventories in the channel) and help speed cycle times. Value-added services are the premium services that collaborative hubs provide to continuously drive market liquidity. By providing these services, collaborative hubs can increase site "stickiness," generate multiple revenue streams, and increase competitive barriers to entry. Providing these services is an essential component of a collaborative hub strategy if the collaboration expects to develop a sustainable advantage and be the market leader.

Pure E: Digital Products and Mobile Portals

Clearly, we are entering the Pure "E" decade—an era of digital products. A digital product is one for which the product is made online, stored online, sold online, delivered online, and consumed online. Some first-generation examples are digital music, software, books, and photos. How digital goods will be delivered is already changing. In the future, delivery will come, in many cases, as a service across the Internet (for example, via streaming media) instead of as a packaged product. Even the means for creating digital content is changing. Contributing to the growth of digital products are the proliferation of Internet-access devices (such as set-top boxes, WebTV, and video game consoles), cheap and abundant availability of bandwidth, sub-$500 PCs, growing free PC programs, and industry standardization of application programming interfaces (APIs).

Mobile Portals: New Platforms for Digital Media Delivery

Seemingly overnight, the wireless revolution exploded, intensifying the movement toward mobile commerce. New programming languages, platforms, and protocols are embraced almost with abandon, or at least little consideration, while new partnerships and wireless portals are announced daily. The market for the delivery of Internet services through handheld devices is new and evolving rapidly. The business strategy behind the handheld computing marketing is straightforward. If you take control of the operating system infrastructure, you also control the software applications developed to run on it. As handheld devices are adopted in greater numbers and handheld device applications become integrated into other information appliances, an opportunity exists for these operating-system developers to extend their platforms for use on other handheld devices. The wireless revolution isn't only about handheld devices, though. It's also about the new generation of software infrastructure, which will soon enable the convergence of the Internet and mobile telephony. The next-generation mobile delivery systems include voice browsers and telephony-based speech-recognition systems. Now telephony-based speech recognition is extending to the Web. The business models in this area are in their infancy (Charron, et al., 2009)

This is Real e-Business

Kalakota and Robinson have put together a literal blue print for e-Business success. Not, it's not 1.0, but "2.0"! As more and more "real" or "brick 'n mortar" businesses put their businesses online, there needs to be a clear delineation of what is hype and fiction. What's a fly by night Internet start up and what truly is a distinct "e-Business"? E-Business 2.0 leads the way. This is for companies that want to completely embrace all the Internet has to offer and ensure that their business leverages the opportunities it can provide. "To compete effectively in the e-commerce world, a company must structurally transform its internal foundation. This structural change requires a company to develop an innovative e-business strategy, focusing on speed to market and breakthrough exercises" "What sets the truly great organizations apart is their ability to use state-of-the-art e-commerce processes to transform themselves (Ray, 2000). They do the following three things well.

1. They redefine value for their customers
2. They build powerful e-business designs that outperform the competition
3. They understand customer priorities and consistently raise customer expectations to new heights.

E-Business 2.0 is a business manual for strategically using the tool of the Internet to radically transform how you do business. In "Constructing the e-Business Architecture: Enterprise Apps", Chapter 5 of e-Business 2.0: Roadmap for Success, the authors talk about applications and integration - the technology bedrock of e-Business. By using case studies and examples, e-Business 2.0: Roadmap for Success will give you a bird's eye view of how to acquire e-Business applications and tools for your specific business. If your a CEO, President or some other upper management, and are serious about exploring how e-Business can be for your business, then e-Business 2.0: Roadmap for Success is a must read (Ray, 2000).

Value Drivers in e-Business 2.0

Vincent (2007) researched nine e-Business 2.0 examples--nine Dutch (e-Business 2.0) cases, that were selected from companies listed in the Dutch Web 2.0 Awards that was held in January 2006; over 50.000 people could nominate and select Web 2.0 initiatives. Very interesting companies to have a look at:

Wakoopa

Wakoopa is a social network site for software. People can track what kind of software they use and share it with others and find (better) applications. With Wakoopa users acquire information on what software they use and can share software and opinions. The real value that is created using this site is the sharing experience users get when they share software and (new) applications. Wakoopa has made a platform and tracker to use for this site. The technique is only one part of Wakoopa's function. The other part is the community platform and the incentives to people to contribute on the platform. Wakoopa is not only a creator of the technology and facilitator of the platform, but also a motivator and stimulator in a way it wants people to help collaborate by sharing experiences and knowledge.

Swoot

Swoot is an innovative leader in skinning and transforming web enabled applications for the desktop. Users can build their own browser and can participate in building a new website. There is a Swoot portal where all the developed browsers on many topics can be found, which can be accessed when people install a one time plug-in. Swoot offers a technology platform for, what they call, 'ultimate freedom in design and marketing in a fun online experience.' The idea is that everybody can create and control their own Internet browser, instead of using standard ones, like Firefox and Explorer.

Boomr

Boomr is 'a platform where artists from all genres can share their music with everyone who has access to the Internet.' Boomr is also a place where people can get to know their favourite artists music and personal matters. Value is created for the artists on Boomr by enabling a connection to exist with potential supporters and vice versa, value is created for the listener who is able to find music they like. Boomr is free to use and focuses on the non-familiar artists, as well. The value is created by users and artists who contribute and participate on the platform. There is an artist community and a user community. The user community is based on voluntary contributions, like reporters (enthusiastic fans of an artist) that write about concerts. Boomr's artist and user communities are growing and are of significant value to this initiative and helps create a lock-in.

Buurtlink.nl

Buurtlink.nl is part of the Buurtlink foundation and its goal is to increase social cohesion within the Netherlands and to become the largest district website based on zip codes. Buurtlink.nl creates its own value by having a large base of active users. Neighbours can communicate on Buurtlink.nl and can keep their own district website active and relevant. Since facilitating the platform alone is not enough, Buurtlink.nl makes a distinction between 'Buurtlinkers' and users. A 'Buurtlinker' is an active user, like an ambassador or correspondent, and delivers content and promotes the website in the neighbourhood. This motivates neighbours to participate and in creating a stronger collaboration, Buurtlink.nl gives incentives to 'Buurtlinkers' by yearly activities and free gadgets. Besides 'Buurtlinkers', there are users that live in the neighbourhood who can also participate and generate content on the platform. Everyone can give their opinion on the website or can talk/work together with their neighbours. The founders of Buurtlink.nl try to deliver less content as possible on the platform; they have a facilitating and motivating task. Besides collaboration with the users of the website, Buurtlink.nl works together with several partners. These partnerships can have local goals, but also national goals, like regional news stations, digital marketplaces, and local weather forecast agencies.

Watvindenwijover.nl

Watvindenwijover.nl is a free service platform to easily save interesting web pages on the Internet. There are several features of the site that are new and related to Web 2.0 technologies. For example, users can make their own notes on the site while easily organizing results by tagging and can share favourite sites and topics with other users. The activities on the platform are also recognized as 'social browsing', which means social searching and sharing. There are several clusters of communities based on interest and Watvindenwijover.nl tries to link people actively by giving recommendations. In this manner, people can collaborate to find more or better information on certain topics. Watvindenwijover.nl is a subset of Winkwaves and is used as a marketing tool and as a playground to experiment. The actual value appropriation with these platforms is done by Winkwaves in a Business-to-Business context and relates more to Enterprise 2.0.

YelloYello

Traditional guides (in this research referred to as e-Business e.g. Goudengids.nl and iLocal.nl) do not answer questions like; where can I find a good plumber? What is the best lawyer in the district? As a user of this website, you often ask recommendations from friends and family.' YelloYello is a company that fills this gap with help of Web 2.0 by 'social local search': YelloYello has local communities and is a social network and guide in one. Everyone can contribute easily by giving reviews, tagging, and upload locations. The company stimulates people to share experiences so the company can create a recommendation list of companies. The community and cluster aspect can be found in the case of YelloYello. The company focus is on places and people. Based on places and interest there are clusters of communities that contribute and add value for other users. The value is created by the users and is a combination of content and the social aspect of the website. Since the business information is already familiar, the new data contributed by the community adds new value.

Fleck

Fleck.com wants to add a new layer of interactivity to the web by adding new tools that allow its users to add information rather than just consuming it. Fleck allows users to interact with pages on the web just as if it were pages in a magazine; People can save annotated page for own purposes, send it to friends or colleagues or use it in their blog.' The value, appropriated on the platform by its users, is created by the users because data on top of the existing webpage is collected by a collaboration of Internet users. When this data is aggregated correctly, new opportunities for value creation arise, but also appropriation may appear, for instance, more efficient search methods, recommendations, and suggestions on websites. Efficiency and complementarities are the most important drivers for Fleck. People use the platform and technology for several purposes, like bookmarking, communication, and page sharing. In the second half of 2007, Fleck will focus more on collaboration and the Long Tail by increasing the 'discovery factor'. According to the founders of Fleck, there is a huge potential for collaboration with Fleck and it will become the most important driver. Fleck tries to enable knowledge sharing within the community. In this way people can efficiently use the information and knowledge other users contributed on websites. All these contributions on websites are collected in a database. Not only will the popular website be collected in this database, but also smaller and unfamiliar WebPages, referred to as the Long Tail, are collected. Fleck uses the collective intelligence to create value that is contributed by its users.

Hyves

Hyves is one of the most used e-Business 2.0 pure players in the Netherlands and is the most popular social network (Ruigrok NetPanel, 2007). The focus for Hyves is on establishing an online platform, in which people can (re)connect with each other, as they say: 'Always in touch with your friends'. Users can share photos, videos, blogs, and recommendations, but the most added values for users of Hyves are to get reconnected with old friends (Ruigrok NetPanel, 2007). Hyves tries to be the place on the Internet where users share his or her information. Not only can you connect with people, but you can also collaborate and share by using a weblog or gadgets. Integration is also very important to Hyves, like importing an existing weblog on your Hyves page by Web 2.0 technology (RSS), which makes it easy and efficient for users to share. In the near future, Hyves is going to increase their use of AJAX-tools to integrate more easy-to-use applications to create increased value for its users.

Favr

Favr is 'a website platform on which you can save and share your favourites, like websites and articles'. Users can review and recommend

Figure 1. Value drivers in e-Business 2.0. Source: Vincent (2007)

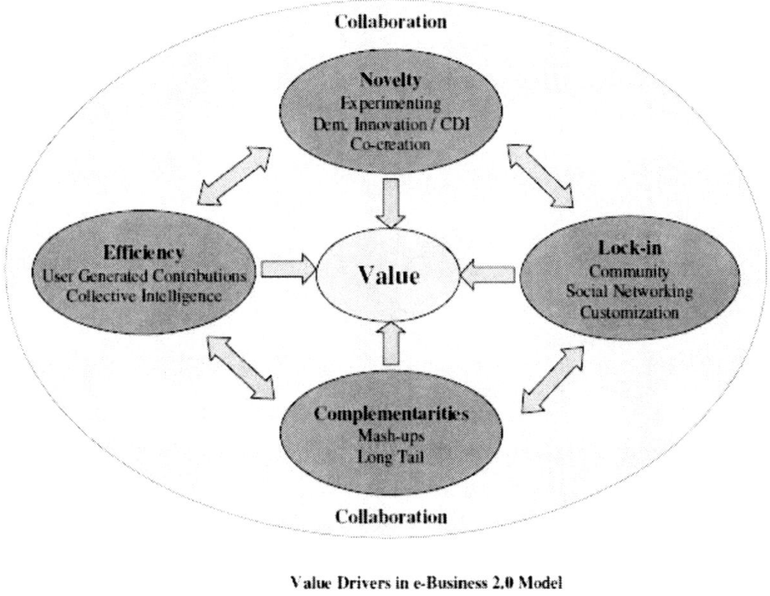

favourites in order to establish a top ranking of favourites. The company wants to create a unique social bookmarking platform, that looks like Delicious, since interest is focused on website level. The community creates value and Favr's role is an intermediary one by which it gives incentives and tools for users to contribute. The community decides what ranking certain websites and articles get and is not influenced by the company. The founder of Favr is also the founder of web-log.nl that was sold successfully to Ilse Media in 2004 (Wiersma, 2004), who started both companies as an experiment. In summarize above, Vincent (2007) proposed a Value Drivers in e-Business 2.0 model as figure 1.

What Does the Study Means with an e-Business 2.0?

This research adopts Forrester's perspective on Web 2.0 (Koplowitz and Young 2007). It allows this research to clearly define the enabler aspect of Web 2.0 technologies that influence companies in e-Business, and allows a development of the concept 'e-Business 2.0'. According to Forrester Research Inc., a renowned technology and market research company,' Web 2.0 is a set of technologies and applications that enable efficient interaction among people, content, and data in support of collectively fostering new businesses, technology offerings, and social structures (Koplowitz & Young, 2007).' Koplowitz and Young (2007) point out that there are three lenses through which to view Web 2.0:

1. Enabling technologies - provide the infrastructure and building blocks for Web 2.0 applications. These supporting technologies are often not as important for marketers, by a lack of knowledge of techniques like AJAX and XML (Derksen, 2007a).
2. Core applications and features - enable people to efficiently interact with other people, as well as, content and data.
3. Forrester Research Inc. calls this 'social computing': Social computing refers to 'easy

Figure 2. Enterprise 2.0. Source: Vincent de la Mar (2007)

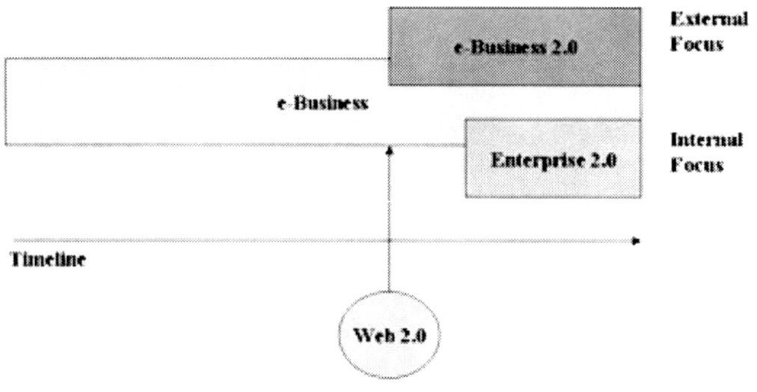

> connections brought about by cheap devices, modular content, and shared computing resources, that are having a profound impact on our global economy and social structure (Koplowitz &Young, 2007).

Individuals increasingly take cues from one another rather than from institutional sources like corporations, media outlets, religions, and political bodies. To thrive in an era of Social Computing, companies must abandon top-down management and communication tactics, weave communities into their products and services, use employees and partners as marketers, and become part of a living fabric of brand loyalists (Charron, Favier et al., 2006).

Many writers and researchers use the term Web 2.0 as the next stage of the Internet and of e-Business. These researchers do not make a clear distinction between the technological enabler aspect and the social aspect. Introducing and developing a concept of e-Business 2.0 and having it implemented in the outmost circle of the figure help provide a better overview and framework for this research.

E-Business 2.0 and Enterprise 2.0

Since the Internet bubble, Web 2.0 with its core applications and enabling technologies has become popular and successful influencing e-Business. Successful start-ups created a new area in e-Business where Web 2.0 was a key factor in creating value. The focus in this research is on these companies that embrace Web 2.0 enabling technologies and core applications that cause a behavioural shift. This research, therefore, develops in scientific literature, the concept of e-Business 2.0 where e-Business companies are actively using Web 2.0 to create and appropriate value from, for, and with stakeholders. Although 'e-Business 2.0' is used in a book from Robinson et al. (1999), the meaning is different. A perspective of van der Sleen (2007) who refers to contact with customers and suppliers, is more related. However, scientific theory on Web 2.0, let alone e-Business 2.0, is scarce. As can be seen in the figure, this research also makes a distinction between an internal and external focus (figure 2).

This research looks at e-Business 2.0 and has an external focus, e-Business 2.0 pure players depend on Web 2.0 to create and appropriate value with a focus to external customers, instead of internal organisations. The latter focus is called 'Enterprise 2.0' and is introduced by McAfee (2006a). McAfee (2006a, p. 23) argues that 'there is a new wave of business communication tools including blogs, wikis and group messaging. There are new digital platforms for generating, sharing and refining information that are already popular on the Internet. These platforms are collectively labeled Web 2.0 technologies. The term 'Enterprise 2.0' focuses only on those platforms in which companies can buy or build in order to make the practices and outputs of their knowledgeable workers visible.' Enterprise 2.0 looks at Web 2.0 technologies and practices within organisations and businesses and is therefore, referred to as internal focus. McAfee (2007, p. 52) simply and concisely defines Enterprise 2.0 as 'the emerging use of Web 2.0 technologies like blogs and wikis within the Intranet'.

Next to e-Business 2.0 pure players, companies that acquire parts of e-Business 2.0 characteristics and regular e-Business (e.g. e-Commerce) companies are also active on the Internet. Larger companies can learn from these, often smaller, e-Business 2.0 companies who display themselves as early adopters (Rogers, 1995) and use it to adopt to market changes and/or to Enterprise 2.0. The concept of e-Business 2.0 highlights that e-Business is evolving. E-Business 2.0 is a part of e-Business and can also be referred to as a new stage in e-Business that will become more prominent in the next few years. E-Business will adopt more e-Business 2.0 aspects and this is in correspondence with Van der Vlist et al. (2007), who argue that the e-Business and the Internet have reached a stage where its growth would slowly start to decline. Traditional media producers controlled the Internet and mergers and acquisitions signified that the Internet industry had started its consolidation phase. From a social perspective, the Internet was mostly used to read. This was however, not the meaning of the World Wide Web (www) and was not the case at the beginning of the Internet. The Web was originally designed as a medium where scientists could easily share their documents (Leiner & Cerf, et al., 2003). According to van der Vlist et al. (2007) this was still the case when publishing home pages and editing was still easy because of simple technology and a smaller group of participants. In the last decade, the Internet has had more difficult tools and technologies added and more people were interested in using the Internet, which resulted in a passive Internet usage. With simple Web 2.0 technologies the Internet is becoming a read/write web again. Web 2.0 enables Internet users to participate and share contributions again in a simple manner.

Recent research shows that this changed the way we use the Internet completely; 'nearly half of online consumers participate in at least one Web 2.0 activity with 13% coming from creators (e.g. publish WebPages or blogs, upload photos), 19% from critics (e.g. comment rate or review), 15% collectors (e.g. use RSS or tag WebPages), 19% from joiners (e.g. use social networking sites), and 33% from spectators (e.g. read blogs, watch peer-generated videos and listen to podcasts)' (Forrester Research, 2006a). Although research reveals that a low number of Internet users are familiar with the definition of Web 2.0, many people do use it (Ruigrok, NetPanel 2007). By several experienced people, it is already pointed out that Web 2.0 changes our economy and business perspective. For instance, Charron, Favier et al. (2006a) argues that top down-management must be abandoned; Hinchcliffe (2007) points out to focus on communication in the form of conversation, instead of a monologue; and Sturgeon (2006) writes about new levels of interactivity. This research tries to extend this by providing first insight in companies that already take advantage of Web 2.0. (Vincent, 2007)

Vincent (2007) indicated this research tries to give first answers to problems that are argued: Our first problem from a theoretical approach is that theory on value creation in e-Business is relatively scarce. This is related to a more practical problem that companies could make incorrect decisions, because of scarce theory. With the upcoming of new developments of Web 2.0 a second problem arises and results in the fact that extending theory on value drivers in e-Business becomes even more relevant: Previous theory on value creation in e-Business might not be applicable anymore. Amit and Zott (2001) research value drivers in e-Business companies before 2001. With new aspects of Web 2.0 these results might not be up to date anymore. Therefore the objective of this research is to further develop Entrepreneurship and Strategic Management Theory on value creation in e-Business, by providing first insights in value drivers in e-business companies that use Web 2.0. To reach this goal this research tries to give first answers to the central research question, if value drivers associated with Web 2.0 are different from known value drivers in e-business?

Leveraging Enterprise Web 2.0 for Competitive Advantage

What is Enterprise Web 2.0?

For the last 3 years, web 2.0 and social networking have been all the rage in the Internet community. This is where the VC money is going, the media attention is focused and users are spending much of their time. Businesses are still trying to figure out what does it mean for them. Applying web 2.0 principals and attitudes to business and the enterprise can be called enterprise web 2.0. Many tend to think that becoming a 2.0 organization as the use of flashy interfaces, communities, blogs, wikis and user generated content and tried to jump on the bandwagon by adding these to their sites without comprehending the deeper and more fundamental cultural changes that make these tools effective, and have seen little gain. Web 2.0 is about attitudes and a new way of interaction with all constituents, customers, employees, and partners. With all its hype, cool startups and sexy conferences, web 2.0 still baffles many business people who see it as a playground for kids (MySpace, Facebook, YouTube) or a get-rich scam for young entrepreneurs and VC's. Many who have been through Bubble 1.0 would rather wait until the web 2.0 fads disappear to see what is left standing. Tim O'reilly has provided what many see as the most comprehensive definition of web 2.0. And while his explanation is very thorough, it is also technical in nature (Fishler, 2008).

The definition comes from Ian Davis who wrote: "Web 2.0 is an attitude, not a technology. It's about enabling and encouraging participation through open applications and services. By open I mean technically open with appropriate APIs but also, more importantly, socially open, with rights granted to use the content in new and exciting contexts." Web 2.0 is indeed defined as an attitude that can be personal or organizational. A web 2.0 organization adds specific terms and values to its code of conduct and sets priorities and incentives to promote them. The study sees web 2.0 attitudes, or to call the web 2.0 spirits, as made of the following attitudes (Ori Fishler, 2008):

A. **Open:** you don't have to share your source code to be open but from the application to the users, the approach is open. Easy to integrate with, easy to add to. Built on Sharing. Open to new ideas, Flexible, Agile, Simple, and Diverse. Interactive: the interaction among users and active participation is a core element of Web 2.0. The ability of customer and partners to respond and engage in discussions, post reviews, comments, thoughts and ideas. Agree and disagree. Provide a different point of view. Support and promote.
B. **Transparent:** Do not hide, lie, spin, manipulate, threat, or intimidate. The Internet walls are nonexistent and everything you say or do, internally or externally will be exposed. Therefore: Share as much information as possible, acknowledge mistakes, and explain decisions.
C. **Collaborative:** Listen, encourage opinions and group decisions. True collaboration is a tremendous thing producing a result much greater than the sum of the parts. It can only flourish in a nurturing environment. Social: Web 2.0 is about building relationships, trust, playing well with others, give and take, respect of each player and of the social order that is in place. Social corporate responsibility, caring about the environment

and about the local community are very important as well.

Andrew McAfee at Harvard likes to add the term Emergent, noting that out of many local interactions as web 2.0 facilitates, comes higher level structures. I'll expand that definition to include emergence of order and structure out of the seemed chaos that is online interaction. It is the transcendence of web 2.0 communities that created Wikipedia.

What can be Gained?

Enterprise web 2.0 promises substantial incentives for early adopters (Fishler, 2008):

A. Enhanced brand image, exposure and buzz. As influence circles expand, using new methods for communication and data distribution will reach an ever-expanding user base.
B. Improved customer relationships and increased loyalty. Customers will appreciate the new approach that respects and listens to them.
C. Faster feedback cycle and agile response to market opportunities. By providing real avenues for customer collaboration and listening to chatter and monitoring usage, companies can create faster release cycles and quicker response methods.
D. Improved utilization of internal creativity and innovation. When employees at all level are engaged is collaboration and discussion, great ideas and solutions can quickly surface, get reviewed and implemented
E. Better lead generation and inbound traffic. Beyond search, activity in the social web can be a great source of traffic and referrals.
F. New business channels. Whether it is finally establishing a DTC channel to leveraging social commerce applications, the new landscape provides new opportunities and new potential partnerships.

Adoption Challenges

So now, show of hands. Has your organization embraced the web 2.0 spirit? Chances are that unless you are working for a web 2.0 startup, the most you have seen is the introduction of a limited corporate blog or a Wiki's coming up on your intranet. Many companies have a deep-rooted problem with the web 2.0 spirits. It contradicts some of the fundamental principles of corporate mentality and therefore risky to undertake. In my experience very few companies have truly bought into this attitude and at the most are paying lip service by implementing some basic enterprise 2.0 applications to replace their failed and unused Intranets and KM systems. Bob Warfield provided a very insightful discussion as to the reasons companies are wary of embracing web 2.0:

The headlong rush the Web brings to expose everything to everyone scares the heck out of most corporate types. Their two biggest requests for Web 2.0 initiatives are Governance and Security, and the reasons for it are exactly what we've been discussing. It isn't just that they have "control issues". There are sound business reasons why controls have to be in place (Ori Fishler, 2008).

A. **Morale:** Do we really want everyone to know how poorly some initiative is going? How will it help to tell those who can't make a difference and would only be depressed by the knowledge? Is it fair to expose some internal squabble that was mostly sound and fury signifying nothing? Won't that just unfairly tarnish some otherwise good people's reputations and make them less effective?
B. **Governance:** Is the information legal and appropriate for everyone to know in this age of SOX and Securities Laws?
C. **Competitive Advantage:** Do I want to risk giving my competitors access to key information because I've distributed it too broadly?

Still, the web 2.0 spirit as reflected in the actions, habits and expectations of users will impact the way companies do business. Some of the most important trends include:

A. **Loss of control:** as mentioned above, companies no longer have absolute control over their brand, products and services and how they are portrayed. From rumor sites to product reviews and fake commercials, people have many more ways to learn about you and form opinions.
B. **Opinions matter:** 68% of shoppers read products reviews before making a purchase.
C. **Wider influence circles:** Information (good and bad) can quickly spread through influence and social circles. Transparency is expected and recent cover-up attempts by companies like Merck and Bear Stearns were not tolerated. Companies will have to adapt because the old practices are getting them in trouble and new opportunities for leadership position are being lost due to lack of clear web 2.0 corporate strategy or what we would call enterprise web 2.0

By embracing the new enterprise web 2.0 paradigms, businesses can create long lasting changes that will truly resonate with audiences beyond the quick fix of adding a marketing blog to the web site and some promotional videos. As these changes take time to implement, early adopters and market leaders can create a significant competitive advantage by differentiating themselves and reaping the benefits (Ori Fishler, 2008).

Enterprise Web 2.0

A Butler Group Report

In some circles, the terms 'Enterprise Web 2.0' and 'Enterprise 2.0' are used interchangeably to describe the application of Web 2.0 ideas and technologies in the enterprise; however, Butler Group believes that a clear distinction exists between the use of these two terms, and that this differentiation is important to maintain, as it enables a more meaningful discussion to be had when examining the future role of IT within the business (butlergroup, 2008).

Enterprise 2.0

Professor McAfee at Harvard (2006) argues there is a new wave of business communication tools including blogs, wikis and group messaging. There are new digital platforms for generating, sharing and refining information that are already popular on the Internet, where they are collectively labeled Web 2.0 technologies. The term "Enterprise 2.0" focus only on those platforms that companies can buy or build in order to make visible the practices and outputs of their knowledge workers. Enterprise 2.0 is all about Web 2.0 technologies and practices within organisations and businesses. Andrew McAfee provides a clear, clean explanation of Enterprise 2.0; the emerging use of Web 2.0 technologies like blogs and wikis within the Intranet (McAfee, 2007). He has introduced his "SLATES" mnemonic to help guide those creating or acquiring Enterprise 2.0 software. SLATES describes the combined use of effective enterprise search and discovery, using links to connect information together into a meaningful information ecosystem using the model of the Web, providing low-barrier social tools for public authorship of enterprise content, tags to let users create emergent organizational structure, extensions to spontaneously provide intelligent content suggestions similar to Amazon's recommendation system, and signals to let users know when enterprise information they care about has been published or updated, such as when a corporate RSS feed of interest changes (McAfee, 2006).

As in previous innovation cycles, whenever multiple point capabilities converge – such as wireless, pervasive broadband, and online collaboration – many new applications become possible.

In these cases, consumers tend to adopt the new services and products before the enterprise, but in the end the enterprise market is usually far larger and more profitable. In McKinsey's and Sand Hill Group's Software Industry Report 2006 state that the hype around "Web 2.0" for consumers – with its rapid innovation in content tools (e.g., blogs, wikis, user editing and tagging) heralds a much larger opportunity to put these innovations to work in the enterprise. Many innovations, collectively termed Web 2.0, will fully reach the enterprise – as in previous cycles, innovation developed for individual users will translate into substantial enterprise opportunities (Berryman & Jones, et al., 2006).

CASE STUDIES

Enterprise 2.0 for IBA, a Belgian Fast Growing Company

IBA is a worldwide company based in Belgium and active in the cancer diagnosis. It currently counts 2500 employees and has doubled its staff in less than 2 years. This fast growth makes IBA facing new organisational challenges around knowledge, innovation and collaboration management. In that context, Early Stage was in charge of auditing the company structure and the way the multiple BU's are currently collaborating. Through its proprietary methodology, made of workshops and internal structured analysis, Early Stage submitted its recommendations on the following topics (Early Stage, 2009):

1. IBA's maturity in terms of Enterprise 2.0
2. The potential social software set that best matches IBA's strategic objectives and environmental context
3. The possible locations where pilot projects can be deployed
4. The User Adoption Plan (UAP) around the pilot projects and the further deployments
5. An Enterprise 2.0 roadmap for the next 24 months

IBA is actually a challenging Enterprise 2.0 business case, for several reasons:

1. IBA is present on 4 continents and the top management must deal with different cultures and work organisations
2. The core business covers different activities around cancer diagnosis, and each one runs its own methodology, serves its own market and has its own legacy
3. The IBA staff is a mix of young engineers (Generation Y) and experienced professionals (Generation X)

In this context, a few months after the launch, Early Stage will be proud to demonstrate, thanks to a detailed KPI analysis, how collaboration platforms (and related HR management) can drastically improve the global performance of an international group (Early Stage, 2009).

Belgian Government: E-Fov 2.0 Study

In 2008-09, Early Stage run an analysis of interactive tools used for eGov 2.0 projects for the Belgian Government together with the development of a web governance model for the new Belgian federal portal. This mission had as ultimate goal the development of the basis for an "e-Government Maturity Model" (eGMM) for the Belgian government and this on the following levels: the interactivity in the service delivery, the multi-channel distribution and the compilation of available data to deliver personalised information with added value. The most evolved layers of such a model foresee notions such as « co-governance » (participative democracy) and the legal dialogue in real time with the citizen. Early Stage has developed his own maturity model for this project that is simple, flexible and adaptable.

It can be used during benchmark and audit studies but also to formulate recommendations and to develop roadmaps. The goal to apply this model consisted in the development of a roadmap but also in an e-Governance that specified the roadmaps founding principles and its sustainability. If the roadmap was intended to evolve together with the standards and best practices we know in the web-universe then it was clear that it also had to follow a strategic course that would ensure the validity of the model throughout the time and that is exactly the goal that was achieved with this e-Governance model (Laurent, 2008).

The maturity model was also based on specific fundamental values that were considered "key" in a performing and globally adopted e-delivery of the public service. These values commonly refer to the following goals:

1. Simplification
2. Transparency
3. Respect for the private life
4. Citizen's engagement
5. Distribution of the information

Another goal was also to align the different relations:

1. Align the e-Gov strategy with the "Gov" strategy (to avoid that one would not be aligned with the other one so that both are aligned)
2. Align the e-Gov strategy with the citizen (Offer interactive services that take into account the current evolutions so that they are accessible, understood and available for all the citizens. Take into account the penetration of certain equipment and the evolution of the common habits in our country. What is OK for the States is not necessarily ok for Belgium.
3. Align the e-Gov strategy with the public servant (to avoid that the public service delivery will be wrongly understood or badly handled due to the public servant's intervention in the process).
4. Align the e-Gov strategy with the existing infrastructure (make it so that the roadmap is actually implementable on the current technical infrastructure).

For this mission, Early Stage has analysed over 200 sites oriented towards e-Gov 2.0 in the whole world in order to find the "best practices". These practices have been filtered and adapted to the Belgian situation and finally led to a web governance model for the future Belgian federal portal (Laurent, 2008).

FUTURE RESEARCH DIRECTION

Enterprise 2.0 is the term used to describe how a Web 2.0 approach can be used to work more collaboratively together in business. Harvard professor Andrew McAfee coined the phrase Enterprise 2.0, defining it: the use of emergent social software platforms within companies or between companies and their partner or customers. However Enterprise 2.0 is much more than just 'Web 2.0 for business'.

Enterprise 2.0, being more a philosophy than a technology, can truly create huge added value for organizations in any sector and it is often remarkable to see in what way the Enterprise 2.0 methods are used to solve specific problems. In the near future the study will to further propose applications of Enterprise 2.0 projects in specific sectors.

CONCLUSION AND RECOMMENDATIONS

Conclusion

This research adopts Forrester's perspective on Web 2.0 (Koplowitz and Young 2007). It allows this research to clearly define the enabler aspect of Web 2.0 technologies that influence companies in e-Business, and allows a development of the concept 'e-Business 2.0'. According to Forrester Research Inc., a renowned technology and market research company,'Web 2.0 is a set of technologies and applications that enable efficient interaction among people, content, and data in support of collectively fostering new businesses, technology offerings, and social structures (Koplowitz &Young, 2007).

Enterprise 2.0 describes the introduction and implementation of Web 2.0 technologies within the enterprise, including rich Internet applications, providing software as a service, and using the web as a general platform. This topic will track the latest Enterprise 2.0 developments. According to Earlystage (2009), businesses have incumbent technology platforms, multiple data sources and many regulations and policies. Employees are drowning in a sea of information and are often unable to access the people and knowledge they need. Enterprise 2.0 is an evolutionary step forward releasing employees from the constraints and limitations of the legacy communication and productivity tools. If people feel like they can make a difference, they will. The Enterprise 2.0 approach promotes open communications that encourage respect and participation, even across geographic and cultural boundaries. Access to knowledge empowers and motivates people to strive towards common goals together. Enterprise 2.0 addresses 'knowledge silos' by enabling a common space for knowledge capture and sharing. Unlike information locked-up in email and discrete documents, this centrally captured knowledge is easier to find and use when people actually need it. It is more likely to be up to date, and it can be fully searched by all who have access.

High calibre people are attracted to companies using cutting edge technology. This is particularly true for 'Generation Y' people (today's 18–25 year olds) who already use Enterprise 2.0 technologies in their everyday lives and expect to be able to use them in the workplace too. As with many things, it takes the passing of the older generation from executive status into retirement before a true shift can occur. Over the next three years, millions of baby boomers will retire and the younger workers brought in to fill the void will not only want, but will expect similar tools in the office as those they use at home in their personal lives. The whole business world is about to face a series of new fundamental challenges that go deep into the companies' DNA and organisation. Companies will need to be guided through the fog, turning their traditional e-business masterpieces into genuine interconnected systems. Organisations who disregard those fundamental changes, don't take the necessary actions or underfund such projects will face huge corporate-wide problems.

The world is in constant evolution, everybody knows it. Most recent trends in the human behaviour and in the latest technological evolutions will allow companies and organisations to leverage the potential of a collective intelligence (and therefore the overall efficiency) thanks to adapted tools, processes and mindset. People who're about to enter the business today have grown up digital, with connected computers and mobile phones in their young hands. Social Networks leverage Social Intelligence: Social Networks are both symptoms and results of the Digital Native demographic move, and they can be put to work for business. New trends of Web technology clearly show the way towards the Web as a platform and widespread SaaS. Enterprise 2.0 enables a diverse, distributed workforce to work together efficiently on projects. Information is more accessible, and subject-matter-experts can be found quickly. This avoids duplicated effort and saves time, leading to greater efficiency and improved productivity. Enterprise 2.0 technologies are not really "new" technologies but more the combination of already existing ideas in a professional environment. The Enterprise 2.0 market (also known as the Social software market) is fully exploited by established firms but also by start-ups who are trying to position themselves in this new market. However, at this time, there is no real leader yet.

Forrester Research predicts in a recent report that enterprise spending on Web 2.0 technologies will reach $4.6 billion by the year 2013. External Web 2.0 expenditure will dwarf internal spending, by 2013, by a billion dollars. Internally, companies will spend money on internal social networking, blogs, wikis, and RSS; externally, the spending patterns will be very similar. Social networking tools that provide customer interaction, allowing customers the ability to create profiles, join discussion boards, and company blogs, for example, will receive more investment and development over the next five years. One of the main challenges of getting Web 2.0 into the enterprise will be getting past the gatekeepers of traditional I.T. Businesses have been showing interest in these new technologies, but, ironically, the interest comes from departments outside of I.T. Instead, it's the marketing department, R&D, and corporate communications pushing for the adoption of more Web 2.0-like tools.

Recommendations

Enterprise 2.0 still suffers from a couple of myths coming from the "2.0" label. But, far from being a hype word applying Web 2.0 concepts to professional organisations, it refers to a tangible reality. Earlystage (2009) shatter a few myths as follows:

One tends to consider that any concept with a '2.0' timestamp refers to a hyped-buzz reality, originating from young entrepreneurs' creativity but whose added-value is questionable or inapplicable to existing infrastructures. However, Enterprise 2.0 covers a tangible reality that goes beyond technology and tools: it answers some important challenges for companies, such as collaboration and sharing, knowledge management, mobility or work-life balance – and leverages the power of collective intelligence. Enterprise 2.0 is beyond technology – it is business-related. Most of the tools do not require big bangs and are compliant with existing frameworks on which implementation is layered on top. Most of the collaboration and knowledge management concepts proposed by recent traditional software are built-upon "features", while native Enterprise 2.0 tools put them at the heart of their philosophy. On top of that, they are most of the times compatible with existing major software.

Enterprise 2.0 puts collaboration, knowledge sharing and social intelligence at the center of the organisation's relationships. Doing so, it refers to work organisation rather than to specific skills, processes or professions, and impacts any business at any level.

The different paradigms that lead to consider Enterprise 2.0 solutions do not come from corporations' strategic decisions: they come from the evolutions of the human society and demography, putting any organisation in the line of fire. Enterprise 2.0 relies on SaaS principle, which is considered as the future of IT by most leader analysts. Security and privacy is one of the most serious components of such tools. If needed, they can even be installed on-site. Enterprise 2.0 tools are almost always cheaper than traditional products whose license costs are often high. Besides, they allow scalability as they are often billed according to the number of users. On the other way, the overall cost for the organisation should include the productivity gain and loss, and the goodwill it would gather while encouraging collaboration, knowledge sharing and collective intelligence. The part of technology in the total balance is less important than you can think.

According to Earlystage (2009), Markets & Professions Although solutions such as Wiki's, Blogs and collaboration spaces are often seen as "generic" solutions that can be implemented in any organization it is interesting to see how these tools can help organizations in specific sectors. Some examples are as follows:

1. **Finance, Bank & Insurance:** New collaboration tools are improving the transparency

of the internal workings and allow the organization to keep better track of investment portfolios and to improve risk management.
2. **Healthcare:** R & D departments can use Enterprise 2.0 tools to improve knowledge sharing and shorten research cycles for new products.
3. **Political Organisations:** Often scattered on the whole territory in local federations, E2.0 tools will help them to better communicate internally, synchronise actions, remotely collaborate on dossiers, and make members relationships easier.
4. **Strategy & Watch:** Concatenation of customized RSS feeds on monitored topics, automatically imported in a strategy dashboard, makes strategic watches easier.
5. **Universities:** Enterprise 2.0 techniques facilitate fundamental research within and between universities through collaboration authoring tools or by creating students' project teams around courses.

REFERENCES

Benkler, Y. (2002). *The wealth of networks: How social production transforms markets and freedom*. Yale University Press. Retrieved from http://www.benkler.org/Benkler_Wealth_Of_Networks.pdf

BlogSpot. (2009). *Value drivers in Web 2.0*. Retrieved from ValueWeb2.BlogSpot.com

Butlergroup. (2008). *Enterprise Web 2.0: Building the next generation workplace*. Retrieved from http://www.butlergroup.com/research/reportHomepages/EntWeb.asp.

Charron, C., Favier, J., & Li, C. Joseph, J., Neurauter, M., Cohen, S.M., et al. (2006). *D. Richard Dance, a book review: CPA and principal of Soft Resources LLC*. Retrieved from http://www.forrester.com/Research/Document/Excerpt/0,7211,38772,00.html

Charron, F. (2006a). *Social computing: How networks erode institutional power, and what to do about it*. Forrester Research.

de la Mar, V. (2007). *Value drivers in e-Business 2.0: How Web 2.0 is changing the landscape of e-Business*. Retrieved from http://valueweb2.blogspot.com/2007_03_01_archive.html

Derksen. (2007a). *Update Web 2.0*. Retrieved from http://www.upstream.nl/comments.php?id=496_0_1_0_C.

Earlystage. (2009). *Enterprise 2.0: Myths*. Retrieved from http://www.earlystage.be/enterprise20/myths.php

Fishler, O. (2008). *Leveraging Enterprise Web 2.0 for competitive advantage*. Edgewater Technology Weblog. Retrieved May 1, 2008, from http://edgewatertech.wordpress.com

Hinchcliffe, D. (2006a). *Welcome to the Web 2.0 world of Flickr,* del.icio.us, *Writely, Basecamp, Digg, and many others*. Retrieved October 13, 2006, from http://www.web2journal.com/read/178008.htm

Hinchcliffe, D. (2007). *Social media goes mainstream*. Retrieved March 14, 2007, from http://web2.socialcomputingmagazine.com/social_media_goes_mainstream.htm

Jaokar, A., & Fish, T. (2006). *Mobile Web 2.0 - The innovator's guide to developing and marketing the next generation wireless/mobile applications*. London: Futuretext Limited.

Kalakota, R., & Robinson, M. (2001). *e-Business 2.0: Roadmap for success (2nd ed.)*. Addison-Wesley Information Technology Series. Longman, Inc.

Kalakota, R., & Robinson, M. (2009). *e-Business 2.0: Emerging business models*. Indianapolis: Informit.

Koplowitz & Young. (2007). *What is Web 2.0? And how are businesses making use Of Web 2.0 tools and techniques?* Retrieved from http://www.forrester.com/rb/teleconference/what_is_web_20_and_how_are/q/id/1846/t/1

Laurent. (2008). *Belgian government: e-gov 2.0 study*. Retrieved October 2, 2008, from http://www.earlystage.be/belgian-government-e-gov-20-study

Leiner, B. M., Cerf, V. G., Clark, D. D., Kahn, R. E., Kleinrock, L., & Lynch, D. C. (2003). *A brief history of the Internet, version 3.32*. Internet Society.

MacManus, R., & Porter, J. (2005). *Web 2.0 for designers*. Digital Web Magazine.

McAfee, A. (Spring 2007). The future of the Web. *MIT Sloan Management Review*, 49-64.

McAfee, A. P. (2006). *Enterprise 2.0: The dawn of emergent collaboration*. MIT Sloan Management Review.

McAfee, A. P. (2006a). *I can quote them*. The Business Impact of IT.

O'Reilly, T. (2005). *What is Web 2.0: Design patterns and business models for the next generation of software*. Retrieved September 12, 2006, from http://www.oreillynet.com/pub/a/oreilly/tim/news/2005/09/30/what-is-web-20.html

Perez, C. (2002). *Technological revolutions and financial capital: The dynamics of bubbles and golden ages*. Cheltenham, UK: Edward Elgar.

Ray, R. (2000). *This is real e-Business*.

Robinson, M., Tapscott, D., et al. (1999). *e-Business 2.0: Roadmap for success*. Boston: Addison-Wesley Professional.

Rogers, E. M. (1995). *Diffusion of innovations* (5th ed.). NY: Free Press, Simon & Schuster.

Ruigrok NetPanel. (2007). *Web WHAT? - Web 2.0 research*. SlideShare Inc.

Stage, E. (2009a). *Enterprise 2.0 for IBA, a Belgian fast growing company*. Retrieved from http://www.earlystage.be/success-stories/

Stage, E. (2009b). *Challenges of the Enterprise 2.0: Ten facts*. Retrieved from http://www.earlystage.be/challenges/

Sturgeon, W. (2006). *Cheat sheet: Web 2.0. What on earth is it and should you care?* Retrieved from http://networks.silicon.com/webwatch/0,39024667,39161662,00.htm

Surowiecki, J. (2005). *The wisdom of crowds: Why the many Are smarter than the few, and how collective wisdom shapes business, economies, societies*. Random House.

van der Sleen, G. (2007). *Nu alles 2.0! Web, e-Business, enterprise en meer?* Retrieved August 19, 2007, from http://the-efuture.blogspot.com/2007/03/nu-alles-20-web-e-business-enterprise.html

van der Vlist, E., & Vernet, A. (2007). *Professional Web 2.0 programming*. Indianapolis: Wiley Publishing, Inc.

Yin, V. (2009). New *Web: mainstream Web 2.0*. Verecom Web design blog. Retrieved from http://www.verecom.com.au/verecomblog/wordpress/new-web-mainstream-web-20-what-is-e-business-20/2009/02/

ADDITIONAL READING

Allindialive. (2009). *Enterprise 2.0: e-business transformation*. Retrieved from http://toostep.com/insight/enterprise-2-0-ebusiness-transformation?t=online-business

Cawthorne, J. (2010). *Evaluating SharePoint 2010 as an Enterprise 2.0 platform*. Retrieved from http://bx.businessweek.com/enterprise-20/view?url=http%3A%2F%2Fwww.cmswire.com%2Fcms%2Fenterprise-20%2Fevaluating-sharepoint-2010-as-an-enterprise-20-platform-007417.php

Davila, T., Epstein, M. J., & Shelton, R. (2006). *Innovation: Creating long-term value in new business models and technology*. Wharton School Publishing.

de Pasquale, F. & Siemens (2010). *Innovation in an Enterprise 2.0 world*. Retrieved from http://bx.businessweek.com/enterprise-20/view?url=http%3A%2F%2Ffeedproxy.google.com%2F~r%2FFrontEndOfInnovationBlog%2F~3%2Fwct4x6YMbX0%2Ffei2010-innovation-in-enterprise-20.html

Elphick, K. (2010). *Approaching Enterprise 2.0, beware your mindset*. Retrieved from http://bx.businessweek.com/enterprise-20/view?url=http%3A%2F%2Fdigitalbridges.wordpress.com%2F2010%2F05%2F04%2Fapproaching-enterprise-2-0-beware-your-mindset%2F

Haque, U. (2009). *Why ideals are the new business models*. Harvard Business Publishing.

Morgan, J. (2010a). *Implementing Enterprise 2.0 at Océ, part one: Business, drivers, http*. Retrieved from //www.jmorganmarketing.com/implementing-enterprise-2-0-at-oce-part-one-business-drivers/

Morgan, J. (2010b). *Implementing Enterprise 2.0 at Océ, part two: Making the push*. Retrieved from http://www.cloudave.com/link/implementing-enterprise-2-0-at-oce-part-two-making-the-push

Scarpazza, D. P. (2009). *High performance computing: Is Larrabee for the rest of us?* Retrieved from http://www.drdobbs.com/high-performance-computing/221601028;jsessionid=RLHRYH3UZFBKNQE1GHRSKHWATMY32JVN

Thompson, M. (2010). *Creating a typology of Enterprise 2.0 use cases*. Retrieved from http://bx.businessweek.com/enterprise-20/view?url=http%3A%2F%2Fwww.headshift.com%2Fblog%2F2010%2F04%2Funderstanding-enterprise-20-us.php

Viscio, A. J., & Pasternack, B. A. (1996). *Toward a new business model: Strategy & business, global commercial consulting firm*. Booz & Company.

KEY TERMS AND DEFINITIONS

Web 2.0: In the simplest terms Web 2.0 is the phrase being applied to 'the second coming' of the Internet. The 2.0 name is a clear allusion to the naming convention of software updates; this is the Internet version 2.0 (Sturgeon 2006).

Software as a Service (SaaS): Web 2.0 service is a combination of software and data. Individual, the software and the databases are of limited value, but together they create a new type of service. In this context, the value of software lies in being able to manage the (vast amounts of) data. The better it can do, the more valuable the software becomes.

Mashup: Web 2.0 website are often a combination of data from two or more sources into one experience, this is called a mashup. According to O'Reilly (2005) the race is on to own certain classes of core data.

E-Business 2.0: Although 'e-Business 2.0' is used in a book from Robinson et al. (1999), the meaning is different. A perspective of van der Sleen (2007) who refers to contact with customers and suppliers, is more related. e-Business 2.0 has an external focus, e-Business 2.0 pure players depend on Web 2.0 to create and appropriate value with a focus to external customers, instead of internal organisations. The concept of e-Business 2.0 highlights that e-Business is evolving. e-Business 2.0 is a part of e-Business and can also be referred to as a new stage in e-Business that will become more prominent in the next few years.

Enterprise 2.0: The term "Enterprise 2.0" focus only on those platforms that companies can buy or build in order to make visible the practices and outputs of their knowledge workers. Enterprise 2.0 is all about Web 2.0 technologies and practices within organisations and businesses. Andrew McAfee provides a clear, clean explanation of Enterprise 2.0; the emerging use of Web 2.0 technologies like blogs and wikis within the Intranet (McAfee 2007). McAfee (2006a: 23) argues that 'there is a new wave of business communication tools including blogs, wikis and group messaging. There are new digital platforms for generating, sharing and refining information that are already popular on the Internet. These platforms are collectively labeled Web 2.0 technologies. The term 'Enterprise 2.0' focuses only on those platforms in which companies can buy or build in order to make the practices and outputs of their knowledgeable workers visible.' Enterprise 2.0 looks at Web 2.0 technologies and practices within organisations and businesses and is therefore, referred to as internal focus.

Social Computing: Orrester Research Inc. refers social computing to 'easy connections brought about by cheap devices, modular content, and shared computing resources, that are having a profound impact on our global economy and social structure (Koplowitz and Young 2007).

Chapter 2
Management 2.0:
Managing Knowledge Workers in the 21st Century

Moria Levy
Israeli Knowledge Management Forum, Israel

ABSTRACT

"The most important, and indeed the truly unique, contribution of management in the 20th Century was the fifty-fold increase in the productivity of the manual work in manufacturing. The most important contribution management needs to make in the 21st Century is similarly to increase the productivity of knowledge work and the knowledge worker."

Peter Drucker, 1999

The world has changed a great deal since modern management principles were established one hundred years ago, at the turn of the 20th century. This chapter suggests a new management framework for managing today's knowledge workers. This framework is based on three perspectives: analyzing the manager's tasks; observing the knowledge worker's behaviors and expectations; and management recommendations via suggested underlying guiding principles. Together these construct a framework for the new era's manager, defined here as the 2.0 manager.

DOI: 10.4018/978-1-60960-129-4.ch002

WHY IS A NEW MANAGEMENT FRAMEWORK REQUIRED?

Background

While implementing new business models in organizations may always have seemed like a good idea, nowadays it is a must. What has changed? Why do we need new business models?

Modern management paths date back to the 18th century, when Adam Smith (1776) in *The Wealth of Nations* set out the first theory of management principles, dealing with labor specialization. Much later, at the turn of the 20th century, the world was fascinated by the new management and business ideas presented by Frederick Taylor (1911) in *The Principles of Scientific Management*. Both books, and many publications in between, focus on production organizations and posit efficiency of production work as the main goal of the manager in these organizations (Drucker, 1954).

Era of Information and Knowledge

Where do we stand today? What makes the 21st century different from preceding decades? A simple tour in any organization, observing the overload of computer workstations, provides a glimpse of the new organization. We are now in an era of information and knowledge. Production work is no longer the primary job in many organizations; more and more organizations' work and wealth is based on knowledge workers.

The Knowledge Worker

The term "knowledge worker" was first coined by Drucker already in 1957, as he identified the new developing worker in *The Landmarks of Tomorrow*. "A knowledge worker is no more a sub-ordinate, as managers and organization were used to handling them. A knowledge worker is nowadays an associate" (Drucker, 1999, p. 18), "a person that thinks for a living" (Davenport, 2005, p. 10), a person whose knowledge is central to the job. A knowledge worker does not have to work solely with brainpower, but can also, like a surgeon or furnishing designer, perform manual work. What makes these people knowledge workers is both the portion and the importance of information, knowledge and thinking to their job.

If we examine the emergence of job definitions, we will probably find that most job definitions have changed over the past ten years. There are professions - like teaching - that were always knowledge, information and thinking oriented. Teaching involves knowing and thinking about how to best pass the knowledge on to the student. In many other jobs, however, computers and robots took over the manual production portions of the work. The new worker has to know how to operate these in different modes for different needs, how to understand why they do not work when they malfunction, and how to fill in the gaps with thinking that machines cannot do.

Knowledge Workers' Characteristics

Volumes can be written about the knowledge worker (e.g. *Thinking for a Living* by Tom Davenport (2005)). Of all the attributes describing the knowledge worker, the following were chosen, emphasizing the need for a new management paradigm:

The knowledge worker chooses where to work and when to leave one place of work in order to start somewhere else. The manager is no more the "big boss" who will have the last word no matter what he/she says and does. He/she has to be aware that people will not stay regardless of the conditions. Alternatives exist, and it is normal to see people moving from job to job and even changing careers. Drucker (1999) claims that these employees, the new knowledge workers, have to be managed as if they were volunteers (pp. 20-21).

People seek meaning and significance in life and in work. [We are in] "'a gradual shift from 'materialist' values (emphasizing economic and physical security above all) towards 'post-materialist' priorities (emphasizing self expression and the quality of life). Whatever we call it - the 'Fourth Great Awakening', 'post-materialist' values, 'meaning want'- the consequences are the same. Meaning has become a central aspect of our work and our lives[1]" (Pink, 2005, p.219). Maslow in his 1943 paper "A Theory of Human Motivation," based on generalizations made about exemplary people such as Albert Einstein, Jane Addams, Eleanor Roosevelt and Frederick Douglass, described the grounds for human motivation that enable extraordinary achievements: People seek more than physical solutions, such as making a living. They seek love and belonging, self-esteem, achievement, respect, and self-actualization. Once this theory included extraordinary people, who would seek these needs in other places; nowadays, this is a concern of most knowledge workers. These needs must be fulfilled not only in life but also specifically at work. Fulfilling these needs is one of the manager's tasks.

Knowledge workers consume knowledge and information in order to perform their jobs. "For the knowledge worker in general, and especially for executives, information is their key resource" (Drucker, 1999, p. 123). They are exposed to massive volumes of knowledge and information available in many channels, above all on the web. These workers can, and sometimes do, know more than their managers regarding their jobs. The authority of the manager is no longer based on knowledge, even though we are dealing with knowledge workers.

One more attribute, interesting in the management perspective, has to do with the autonomy of knowledge workers. Knowledge workers like autonomy in their work, and like to be independent in their decision-making (Davenport, 2005, pp. 15-16). Managers cannot give up the role of managing, yet should find new alternatives for controlling decisions and managing the knowledge workers making them.

The Need for New Management Paradigms and Frameworks

In the past few years, we find more discussion about these changes and the corresponding new management paradigms and frameworks required. Some speak of ending the era of management, others about a revolution. The modest, like Hamel, speak about the need of climbing and reaching a new peak in modern management (Hamel, 2007, pp. 7-8).

Hamel, in "Moon shots for Management," describes the gathering of renowned scholars and business leaders in May 2008, as they aimed to lay out an agenda of reinventing management in the 21st century. The group came to several conclusions, the main one being that that the management methods used today, invented back at the end of the 19th century, are now "seriously out-of-date." The group therefore set a goal of reinventing management so as to make large organizations fundamentally more adaptable, more innovative and more inspiring places to work (Hamel, 2009).

To accomplish these goals, a new management methodology and framework should be devised, which suggests methods that take into consideration the knowledge workers' behavior and expectations. It should be a framework for managing, where a new relationship is forged between managers and employees; a framework that gives the manager tools for empowering the knowledge worker even though that worker may know more than the manager may and desires autonomy. Indeed, despite his/her knowledge, this employee should be trained, developed professionally, and be guided in finding the path for self-esteem, confidence, achievement, respect and maybe even for self-actualization.

THE NEW 2.0 MANAGER

Management 2.0

The term 2.0 is well-known today, and has its root in the term Web2.0. The concept of "Web2.0" began with a conference brainstorming session between O'Reilly and MediaLive International back in 2004, two years after the dot-com bubble crash, which, from March 2000 to October 2002, wiped out $5 trillion in market value of technology companies. The public did not believe the Web could ever return to its glory days. A change in mindset, one may say a revolution, was needed. The term Web2.0 was coined symbolizing a new era: what was, should remain in the past. Now is the time for a new concept, a new future. Web2.0 turned out to be the revival of the Web.

Web2.0 is based on a set of concepts and tools. Concepts as user centric; the wisdom of the crowds; and harnessing collective intelligence; Tools as social networks; blogs; wikis; and twitters (Oreilly, 2005).

The term 2.0 was first used out of the context of Web2.0 to symbolize the use of Web2.0 concepts and/or tools in other contexts: Enterprise2.0, for example, deals with use of blogs, wikis and social networks within the enterprise for organizational needs. Knowledge Management2.0 involves both usage of tools and concepts for sharing purposes within the organization (Levy, 2009, p. 131).

However, the term 2.0 is currently used to also express a broader idea of revival of paradigms, especially, but not only, being user centric. Web1.0 spoke about content ("content is the king" (Walsh, 2006)); Web2.0 is about users. It is common to find terms like Management2.0, Sales management 2.0, Marketing2.0. Some even speak about love2.0.

Management2.0 is the expression for a renewed way of thinking about management, in contrast to the existing Taylor etc. paradigm (hereby referred to as Management1.0). Management2.0 is a revival management paradigm, based on the employee (the knowledge worker) occupying the focal spot, and management taking into account the employee's enhanced needs, behaviors and expectations.

Framework

Management functions include three major-level interconnected management issues, which have not changed over the years, illustrated below:

Managers must concern themselves wit three major-level issues:

- Managing the employees.
- Managing the work, ensuring that it is accomplished (within budget) and that targets are reached.
- Managing the relations with external groups, people and entities.

All three aspects are influenced by the huge changes in the economy, by the technology leap and by the information and knowledge presently required for success. This article focuses on a management framework reflecting on all three aspects.

MANAGING EMPLOYEES

The renewed framework can be designed dealing with management through various perspectives.

Figure 1. Management major functions

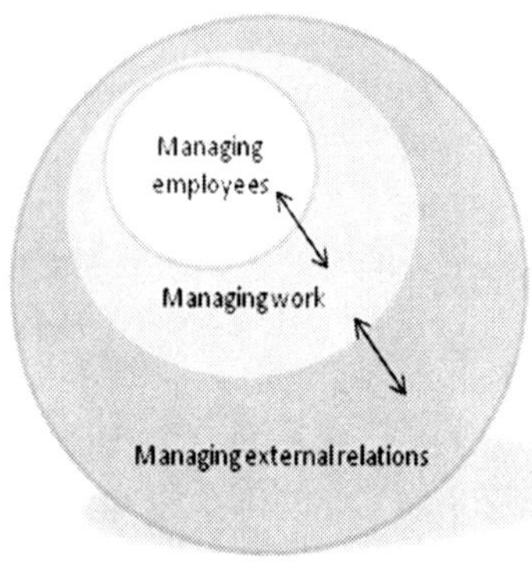

one perspective includes analyzing the desired behavior of the new manager in his/her routine functions: hiring a new employee; risk management; employee evaluation and feedback; and employees leaving work.

A different perspective involves analyzing the characteristics of the knowledge worker, and, in response, recommending actions for the manager. Examples of the knowledge worker's characteristics include: the desire for autonomy; having certain knowledge that exceeds that of the manager, etc.

A third perspective entails examining the underlying guiding principles of management, and how these are reflected in the relations between the manager and the knowledge worker. Examples of underlying guiding principles include: democracy in management; the place of values in management; emotional vs. rational management, etc.

Interconnections between the three perspectives do exist. Describing all three in the suggested management framework, however, provides a richer understanding of management in the new era.

The three perspectives and their interrelations are illustrated in the following figure:

As defined above, all three perspectives are focused within this work on managing the employee.

Figure 2. Management perspective and interrelations

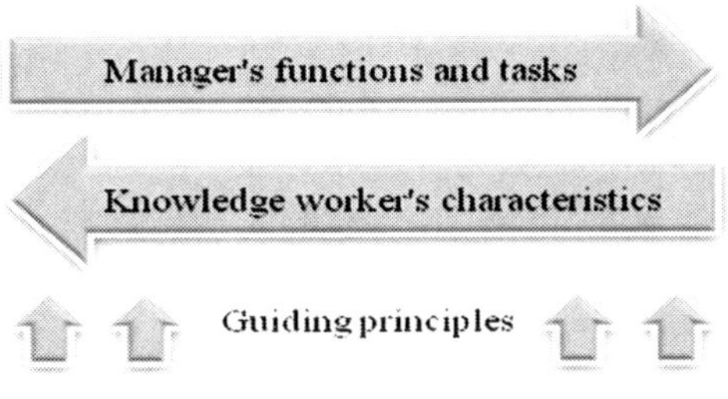

The Manager's Functions and Tasks

No single article can cover all of the manager's functions and tasks; thus this work focuses on one of the three major management functions, employee management, leaving the others out. Furthermore, managers differ each from each other, based on the specific profession, organizational structure, employees' knowledge and seniority, etc., and, therefore, it is not pertinent to cover all management tasks. The suggested framework covers universal core functions and tasks, shared by most managers in most organizations. These functions include:

1. Hiring: Examining potential new employees for job.
2. Recruiting and absorption.
3. Controlling work of employee.
4. Rewarding
5. Yearly Evaluation
6. Employee Leaving work

For each management function or task, a concise comparison emphasizes the differences between the typical actions of a Management 1.0 manager and those actions recommended in Management 2.0: (Table 1)

The table emphasizes the complexity of the manager's functions and tasks. We live in a dynamic era of information and knowledge. The knowledge worker has to know how to learn, and the manager has to understand that he/she will not be able to know all that their employees know. Therefore, choosing a new employee is not an easy task, and involves anticipating not only what the potential knowledge worker knows now, but also what s/he will know in the future. Managing the progress in work achieved by the knowledge worker is even more challenging. Feedback and questioning techniques are offered. When the user leaves, accumulated information and knowledge have to be transferred. As these become more essential to business success, and, as the knowl-

Table 1. Management 2.0 recommendations for fulfilling functions and tasks

Function / task	Management 1.0	Management 2.0
Hiring: Examining potential new employees for job	Main parameters for choosing the new employee: o Knowledge and skills. o Salary and social security conditions	In addition: o Ability of K.W.[2] to learn (Davenport, 2005, pp. 159-160). o Ability of K.W. to work in a team (Davenport, 2005, pp. 12, 168). o Fit between K.W.'s desires for self esteem and self-actualization to the company's organizational culture and values (Maslow, 1943, pp. 379-380).
Recruiting and absorption	Includes: o Absorption - as short as possible. o Training	In addition: o Matching expectations with employee as to a length of absorption (in many cases, one year). o Continually coaching, and understanding and filling knowledge gaps (Leonard & Swap, 2005, pp. 192-199).
Controlling work of employee	o Telling the employee how to do things correctly. o Explaining.	o Using questioning technique to understand why decisions were taken by K.W., and further guiding him/her how to better do the job.
Rewarding	o Salary was the main incentive component. Rewarding existed, and was not to complicate to decide who deserves it.	o People seek meaning in work. Incentives and rewards are some of the most powerful management tools available (Davila, Epstein & Shelton, 2006, p. 179). o Putting efforts in the decision who to reward: Understanding who is to be rewarded can be a complicated task, as the manager's knowledge of ones work and success is partially depended on what the K.W. updates. Rewarding is not simple as measurement of work and success are not trivial. Nevertheless, rewarding should be clear and regarded as "fair" in order to be organizational effective. o Rewarding should be more "soft" oriented, answering needs of honor, esteem, respect and appreciation of the K.W. (Maslow, 1943, p. 379).
Yearly Evaluation	o Reflective evaluation as to strengths and weaknesses.	o Feedback concentrating on 2-3 topics, in which manager decides that change is required and applicable.
Employee Leaving work	o Appointment of tasks to other people. o Knowledge transfer.	In addition: o Knowledge retention program, especially for retiring K.W.s (Delong, 2004).

Notes:

a. The main management functions or tasks have not changed as society has moved from the production era to the knowledge and information era.

b. In some areas, the change involves the addition of new actions and is a sub-task to previous actions.

edge becomes more complicated (Delong, 2004, pp. 16-18), this task is not as easy as one might wish.

The above table does not provide the full, rich picture of Management2.0. In order to understand the suggested framework, two additional perspectives of management are described.

The Knowledge Worker's Characteristics

The knowledge worker's characteristics are influenced by the changes that accompany the information and knowledge era. These changes are no revolution; they have occurred gradually over the past twenty to thirty years. The accumulative shift, though, is significant. Management techniques, which were designed by Taylor etc. and served us all, are not sufficient in the 2.0 era.

Main characteristics of the employee in the 2.0 era, include:

1. The knowledge worker chooses where to work and when to leave.
2. The knowledge worker seeks meaning and significance in work.
3. The knowledge worker consumes knowledge and information in order to perform his/her job. Information volume is high, and knowledge and information are significant to organizational and business success.
4. The knowledge worker knows more than the manager regarding the job.
5. The knowledge worker likes autonomy.

Management 2.0 techniques dealing with these characteristics include: (see Table 2)

This table analyzes the 2.0 managers recommended actions and behaviors from the perspective of the knowledge worker and his/her characteristics. The main change the manager has to deal with can be summarized in one sentence: If in the past the manager's main concern was the work, nowadays the 2.0 manager's concern is both the work as well as the knowledge workers. Managers that deal with workers as a technical resource only will find it hard to survive in the long term. Managing the knowledge worker is not only essential, it is complicated, It is complicated as the knowledge worker has needs other than money (requiring the manager to deal with resources with which /she he is less familiar); as the knowledge worker knows many times more than the manager; and as the knowledge worker wants his/her autonomy in work. Management has to be performed differently than in the past. Management underlying guiding principles hold a significant role in the difference.

Table 2. Management 2.0 recommendations as to knowledge worker's characteristics

Employee in the 2.0 era- K.W. characteristics	**Employee in the 1.0 era**	**Management 2.0**
The K.W. chooses where to work and when to leave (Davenport, 2005, p. 198)	Employees usually worked in one place and rarely had more than one career	The manager has to focus not only on achieving work and controlling its accomplishment on time, on budget and according to quality standards, but also s/he must verify that the K.W. is satisfied with doing the work. Drucker defines new management in this context as volunteer management (Drucker, 1999. pp. 20-21).
The K.W. seeks meaning and significance in work (Maslow, 1943, p.378-380); (Dychtwald, Erickson & Morison, 2006, pp. 207-227)	Employees regarded the organization as a place that only supplies money and means for earning a living.	The manager has to develop ways to empower the K.W., enabling the fulfillment of the K.W.'s needs: 1. Love and belonging- providing a sense of team and organization loyalty, and place for each employee to feel part of it. 2. Esteem- providing the K.W. with feedback that not only advances tasks, but also gives the employee a sense of respect and self-esteem. Making decisions in a way that employees feel respected; etc. 3. Self actualization- helping the K.W. find a path for fulfilling her/his personal vision, while still advancing the organizational vision. Dychtwald, Erickson and Morison (2006) suggest providing the K.W. with stimulation, variety, edification, connection, control and value. These can help in the development of meaningful work and engaged workers (pp. 207-227).

continued on following page

Table 2. continued

Employee in the 2.0 era- K.W. characteristics	Employee in the 1.0 era	Management 2.0
The K.W. consumes knowledge and information in order to perform his/her job. Information volume is high, and knowledge and information are significant to organizational and business success (Davenport, 2005, p. 124)	Employees did consume information and even knowledge, yet: 1. Not all employees consumed information and knowledge for their job. 2. The information and knowledge were rather static. 3. The volumes of information and knowledge were not high. 4. The information and knowledge were not as significant to organizational and business success.	The manager: 1. Has to provide time for reading and learning. 2. Has to enable social networking of the K.W. outside the team and/or organization boundaries, enabling him/her to ask but also to answer others' queries and requests (Leonard & Swap, 2005, pp. 230-244) 3. Has to provide means for documentation and content organization.
The K.W. knows more than the manager regarding the job	In many cases, the manager performed similar work to that of the employee in his/her past. The information and knowledge required for performing the job rarely changed, and the manager therefore knew all the employee knew, and even more (being more senior). The manager was often a professional authority.	Rapid change of knowledge and information influence the 2.0 manager's ability to remain a professional authority if s/he is not connected to field work. The manager: 1. Should continue performing limited, focused fieldwork as means for maintaining professionalism. 2. Should recognize and admit that the K.W. may know more than him/herself. 3. Should seek alternative sources of authority, as knowledge based authority is no longer sufficient. 4. Should develop alternative techniques for controlling the work and worker; should develop techniques for empowering the K.W. professionally. All this should be done in the paradoxical situation where the manager has less specific knowledge than the K.W.
The K.W. likes autonomy (Drucker, 1999, pp.145-146); (Davenport, 2005, pp. 15-17).	Employees had no or very limited autonomy in their work.	The 2.0 manager has to respect the desire for autonomy, yet is not less responsible for the work and its accomplishment on time, on budget and according to quality standards. It is recommended that the 2.0 manager should: 1. Delegate limited responsibility to the K.W. as a condition for receiving the desired autonomy. 2. Distribute autonomy where risk is not too high and can be controlled, understanding this is not only a wish of the K.W. but also a way of empowering him/her professionally. 3. In appropriate places, centralize the decision of what to do (leaving it to the manager) and distribute the decision of how to carry it out to the K.W.

Underlying Guiding Principles

In the previous paragraph, the knowledge worker was described as one that likes autonomy. One of the corresponding recommendations was to continue centralizing the "what," while distributing the "how." Distinguishing the "what" from the "how" may serve as a useful tool for explaining the suggested changes in the management2.0 framework. Most of the manager's traditional functions and responsibilities have remained; some have been added, none can be spared. The main differences between the 1.0 manager and the 2.0 manager are in the "how." The list of guiding principles is long. The following includes representative guiding principles on how to manage in the 21 century:

1. Combined emotional and rational management.
2. Democracy.
3. Innovation encouragement
4. Social involvement.

5. Social involvement.

Explanation of these guiding principles: (see Table 3)

Five guiding principles for the 2.0 manager were described: combined emotional and rational management; democracy; innovation encouragement; values; and social involvement. Each guiding principle can be adopted by all managers, even those without knowledge workers to manage. Each guiding principle is a representative example, guiding the manager as to the distance management has come, and the revolutionary way of thinking that the 2.0 manager should adopt, as compared to the period in which management 1.0 frameworks and methods were published.

To summarize the renewed framework for managing employees, management can be described and defined through various perspectives. Three perspectives were chosen here, and the issue of employee management was defined accordingly:

1. Understanding management through examining universal, typical employees' management tasks;
2. Understanding management through analyzing knowledge workers' characteristics, and deriving recommendations for managing them.
3. Understanding management through underlying guiding principles for the 2.0 manager.

MANAGING WORK

The previous sections defined a renewed framework for managing the employees - the knowledge workers. Managing, however, involves more than managing employees. Management functions include three major-level interconnected management issues: managing employees; managing work; and managing external relations.

If we compare work areas to one hundred years ago, when existing management 1.0 methods were established, we find the same fields exist: Doctors and teachers existed in the past and will continue to exist in the future; this is true also of factory workers. Engineers, scientists, builders, judges, bankers, consultants and most other professions have served society for hundreds and even thousands of years. We are exposed to new professions, such as high-tech professionals, but these are in the minority; management as a paradigm will not change just because several new professions have emerged.

However, the work in each profession has developed, and, more importantly, the manager's knowledge of each and every topic and assignment is far less deep than in the past. Employees know more and have more autonomy in their work; this means that the manager knows less. Nevertheless, the manager remains responsible for completing the work. This may seem contradictory. On one hand, the manager lacks some levels of understanding, as opposed to the past, when s/he knew and experienced the field. Even if the manager grew from the same position as his/her employees, the field constantly and rapidly changes, and the knowledge grows greater every year, leaving the manager's knowledge incomplete. Furthermore, knowledge workers enjoy autonomy in their work and like to be independent (Davenport, 2005, pp. 15-16). The manager's task of knowing what is happening and actually managing the work is not simple. On the other hand, the level of responsibility has not changed at all. The manager must make decisions and ensure that work is completed within the given resources (time, money and personnel) and with the highest quality.

The 2.0 manager has to emphasize some aspects of the known techniques, enabling achievement of classic management goals while having limited knowledge. Following are the manager's main functions:

1. Decision making
2. Time management
3. Budget management

Table 3. Management 2.0 underlying management principles

Guiding principle	Explanation
Combined emotional and rational management	Importance of rational decision making is well known and understood; less understood is the place and significance of emotional decision making. Tversky and Kahneman (1981) have suggested the prospect theory as a way to understand how people take decisions in conditions of uncertainty, proving that subjective judging is common (especially when low probabilities exist). Leonard and Swap (2004) explain that what we consider "gut-feeling" decision making may be expressed as intuition or insight that might "accurately reflect the expert's knowledge" (pp. 60-62). The 2.0 manager, who deals not only with work but also with workers: 1. Must understand that pattern recognition, observed as intuition, is a technique assisting the expert to best handle the mass volumes of knowledge and information (Leonard & Swap, 2004, pp. 195-196). 2. Can benefit from combining the emotional and rational decision-making about work and workers, recognizing that intuition is more than "gut feeling." 3. Can benefit from combining the emotional and rational decision-making about work and workers, recognizing the place of emotional intelligence in business and life (Goleman, 1995).
Democracy	Organizations are not democracies, although it may be wise for the 2.0 manager to include democracy in his/her guiding principles, used selectively where appropriate: 1. Democracy can play a positive role in engaging the employee to work. As stated earlier, the K.W. chooses where to work and when to leave, and the K.W. seeks meaning and significance in work. Having the K.W. share in decision making processes can have a positive influence on his/her sense of self-esteem, confidence, achievement, respect and self-actualization. 2. Professionally, it is better to make some decisions after consulting with many people. This claim is known as "the wisdom of the crowds," a term coined by James Surowiecki in 2004. The idea is that, in defined conditions, consulting more people and asking for their opinion, results in better decisions. It is important to understand the conditions under which this claim proves to be true: a. Asking people with diverse knowledge and opinions. b. Independence of each person consulted (no or minimal tribe and herding effects). c. Aggregation mechanism of collecting the various opinions and integrating them into one decision (Surowiecki, 2004, pp. 78-79). It must be noted that democratic decisions are resource consuming (mainly time consuming) and can potentially put the manager's authority at risk. It is therefore recommended to prefer democracy when time is not significant and/ or in strategic and innovative situations where decisions are neither critical nor trivial.
Innovation encouragement	For many years, innovation was the property of focused groups in organizations: marketing, strategies and R&D. In the knowledge and information era, innovation can and should develop everywhere in the company (Davila, Epstein & Shelton, 2006, p. 10). The 2.0 manager should: 1. Know that innovation may be operational, but may also be connected to products and/ or services, strategy and even to management itself (Hamel, 2007, p. 32); "integrate innovation into the company's basic business mentality" (Davila, Epstein & Shelton, 2006, p. 11). 2. Understand that innovation can stem from each worker. The manager should enable it to develop, and communicate these expectations to the knowledge workers. 3. Enable and nurture working in teams. Small teams facilitate discussion and strengthen innovation (Davila, Epstein & Shelton, 2006, p.137). 4. Work with temporary constellations of people: Mixed heterogeneous teams, assigning different people to different tasks with different teammates. (Surowiecki, 2004, pp. 40-65); (Hedlund, 1994).
Values	Volumes have been written on the importance of vision, mission and values. Collins and Porras (1997) have researched eighteen visionary companies, seeking the cooperative elements that turn them to lasting, excellent companies. "Our research showed that a fundamental element in the 'ticking clock' of a visionary company, is a *core ideology* - core values and sense of purpose beyond just making money, that guides and inspires people the organization and remains relatively fixed for long periods of time" (pp. 46-79). Values were important to business success before the knowledge and information era; their significance, however, has increased as the K.W. seeks meaning and significance in work. The 2.0 manager should: 1. Ensure values exist and are incorporated into business processes and decision-making. 2. Try promoting combined organizational and personal vision and values (Senge, 1990, pp. 191-215).

continued on following page

Table 3. continued

Guiding principle	Explanation
Social involvement	Social involvement is an important value in life, but is naturally tagged with "after work" hours, as a decision of the individual rather than of the organization. In the past few years, many organizations have joined the social involvement movement and are contributing money or employees' time to assist those people or causes needing help. Social involvement of organizations is a win-win-win situation. Those who need the help obviously win. However, the organization also benefits. Knowledge workers are seeking meaning and significance, and social involvement is a noble instrument through which the organization can provide this meaning. The K.W. benefits as well. Pink, in *A Whole New Mind*, explains how volunteering is a great way to develop empathy. Empathy- defined by Pink as one of the six senses possessed by right-brainers – is a factor in the success of those people in and out of the business world with exceptional abilities and leadership qualities (Pink, 2005, p. 184).

4. Quality management
5. Planning
6. Risk management
7. Measuring

The following table explains the type of emphasis needed for each task in the 2.0 management era: (see Table 4)

Management work has not changed. Change is driven by the softness of tasks and of defining business success, by the manager not always being proficient in details and by rapid changes in the market These turn the classic management tasks of decision making, time management, budget management, quality management, planning, risk management and measuring into sophisticated tasks. The 2.0 manager has to think wisely in order to perform them properly.

MANAGING EXTERNAL RELATIONSHIPS

Managers always had to manage relations with customers and suppliers, but certain characteristics of the 21st century are changing the way organizations observe external relationships:

1. Customers.
2. Noncustomers.
3. Competitors.

External relationships always existed and will always exist. The boundaries between the different types of external groups are not as sharply drawn as in the past. 2.0 managers have to invest more effort in customers as well as in non-customers, trying to add them to customer lists.

TECHNOLOGY

Technology has a great impact on the 2.0 manager's capabilities. Below are a few examples of software technologies and a description of their benefit to the 2.0 manager. It should be noted that some software technologies are new (web2.0 oriented), while others may be serving already for several decades, yet remain important.

1. **Email**: The most popular channel for transferring and sharing knowledge. The "cc" option added to every email client software enables managers to be more informed and involved compared to other knowledge transfer alternatives.
2. **Business Intelligence platforms and applications**: Enabling the 2.0 manager to manage the huge masses of data, and make decisions based on thereon (Davenport, 2005, pp. 89-90).
3. **Knowledge Management enterprise solutions (portals, ECM systems[3], communi-**

Table 4. Management functions: Emphasis in the 2.0 era

Management Function	Emphasis
Decision making	The manager cannot make all decisions alone. Furthermore, s/he cannot even be involved in all decision making processes. In the knowledge era, many decisions have to be made almost every day, and the 2.0 manager does not possess all knowledge. The manager has to decide in which areas and at which levels decisions will be made by the K.W. and where s/he as a manager will intervene. This was true in the past century for high-level managers (managing other managers); today it is true also for line managers (managing knowledge workers). As to decisions taken by the manager, it is almost impossible to know all the relevant information influencing the decision making process. Accepting the recommendation of the K.W. is not an alternative either, as it brings the manager to a place of not making the decision independently at all. Managers should request that employees describe the pros and cons of each alternative. These advantages and disadvantages, even if described by a subjective employee, can provide the manager with the tools to objectively understand the complexity of the issue, and make the proper decision. Drucker (1999) describes the new decisions to be made as "risk-taking decisions." Thus, as business success is nowadays based on the creation of value and wealth, "it requires strategic decisions based on new certainties.... These decisions are the true top management tasks" (Drucker, 1999, p. 85).
Time Management	As described earlier, knowledge oriented tasks are not as easily defined as industrial classic ones. Allocating time for each mission is not always possible. Furthermore, there is evidence that differences exist in knowledge workers' efficiency and in their ability to handle several projects or tasks simultaneously. As K.W.s are fond of autonomy (Davenport, 2005, pp. 15-16) and seek self-esteem (Maslow, 1943, pp. 379-380), the new 2.0 manager may decide to ask the K.W. to define the time needed for every task. The manager will control performance in time, synchronization between various K.W.s and their tasks, and solve conflicts when these do not line up together.
Budget Management	Budget management techniques do not seem to be affected by the knowledge era and the work of knowledge workers. This new century, though, is characterized as a fast-changing market, making it difficult to congregate within a defined budget. 2.0 organizations and managers should consider changing the budget planning routine: 1. Defining long-term plans for no more than three years. 2. Working with six-month budgets, instead of annual budgets.
Quality Management	Business success drives are changing over the years. Drucker claims, "business success is nowadays based on the creation of value and wealth" (Drucker, 1999, p. 85). Pink writes about the importance of design: where once we seized functionality, we now seek design (Pink, 2006, pp. 68-99). Quality, in these terms, may be subjective, and quality management is less obvious. Quality paradigms have been dealing with these issues over the past twenty years, suggesting frameworks for quality ISO, CMMI, etc.), yet leaving the decision of what comprises quality to the organization itself. 2.0 managers can adopt the same idea: define the framework for quality, yet leave the knowledge workers the autonomy to interpret quality in their job, and to decide how quality is to be obtained. K.W.s seek meaning in their work and their incentive for quality might be higher than that of the industrial employees of the past century, thus easing the task of the manager.
Planning	Planning takes place as part of organizations' and people's efforts to ensure that targets can be reached. Without planning, success may be coincidental. Planning in the 21st century, however, is less trivial than in the past: Technology has turned the global business market into one huge market. Changes on one side of the globe affect businesses everywhere. Furthermore, the world is rapidly and frequently changing.. All this makes the planning process one of the more difficult tasks of the 2.0 manager. As with budget management, planning can be dealt with through time definitions. Handling frequent audits and discussions regarding current plans and future changes is a possible solution for the 2.0 manager. Organizations should enable the updating process of the plan as part of the regular organizational plan process. Flexible plans should be standard rather than exceptional.

continued on following page

Table 4. continued

Management Function	Emphasis
Risk Management	The 21st century may be regarded as a century of risks: On one hand, information and knowledge are available, easing the ability of the 2.0 manager to objectively make decisions based on facts (Davenport & Harris, 2007). On the other hand, rapid changes and subjectivity of value increase the risk level. Furthermore, many of the managers do not yet make enough decisions based on facts, and the number of managers competing on data and its analytics is still small (Davenport & Harris, 2007). Risk may seem increased as managers are unaware of all details of the work performed by the knowledge workers, leaving them in uncertainty. Risks need to be managed by the 2.0 manager. The techniques may be those used for decades, yet the manager cannot absorb this task alone; risk management should be performed by the manager with the assistance of the K.W.s.
Measuring	Measurement is an essential task of management: "What gets measured gets done" (Davila, Epstein & Shelton, 2006, p. 144). Measurement is, in many cases, however, a complicated task, as neither the knowledge worker's tasks nor the organization's business success can always be defined sharply. The 2.0 manager should not abandon the measurement task, rather develop techniques for measuring work with which s/he may not be completely familiar, while the work may be defined as "soft" or as having "soft" value. One technique, for example, involves focusing more on qualitative measuring. Another technique, relevant for measuring the process of pre-evaluations, is the measurement of the cost of error (Hubard, 2007).

Table 5. External relationships in the 2.0 era

Group	Relationship
Customers	Drucker discusses the growing importance of customer in the 21st century: "The starting point has to be what customers consider value… What customers consider value is always something quite different from what is value or quality to the supplier." (Drucker, 1999, p. 25). This implies close relationships - far closer than in the past - with the market, with potential customers and with customers. One technique for handling such relationships is via shared social networks, having both the manager, the customers and knowledge workers share these networks.
Noncustomers	Organizations have many more noncustomers than customers. "Even the biggest enterprise (other than a government monopoly) has many more no-customers than it has customers… And yet very few institutions know anything about the noncustomers- very few of them even know that they exist, let alone know who they are. Even fewer know why they are not customers. Yet it is with the noncustomers that change always starts." (Drucker, 1999, p. 25) Noncustomers were always important. The changes of the 21st century, turning us all into one global market, bring organizations to a new situation: more noncustomers, with the potential to be customers, and more far away, unknown noncustomers. The 2.0 manager has to define a strategy how to wisely know these noncustomers and turn them into customers.
Competitors	Competition has changed its flavor in the past 20 years. In the past, a competitor was always a competitor. Nowadays, managers find themselves competing with some organization on one project, yet having an alliance with the same organization on a different project, whether as a supplier, a partner or even a customer. The partial mergers and acquisitions of companies bring about a new situation in which two competing companies find themselves helped by the same mother company, which holds a 51 percent share. All these situations are possible and even common, and the 2.0 manager has to know how to handle them. There is no one right strategy for handling these situations. 2.0 managers have to be aware of them and of the possibility that they may occur at any time...

ties of practice, etc.): (Davenport, 2005, pp. 90-91, 193): These platforms are designed mainly for the knowledge worker. The 2.0 manager must recommend constructing these solutions that improve both the efficiency and quality of the knowledge workers s/he manages. The 2.0 manager also has the responsibility to encourage the knowledge workers to start using new knowledge management enterprise solutions.

4. **Social Networks:** Social networks serve as a main channel of relationships between the knowledge worker and his/her colleagues outside the organizational (or division) boundaries (Davenport, 2005, p. 206); (Leonard & Swap, 2005, pp. 230-244). If enterprise communities of practice deal with the enterprise (closer) colleagues, the social network is based on weekly connections with larger groups of interest, mainly outside the organization. The manager's responsibility is to encourage the knowledge worker to use this channel to share knowledge and consult. Social networks can serve also within very large enterprises.
5. **Blogs:** Blogs are a productive way for managers to communicate ideas, thoughts and messages to their employees. They are more popular within large enterprises where there is no direct contact between the manager and the employees. However, even in small organizations, these types of messages can often only be passed through this channel. The daily routine dictates concentrating on operational and professional issues, and less on managerial ones (Scoble & Israel, 2006).
6. **WIKIs:** Enterprise WIKIs are a part of the knowledge management tools each organization may choose to build according to specific business needs. WIKIs are useful in areas such as collective wisdom and content-entities-and-relations management. WIKIs should be dealt with like all other knowledge management solutions.
7. **Twitters**: Twitters are technically micro blogs, yet they serve differently from blogs. Twitters are a convenient tool for sending mini messages as an alternative to the organizational bulletin board placed on the organizational or professional portal. The twitter can serve 2.0 managers of large organizations. In small to medium organizations, the alternative channels for messages are often simpler and more efficient.

Technologies do indeed play a role in assisting the 2.0 manager manage knowledge workers under his/her responsibility, and in helping them work more efficiently. Every 2.0 manager should remember, however, that this potential enabler can backfire when data overflow (in case of BI technologies) or information and knowledge overflow (in case of other mentioned technologies) occur. One of the manager's responsibilities is to see to that data, information and knowledge are well organized and utilized (Davenport, 2005, p. 135).

It must also be noted that technology is only an enabler. The challenge of the 2.0 manager involves managing people and their emotions, needs and desires, as well as managing the work conducted by these knowledge workers and managing the external relations with suppliers, customers and other partners. In these areas, technology may be helpful, yet not main.

CHALLENGES

Management2.0 is a management paradigm, based on the employee occupying the focal spot. Thus, the management 2.is a challenge, by definition, as management is defined serving organizations' needs. 2.0 Managers have to balance between these two polar aspects of organization and individual. The suggested framework includes specific techniques for handling the challenge, and these were emphasized in the sections above. In addition, supporting technologies were suggested, easing the 2.0 manager as s/he handles the management2.0 challenge.

Yet, these do not supply a full solution, as more challenges do exist. Hereby are three examples of possible challenges and how 2.0 managers can deal with them:

1. There is and probably cannot be any predefined cookbook for management. Every manager has to be aware of the guidelines, and learn for him/herself, through self-experiencing, how to correctly manage their employees.
2. In life, contradictions may appear, as situations are multi-dimensional, not flat. Contradictions can take place between planning and rapid changes of information and knowledge; between democracy and asking questions as a supervision technique, etc. Common sense is the most effective way to decide among contradicting guidelines.
3. The manager operates in a defined environment, yet does not obtain all information on each situation, and therefore cannot always know what the right recommendation is at each specific scenario. Furthermore, the manager cannot control all partners, only him/herself. In many cases, the employee or customer can act in an un-expected manner, whether on a rational or emotional basis. The manager has to consider and re-consider his/her behavior as to the partners' one.

SUMMARY

One hundred years ago, management started to flourish, and management frameworks and methodologies arose. The world has dramatically changed since. The knowledge and information era, in which we live and work, took us a step further, and many of the employees turned to be knowledge workers. These workers are different to employees of the past, and these differences influence the relations between the typical knowledge worker and his/her manager, influence the way work is controlled, and influences the way managers develop and maintain external relations. All these result in having new paradigms to define management necessary. The new management, called "management 2.0," is employee-centric, yet retains responsibility of the manager for the employee, for the work and for external relations.

To summarize all in one sentence, one might say: Management 2.0 has to do with transforming from a boss into a leader.

FURTHER RESEARCH DIRECTIONS

Naturally, more research in this field is required. Further research directions may include management2.0 focused on productive work (as in Davenport's (2005)*Thinking for a living*); management2.0 should be further researched focused on the relationships with directorates, potential customers, customers, suppliers, colleagues and the public. This area is now in first stages of research, and much yet has to be learned in order to maximize the potential profits as from these relations.

In this work, Management2.0 was researched reflecting one of the main changes: us living in an information and knowledge era. Further research can be conducted, reflecting other changes, as new technology, dynamics of changes, wealth, etc.. These can shed more light on the management2.0 issue, adding new insights and implementation recommendations, teaching us how to better live and work in this new era.

REFERENCES

Collins, J. C., & Porras, J. I. (1994). *Built to Last: Successful habits of visionary companies*. NY: HarperCollins Publishing Inc.

Davenport, T. H. (2005). *Thinking for a living: How to get better performance and results from knowledge workers*. Boston: Harvard Business School Press.

Davenport, T. H., & Harris, J. G. (2007). *Competing on analytics: The new science of winning*. Boston: Harvard Business School Press.

Davila, T., Epstein, M. J., & Shelton, R. (2006). *Making innovation work: How to manage it, measure it, and profit from it*. Pearson Education Ltd.

Delong, D. W. (2004). *Lost knowledge: Confronting the treat of an aging workforce*. New York: Oxford University Press.

Drucker, P. F. (1954). *The practice of management*. New York: Harper & Row, Publishers Inc.

Drucker, P. F. (1957). *The landmarks of tomorrow*. New York: Harper & Row, Publishers Inc.

Drucker, P. F. (1999). *Management challenges for the 21st century*. New York: HarperCollins Publishers, Inc.

Dychtwald, K., Erickson, T. J., & Morison, R. (2006). *Workforce crisis: How to beat the coming shortage of skills and talent*. Self-published.

Goleman, D. (1995). *Emotional intelligence*. New York: Bantam Books.

Hamel, G. (2007). *The future of management*. Self-published.

Hamel, G. (2009). Moon shots for management. *Harvard Business Review*, (February): 2009.

Hedlund, G. (1994). A model of knowledge management and the n-form corporation. *Strategic Management Journal*, *15*(2), 73–90. doi:10.1002/smj.4250151006

Hubard, D. W. (2007). *How to measure anything: Finding the value of intangibles in business*. Hoboken, NJ: John Wiley & Sons, Inc.

Leonard, D., & Swap, W. C. (2005). *Deep smarts: How to cultivate and transfer enduring business wisdom*. Boston: Harvard Business School Publishing Corporation.

Levy, M. (2009). WEB2.0 Implications on Knowledge Management. *Journal of Knowledge Management*, *13*(1), 120–134. doi:10.1108/13673270910931215

Maslow, A. H. (1943). A theory of human motivation. *Psychological Review*, *50*(4), 370–396. doi:10.1037/h0054346

O'reilly, T. (2005). *What is WEB2.0- design patterns and business models for the next generation of software*. Retrieved August 12, 2009, from http://oreilly.com/web2/archive/what-is-web-20.html

Pink, D. H. (2005). *A whole new mind: Why right-brainers will rule the future*. New York: Riverhead Books.

Scoble, R., & Israel, S. (2006). *Naked conversations: How bogs are changing the way businesses talk with customers*. Hoboken, NJ: John Wiley & Sons, Inc.

Senge, P. M. (1990). *The fifth discipline: The art & practice of the learning organization*. Doubleday, Random House, Inc.

Smith, A. (1776). *The wealth of nations*. New York: Classic House Books.

Surowiecki, J. (2004). *The wisdom of the crowds: Why the many Are smarter than the few and how collective wisdom shapes business, economies, societies and nations*. New York: Anchor Books, Random House.

Taylor, F. W. (1911). *The principles of scientific management*. New York: W.W. Norton & Company.

Tversky, A., & Kahneman, D. (1981). The framing of decisions and the psychology of choice, *Science. New Series*, *211*(4481), 453–458.

Walsh, B. (2006). *Content isn't King*. Retrieved August 12, 2009, from http://thepartycow.com/2006/10/content-isnt-king.html

ADDITIONAL READING

Emotional Intelligence (Goleman, 1995).

http://managing-knowledge.blogspot.com

Management Challenges for the 21st century (Drucker, 1999).

The Fifth Discipline. (1990). *The Art & Practice of the Learning Organization*. Senge.

The future of Management (Hamel, 2007).

Thinking for a living: How to get better performance and results from knowledge workers (Davenport, 2005).

Whole New Mind, A. (2005). *Why Right-Brainers Will Rule the Future*. Pink.

KEY TERMS AND DEFINITONS

Knowledge Worker: A person whose knowledge is central to his/her job.

Management 2.0: Renewed paradigms regarding management.

Knowledge Management: Retaining, sharing, developing and structuring knowledge using methodologies and tools, while focusing on improving organizational and business targets.

ENDNOTES

1 It should be noted that Pink refers to the present era as a post knowledge worker era. In this work the present is defined as part of the same developing era.

2 K.W: Knowledge Worker

3 ECM- Enterprise Content Management; advanced document management systems.

Chapter 3
The CSFs Methodology and Modified DEA Approach to Construct a New Business Model to Evaluate Operational Performance of all International Tourist Hotels in Taiwan

Chieh-Heng Ko
Chung Hua University, Taiwan

ABSTRACT

This chapter evaluates the operational performance of International Tourist Hotels in Taiwan, and explores the critical success factors that contribute to good performance. This research initially adopted data envelopment analysis (DEA) to measure the relative operational efficiency of 57 international tourist hotels in Taiwan. However, the DEA approach can only determine relative operational efficiency but does not identify the factors that give rise to inefficiency or lead to efficiency. Furthermore, DEA only calls attention to those hotels in which efficiency and inefficiency exist, but cannot provide suggestions on how to improve operational efficiency. A qualitative approach is a good way to address this limitation of DEA. Thus, after using DEA to evaluate hotel's operational efficiency, this research used a qualitative approach to further explore the critical success factors that contribute to hotels having good performance in Taiwan. Through determination of these factors, this research provides hotel managers with a list of advice and recommendations to develop effective strategies to meet a highly competitive environment.

DOI: 10.4018/978-1-60960-129-4.ch003

INTRODUCTION

The hotel industry in Taiwan is encountering a highly competitive environment due to the rapid expansion of hotels. For example, the total number of international tourist hotels has increased from 44 in 1985 to 60 in 2005 (Taiwan Tourism Bureau, 2007). However, due to inappropriate hotel management (Sun & Lu, 2005; Hwang & Chang, 2003), eight international tourist hotels have closed down over the last six years. Average occupancy rate has decreased from 73% to 69% between 2005 and 2006 which is surprising given the surge in new demand entering the market.

Hwang and Chang (2003) noted that Taiwanese hotels have adopted two ways to respond to competition. First, by targeting international travelers and domestic tourists to increase the source of customers. Second, to join franchise-chains, outsourced management and acquired membership in international hotel associations to introduce international management systems and improve their managerial capacities. Even so, it has still been hard for these hotels to improve their performance. According to monthly report on international tourist hotel operations in Taiwan in 2006, the occupancy rate and average room rate of international hotels in 2006 were 69% and US$ 95 respectively, (Taiwan Tourism Bureau, 2007a). Compared with Hong Kong (87%, US$ 140) (Hong Kong Tourism Board, 2007), the occupancy rate and average room rate in Taiwan is much lower. Most of the hotel owners were not satisfied with this result. Furthermore, according to Taiwan Tourism Bureau, 43 hotels and approximately 12165 rooms have been scheduled to open between 2007 and 2010. This will make the hotel industry in Taiwan encounter a highly competitive environment.

Facing this situation, the formulation of competition strategy, strengthening operational efficiency, and developing corporate advantage are essential for hotel operations. When formulating any strategy, it is necessary to have a sound knowledge of the operating efficiency of a given hotel relative to the entire industry (Hwang, Chang, 2003).

Efficiency was defined by Jones and George (2003) as a measure of how well or how productively resources are used to achieve a goal. Organisations are efficient when managers minimize the amount of input resource or the amount of time needed to produce a given output of goods or service. A manager's responsibility is to ensure that an organisation and its members perform as efficiently as possible. The fewer the inputs required to produce a given output, the higher will be the efficiency of the production system. Therefore, it is very important for managers to evaluate organisational efficiency, and a number of different approaches and techniques have been employed to conduct such evaluations. However, the often-used mechanisms for measuring and analyzing efficiency of organisations have remained too narrow in their focus to capture the broad spectrum of factors that actually contribute to an organisation's success (Reynold, 2003). One approach that has been successful is data envelopment analysis (DEA), used in this research as it can integrate multiple input and output variables and remedy this shortcoming.

Moreover, one of the issues which hotel managers are most concerned about is the differences in performance levels that exist between different hotels and what possible factors may justify those differences. Therefore, based on the results of efficiency evaluation, this study will use a qualitative approach to identify the critical success factors contributing to efficient hotel operations to assist hotel managers to develop strategy and enhance operational performance. The objectives of this study are:

1. To evaluate the operational efficiency of international tourist hotels in Taiwan.
2. To identify the critical success factors contributing to good performance.

3. To identify which hotels have good performance and have become a benchmark for other hotels; and which hotels are inefficient and should improve their operation.
4. To analyze the reasons why benchmarking hotels are doing well and how inefficient hotels can improve their performance.
5. To determine the strategies that are more effective in the highly competitive environment.

LITERATURE REVIEW

Performance Measurement in the Hotel Industry

As with other industries, the hotel industry has its own particular characteristics associated with the provision of the "hotel product" and, therefore, the measures used to assess hotel performance should reflect the specific activities and kinds of products and services offered. Similarly, although performance measures have an important role in monitoring past achievements and providing the basis for planning and control decisions, unless they are related to the particular kind of business, performance evaluation is undermined. Thus, when reviewing performance management systems, it is critical to recognise the fundamental "orientation" and "industry context" of an organisation (Kotas, 1975; Fitzgerald *et al.*, 1991). In addition, it is also vital for performance measurement systems to reflect the complex nature of the service delivery process within hotels – including such typical characteristics as high degrees of perishability, intangibility, heterogeneity and simultaneity (Jones and Lockwood, 1989; Fitzgerald *et al.*, 1991).

Additionally, productivity is used to reflect company performance, because productivity determines the ratio of outputs over inputs, with larger values indicating better performance. However, productivity measurement in hospitality faces additional difficulties due to the specific characteristics of service and that in turn creates problems such as labour and process scheduling, consistency and demand (Sigala, 2004; Witt & Witt, 1989). Indeed, several researchers (Sassers, Olsen & Wyckoff, 1978; Jones & Lockwood, 1989; Witt & Witt, 1989) argue that productivity management and measurement has been limited in the hospitality sector by the features and characteristics of services. Specifically, the intangible nature of hospitality service suggests that it is difficult to define objectively and measure the service output being provided such as number of guest-nights versus number of satisfied guests. The measurement and management of hospitality input and output is also complicated because of the simultaneous production and consumption of the hospitality services, along with their perishability and heterogeneity, as service encounters are experienced differently by people or even by the same people in different circumstances.

Traditional Performance Measurement

Conventionally, average occupancy rates and average room rates have been used as indicators of hotel performance. Coltman (1978) and Fay, Rhoads and Rosenblatt (1971) used a cost-volume-profit approach to analyse individual hotel performance. Kimes (1989) employed the perishable asset revenue management concept to evaluate hotel industry performance. Weatherford and Bodily (1992) developed a classification for length of stay and Weatherford (1995) provided a length of stay decision rate for perishable asset revenue management. Van Doren and Gustke (1982) used lodging industry sales receipt information to assess hotel industry performance. Wijeysinghe (1993) applied a method for calculating breakeven room occupancy that provided accurate calculations together with a system of effective management.

Despite the above research which attempted to accurately assess the efficiency of the hotel industry and provide robust firm-specific performance measures, managers are still faced with a dilemma when making strategic decisions. The major reason is that most previous studies employed ratio analysis and aggregated indices to evaluate performance. Ratio analysis is an effective method for evaluating the relationship between just two variables, but it is inadequate in the multi-output, multi-input setting that characterizes real-world organizations. In such a situation, ratio analysis results in a nebulous set of ratios that, at best, provide no clear indication of true efficiency and, at worst, produce conflicting indications (Sexton, 1986).

Financial performance measures are commonly used measures of managerial performance. Whilst there is nothing inherently wrong with the use of earning and profitability as determinants of business performance, over emphasis on financial measures such as earnings per share (EPS), return on investment (ROI), and return on capital employed (ROCE), can produce myopic behavior (Phillips, 1999). Atkinson and Brown (2001) also noted that financial performance measures have limitations in their accuracy and neutrality, causing a focus dominated by results rather than determinants and only stress past achievements while largely ignoring the drivers of future performance.

Data Envelopment Analysis (DEA)

To overcome the shortcomings mentioned above new techniques have been developed that have the ability to compare the efficiency of similar service organizations by explicitly considering the use of multiple inputs to produce multiple outputs. This new efficiency technique is data envelopment analysis (DEA).

DEA is a linear programming based method that integrates several relatively disparate input and output variables simultaneously. It then produces a single productivity index that compares all units to the most-efficient units in the sample, helping analysts to identify which unit is most efficient given its own set of variables, which are then compared with others in the set (Raynolds, 2003).

Apart from the measure of the relative efficiency of each unit, DEA also distinguishes the most productive unit or units within the competitive set, describes the relatively less-productive units, and calculates the excess resources used by each of those less-productive operations (Anderson et al., 2000). As such DEA has become increasingly popular as a tool for assessing the relative productivity efficiency of companies, including hotels.

Morey and Ditmam (1995) were the first researchers to apply the DEA approach in the hotel industry. They employed DEA to analyze the efficiency of 54 hotels in the United States, and found that managers were operating at 89% efficiency and the least efficient hotels were 64%. Consequently, the results deemed the lodging market to be operating efficiently in U.S.A. Using the DEA approach, Anderson et al. (2000) measured the managerial efficiency of 48 hotels in the United States and provided evidence that the hotel industry was operating inefficiently with a mean overall efficiency measure of 42%. Huang and Chang (2003) also adopted DEA to analyze the efficiency of 45 international tourist hotels in Taiwan in 1998. The results indicated that managers were operating at 79.16% efficiency with only 20 of the 45 hotels improving their managerial efficiency over time. Consequently, the market for lodging services seemed to be operating efficiently in Taiwan.

Research Gap

Although DEA has been used in previous research to evaluate hotel operational efficiency, the results only focus on efficiency scores; benchmarking hotels and inefficient hotels; the research thus far does not explore the reason why benchmarking hotels are doing well. In other words, they only answer "how well a hotel is doing"; and "which hotel is doing well"; but they ignored the most important question "why are certain hotels doing well". The real aim of applying DEA is to identify what factors contribute to efficiency and what factors result in inefficiency. Berro (2005) also noted that DEA does not identify the factors that give rise to inefficiency and only calls attention to those units in which inefficiency exists. That is the limitation of DEA and most of the previous research that did not further explore the causes of inefficiency.

Evaluating hotel efficiency is to develop effective strategies to improve hotel operational performance. Johns and Wheeler (1991) proposed expansive and contractive productivity management strategies. The aim of the latter is to reduce inputs while increasing or maintaining output, while the aim of expansive strategy is to improve output while trying to keep inputs fixed. However, most of the previous DEA research did not discuss these issues and that will reduce the value of the research results. In fact, if these strategies are adopted, contractive strategies may be suitable for the back of the house in hotels such as housekeeping and executive office; and expansive strategies are better applied to front of the house such as front office and restaurants, to increase hotel sales and revenues.

Furthermore, most of the previous studies using the DEA approach only measured physical items. As a result, many of the other features of the hotel sector, such as service and atmosphere have been ignored. In addition, because each transaction with each customer can be regarded as unique, a quality factor should also be considered. In fact, performance measurement becomes more complex when one also examines the array of hotel characteristics such as the simultaneous production and consumption of the hospitality service as well as their perishability and heterogeneity. Consequently, this research further investigates the critical success factors (CSFs) contributing to good hotel performance in Taiwan in order to determine why the hotel is doing well.

Critical Success Factors

Critical success factors (CSFs) were first proposed by Daniel in 1961 as a means to classify critical information needs of managers, but it is generally considered that Rockart (1979) popularized the CSFs approach in the field of management information systems. Indeed, CSFs has a long history of application to the information systems field (Ghym & King, 1976; Rockart, 1979; Davis, 1979; Brotherton & Leslie, 1991; Robson, 1994). Until the last 20 years its application has been extended beyond this field as a more generic approach to management, particularly within the strategic and operational management fields (Devlin, 1989; Grunert & Ellegaard, 1993). Now the identification of CSFs has been used to identify information needs, to list and describe elements critical to system success, and help define and focus management's responsibilities and efforts (Munro & Wheeler, 1980).

CSFs are defined as the limited number of areas in which results, if they are satisfactory, will ensure successful competitive performance (Rockart, 1979). Digman (1990) also defined CSFs as the areas where things must go right for the business to flourish. Oakland (1995) regarded them as what the organization must accomplish to achieve the mission by examination and categorization of the impacts. He adds that they are the minimum key factors or sub-goals that the organization must have or need, and which together will achieve the mission. Kanji & Tambi (1999) stated that CSFs are the few things that must go well to ensure success for a manager and/or organization. They represent those managerial areas that must be given special and continual attention to cause high performance. These definitions see CSFs as points, areas, or goals that have to be given extensive attention and support by the management to achieve the mission, quality and high performance. Consequently, these areas have to be defined and measured before the organisation starts implementing any project.

Figure 1. Research model for hotel performance measurement

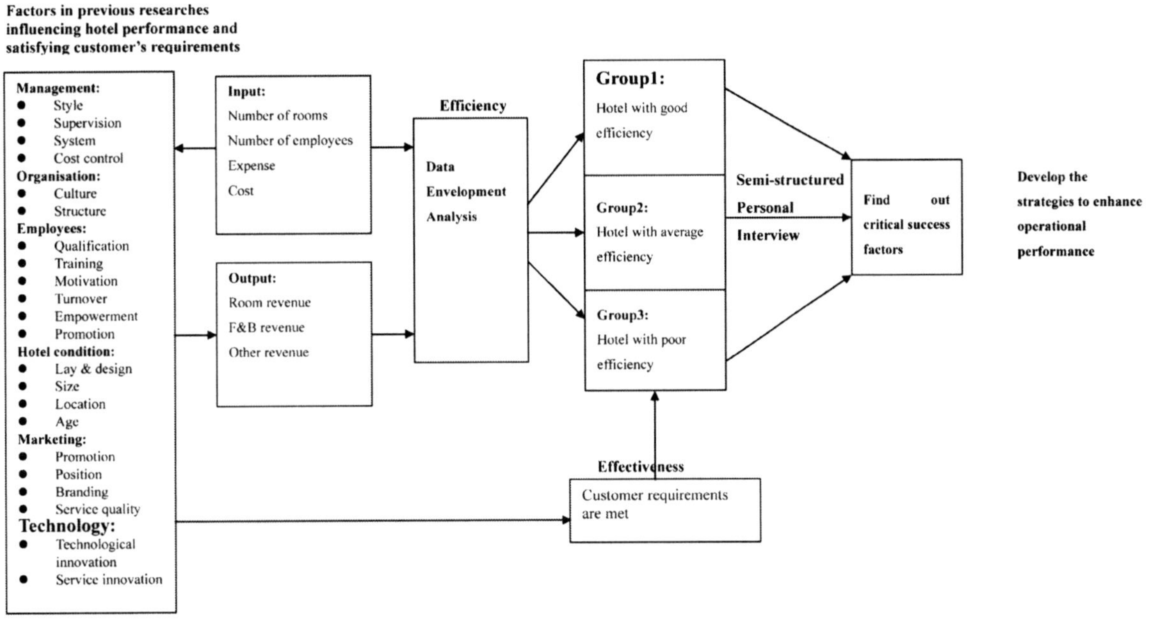

Attraction of the CSFs approaches is its pragmatic benefits. Researchers and consultants have often found direct and immediate applications for the results of their investigations (Brotherton & Shaw, 1996). Jenster (1987) found companies that identified CSFs and implemented their usage, through proper measurement, feedback and management, received a higher return on equity when compared to companies that did not employ CSFs methodology. Owing to the advantages of CSFs mentioned above, this research does not only evaluate the efficiency of Taiwan international tourist hotels but further investigate the CSFs contributing to good performance hotels to find out the reason why these hotels are doing well.

Construction of the Research Model

According to abovementioned, this research will construct a new business model to evaluate operational efficiency of all international tourist hotels in Taiwan. The model of this research is depicted in Figure 1.

Kolter (1984) indicated performance measurement could be regarded as the process of quantifying the efficiency and effectiveness of action. Organisations achieve good performance by satisfying their customers with greater efficiency and effectiveness than their competitors. In this context, effectiveness refers to the extent to which customer requirements are met, while efficiency is a measure of how economically the firm's resources are utilized when providing a given level of customer satisfaction.

Hotels were divided into three groups: good efficiency, average efficiency and poor efficiency due to the results of DEA. A selection of hotels was chosen from each group as sampled hotels, then semi-structured personal interviews were conducted with managers of each sampled hotel. The data collected from interviews were analysed by qualitative approach to identify the critical success factors leading to hotels with good performance and to further develop strategies to enhance hotel operational performance.

Therefore, this research model utilized the DEA (efficiency) and the factors in previous researches satisfying customer's requirements (effectiveness) to explore the critical success factors contributing Taiwanese hotels to have good performance.

METHODOLOGY

Research Design

This research will be conducted in five stages.

Stage 1: Pilot Testing

Prior to conducting this research, a pilot testing was carried out to test the relevance of the language of the interview protocol, and the appropriateness and completeness of the contents of the interview protocol in relation to its subject domain and purpose. The researcher was unsure about the responses obtainable, and therefore felt that the pilot testing could serve as a guide. The pilot testing was conducted in a way that would allow for refinement of the language and procedures as the testing proceeded.

Six hotel managers and two university assistant professors from a hospitality faculty were recruited to participate in the study as the pilot testing. In the beginning, they were asked to review the draft interview protocol without help from the researcher. They were first asked to comment on their understanding of the interview questions and to comment on the relevance of the questions to the research issues. Then, they were asked to answer the questions to test whether respondents could and would answer the questions asked during the course of the interview and whether the interview protocol appeared to be appropriate for examining the research questions. After interviewing the participants, feedback was obtained pertaining to the nature of the questions asked, so as to help the researcher refine the interview protocol. A few of the interview questions had been modified for better and easier understanding. With the positive feedback, the researcher was able to proceed with the research.

Stage 2: Efficiency Evaluation

To understand the operational efficiency of Taiwan international tourist hotels, this research will adopt DEA, developed by Charnes, A. et al. (1978), using multiple inputs and outputs to measure the relative operational efficiency of 60 international hotels in Taiwan. At the same time, the research will use the Malmquist productivity approach expressed by Färe, R. et al (1992) to measure the operational efficiency change of these international tourist hotels. By comparing annual changes in the operational efficiency of individual hotels, it is possible to identify general trends in the efficiency of the hotel industry as a whole and to identify individual hotel exhibiting pattern of change in efficiency that differ from the rest of the industry. The data necessary for this analysis is to be collected from " *The Annual Operation Report of the International Tourist Hotels in Taiwan*" published by the Taiwan Tourism Bureau.

Stage 3: Efficiency Analysis

According to the results of DEA, 60 hotels will be divided into three groups. The first group is the hotels with good efficiency. Their efficient score is high and become best practice hotels. The second group is comprised of hotels with an average efficiency score. The last group is comprised of hotels which are scored as inefficient and need to improve their efficiency.

Stage 4: In-Depth Interviews

Based on the three groups categorized above, this study will chose two hotels as sample from each group, then conducting the semi-structure personal interview with managers of each sample hotel. This interview will use open-ended questions to identify the perceptions of manager as to what they believe are important in increasing operational efficiency.

Stage 5: Qualitative Analysis

Interview data was analysed by way of constant comparative method. In this approach to the analysis of qualitative data, the theory is generated from the data, or if existing theories seem appropriate, then these may be elaborated and modified as incoming data are compared against them (Denzin & Lincoln, 1994, p. 643). Researchers can also carry into current studies any theory based on their previous research, being careful to constantly match their a priori theories against the incoming data (Glaser, 1965). Through the analysis of qualitative data, critical successful factors contributing to hotels having good performance have been identified.

Data Envelopment Analysis (DEA)

The Concept of DEA

DEA is a linear-programming-based benchmarking technique initially developed by Charners, Cooper and Rhodes (1978) to evaluate multiple outputs and inputs, producing a single measure of performance. In contrast to parametric approaches whose purpose is to optimize a single regression plane through the data DEA optimizes on each individual observation with an objective of calculating a discrete piecewise frontier occupied by the most efficient units. This frontier—and the associated measure for each unit, which is generally referred to as relative efficiency or productivity—has particular managerial relevance in that it allows for comparison of disparate operating units (Reynolds & Thompson, 2007). The term "relative" is rather important here since an organisation identified by the DEA technique as an efficient unit in a given set may become an inefficient one when evaluated in another set of organisations.

There are different mathematical forms of the DEA model. The model used in this study is CCR input-oriented model developed by Charners, Cooper and Rhodes in 1978. According to their model, the formulation is based on the following form:

$$\text{Maximize } E_k = \frac{\sum_{r=1}^{s} u_r y_{rk}}{\sum_{i=1}^{m} v_i x_{ik}}$$

Subject to:

$$\frac{\sum_{r=1}^{s} u_r y_{rj}}{\sum_{i=1}^{m} v_i x_{jk}} \leq 1 \text{ for } j=1,2,\ldots,n$$

$$u_r, v_i \geq \varepsilon \geq 0 \; r=1,\ldots,s \; i=1,\ldots,m$$

Where y_{rj} = observed quantity of output r produced by hotel j

x_{ij} = observed quantity of input i produced by hotel j

u_r = the weight given to output r by the hotel j

v_i = the weight given to input i by the hotel j

ε = non-Archimedean quantity, a sufficiently small positive number

The linear fractional programming model above can be transformed into an ordinary linear programming model by letting $u_r = t u_r$ and $v_i = t$

v_i, where $t^{-1} = \sum_{i=1}^{m} v_i x_{jk}$. Then the equivalent DEA model can be stated as follows.

Maximize $E_k = \sum_{r=1}^{s} u_r y_{rk}$

Subject to

$$\sum_{i=1}^{m} v_i x_{ik} = 1 \qquad (1)$$

$$\sum_{r=1}^{s} u_r y_{rj} - \sum_{i=1}^{m} v_i x_{ij} \leq 0 \text{ for } j=1,2,\ldots,n$$

$$u_r, v_i \geq \varepsilon \geq 0 \; r=1,\ldots,s \; i=1,\ldots,m$$

The DEA model above has the following interpretation within the context of hotels. There are n hotels in the observation set K, each of which producing r different outputs using i different inputs and we are interested in determining the relative efficiency E_k of hotel $k \in K$ with respect to all other hotels in the set K. The relative efficiency E_k is nothing but the ratio of outputs of the hotel k to its inputs. Such a definition of efficiency transforms the multidimensional nature of input and outputs into a single scalar ratio of single output to a single input.

For computational convenience, the efficiency of any hotel, j, can be solved by the dual of (1). The dual of (1) can be written as follows:

$$\text{Minimize } E_k = \theta - \varepsilon\left(\sum_{i=1}^{m} s_i^- + \sum_{r=1}^{s} s_r^+\right) \qquad (2)$$

Subject to

$$\sum_{j=1}^{n} \lambda_j x_{ij} - \theta x_{ik} + s_i^- = 0, i= 1,\ldots,m$$

$$\sum_{j=1}^{n} \lambda_j y_{rj} - s_r^+ = y_{rk}, r= 1,\ldots,s$$

$$\lambda_j, s_i^-, s_r^+ \geq 0 \; j= 1,\ldots,n \; i= 1,\ldots,m \; r=1,\ldots,s$$

θ unconstrained

An analysis provides the following type of information for decision making purposes.

1. Each hotel being evaluated will have a value E_k, $0 < E_k \leq 1$, obtained from the DEA model indicating its efficiency level. If E_k <1, the hotel is inefficient compared to 'best practice' units in the observation set K. If E_k =1, this is a relatively 'best practice' hotel and therefore is identified as an efficient one.
2. The DEA model will identify, from the viewpoint of a hotel k, the 'efficiency reference set' K_k or 'efficient frontier' which is a subset of K that includes only those hotels with E=1 from the observation set K. The hotel k is compared against the hotels in K_k to find the sources of its inefficiency. This is allows a hotel manager to locate and understand the nature of the existing inefficiencies by comparing his/her hotel with a select subset of more efficient hotels. It therefore avoids the need to investigate all hotels to understand the existing inefficiencies, and consequently helps allocate limited managerial resources to areas where efficiency improvements are most likely to be achieved.
3. The above model hence produces information with which managerial measures (reducing the inputs used, or increasing the outputs produced) can be formulated to make an inefficient hotel relatively efficient. For example, the necessary and sufficient conditions for any hotel, j, to reach efficiency are

$K_j = \theta = 1$, $s_{ij}^- = s_{rj}^+ = 0$; therefore, the efficiency score is 1, and there are no input surpluses or output shortfalls. On the contrary, if a hotel j does not achieve 100% efficiency, then an improvement, $x'_{ij} = \theta x_{ij} - s_{ij}^-$, $y'_{rj} = y_{rj} + s_{rj}^+$, could be applied so that a 100% efficient hotel can be achieved. That is, the input is decreased by $\Delta x_{ij} = x_{ij} - x'_{ij}$ and the output is increased by $\Delta y_{rj} = y'_{rj} - y_{rj}$.

Input and Output Data

Using DEA to evaluate efficiency requires data that measures each of the relevant outputs and each of the inputs used to produce these outputs over a common time period. The outputs would include those outcomes that management believes are basic to the purpose of the organization, such as revenue. The inputs should reflect the resources that are required to produce the outputs such that an increase (decrease) in output levels is expected to result in an increase (decrease) in the amount of inputs used (Charnes, et al. 1978).

The primary output of a hotel is revenue. There are two kinds of revenue for international tourist hotels in Taiwan: accommodation and meals. These constitute more than 80% of total hotel revenue. Other revenue includes revenue from laundry, lease of store space, night clubs, service fee, all of which do not exceed 20% of total revenue. The three revenue output data used in this research are:

- **Room revenue:** refers to revenue from lease of rooms.
- **Food and beverage revenue:** the total revenue generated from all food and beverage revenue.
- **Other revenue:** the total revenue excluding the room and food and beverage revenue (e.g. laundry, telephone, conference room).

On the other hand, input resources for international tourist hotels management include input material, staff, capital and equipment. These resources produce tangible and intangible services through front office and back office operations. Therefore, among input factors, numbers of employees are used to represent input manpower, total floor area of food and beverage department, and the number of rooms is used to represent capital investments of hotel and operating expenses are used to represent cost of input changes. Therefore, the four input data used in this research are as following:

- **Guest rooms:** the number of each hotel rooms.
- **Food and beverage capacity:** the total space of all food and beverage outlets in each hotel.
- **Number of full-time employees:** refers to hired employees.
- **Operating expenses:** including employee salaries, rooms costs, food and beverage cost and other relevant operating costs.

The data used in this study was collected from the Annual Operation Report of the International Tourist Hotels in Taiwan 2005 published by Taiwan Tourism Bureau (2007a). The reason for covering the year 2005 is that this was the most recently published data available prior to the collection of the interview data in 2007.

Qualitative Methods

Using DEA to measure the operational efficiency of hotels can only reveal the efficiency score and cannot identify what factors lead to efficiency and what factors result in inefficiency. Therefore a qualitative approach was adopted to address this limitation. The emphasis in this research is on identifying critical success factors contributing to hotels having good performance via semi-structured personal interviews with senior hotel executives. This research has tended to be exploratory and descriptive because the researcher wanted to understand the critical factors in the hotel operation in Taiwan as seen through the eyes of managers in the industry, rather than only through the lens of macro analysis of industry statistics and profiles. This research asked a series of questions which were open-ended and which the respondents could answer in any way they wished. While their descriptions may be incomplete when put in the macro context, they are important because the perception and ideas that are in the minds of managers in the industry are what drive their actions and their responses to the challenges surrounding them. Their understanding and perceptions are critical in developing a more complete picture about hotel operational performance compared with the recommendations and advice contained in academic and industry research and commentary.

Data Analysis

Efficiency Evaluation

To understand the performance of international tourist hotels in Taiwan, this research used DEA to evaluate operational efficiency of 57 international tourist hotels. To find the DEA results, one computer software, DEAP 2.1 developed by Tim Coelli (1996), was used to handle the data in this research. This program was used to construct DEA frontier for the calculation of efficiency and also for the calculation of Malmquist productivity index. As DEAP 2.1 is a DOS program, to make it easier use in the Windows environment, this research also used a program, Win4DEAP, which provides a convivial Windows front end for DEAP. This program provides a spreadsheet-like interface to enter input and output data which DEA requires. After entering all data, the executive function was used to calculate the DEA score and Malquest productivity index. Through the DEA analysis, the benchmarking hotels and an individual hotel's operational efficiency can be identified. Moreover, by comparing the Malmquist Index, it is possible to identify general trends in the efficiency of the hotel sector as a whole and to identify individual hotel exhibiting pattern of change in efficiency that differ from the rest of the industry.

Critical Success Factors Leading to Hotel Performance

To explore critical success factors contributing a hotel to have good performance, this research utilizes qualitative in-depth interview with hotel managers to identify the perceptions of the managers on what they believed are important to increasing operational efficiency. Interview data was analysed through constant comparative method (CCM) developed by Glaser and Strauss (1967). CCM is an analysis tool in grounded theory. By comparing, the researcher is able to do what is necessary to develop a theory more or less inductively, namely categorizing, coding, delineating categories and connecting them (Boeije, 2002).

DATA ENVELOPMENT ANALYSIS (DEA) FINDING

To estimate the operational efficiency of 57 international tourist hotels in Taiwan, this study used input-output data on 57 hotels for the year 2005. The data was obtained from "*Annual Operation Report of the International Tourist Hotels in Taiwan (2005)*" published by Taiwan Tourism Bureau. Results, in order of relative operational efficiency, reference hotel and frequency with which each hotel is in the reference hotel groups, are shown in Table 1. A hotel with the value of 1 is a relatively 'best practice' hotel, and therefore is identified as an efficient one. On the contrary, a hotel with a value of less than one is inefficient compared to the 'best practice' hotels. The efficiency score of the Howard Hotel Taipei, for example, is 0.916, which means that the Howard Hotel Taipei has

Table 1. Operational efficiency of international tourist hotel in 2005 through DEA

No	Hotel	Efficiency	Reference Hotels				Frequency as Reference Hotels	Rank
H21	Grand Formosa Hotel Taipei	1.000	H21				37	1
H7	Caesar Park Hotel Taipei	1.000	H7				23	1
H20	Grand Hyatt Hotel	1.000	H20				9	1
H22	Sherwood Hotel	1.000	H22				7	1
H2	Ambassador Hotel Taipei	1.000	H2				5	1
H54	Tainan Hotel	1.000	H54				4	1
H43	Lalu Hotel	1.000	H43				2	1
H23	Shangri-La's Hotel	1.000	H23				1	1
H10	Brother Hotel	1.000	H10				1	1
H24	Westin Hotel	1.000	H24				0	1
H48	Royal Hotel Chipen	1.000	H48				0	1
H46	Caesar Park Hotel Kenting	1.000	H46				0	12
H14	Sheraton Hotel	0.990	H20	H21	H10		0	13
H4	Gloria Prince Hotel	0.987	H21				0	14
H12	Landis Hotel Taipei	0.960	H2	H22	H20		0	15
H18	Howard Hotel Taipei	0.916	H21	H20	H22		0	16
H34	Evergreen Laurel Hotel	0.876	H21	H20			0	17
H47	Howard Hotel Kenting	0.871	H48	H20			0	18
H35	Howard Hotel Taichung	0.860	H21	H54	H7		0	19
H29	Howard Hotel Kaohsiung	0.844	H7	H21			0	20
H17	Royal Hotel Taipei	0.838	H7	H21			0	21
H8	Golden China Hotel	0.837	H21	H7			0	22
H50	Taoyuan Hotel	0.835	H22	H20	H7		0	23
H38	Marshal Hotel	0.821	H21	H7			0	24
H27	Ambassador Hotel Kaohsiung	0.818	H21	H2			0	25
H28	Grand Hi-Lai Hotel	0.802	H21				0	26
H6	Riverview Hotel	0.800	H21	H7			0	27
H42	Landies Resort Yanminsan	0.788	H22	H43	H21		0	28
H9	San Want Hotel	0.788	H2	H22	H21		0	28
H13	United Hotel	0.783	H2	H22			0	30
H5	Emperor Hotel	0.779	H13				0	31
H33	Plaza Int'l Hotel	0.776	H21	H7			0	32
H55	Tayih Landis Hotel Tainan	0.771	H7	H21			0	33
H36	Splendor Hotel Taichung	0.767	H21				0	34
H31	Han-Hsien Hotel	0.760	H21				0	35
H1	Grand Hotel Taipei	0.753	H21	H23			0	36
H39	China Trust Hotel Hwaleng	0.750	H21	H20			0	37
H41	Farglory Hotel	0.749	H7	H21	H20		0	38
H51	Ta Shee Resort	0.742	H21	H43			0	39

continued on following page

Table 1. continued

No	Hotel	Efficiency	Reference Hotels				Frequency as Reference Hotels	Rank
H3	Imperial Hotel	0.729	H21	H7			0	40
H16	Holiday Inn Hotel	0.719	H48	H21	H20		0	41
H53	Ambassador Hotel Hsinchu	0.716	H21				0	42
H52	Royal Hotel Hsinchu	0.716	H48	H7	H21		0	42
H30	Splendor Hotel Kaohsiung	0.712	H21	H7			0	44
H26	Holiday Garden	0.708	H21	H7	H13		0	45
H40	Parkview Hotel	0.679	H21	H13	H7		0	46
H32	Hotel National	0.665	H7	H54	H21		0	47
H25	Kingdom Hotel	0.660	H7	H54	H21		0	48
H56	Evergreen Plaza Hotel	0.659	H7	H21			0	49
H45	Grand Hotel Kaohsiung	0.658	H2	H21			0	50
H15	Fortuna Hotel	0.652	H7	H13			0	51
H57	Naruwan Hotel	0.632	H21	H13	H7	H18	0	52
H19	Crown Plaza Hotel	0.627	H13	H22	H21		0	53
H37	Astar Hotel	0.621	H46	H54			0	54
H11	Santos Hotel	0.603	H7	H13			0	55
H49	Grand Formosa Taroko	0.594	H7	H21	H13		0	56
H44	Hibiscus Resort	0.477	H21	H13	H7		0	57

only attained about 92% efficiency in relation to the most efficient hotels.

Due to the DEA results coming from comparing different units, for each inefficient unit DEA can identify a set of corresponding efficient units that are said to form a reference group for the inefficient unit. Each reference unit will become the exemplar for the corresponding inefficient unit. For example, through DEA, we find that the reference groups of the Landies Hotel Taipei include the Caesar Park Hotel Taipei, Sherwood Hotel and Grand Hyatt Hotel, and these three hotels become the benchmark for the Landies Hotel Taipei.

In many practical DEA assessments one needs more than the mere mathematical results to communicate to a relatively inefficient unit that their performance could improve. Reference units can prove helpful in this respect (Boussofiane et al, 1991). Merely contrasting the input/output levels of the relatively inefficient hotel with those of its reference hotels often helps to highlight inadequacies in the performance of the relatively inefficient hotel. Also, given the fact that the reference hotels are relatively efficient and have a similar input/output orientation, they can provide examples of good operating practice for the inefficient hotel to study. They may also provide suitable targets for it, particularly where some reference hotels are of a similar size to the inefficient hotel. The higher the frequency a relatively efficiency hotel has been referred to by other hotels, the higher is its chance of being a benchmark hotel.

The DEA results show that there are 12 hotels with an efficiency score of 1, including the Grand Formosa Hotel Taipei, Caesar Park Hotel Taipei, Royal Hotel Chipen, Grand Hyatt Hotel, Sherwood Hotel, Ambassador Hotel, Tainan Hotel, Lalu

Hotel, Shangri-La's Hotel, Brother Hotel, Westin Hotel and Caesar Park Hotel Kenting. These were the most efficient hotels in Taiwan in 2005. Among these hotels, the Grand Formosa Hotel is referred by hotels with poor efficiency 37 times, and became the best hotel with good efficiency. Moreover, among the hotels with good efficiency, 9 are business hotel and 3 resort hotels. As for location, 8 hotels are located in Taipei and 4 are located in other areas in Taiwan. The primary sources of customers for 9 hotels are foreign customers, and the remaining 3 are local customers. 11 hotels focus on individual customers and only one hotel has a focus on groups of customers. Eight hotels are the members of chain operation while 4 hotels are independently managed and operated (see Table 2).

Among these hotels, 5 hotels are also members of the Top 10 hotels with the highest average room rate in Taiwan (see Table 3).

From these analyses, it can be concluded that hotels with good operational efficiency have the following common features:

- business hotels
- located in Taipei
- focusing on foreign customers and individual customers
- chain operations
- providing top level, luxurious facilities and charging expensive room rates.

INTERVIEW FINDING

Owner's Attitude and Emphasis Play a Key Role to Hotel Performance

Research results showed that there are 13 critical success factors for enhancement of hotel performance. However, whether every factor can be supported and effectively executed still depends on the owner's attitude. No matter what management model, the hotel owners always dominate financial resources and ultimate decisions. Implementation of all investment plans or significant decisions should still be approved by the hotel owners. If the owner is reluctant to provide support, even a good program or a highly competent manager cannot effectively improve the hotel's performance. Thus, the owner's attitude and emphasis play a key role to hotel performance.

This research indicated that Taiwanese hotel owners were unwilling to accept the advice of professional managers, and insisted on their own personal views. Moreover, some Taiwanese hotel owners tend to be short-term profit oriented. If they cannot gain profits or as much as expected from their hotel business, they will begin to intervene in the management; start cutting on service and will not spend enough for maintenance and improving customer service. This kind of management model does not only hurt the hotel's image, but also attacks the hotel's performance. To hotel owners, great service without profit is nothing. However, running a hotel is a long-term and persistent investment. To make profits, hotels need to persistently improve their services and maintain a comfortable environment. Only by doing so can they attract customers at all times. Without understanding of this characteristic of the hotel sector, they can hardly make their operations run on a right track.

Respect and Support for Professional Knowledge is an Indispensable Element in Hotel Management

In Taiwan, most hotels are not run by hotel owners with professional knowledge. Some entrepreneurs established hotels simply because they have lands and sufficient capital, and these hotel owners are very involved in management and are characterized by stringent supervision and control. This tendency of hotel owners to rely on their past experience as the platform for management, and therefore accepting advice from professional managers is something they are reluctant to do.

Table 2. Comparing DEA with location, hotel type, management type and major source of customer

No	Hotel	Efficiency	Location	Hotel Type	Management Type	Major Source of Customer	Customer Type	
							FIT	Group
H21	Grand Formosa Taipei	1.000	Taipei	Business	Local Chain	Foreign	61%	39%
H7	Caesar Park Hotel Taipei	1.000	Taipei	Business	Local Chain	Foreign	60%	40%
H20	Grand Hyatt Hotel	1.000	Taipei	Business	Int'l Chain	Foreign	67%	33%
H22	Sherwood Hotel	1.000	Taipei	Business	Independent	Foreign	100%	0%
H2	Ambassador Hotel Taipei	1.000	Taipei	Business	Local Chain	Foreign	41%	59%
H54	Tainan Hotel	1.000	Tainan	Business	Independent	Foreign	93%	7%
H23	Shangri-La's Hotel	1.000	Taipei	Business	Int'l Chain	Foreign	70%	30%
H10	Brother Hotel	1.000	Taipei	Business	Independent	Foreign	72%	28%
H24	Westin Hotel	1.000	Taipei	Business	Int'l Chain	Foreign	69%	31%
H48	Royal Hotel Chipen	1.000	Taitung	Resort	Local Chain	Local	83%	17%
H43	Lalu Hotel	1.000	Sun Moon Lake	Resort	Independent	Local	78%	22%
H46	Caesar Park Hotel Kenting	1.000	Kengting	Resort	Local Chain	Local	70%	30%
H14	Sheraton Hotel	0.990	Taipei	Business	Int'l Chain	Foreign	62%	38%
H4	Gloria Prince Hotel	0.987	Taipei	Business	Int'l Franchise	Foreign	52%	48%
H12	Landies Hotel Taipei	0.960	Taipei	Business	Local Franchise	Foreign	100%	0%
H18	Howard Hotel Taipei	0.916	Taipei	Business	Local Chain	Foreign	87%	13%
H34	Evergreen Laurel Hotel	0.876	Taichung	Business	Local Chain	Local	86%	14%
H47	Howard Hotel Kenting	0.871	Kenting	Resort	Local Chain	Local	61%	39%
H35	Howard Hotel Taichung	0.860	Taichung	Business	Local Chain	Local	85%	15%
H29	Howard Hotel Kaohsiung	0.844	Kaohsiung	Business	Local Chain	Foreign	65%	35%
H17	Royal Hotel Taipei	0.838	Taipei	Business	Local Chain	Foreign	100%	0%
H8	Golden China Hotel	0.837	Taipei	Business	Independent	Foreign	31%	69%
H50	Taoyuan Hote	0.835	Taoyuan	Business	Independent	Foreign	18%	82%
H38	Marshal Hotel	0.821	Hwaleng	Resort	Independent	Local	26%	74%
H27	Ambassador Kaohsiung	0.818	Kaohsiung	Business	Local Chain	Local	59%	41%
H28	Grand Hi-Lai Hotel	0.802	Kaohsiung	Business	Independent	Local	74%	26%
H6	Riverview Hotel	0.800	Taipei	Business	Independent	Foreign	7%	93%

continued on following page

Table 2. continued

No	Hotel	Efficiency	Location	Hotel Type	Management Type	Major Source of Customer	Customer Type	
							FIT	Group
H42	Landies Resort Yanminsan	0.788	Yanminsan	Resort	Local Franchise	Local	73%	27%
H9	San Want Hotel	0.788	Taipei	Business	Independent	Foreign	79%	21%
H13	United Hotel	0.783	Taipei	Business	Independent	Foreign	65%	35%
H5	Emperor Hotel	0.779	Taipei	Business	Independent	Foreign	100%	0%
H33	Plaza Int'l Hotel	0.776	Taichung	Business	Independent	Local	73%	27%
H55	Tayih Landis Hotel Tainan	0.771	Tainan	Business	Local Franchise	Local	85%	15%
H36	Splendor Hotel Taichung	0.767	Taichung	Business	Local Franchise	Local	76%	24%
H31	Han-Hsien Hotel	0.760	Kaohsiung	Business	Independent	Local	65%	35%
H1	Grand Hotel Taipei	0.753	Taipei	Business	Local Chain	Foreign	31%	69%
H39	China Trust Hotel Hwaleng	0.750	Hwaleng	Resort	Local Franchise	Local	62%	38%
H41	Farglory Hotel	0.749	Hwaleng	Resort	Independent	Local	63%	37%
H51	Ta Shee Resort	0.742	Ta Shee	Resort	Independent	Local	49%	51%
H3	Imperial Hotel	0.729	Taipei	Business	Independent	Foreign	47%	53%
H16	Holiday Inn Hotel	0.719	Taipei	Business	Int'l Franchise	Foreign	59%	41%
H53	Ambassador Hotel Hsinchu	0.716	Hsinchu	Business	Local Chain	Foreign	94%	6%
H52	Royal Hotel Hsinchu	0.716	Hsinchu	Business	Local Chain	Foreign	93%	7%
H30	Splendor Hotel Kaohsiung	0.712	Kaohsiung	Business	Local Franchise	Local	65%	35%
H26	Holiday Garden	0.708	Kaohsiung	Business	Independent	Local	27%	73%
H40	Parkview Hotel	0.679	Hwaleng	Resort	Independent	Local	57%	43%
H32	Hotel National	0.665	Taichung	Business	Independent	Local	63%	37%
H25	Kingdom Hotel	0.660	Kaohsiung	Business	Independent	Local	48%	52%
H56	Evergreen Plaza Hotel	0.659	Tainan	Business	Local Franchise	Local	77%	23%
H45	Grand Hotel Kaohsiung	0.658	Kaohsiung	Resort	Local Chain	Local	60%	40%
H15	Fortuna Hotel	0.652	Taipei	Business	Independent	Foreign	69%	31%
H57	Naruwan Hotel	0.632	Taitung	Resort	Independent	Local	81%	19%
H19	Crown Plaza Hotel	0.627	Taipei	Business	Int'l Franchise	Foreign	76%	24%
H37	Astar Hotel	0.621	Hwaleng	Resort	Independent	Local	46%	54%
H11	Santos Hotel	0.603	Taipei	Business	Independent	Foreign	10%	90%
H49	Grand Formosa Taroko	0.594	Taroko	Resort	Local Chain	Local	65%	35%
H44	Hibiscus Resort	0.477	Nansi	Resort	Independent	Local	57%	43%

Source: Taiwan Tourism Bureau 2007a

Table 3. Top 10 hotels with the highest average room rate

Rank	Hotel	Efficiency	Average Room Rate Unit: US$
1	Lalu Hotel	1.000	253
2	Shangri-La's Hotel	1.000	172
3	Westin Hotel	1.000	171
4	Grand Hyatt Hotel	1.000	163
5	Landies Resort Yanminsan	0.788	159
6	Farglory Hotel	0.749	135
7	Royal Hotel Chipen	1.000	130
8	Sheraton Hotel	0.990	125
9	Landies Hotel Taipei	0.960	119
10	Howard Hotel Taipei	0.916	117

Source: Taiwan Tourism Bureau 2007a

As a result, most professional managers would rather follow an owner's opinion than create a new idea. In this era of emphasizing professionalism and efficiency, such an approach will have negative impacts on hotel operations. Moreover, the management team in some hotels is composed of the owner's family members, close relatives or friends. It was observed through the interviews that these people have high loyalty and can be trusted by the owners. However, these people have no professional background and there is not a sound management system in this kind of hotels. Management is highly dependent on people, not systems. All the decisions are in the hands of family members and many have been made without appropriate attention to the facts. Professional knowledge is not respected in these hotels. As a result, the operational performance is poor.

Hotels are a highly professionalised and delicate business. Hotel owners do not necessarily have to be experts on hotel management, because they can get out of conventional frameworks and introduce new ideas into this industry. However, operating a hotel requires professional knowledge and skills. Owners still have to rely on professional managers. Running a hotel, after all, is professional and complicated. It cannot be done simply with the owner's personal ideas or reliance on trustworthy family members. The research results indicated that most owners of high-performance hotels are clear with their limits and willing to delegate their power to professional managers. Therefore, respect for professional knowledge and management experience is still an indispensable element in hotel management.

Positive Corporate Culture is a Motivating Power to Enhance Hotel Performance

This research revealed that a strong positive corporate culture is one of the key factors contributing to hotels having a sustained high performance. A special phenomenon is that in Taiwan, hotel owner's concepts of and attitudes toward hotel management can significantly influence the development of hotel's corporate culture. As most Taiwanese hotels belong to independent operators, hotel owners are usually deeply involved in hotel operation including operative strategy, management style and personnel matters. In this situation, even though professional managers may have their own views, they are constrained and can only follow the owner's ideas. Otherwise, they cannot work in this hotel. After a period of time, this situation makes a strong influence on hotel's corporate culture. Thus, if a hotel owner has innovative ideas and proactive attitudes, it is easy for this hotel to have positive corporate culture. On the contrary, if hotel owner's mind is negative, hotel's corporate culture will turn to negative. The reason for this is that owners with a proactive attitude will naturally form a force propelling employees to work hard. If any employee cannot attain standard, they are not likely to survive in the hotel. This attitude has a positive effect on hotel performance. In contrast, passive and conservative owners seldom show support to their managers, even if they have done certain jobs that contribute to hotel performance. In the long run, employees will also become passive and conservative. The hotel's performance will certainly be affected. This implies that corporate culture is an important factor affecting hotel performance, but formation of corporate culture is critically affected by hotel owner's attitude. Therefore, hotel owners should shape a positive corporate culture and internalise it into the mind of employees. This corporate culture, once internalized, becomes a motivating power, which drives employees to be more devoted to their jobs to enhance hotel performance.

Innovation and Renovation are Important Strategies for Hotel to Enhance Competitiveness

When asked about the strategies to increase hotel's competitive advantage, many interviewees revealed that innovation, physical facilities and renovation are the key factors to attract customers. The main reason is that in the face of a hotel environment where customer preferences are changing rapidly, where competition is intense, and where differentiation is limited, innovation seems to be an important strategy for hotels to stay competitive. Moreover, compared with intangible service, service quality is a subjective perception, which varies from one customer to another. Services widely rated as satisfactory may still induce customer compliants. However, physical facilities are tangible and can be more objectively evaluated. Through improvement of physical facilities, an attractive environment can be easily created. Customers today do not exhibit, as in past decades, a truly brand loyal behavior. Customers instead are choosing to patronize hotels that offer the best value proposition under existing budgetary constraints. The best way to make customers feel their expenditure is justified is to provide the innovative products and the best physical facilities.

According to the research, a number of customers come to a hotel for more than accommodation or dining. They also come to experience the atmosphere presented in the hotel. Therefore, hotels need to constantly be innovative to maintain the design of their environment to retain customers. Moreover, with the elapse of time, physical facilities will gradually become old, consumer's feeling of freshness will naturally fade, and the hotel's revenue and profits will be influenced. Therefore, physical facilities should be renewed on a regular basis. Although it is necessary for hotel to conduct innovation and renovation, this research indicated that only a small portion of hotels in Taiwan are proactively engaged in innovation and renovation, and this is mainly due to the reluctance of hotel owners. No matter what innovation or renovation, hotel requires a considerable amount of investment, but issues such as whether this investment can generate more revenue and when it can be repaid are not foreseeable. Thus, many owners are unwilling to undertake this risk. Senior owners, in particular, always think that broken facilities should be repaired rather than directly renewed. Some even argue that the best facilities should be used in the beginning, believing that they can be more durable and problem-free in the future. However, modern society does not renew a facility because it is broken but because it is out of style. Consequently, Taiwanese hotel owners do not fully realize the importance of renovation as an effective marketing tool, and its potential to attract new customers. In turn, renovation is used in the Taiwanese hotel on the maintenance level in terms of extending the useful life of the property rather than to reposition the property and increase its competitiveness.

It is revealed from the research that in the current competitive environment of Taiwanese international tourist hotels, it is hard to attract customers just through intangible service. In this hotel market, competitors are numerous but services are similar across competitors. Innovative products and regular renovation seem to have become indispensable factors that determine whether a hotel can outperform its rivals and win customer's trust.

Successful innovation and regular renovation can raise awareness of the hotel, improve image of hotel, enhance customer loyalty, and attract new customers. Moreover, they do not only offer a competitive advantage but also deliver their benefits and unique features to establish a distinct positioning in the customers' mind. Therefore, to maintain competitive advantages, hotels need to have prospective visions to accurately predict customer expectations and satisfy them with creativity. Then, they can prosper in the highly competitive market.

Quality Employees are the Important Assets to Increase Hotel Performance

From a strategic perspective, hotels are not just in the business of selling accommodation, food and beverages, but rather in the business of providing people with memorable experiences of service. This experience is enhanced by hotel employees. Although high technology and information system have replaced many traditional and administrative functions, it is not possible to replace service employees in an intensive "hands on" customer service culture in the hotel sector. Therefore, quality employees will continue to be an important factor to enhance hotel operational performance. However, many hotel owners in Taiwan are product-oriented and regard physical facilities as the way to gain competitive advantage when they reluctantly invest in hotel improvements. They are more likely to make investments in physical facilities because they are more likely to think luxurious amenity is attractive to customers. It seems that they do not realise that physical facilities can be imitated easily and usually results in many similar, often easily substitutable service offerings. Moreover, due to the particular characteristics of the hotel sector, it is important that the employees' personality can fit in the industry. Long working hours, hard working loading, shifts, and relatively low payment make the hotel sector an unattractive working environment. Employees must be happy and enjoy working in the hotel sector, otherwise, they will exit quickly. Under this situation, this research found that the way to attract and retain the good employees is to provide them with opportunities for continuous learning and growth and create a work environment where they are allowed a space to fulfill their ideals and feel taken care of by the hotel.

Well-Trained Employees can Increase Hotel's Productivity

In terms of providing opportunities for continuous learning and growth, training can be viewed as an indication that the hotel is willing to invest in its employees and cares about them; thus training may enhance their commitment to the hotel. In addition, hotels need high-levels of professionalism and care about details. Employees who have not received stringent training are unable to provide professional services. Today, customer's expectations are more unpredictable. Hotel attendants need to please customers holding more critical standards, and the difficulty of delivering service value is much higher. Employee training is thought to be critical in improving the level of service and operational efficiency, and to increase customer satisfaction and loyalty. Well-trained employees can increase the productivity of a hotel, because they can finish their works fast with fewer mistakes and they can indirectly reduce the burden on managers.

Since training is necessary and significant for hotel operation, we expect to see the hotel sector spending relatively high levels on training in Taiwan. However, several Taiwanese hotels still do not put emphasis on training. The reason for this is that the costs of training are upfront and obvious, while the benefits appear to be remote and immeasurable. In Taiwan, a number of hotel owners regard training as an operating expense rather than an investment. They rationalize large investment in physical assets such as new technology and product development which can generate money directly, yet it is hard for them to see spending in employee training as an investment. To convince hotel owners to implement employee training, there must be a recognisable benefit to the training activity, and if direct benefit and value cannot be identified then hotel owners will not spend money in training. In fact, the money spent on training can be earned from training effect and even create more profit. Moreover, training can save labour, hire less employees and at the same time provide efficient customer service. In addition, although training is costly, through technology application, training cost can be reduced and increase efficiency. Therefore, hotel cannot stop training employees simply because training is costly and not likely to bring immediate return. The loss of not providing training will be much greater.

Empowerment Allows Employees to Quickly Respond to Consumer Needs and Increase Customer Satisfaction

Empowerment is a substantial way to allow employees to demonstrate their capabilities and fulfill their ideals. Findings from this research suggested that empowerment is a kind of recognition of employee's competence. Employees know that they are empowered because they are trusted. Likewise, empowerment allows employees to win customer trust, because customers know their problems can be immediately addressed by employees. For hotel employees, it is the highest honor to win the trust of hotel and customers at the same time.

In the hotel sector where speed and efficiency are critical, empowerment is absolutely necessary. In the handling of customer compliant, if the customer's needs can be immediately satisfied, hotel may potentially overturn the customer's negative attitude and even receive compliment on service efficiency. In addition, empowerment can increase employee's sense of responsibility. Because when employees are given the information and authority required to handle customer issues, they cannot avoid assuming responsibility. Such an increase in responsibility will give them a sense of having ownership in the hotel. The result of which may create more positive employees and enhance operational performance.

Although empowerment can increase hotel's service quality, customer's satisfaction and operational efficiency, several of Taiwanese hotels still avoid empowering their employees. The major reason is that hotel owners are afraid that due to employee's promising more than it is cost-effective for the hotel to deliver, the hotel will suffer a loss. In fact, this problem can be prevented through proper design of the system and employee training. Through system design, the power of each level of employees can be clearly defined, and employees are also trained to properly use their power. Therefore, if there is an urgent need, employees can help customers solve problems in the first time without the decision of the supervisor.

This decentralized decision-making will help employees develop and grow in the job, and is claimed to be a technique which will both encourage the necessary level of commitment to organisational goals and provide the necessary discretion and autonomy to generate the level of customer service required (Lashley, 1995). Hotels should make good use of empowerment and become their advantage to increase their operational performance.

Providing Good Work Environment Will Make Employees Present the Best in Return

In the hotel sector, most of the operations and services rely on employees. Since employees are involved in hotel operation, the performance of these operations may be easily affected by human emotions. If a hotel manages to look after employees sincerely then employees will serve customers wholeheartedly, and customers may have a positive experience and feed that back to the hotel. This would be a virtuous circle. Therefore, employees should be regarded as one of the important assets, and a hotel should take good care of its employees.

The managers interviewed indicated that employees are internal customers of the hotels. A hotel should build a work environment where employees are treated like customers, and employees' personal affairs are viewed as matters of high importance by the hotel. The more concern the hotel shows in taking care of employees' personal affairs, the more they can perceive the concern of the hotel. Employees will also have a stronger sense of cohesion, which is contributive to hotel performance. Only happy employees will generate more happy customers. This relationship is the fundamental principle needed in an effective and sustainable customer service culture. Therefore, hotel cannot ignore the importance of providing its employees with good working environment.

This research revealed that those hotels suffering from low performance, usually treat employees as simply people hired to work for the hotel owners. These hotel owners do not deem taking care of employees and providing a good work environment as important. Some of them even regarded employees as substituent labour and do not mind if employees dislike their jobs, because they think a long line of applicants are waiting for their positions. If the hotel treats employees like this, its employees may take a passive attitude toward their jobs and hotel's performance will be influenced.

Although superior facilities are the foundation of a quality delivery system, it is the front-line employees who deliver the competence, convenience, respect, care, and integrity that convert the facility into true value for the customer. With competent and motivated employees, great service is possible; without it great service is a "pipe-dream" (LeBoeuf, 1987). To sum up, hotels should view employees as an important asset, and give full support and a good work environment with proper care for them. Then, they will be pleased to present their best to the hotels in return.

FUTURE RESEARCH DIRECTIONS

As mentioned earlier in this research, the policy that allows Chinese tourists to come to Taiwan has been concerned by local hotel operators but delayed for a long time. This policy finally took effect in July 2008. However, since implementation of this policy, there has been a large gap between the actual number and the expected number of Chinese visitors to Taiwan. Whether this policy can really bring positive effects on local hotels' performance as many have expected should be continuously followed in future research. In addition, in the last five years, motels and home-stays in Taiwan have become the favorite of many consumers due to their creative features and operating model. Their rapid growth has even threatened the business of international tourist hotels. Thus, the critical success factors of Taiwanese motels and home-stays can also be a focus of future researchers. Through research of their success factors, some useful information might be obtained as tips for international tourist hotels.

CONCLUSION

The main objective of measuring hotel operational efficiency was to gain an insight into how a hotel is evaluated and how it can improve efficiency with its current resource base or a change of resource allocation. The major problem in measuring lies on the incommensurability of different output measurements as well as input measurements. This problem can be solved by the DEA approach. However, DEA approach can only determine relative operational efficiency but cannot identify the factors that give rise to inefficiency or lead to efficiency. Furthermore, DEA only calls attention to those hotels in which efficiency and inefficiency exist, but cannot provide suggestions on how to improve operational efficiency. In other words, DEA only answers "how well a hotel is doing"; "which hotel is doing well"; but it ignores the most important question "why this hotel is doing well". The real aim of applying DEA is to identify what factors cause efficiency and what factors result in inefficiency.

In addition, using DEA to evaluate hotel operational efficiency can only measure quantitative data and often overlook intangible issues such as hotel location, employee's ability or hotel age. These issues may be external to the control of management but can crucially affect hotel operational efficiency. As Morey and Dittman (1995, p.21) observed, "sometimes one must look past the numbers and take into account qualitative factors". Lucas and Deery (2004) also indicated that qualitative research inquires have great potential when exploring issues in the field of hospitality. Therefore, qualitative approach may be a good way to address this limitation of DEA. This would involve the collection and analysis of verbal data by in-depth interviews with hotel managers, and to develop critical success factors contributing to hotels having good performance. Through the exploration of critical success factors, this research helps managers understand the factors determining the operational efficiency; develop effective strategies to meet a highly competitive environment; and provide hotel managers with a list of recommendations to enhance hotel performance.

It is noted that previous research demonstrated that in Taiwan, hotels belonging to an international chain have better performance than independent hotels (Hwang and Chang, 2003). However, this research found that joining an international chain is only effective in Taipei, because there are many foreign travelers in Taipei, they have higher brand loyalty, and they will choose familiar international chains. If the hotel is located elsewhere, the number of foreign guests is small, and local customers usually have no brand awareness. Therefore, the effect of an international chain membership will be minimal. This implies that even international chain hotels have sounder management system, better brand image. It cannot be denied that the location factor has a great influence on hotel operation and are outside the control of hotel management. Taiwan is small, but customer type, consumer habit, market characteristic, and even competitive situations all vary from one region to another. It is not possible to apply a fixed management model to all the regions. This is also the reason why several chain hotels have good performance only in their Taipei branch. Therefore, all hotels should thoroughly evaluate the characteristics of their market and make use of their exclusive conditions and resources to develop strategies that meet the needs of their local markets.

This research was intended to generate data and insights that are relevant to operational performance of Taiwanese international tourist hotels. However, there are some limitations regarding the generalisation of the results presented here. The target of this research was international tourist hotel, which total 57 establishments in Taiwan. However, in Taiwan, a large number of hotels do not apply to Taiwan Tourism Bureau to be recognised as an international tourist hotel. These hotels are not necessarily inferior to international tourist hotels whether in terms of scale, facilities or services. Some of them are even superior. However, they were not included in the sample of this research, because unlike international tourist hotels, their business data, such as occupancy rate, average room rate, business income, business expenditure could not be accessed from the annual operation report published by Taiwan's Tourism Bureau. Without sufficient data of these hotels, we had no choice but to exclude them in the DEA analysis.

Data used in the DEA analysis were mainly extracted from the *Annual Operation Report of the International Tourist Hotels in Taiwan 2005* published by Taiwan Tourism Bureau in 2007. This was also the latest operation data of international tourist hotels in Taiwan to date. However, the data were collected three years ago. Over the last three years, with the constant variation of the market, the 57 international tourist hotels included in this report could have made some changes to their operations. Therefore, a certain gap could exist between the results of analysis made the basis of data of three years ago and practical operations of these hotels.

In our qualitative in-depth interview, all of the respondents were hotel managers. Although the information they provided were representative of professional opinions, if opinions of entry-level employees and customers could also be collected, the research data may be more comprehensive.

In the face of strong growing competition, the performance of hotel operations and management plays a crucial role to determine a hotel's profitability and even its survival. Performance measurement can provide hotel managers with benchmarking information and further insight on the improvement of hotel operation. This thesis adopted the DEA to measure the operational efficiency of 57 international tourist hotels in Taiwan. By comparing relative efficiency, the benchmarking hotels and an individual hotel's competitiveness can be identified. Further analysis of the critical success factors contributing to hotels having good performance help managers understand the factors determining the good operational performance. In this thesis, the linkage between performance measurement and critical success factors were illustrated by Taiwanese international tourist hotels. It was expected that this thesis will provide useful information for future related research as well as identifying hotel management needs.

REFERENCES

Anderson, R. I., Fok, R., & Scott, J. (2000). Hotel industry efficiency: An advanced linear programming examination. *American Business Review*, *18*(1), 40–48.

Atkinson, H., & Brown, J. B. (2001). Rethinking performance measures: assessing progress in UK hotels. *International Journal of Contemporary Hospitality Management*, *13*(3), 128–135. doi:10.1108/09596110110388918

Barros, C. P. (2004). Productivity in the tourism industry. *International Advances in Economic Research*, *10*(3), 215–226. doi:10.1007/BF02296216

Barros, C. P. (2005). Evaluating the efficiency of a small hotel chain with a Malmquist productivity index. *International Journal of Tourism Research*, *7*(3), 173–184. doi:10.1002/jtr.529

Charnes, A., Cooper, W. W., & Rhodes, E. (1978). Measuring the efficiency of decision making units. *European Journal of Operational Research*, *2*(6), 429–444. doi:10.1016/0377-2217(78)90138-8

Coltman, M. M. (1978). *Hospitality management accounting*. Boston: CBI Publishing Co., Inc.

Fay, C. T., Rhoads, R. C., & Rosenblatt, R. L. (1971). *Managerial accounting for hospitality service industries. Dubuque, IO: William C.* Brown Publishers.

Fitzgerald, L., Johnston, R., Brignall, T. J., Silvestro, R., & Voss, C. (1991). *Performance measurement in service businesses*. London: The Chartered Institute of Management Accountants.

Harris, P. J. (1999). *Profit planning* (2nd ed.). Oxford: Butterworth-Heinemann.

Hong Kong Tourism Board, (2007). *Monthly operation report of hotel in December 2006.*

Hwang, S., & Chang, T. (2003). Using data envelopment analysis to measure hotel managerial efficiency change in Taiwan. *Tourism Management, 24*(4), 357–369. doi:10.1016/S0261-5177(02)00112-7

Jones, G. R., & George, R. W. (2003). *Contemporary management* (3rd ed.). New York: McGraw-Hill Companies, Inc.

Kimes, S. E. (1989). The basics of yield management. *The Cornell Hotel and Restaurant Administration Quarterly, 30*(3), 14–19. doi:10.1177/001088048903000309

Kotas, R. (1975). *Market orientation in the hotel and catering industry*. Guildford, UK: Surrey University Press.

Morey, R. C., & Dittman, D. A. (1995). Evaluating a hotel GM's performance. *The Cornell Hotel and Restaurant Administration Quarterly, 36*(2), 18–32.

Morey, R. C., & Dittman, D. A. (2003). Update and extension to 'Evaluating a hotel GM's performance'. *The Cornell Hotel and Restaurant Administration Quarterly, 44*(5), 60–68. doi:10.1016/S0010-8804(03)90108-X

Phillips, P. A. (1999). Performance measurement systems and hotels: A new conceptual framework. *International Journal of Hospitality Management, 18*(2), 171–182. doi:10.1016/S0278-4319(99)00016-X

Reynolds, D. (2003). Hospitality-productivity assessment using data-envelopment analysis. *The Cornell Hotel and Restaurant Administration Quarterly, 44*(2), 130–137.

Reynolds, D., & Thompson, G. M. (2007). Multiunit restaurant productivity assessment using three-phase data envelopment analysis. *International Journal of Hospitality Management, 26*(1), 20–32. doi:10.1016/j.ijhm.2005.08.004

Sasser, W. E., Olsen, P. R., & Wyckoff, D. D. (1978). *Management of service operations*. Boston: Allyn and Bacon.

Sexton, T. R. (1986). The methodology of data envelopment analysis. In Silkman, R. H. (Ed.), *Measuring efficiency: an assessment of Data Envelopment Analysis* (pp. 115–130). San Francisco: American Evaluation Association.

Shoemaker, S., Lewis, R. C., & Yesawich, P. C. (2007). *Marketing leadership in hospitality and tourism: strategies and tactics for competitive advantage (4th ended.)*. New Jersey: Pearson Prentice Hall.

Sigala, M. (2004). Using data envelopment analysis for measuring and benchmarking productivity in the hotel sector. *Journal of Travel & Tourism Marketing, 16*(2/3), 39–60. doi:10.1300/J073v16n02_04

Sun, S., & Lu, W. M. (2005). Evaluating the performance of the Taiwanese hotel industry using a weight slacks-based measure. *Asia-Pacific Journal of Operational Research, 22*(4), 487–512. doi:10.1142/S0217595905000595

Taiwan Tourism Bureau. (2005). *Annual operation report of international tourist hotels, 2004.* Taipei: Republic of China Press.

Taiwan Tourism Bureau. (2007). *Monthly operation report of international tourist hotels, Dec. 2006.* Taipei: Republic of China Press.

Taiwan Tourism Bureau. (2007a). *Annual operation report of international tourist hotels, 2005.* Taipei: Taiwan Tourism Bureau Press.

Van Doren, C. S., & Gustke, L. D. (1982). Spatial analysis of the U.S. lodging industry. *Annals of Tourism Research, 9*(4), 543–563. doi:10.1016/0160-7383(82)90072-X

Weatherford, L. R. (1995). Length of stay heuristics: do they really make a difference. *The Cornell Hotel and Restaurant Administration Quarterly, 36*(6), 70–79.

Weatherford, L. R., & Bodily, S. E. (1992). A taxonomy and research overview of perishable-asset revenue management: yield management, overbooking and pricing. *Operations Research*, *40*(5), 831–844. doi:10.1287/opre.40.5.831

Wijeysinghe, B. S. (1993). Breakeven occupancy for a hotel operation. *Management Accounting*, *71*(2), 32–33.

Witt, C. A., & Witt, S. F. (1989). Why productivity in the hotel sector is low. *International Journal of Contemporary Hospitality Management*, *1*(2), 28–34. doi:10.1108/EUM0000000001669

Yasin, M. M., Andrew, J. C., & Jeffrey, J. D. (1996). Breakeven occupancy for a hotel operation. *Management Accounting*, *7*(12), 32–33.

ADDITIONAL READING

Alexander, M., & Young, D. (1996). Outsourcing: where the value is. *Long Range Planning*, *29*(5), 728–730. doi:10.1016/0024-6301(96)00069-6

Anderson, R. I., Fish, M., Xia, Y., & Michello, F. (1999). Measuring efficiency in the hotel industry: A stochastic frontier approach. *International Journal of Hospitality Management*, *18*(1), 45–57. doi:10.1016/S0278-4319(98)00046-2

Baker, M., & Riley, M. (1994). New perspectives on productivity in hotels: some advantages and new direction. *International Journal of Hospitality Management*, *13*(4), 297–311. doi:10.1016/0278-4319(94)90068-X

Berry, L. L. (1986). Big ideas in service brand equity. *Journal of the Academy of Marketing Science*, *28*(Winter), 128–137.

Brotherton, R., & Leslie, D. (1991). Critical information needs for achieving strategic goals. In Teare, R., & Boer, A. (Eds.), *Strategic hospitality management: Theory and practice for the 1990s* (pp. 33–44). London: Cassell.

Brymer, R. A. (1991). Employee empowerment: a guest driven leadership strategy. *The Cornell Hotel and Restaurant Administration Quarterly*, *32*(1), 58–68.

Buick, I., & Muthu, G. (1997). An investigation of the current practices of in-house employee training and development within hotels in Scotland. *The Service Industries Journal*, *17*(4), 652–668. doi:10.1080/02642069700000039

Cacioppe, R. (1998). Structured empowerment: an award-winning program at the Burswood Resort Hotel. *Leadership and Organisation Journal*, *19*(5), 264–274. doi:10.1108/01437739810234332

Dube, L., Enz, C. A., Renaghan, L. M., & Singuaw, J. A. (2000). Managing for excellence. *The Cornell Hotel and Restaurant Administration Quarterly*, *41*(5), 326–380.

Easinwood, C. J., & Mahajan, V. (1989). Positioning of financial services for competitive strategy. *Journal of Product Innovation Management*, *6*(3), 207–219. doi:10.1016/0737-6782(89)90032-5

Espino-Rodríguez, T. F. (2004). The tendency to outsource hotel operations: strategic reasons and relationship to activity, performance, and size. *Tourism Review*, *59*(2), 17–25. doi:10.1108/eb058432

Eyster, J. J. (1977). Owner and operator bargaining power factors in hotel management contract negotiations. *Cornell Hospitality Quarterly*, *18*(1), 57–63.

Guilding, C. (2003). Hotel owner/operator structures: implications for capital budgeting process. *Management Accounting Research*, *14*, 179–199. doi:10.1016/S1044-5005(03)00049-0

Hassanien, A. (2006). Exploring hotel renovation in large hotels: a multiple case study. *Structural Survey*, *24*(1), 41–64. doi:10.1108/02630800610654414

Herzberg, F., Bernard, M., & Narnara, S. (1959). *The motivation to work* (2nd ed.). NY: John Wiley and Sons, Inc.

Jiang, W., Dev, C. S., & Rao, V. R. (2002). Brand extension and customer loyalty: Evidence from the lodging industry. *The Cornell Hotel and Restaurant Administration Quarterly*, *43*(3), 5–16. doi:10.1016/S0010-8804(02)80037-4

Jogaratnam, G., & Tse, E. C. Y. (2004). The entrepreneurial approach to hotel operation. *The Cornell Hotel and Restaurant Administration Quarterly*, *45*(3), 248–259. doi:10.1177/0010880404266192

Klidas, A., Berg, P. T., & Wilderom, C. (2007). Managing employee empowerment in luxury hotels in Europe. *International Journal of Service Industry Management*, *18*(1), 70–88. doi:10.1108/09564230710732902

Lewis, R. C. (1990). Advertising your hotel's position. *The Cornell Hotel and Restaurant Administration Quarterly*, *31*(2), 84–91. doi:10.1177/001088049003100213

Mazanec, J. A. (1995). Positioning analysis with self-organizing maps: an exploratory study on luxury hotels. *The Cornell Hotel and Restaurant Administration Quarterly*, *36*(6), 80–95.

Ottenbacher, M. (2007). Innovation management in the hospitality industry: different strategies for achieving success. *Journal of Hospitality & Tourism Research (Washington, D.C.)*, *31*(4), 431–454. doi:10.1177/1096348007302352

Teng, J., Cheon, M., & Grover, V. (1995). Decisions to outsource information system functions: testing a strategy-theoretic-discrepancy model. *Decision Sciences*, *26*(1), 75–103. doi:10.1111/j.1540-5915.1995.tb00838.x

Tidball, K. H. (1988). Creating a culture that builds your bottom line. *The Cornell Hotel and Restaurant Administration Quarterly*, *29*(3), 63–69. doi:10.1177/001088048802900118

Victorino, L., Verma, R., Plaschka, G., & Chekitan, D. (2005). Service, innovation, and customer choices in the hospitality industry. *Managing Service Quality*, *15*(6), 555–576. doi:10.1108/09604520510634023

KEY TERMS AND DEFINITIONS

Benchmarking: A continuous systematic process for evaluating the products, service and work of organisations that are recognized as representing best practices for the purpose of organisational improvement (Spendolini, 1992).

Critical Success Factors: Defined as what the organization must accomplish to achieve the mission by examination and categorization of the impacts. They are the minimum key factors or sub-goals that the organization must have or need, and which together will achieve the mission (Oakland, 1995).

Efficiency: Defined as a measure of how well or how productively resources are used to achieve a goal. Organisations are efficient when managers minimize the amount of input resource or the amount of time needed to produce a given output of goals or service (Jones and George, 2003).

Financial Performance: The use of earnings and profitability as the indicator of business performance such as earning per share (EPS), return on investment (ROI), and return on capital employed (ROCE) (Phillips, 1999).

Heterogeneity: The inconsistent delivery of service levels provided by many different employees, affected by many different customers. Owing to human-intensive nature of providing a service, the fluctuation in service are a result of individual differences among employees and among customers themselves as well as customers' perceptions of these differences (Shoemaker et al., 2000).

International Tourist Hotel: According to the Taiwan Tourism Bureau (TTB), the hotel industry in Taiwan can be divided into international tourist hotels and standard tourist hotels. The plum-grading system is issued by TTB for hotel grading. This plum-grading system is similar to the star-grading system used by many countries in the world. A hotel with more plums means that it has more quantity of hotel facilities. An international tourist hotel is a hotel with five or four plums.

Intangibility: The attribute of services that the customer cannot grasp with any of the five senses; that is, customers cannot taste, feel, see, smell, or hear a service until they have consumed it, and one cannot easily grasp it. Services are experienced, rather than possessed. There is no passing of title when service is purchased. Buyers have nothing to be displayed, to be shown to friends or family, to put on the shelf, or ever to use again. In sum, buyers leave the transaction empty-handed. They do not, however, go away empty-headed. They have memories of the experience that they can recall and share with associates and friends (Shoemaker et al., 2000).

Non-Financial Performance: Is using the factors not relative to finance to evaluate business performance such as service quality, customer satisfaction (Eccles, 1991).

Perishability: The life cycle of the hospitality service. For example, a room is only available for a 24-hour period and cannot be stored and sold the next day. If is not sold on a particular night, the opportunity to sell it is gone forever (Shoemaker et al., 2000).

Performance Measurement: The process of quantifying action, where measurement is the process of quantification and action leads to performance. In other words, performance measurement can be regarded as the process of quantifying the efficiency and effectiveness of action (Neely, Gregory and Platts, 1995).

Productivity: Gummesson (1998) defined the productivity as a ratio between output and input; but further referred to the interconnection between productivity, quality and profitability and discussed the role of customers in impacting productivity and quality.

Chapter 4
Knowledge Management Approach as Business Model:
Service Industry Prospective

Viju Mathew
College of Applied Sciences Salalah (MOHE), Sultanate of Oman

ABSTRACT

Knowledge management (KM) has been sprouting as one of the outstanding conversant factor strongly in trust, and trust is a critical precondition to knowledge learning and sharing management concepts (Mathew, 2008). The chapter intended to bring forward various KM strategies specially framed for the service industries looking forward for the global market and need to create advantage in providing customer satisfaction and enhancing the growth prospects, applications in organizations, indicate how to improve knowledge based performance and act a base for the service industry for developing innovation, creating global opportunities for better service. The case study highlighting knowledge strategies is designed to achieve the required knowledge sharing and output. Open-ended and closed-ended strategies plays a significant role in collaborative learning, development, building the potential and providing the knowledge creation and sharing capacities needed for strategic formulation and decision making to create competitiveness.

INTRODUCTION

Sharing of knowledge is extremely important that the organization should be encouraged through various means and method enabling to depend on its own sources. Knowledge sharing within the organization enables the employers to share insight which help them to adopt appropriate faster and cost effective move towards the achievement of organizational goals. Organization exist due

DOI: 10.4018/978-1-60960-129-4.ch004

to people, process and profit which are the most essential elements guiding different terms like organizational growth, competitive advantage, and development. Some of the analysts believe that the information and technology are the key drivers for the today's business and plays a vital role affecting both individual and organization. Ages back, information has been extremely important that creates benefits to the organization. The organization looks for the information which can be used by the people, for the process to gain profit and advantage. Information system transformed to knowledge system in last decades where knowledge are the source for gaining advantages. Knowledge and its management is not just technology based but also have human factor. Information technology is a key driver for knowledge management (Soliman & Spooner, 2000).

Knowledge management has become an important area of focus for many organizations in order to be successful in today's business environment. There are many reasons for this; the foremost is the difficulty in establishing regular improvement system and loss of knowledge in an undertaking. Secondly, finding the cause and effect about the management process and finding business outcome. The number of steps required to show a connection to relate the knowledge management benefits and business outcomes can be highlighted as:

1. Need to be a strategy assessment with respect to knowledge management
2. Knowledge audit
3. Strategy needs to be aligned with the business strategy
4. Identify any gaps.
5. Searching new opportunities for knowledge programs
6. Build justification

BACKGROUND

Importance of KM Initiatives

The increasing globalization, efficiency in process, competitive advantage, organizational learning, and development of technology (Davenport & Prusak, 1998) has pressured to gain knowledge assets within the organization for improving its system. It has been said knowledge has become the key economic resource and the dominant source of competitive advantage (Drucker, 1995). Salleh and Goh's (2002) defined knowledge management as process of leveraging knowledge as means of achieving innovation in process and products/services, effective decision-making, and organizational adaptation to the market for creating business value and generating a competitive advantage to organizations. If the above statement is true, then it is extremely important that an efficient knowledge-intensive process must be established to meet the demands of improved enterprise performance (Quinn et al., 1996).

'Knowledge' is considered to possess key properties like experience, truth and decision making, and is typically associated with so-called knowledge- intensive firms (Alvesson, 1995, p. 6). Sharing of knowledge is considered as the most important in KM process. Effective flow of knowledge is only possible through the people through appropriate technology and mutual understanding (Egan, 2003; Geraint, 1998). People remain vital in the knowledge sharing and because lack of these factor knowledge management initiatives fail (Carter & Scarborough, 2001). Knowledge based business establishment tries to create a knowledge culture where learning through various methods has been established. The people and technology are combined to share and flow of knowledge. KM is dependent directly on people and at some percent on technology. Knowledge officers play a major role in contribution of knowledge process and determine the knowledge flow. Hislop (2003); Greengard (1998b) recommended that each functional departments have their own responsibility in knowledge flow, transfer and process. It has been tremendously important that the organization should be encouraged through various means and method for knowledge sharing which will enable the organization to depend on its own sources. Information and communication technology plays a crucial role in organizing knowledge, both in order to enable sharing and collaboration, categorizing, disseminating and storing of different knowledge which can later be retrieved and accessible as meaningful across different contexts.

Individuals knowledge (termed as tacit knowledge by Nonaka & Takeuchi, 1995) came from various factor can be means of problem solving criteria or organizational knowledge which can be combined with explicit knowledge for KM process. The storage of explicit knowledge in form of meeting minutes, committee, discussion and other forums should be transmitted in the form of filtered documents and shared within the organization.

KNOWLEDGE AND KNOWLEDGE MANAGEMENT

Knowledge sharing within the organization enables the employers to share insight (Mathew *et al.* 2008) which help them to adopt appropriate ideas and allows faster and cost effective move towards the achievement of organizational goals. Employees coming from the different background and experience create cost effective and time saving process which can be captured, stored and shared by much other recreating better process. Appropriate knowledge transfer culture will support the organization to draw up the experience of other in their pursuit of finding cost effective and result oriented solution to the organizational problems. Various strategies and policy will motivate the organization to support organizational culture in practice.

"The capability of an organization to create new knowledge, disseminate it throughout the organization and embody it in products, services and systems." Nonaka & Takeuchi, 1995

"An integrated systematic approach to identifying, managing and sharing an organization's knowledge and enabling persons to create new knowledge collectively and thereby help achieving the objectives of organization" (Mathew et al. 2008).

The following definitions might help to gain the perspectives of knowledge:

1. Awareness, consciousness or familiarity gained by experience or learning.' (Collins English Dictionary)
2. Information and skills acquired through experience and education. (Oxford English Dictionary, Oxford University Press, 2002, p. 786)
3. Knowledge is understanding of why, what, how, who, when, and relative to taking some action. Knowledge is the product of organization and reasoning applied to raw data (Knowledge Management in ADB, Asian Development Bank, June 2004, p. 3)
4. Knowledge is a fluid mix of framed experience, values, contextual information, and expert insight that provides a framework for evaluating and incorporating new experiences and information. It originates and is applied in the minds of knowers. In organizations, it often becomes embedded not only in documents and repositories but also an organizational routines, processes, practices and norms.' (Davenport, T and Prusak, L. – Working Knowledge: How Organizations Manage What They Know. Cambridge, MA Harvard University Press, 1998, p. 5)
5. Knowledge is intrinsically a human characteristics manifested in the thinking,

learning, artistic, behavioral, and problem solving capabilities of human beings acting in a social context (Sami AlBanna – Knowledge Management and Strategies for Development in a Rapidly Changing Global Environment)

The components of knowledge management (Binwal, 2001) are:

1. **People management:** recognition of the skills of people
2. **Process management:** links into the identification and deployment of practices may be associated with business process reengineering.
3. **Information management:** knowledge, and not just information and data, should be available from wherever it is needed to all those authorized to receive it. The language should be simple and appropriate making both input and output easy.

Knowledge Management is a systematic process that uses knowledge and continuously transfers knowledge from individual, groups, functional units and other related areas for the benefit of the entire organization creating learning and knowledge sharing culture (Mathew, 2008). It is the systematic capture, sharing, dissemination and use of various applications to maximize organizational performance and effectiveness. The core of knowledge management is to leverage knowledge resources into best practices for competitive and other advantages. Knowledge can be acquired. It includes understanding, familiarity, awareness and perceptive gained through experience or study, and results from making comparisons, identifying consequences, and making connections. KM can also be explained as systematic arrangement of information which provide and support organization development and decision making creating value. In organizational terms, knowledge is generally thought of as being "know how", or "applied action" or "know what".

Denning's (2000) Knowledge Management framework reviews of the work originally done by Van der Spek and de Hood in which he covers such issues as:

- Identifying what knowledge assets a company possesses
- Analyzing how the knowledge can add value
- Specifying what actions are necessary to achieve better usability and added value
- Reviewing the use of the knowledge to ensure added value.

Sveiby (2001) considers that KM is the added value creation capability through organization intangible assets. He explained that the basic components of KM are the people, process, information and technology that turn into knowledge data and information. Andreu and Sieber (1999) explained knowledge management as a "continuous process to ensure practical development at the organization in order to improve organization problems solution capability and contribute competitive advantages support". Waltz (2003) argues that KM refers to different organizational disciplines, processes and technology information applied to acquire, create and spread knowledge to get companies mission and its strategies and targets business. Gurteen (1998) reflected "Knowledge Management is an emerging set of organizational design and operational principles, processes, organizational structures, applications and technologies that helps knowledge workers dramatically leverage their creativity and ability to deliver business value".

Knowledge sharing–Is the exchange of knowledge and information which the people has gained of experiences, education, training, thoughts and sharing through social interaction, coordination and cooperation. Three basic prerequisites of knowledge sharing are: people related factor includes people attitude, motivation, values, skills, trust, and roles etc. Second, organizational related factor includes policies, strategies, structure, systems, and style and shared values in organizations. Thirdly, resource factor includes human, technology, knowledge repository, collaboration, knowledge route map, and cooperation strategies for sharing knowledge.

Knowledge transfer – Knowledge transfer can be explained as the process of transferring knowledge through sharing and collaboration. It involves the use of resources and technological aid supporting the transfer process. It involves sharing of knowledge to a potential recipient, and understanding the send knowledge for contributing and enhancing recipient's performance.

KM ADVANTAGES

Other than capturing, sharing knowledge of best practices, training, collaboration, corporate learning, effectively managing customer relationships, and delivering competitive intelligence. Attain level of performance by ensuring continuity and consistency; promote transparency in decision making; disseminating the information in various functional units; focuses on enabling, empowering, directing, and energizing employees (Wing, 1999); creates networking to enable people to access knowledge resources developed by others; provides flexible sustainable information base and protects capital resources, support in decision making, problem solving; developing the level of performance; future forecasting improvement and productivity; Less error, less redundancy, quicker problem solving, better decision making, reduced R&D costs; learning; forming group decision and opinions; optimize resources in making decisions; increased worker independence, enhanced customer relations, and improved service (Fernandes & Usher, 1999); system of management decision making by supporting the functional activities to make use of existing information and link with other functional department for the overall coordination and growth (Mathew, 2008); Reducing cost, maximize organization's potential; supports strategic planning, policy formulation, forecasting and generating viable alternatives for measured activities to achieve desired results are the other advantages of KM in an organisation.

The main features of KM are as follows:

1. KM adds value to the organizational goals through constant review and updates
2. KM depends on the competencies, organizational culture, learning, motivation, attitude and trust among human resources.
3. KM is continuous and flexible in nature.
4. KM is systematic process which enhances organizational efficiency and effectiveness of organization.
5. KM supports organizations to achieve their goal by managing and using information (creating, obtaining, analyzing, verifying, storing, preserving, retrieving and disseminating)
6. KM supports the management by supplying critical knowledge for decision making

FUNCTIONS OF KNOWLEDGE MANAGEMENT

The function of knowledge is to make a change in the overall organizational performance and leads to higher productivity. Knowledge is high-value resource that is integrated to apply for making organizational decisions and taking productive actions. It includes data, information, ideas, experience, insights and awareness. It is the combination of information or what we know or the state of knowing in-depth.

The main features include:

- Collective capabilities to understand, apply skills and accessing knowledge resources and experience.

- The core function of knowledge management in an organization is the ability to identify critical knowledge resources and use them objectively in improving competency, creating efficiency, developing self-confidence; enhance competitiveness and leads to productivity.
- Enhancement of knowledge support continuous and meaningful application of skill, continuous learning, social interaction and analyzing performance results.
- KM is significant in problem solving, decision making, integrating, goal accomplishment and improving and evaluating the performance.
- Knowledge Management process function is to gain through sharing, education, training, work experience, dialogue, participation and group interactions both internally and externally.
- Knowledge should be regularly reviewed and updated to make it relevant and effective.
- Knowledge supports solving problems and contributes to productivity and sustainable development and improvement.

CRITICAL SUCCESS FACTORS FOR KNOWLEDGE MANAGEMENT

The critical success factors for KM in a service organisation can be broadly classified as into four divisions- People, Processes, Technology & Sustainable development.

Standardized Processes: includes standard procedure for knowledge-contribution, content management, retrieval, communities of practice, implementation, project management, methodology & standard formats to document best-practices & case studies, etc. It is necessary by various stakeholders to understand and support the implementation of standard procedure of KM

People: Major contribution in KM process is based on people for "Knowledge-hoarding" to "knowledge-sharing" and "knowledge development". People are considered as the major participant contributing through knowledge sharing, collaboration and re-use to achieve business results. This is achieved through a combination of motivation / recognition & rewards performance appraisal systems, and other measurement systems.

Technology: KM technology (both information technology and communication) solutions provide functional support for knowledge-sharing, collaboration, workflow, document-management, etc. across the enterprise and beyond into the extended enterprise. Technology is a key enabler to KM ensuring technological solution and focus business issues and is user-friendly used for exchange information, share knowledge and guide each other and the organization to better decisions.

Sustainable development: KM supports success and provides sustainable development committed to continuous improvement.

Davenport et al. (1998) have identified eight knowledge management success factors such as: technology infrastructure; organizational infrastructure; balance of flexibility, evolution and ease-of-accessibility to knowledge; shared knowledge; knowledge-friendly culture; motivated worker who develop, share and use knowledge; means of knowledge transfer using various information technology infrastructures; and senior management support and commitment. The most comprehensive list of success factors by Moffett et al. (2003) has presented ten key components to successful knowledge management as: a friendly organizational culture; senior management leadership and commitment; employee involvement; employee training; trustworthy teamwork; employee empowerment; information systems infrastructure; performance measurement; benchmarking and knowledge structure.

PREREQUISITES FOR KNOWLEDGE TRANSFER

Building Trust in the Organization

Knowledge transfer is directly linked on trust among the people building confidence about sharing experiences, ideas, and relationships within the organization

Creating the Culture to Accommodate Change

Creating the organization culture through mission, values, policies, strategies and developing practices to accommodate changes will support the organization to achieve performance. Leadership, operational practices, policies, structure and management plays a vital role in accommodating change.

Infrastructure for KM

The organization need to have KM supporting infrastructure to gather, process, storage, retrieval, dissemination and collaboration

Knowledge Workers

The people are the base line of KM process and teamwork required for effective functioning of the process. The organization need knowledge workers supporting the implementation of KM policies and strategies, gather, process, storage, retrieval, disseminate, collaborates and regularly improve the knowledge within the organization for achieving knowledge result.

Collaboration, Cooperation and Teamwork

The organizational functional department, units, employees and organization need to be supportive to KM processes in terms of collaboration, cooperation and teamwork for knowledge sharing and transfer within the organization and other related components.

FACTORS FOR KNOWLEDGE MANAGEMENT IMPLEMENTATION

Employee Involvement

Employee involvement for sharing knowledge contributes to meet organizational objectives. Employee involvement is a sequential process aimed at sharing information, knowledge, rewards and authority (Steinecke, 1993). The focus of KM application is to provide a surrounding in which knowledge workers can create new knowledge and share.

Information Systems Infrastructure

Well developed information systems infrastructure is necessary for the organization to implement the knowledge management process. Information system and network technology infrastructure supports storage, analysis, dissemination, and sharing of knowledge which forms an important element of KM process.

Employee Training

Greco (1999) explains that the key elements of successful KM is education to help employees recognize what knowledge is valuable, and therefore merits sharing. The training capabilities for any organizations should be well recognized, especially for those agents concerned with preserving intellectual capital (Carneiro, 2001). Training provides skills and necessary knowledge to fulfill their responsibilities.

Teamwork

Teamwork is an essential source of the knowledge generation process (Choi, 2000). Teams are the units that actually carry out the work in many knowledge-intensive organizations (Mohrman et al., 1995). A well-staffed team is crucial for successful implementation of knowledge management (Civi, 2000).

Performance Measurement

KM process should be measured in terms of performance understanding expansion, innovation, development, quantity of intellectual capital and productivity. Measuring intangible assets help the organization to develop efficiency.

Employee Empowerment

Employee empowerment is one of the critical factors for knowledge management implementation success. Employee's empowerment will enable them to comprehend and contribute to the performance of the organization (Bowen & Lawler, 1992) and this fact initiate to take extra responsibilities to solve organizational problems by learning new skills in their jobs (Anahotu, 1998).

Leadership of Top Management

Leadership is very essential for successful KM process. Leadership is responsible for creating the knowledge vision of the organization, and building a knowledge culture maintaining employees' morale for KM process.

Benchmarking

Benchmarking is the most effective tools for developing knowledge management process. Effective and continuous application of benchmarking in KM process will help the organization to support competitive advantage. Benchmarking insists on developing knowledge strategy in order to capture, share and manage organizational knowledge.

Knowledge-Friendly Culture

Organizational culture acts as fundamental concept managing organizational development and change. Organizational culture reflect organizational outlook facilitating both learning, innovation and change encouraging organization to adopt KM process building knowledge as support for adding value and change.

Principles of Knowledge Management

1. Connectivity and collaboration can be used as the major tool for KM
2. Knowledge process should be linked and hold together:
3. Knowledge systems should include collective knowledge contents
4. Knowledge management systems should focus on both individual and group within the same system.
5. Knowledge should be 'pulled' from its source using various KM techniques, rather than 'pushed' to central repositories.
6. Knowledge process systems should capture and develop in usable form
7. Knowledge processes add value
8. Knowledge should be provided in the context of existing business processes
9. Knowledge should be self-managed by its authors and users.
10. Knowledge systems should adapt themselves to the organization's culture and information
11. Knowledge systems should enable users/customers to find needed experts and connect with them expediently:
12. Knowledge change management need to acquire knowledge based on need of the organization
13. Knowledge management tools should be simple and provide insight

14. Knowledge needs should be specified in terms of requirement of the user

TECHNIQUES TO ADMINISTER KNOWLEDGE

Literature related to the KM suggests various techniques for managing knowledge within the organization are as follows:

1. Balanced scorecards (Kaplan & Norton, 1996),
2. Modeling languages (Mayer, Cullinane, de Witte, Knappernberger, Perakath, & Wells, 1992)
3. Other knowledge-based applications (Benus, 1993; Schreiber, Akkermans, Anjewierden, De Hoog, Van De Velde, & Wielinga, 1998)
4. Role Activity Diagrams (Ould, 1993);
5. SWOT (Strengths Weaknesses Opportunities Threats) analysis,

Knowledge sharing is one of the most difficult and time consuming activity. The employees in fear of losing advantage are less incline to share their knowledge with others. It is also difficult to determine the solution on which the organization tries to solve the problems.

Various obstacles for sharing knowledge in an organization are:

1. Lack of knowledge sharing strategies to encourage individual, group, functional and organizational knowledge sharing and exploring employees related to knowledge.
2. Knowledge among the employees which are hindered (Gonam, 2002) reducing their advantage and can impede their ability (Bender & Fish, 2000).
3. Lack of trust, understanding & collaboration among employees.
4. Knowledge sharing is time consuming & costly.
5. Competition among different functional unit leads to unwilling to share their knowledge
6. Lack of technology, infrastructure
7. Lack of motivation
8. Lack of open communication
9. Lack of trustworthiness
10. Lack of top management support

KNOWLEDGE SHARING STRATEGIES: DESIGNED AS SOLUTION

Knowledge sharing among the employees and to develop a knowledge sharing culture needs strategies. The strategies include:

1. Open strategies
2. Closed strategies

1. ***Open strategies:*** Organization have defined set of rules and regulation guiding communication, knowledge sharing, transfer and other purposes. The open strategies have been described as the strategies adopted by the organization including rules and policies which will be open to all and can be used for getting connected for the organizational resources and reasons. This includes:
    a. Interaction among employees (Smith, 2003)
    b. Mentorship (Cope, 1998)
    c. Management support (Geraint, 1998; Goman, 2002)
    d. Technological usage (Smith, 2003)
    e. Knowledge sharing and culture
2. ***Closed strategies:*** The limited activities in which employees are involved and specified based on certain criteria providing sharing of knowledge in an organization. This includes:

a. Reward system (Desouza & Awazn, 2003)
b. HR development (Hislop, 2003)
c. Structural matching (Bhatt, 2001; Hwang, 2003)

KNOWLEDGE MANAGEMENT: CASE ANALYSIS

Collaborative Learning: Knowledge Strategies of KYC[1] Medical Centre

Medical activities are recognized as one of the most crucial task world over. This field and its activities are related to collaborative work and many other including trust, dedication, motivation, experience, service, care so on. It is entirely different from that of general task in service industry, business, art, domestic etc and involves a sequence of anticipated tasks at the right time. Medical field is the chain of tasks and the knowledge associated with the course of infirmity of a patient. Factor that influences the complexity of medical work is its richness and muddled character includes patient's case work and keeping patient's continuous improvement.

KYC Medical Centre

KYC medical centre has gained high repute in various specializations and receives thousand of patience within and outside the country for the treatment. The medical centre has formal structure which is directly two steps to reach the board. The medical centre have collaborative link with organization in Malaysia, Australia, UAE, USA, Canada, Philippines and other countries for consultancy and sharing. The centre extends the supportive help to other medical centre within the country and offers all type of specialization to the patience's with high standards.

KYC Learning

After eight years of opening the medical centre the KYC board has recognized that the doctors who are performing well and known to be leading practitioners in there respective specialization are not much inclined towards the sharing of the knowledge to their subordinate doctors and reluctant to discuss various cases in general and specific. Most of the doctors under the same line have in-depth experience in their own specialization. Also, the handful of doctors plays major role in the KYC reputation and has great market acceptability among patience and honored with number of awards.

During the same period KYC board has made policy decision to install ultra modern micro cameras with voice recognition facility and record inside the operation theatre, doctor patience consultation room to gather knowledge and develop knowledge sharing process. The board was aware that this will cost high and requires additional staff. The policy started to be implemented arranging all areas in collaboration with the suppliers and separated a block to administer the technological advancement.

Early phases of the instrument installation doctors and nurses are very reluctant and put forward the issue of privacy and confidentiality of the issues and thought for the checking their activity inside the medical centre. This has become major issue for more than 25 days and affected the medical centre working [Refer above obstacle 2, 4, 7, 10]. The Chairman addressed the doctors with the advantages and implication for installation [refer Open strategy b, c]. The basic objective of the installation of the technology is to assist the doctors and nurses thousand kilometers far and have collaboration and learning with the KYC [refer Open strategy a) and e)]. The doctors were addressed by the top management [refer Open strategy b, c] every week end related to various issues and addressing the future scope for technological advancement.

To support the staff and motivate the employees, the management has decided to provide the increment [refer Closed strategy a] for the members for external consultation, discussion and collaborative learning. The doctors were provided with all sort of technological equipment [refer Open strategy d] and supportive staff in information and communication technology (ITC). The medical centre spends huge cost and approximately years of time [refer obstacle 5] to get the thing started for collaboration learning. The management has yet to do lot of work on the basic level to get the problem solved and achieve the objectives. The technological mistake can cost the life of patient and reputation within the collaboration and market. The fundamental activity is to capture the tacit knowledge which is provided by the doctors during operation, consultation and other daily activities [refer Open strategy e]. To capture the service provided by the nurses creating the competitiveness being very important in the service industry. The technological support provides help to capture the operation and the procedure while consultation and prescription being given by the doctors are recorded first hand.

What next?

This tacit knowledge is to be converted into explicit knowledge support the learning for the subordinates within and outside. The management has appointed intern doctors for doing translating the operation code into simple explicit technical language. The intern doctors being trained [refer Closed strategy b] for adopting the high level operation and learn the lesson being carried out by the process. The knowledge is being transferred from the doctors to doctors at different levels. Interns are supposed to be shifted to the wards for normal routine and next interns have been put in the place on regular basis. The application of the case is done with the specialized doctors assisting them in the similar type of job. The process of rotation of interns and other staff maintained for the tacit knowledge being transferred itself while in other tacit knowledge being transferred as explicit also. The shift of the manual based storage to the technological based storage has been the great achievement. The later stage doctor also realized the importance by looking the videos and the footage of operation from the specialized doctors gained important insight and started giving valuable comments to improve the process of operation and process of handling.

Collaboration, Sharing and Learning in KYC

Knowledge Sharing

Knowledge sharing is integrating of activities within the organization taking place when the components related in the organization share experience and problems. Knowledge sharing in KYC is considered crucial within organizational settings characterized with the division of activities based on structure. The knowledge generated from members within and outside, KYC facilitates the integration, specialized, and asymmetrically distributed among various components [refer Closed strategy c] in the network.

For effective integration and knowledge sharing KYC organizes annual conferences in various field of medicine which will extends the sharing among different components associated with KYC. Also various workshops, seminars and other related knowledge sharing programs are conducted within the system for transfer of knowledge among the employees, improve efficiency and effectiveness related to managing the knowledge for sharing; and value issues. The collaboration among the components provides effective implementation and feedback. The crucial feedback between the internal and external partners supports improvement in function. Collaboration will determine the components that are most useful and have maximum market value.

KM Problems Faced by KYC

KYC faces many challenges connected with identifying knowledge and implementing KM process. KYC take maximum care for the need to:

- Create an organization culture that encourages knowledge sharing among different people involved
- Create knowledge sharing culture which will support the overall improvement and development
- Ensure that the correct knowledge should be created, stored and used.
- Identify, model and explicitly represent the knowledge to its employees.
- Implement support that identify, capture, analyze, represent, verify, store and disseminate and reuse of the knowledge in the organization day to day applications.
- Produce systematic approaches to designing and building knowledge-based application.
- Share and re-use their knowledge among its employee for the achievement of it objectives and also for future strategic formulations

KM is supportive and is capable to address the issue of improvement and development in the organisation. Knowledge in an organisation is formed from various inputs and executed despite massive investments in the process. KYC implemented KM to get better pay back for the opportunity. There are various reasons that KYC revealed about the precaution they took from various reasons they perceived for the failure of KM despite:

1. The past few years KYC lack behind to take the initiative because of the organization have no alternative and implementation during the introduction stage will create extra efforts and cost.
2. KM initiatives are mostly framed but required amount of efforts have not been put for effectiveness both in terms of time, money and specialization.
3. KM relies on technology, information system and communication in the organization which may fails to address the common issue of knowledge sharing
4. Design and strategic formulation and embedding it in the policy are not integrated in case of KYC in such a way that allowed stakeholders to access and analyze the implementation.

Since the installation of KM application the knowledge has been greatly captured, transformed and transferred to the subordinates by the process reduces the risk of getting knowledge loss and purpose of achieving competitive advantage. KYC achieve the competitive advantage over the other in terms of effectiveness and efficiency in the field of health care.

Knowledge Development as Strategic Solution at KYC

The KYC implementing the KM deals with the organisation's most imperative issues to synchronizing the KM goals with the organizational strategies. This creates a close coordination between the KM strategies and the organization objective which is directly and indirectly affected by the process. The knowledge sharing in the network acts as the major solution for the effective flow and transfer of knowledge leading to learning and effective implementation of knowledge strategies at KYC. It has also been found that the KM initiatives in the KYC are combined with the overall organizational strategies and framed to undertake and articulate with the objectives in the long run. This advantage of linkage of knowledge strategy and the organizational strategy show the way to create the advantage for becoming a 'learning and development organization' using knowledge for the improvement and also to develop the goals into strategic action. This has been a great achievement that the collaborative knowledge and learning within the network achieves results in long run. Organizational learning and knowledge management at KYC facilitates trust, interest, and shared language fostering access to knowledge and a culture marked by autonomy, redundancy, requisite variety, intention, and fluctuation which stays true in case of KYC within the network.

Knowledge as Solution for the Business Strategy and Development

Strategies at KYC are the guiding factor for the achievement of the objectives. KM and its application play a significant role in building the potential and providing the knowledge creation and sharing capacities to build knowledge organization needed to support the ongoing strategy formulation. KM based strategy at KYC supports and seeks to create sustainable competitive advantage developing the organization for competency (learning) and improving the performance. KM strategy develops and improves core capabilities (Martin, 2000) build capabilities to develop market, product and services adapting innovation needed for the future.

This strategic knowledge designed for the problem solving and decision making at KYC support to gain strategic advantage in following forms:

- ***Innovation:*** KM process at KYC identifies new opportunities for innovation, improvement in value by solving the problems and redefining business to innovate and add strength to the core capabilities. Process innovation enables the KYC to support the knowledge flow and transfer among individuals, groups, functional units and network as a whole. Innovative knowledge based process with the external and internal support collaborative learning and provides customized solutions to unique medical problems.
- ***Analyses:*** Knowledge based process will help the organization to analyze and understand the change within the internal and external factor. These factors which are affecting the organization can be determined and design to provide productivity. Competition being the major contributor to change can be analyzes and appropriate steps can be taken for advantage.
- ***Strategic Intent:*** Becoming more analytical, adaptive, flexible help KYC to innovate the product and services. KYC develops the strategic intent to determine the future objectives which can be achieved effectively and efficiently. Creating new knowledge about technological change, markets, society, proposes strategies and process changes, developing new competencies.

KYC addresses the major purpose of knowledge management at KYC is to:

- Capture knowledge from experts giving subjects accessibility and in-depth research development.
- Collect input data and deliver the output to the end user, update data records; check for the process through collected data. This allows the user to access the information in a quick and easy way.
- Connect each component of knowledge with a set of experts and develop an active database of such experts for problem solving, collaborative research and supporting decision making.
- Develop collaborative links with resources both physical through institutions and individuals either electronically or through data transfer.
- Develop strategy, structure, and culture of the enterprise into a learning system.
- Encourages double loop learning (practice and literature learning) in which learning informs and impacts on strategic directions

- Facilitates participative and innovative development with and between people and institutions commercially, technologically, and socially.
- Gain significant returns from the data and information which they produce during various processes and utilizing this information for further improvement.
- Has as its primary aim rapid and continual regeneration of the total organization depending on rapid and continual learning.
- Responds to changes in the internal and external environment of the organization by detecting and correcting error.
- Retrieving as much knowledge needed for future research.
- Support learning of all its members and continuously transforming itself,
- Train subordinates and staff accessing knowledge and guide them to the appropriate resource.

Knowledge Management Acting as a Support for Strategic Service Management

KM and knowledge based strategies addresses specific business needs and focus on adding value and innovation with the capability of knowledge support which enhances the stand for creating enhanced products and services for added advantage. These advantages in terms of the case can be represented in terms of performance and productivity by: develop trust, interest and motivation; development by capturing, sharing and delivery of required knowledge; encourage learning culture; facilitate information linkages throughout many processes and functions; facilitate processes by ensuring the right knowledge transfer; facilities innovation; focuses on the creation of knowledge; improve quality; improved customer information and networking; improved customer service; promote sharing; reduce duplication by providing required informational support; strengthening strategic position support knowledge sharing; systematic application of knowledge for strategic planning;

KYC Case Summary

The knowledge in an organization is vital for organizational change and development. The knowledge sharing in an organization depends on various factors and ensures appropriate transfer of knowledge. The obstacles for the knowledge flow and transfer can be removed by various strategies. The strategies include open ended and closed ended strategies which give particular solution to the organization and fasten the knowledge flow and sharing. KM at KYC initiatives linked with the overall organizational strategies and framed to undertake and articulate the objectives in the long run. The case study of KYC being implementing knowledge management based strategies achieves higher level of performance and productivity. The KM process at KYC supports the organization for the strategic decision making and solution to create advantage. The KM strategic solution creates collaboration, learning, improves performance, process development, productivity, product and service facility which creates the sustainable competitive advantage over the factor which is affecting directly and indirectly in the organization and its goals.

KM IN EDUCATION

The application of KM tools and techniques can be used education scenario as a success factor as in the corporate and business. Despite the short coming KM application can be used for creating competitive advantage for education system. The system should adopt various models and techniques for success in global competition. KM has become a strategic tool for academics development in most of the developed countries and adopted by developing countries based on improved information system and technology which help the industry to store, retrieve and assess to resources effectively from inside and outside the organisation. This transmission of knowledge with the idea has developed and transforms the academic organisation and the system. The traditional system of knowledge transfer through classroom teaching has been changed in many other form easy to accessed and gain. Due to the increasing cost, expenditure and maintenance of IT infrastructure some have adopted other way solution. The infrastructure and access to the information technology, communication technology and knowledge resources should be developed. Simultaneously, the mode of knowledge transfers and management in educational institution has been changing with the industry concentrating more on knowledge management and the reuse for competitive advantage. In much of the knowledge management research, the term learning organization and knowledge organization are used interchangeably to reflect workplaces that "are continuously seeking data from the environment, are fluid and adaptable, and learn from their previous experiences. They share knowledge and contain systems and process for sharing knowledge" (Johnson, 2002, pp. 242).

KM PRINCIPLES IN MANAGEMENT EDUCATION

Some of the reasons for applying KM in Management Education in India are:

1. Competitive reason
2. Administrative reasons

- *Competitive reason:* The adoption of KM tools and techniques will help the overall competitive stand among national and international stand. Knowledge management strategies will be adopted to facilitate the usage and sharing of resources and experiences in much education institution.

The education institution looks for improving overall ranking affecting student's placements, accreditation, performance, admission, brand name which are evaluated by the regulatory body to ensure efficiency and quality. Main reason among the institution making significant investments in infrastructure and information technologies initiatives is to meet the future objectives of the institution and to improve efficiency and effectiveness in the system. Infrastructure development in terms of technological development will help the management institution for creating cutting edge in the rapid changing competition.

- *Administrative reason*: Administrative reasons includes: Planning; administrative issues; collaboration; customer focus; employees development; information development; internal documentation; operation management; process management; program development; research and publication; strategy formulation; teaching-learning excellence; others. Administrative issues also includes processed knowledge about students, faculty and staff, research, project, collaboration, system, infrastructure, organizational human resources, programs, courses, lectures details, changes, competition, appraisal and so on serves as a strategic input for improving overall teaching – learning education

FACTORS AFFECTING KNOWLEDGE MANAGEMENT IN EDUCATIONAL INSTITUTION

Various factors affecting knowledge management in educational institution affecting the process issues are: integration and balancing of leadership, organization, learning and technology; culture and management; organizational innovation; organizational culture, process, technology; knowledge sharing process etc

CHALLENGES OF KM APPLICATION IN EDUCATION

Knowledge sharing within the educational organization enables the employers and employees to share insight (Mathew, 2009) helping them to adopt appropriate ideas and allows faster and cost effective move towards the achievement of organizational objectives. Various challenges which are predicted of applying KM in education institutions are:

Personal Constraints

Despite the revolution in information and communication technology, the social background has not yet changed. Social system of greeting, face to face interaction, discussing, and environmental condition are common elements of the society which has not got the momentum to change which restrict the KM process acting as constraints within the individual level. The dynamic change in information, technology and communication, appears drastically in terms of KM technology has not occurred in personal customs and culture constraints. People working in the organization are not inclined to disseminate the information due to various reasons acting as personal constraints to implement KM process.

Cost Constraint

The implementation of KM at initial stages needs to have knowledge workers, resources and infrastructures which insure high cost. Also, people are rigid to transfer knowledge due to various factors which need to be solved using different tools and techniques like incentive leads to cost constraints. Creating infrastructure for the application and setting all components and common elements for sharing and dissemination of knowledge will create cost constraints (Mathew, 2009).

Face to Face Learning

Face to face interaction related to trust and ambiguity that surrounds identity in the virtual world are most easily overcome (Hildreth et al, 1998; Kimble et al, 2000). The psychological effect that face to face learning create deeper and long term effect on the learner and encourages to discussion inclining towards more learning and understanding. Reducing the distance between he teacher and learner but face to face interaction will be rarely possible as that of classroom teaching.

Differentiation and Integration

The community among the learner having the consequences of being differential based on system, culture, language, social setup, personal interaction etc leading to be constraints for sharing knowledge among distance learners.

The integration among different group of people having different background, specialization, experience etc will be difficult to serve under same programs give only the technical aspects trough distance learning.

Trust, Collaboration and Cooperation Constraints

Lack trust, collaboration and cooperation, virtual interaction among the employees in the organization and potential knowledge provider and learners leads to constraints and restrict sharing of knowledge.

KM AS TOOL

KM tool allows the learners to gain access to the source of knowledge beyond the boundaries and context creating favorable environment that improve shared understanding among different user in the teaching learning process of distance education. Various combinations of technological advances like video conferencing, online video chatting, will help the user to be interacting with concern department and experts and facilitate access to source of knowledge and enables interaction among teacher and learner. KM tool allows the institution to solve the constraints at maximum level by establishing trust and allows collaboration with the potential learner.

ORGANIZATIONAL KM CULTURE AND CHANGE

The KM culture in an organization has been explained from various researchers and practitioners with model. Alavi & Leidner, 2001; Karlsen & Gottschalk, 2004 explained it in three basis in KM process. They are: (a) Information-based; (b) technology-based; and (c) culture-based. Wilkins and Dyer (1988) put forward that culture "is [composed] of the values, competencies, and beliefs of a group of people that strongly influence whether and how organizational strategies are implemented. (p. 522)."

KNOWLEDGE MANAGEMENT SYSTEM FOR ORGANIZATIONAL CHANGE

The major challenge for the organization is to adapt to the constantly changing environment in terms of innovation. Most of the organization innovate with the input taken from the environmental factors and constantly deliver the product and services. It is relatively long term and every functional unit in an organization play vital role for knowledge management process. Adopting knowledge transfer will reduce the knowledge gap within the organization. KM system in an

Figure 1. Modified KM integration for change

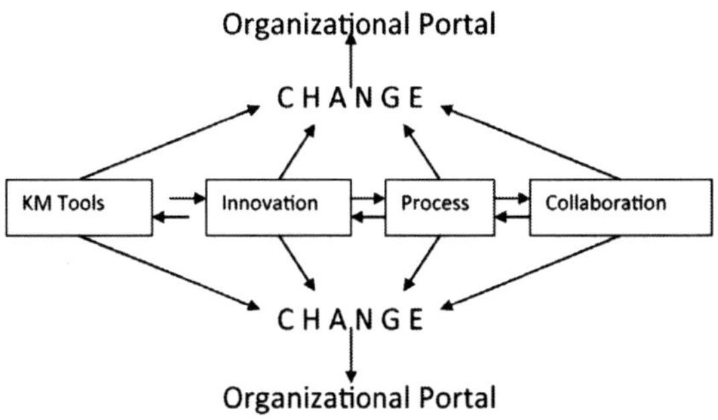

organization creates such an innovative culture to bridge the gap. The adoption of knowledge transfer culture helps the organization to improve value issues in marketing, production, research and so on can be captured and used for adding value contributing to the overall value creation.

Knowledge Management is influenced by human factor and technological aspect will support and perform function contributing to the KM implementation having accountability as HR factor. The use of information and technology (IT) will support adopting the KM approach as prerequisite for capturing, sharing, disseminating and innovating and retrieval for the further use. Various factor integrating (Mathew, 2008) the KM for adopting with the change can be collaboration, process Management, innovation, e- transfer, and other KM tools as shown in Figure 1.

KNOWLEDGE MANAGEMENT TO CHANGE MANAGEMENT

Adopting technology and knowledge workers resources will not suffice and solve the KM issues to adopt change in the organization. Knowledge culture need to be imbibed and should be created within the organization. The top management should motivate human resource to transfer knowledge. The management should emphasis innovation with the application of knowledge in daily process as "Change is continuous". The orga-

Figure 2. Process systems to change system with KM (Mathew, 2008)

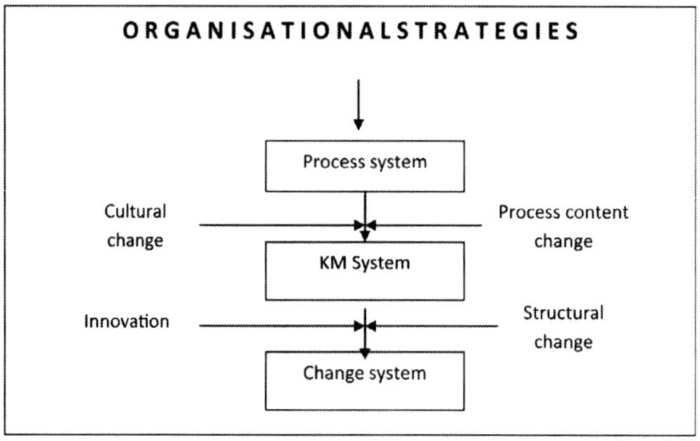

nization should look for the change factors using the knowledge management tools and techniques for the process evaluating existing and required competencies. The system incorporate the value addition with innovation and builds the structural framework for active innovation actively use and practice innovation as organizational culture to adopt change and steer in the desired strategic direction of the organization (Mathew, 2008). The Figure 2 highlights the process development.

KNOWLEDGE MANAGEMENT AND ORGANIZATIONAL CULTURAL CHANGE

Implementing knowledge management will support the new change culture and strategic development adopting the organizational objectives. The knowledge gap can be reduced providing support to the organization change process as shown in Figure 3.

In most of the traditional organization, KM system is very rarely followed which leads to the knowledge gap in different functional and management process. KM system is used by the employees with the process change aimed for improve the organizational performance and support innovation. The implementation of the KM tools and techniques will enable structural, technological and functional change for required gaining competencies. This change incorporating the environmental factor will support the organization to create knowledge transfer culture. At this point of transaction incorporating the change and developing the knowledge transfer culture, organization achieves the objective with the set criteria to take advantage of the available knowledge for creating competencies. The complete approach will be institutionalized for the change in the organization. The positive change system will focus on the innovation for further improvement of products, services and competitive advantage.

CONCLUSION

Knowledge management has become an important area of focus in order to be successful in today's business environment. Knowledge based business establishment tries to create a knowledge culture where learning through various methods has been established. Knowledge is high-value resource that is integrated to apply for making organizational decisions and taking productive actions. It includes data, information, ideas, experience, insights and awareness. It is the combination of information or what we know or the state of knowing in-depth. The critical success factors for KM in a service

Figure 3. Knowledge culture for organizational change

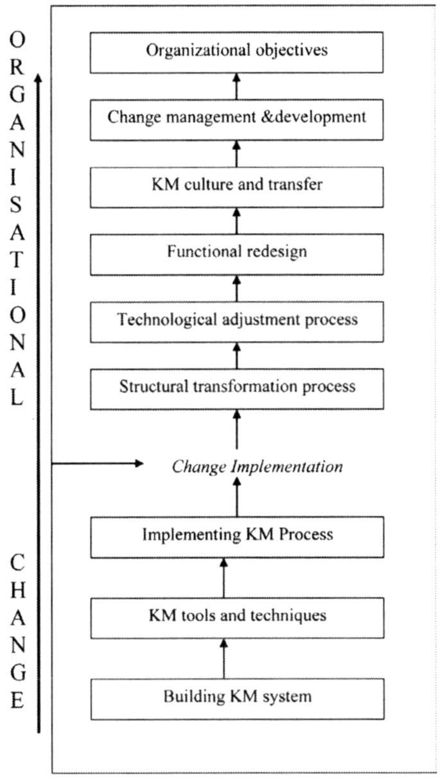

organisation can be broadly classified as into four divisions- People, Processes, Technology & Sustainable development. Various principles, techniques, obstacles, strategies has been used for implementing KM. The case of KYC explains the effective knowledge use for development. This paper highlights the implementation of KM in education providing KM strategies for organization change for effective implementation and achievement of organizational objectives.

FUTURE RESEARCH DIRECTIONS

In today's world of global competition and service delivery the managers are facing unprecedented challenges caused due to change in the external environment namely change in technologies, financial policies, HR practices, etc giving hard time to create advantage and to sustain that advantage. The emerging discipline of KM provides systematic management of knowledge that evolves with the enterprise for creating advantage among the business and industry. Most of the organizations are taking innovative steps to develop its knowledge for improving competitiveness, performance and service delivery. The integration of technologies into business processes has created wide impact on the development and creating efficiency in business performance creating new paradigm shift leading to provide services and pays crucial role in the industries

It can be further explored and developed that the use of KM in other areas in new ways is an opportunity which exists with the development of business system and delivery. KM strategies can now be used as basic framework focusing more on organizational processes and the creation of new knowledge in order to provide effective service delivery and remain ahead of its competitors. Researches have to play a greater role in identifying effective ways for utilizing existing knowledge and to create new knowledge using technological advancement for improving process application. Organizations have to find the ways and method for knowledge sharing and transfer externally and internally more competently and learn to adapt the changes more quickly which occurs in order to retain their competitive advantage. KM process models and structure can be broken down into the simplest manageable parts that can cost effective and influential to be used as essential feature of business system. While technology can plays vital role in facilitating communication and collaboration among knowledge workers which is essential for KM process. The future research can explore "comprehensive business drivers" adopting change within the process drivers and create relationship with emerging knowledge management systems to compete in the new global service delivery.

REFERENCES

al Banna, S. (2000). *Knowledge Management and strategies for development in a rapidly changing global environment*. (p. 12)

Alavi, M., & Leidner, D. E. (2001). Review: Knowledge Management and Knowledge Management systems: Conceptual foundations and research issues. *Management Information Systems Quarterly*, *25*(1), 107–136. doi:10.2307/3250961

Alvesson, M. (1995). *Management of knowledge-intensive companies*. Berlin: Walter de Gruyter.

Anahotu, N. D. (1998). Empowerment and production workers: a knowledge-based perspective. *Empowerment in Organisations*, *6*(7), 177–186. doi:10.1108/14634449810242611

Andreu, R., & Sieber, S. (1999). *Knowledge and problem solving: A proposal for a model of individual and collective learning*. Barcelona: IESE Publishing.

(2004). *Asian Development Bank* (p. 3). Knowledge Management in ADB.

Bender, S., & Fish, A. (2000). The transfer of knowledge and the retention of expertise: The continuing need for global assignments. *Journal of Knowledge Management*, *4*(2), 125–137. doi:10.1108/13673270010372251

Benus, B. (1993). *Organizational modeling and Knowledge Management*. Department of Social Science Informatics, University of Amsterdam.

Bhatt, G. (2001). Knowledge Management in organisations: Examining the interaction between technologies, techniques, and people. *Journal of Knowledge Management*, *5*(1), 68–75. doi:10.1108/13673270110384419

Bhatt, G. D. (2000). Organising knowledge in the knowledge development cycle. *Journal of Knowledge Management*, *4*(1), 15–26. doi:10.1108/13673270010315371

Bhatt, G. D. (2002). Management strategies for individual knowledge and organisational knowledge. *Journal of Knowledge Management*, *6*(1), 31–39. doi:10.1108/13673270210417673

Binwal, J. C. (2001). Knowledge Management. *IASLIC Bulletin*, *46*(2), 65–78.

Bowen, D. E., & Lawler, E. E. (1992). The empowerment of service workers: What, why, how and when. *Sloan Management Review*, (Spring): 31–39.

Carneiro, A. (2001). The role of intelligent resources in Knowledge Management. *Journal of Knowledge Management*, *5*(4), 358–367. doi:10.1108/EUM0000000006533

Choi, Y. S. (2000). *An empirical study of factors affecting successful implementation of knowledge management*. Unpublished academic dissertation, University of Nebraska.

Civi, E. (2000). Knowledge management as a competitive asset: A review marketing intelligence and planning. *Journal of Knowledge Management*, *18*(4), 166–174.

Collins English Dictionary. (2004).

(2002). *Concise Oxford English Dictionary*. Oxford University Press.

Cope, M. (1998). Developing a working definition. *Knowledge Management Review*, *1*(1), 26–31.

Davenport, T., & Prusak, L. (1998). *Working knowledge: How organizations manage what they know* (p. 5). Cambridge, MA: Harvard University Press.

Davenport, T. H., & Prusak, L. (1998). *Working knowledge: Managing what your organization knows*. Boston: Harvard Business School Press.

Denning, S. (2000). *The springboard: How storytelling ignites action in knowledge-era organizations*. Boston: Butterworth Heinemann.

Desouza, K., & Awazu, Y. (2003, November). Knowledge Management. *HRMagazine*, 107–112.

Egan, M. (2003). Creating a knowledge bank. *Strategic Human Resource Review*, *2*(2), 30–34.

Fernandes, J., & Usher, J. M. (1999). An object-oriented application of tool selection in dynamic process planning. *International Journal of Production Research*, *37*(13), 2879–2894. doi:10.1080/002075499190329

Geraint, J. (1998). Share strength. *People Management*, *4*(16), 44–47.

Goman, C. (2002). What leaders can do to foster knowledge sharing. *Knowledge Management Review*, *5*(4), 10–11.

Greco, J. (1999). Knowledge is power. *The Journal of Business Strategy*, *20*(2), 18–22. doi:10.1108/eb039990

Greengard, S. (1998a). Will your culture support Knowledge Management? *Workforce*, *77*(10), 93–94.

Greengard, S. (1998b). Storing, shaping, and sharing collective wisdom. *Workforce*, *77*(10), 82–87.

Gurteen, D. (1998). Knowledge, creativity and innovation. *Journal of Knowledge Management*, *2*(1), 513–522. doi:10.1108/13673279810800744

Hislop, D. (2003). Linking human resource management and Knowledge Management via commitment. *Employee Relations*, *25*(2), 182–202. doi:10.1108/01425450310456479

Hwang, A. (2003). Training strategies in the management of knowledge. *Journal of Knowledge Management*, *7*(3), 92–104. doi:10.1108/13673270310485659

Kaplan, R. S., & Norton, D. P. (1996). *Balanced scorecard: Translating strategy into action*. Boston: Harvard Business School Press.

Kidwell, J. J., Van der Linde, M. K., & Johnson, L. S. (2000). Applying corporate Knowledge Management practices in higher education. *EDUCAUSE Quarterly*, *4*, 28–33.

Mathew, V. (2008). K-C Management: Building knowledge culture in the business organization for managing change. [Special KM edition]. *Effective Executive*, *6*(6), 68–78.

Mathew, V. (2008). Knowledge Management progression, issues, and approaches for organizational effectiveness in manufacturing industry: An implementation agenda. *ICFAI Journal of Knowledge Management*, *6*(1), 20–45.

Mathew, V. (2009). Virtual knowledge sharing and collaborative learning in organization. Paper accepted for First Virtual Conference on Business Management 2009 (VCOBAM 2009) conference.

Mathew, V., & Kavitha, M. (2008). Critical knowledge transfer in an organization: approaches. *ICFAI Journal of Knowledge Management*, *6*(4), 25–40.

Mayer, R., Cullinane, T., De Witte, P., Knappernberger, W., Perakath, B., & Wells, S. (1992). *ICCE IDEF3 process description capture method report (al/tr-1992-0057). Technical report.* Air Force Systems Command.

Moffett, S., McAdam, R., & Parkinson, S. (2003). An empirical analysis of Knowledge Management applications. *Journal of Knowledge Management*, *7*(3), 6–26. doi:10.1108/13673270310485596

Mohrman, S. A., Cohen, S. G., & Mohrman, A. M. Jr. (1995). *Designing team-based organizations: New forms for knowledge work*. San Francisco: Jossey-Bass Publishers.

Nonaka, I., & Takeuchi, H. (1995). *The knowledge-creating company*. New York: Oxford University Press.

Nonaka, I., & Takeuchi, M. (1995). *The knowledge creating company – How Japanese companies create the dynamics of innovation*. Oxford: The Oxford University Press.

Ould, M. (1993). Strim/rads. *Iopener, 1*(5), *2*(1&3).

OXFAM. Scarborough, H., & J. Swan. (2003). Discourses of Knowledge Management and organizational learning, their production and consumption. In M.E. Smith & M. Lyles (Eds.), *The Blackwell handbook of organizational learning and Knowledge Management*. Oxford: Blackwell Publishing.

Pan, S. L., & Scarbrough, H. (1999). Knowledge Management in practice: An exploratory case study of Buckman Labs. *Technology Analysis and Strategic Management, 11*(3), 359–374. doi:10.1080/095373299107401

Quinn, J., Anderson, P., & Finkelstein, S. (1996). Managing professional intellect. In *Harvard Business Review on Knowledge Management*. Boston: Harvard Business School Publishing.

Salleh, Y., & Goh, W. K. (2002). Managing human resources toward achieving Knowledge Management. *Journal of Knowledge Management, 6*(5), 457–468. doi:10.1108/13673270210450414

Schreiber, A. T., Akkermans, J. M., Anjewierden, A. A., De Hoog, R., Van De Velde, W., & Wielinga, B. J. (1998). *Engineering of knowledge: The common KADS methodology*. University of Amsterdam.

Smith, H. (2003). Instilling a knowledge-sharing culture. (p. 1-17). Retrieved from www.business.queens.ca/kbe

Soliman, F. & Spooner, K. (2000). Strategies for implementing Knowledge Management: Role of human resource management. *Journal of Knowledge.*

Soo, C., Devinney, T. M., & Midgley, D. F. (2002). Knowledge creation in organizations: Exploring firm and context specific effects. *INSEAD*, 1-34. Retrieved May 19, 2005, from www.knoweldge.insead.edu

Steinecke, C. (1993). *The federal total quality management handbook: Employee involvement and quality management in the federal government*. Washington, D.C.: U.S. Government Printing Office.

Stonehouse, G. H., & Pemberton, J. D. (1999). Learning and Knowledge Management in the intelligent organization. *Participation & Empowerment: An International Journal, 7*(5), 131–144. doi:10.1108/14634449910287846

Sveiby, K. E. (1997). *The new organizational wealth. Managing and measuring knowledge-based assets*. San Francisco: Berret-Koehler Publishers Inc.

Waltz, G. (2003). *Knowledge Management in the intelligence enterprise*. Boston: Artech House Inc.

Wing, K. (1999). What future knowledge management users may expect. *Journal of Knowledge Management, 3*(2), 155–165. doi:10.1108/13673279910275611

ADDITIONAL READING

Alavi, M., & Leidner, D. E. (2001). Review: Knowledge Management and Knowledge Management systems: Conceptual foundations and research issues. *Management Information Systems Quarterly, 25*(1), 107–136. doi:10.2307/3250961

Alvesson, M. (2001). Knowledge work: ambiguity, image and identity. *Human Relations, 54*(7), 863–886. doi:10.1177/0018726701547004

Anonymous,. (2003). Caterpillar capitalizes on virtual communities: Knowledge sharing provides competitive edge. *Human Resource Management International Digest*, *11*(6), 16–18. doi:10.1108/09670730310494610

Barth, S. (2003). A framework for personal knowledge management tools. *KM World*, 20-21.

Branin, J.J. (2003). Knowledge Management in academic libraries: Building the knowledge bank at the Ohio State University. *The Journal of Academic Librarianship For Publication*, 1-17.

Brown, J. S., & Duguid, P. (2000). Balancing act: How to capture knowledge without killing it. *Harvard Business Review*, (May-June): 73–80.

Cope, M. (1998). Developing a working definition. *Knowledge Management Review*, *1*(1), 26–31.

Davenport, T. (1998). *Knowledge Management at Hewlett-Packard, early 1996*. Austin, TX: University of Texas.

Davenport, T., Delong, D., & Beers, M. (1998). Successful Knowledge Management projects. *Sloan Management Review*, *39*(Winter), 43–57.

De Long, D. W., & Fahey, L. (2000). Diagnosing cultural barriers to Knowledge Management. *The Academy of Management Executive*, *14*, 113–128.

Drucker, P. (1991). The new productivity challenge. *Harvard Business Review*, *69*(6), 69–79.

Kaplan, R. S., & Norton, D. P. (1996). *Balanced scorecard: Translating strategy into action*. Boston: Harvard Business School Press.

Malhotra, Y. (1998). *Knowledge Management, knowledge organizations & knowledge workers: A view from the front lines*. Retrieved August 29, 2007, from http://www.brint.com/interview/maeil.htm

Mathew, V. (2006). Knowledge management and value. *University of Gondar Journal*, *3*(3), 209–213.

Mathew, V. (2008). K-C Management: Building knowledge culture in the business organization for managing change. [Special KM edition]. *Effective Executive*, *6*(6), 68–78.

Mathew, V. (2009). *Knowledge Management in higher education: Implementation agenda in distance learning*. Paper presented at the International Conference on Distance Education and Open Learning (DEOL 2009).

Mathew, V., & Kavitha, M. (2008). Knowledge Management-model, myths and success factors. *Business Review (Federal Reserve Bank of Philadelphia)*, *1*(1), 4–15.

Mathew, V., & Kavitha, M. (2009). Implementing Knowledge Management, knowledge mapping, matrix and supports. *Journal of Knowledge Management Practice*, *10*(1).

Na Ubon, A., & Kimble, C. (2002). Knowledge Management in online distance education. In *Proceedings of the 3rd International Conference Networked Learning 2002*, University of Sheffield, UK. (pp.465-473).

Nonaka, I. (1994). A dynamic theory of organizational knowledge creation. *Organization Science*, *5*(1). doi:10.1287/orsc.5.1.14

Nonaka, I., & Takeuchi, M. (1995). *The knowledge creating company-how Japanese companies create the dynamics of innovation*. Oxford: The Oxford University Press.

Nonaka, I., Toyama, R., & Konno, N. (2001). SECI, Ba and leadership: a unified model of dynamic knowledge creation. In Nonaka, I., & Teece, D. (Eds.), *Managing industrial knowledge: Creation, transfer and utilization* (pp. 13–43). London: Sage Publications.

Polanyi, M. (1997). Tacit Knowledge. In Prusak, L. (Ed.), *Knowledge in Organizations*. Boston: Butterworth-Heinemann.

Prusak, L. (2001). Where did Knowledge Management come from? *IBM Systems Journal*, *40*(4), 1002–1006. doi:10.1147/sj.404.01002

Rowley, J. (2000). From learning organisation to knowledge entrepreneur. *Journal of Knowledge Management*, *4*(1), 7–14. doi:10.1108/13673270010315362

Warne, L., Ali, I. M., & Pascoe, C. (2003). Team building as a foundation for Knowledge Management: Findings from research into social learning in the Australian Defence Organization. *Journal of Information & Knowledge Management*, *2*(2), 93–106. doi:10.1142/S0219649203000024

ENDNOTE

1 Identification code given for the organization

Chapter 5
Role of Small and Medium Sized Enterprises in E-Supply Chain Management:
A Case Study

Fang Zhao
American University of Sharjah, UAE

ABSTRACT

This chapter studies the role that small and medium-sized enterprises (SMEs) play in the e-supply chain management. It has two objectives: (1) it explores how a SME embraces and implements electronic supply chain management (e-SCM) and the challenges facing it, and (2) it develops strategy to deal with the challenges. The chapter draws upon a case study of IFC Global Logistics (IFC), a small-to-medium-sized third party logistics provider. The case study illustrates how the SME embraces enabling technologies, the Internet, and modern business practices to integrate its supply chain management processes and to create for itself differentiation and a competitive advantage in the tough logistics industry. Based upon a literature review and the case study, the chapter explores effective strategy for SMEs in e-supply chain management.

INTRODUCTION

There is a general census amongst practitioners and academia that SMEs are playing an increasing important role in the technology-driven economy of both developed and developing countries. The old supply chains have evolved into electronically powered networked supply chains that rapidly link optimal supply chain members with the right com-

DOI: 10.4018/978-1-60960-129-4.ch005

ponents, technology, and services for customers (McCormack et al., 2003). In this regard, information technology (IT) is an important enabler to achieve supply chain performance (Fawcett et al., 2007, Chandra et al., 2007, Yee, 2005). The issues in electronic supply chain management (e-SCM) take on a different perspective when the enterprises involved are in the SME sector. The literature review for the present study found that research in the current literature tends to focus more on e-supply chain management of large firms but not on SMEs from which they outsource raw materials, intermediates, parts, components and services (Sastry, 1999; Hong and Jeong, 2006). To fill the knowledge gap, this chapter studies the role of SMEs in the e-supply chain management. It has two objectives: (1) it explores how a SME embraces and implements e-SCM and the challenges facing it, and (2) it develops strategy to deal with the challenges.

The chapter starts with background information which provides definitions of the key concepts to be discussed in this chapter and reports the main themes in the study fields. Followed by that, the chapter presents a case study which illustrates how a SME embraces enabling technologies, the Internet, and modern business practices to integrate its supply chain management processes and to create for itself differentiation and a competitive advantage in the tough logistics industry. Based upon a literature review and the case study, the chapter explores effective strategy for SMEs in e-supply chain management. The chapter concludes with proposing future directions for research.

BACKGROUND

E-Supply Chain Management (e-SCM)

E-supply chain management is viewed as the most recent stage of development of the concept of supply chain management (Ross, 2003; Johson, 2006). The focus of management is placed primarily on the application of the Internet to the SCM concept and SCM synchronization. From an operational perspective, there are two major activities in e-SCM: the flow of materials and the development of information systems. E-SCM is likely to offer competitive advantage in better lead times, customer service and supply chain synergy (Burgess, 1998, Nguyen, 2004) and therefore it represents an effective strategy for many manufacturers and service providers. Networked and multi-enterprise supply chains have become a popular organizational design. As Ross (2003, p. 11) describes, "SCM has evolved, through the application of e-business technologies, into a powerful strategic function capable of engendering radically new customer value propositions through the architecture of external, Internet-enabled collaborative channel partnerships". In this regard, e-supply chain management is concerned largely with the management of such "Internet-enabled collaborative channel partnerships" called e-collaboration (van Hoek, 2001).

e-SCM and E-Collaboration

Generally speaking, e-collaboration refers to the use of electronic technologies (like the Internet and/or Internet-based tools) among business partners beyond market transactions (Kock, 2007; Davis and Spekman, 2004).The term is often used in the context of supply chain. E-collaboration is identified as one of the new areas of optimizing the relationship between suppliers and original equipment manufacturers (OEM) via the Internet (Radjou, 2004). It is an Internet-supported, enterprise-spanning cooperation which is seen as crucial during the development and construction process (the so called e-engineering process) (Kersten et al., 2004). E-collaboration aims to facilitate coordination of various supply chain activities and decision-making processes. Therefore, the fundamental construct of e-SCM is to foster an e-collaboration environment where members in supply chains can work together in a more efficient and effective way by using Internet technology. In a Web-based supply chain environment, it is viewed as one of the main players in achieving a sustainable competitive edge (LeFefebvre et al., 2003).

E-collaboration and e-SCM often means mutual exchange of information amongst members in the supply chain. In addition to information sharing, e-collaboration provides opportunities for collaborative planning and new product development (Kock et al., 2006). By resorting to e-collaboration and Web technologies, supply chain partners can exchange product forecasts and replenishment plans and then develop new plans that meet market demand in a timely and effective way. Ultimately, the primary goal of e-SCM is to achieve, through effective e-collaboration, the overall efficiency and competitiveness of the supply chain and enhance customer satisfaction.

Main Potential Benefits of e-SCM to Businesses Including SMEs

There is a consensus among practitioners and industry experts that the real value and benefits generated through e-business is not about automation but the abundant opportunities that e-business provides for organizations and businesses to e-collaborate (Ross, 2003; Lee & Whang, 2002). As more and more integrated supply chain management and collaborative commerce initiatives are being implemented, the development and management of long-term strategic supply chain partnerships are becoming important (Angeles & Nath, 2004). The following summarizes the main potential benefits that e-SCM and e-collaboration can bring to businesses including SMEs, according to previous studies published in the literature. The potential benefits are:

- Streamlining the supply chain by moving business processes online;
- Facilitating access to an extended network of suppliers, manufacturers, retailers and customers;
- Simplifying procurement, reducing inventory costs and shortening product-development cycles (Kuglin & Rosenbaum, 2001; Lagrosen, 2005);
- Giving customers access to a wide range of services and technologies that a single company simply could never deliver by itself;
- Helping leverage the combined strengths and skills of multiple smaller companies who often lack the critical mass to compete in the world market (Zhao, 2006);
- Serving customers in foreign markets through local partners in the e-supply chain;
- Expanding customer base and securing future markets; and
- Facilitating the implementation of multi-channel strategies through horizontal integration in the e-supply chain (Kock, 2007; Kock, et al., 2006).

SMEs and e-SCM

It has been a well-known fact that the majority of suppliers in the supply chain are SMEs, in particular when it comes to the Fast Moving Consumer Goods (FMCG) sector and the automobile industry. Therefore, it is important to look into their role in the context of e-SCM.

There are various definitions of small and medium sized enterprises (SMEs). The common criteria for categorization of enterprises are based on the maximum number of staff and annual turnover of a company. European Union defines SMEs as enterprises with a workforce of 1-250 employees. Australian Bureau of Statistics defines SMEs as companies employing between 1-199 people, wherein companies with 5-19 staff are termed 'small companies', while those with 20-199 employees are termed 'medium companies'. In this study, the Australian definition is used, as the case company is Australia-based.

According to the literature review for the present study, compared with large enterprises, SMEs demonstrate the following distinctive features and behavior in terms of embracing information technology and the e-SCM:

- SMEs are often strongly associated with the CEO/owner's background, knowledge and skills base. In such circumstance, the imperative remains in the marketplace, while the question of whether the company embraces the latest technology and participates in the e-business evolution depends largely on personal preferences of the CEO/owner (Zhao & Dalrymple, 2002).
- Many SMEs are struggling to see the business value of innovations of information technology to them and are often limited their use of IT to the basic functions of word processing, accounting and stock management (Schlenker & Crocker, 2003, Temperley et al,, 2004). This is largely due to difficulties in gaining access to appropriate technologies and information on available techniques as well as constraints on their financial and skill/knowledge resources (Thakkar, Kanda & Deshmukh, 2009). This is one of the key reasons that SMEs are reluctant to participate in e-SCM.
- SMEs' plans to exploit information technology are often directed towards the promotional and market communications aspects rather than the wider supply chain management aspects (Ritchie & Brindley, 2000; Schlenker & Crocker, 2003).
- Individual SMEs often find it hard to achieve economies of scale in the purchase of inputs such as software and other technologies for e-SCM and related consulting services (Thakkar et al., 2009).

Small- and Medium-Sized Logistics Companies

The case company in this study is a small-to-medium-sized third party logistics (3PL) provider. A brief review of related literature helps better understand the specific nature and operational context of 3PL providers including small and medium-sized 3PL companies. Over the past decade, to achieve logistics efficiency and cost-effectiveness, many companies started outsourcing their logistics to specialized logistics service providers, of whom the majority are SMEs (Halley & Guilhon, 1997, Gelinas & Bigras, 2004). As a result, single-party self-managed logistics has developed into multi-party logistics such as 3PL and 5PL which are powered by e-logistics networks that expand to global operations. The study by Gunasekaran and Ngai (2003) found that although SMEs are playing a key role in the trend of 3PL, there are few studies focusing on small and medium-sized logistics companies. They also found that lack of strategic planning and management capacity to take advantage of IT and e-logistics are the primary issues facing SMEs operating in the 3PL. Other than that, the SMEs in the logistics industry exhibit the same features in embracing IT and are constrained by their very limited resources as shown above.

METHODOLOGY

This study follows a case study design by Yin (2003), taking a SME as a unit of analysis. Although it does not prelude a capacity for generation, case study can provide detailed illustration of specific issues and answer specific questions of "how" and "why". This is why case study method is chosen for the present study to examine and illustrate how a SME takes initiative to implement e-SCM. The selection of the case company is based largely on its success and rich experience in e-SCM and the open support of the senior managers of the company for this study.

Data was collected and triangulated from various sources and methods for the case study. By using triangulation, a generally commendable mode of research, the weakness in a single method and single source of data can be compensated by the strength of another method and/or another source of data (Creswell, 2003). Observation through field visits to the case company as well as semi-structured informant interviews with two senior managers in late 2008 form the major sources of data for this study. Complemented with that is the collection of the company documents about the company's operations and in particular its endeavours in implementing e-SCM.

To maintain originality and precision, content analysis was employed to analyze the interview data and company documents. To guard against superficial face validity of content analysis, this researcher gave greater weight to the analysis of latent content or meaning conveyed rather than merely an interpretation of the surface or literal contents (Berg, 1995). Furthermore, triangulation of methods and sources of data for the present study helps check out the consistency of the findings and improves validity as multiple sources of information were used to converge the inquiry. Triangulation also helps minimize the risks and effects of the researcher' and informants' biases in this study.

CASE STUDY

This chapter draws upon a case study to illustrate how a SME embraces the concept of e-SCM to enhance its services and performance through e-SCM. The case company, IFC Global Logistics (IFC) with a workforce of around 80 employees, was established in 1991. It is a Melbourne-based transport logistics company in Australia, specializing in end-to-end planning and execution of logistics services. The company offers a portfolio of supply chain services that incorporates ocean freight, airfreight, customs clearance, domestic transportation and 3PL warehousing and distribution (IFC, 2008).

IFC's service offerings rely largely on e-collaboration amongst its key agents both in Australia and abroad in the supply chain. To meet the growing demands of its key clients in the supply chain for real-time supply chain information and end-to-end supply chain management services, IFC developed its own web-based freight tracking system known as Freight Supply Chain (FSC). Taking into account, in particular, the financial constrains of SMEs in the supply chain, IFC Global Logistics designed and developed the low-cost FSC. The FSC system has been integral in IFC's strategic pursuit for e-SCM, enabling its SME clients and partners to collaborate effectively and have full visibility of their products throughout the supply chain. The FSC system speeds up the process of supply chain communication, linking point of production with point of delivery, and thus allowing supply chain members and their own trading partners to move from existing conventional supply chain activities and methodologies to e-SCM. This e-SCM has engendered continuous improvements of existing processes, both internal and external to IFC, and has enabled higher levels of trust and longer term relationships between stakeholders, according to the interviews with the senior managers from the case company (Interview data, 2008). The e-SCM provides the integrated approach necessary for success when managing and executing end-to-end logistics solutions for clients. The key benefits generated from the e-SCM have enabled IFC's SME clients and partners to:

- address more effectively fluctuations in supply and demand;
- leverage on information to learn and engineer their supply chains so to monitor supplier responses and lead times, maximize container loads, and shift volumes via the best routes;
- create meaningful performance measurement indicators;
- help answer queries on status of orders and times of delivery;

- decrease to almost nil the level of paperwork required for legislative retention;
- leverage on the information trail that follows the product's physical trail;
- enjoy shorter cycle times; and
- help make better business decisions (Interview data, 2008).

According to Dumas (2008), FSC plays a central role in connecting the supply chain members of the case company and serves as a catalyst and a driver of the e-supply chain management.

Key Technology Challenges

However, the case company and its SME partners in the supply chain face a number of issues and challenges in implementing the e-SCM. For example, system failure is a main threat to e-collaboration amongst SME supply chain members and their e-business both in the short and long terms. According to the case company, the tremendous complexity of information technologies remains a huge hurdle to SMEs' implementation of e-SCM, affecting their entire management strategy, process, structure, and most importantly, business bottom line results (Interview data, 2008). This study found that the main technological issues are associated with SMEs' existing IT infrastructure, and managers' and operatives' knowledge and skills in e-SCM. The following constitutes some of the key technological issues facing SMEs in e-SCM in general:

- Process and system alignment and integration;
- Interoperability of systems;
- Accessibility and security of IT systems;
- Investment in new e-SCM applications, for example, collaborative technologies (i.e. partner relationship management [PRM] tools);
- Transferring and sharing technical information and knowledge between SMEs and building integrated information systems (for example, establishing a private portal where partners can co-plan and share information in real time) (Li et al., 2005);
- Effectiveness and efficiency of real-time reporting system;
- Building and sustaining an effective virtual network structure amongst e-supply chain partners; and
- Sustained IT support and resources.

Key Organizational and Management Challenges

Compounded with the technological challenges are the challenges of people and organizational management for the case company and other SMEs in the implementing e-SCM which include:

- Higher investment risks associated with e-SCM implementation given the extremely tight resources available to SMEs;
- Fostering and maintaining an innovation and forward-thinking organizational culture;
- Individual and organizational (top management) commitment to e-SCM;
- Taking e-SCM as a core element of a SME's business model or as a built-in corporate strategy;
- Joint business planning and development with supply chain partners for mutual interest and benefit;
- Educating and training employees to understand the concepts and goals of e-SCM;
- Effective and efficient ongoing monitoring and measurement metrics and systems; and
- Quality and effective networking and continuous improvement of communication (Zhao, 2008; Zhuang, 2005).

STRATEGIES

This section explores and develops effective strategies to address the above challenges identified facing SMEs in e-supply chain management. The author considers that the critical factors for e-SCM concern both IT and inter-organizational interfaces. Although collaborative technology infrastructure capacities required may vary in different supply chains and e-collaboration contexts, along with the role and size of each SME, the following presents fundamental and broad strategies for establishing and maintaining an effective e-infrastructure for e-collaboration in the supply chain.

The author recommends that simplified and standardized solutions for e-supply chain collaboration based on common technology architecture be instigated, which may include trading partner processes, multiple levels of connectivity amongst trading partners, internal infrastructure and system reengineering to ensure e-supply chain interoperability (that is, the ability to be fully compatible and capable of being integrated with each other in e-collaboration), and e-application architecture (Ross, 2003; Kotzab, Skjoldager, & Vinum, 2003). Given the fact that many SMEs now operate in more than one electronic supply chain, multiple IT integration becomes paramount to their business operations. Interoperability can be achieved through process standardization and information standards (e.g. EDI and RosettaNet Standards). Studies show that the achievement of multiple IT integration brings significant benefits to the companies that implement it (Davis & Spekman, 2004).

Given the constraints of SMEs in various aspects, it is imperative to establish simple and low-cost connectivity to ensure that smaller firms are able to access, and participate fully in, a collaborative infrastructure without having to make a major investment. For example, SMEs should have access to networked SCM applications which are browser-based through broadband Internet connections or virtual private networks. This researcher recommends that a common data model for data storage across the supply chain be established and implemented, which would be a simpler, faster, and far more efficient than integrating all the various data models.

As noted in the chapter, the success of e-SCM is concerned largely with the management of e-collaboration in the supply chain. It often involves sharing information and knowledge on which joint supply chain decisions can be made. Information that needs to be shared amongst supply chain partners often include sales data, inventory status, production schedule, promotion plans, demand forecasts, shipment schedule, and new product introduction plans (Huang & Gangopadhyay, 2004). Therefore, it is important to develop high-level self-service technologies which enable supply chain members to not only track orders, obtaining logistics and billing information but also automatically configure products, make payments and resolve disputes earlier on. Developing business intelligence technologies to analyze the ongoing flow of information drawn from the entire supply chain helps SMEs make improvements in internal operations and collaborative capabilities on an ongoing basis. In fact, applying business intelligence into e-business processes provides enormous opportunity for value creation in the supply chain and enhances SCM practices (Horvath, 2001; Mattsson, 2003).

To address the organizational and management challenges identified in this chapter, this author considers that focus should be placed primarily on leadership of SMEs, considering the dominating role that CEO/owner plays in a SME. According to the studies of SME innovation, the CEO/owner is the key driver and factor to the success of SME innovation (Laforet & Tann, 2006). The value, belief, attitude and commitment of a CEO/manager and his/her management team have a direct impact on the organizational culture and behavior of their company. For example, investment in skills and people, and allocation of much-needed resources to support e-SCM initiative and implementation are all at the hands of CEC/owner of a SME. An effective and committed leader with vision, passion and strategic thinking is the main resource for a SME to succeed in addressing the challenges of embracing e-SCM and gaining a competitive advantage from it. In addition to the effective leadership and innovative organizational culture of SMEs, effective processes and mechanisms should be in place to manage and monitor e-SCM implementation systematically.

Compared with large companies, SMEs have the advantages of flexibility, short communication lines, close relations with customers, and less bureaucracy. All of these advantages can facilitate the implementation and integration of e-SCM. This study found that one of the key success factors of the case company lies in its closeness to, and agility in responding to, its clients and other supply chain members' needs.

FUTURE RESEARCH DIRECTIONS

The future trends for e-supply chain management concerning SMEs will be characterized largely by:

- More needs for devising and popularizing e-supply chains due to the needs for integrating the flow of information with the flow of goods; and
- Greater pressure for SMEs to achieve business sustainability through information technology, due to a more competitive and uncertain economic environment, the increasing complexities of new technologies, and the more globalised economy.

The implication is that SMEs need to incorporate e-SCM concept into their overall business strategy. The alignment and integration of information systems and processes and the effective use of various inter-organizational information systems and Web technologies amongst SME supply chain members are only part of the challenges to make e-SCM work. Effectively dealing with flexibility, innovation, entrepreneurship, human, and cultural factors and reducing potential financial, commercial and legal risks associated with e-SCM implementation exceed the complexities of information and communication technologies in building and supporting e-collaboration amongst supply chain members. Thus, managing e-SCM requires more than the navigation of technological hurdles and complexity. It also requires strategy to deal with soft issues of how to manage a high-tech and high-touch international e-supply chain. This study is only the first step towards solutions to the issues. More empirical and theoretical studies are needed to study the issues facing SMEs in the inexorable trends of e-supply chain management.

CONCLUSION

With the rapid development of e-supply chain, taking up, and participating in, e-SCM is no longer an option but an imperative for SMEs to be competitive and sustainable in today's digitalized economy. Compared with traditional supply chains, e-supply chains are extremely dynamic, allowing for companies including SMEs to be included or excluded based upon technological advances, product life cycles, and customer preferences (Kuglin & Rosenbaum, 2000). These complex and volatile supply networks call for businesses to seek greater flexibility, agility and responsiveness. As shown in the case study of this chapter, in order to survive, SMEs are more likely and willing to meet the demand by taking advantage of their small size which makes them more flexible and responsive to the environmental changes.

By exploring the role that SMEs play in the e-supply chain management through a case study, this chapter contributes to a better understanding of the crucial issues in SME's adoption and implementation of e-SCM system and processes, and to effective strategy development to deal with the challenges.

In spite of the contribution and significance stemming from this study, limitations need to be acknowledged in terms of being a single case study and relying largely on the information provided by the senior managers and the company. In view of the limitations, this study treated the data as illustrative rather than definitive. The next stage of the study will focus on how to implement the strategies proposed by this study. Multi-case studies and quantitative methodology will be taken to identify specific issues raised in the implementation. The author wishes to see more rigourous empirical studies on how to help SMEs, specifically and in practice, take on e-SCM to benefit their business in the literature.

ACKNOWLEDGMENT

This author wishes to acknowledge the contributions made by Joe Dumas, the Head of the IT Division at IFC Global Logistics to the case study in this chapter. An extended case study of IFC Global Logistics can be located in Volume 2, Issue 2 of the *International Journal of e-Business Management* (ISSN: 1835-5412) at http://www.rmitpublishing.com.au/ijebm.htm.

REFERENCES

Angeles, R., & Nath, R. (2003). Electronic supply chain partnerships: Reconsidering relationship attributes in customer-supplier dyads. *Information Resources Management Journal, 16*(3), 59.

Berg, B. L. (1995). *Qualitative Research Methods for the Social Sciences*. Boston: Allyn and Bacon.

Burgess, R. (1998). Avoiding supply chain management failure: lessons from business process re-engineering. *International Journal of Logistics Management, 9*, 15–23. doi:10.1108/09574099810805717

Chandra, C., Grabis, A., & Tumanyan, A. (2007). Problem taxonomy: a step towards effective information sharing in supply chain management. *International Journal of Production Research, 45*(11), 2507–2544. doi:10.1080/00207540601020486

Creswell, J. W. (2003). *Research design: Qualitative, quantitative, and mixed method approaches* (2nd ed.). Thousand Oaks, CA: Sage.

Davis, E. W., & Spekman, R. E. (2004). *The extended enterprise: gaining competitive advantage through collaborative supply chains*. Upper Saddle River, NJ: Prentice Hall.

Dumas, J. (2008). IFC Global Logistics: Our successful story. *International Journal of e-Business Management, 2*(2), 47-51.

Fawcett, S. E., Osterhaus, P., Magnan, G. M., Brau, J. C., & McCarter, M. W. (2007). Information sharing and supply chain performance: The role of connectivity and willingness. *Supply Chain Management, 12*(5), 358. doi:10.1108/13598540710776935

Gelinas, R., & Bigras, Y. (2004). The characteristics and features of SMEs: Favorable or unfavorable to logistics integration? *Journal of Small Business Management, 42*(3), 263–278. doi:10.1111/j.1540-627X.2004.00111.x

Global Logistics, I. F. C. (2008). *About us–IGC Global Logistics*. Retrieved on March 7, 2007, from http://www.ifc.com.au/about_us.html

Gunasekaran, A., & Ngai, E. W. T. (2003). The successful management of a small logistics company. *International Journal of Physical Distribution & Logistics Management, 33*(9), 825–842. doi:10.1108/09600030310503352

Halley, A., & Guilhon, A. (1997). Logistics behaviour of small enterprises: Performance, strategy and definition. *International Journal of Physical Distribution & Logistics Management, 27*(8), 475–495. doi:10.1108/09600039710182644

Hong, P., & Jeong, J. (2006). Supply chain management practices of SMEs: From a business growth perspective. *Journal of Enterprise Information Management, 19*(3), 292–302. doi:10.1108/17410390610658478

Horvath, L. (2001). Collaboration: The key to value creation in supply chain management. *Supply Chain Management: An International Journal, 6*(5), 205–207. doi:10.1108/EUM0000000006039

Huang, Z., & Gangopadhyay, A. (2004). A simulation study of supply chain management to measure the impact of information sharing. *Information Resources Management Journal, 17*(3), 20–32.

Interview data (2008). The data was collected by the author from her interviews with senior managers at IFC, Melbourne in 2008.

Johnson, M. E. (2006). Supply chain management: technology, globalization, and policy at a crossroads. *Interfaces, 36*(3), 191–195. doi:10.1287/inte.1060.0214

Kock, N. (2007). Global funding of e-collaboration research: Challenges and opportunities. *International Journal of e-Collaboration, 3*(2), 1–5.

Kock, N., Lynn, G. S., Dow, K. E., & Akgun, A. E. (2006). Team adaptation to electronic media: Evidence of compensatory adaptation in new product development teams. *European Journal of Information Systems, 15*(3), 331. doi:10.1057/palgrave.ejis.3000612

Kotzab, H., Skjoldager, N., & Vinum, T. (2003). The development and empirical validation of an e-based supply chain strategy optimization model. *Industrial Management & Data Systems, 103*(5), 347–360. doi:10.1108/02635570310477406

Kuglin, F. A., & Rosenbaum, B. A. (2001). *The supply chain network at Internet speed: Preparing your company for the e-commerce revolution.* New York: Amacom.

Laforet, S., & Tann, J. (2006). Innovative characteristics of small manufacturing firms. *Journal of Small Business and Enterprise Development, 13*(3), 363–380. doi:10.1108/14626000610680253

Lagrosen, S. (2005). Effects of the internet on the marketing communication of service companies. *Journal of Services Marketing, 19*(2), 63–70. doi:10.1108/08876040510591376

Lee, H. L., & Whang, S. (2002). Supply chain integration over the Internet. In Genunes, J. (Eds.), *Supply chain management: Models, applications, and research directions* (pp. 3–18). Bordrecht, The Netherlands: Kluwer Academic Publishers.

Lefebvre, E., Cassivi, L., Lefebvre, L. A., & Loger, P. (2003). E-collaboration within one supply chain and its impact on firms' innovativeness and performance. *Information Systems and E-business Management, 173*(2).

Li, G., Yan, H., Wang, S., & Xia, Y. (2005). Comparative analysis on value of information sharing in supply chains. *Supply Chain Management, 10*(1), 34. doi:10.1108/13598540510578360

Mattsson, L. (2003). Reorganization of distribution in globalization of markets: The dynamic context of supply chain management. *Supply Chain Management, 8*(5), 416–427. doi:10.1108/13598540310500259

McCormack, K. P., Johnson, W. C., & Walker, W. (2003). *Supply chain networks and business process orientation: Advanced strategies and best practices.* New York: St. Lucie Press.

Nguyen, H. M., & Harrison, N. J. (2004). Electronic supply chain orientation and its competitive dimensions. *Production Planning and Control, 15*(6), 596–607. doi:10.1080/09537280412331283946

Radjou, N. (2004). The Internet invigorates supply chains. *Industrial Management (Des Plaines), 46*(1), 13–18.

Ritchie, B., & Brindley, C. (2000). Disintermediation, disintegration and risk in the SME global supply chain. *Management Decision*, *38*(8), 575–583. doi:10.1108/00251740010378309

Ross, D. F. (2003). *Introduction to e-supply chain management: Engaging technology to build market-winning business partnerships*. Boca Raton, FL: St. Lucie Press.

Sastry, T. (1999). Supply chain strategies for small firms facing high demand uncertainty and seasonality. *Vikalpa*, *24*(4), 7–15.

Schlenker, L., & Crocker, N. (2003). Building an e-business scenario for small business: The IBM SME Gateway project. *Qualitative Market Research: An International Journal*, *6*(1), 7–17. doi:10.1108/13522750310457339

Temperley, N. C., & Galloway, J. (2004). *SMEs in Australia's high-technology sector: Challenges and opportunities*. AEEMA.

Thakkar, J., Kanda, A., & Deshmukh, S. G. (2009). Supply chain management for SMEs: A research introduction. *Management Research News*, *32*(10), 970–993. doi:10.1108/01409170910994178

van Hoek, R. (2001). E-supply chains–virtually non-existing. *Supply Chain Management: An International Journal*, *6*(1), 21–28. doi:10.1108/13598540110694653

Yee, S. T. (2005). Impact analysis of customized demand information sharing on supply chain performance. *International Journal of Production Research*, *43*(16), 3353–3373. doi:10.1080/00207540500095779

Yin, R. K. (2003). *Case study research: Design and methods* (3rd ed.). Thousand Oaks, CA: Sage.

Zhao, F. (2006). *Maximize Business Profits through E-partnerships*. Hershey, PA: IDEA Group Publishing.

Zhao, F., & Dalrymple, J. (2002). E-partnerships in information era: Issues of information management. Organizational excellence: Managing information. *Proceedings of the 3rd Multinational Alliance for the Advancement of Organizational Excellence Conference,* Scotland.

Zhao, F., McMurray, A. J., & Toomey, M. (2008). Effectiveness of Information Technology governance: Perceptions of board directors and senior managers. In Zhao, F. (Ed.), *Information Technology Entrepreneurship and Innovation*. Hershey, PA: IDEA Group Publishing. doi:10.4018/9781599049014.ch004

Zhuang, Y. (2005). Does electronic business create value for firms? An organizational innovation perspective. *Journal of Electronic Commerce Research*, *6*(2), 146–156.

ADDITIONAL READING

Ackermann, I. (2003). Using the balanced scorecard for supply chain management–prerequisites, integration issues, and performance measures. In Seuring, S., Muller, M., Goldbach, M., & Schneidewind, U. (Eds.), *Strategy and organization in supply chains* (pp. 289–304). New York: Physica-Verlag.

Arend, R. J., & Winser, J. D. (2005). Small business and supply chain management: Is there a fit? *Journal of Business Venturing*, *20*, 403–436. doi:10.1016/j.jbusvent.2003.11.003

Auramo, J., Aminoff, A., & Punakivi, M. (2002). Research agenda for e-business logistics based on professional opinions. *International Journal of Physical Distribution & Logistics Management*, *32*(7), 513–532. doi:10.1108/09600030210442568

Cammaerts, B. (2006). The eConvention on the future of Europe: Civil society and the use of internet in European decision-making processes. *European Integration*, *28*(3), 225–245. doi:10.1080/07036330600744431

Cheng, W. L. E., Li, H., Love, E. D. P., & Irani, Z. (2001). An e-business model to support supply chain activities in construction. *Logistic Information Management*, *14*(1/2), 68–78. doi:10.1108/09576050110363239

Chinho, L., Hsiang-Chin, H., June-Yie, W., & Binshan, L. (2002). A Knowledge Management architecture in collaborative supply chain. *Journal of Computer Information Systems*, *42*(5), 83.

Damien, P. (2005a). Implementation and use of B2B-enabling technologies: Five manufacturing cases. *Journal of Manufacturing Technology Management*, *16*(5/6), 554.

Damien, P. (2005b). Strategy development processes as determinants of B2B e-commerce performance: A comparative model in a supply chain management context. *Internet Research*, *15*(5), 557. doi:10.1108/10662240510629493

David, J. K. Jr, & Hult, G. T. M. (2007). Bridging organization theory and supply chain management: The case of best value supply chains. *Journal of Operations Management*, *25*(2), 573. doi:10.1016/j.jom.2006.05.010

Davis, E. W., & Spekman, R. E. (2004). *The extended enterprise: Gaining competitive advantage through collaborative supply chains*. Upper Saddle River, NJ: Prentice Hall.

Dimitris, F., Vicky, M., Marianna, S., & Maro, V. (2004). Evolution of a supply chain: cases and best practices. *Internet Research*, *14*(4), 274. doi:10.1108/10662240410555298

Fink, L. (2007). Coordination, learning, and innovation: The organizational roles of e-collaboration and their impacts. *International Journal of e-Collaboration*, *3*(3), 53–71.

Jaana, A., Jouni, K., & Kari, T. (2005). Benefits of IT in supply chain management: An explorative study of progressive companies. *International Journal of Physical Distribution & Logistics Management*, *35*(2), 82. doi:10.1108/09600030510590282

Kersten, W., Schroeder, A. K., & Schulte-Bisping, A. (2004). Internet-supported sourcing of complex material. *Business Process Management Journal*, *10*(1), 101–114. doi:10.1108/14637150410518356

Luc, C., Pierre-Majorique, L., & Pierre, H. (2005). Electronic commerce and supply chain integration: the case of the telecommunication equipment industry. *Business Process Management Journal*, *11*(5), 559. doi:10.1108/14637150510619885

O'Toole, T. (2003). E-partnerships–emergence and the small firm. *Marketing Intelligence & Planning*, *21*(2), 115–122. doi:10.1108/02634500310465434

Ross, D. F. (2003). *Introduction to e-supply chain management: Engaging technology to build market-winning business partnerships*. Boca Raton, FL: St. Lucie Press.

Samaniego, M. J. G., Arranz, A. M. G., & Cabezudo, R. S. J. (2006). Determinants of Internet use in the purchasing process. *Journal of Business and Industrial Marketing*, *21*(3), 164. doi:10.1108/08858620610662813

Sean, L., David, C. Y., & Cheng-Yuan, K. (2006). E-supply chain management: an evaluation of current web initiatives. *Information Management & Computer Security*, *14*(2), 167. doi:10.1108/09685220610678613

Sierra, M. C. D. L. (1994). *Managing global alliances: Key steps for successful collaboration*. Addison-Wesley Publishing.

van Hoek, R. (2001). E-supply chains–virtually non-existing. *Supply Chain Management: An International Journal*, *6*(1), 21–28. doi:10.1108/13598540110694653

Walters, D. (2002). *Operations strategy*. Sydney: Palgrave.

KEY TERMS AND DEFINITIONS

E-Supply Chain Management (e-SCM): E-supply chain management is viewed as the most recent stage of development of the concept of supply chain management (Ross, 2003, Johson, 2006). The focus of management is placed primarily on the application of the Internet to the SCM concept and SCM synchronization. Networked and multi-enterprise supply chains have become a popular organizational design in the e-SCM. It is concerned largely with the management of Internet-enabled collaborative channel partnerships.

E-Collaboration: Generally speaking, e-collaboration refers to the use of electronic technologies (like the Internet and/or Internet-based tools) among business partners beyond market transactions (Kock, 2007; Davis and Spekman, 2004).The term is often used in the context of supply chain. E-collaboration is identified as one of the new areas of optimizing the relationship between suppliers and original equipment manufacturers (OEM) via the Internet (Radjou, 2004). It is an Internet-supported, enterprise-spanning cooperation which is seen as crucial during the development and construction process (the so called e-engineering process) (Kersten et al., 2004).

Small and Medium Sized Enterprises (SMEs): There are various definitions of small and medium sized enterprises (SMEs). The common criteria for categorization of enterprises are based on the maximum number of staff and annual turnover of a company. European Union defines SMEs as enterprises with a workforce of 1-250 employees. Australian Bureau of Statistics defines SMEs as companies employing between 1-199 people, wherein companies with 5-19 staff are termed 'small companies', while those with 20-199 employees are termed 'medium companies'.

Third Party Logistics Provider (3PL): According to the definition of the Council of Supply Chain Management Professionals (http://cscmp.org/), a third party logistics provider refers to "a firm that provides multiple logistics services for use by customers. Preferably, these services are integrated, or 'bundled' together, by the provider. Among the services 3PLs provide are transportation, warehousing, cross-docking, inventory management, packaging, and freight forwarding." Over the past decade, to achieve logistics efficiency and cost-effectiveness, many companies started outsourcing their logistics to specialized logistics service providers, of whom the majority are SMEs (Halley and Guilhon, 1997, Gelinas and Bigras, 2004). As a result, single-party self-managed logistics has developed into multi-party logistics such as 3PL and 5PL which are powered by e-logistics networks that expand to global operations.

Business Intelligence (BI): Business intelligence is often defined as capturing and analyzing hidden, inherent and decision-relevant contexts in stored data warehouses, operational databases, and/or ERP systems (Hameed, 2004). Developing business intelligence technologies to analyze the ongoing flow of information drawn from the entire supply chain helps make improvements in internal operations and collaborative capabilities on an ongoing basis.

Integration: Integration refers to collaborative planning and control, decision integration, information integration and business process integration between inter-firm partners, using information technologies and systems. With an e-procurement system, for example, it is important that the system should be integrated with the internal systems of the buyer partners and external order information from this system would be easily transferable to the supplier partners (Zhao, 2006).

Interoperability: Interoperability refers to the ability to be fully compatible and capable of being integrated with each other in the e-supply chain. Interoperability requires enhancement of the existing systems to transfer them into a cross-firm mode.

Chapter 6
Taiwan's Corporate Governance:
Explorations from the Ethical Corporate Governance Model

Hsiang-Yi Lin
Ching Yun University, Taiwan

Li Lin
Tamkang University, Taiwan

ABSTRACT

This chapter discusses the meaning and internal and external mechanisms of Taiwan's corporate governance, explains why this kind of mechanism cannot prevent the agency problem, and demonstrates the importance of business ethics by looking at the flaws in Taiwan's corporate governance. Other questions addressed in this study include what limitations are in the internal and external mechanisms of Taiwan's corporate governance, what makes the agency problem seem inevitable, and whether business ethics may compensate for the shortcomings in Taiwan's corporate governance. In this chapter, the correlation between business ethics and corporate governance is reviewed and organized in order to demonstrate how this topic was viewed by previous scholars along with a proposal of how these two topics can be joined together. The question of how the agency problem in corporate governance emerges is then examined, followed by a literature review of past studies on the influences of introducing business ethics on the agency problem as well as their relationship. The findings of the new business model are discussed in the section V.

DOI: 10.4018/978-1-60960-129-4.ch006

INTRODUCTION

The corporate problems revealed by the aforementioned incidents indicate many major flaws with Taiwan's enterprises. These problems not only seriously undermine minor shareholders' interests but also hinder the public's confidence in investing in Taiwan. In modern corporations where stock ownership is very scattered, an important task is to have complete corporate governance. Ye (2002) believes the purpose of corporate governance is to reinforce a corporation's social obligations, and pointed out the cases of failed corporate governance also demonstrate serious problems in corporate trust (B. Ye, 2002, 70-72). Further, Ye (2005) takes the business ethics and personality trait approaches and stresses that more attention should be placed on a director's credentials and abilities. For the sake of complete corporate governance, each director should be required to have relevant experiences and skills and a broad perspective in order to effectively manage a company, make professional judgments and careful decisions, and lead the company to grow and develop steadily. Therefore, a CEO must have the traits of a leader and managerial skills as well as dignity and communication skills in order to help the organization earn trust and develop talents (B. Ye, 2005, p.239).

LITERATURE REVIEW

C. Stone (1993) pointed out why law cannot replace ethics through three aspects. The first aspect is that the legislation of a new law often only takes place after a certain issue has emerged quite a while ago and thus lags behind. The second aspect is with the legislative process, in which legislatures may have different or insufficient legislative knowledge, and passed bills are often compromised. Lastly, the procedures of reaching a verdict and enforcing the law are all expensive expenditures, and even law enforcers themselves may get slothful on their job (Stone, 1993, 162-166). J. Bentham (1987) conducted an in-depth discussion on what kinds of behavior should be intervened by the law and which behaviors should stay in the domain of morality and ethics. Bentham believes when the cost of law enforcement outweighs the benefits to the society, intervention should be done through the domain of morality and ethics instead of the law; the same goes for offenses that cannot be clearly defined (Bentham, 1987, 62-63).

Hsu (2004) further pointed out that though the law upholds the bottom-line of morality, it is also based on the moral foundation; therefore, he defines the relationship between the law and morality as "interdependence" and "pushing and pulling (Hsu, 2004)." From the above discussions we can see that the law and the domain of morality and ethics are complementary and interdependent. Therefore, a topic that interest many scholars is to contemplate on the issue of corporate governance from the perspective of business ethics that is not a part of the corporate governance law (please see Table 1 for details).

Hitt, Ireland, Hoskisson (2003) mentioned there are strong relationships between ethical behaviors and corporate governance, thus the board of directors should clearly instruct their authorized agents (high-level managers) on the expectations of ethical business decisions and looking after all stakeholders' interests and ask the CEO to lead the employees by example in terms of ethical behaviors(Hitt, Ireland and Hoskisson, 2003, 332-333). S. P. Robbins (2005) believe the corporate governance incidents of false accounts and manipulated financial reports in Enron WorldCom demonstrate the importance of "trust," whose values include integrity, competence, consistency, loyalty, and openness -- important traits in a leader (Robbins, 2005, 356-357). A. Davies (1999) also mentioned that the foundation and effective operation of all forms of governance require "trust," and thus classifies trust as a key topic in corporate governance (Da-

Table 1. Relationships between law and ethics and morality

Scholar	Proposal
Bentham (1987)	1. When the cost of law enforcement outweighs the benefits to the society, intervention should be done through the domain of morality and ethics instead of the law; 2. Offenses that cannot be clearly defined should also be handled by the domain of morality and ethics.
Stone (1993)	1. Legislation often lags behind. 2. In the legislative process, legislatures may have the legislative knowledge gap, and passed bills are often compromised. 3. Reaching a verdict and enforcing the law are all expensive expenditures, and even law enforcers themselves may get slothful on their job.
Hsu (2004)	1. The law upholds the bottom-line of morality and is also based on the moral foundation 2. Defines the relationship between the law and morality as "interdependence" and "pushing and pulling."

Source: Compiled by the Researcher of this Study

vies, 1999, 14-17). Though J. L. Colley, Jr., J. L. Doyle, G. W. Logan, W. Stettinius (2003) have not directly discussed the agency theory, they also treat those who are the opposite of shareholders as trustees and proposed that ethics and morality not only have to be included in national governance but also in corporate governance as well, and stressed the importance of values such as integrity in corporate governance (Colley, Doyle, Logan, & Stettinius, 2003: x, 6, 230).

Micklethwait & Wooldridge (2003) mentioned that problems such as the Enron scandal will only repeat themselves, and the rule of regularly changing accountants specified in The Sarbanes-Oxley Act of 2002 will not be as effective as regularly changing accounting firms in terms of eliminating financial scandals; in addition, whether a corporate leader has a noble soul and whether trust is established are also important issues (Micklethwait & Wooldridge, 2003, pp. 189-192). O. C. Ferrell, J. Fraedrich, L. Ferrell (2005) assigned one task to each decade of business ethics since the 1960s and believe that the focus and task in the 21st century is the topic of business ethics in corporate governance and the importance of loyalty and trust in ethical climate. They also mentioned that not only the New York Stock Exchange requires all publicly traded corporations to formulate ethics rules, the European Union, North American Free Trade Agreement, Common Market of the Southern Cone, and the World Trade Organization all emphasize on ethical norms in global business activities, thus the "Principles For Business" introduced in "The Caux Round Table" will receive more attention (Ferrell, Fraedrich, & Ferrell, 2005, pp. 9-14).

R. Kreitner & A. Kinicki (2004) also believe organizational culture and ethic climate may help reduce problems such as the Enron scandal (Kreitner and Kinicki, 2004, pp. 76-78). A. B. Carroll & A. K. Buchholtz (2006) take the social contract approach and treat corporations as corporate citizens who have the Corporate Social Responsibility (CSR). In the topic of business ethics, the approach is how social stakeholder can regulate businesses' behaviors that are harmful to the society. Regarding corporate governance, Carroll & Buchholtz defined "social stakeholders" as "owner stakeholders" and believe the management level's most important duty is "full disclosure" and "information transparency," whereas owner stakeholders should work as active supervisors such as actualizing shareholder activism in order to reduce agency problems (Carroll and Buchholtz, 2006, pp. 19-20, 612-622).

R. W. Mondy & R. M. Noe (2005) also took the social contract and stakeholder approach to observe corporate governance, and indicated that due to the modern social atmosphere and public's expectation, CSR and business ethics-related bills are passed, and there is a clear direction for the aforementioned legislation of business ethics and moral norms (Mondy and Noe, 2005, p. 27). When discussing the issue of agency cost caused by agency problems in the cost of transaction, J. F. Hennart (1991) stated that cost increases when employees demonstrate behaviors such as deception, laziness, and dereliction of duty (Hennart, 1991). Lin (2004) suggested that agency problems can be reduced if corporate managers have self-discipline and self-control (Lin, 2004). In this present study, past literatures on the relationships between the agency problem and business ethics are listed in Table 2.

In Lin's(2004) study of the board of directors' duties and entrepreneurship in three publicly-traded companies in Taiwan – TK3C, AUO, and Tong Lung Metal Industry, he stresses that a corporate manager must have self-discipline and self-control in order to reduce the agency problem caused by transaction costs and in turn protect the interests of shareholders and stakeholders (Lin, 2004). Wu (2006) also stresses that good corporate governance is achieved when a company fulfills its social obligations through transparency and trust (Wu, 2006). Wu (2002) also stresses that corporate governance should be based on ethical leadership and include a mechanism that promotes ethical conduct and encourages employees to demonstrate moral conducts. In addition, Wu also stated that the purpose of corporate governance is to rebuild the public's trust in enterprises, which can be achieved by improving existing flaws. Wu also proposed achieving business ethics through corporate governance, and ethics is an essential element in corporate governance. Wu used Shiseido (Japan) as an example: in this corporation, corporate governance equals business ethics, the purpose of corporate governance is to improve employees' qualities, and all employees are expected to treat themselves as good citizens (Wu, 2002, pp. 120-121).

Ye, Li, and Ke (2002) especially stress that a manager's integrity is the key to the success of corporate governance since a lack of integrity would result in corporate governance not being able to express its features in a timely fashion. This is why the corporation law around the world requires company owners to exercise due care in order to ensure high-level managers would not turn their backs on their fiduciary duty given by shareholders. The scholars believe the most effective way to achieve this is through a manager's self-discipline and self-integrity (Ye, Li, and Ke,

Table 2. Relationship between the agency problem and business ethics

Scholar	Proposal
Katz (1964)	A company's members may sometimes demonstrate behaviors that benefit the organization when playing their designated roles.
Hennart (1991)	The cost of transaction increases when employees demonstrate behaviors such as deception, laziness, and dereliction of duty in the issue of agency.
Davies (1999)	The foundation and effective operation of all forms of governance require "trust," and thus classifies trust as a key topic in corporate governance.
Donaldson & Dunfee (1994 & 1999)	1. In ISCT, the "microsocial contract" for special groups is based on the mutually-agreed goals, values, and norms among community members (1994). 2. The loyalty demonstrated through the extra-role behaviors by an organization's members is consistent with the "authentic ethical norm" defined by Donaldson & Dunfee. It is not only the third principle in Küng's Global Ethic but also the source of substantive hyper-norm in the macro-social contract (1999).
Hitt, Ireland, & Hoskisson, 2003)	The board of directors should clearly instruct their authorized agents (high-level managers) on the expectations of ethical business decisions and looking after all stakeholders' interests and ask the CEO to lead the employees by example in terms of ethical behaviors.

continued on following page

Table 2. continued

Scholar	Proposal
Colley, Doyle, Logan, & Stettinius (2003)	1. Treat those who are the opposite of shareholders as trustees. 2. Proposed that ethics and morality not only have to be included in national governance but also corporate governance as well, and stressed the importance of values such as integrity in corporate governance.
Micklethwait & Wooldridge (2003)	1. The rule of regularly changing accountants specified in The Sarbanes- Oxley Act of 2002 will not be as effective as regularly changing accounting firms in terms of eliminating financial scandals. 2. Whether a corporate leader has a noble soul and whether trust is established are also important issues.
Lin, H. (2004).	Agency problems can be reduced if corporate managers have self-discipline and self-control.
Kreitner & Kinicki (2004)	Organizational culture and ethic climate may help reduce problems such as the Enron scandal.
Mondy & Noe (2005)	The modern social atmosphere and public's expectation are the reason why CSR and business ethics-related bills are passed and there is a clear direction for the legislation of business ethics and moral norms.
Ferrell, Fraedrich, & Ferrell (2005)	1. The task at hand after entering the 21st century is business ethics and organizational loyalty and trust. 2. New York Stock Exchange, European Union, North American Free Trade Agreement, Common Market of the Southern Cone, and the World Trade Organization all emphasize on ethical norms and business ethics.
Robbins (2005)	1. The value of "trust" should be emphasized. 2. The values of "trust" include integrity, competence, consistency, loyalty, and openness, and they are important traits in a leader.
Carroll & Buchholtz (2006)	1. Take the social contract approach and treat corporations as corporate citizens who have the Corporate Social Responsibility (CSR). 2. In the topic of business ethics, the approach is how social stakeholder can regulate businesses' behaviors that are harmful to the society. 3. Regarding corporate governance, "social stakeholders" are defined as "owner stakeholders." 4. The management level's most important duty is "full disclosure" and "information transparency," whereas owner stakeholders should work as active supervisors.
Chiang, T., Cheng, B., Wu, T., and Cheng, C. (2006)	Extra-role behaviors sometimes reduce agency problems, thus employee loyalty is an alternative to the principal's contract that regulates the agent.
Hill & Jones (2006)	1. When a company's manager puts his/her interests above those of the stakeholders, immoral behaviors rooted in the agency problem may emerge and may be reflected by his/her self- dealing and information manipulation. 2. Corporate managers should ensure ethical decision-making.
Pearce II & Robinson (2007)	A manager with an ethic attitude would treat business ethics as the core values when dealing with the interactions between the society and all the stakeholders, and would reach a balance between shareholders' interests and the interests of the company's stakeholders.

Source: Compiled by the Researcher of this Study

2002, p.307). Tai (2006) also mentioned that Taiwan's industries, government, and academic societies are coming up with regulations and auditing systems to achieve improvements. However, even if such efforts are complete, the key to eliminating financial scandals still lies inside people's minds. In other words, financial order can only be achieved through self-control, ethics management, and improving the social atmosphere (Tai, 2006, p.21). Sun (2000) believes the failure of corporate governance involves three aspects: morality and ethics, law and systems, and governmental interventions. A corporation can only have the same goals as the society when it obeys the law and is operated properly, and only then can an individual's pursuit of profits be supported by ethics (Sun, 2000, p.4).

Wu believes the reason why a company's controlling shareholders have the opportunity to commit crimes for selfish gains is mostly because the company's internal control is mostly at the disposal of the controlling shareholders. They have control over the company's internal audits, the board of directors' functions, supervisors' tasks, and even accountants' certification. In other words, the supervision and monitoring in corporate governance are under the grasp of the controlling shareholders, thus seriously undermining the interests of minor shareholders(Wu, 2004, pp. 26-27).

CORPORATE GOVERNANCE AND SHAPES OF VIOLATIONS AMONG PUBLICLY-TRADED CORPORATIONS

In the discussion on corporate governance, many scholars also include the issue of "agency" and view it as the main cause behind problems in corporate governance. Chen (2004) pointed out that the focus on corporate governance is not only to enhance shareholders' long-term values and returns but also to look after the interests of stakeholders and solve the agency problem in order to avoid the conflict of interest among managers after the ownership and the managerial control over a business are separated (Chen, 2004, p.20). E. F. Fama & M. C. Jensen (1983) and A. Schleifer & R. Vishny (1997) all believe the agency problem is inevitable in corporate governance (Fama and Jensen, 1983; Shleifer and R. Vishny, 1997). Fama & Jensen (1983) further argue that there is a close relationship between the agency problem and the board of directors' failure to fulfill its role as the general manager (Fama and Jensen, 1983); therefore, Fama (1980) believes that the agency problem is less likely to occur when the president of a company is able to intervene in its managerial control while the general manager has less power (Fama, 1980). Ye et al. (2002) believe there are conflicts of interest between a company's managerial level and the stakeholders, which lead to problems in corporate governance; when major shareholders also work as managers, the problem of agency becomes a part of the problem of corporate governance (Ye, Li and Ke, 2002, p.23). B. K. Boyd (1995) also believes this practice of "dual-identity" would only cause the board of directors to lose the supervisory capacity and mechanism and does not help solve the agency problem (Boyd, 1995).

In their work "Observing the agency Issue from the Shareholder Structure in Corporate Governance, M. C. Jensen & W. Meckling (1976) mentioned that when share ownership is concentrated on a few major shareholders, a company's managerial decisions will have a tremendous amount of influences on these shareholders' interests; therefore, they are more likely to heavily supervise the company's managerial level (agency) and can better reduce the agency problem (Jensen & Meckling, 1976). M. C. Jensen & R. S. Ruback (1983) further argue that when shares are mostly owned by a handful of major shareholders, they are able to pass resolutions that are in their favor at the expense of minor shareholders' interests (Jensen & Ruback, 1983). Also examining the agency problem from the perspective of the shareholder, Huang (2001) pointed out that the focus of future corporate governance problems is not the scattered shareholder structure but the concentrated shareholder structure, and under the spotlight is the relationship between powerful major shareholders and the rest of the weaker minority. An urgent issue to be addressed in Taiwan is how the corporate governance system can prevent moral hazard and keep a few controlling shareholders from infringing the interests of the general shareholders (Huang, 2001, pp. 12-17, 24).

In the discussion on the agency theory, Yang (2007) stressed that there is really no way for a company principal to be fully aware of the behaviors of the agent, and improving the information transparency can only solve half of the agency problem. The only solution is having complete and accurate information, and what Yang stressed is the quality of information. It is, however, very difficult to reach this goal. To allow better corporate governance, the board of directors has to invest more in the company's major managerial decisions, and its decisions-making process also needs to be more revealed to the shareholders (Yang, 2007, p.428). J. A. Pearce & R. B. Robinson (2007) believe the agency relationship between a company's shareholders and the CEO leads to the following problems: (1). The CEO only pursues the company's growth and neglects the shareholders' deserved returns, (2) the CEO affected the shareholders' returns when diversifying or avoiding risks for the company, and (3). the CEO pursues maximum personal returns and strengthened personal status and does not care about the shareholders' deserved returns. (PearceII and Robinson, 2007, 37-38)

C. W. L. Hill & G. R. Jones (2007) reminded that in corporate governance, the agency problem is not limited to the relationship between a company's high-level managers and the shareholders but may also occur in the relationship between high-level managers and their subordinates, and even between the subordinates and their own subordinates. This is because a subordinate may provide false performance reports through his/her grasp of information for the purpose of getting more rewards or resources from the company (Hill & Jones, 2007, p.385). M. A. Hitt, R. D. Ireland, R. E. Hoskisson (2003) pointed out that "managerial opportunism" often exists in the agency relationship in corporate governance, and many agency problems emerge as a result of fraud committed by this kind of agent who looks after their own interests (Hitt, Ireland & Hoskisson, 2003, p.312). J. Micklethwait & A. Wooldridge (2003) believe problems in the corporate governance in corporations such as Enron, WorldCom, and Xerox imply the relapse of the agency problem regarding the interests of managers and owners, and pointed out the main contribution from The Sarbanes-Oxley Act of 2002 is to redefine the duties and obligations of the accounting sector and to once again manifest the fundamental principles in the American capitalism (Micklethwait & Wooldridge, 2003, 155-158).

In the discussion on the agency problem, K. M. Eisenhardt (1989) pointed out that moral hazards, reverse selection, and risk aversion may occur between a principal and an agent, and thus believe that the principal and the agent may a sign a contract that regulates the agent through behaviors or outcomes in order to fully stay on top of the agent's behaviors and avoid agency problems (Eisenhardt, 1989). D. Katz (1964), however, proposed that a company's members may sometimes demonstrate behaviors that benefit the organization when playing their designated roles (Katz, 1964). This kind of extra-role behavior sometimes reduces agency problems. Therefore, Chiang, T., Cheng, B., Wu, T., and Cheng, C. (2006) mentioned that employee loyalty is an alternative to the principal's contract that regulates the agent. In this present study, the agency problems in corporate governance are listed in Table 3.

Wu divides different shapes of corporate governance failure based on their characteristics along with their solutions into 10 categories. Problems caused by the failure of directors and supervisors to carry out their supervisory duties include Shape B, C, E, and D; those caused by accountants' failure to verify financial reports include Shape A, D, G, E, and I. Those due to a company's management level hiding transactions and having false financial reports include Shape E, F, G, I, and J. Other shapes worth mentioning include controlling shareholders embezzling corporate funds, controlling shareholders selling their per-

Table 3. Agency problems in corporate governance

Scholar	Proposal
Jensen & Meckling (1976)	When share ownership is concentrated on a few major shareholders, they are more likely to heavily supervise the company's managerial level (agency) and thus reduce the agency problem.
Fama (1980)	The agency problem is less likely to occur when the president of a company is able to intervene in its managerial control while the general manager has less power.
Fama & Jensen, 1983)	1. The agency problem is inevitable in corporate governance. 2. There is a close relationship between the agency problem and the board of directors' failure to fulfill its role as the general manager.
Jensen & Ruback (1983)	When shares are mostly owned by a handful of major shareholders, they are able to pass resolutions that are in their favor at the expense of minor shareholders' interests.
Eisenhardt (1989)	1. Moral hazards, reverse selection, and risk aversion may occur between a principal and an agent. 2. The principal should sign a contract with the agent that regulates the latter and avoid agency problems.
Boyd (1995)	When major shareholders also work as managers, the board of directors will lose the supervisory capacity and mechanism, which does not help solve the agency problem.
Schleifer & Vishny, 1997)	The agency problem is inevitable in corporate governance.
Huang (2001)	The key to solve problems in corporate governance lies in the concentrated shareholder structure. Moral hazards need to be prevented in order to keep a few controlling shareholders from infringing the interests of the general shareholders.
Ye (2002)	1. There are conflicts of interest between a company's managerial level and the stakeholders, which lead to problems in corporate governance 2. When major shareholders also work as managers, the problem of agency becomes a part of the problem of corporate governance.
Hitt, Ireland, & Hoskisson (2003)	"Managerial opportunism" often exists in the agency relationship in corporate governance, and many agency problems emerge as a result of fraud committed by this kind of agent who looks after their own interests.
Micklethwait & Wooldridge, 2003)	1. Problems in the corporate governance in corporations such as Enron, WorldCom, and Xerox imply the relapse of the agency problem regarding the interests of managers and principals. 2. The main contribution from The Sarbanes-Oxley Act of 2002 is to re-define the duties and obligations of the accounting sector and to once again manifest the fundamental principles in the American capitalism.
Chen (2004)	The focus on corporate governance is not only to enhance shareholders' long-term values and returns but also to look after the interests of stakeholders and solve the agency problem in order to avoid the conflict of interest among managers after the ownership and the managerial control over a business are separated.
Hill & Jones (2006)	The agency problem exists between a company's high-level managers and the shareholders, between high-level managers and their subordinates, and between the subordinates and their own subordinates. A subordinate may provide false performance reports through his/her grasp of information for the purpose of getting more rewards or resources from the company.
Yang (2007)	1. Improving the information transparency can only solve half of the agency problem. The key is the quality of information. 2. The board of directors has to invest more in the company's major managerial decisions, and its decisions-making process also needs to be more revealed to the shareholders.
Pearce & Robinson (2007)	The agency relationship between a company's shareholders and the CEO leads to the following problems: (1) The CEO only pursues the company's growth and neglects the shareholders' deserved returns, (2) the CEO affected the shareholders' returns when diversifying or avoiding risks for the company, and (3) the CEO pursues maximum personal returns and strengthened personal status and does not care about the shareholders' deserved returns.

Source: Compiled by the Researcher of this Study

sonal properties to the company at high prices as a way to seize corporate funds, controlling shareholders seizing corporate funds through forged documents, the management level selling stocks at low prices, and the management level's illogical and unnecessary advanced payments. The above violations are listed in Table 4 (Wu, 2004, pp. 17-20).

The solutions proposed by Wu indicate that some problems are caused by the accountant's failure to fully carry out an audit, and Wu has repeatedly stressed the importance of having an independent director/supervisor system. Of the ten cases of corporate governance violation (from A to J), the main cause is the controlling shareholders having control over the board of directors/supervisors and prohibiting them from carrying out their duties, resulting in a total failure of the corporate governance mechanisms. Whether a company's controlling shareholders have business ethics and dignity is intertwined with the flaws in Taiwan's corporate governance when the internal mechanism is controlled by the former and thus disabled.

When discussing the roles of and regulations over accountants in corporate governance, Huang (2003) mentioned that an accountant's social obligation is not only to comply with audit-related standards but also to respect the interests of the client and third-parties in order to maintain his/her reputation. An accountant's characteristics are critical since they affect his/her professional judgments. Huang believes when making professional judgments, an accountant must stay independent, objective, and honest and must never succumb to the client's management level (Huang, 2003, pp. 30-33). Therefore, when an accountant can stay independent, objective, and honest and maintain his/her role as the pillar of the external mechanism of corporate governance despite the pressure from the company's controlling shareholders, the latter would not be able to fully seize all the internal and external mechanisms of corporate governance. This is consistent with Wu's solutions as discussed earlier and demonstrates the accountant's business ethics is directly correlated with the success of corporate governance.

THE CASE STUDY: THE CHARACTERISTICS IN TAIWAN'S CORPORATE GOVERNANCE

When further considering the influences of cultures and regions on Taiwan's corporate governance, Liu also pointed out that corporate governance is closely connected to the cultural background and geography. As a result, Taiwan's corporate governance has diverse and complex characteristics. Lu mentioned that Taiwan's corporate governance may be influenced by the following: (1) A family-owned, publicly-traded corporation in the Chinese society. (2) The family-based stock ownership is deeply influenced by the U.S. when the high-tech industry is promoted through entrepreneurship and engineers are becoming the technology upstarts. (3) The government has led the financial system for years and encourages people to save their money at banks, yet banks' development is suppressed due to the concern for problems. The capital market that used to be treated as a casino now recovers after the curfew is lifted, resulting in the trend of direct finance taking over indirect finance. (4) While advertising the necessity and importance of corporate governance, the government actually intervenes in the stock market through the four major funds and the National Stabilization Fund; privatization is also lagging behind. (5) Taiwan's legal workers undergo stringent and standard legal training and stress formalism. As a result, their understanding of the knowledge and actual practice of finance is not as strong. They stress fairness and justice but lack the understanding of and confidence in the market. (6) Taking advantage of Taiwan's policy of avoiding direct contact with mainland China and reduced foreign exchange control, Taiwanese enterprises have been investing in China through affiliated companies. This

Table 4. Shapes of violations among publicly-traded corporations and suggested solutions

	Shape	Characteristic	Suggestion
A	Removing corporate funds -- The company owner transfers overseas branch offices' losses to the parent company through unconventional stock transactions.	The accountant verifies financial reports for problems. The board of directors' resolution does not comply with business norms.	Establish an independent director/supervisor system. Reinforce an accountant's audits over major stakeholders.
B	Removing corporate funds -- In order for a company to maintain its stock prices, its major shareholders and the subsidiary company intervene in the stock market and purchase the company's stocks through credit expansion. The continued drop of stock prices results in major losses for the major shareholders and the subsidiary company and major investment losses recognized by the parent company.	Major shareholders embezzling corporate funds. Major shareholders sell their personal properties to the company at high prices in order to seize corporate funds. Incomplete internal control. Directors and supervisors fail to carry out supervisory duties.	Reinforce audits over stakeholders' transactions and investments. Reinforce a corporation's internal control over its stakeholders' transactions. The account must carry out audits in an independent and professional manner. Prompt corporations to value and actualize corporate governance. Actualize the "Securities Investors Protection Act."
C	Removing corporate funds — The company owner sells the company stocks owned by him/herself and his/her family members that have lost their values back to the company, resulting in the removal of corporate funds and payments made by the company's clients.	The procedures of asset-acquisition violate the rules. Insufficient asset-protection measures. Directors and supervisors fail to carry out supervisory duties.	Reinforce audits over stakeholders' transactions and investments. Establish the independent director/supervisor system. The account must carry out audits in an independent and professional manner. Prompt corporations to value and actualize corporate governance. Actualize the "Securities Investors Protection Act."
D	Embezzling corporate funds — The company owner embezzles corporate funds to manipulate stock prices; however, the stock prices continue to drop, and the company faces a financial crisis and is thus suspended due to a lack of cash flow.	The company owner embezzles corporate funds through forged documents. The accountant fails to pay professional attention.	Establish an independent director/supervisor system. Reinforce the accountant's audit duties. Reinforce audits over advanced payments and stakeholders' transactions.
E	Embezzling the funds of the company and affiliated companies — The company owner transfers the corporate funds into the subsidiary company, and the subsidiary company and the affiliated company then transfer the funds to a private investment company established by the owner. The company and the subsidiary company then use short-term notes as collaterals for the owner's private investment company to issue commercial promissory notes.	Incomplete internal control. The management level hides the transactions, resulting in repeated financial report revisions. Directors and supervisors fail to carry out supervisory duties.	Establish an independent director/supervisor system. Reinforce the accountant's audit duties. Reinforce the management of a corporation's capital loans and endorsement.
F	Removing corporate funds — A company's stocks are purchased through the group's cross holdings, stakeholders, or affiliated companies for the purpose of arranging the group's capital for manipulating the stock prices, which in turn allows the manipulation of the profits/losses of the group's corporations and illegal stock transactions by the group's members.	The group has crossing holdings and a high percentage of mortgage clause. Provide false reports of bloated earnings. Disclosure of off-balance sheet transactions.	Reinforce audits over stakeholders' transactions and investments. Beware of the content of disclosed information outside the balance sheet. Establish the independent director/supervisor system. Prompt corporations to value and actualize corporate governance. Actualize the "Securities Investors Protection Act."

continued on following page

Table 4. continued

	Shape	Characteristic	Suggestion
G	Removing corporate funds — The company conducts a capital increase, sells debenture stocks to acquire capital, conducts actions outside the planned capital-increase, or uses its assets to manipulate stock prices.	False prospectus. False financial reports. The accountant's negligence. Directors and supervisors fail to carry out supervisory duties.	Reinforce audits over stakeholders' transactions and investments. Reinforce a corporation's internal control over its investments. Beware of the content of disclosed information outside the balance sheet. The account must carry out audits in an independent and professional manner. Establish the independent director/supervisor system. Prompt corporations to value and actualize corporate governance. Actualize the "Securities Investors Protection Act."
H	Capital embezzlement — The company owner withdraws payments made by other companies through stakeholders' transactions, resulting in huge losses for the company; the company sells a large amount of goods in stock to a stakeholder at low prices, committing offenses such as Non-arm's Length Transaction or embezzlement of corporate funds.	Selling goods to a stakeholder at low prices. Embezzlement of corporate funds. Having unconventional stock transactions with stakeholders.	Actualize the "Securities Investors Protection Act."
I	An advanced payment is involved with Non-arm's Length Transaction —The company makes a large advanced payment for goods but does not actually take them in, does not sign relevant contracts, or does not seem rational in the decision-making process; the advanced payment does not seem rational or necessary; the authenticity of the transaction and the capital-flow seem suspicious.	Improper capital flow. Irrational decision-making process regarding the advanced payment. The advanced payment does not seem rational and/or necessary. The cash-flow process seems suspicious.	Reinforce audits over stakeholders. The account must carry out audits in an independent and professional manner. Prompt corporations to value and actualize corporate governance.
J	The prospectus involves false/hidden or embezzled capital funds – Information disclosure does not comply with the regulations, and/or the corporate funds are used to buy/sell stocks through a subsidiary company.	False prospectus. Corporate funds are embezzled or diverted.	Reinforce the company managers' legal education. Prompt corporations to value and actualize corporate governance.

Source: Based on the work by Wu (2004, 17-19)

kind of non-transparency is not consistent with the principle of corporate governance, yet it is a result of the national policies. Therefore, the competitions between Taiwan and China will be reflected by the corporate governance systems in the future (Liu, 2002, pp. 70-85).

Therefore, Liu believes it is inevitable for Taiwan's corporate governance to take on the characteristics of family-owned businesses, and the co-existence of socialism and capitalism is also rich in formalism. The system not only has independent directors but supervisors as well. Taiwan's unique corporate governance includes a mixture of the British, American, German, and Japanese corporate governance systems and the British-American-French and the continental legal systems, thus often resulting in the issue of formalism, which is closely correlated with the culture of dummy accounts (Liu, 2002, p.78).

Despite the efforts to improve Taiwan's corporate governance (Table 5), incidents such as the embezzlement in Re-bar (occurred on

Table 5. Recent efforts to improve Taiwan's corporate governance

Number	Name/content of Measure	Expected Results
1	Ask publicly-traded corporations to establish internal control systems and reinforce management over investments.	Helps improve internal supervision and provides early warning.
2	Provides combined financial reports as requested by affiliated companies.	Improves information transparency in affiliated companies.
3	Revise the Corporation Law, the Securities Exchange Act, and the Merger and Acquisition Law, forcing company owners to exercise due care and prohibiting transmission of interests.	Promotes the legalization of ethics and prevents illegal stakeholder transactions.
4	A company applying for incorporation must have 2 independent directors and 1 independent supervisor.	Improves the independence of directors and supervisors.
5	Formulate rules over how the annual report and the prospectus should be prepared; mandatory disclosure of whether independent directors/supervisors are available.	Methods such as "co-operation" and "exposure" push the establishment of independent directors/supervisors in corporations.
6	Revise regulations over endorsement, handling of assets, extensive financial products, and capital loans for corporations.	Provides additional disclosure for investors to evaluate risks.
7	Establish the HR bank of independent directors/supervisors and ask corporate staff to take additional training before and after the incorporation.	Achieves qualitative changes through quantitative changes by developing needed talents.
8	Following the U.S. SEC's EDGAR (Electronic Data Gathering and Retrieval) system, TWSE establishes a single-track financial report online system for corporations.	Avoids information blind spots and promotes transparency and accessibility.
9	TWSE establishes an information observation station with an English interface.	Reinforces diplomatic information and prevents foreign corporate governance research institutes (such as CLSA or S&P) from having too little information to correctly interpret the situation or to implement changes.
10	Actively participate in international seminars such as OECD and APEC.	Helps the world understand the current status and future tasks of Taiwan's corporate governance and clarifies misunderstandings.
11	Formulate the Merger and Acquisition Law, revise the Corporation Law, the Fair Trade Act, and the Securities Exchange Act regarding restructuring, investments, and mergers.	Establishes the legal basis that facilitates business mergers, which in turn promotes corporate governance.
12	Establish an information disclosure evaluation system.	Promotes the supervision over the information system and improves the quality of disclosure.
13	Relax regulations over share ownership in independent directors/supervisors.	Avoids hindering the tasks of independent directors/supervisors caused by regulations on the minimum share ownership in directors/supervisors.
14	Assist in the establishment of private corporate governance organizations.	TCGA has been established to promote the corporate governance culture and the training of auditors, allowing future evaluations.
15	Regularly update the websites of SFB, TWSE, Gre-Tai Securities Market, and Securities & Futures Institute.	Improves domestic and overseas promotion and communication.
16	Formulate plans to revise the Securities Exchange Act in order to have the legal basis for enforcing independent directors/supervisors.	Completely solves disputes such as whether a legal basis is lacking or whether the Constitution is violated.
17	Revise the Corporation Law and prohibits cross holding.	Avoids stock manipulation and increases transparency.
18	Revises rules regarding general companies and financial organizations' prospectus, annual reports, incorporation standards, and the requirement for a substantial owner.	Investigations into individuals behind the curtain help promote corporate governance, bank governance, and financial reform.
19	Formulate the "Rules Governing the Actual Practice of Corporate Governance in Corporations."	Establishes a set of standards for the optimal actual practice of corporate governance that enhances the actual practice of governance.
20	Require investment and credit companies to specify and explain the daily stock transactions and review the situation when an investor's stocks are suffering losses to a certain degree.	Improves transparency and responsibility that also enhance fund governance.

Source: Liu (2002:155)

2007/1/27) and false financial reports in YHi (occurred on 2007/3/21) make us further realize that the success and failure of corporate governance is intertwined with the cultural background no matter how complete the law and anti-corruption measures may seem, and this further demonstrates the invaluable role of business ethics in Taiwan's corporate governance.

THE NEW BUSINESS MODEL: ETHICAL CORPORATE GOVERNANCE MODEL

It is natural for us to also think about business ethics after discussing the importance of employee loyalty and values in the previous sections. When explaining their ISCT, Donaldson & Dunfee (1994) mentioned that the "microsocial contract" for special groups is based on the mutually-agreed goals, values, and norms among community members (Donaldson and Dunfee, 1994). The loyalty demonstrated through the extra-role behaviors by an organization's members is consistent with the "authentic ethical norm" (Donaldson and Dunfee, 1999, pp. 35-38) defined by Donaldson & Dunfee (1999). Authentic ethical norm such as loyalty is not only the third principle in Küng's Global Ethic, "the commitment to a culture of tolerance and a life of truthfulness," but also the source of substantive hyper-norm in the macro-social contract defined by Donaldson and Dunfee (1999) (Donaldson and Dunfee, 1999, p.69; Küng, 1998, pp. 110-111).

Therefore, after discussing corporate governance and the agency problem, Pearce & Robinson (2007) discussed the importance of ethics management and pointed out that a manager with an ethic attitude would treat business ethics as the core values when dealing with the interactions between the society and all the stakeholders, and would reach a balance between shareholders' interests and the interests of the company's stakeholders(PearceII & Robinson, 2007, pp. 64-66). Hill & Jones (2006) stated that when a company's manager puts his/her interests above those of the stakeholders, immoral behaviors rooted in the agency problem may emerge and may be reflected by his/her self-dealing and information manipulation – two common causes of accounting-related scandals in American enterprises. The scholars proposed that corporate managers should meet the following seven rules in order to ensure the implementation of ethic decision-making. The seven rules are: (1) Ethic or moral individuals should have the priority in being promoted, (2) establish an organizational culture that highly acknowledges business ethics, (3) corporate leaders must be as good as their words in terms of ethic behaviors, (4) appropriate, ethical decision-making models should be considered, (5) hire ethical individuals as managers, (6) improve corporate governance procedures, and (7) encourage the moral courage (Hill & Jones, 2007, pp. 397-399, 403-406).

Ye (2005) pointed out that although cases of failed corporate governance in Taiwan and other countries also show reduced corporate competitiveness, most of the problems are caused by a lack of honesty in the controlling shareholders (Y. Ye, 2005, p.176). Ye thus determined 10 "Warning Signs" of a company in financial distress: (1) continued decline of the ratio of controlling shareholders, (2) internalization of the board of directors, and a widening gap between the controlling shareholders' power and their commitment, (3) major shareholders and investors selling their shares, (4) frequent resignation of the directors, supervisors, and financial managers, and frequent change of accountants, (5) having too many long-term investments, investment companies, or complex overseas investments, (6) having too many major and abnormal stakeholder transactions in the company, (7) major shareholders and directors having too many stock collaterals or showing the tendency of intervening in the stock market, (8) frequent changes of financial forecast, (9) the managers radically acknowledging profits, and (10) an abnormally high percentage of stock

Figure 1. Evaluation of controlling shareholders' trust structure. Source: Ye (2005, p.178)

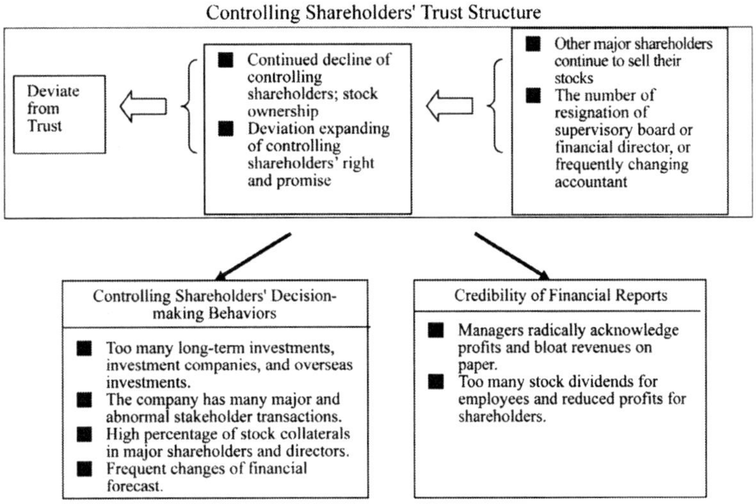

dividends for employees (Y. Ye, 2005, pp. 179-196). See Figure 1 for the above discussion.

Warning Sign 1 and 2 are elements through which the inner-most level influences the shareholders' trust structure. The controlling shareholders are no longer confident in the company's growth or willing to go through the company's future growth or disasters. The board of directors is now mostly consisted of the owner's family members or inner circles, meaning the board of directors (principal) that is supposed to be the supervisor is now colluding with managers. At this time, the internal mechanism of corporate governance is lost, the board of directors has turned its back on the shareholders, thus violating the duty as a good manager as well as the duty of exercising due care (Y. Ye, 2005, pp. 179-182). Among the elements that reflect the controlling shareholders' trust structure, the major shareholders and investors are selling their stocks, and the high turn-over rate of the directors, supervisors, financial managers, and accountants indicates the controlling shareholders and managers are no longer confident in the company and cannot fulfill their duties, and the company's financial status may have problems, thus reducing its financial transparency and making it difficult for people to trust in the controlling shareholders and managers (Y. Ye, 2005, pp. 183-185).

In the third level, Ye believes the honesty of the controlling shareholders can be observed by examining whether they are demonstrating behaviors that damage the company's values. For example, if a company has too many long-term investments, the controlling shareholders still insist on establish too many investment companies or engaging in complex overseas investments when the company's profit is regressing and overseas investments are yielding losses, it will be natural for one to suspect whether they are embezzling the company's capital at the cost of other shareholders' interest. On the other hand, one may also suspect illegal transfers of capital when the company has too many major and abnormal transactions, as these could be used to transfer interests or make false reports of profits, looses, and assets. Major shareholders and directors having too many stock collaterals or the tendency of intervening in the stock market indicate not only the company's funds have been embezzled but its assets could have been taken away by the controlling shareholders and managers. Frequent changes made to financial forecast not only indicate problems of the managers' honesty but also a lack of information

Figure 2. The ethical corporate governance model. Source: Ye (2005, p.178) and compiled by the researcher of this study

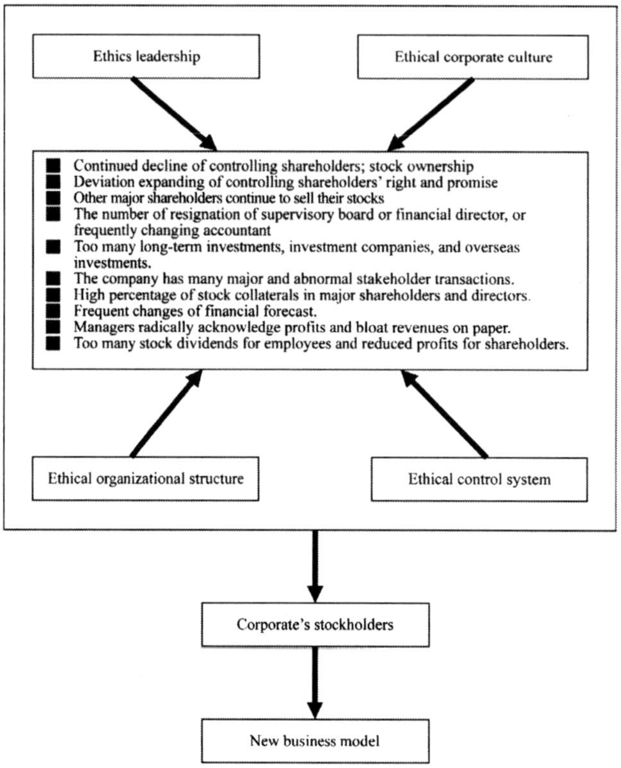

transparency (Y. Ye, 2005, pp. 189-192). As for the fourth level, Ye believes that if the managers radically acknowledge profits and give too many stock dividends to their employees, this would not only result in bloated profit reports but the after-tax profits will not be entirely given to the shareholders, thus damaging minor shareholders' interests (Y. Ye, 2005, pp. 192-201).

Proposals by M. C. Jensen & W. Meckling (1976), R. La Porta, F. Lopez-de-Silanes & A. Shleifer (1999), and Lin (2007) (Jensen & Meckling, 1976, pp. 305-360; La Porta, Lopez-de-Silanes & Shleifer, 1999, pp. 471-571; Lin, 2007, pp. 180-183) also provide the following warning signs for a company in financial distress: the percentages of stock ownership in major and minor shareholders, managerial control reflected by stock ownership and cash flow, asymmetrical information reflected by the pyramid structure, overseas investments, and cross ownership, shareholders' stock collateral ratios. These indicators help us observe companies with failed corporate governance. In figure 2 the ten above warning signs are discussed in order to analyze the cases selected for this study, and establish a new business model.

From the previous discussions we see that the agency relationship will always exist in the current corporate system of separated ownership and managerial control; therefore, the agency problem in corporate governance has become an inevitable challenge. Fama's proposal of a president actively intervening in management will eliminate the agency relationship, turn the system closer to "single-principal," and the agency relationship is naturally removed. Eisenhardt's proposal of a principal regulating the agent through a contract deserves attention in the discussion on the feasibility of the most appropriate contract. In addition,

Figure 3. The new business model- The corporate governance model under Business ethical climate. Source: by the researcher of this study

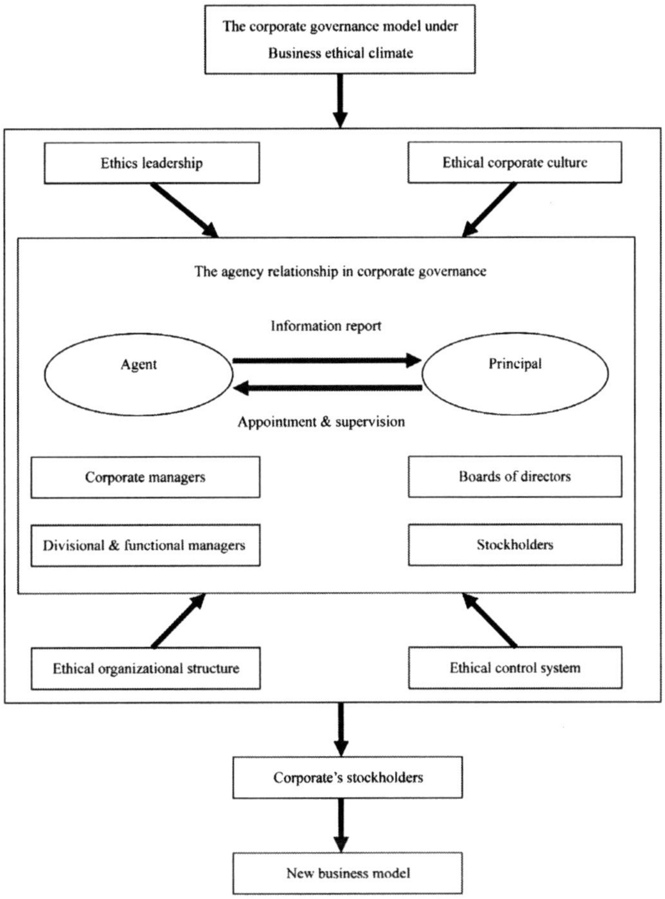

although past studies all indicate that the agency problem is inevitable in corporate governance, this problem is actually rare when corporate governance is approached from transaction cost and information asymmetry, and future researchers are encouraged to examine this issue.

Eisenhardt (1989) advised company principals to use conditions in their contracts to avoid the agency problem (Eisenhardt, 1989). Regarding this practice, Cheng (2006) suggested that employee loyalty is an alternative to regulate agencies with contracts (Chiang, Cheng, Wu, & Cheng, 2006, p.152). Besides Cheng, many other scholars (Katz, 1964; Hennart, 1991; Davies, 1999; Donaldson & Dunfee, 1994 &1999; Hitt, Ireland, & Hoskisson, 2003; Colley, Doyle, Logan, & Stettinius, 2003; Micklethwait & Wooldridge, 2003; Lin, 2004; Kreitner & Kinicki, 2004; Mondy & Noe, 2005; Ferrell, Fraedrich, & Ferrell, 2005; Robbins, 2005; Carroll & Buchholtz, 2006; Hill & Jones, 2007; Pearce & Robinson, 2007) all supported the idea that certain norms in business ethics and the values they reflect can help reduce the agency problem, thus ethical values such as trust, loyalty, honesty, consistency, and openness have all been emphasized. The idea of ethic climate is thus proposed when the above ethical values are treated as a part of the organizational culture. The study tries to use the concept and means of corporate governance under ethic climate to build a new business model. Please see figure 3.

CONCLUSION

Liu's analysis of the functions of the board of directors and each director's duties and obligations and the 10 warning signs proposed by Ye help us understand that the core of corporate governance is the board of directors, and cases of failed corporate governance are mostly due to major problems in controlling shareholders' honesty, suggesting the inseparability between a company's system and its business ethics.

The above discussion reveals that the problems in the internal and external mechanisms of corporate governance are correlated to the agency costs such as morality hazards and agency risks in the agency problem. From the perspective of stakeholders, the loss of auditor independence and accountants failing to carry out duties given by their superiors and public investors are also a form of the agency problem in a broad sense, and business ethics is correlated with reduced agency cost to a certain degree.

In the previous discussions it is evident that past studies have revealed the limitations of the law, which is separated from, interdependent with, and pushes and pulls the domain of morality and ethics; therefore, morality and ethics have an irreplaceable role. Moreover, despite the width of the topic of corporate governance, the focus of this present study is the agency problem; the literature review indicates the agency problem in corporate governance has indeed been the focus in past studies and is an inevitable problem in corporate governance. Some researchers who study the agency problem, however, have shifted from the focus on the agency relationship between company principals and managers to that of a company's entire owners, managers, and stakeholders, including Ye (2002), Huang (2001), and Hill & Jones (2007) (Ye, Li & Ke, 2002, p.23; Huang, 2001, pp. 12-17, p. 24; Hill & Jones, 2007, p. 385). Fama (1980), on the other hand, examined the topic from the single-owner perspective and stresses that the president's active intervention would effectively reduce the agency problem (Fama, 1980). Since most past studies focus on the agency relationship between a company's entire owners and the managers rather than on the agency relationship with the entire stakeholders, therefore Lin (2007a, 2007b, 2009a, 2009b, 2009c) used the declaration and principles in Küng's Global Ethic as the source for constructing the social responsibilities and substantive hypernorm in the social contract for business ethics, and the agency problem involving stakeholders is also included in our discussion on the agency problem in corporate governance – a topic that has not been addressed in past studies and is the focus of Lin (2007, 2009). The discussions in the future on the relationships between the agency problem and business ethics are based on the implications of stakeholder ethics.

Mondy & Noe (2005) observed that the legalization of business ethic norms makes this trend more prominent due to the social atmosphere and public anticipation (Mondy & Noe, 2005, pp. 37-38). These two scholars, however, did not explore deeper into the legalization of business ethics, and future researchers could examine The Sarbanes-Oxley Act of 2002, through which moral norms are legalized and become a part of corporate governance, in order to uncover other significant findings.

REFERENCES

Bentham, J. (1987). *The theory of legislation*. Littleton, CO: Fred B. Rothman & Co.

Boyd, B. K. (1995). CEO duality and firm performance: A contingency model. *Strategic Management Journal*, *16*(4), 301–312. doi:10.1002/smj.4250160404

Carroll, A. B., & Buchholtz, A. K. (2006). *Business and society: Ethics and stakeholder Management*. (pp 19-20, 612-22). Ohio: South-Western.

Chen, C. (2004). *Corporate governance law and prospect of its actual practice* (p. 20). Taipei: Sharing Culture Enterprise.

Chiang, T., Cheng, B., Wu, T., & Cheng, C. (2006). Organizational loyalty. In Cheng, B. & Chiang, T., et al. (Eds.), *Chinese organizational behaviors–topics, methods, and publication*. (p. 152). Taipei: Hua-tai.

Colley, J. L. Jr, Doyle, J. L., Logan, G. W., & Stettinius, W. (2003). *Corporate governance* (pp. x, 6, 230). New York: McGraw- Hill.

Davies, A. (1999). *A strategic approach to corporate governance* (pp. 14–17). Hampshire, UK: Gower House.

Donaldson, T., & Dunfee, T. (1994). Toward a unified conception of business ethics: Integrative social contract theory. *Academy of Management Review*, *19*(2), 262. doi:10.2307/258705

Donaldson, T., & Dunfee, T. (1999). *Ties that bind-a social contract approach to business ethics*. (pp. 34-38, 69). Cambridge, MA: Harvard Business School Press.

Eisenhardt, K. M. (1989). Agency theory: An assessment and review. *Academy of Management Review*, *14*(1), 57–74. doi:10.2307/258191

Fama, E. F. (1980). Agency problems and theory of the firm. *The Journal of Political Economy*, *88*(2), 288–307. doi:10.1086/260866

Fama, E. F., & Jensen, M. C. (1983). The separation of ownership and control. *The Journal of Law & Economics*, *26*, 301–325. doi:10.1086/467037

Ferrell, O. C., Fraedrich, J., & Ferrell, L. (2005). *Business ethics: Ethical decision making and cases* (pp. 9–14). Boston: Houghton Mifflin.

Hennart, J. F. (1991). Control in multinational firms: The role of price and hierarchy. *Management International Review*, *31*, 71–96.

Hill, C. W. L., & Jones, G. R. (2007). *Strategic management theory* (pp. 385, 397–399, 403–406). New York: Houghton Mifflin.

Hitt, M. A., Ireland, R. D., & Hoskisson, R. E. (2003). *Strategic management-competitiveness and globalization* (pp. 312, 332–333). Ohio: South- Western.

Hsu, K. (2004). Virtue, intervention, and personal freedom. *Poultry Science Reviews*, *20*, 9–16.

Huang, H. (2003). *A discussion on the accountant's role and regulations from the perspective of corporate governance*. (pp. 30-33). Unpublished Master's thesis, Department of Law, National Taipei University.

Huang, M. (2001). *The law for publicly-traded corporations and corporate supervision*. (pp. 12-17, 24). Taipei: Angle Publication.

Jensen, M. C., & Meckling, W. H. (1976). Theory of the firm: Managerial behavior, agency costs and ownership structure. *Journal of Financial Economics*, *3*, 305–360. doi:10.1016/0304-405X(76)90026-X

Jensen, M. C., & Ruback, R. S. (1983). The market for corporate control: The scientific evidence. *Journal of Financial Economics*, (May): 5–50. doi:10.1016/0304-405X(83)90004-1

Katz, D. (1964). The motivational basis of organizational behavior. *Behavioral Science*, *9*, 131–146. doi:10.1002/bs.3830090206

Kreitner, R., & Kinicki, A. (2004). *Organizational behavior* (pp. 76–78). New York: McGraw- Hill.

Küng, H. (1998). *A global ethic for global politics and economics* (pp. 251–253, 274–275). New York: Oxford University Press.

Lin, H. (2004). *A study of corporate features, entrepreneurship, organizational performance, and capacity of the board of directors*. Unpublished doctoral thesis, Department of Technology Management, Chung Hua University.

Lin, H.-Y. (2007a). Business ethics under the framework of Hans Küng's global ethic theory. *The Journal of Global Business Management*, *3*(1), 38–45.

Lin, H.-Y. (2007b). *Using Hans Küng's global ethic to construct a set of business ethics to research the agency problems within corporate governance.* Unpublished doctoral thesis, Graduate Institute of European Studies, Tamkang University.

Lin, H.-Y. (2009a). Correlation between universal ethic and business ethics–explorations from the perspective of Hans Küng's global ethic. *Journal of International Management Studies*, *4*(1), 182–188.

Lin, H.-Y. (2009b). Universal ethic factors and Hans Küng's global ethic in contemporary capitalist values. *The Journal of Global Business Management*, *5*(1), 12–19.

Lin, H.-Y. (2009c). From Hans Küng's global ethic to value community–re-thinking the construction of business ethics theory. *The Journal of Human Resource and Adult Learning*, *5*(1), 10–18.

Lin, S. (2004). A *study of corporate features, entrepreneurship, organizational performance, and capacity of directors.* Unpublished doctoral thesis, Department of Technology Management, Chung Hua University.

Liu, S. (2002). *From Chuang-zi to Enron-A+ corporate governance* (pp. 70–85). Taipei: Common Wealth.

Micklethwait, J., & Wooldridge, A. (2003). *The company*. (pp. 155-58, 198-92). New York: Random House.

Mondy, R. W., & Noe, R. M. (2005). *Human resource management* (p. 27). New Jersey: Prentice Hall.

Pearce, J. A., II, & Robinson, R. B. (2007). *Formulation, implementation, and control of competitive strategy*. (pp. 37-38, 64-66). New York: McGraw- Hill.

Robbins, S. P. (2005). *Organizational behavior*. New Jersey: Prentice Hall.

Shleifer, A., & Vishny, R. (1997). A survey of corporate governance. *The Journal of Finance*, *52*, 737–783. doi:10.2307/2329497

Stone, C. (1993). Why the law can't do it. In Beauchamp, T. L., & Bowie, N. (Eds.), *Ethical theory and business* (3rd ed., pp. 162–166). New Jersey: Prentice Hall.

Sun, C. (2000). *An exploration into problematic companies and financial organizations in Taiwan after the financial crisis.* (p. 4). Taipei: The Sun Yun-suan Academic Foundation.

Tai, T. (2006). Economic life and social obligations. Hu, G., et al. (Eds.), *Universal values and local care.* (p. 21). Taipei: KuanhChi Cultural Group.

Wu, C. F. (2002). *The practice of business ethics* (pp. 120–121). Taipei: Chien Cheng Publishing Co.

Wu, C. H. (2006). The key to a corporation's social responsibilities-corporate governance. *Gre-Tai Securities Market Monthly*, *116*, 22–28.

Wu, D. (2004). *Corporate governance-theories andpractice.* (pp. 17-20, 26-27). Taipei: Securities & Futures Institute.

Yang, C. (2007). *Strategic management-theories and practice.* (p. 428). Taipei: Hua-tai.

Ye, B. (2002). *Constructing businesses' social contracts* (pp. 70–72). Taipei: National Open University.

Ye, B. (2005). [). Taipei: Wu-Nan Book Inc.]. *Business Ethics (Oxford, England)*, 239.

Ye, Y. (2005). *Disappeared controlling shareholders-be the first to detect risks* (pp. 176, 178–196). Taipei: Business News Publishing Ltd.

Ye, Y., Li, T., & Ke, C. (2002). *Corporate governance and the evaluation system* (p. 307). Taipei: Business News Publishing Ltd.

Ye, Y., Li, T., & Ke, C. (2002). *Corporate governance and the evaluation system* (p. 23). Taipei: Business News Publishing Ltd.

ADDITIONAL READING

Akerlof, G. (1970). The market for lemons. *Journal of Economics*, *84*, 175–187.

Barnea, A., Haugen, R. A., & Senbet, L. W. (1981). Market imperfections, agency problems, and capital structure, a review. *Financial Management*, (Summer): 7–21. doi:10.2307/3665045

Berkovitch, E., & Kim, H. (1990). Financial contracting and leverage induced over-and-under-investment incentives. *The Journal of Finance*, (July): 765–794. doi:10.2307/2328792

Buchanan, J.M. (1983). The public choice perspective. *Economia delle scelte Publiche, January*, 7-15.

Carroll, A. B. (1991). The pyramid of corporate social responsibility: Toward the moral management of organizational stakeholders. *Business Horizons*, (July-August): 39–48. doi:10.1016/0007-6813(91)90005-G

Coase, R. H. (1937). The nature of firm. *Economica*, *4*(16), 386–405. doi:10.1111/j.1468-0335.1937.tb00002.x

Coase, R. H. (1960). The problem of social cost. *The Journal of Law & Economics*, *3*, 1–44. doi:10.1086/466560

Dahlman, C. J. (1979). The problem of externality. *The Journal of Law & Economics*, *22*, 135–148. doi:10.1086/466936

Dietze, E. von. (1998). Hans Küng's paradigm theology and some educational implications. *Religious Education, Decatur, Winter*, 65.

Donaldson, T., & Dunfee, T. (1985). Integrative social contract theory: A communitarian conception of economic ethics. *Economics and Philosophy*, *11*, 85–112. doi:10.1017/S0266267100003230

Drago, R., & Wood, J. S. H. (1995). The choice of payment schemes: Australian establishment date. *Industrial Relations*, *34*(4), 507–531. doi:10.1111/j.1468-232X.1995.tb00386.x

Fama, E. F. (1978). The effects of firm's investment and financing decisions on the welfare of its security holders. *The American Economic Review*, (June): 272–284.

Fama, E. F., & Jensen, M. C. (1983a). Agency problems and residual claims. *The Journal of Law & Economics*, *26*, 327–349. doi:10.1086/467038

Fama, E. F., & Jensen, M. C. (1983b). The separation of ownership and control. *The Journal of Law & Economics*, *26*, 301–325. doi:10.1086/467037

Foster, A. D., & Rosenzweig, M. R. (1994). A test for moral hazard in the labor market: Contractual arrangements, effort, and health. *Economie & Statistique*, *72*(2), 213–227.

Frederick, W. C. (1986). Toward CSR3: Why ethical analysis is indispensible and unavoidable in corporate affairs. *California Management Review*, (Winter): 126–141.

Friedman, M. (1970). The social responsibility of business is to increase its profits. *New York Times Magazine, September*, 13-33.

Gaynor, M., & Gertler, P. (1995). Moral hazard and risk spreading in partnerships. *Journal of Economics*, *26*, 591–613.

George, W. P. (1996). Looking gor a global ethic? Try international law. *The Journal of Religion*, *76*(3), 359–382. doi:10.1086/489800

Gravelle, H., & Waterson, M. (1993). No win, no fee: Some economics of contingent league fees. *The Economic Journal*, *103*(420), 1205–1220. doi:10.2307/2234246

La Porta, R., Lopez-de-Silanes, F., & Shleifer, A. (1999). Corporate ownership around the world. *The Journal of Finance*, *54*(2), 471–517. doi:10.1111/0022-1082.00115

Lambert, R. A. (1983). Long term contracts and moral hazard. *The Bell Journal of Economics*, *14*, 441–452. doi:10.2307/3003645

Lin, H. Y. (2010). A discussion on the correlations between Küng's global ethic and business ethics-a critical review. *The Journal of Global Business Management*, *6*(1).

Mork, R., Shleifer, A., & Vishny, R.W. (1988). Management ownership and markets valuation: An empirical analysis. *Journal of Financial Economics, January/March*, 293-316.

Moyer, R. C., Chatfield, R. E., & Sisneros, P. M. (1989). Security analysts monitoring activity: Agency costs and information demands. *Journal of Business Finance & Accounting*, (Summer): 385–398.

Oviatt, B. M. (1988). Agency and transaction cost perspectives on the manager- shareholder relationship. *Academy of Management Review*, *13*, 214–225. doi:10.2307/258573

Rasmusen, E. (1989). Games and information—an introduction to game theory. *Academy of Management Review*, *25*(1), 77–87.

Rosenman, R. E., & Wesley, W. W. (1991). Quality differentials and prices: Are cherries lemons? *The Journal of Industrial Economics*, *39*(6), 649–658. doi:10.2307/2098667

Salop, J., & Salop, S. (1976). Self-selection and turnover in the labor market. *Journal of Economics*, *90*(4), 619–627.

Schwartz, A. (1973). Moral neutrality and primary goods. *Ethics, 83*, 294-307, 301.

Shaeffer, P. (1998). Encyclical wins cautious praise. *National Catholic Reporter*, *10*, 3–5.

Smith, C. W., & Warner, J. B. (1979). On financial contracting—an analysis of bond covenant. *Journal of Financial Economics*, *7*, 117–161. doi:10.1016/0304-405X(79)90011-4

Stiglitz, J. E. (1975). The theory of "screening", education, and the distribution of income. *The American Economic Review*, *65*(3), 283–300.

Stiglitz, J. E. (1979). Equilibrium in product markets with imperfect information. *The American Economic Review*, *69*(2), 339–345.

Stulz, R. M., & Johnson, H. (1985). An analysis of secured debt. *Journal of Financial Economics*, *14*, 501–521. doi:10.1016/0304-405X(85)90024-8

Tullock, G. (1967). The welfare costs of tariffs, monopolies, and theft. *Western Economic Journal*, *5*, 224–232.

Williamson, O. E. (1983). Credible commitments: Using hostages to support exchange. *The American Economic Review*, *73*(4), 32–38.

KEY TERMS AND DEFINITIONS

Agency Problem: In political science and economics, the principal–agent problem or agency dilemma treats the difficulties that arise under conditions of incomplete and asymmetric information when a principal hires an agent, such as the problem that the two may not have the same interests, while the principal is, presumably, hiring the agent to pursue the interests of the former.

Business Ethics: Business ethics (also known as Corporate ethics) is a form of applied ethics or professional ethics that examines ethical principles and moral or ethical problems that arise in a business environment. It applies to all aspects of business conduct and is relevant to the conduct of individuals and business organizations as a whole. Applied ethics is a field of ethics that deals with ethical questions in many fields such as medical, technical, legal and business ethics.

Corporate Governance: Corporate governance is the set of processes, customs, policies, laws, and institutions affecting the way a corporation (or company) is directed, administered or controlled. Corporate governance also includes the relationships among the many stakeholders involved and the goals for which the corporation is governed. The principal stakeholders are the shareholders, management, and the board of directors. Other stakeholders include employees, customers, creditors, suppliers, regulators, and the community at large.

Information Asymmetry: In economics and contract theory, information asymmetry deals with the study of decisions in transactions where one party has more or better information than the other. This creates an imbalance of power in transactions which can sometimes cause the transactions to go awry. Examples of this problem are adverse selection and moral hazard. Most commonly, information asymmetries are studied in the context of principal-agent problems.

Organizational Culture: Organizational culture is an idea in the field of Organizational studies and management which describes the psychology, attitudes, experiences, beliefs and values (personal and cultural values) of an organization. It has been defined as "the specific collection of values and norms that are shared by people and groups in an organization and that control the way they interact with each other and with stakeholders outside the organization."

Shareholder: A mutual shareholder or stockholder is an individual or company (including a corporation) that legally owns one or more shares of stock in a joint stock company. A company's shareholders collectively own that company and are the members of the company by signing the memorandum of association. Thus, the typical goal of such companies is to enhance shareholder value.

Stakeholder: A person, group, organization, or system who affects or can be affected by an organization's actions.

Section 2
Implementing New Business Models in Non-Profit Organizations

Chapter 7
Adopting Web 2.0 in English Writing Course: A Collaborative Learning Approach in NPO Universities in Taiwan

Yuan-Chu Hwang
National United University, Taiwan

Min-Ching Chen
National Chiao Tung University, Taiwan

ABSTRACT

In this chapter, the authors present a Web 2.0 collaborative learning approach that facilitates the English learning process for universities in Taiwan. In traditional English writing course, the lack of intensive interactions between students and teacher may not provide sufficient information for students to improve their writing content. In order to understand how web 2.0 and collaborative peer group facilitate English learning, the authors elaborate the collaborative learning process in both micro view and macro view. The micro view focuses on individual students' viewpoint and their learning stages in web 2.0 collaborative learning. The macro view of learning approach focuses overall interactions between students, teacher and student peer groups. The proposed web 2.0 learning model allows learners to access abundant learning materials from their peer groups. Students can learn though peer interactions and enhance the learning motivation in the collaborative learning environment. By peer learning and competition, students can benefit from various learning resources by adopt web 2.0 concept in the collaborative English writing course.

DOI: 10.4018/978-1-60960-129-4.ch007

INTRODUCTION

Advanced information technology has improved the quality of our life in many ways. The Internet makes the information exchange rapidly in our daily life. The telecommunication technology makes it possible for people to communicate with others crossing geographical distance. As the development of new information technology, our real world has integrated with the cyberspace and become a well-connected environment. The relationships in current era are more complex than the old days. Today, people can interact with others through various information channels and connected with each other easily, that helps people's social networking become a loosely connected environment.

Non-Profit organization (NPO) is an organization that does not distribute its surplus funds to owners or shareholders, but instead uses them to help pursue its goals. Educational institutions in Taiwan are one kind of NPO. In this paper, we will introduce a collaborative learning approach based on Web 2.0 that facilitates the collaborative English learning for universities in Taiwan.

Teaching English writing for universities in Taiwan focuses on traditional writing teaching methods. Usually, teachers try to explain the rules and use the textbooks; and students are just listeners during the writing class. The writing course may be lack of interactions between students and teachers.

Today, the world is a global and high-tech era that people utilize various kinds of information communication technologies to improve their life quality. How teachers utilize the internet in writing course and encourage collaboration between students becomes an important issue in NPO's performance. In this chapter, we will discuss how the emerging Web 2.0 collaborative approach is applied to English writing courses and its performance.

Statement of the Problem

In the past, teaching English writing in the classroom might be limited by time. Teachers might only supply few writing samples to discuss in class. Students may read only parts of writing works from classmates or textbooks, and imitate writing from them. The lack of strong interaction between students and teacher may cause students to obtain limited information about how to write English well. Moreover, there may not be enough information for students to improve their content significantly.

Problems of English Writing Leaning in Current Era

Currently, the model of English writing mainly focuses on the interaction between teachers and students. Imitation and learning between students is restricted by time and place. In addition, there may be difficult in achieving the goal of peer learning. With the trend of combining information technology and English learning, the model of interaction and learning between teachers and students may overcome limitation by the use of information delivery. Moreover, there would be far more interaction between students and teachers. This model is called the "Asynchronous Network Collaborative Learning Model".

In order to teach students to improve English writing efficiently, the learning model combines information technology with English writing. It emphasizes providing more opportunities for students and teachers to have more interaction outside of classroom. Nevertheless, interaction and cooperation between students may not be focused on and may not be managed properly in the age of web1.0. In other words, during the age of web1.0, there might be a lack of interaction between groups. Therefore, the power of cooperation and competition between groups may not be strengthened and not put it into practice.

Power of Peer Review Group

In the past, learning models for English writing gave learners only writing evaluation from a teacher. Learners' writing skills might be learned solely from a teacher's evaluation. The students could not have much time for peer responses (also known as peer review groups) in class. (Reid, 1993) However, the peer review gives students opportunities to read other classmates' writing. At the same time, the peer review can allow readers interaction with the writer. (Freeman & Sperling, 1985; Hillocks, 1982; Nystand,1990; Richard-Amato, 1988) Accordingly, peer review gives students' possibilities to observe classmates' writing essays and evaluate each essay by the criterion of writing evaluation via email and blog.

Benefits of Web 2.0 Collaboration

Web 2.0 has already been applied in various industries and emphasizes the cooperation between users. How this helps to create an innovative English writing learning model will be well defined on this paper.

A learning model utilizing web 2.0 can allow learners to access abundant learning materials throughout learning groups. Most importantly, the students can also learn though peer interaction to enhance the learning motivation. By peer learning and competition, a student can benefit from different learning resources; no matter if it is positive or negative information. Both can provide infinitive references to improve the students' English writing, and may provide greater potential for solving problems that students come across when writing English content because they lack for information.

In addition, utilizing the concept of web2.0, users are not only using the channel of media, but also their essays can be read by all people. Moreover, students' writing works can be widely discussed and analyzed by peers. The weakness of various English writing processes can also be criticized by peers. Capturing plentiful amounts of English writing samples from classmates can be references and information for English writing students.

In the sort of cooperative interactive model that we are describing, we emphasize peer interaction, and our learning model may therefore be quite different from the previous English writing teaching models. Interaction sequences may be adjusted by the environment of web 2.0. Additionally, with a web 2.0 interaction learning model, a teacher's role will be more important. Furthermore, in order to enhance students' learning motivation, teachers' involvement with our interactive model will be arranged significantly by the nature of the web 2.0 environment. The specific interaction model will be explained in the chapter concerning research design.

Statement of Research Aim

In this research, we are going to use the web 2.0 concept in English writing teaching. We select two groups from two classes; in one class, teacher uses the concept of web 2.0 inside the English writing class. The other class, the teacher uses the traditional writing teaching; it means that teacher uses the textbook and teaches students writing skills according to the textbook.

In Web 2.0 period, students can learn or practice English writing via blog. In this essay, the teacher sets up a blog for students to write essays and the teacher put the essays on the blog, and all the students have to give comments for all the articles. This is the way to help students to improve their English writing skills. The purpose of the writing blog helps students have opportunities to have interaction outside of classroom. In addition, students can learn some writing skills according to students' interaction.

LITERATURE REVIEW

The Approaches of Teaching English Writing

English writing teaching nowadays has changed due to the internet era. Students and teachers widely use the email, website and blog in their daily life; accordingly, how to utilize the internet into English teaching is a current issue.

However, in this paper, we are going to discuss the historical perspective to view English writing teaching. There are four theoretical approaches on English writing, it's not only the methods utilized in Native English Speakers, but also its suitable for ESL students. (Johns, 1990) Firstly, we will discuss "The expressivist approach", in this approach, teachers are like the facilitator and design the classroom activities to "promote writing fluency and empower the students." (Reid, 1993, p. 260) The second writing approach is "The cognitive approach". This approach is widely used in English for Academic Purpose (EAP) and English for Specific Purpose (ESP). In cognitive classroom, students still "focus on pattern –model tasks". (Reid, 1993, p. 261). In this writing teaching method, strategy training is still the base in this approach.

Next is "The interactive approach"; in this approach, the writer and reader have to communicate with each other, both of them have responsibility on coherent communication. It means that the writer writes the articles from the reader's expectation, and the reader reads from writer's intention (Shriver, 1992; Zamel, 1992). Nowadays, a lot of intensive writing course combine both reading and writing. As I teach in college in Taiwan, "Reading and Writing" is one course, because the students can learn how to read through the writing class; at the same time, students also can learn how to write from reading a lot of writing articles. Consequently, in this paper, we also will use this method to teach students' writing; just we will combine the tool of "web 2.0 ". Finally, "The social constructionist approach". In this method, writing is "a social act in a specific context". (Reid, 1993, p. 261; Coe, 1987). It means that writing is part of social action in academic purpose.

According to these four different approaches, we will try to combine the previous English writing teaching into the web 2.0. And we will see how it works in our research.

Learning in Web 2.0 Era: The Impact on Power of Users

Advanced information technology has improved the quality of our life in many ways. The Internet makes the information exchange rapidly in our daily life. The telecommunication technology makes it possible for people to communicate with others crossing geographical distance. As the development of new information technology, our real world has integrated with the cyberspace and become a well-connected environment. The relationship in current era is more complex than the old days. Today, people can interact with others through various information channels and connected with each other easily, that helps people's social networking become a loosely connected environment.

The Web 2.0 is one of the most popular topics that highlight the massive interaction between users and their social network relationship. "Web 2.0" refers to the second generation of web development and web design that facilitates information sharing, interoperability, user-centered design and collaboration on the World Wide Web. (Wikipedia) There are several key ideas behind the term "Web 2.0", including: individual production and user generated content, Harness the power of the crowd, Data on an epic scale, Architecture of participation, Network effect, and Openness. (Anderson, 2007).Moreover, the Web 2.0 represents new user oriented e-service that related to social networking and collaborative interaction. The reformation of information exchange in Web 2.0 era highlights the possibility of open collaboration for all individual participants. Users create digital content, contribute personal experience, and exchange their opinions with others autonomously. In web 2.0, user's contributions are treated as valuable ingredients for performing collective wisdom (Hwang & Li, 2009).

The rich contributions from user groups bring tremendous valuable contents, which also enrich the information exchange within the user groups. Today, the Web 2.0 concepts have been utilized for many application domains. For example, the collaborative user generated content such as Wikipedia, the social interaction sites such as Facebook and MySpace. For example, wikis have been used at the University of Arizona's Learning Technologies Centre to help students on an information studies course who were enrolled remotely from across the USA. These students worked together to build a wiki-based glossary of technical terms they learned while on the course (Glogoff, 2006). The concept of Web2.0 collaboration has already used in the education domain. Wiki-style technology has also been used in a tool developed at Oxford University to support teachers with 'design for learning. These collaborative applications are based on the concept of web 2.0 and utilize the power of user groups that contributes huge unique content that make others could have the opportunities to access these information. Users will learn new things from their peer groups and improve the deficiency. Moreover, the quality and the quantity of information exchange for web2.0 e-learning interactions have been improved significantly than traditional face-to-face education environment.

Adopt Web 2.0 Concept in Collaborative Learning Approach

In order to improve the learning outcomes using web 2.0 concepts, the learning approaches should be modified to encourage and accelerate the interactions among students. However, there are some key assumptions before adopting web 2.0 concept in collaborative learning. Before adopting the web 2.0, the role for both teacher and students are quite different than traditional learning process. In web 2.0 collaborative learning environments, which highlights every individual's contribution and requires students interact with other peers actively for massive information/knowledge exchange. Through the information exchanging process, students are encouraged by teacher and other peers to present their own experience and skills they have, others could access these heterogeneous information to impact their own knowledge and make evaluations and judgments. Moreover, not all courses are suitable for collaborative learning, the collaborative course is more suitable for students are already learning something and would like to extend their ability from information exchanging. Teachers should select the suitable materials and organize the teaching in separate lecture. Followings are the major key features in web 2.0 collaborative learning.

In the learning process, all information is created by each participant. Unlike the traditional learning that teacher plays the major role for delivering the knowledge to all students. The information is usually the one-way that from teacher to students, but there is lack of interaction between students. Instead, in the collaborative learning process, teachers are playing as a participant who also join the information exchange and observe the interactive learning process. However, the teachers could also learn how students think and feel via the interaction and this could become a new feedback for teachers to improve the course and make it more suitable for their students.

Active Participation

According to Savin-Williams & Berndt, student peers plays an important role for teenagers, which influences their character development, social adjustment, and behavior models (Savin-Williams & Berndt, 1990). Peer acceptance has been shown to be associated with greater feelings of belonging (Brown & Lohr, 1987). The impact between students is strong and students contribute their ideas to the other classmates. For collaborative learning, students are encouraged to present what they think, how they feel, and provide their personal opinions within the peer group. This participating process provides unique information sources for the peer groups. Massive heterogeneous could bring the opportunities for students to access other's opinions and compare with their own ideas. Their friendship and participation are associated with self-esteem and contribute to form self-image (Azmitia, 2002). The self-adjustment could improve the self-evaluation and make students understand how others think. It also makes students to develop companionship skills through various interactions. However, since students may lose the goal while they discuss with others, teacher could intervene the interaction process appropriately and guide the discussion.

Network Effect

While adopting web 2.0 into collaborative learning process, the social connections of each participants are important factors. Network effect implies the phenomenon whereby a service becomes more valuable; therefore, the numbers of adopters are increased. The collaborative encyclopedia Wikipedia is benefit from a network effect. The theory goes that as the number of editors grows, the quality of information on the website improves, and it also encourages more users to turn to it as a source of information; some of the new users in turn become editors, continuing the process (Wikipedia). Applying to learning environment, students could benefit from the network effect that their interaction targets are not merely limited to the peer students in their classes but extend to all other students who take the same classes in the school. While the number of user exceeds the critical mass peer group, students could benefit from the network effect and get more information while they have interaction in peer groups.

Motivation of Students in Collaborative Learning

Sociologists and anthropologists have long recognized that people can feel close to distant others and develop common identities with distant others who they rarely or never meet (Anderson, 1983; Habermas, 1991). Besides geographical distance, in the e-learning era, we emphasize on personal characteristics. Homophily describes the tendency of individuals to associate and bond with similar one. The principle of proximity and similarity provides the basis for numerous social interaction processes (Hwang, 2009). The basic idea is simple: "people like to associate with similar others." (Aristotle & Rackham, 1934; Lazarsfeld & Merton, 1954; Plato, 1968) The collaborative e-learning environment benefits from the collective efforts of each student in the virtual education environment. Similar student groups are more likely to combine the strength of different individuals to achieve specific objectives.

In the Web 2.0 e-learning environment, the roles in learning activities are quite different from in the traditional classroom. Teachers are no longer the single knowledge source in the learning environment. The student peer groups and other learners from the cyberspace could provide alternative incentives for students to address on their learning interactions. For example, in the study of European project WebLabs, which applies a web-based learning environment for students to learn with others. The teacher is seen as a facilitator and a guide in the knowledge discovery process. (Sendova et. al, 2004). In the e-learning environment, if the participants are not only those familiar classmates, there may have some issues especially when the learning activity is freely open to all internet users. The typical issues include the language as well as the communication capability, these issues would slow the collaborative learning activity for students without suitable communication abilities. In order to facilitate the collaborative learning interactions, learning should focus on specific topics with appropriate communication ability for all participants. Since e-learning is generally based on ICT environment, the operation of learning are related to student's computer operation abilities such as manipulating the communication system, accessing rich multimedia information resources, handling the online social interactions.

After concur the communication problems, the interactions between students are quite interesting. During communication, students acquired specific social experience and were stimulated to build valuable personal skills such as: ability to generate and verbalize ideas; to present their results according to a concrete standard; to share their experience by means of electronic communication; to discuss their work and work in a team; to be critical to the work published in the virtual environment (Nikolov, 2007).

Besides the support of individual's similarity, there are some additional incentives encourage students to learn collaboratively. According to McClintock (1992), when working in *flexible groupings, across ages and locations* students can interact according to their interests, needs, and curiosities and *...learning in the course of shared projects, become commonplace features of educational work, cooperation becomes the prime motivator*.

In this chapter, we combine the learning and the web 2.0 platform to create a collaborative education environment. The similarity of individuals and the cooperation encourages students to work together for their ultimate goals. Various incentives motivate the collaborative interactions within student groups. It also enables the healthy development of the collaborative education environment.

The Role of the Teachers

In the 21st century, due to the high technology era, the language teaching has currently been changed. As Jones, J.F. (2001) has stated that "Language Centre throughout the world know that they cannot do without computer for learning purposes."However, in the past, computer-assisted language learning (CALL) has more focused on self-learning. In one university I have taught in Taiwan, the English program is focused on grade one and grade two students in university, the school set a system which is called "Elite English", students have to practice themselves at school or at home. After the end of semester, the teacher will give students scores which is according to how many lessons the students do and also how many lessons students have passed a certain score.

Moreover, the beginning of "CALL" has focused on "drill and kill". It means that the students have just practiced the questions by listening to the CD, or just watching DVD in classroom. Sometimes it's good that teacher can prepare the DVD which is connected with the topic that students learn today. In my personal experience, students feel fun at the beginning; nevertheless, students have started to feel bored. Besides, students have less motivation to watch DVD in class. However, at a "World CALL conference that took place in Melbourne in July, 199,8", Jones (2001, p. 361) has claimed that "keynote speakers, distinguished by their long experience in the computer's educated applications, made no extravagant claims. Ben Shneiderman has also stated that "computers are no more intelligent than a wooden pencil."

Learning English Writing by Collaboration: A Peer Group Collaborative Learning Approach

The term "collaborative learning" is widely defined by many researchers. According to Dillenbourg (1999), the most broadest (but unsatisfactory) definition is a situation in which two or more people learn or attempt to learn something together. There are three key elements should be further determined in the definition. First, the number of participants can be unfolded into several types, such as a pair, a small group (3-5 students), a class (20-30 students), a community (few hundred students in school), or a society. The term "learning something" could be as "follow a course", "study course material", and "perform learning activities such as problem solving". The term "together" could be interpreted as different forms of interaction: face-to-face or computer mediated, synchronous or asynchronous, etc. We will explain our definition in the research design section.

Individual cognitive systems do not learn because they are individual, but because they perform some activities (reading, building, etc.) which trigger some learning mechanisms (induction, deduction, compilation,...). Similarly, peers do not learn because they are two, but because they perform some activities that trigger specific learning mechanisms (Dillenbourg, 1999). Therefore, in this paper, we adopt the web 2.0 concept to collaborative learning approach in the field of English writing course. The aim of this study is to understand the impact on students' learning outcome by comparing the Web-based computer mediated collaborative learning activities with traditional face-to-face collaborative learning activities.

Moreover, there are two issues should be cared about when process the peer group collaborative learning. First, teachers should specify the roles and its appropriate actions/behaviors in each collaboration scenario. By giving different visual viewpoints, students are able to follow some specific rules for interaction. Second, teacher should monitor and regulate the interactions. This issue is more complex when the peer group size is increasing.

In the next section, we will elaborate the research design and describe the experiment process for web 2.0 collaborative learning.

Criteria of English Writing

How to Grade Scales

Most English writing, no matter, IELTS or TOEFL, even the writing test GEPT in Taiwan, the examiner usually scores the writing paper by these five dimensions. Accordingly, in this paper, we use the same way to score the grade.

In this research, we set the five dimensions and sixteen criteria to give students scores. You can see as follows:

1. Grammar
   - Word form
   - The verb tense
   - S/V subject-verb agreement
   - Fragment (If a sentence does not have both a subject and a verb)
     - Ex; we hungry in the morning. (FRAGEMT)
     - EX; We are hungry in the morning. (CORRECT)
2. Vocabulary
   - Spelling correctly
   - Capitalization
   - Wrong words
3. Punctuation
   - Use the proper punctuation
   - RO(round-on sentences happens when two simple sentences are run together without correct punctuation to separate them)
     - EX: I love Sunday, I can sleep late. (RO)
     - I love Sunday because I can sleep late. (correct)
   - Is there a comma after transition words?
     - (Transitions: first/next/ then/ after that/later/finally/ in the morning/at night/ at ten o'clock)
4. Content
   - A variety of sentences

- Have own opinions
- Topic sentence
- Main idea is clear

5. Organization
   - Well organized
   - Logically order

Evaluation Criteria

No matter in peer review or how teachers evaluate students writing scores by using the criteria below.

Grammar-1=Is the word form accurate?
Grammar-2=Is the verb tense appropriate?
Grammar-3=Is the subject-verb agreement?
Grammar-4=Is there any "fragment" sentence?
Vocabulary1=Is the spelling correct?
Vocabulary3=Are there any wrong words?
Vocabulary2=Is the vocabulary using the correct capitalization?
Punctuation1= Does the author use the proper punctuation?
Punctuation 2= Are there any run-on sentences?
Punctuation 3=Is there a comma after transition words?
Content1= Are there a variety of sentences ?
Content2=Does the author have his/her own opinion?
Content3=Is there any topic sentence?
Content4=Is the any concluding sentence?
Organization1=Is it well organized?
Organization2=Does it have a logical order?

Peer Editing

"Peer editing" means " showing your work to another student is a very useful way to improve your writing". (Zemach, & Rumisek, 2003, p. 21). And throughout the process peer editing, students can read various of writing articles from the classes. In addition, students can find the strong and weak points in classmates' articles. While they mark other classmates' writing articles, they also can find their own problems or learn the good points of classmates. The advantages of peer editing is that "get a reader's opinion about writing" (Zemach, & Rumisek, 2003, p. 22). And "the reader can tell you first, you should add more details or explanation. Second, something is not organized clearly. Third, you have some information that is not relevant. Fourth, there is something that is hard to understand." Moreover, the other advantage is "to share writing with others is for you to read more examples of writing." Reading other's article can "give you more ideas to use yourself in the future" (Zemach & Rumisek, 2003, p. 22)

Teacher's Response and Teacher's Attitude

Because of combining English writing teaching with Computer Assisted Language Learning, language teachers have to change their attitude on teaching writing. In traditional English writing teaching and marking, teacher has only use the English material in the classroom, and the teacher has only one to give students' the score. However, when we utilize the concept of web2.0 inside the writing teaching, the teachers have to be interested in computer assisted and also the group opinion. In other words, if the teachers don't have enough knowledge, they couldn't use this approach in the classroom. Moreover, teachers have to change their attitude on teacher center's classroom. That is said teacher is not only the guide in this writing classroom, all of the students can also participate in classmates' writing comments. In order to make the comments fair and objective, in this research, we also invite the other teacher to mark and give students comments on their articles.

RESEARCH METHODOLOGY

Research Aim

In this paper, we adopt the web 2.0 concept to collaborative learning approach in the field of

English writing course. The aim of this study is to understand the impact on students' learning outcome by comparing the Web-based computer mediated collaborative learning activities with traditional face-to-face collaborative learning activities. Moreover, there are two issues should be cared about when process the peer group collaborative learning. First, teachers should specify the roles and its appropriate actions/behaviors in each collaboration scenario. By giving different visual viewpoints, students are able to follow some specific rules for interaction. Second, teacher should monitor and regulate the interactions. This issue is more complex when the peer group size increased.

Due to the impact of Web 2.0, utilizing the information technology in learning has its new method. The cooperation between learner and learner has become another new information resource in ICT learning model. In the Web 2.0 environment, the information consumers are also the information producers. The aim of observation has focused on the interaction between learner and leaner. In the past, the learning process has emphasized on learner and teacher; however, in the web 2.0 environments, it has focused on the information exchanging and the interaction between leaner and learner.

By utilizing Web 2.0 collaborative leaning platform to promote cooperation between learners, the collaborative peer groups may become the alternative learning resource outside of language teaching classroom. In this study, the observation focuses on the interaction between learners and its efficiency. Therefore, the goal of this research will divide into two parts.

The Learning Effect of Collaborative Learning Approach

In order to understand the learning effect of our proposed learning model, we choose two different groups for observation. In one group, we utilize the web2.0 collaborative platform as the learning channel; in another group, we use the traditional FTF (face to face) teaching method in classroom. We give the students in all groups with the same teaching material and homework. In the first week and last week of the English writing course, we give both two classes students an essay tests to evaluate their English writing ability. By comparing the difference of student improvements, we try to explore the effect of the two teaching methods. In order to increase the inter-rater reliability on this research, we ask a group of teachers evaluate students writing. In addition, each essay is also evaluated by students peer evaluations using the given criteria of English writing evaluation.

Exploring the Guideline to Adopt Web2.0 in English Writing Course

To understand the guideline to adopt Web 2.0 in English writing course, we will explore the role changes for both teacher and student. Also, the success or failure case utilizing web2.0 in learning environment can be further analysis. Through the case study, we would like to give the guidelines of utilizing Web2.0 collaborative learning approach and improve student's learning motivation and learning efficiency.

Research Design

In order to understand how web 2.0 and collaborative peer group facilitate English learning, we will elaborate the learning process in both micro view and macro view. The learning process in micro view and macro view tightly related with each other. The micro view of learning approach focuses on individual students' viewpoint and their learning stages in web 2.0 collaborative learning. The students' cognition and the internal flow of the individuals' learning process are shown in micro view process. The macro view of learning approach focuses overall interactions between students, teacher and student peer groups. All interactions of student and other participants within the web

Figure 1. The Web 2.0 collaborative learning approach

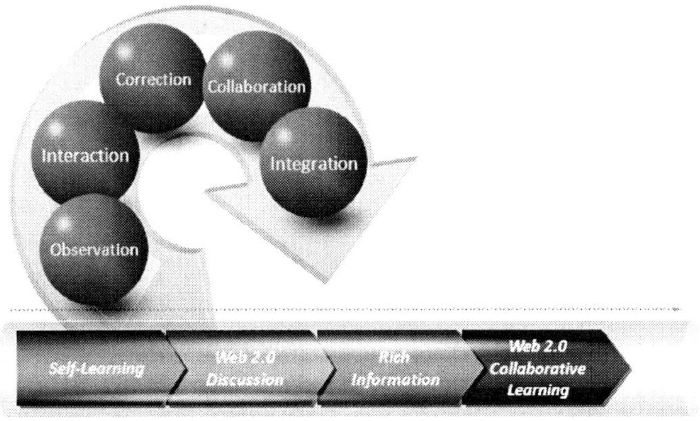

2.0 collaborative learning approach are detailed elaborated in macro view section.

Macro View

The macro view of Web 2.0 collaborative learning approach including four stages of cognitive and interaction processes. The micro view of Web 2.0 collaborative learning approach focuses on five internal processes of interactions, which is shown as upper part of Figure 1.

The macro view of Web 2.0 collaborative learning approach is composed of four steps. The first stage is an internal cognitive process noted as "Self-Learning" stage, which is consisted of five processes. The following process is the information exchange stage noted as "Web 2.0 Discussion" stage. Through the cognitive process, students will obtain rich information and try to adopt them appropriately in their learning process. The "Rich Information" stage provides suitable samples or cases evaluated by peer groups and teachers, those information will also help students to enhance their capability of English writing. Benefits from the previous stages of information exchange, the highly frequent interactions between students will enable the "Web 2.0 collaborative Learning" stage that helps students stay in a healthy learning environment. The macro view highlights the interactions between the individual and their belonging communities.

The Micro View

Different to the macro view that highlights the interactions between users, the micro view focuses on individual cognition and the internal knowledge flow. The internal cognitive process of Web 2.0 collaborative learning is consisted of five parts, including Observation, Interaction, Correction, Collaboration, and Integration. The related learning theory of each part described as follows.

1. **Observation:** Based on social cognitive theory (Miller & Dollard, 1941), an individual's knowledge acquisition can be directly related to observing others within the context of social interactions, experiences, and outside media influences. When students want to know their learning performance, they are seeking for a benchmark. The Web 2.0 collaborative learning approach makes all participating students to learn from their cooperators. The first behavior is observations, which make students find some appropriate channels for new information surrounding them and select suitable target for improving their own abilities. Observations are the

Figure 2. The collaborative learning process

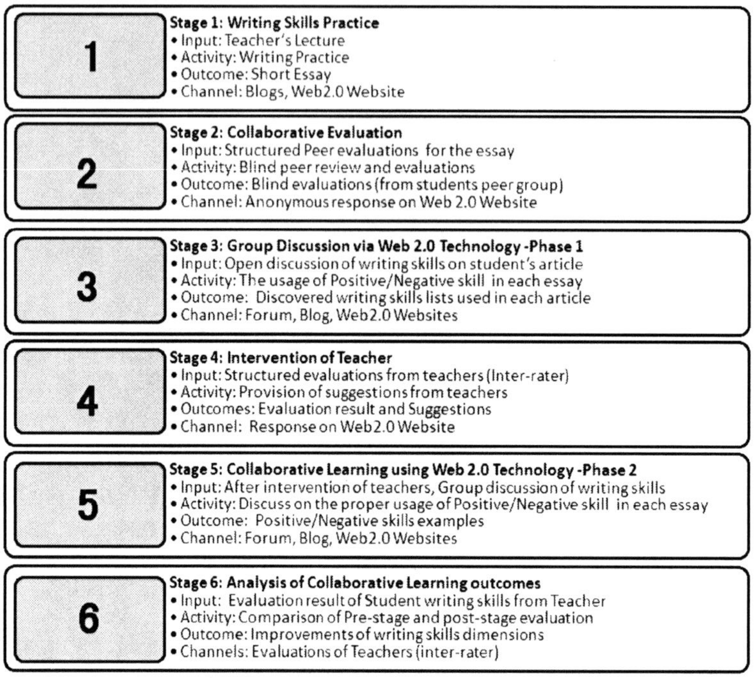

usually belong to one's mental behavior that proceed internally.

2. **Interaction:** According to social learning theory (Bandura, 1977), behavioral learning assumes that people's environment cause people to behave in certain ways. Interaction between student and other student groups is an important issue when adopting web 2.0 collaborative learning. Since the interaction may establish some personal relationships with others, students who could utilize the web 2.0 platform could obtain useful information and benefit from the highly connected student peer groups.
3. **Correction:** Based on social comparison theory (Festinger, 1954), individuals evaluate their own opinions and desires by comparing themselves to others. However, the benchmark must be accurate and appropriate evaluated by reliable authorities. In the Web 2.0 collaborative learning environment, the role of teacher should become the reliable authority that provide accurate information for student and guide them to the right way. The intervention of teacher in collaborative learning platform could monitor the development of collaborative learning process for all participants.
4. **Collaboration:** Since the Web 2.0 collaborative learning platform requires student's participant in and cooperate with others, the atmosphere between all participants will influence the interaction intensity within the collaborative learning group. Collaboration requires some fundamental basis including trustworthy, good intensions, harmonious interactions between all participants.
5. **Integration:** The student peer groups within the Web 2.0 collaborative learning platform could form a tight social group with correcting mechanism that will help students acquire rich useful information facilitate their cognition process. Moreover, the integration of student peer groups could make the Web

2.0 collaborative learning group contribute their ideas and knowledge to the community continuously and form some kinds of "collective wisdom" for all participants.

Collaborative Learning Process

In this research, we set the learning process into a six stages process of each class. The figure is shown as Figure 2. We will describe each stage as follows.

- **On stage one:** Writing Skills Practice, we call it writing skills practice. On this stage, the input is teacher teaches students how to write an essay in class and students brainstorm and discuss in the small group first. The activity on this stage is writing practice: after going back home, each student has to write a short essay by himself/herself. Then the outcome is a short essay. It means all of the students have to put their essays into the class blog.
- **On stage two:** Collative Evaluation, the input is teacher sends each student the evaluation sheet (please see the sub-section 2.7.2), and all students have to do the peer evaluation for all the articles written by all the classmates. The activity on this stage is blind peer review. It means the students give classmates the score, the scale is from 1 to 7. After the students do the peer evaluation, each student sends the result to teacher by email. The outcome is the blind peer evaluation which scales by sixteen dimensions. And students have to give each dimension score from one to seven. From this peer evaluation, we will do the statistics and the result will be discussed in the next chapter.
- **On stage three:** Group Discussion via Web2.0. The input is an open discussion of writing skills on students' articles. At the moment, students have to review all the essays on the blog. The activity on this stage is the students have to give each essay the positive comment and negative comment. The outcome is that students may improve the writing skills from each positive and negative comment. Therefore, on this stage, students may learn some writing skills through reading classmates' essays.
- **On stage four:** Intervention of Teacher. The input is the teacher's structured evaluation. The activity is the suggestion from the teachers. The outcome is the evaluation result and suggestions.
- **On stage five:** Collaborative Learning by Using Web2.0. The input is that students view the teachers' intervention, and also group discussion from the blog. The activity is the students discuss in blog and leave the positive and negative comments, then students can learn writing skills through this kind of activity. The outcome is the feedback from the peer review and teachers' evaluation. The outcome is the positive and negative of the essay.
- **On stage six:** Analysis of Collative Learning Outcomes, the input on this stage is the results from the teachers. It means that the teacher gives the students comments and scores according to the five dimensions---grammar, vocabulary, content, organization and punctuation. The activity is the comparison of pre stage and post stage evaluation. The outcome on this stage is the improvements of writing skill dimensions.

Utilizing ICT in English teaching has been several years. In the past, e-learning has focused on exploring the impact in learning effect or learners himself/herself. The related research has emphasized on learner's individual effect and also focused on the interaction between the teacher and learners by utilizing ICT technology. There are fewer research focuses on the interaction between learners and learners.

Due to the impact of Web 2.0, utilizing the information technology in learning has its new method. The cooperation between learner and learner has become another new information resource in ICT learning model. In the environment of Web2.0, the information customers are also the information producers now. The aim of observation has focused on the interaction between learner and leaner. In the past, the learning process emphasized on learner and teacher; however, in the web 2.0 environment, it has focused on the information exchanging and the interaction between leaner and learner.

By utilizing the platform of Web2.0 to promote the cooperation between learners, it may become the extra learning resource outside of language teaching classroom. Owing to the internet learning circumstance, the observation focuses on the interaction between learners and its efficiency.

Data Collection Procedures

In this section, in the first class, we use the concept of web2.0 in this class. The teacher sets a class blog for students and students give the comments for classmates. The blog is as following: http://afternoontea11.blogspot.com/. Teachers collect students' writing articles by email, then teacher has to put all of the articles onto this blog. And the same week, students have to leave the comments on this class blog. In addition, teacher sends all of the students' writing articles to the other co-worker to check the students' writing. Therefore, the result of the students' writing comments from classmates and two teachers.

Ethical Consideration & Limitations

In the beginning of class, the teacher had already told the students that she would do a research for this class. In addition, the teacher told to students that she would use the students' articles for researching for both classes. Through this research, the teacher has to spend more time on marking students' writing paper. Due to the teacher has to set a blog first, and then put all the articles on the blog. Furthermore, if some teachers have less experiences of using computer or set the blog, they may find its difficult for them

FINDINGS AND DISCUSSION

Introduction

In this section, the teacher will pick up several students' writing from two classes and see what are the differences between one class which teacher uses the concept of web2.0 in the writing class; and the other class, the teacher just give the lecture and let the students give the writing homework after the lesson. We will see which method the students will improve more in writing. In next part "Data Analysis", the first class, we have found out two teachers to evaluate students writing and we will analyze how students get improved according to teachers' comments and classmates' comments. The other class, we will also evaluate how students improve their writing skills according two teachers' evaluation and one classmate's comments.

Analytical Result

The Class which the Teacher Uses the Concept of Web 2.0

Student A

The first writing of student A

My Favorite Vacation

My favorite vacation was travelling in Japan from August 16 to 20 last year. I went to Hokkaido because it had beautiful night view in Hakodate.

The night view of Hokaido was one of the most famous night views in the world. It was especially beautiful in winter because the air was dignified and clear. In addition, there were delicious sea-food, big crabs, milk ice cream and melons and so on. They were eating and drinking what I thought. I expect that I can go abroad every winter and summer vacation during the time I was studying in graduated school. I would like to go to Europe, U.S.A., or New Zealand next time, and go to meet the people who have different custom from us.

The comments and evaluation from the first teacher

1. You write well in this article; moreover, you explain why you like Hokkaido. All the points are excellent.
2. Try to avoid the grammatical error, you can check the dictionary or use the grammar book for your reference.
3. You can use more transition words to make the article clearly.
4. You can try to divide the article into three parts—introduction, body and conclusion.

The comments and evaluation from the second teacher

1. You had a good beginning in developing your article. However, try to express your idea once in one sentence.
2. You may tell me what you did in Hakodate. Did you see any gorgeous views there? Or did you have any special meals there? In that case you can make your article more attractive and organized.

The comments from the classmates--copied from class blog: http://afternoontea11.blogspot.com/2009/08/vacation-3.html

1. Classmate's comment

Grammar
My favorite vacation was travelling in Japan (x)
My favorite vacation had traveled in Japan (O)
It was especially beautiful in winter because the air was dignified and clear.(x)
It is especially beautiful in winter because the air is dignified and clear.(o)

The second writing of student A

The Most Important Person in My Life

The most important person who has black hair, brown eyes, and a caring touch in my life. That's my mom.

First, my mom talks to me about many things. She talks to me about is what will happen when I grow up. One day I had a really bad day with my friends, and she told me what to do about it. Second, my mom and I spend a lot of time together. We play games, bake cookies, and make necklaces. But our favorite thing to do is reading. Our favorite book is If You Give a Mouse a Cookie.

My mom always laughs, and when she laughs she sounds like a hyena gone crazy! She doesn't laugh every day, but when she does, it's hilarious, and I laugh, too!

My mom is the greatest. She always gives me great advice. My mom is more than a mom; she is like my best friend!

The comments and evaluation from the first teacher

1. Try to organize your writing more clearly.
2. Paying more attention to word usage and sentence structure would surely help to make your writing as good as your underlying ideas. Keep trying!!

The comments and evaluation from the second teacher.

1. You explain your feeling about your mom quite well.

2. You show your love with your mom. You and your mom seem to have quite good relationship, that's so nice.
3. It's a well organized article, but pay attention to your verb tense. Keep going!

The comments from the classmates(copied from class blog: http://afternoontea11.blogspot.com/2009/08/vacation-1.html**)**

Classmate's comment

1. The theme is to discuss people, but you seem to discuss a person not existing.
2. I propose that you could use the conjunction in the paragraph and segment narration

Data Analysis of student A's writings

From the student A's two writings, we can see the student has improved the writing. From the aspect of organization, students can write a well organized article. In addition, comparing the student A's first writing and second writing, we can see this student can express more about the feeling for her mom. Moreover, from the perspective of grammar, student A makes less grammatical error from the first article to second article. However, student A has still improved her vocabulary usage. Punctuation is all right in both two articles.

After the using the web 2.0 concept into English writing course, the teacher has found that students have higher motivation to learn English writing, especially the topic is what they are interested in. In addition, while students do the peer reviewing, they have found that they have gained more thoughts about the same topics. At the same time, they also can receive classmates' opinions toward their articles.

Student B

First writing of student B

My Favorite Vacation

There are many vacations in a year. My favorite vacation is the graduated vacation.

My classmates and I were graduated from National Defense University in the summer of 2006 year. We have graduated vacation for two weeks, so we went to PALAU. The dinner of first day was bat soup. Don't be afraid. Actually, it tasted good. The next day we went snorkeling. Trust me, it was the most beautiful scenery I had ever seen. Many fishes were swimming around you. You could discover another world under the water. I will remember the PALAU journey of graduated vacation forever.

The comments from the first teacher

1. You write a well organized article.
2. You have to pay attention on your grammar and the verb tense.
3. You seem to get a quite unforgettable trip in PALAU, don't you?

The comments and evaluation from the second teacher

1. It was a pleasant article.
2. It will be a great travel note if you write more details about the food and special activities there.

Comments from the classmates (copy from class blog: http://afternoontea11.blogspot.com/2009/08/vacation-4.html**)**

Grammar

1. My favorite vacation is the graduated vacation. (change to past tense)
2. We have graduated vacation for two weeks (change to: We had graduated vacation for two weeks)

Second writing of student B

The Most Important Person in My Life

The most important person in my life is my enemy. He is big, strong and invisible. I have never seen him, but I know his existence. Every time I feel tired or depressed, he always encourages me once and once again. He makes my heart stronger and hard to be destroyed. Let me relive from the hell of pain and loneness.

Not only in my losing time, but also in my successful space he would attack me. Because people say that "Extreme pleasure is followed by sorrow." He would remind me to remain humble and polite. It makes me not to lose myself and go toward my target.

So my enemy is the most important person in my life. Without him, I am nothing. Without me, he is disappearing.

The comments and evaluation from the first teacher

1. Your writing has some good insights in it and is very creative.
2. Some sentences could be improved a little bit to make it clearer.

The comments and evaluation from the second teacher

1. You use the vocabulary well and no grammatical error, that's good.
2. Try to write more and make your whole article be more organized.
3. Pay attention to the "punctuation".
4. Anyway, it's true that " there's nothing to fear, but fear itself."

Comments from the classmates (copy from class blog: http://afternoontea11.blogspot.com/2009/08/a4.html**)**

Data Analysis of Student B's writings

According to these two articles which teacher utilizes the web 2.0 concept in the writing class. We can see students improve from the first article to second article. Students can express more on their own opinions and also try to make less grammar error comparing their first and second articles. From the perspectives of vocabulary, student B can use proper words in the end of semester. The punctuation viewpoint, the student seems to keep the same. From the point of view of organization, this student seems to improve a bit.

Moreover, students read more articles comparing with the class that students read less classmates' articles. Therefore, students get more "input" than the other class. In addition, students may compare each other's articles. They will learn the grammar, sentence structure and how to use the different vocabulary from other classmates. Furthermore, students also say that they can see other classmates' writing styles and learn from them. It is also a benefit.

The Class which the Teacher Doesn't use the Concept of Web 2.0

We also can view as following that the teacher doesn't use the concept of web2.0 in the class.

The first article of student A

My favorite vacation

My favorite vacation is summer vacation. Because this vacation have enough time to plan and play. I went to the Yi Lan. I ride the motocycle go to everywhere with my good friend. Guey Shan port is a central in the city. There are more people and many water activity. It's very fun and enjoy in it. Summer vacation can take out my pressure. I can go to everywhere in anytime.

The comments from the first teacher

1. This student makes lots of grammatical error.
2. You have to make your article more organized.
3. The students have some error on sentence structure; for example, My favorite vacation is summer vacation

because we can have more time to relax and go some other places.

The comments from the second teacher

1. The student makes a lot of grammatical error; for instance, I ride the motorcycle go to everywhere with my good friend. It had better change into "My friend and I rode the motorcycle to everywhere."
2. The student also makes the wrong words sentence: There are more people and many water activity. It has to change into "There are a lot of people and many water activities.
3. You can write more and divide into three paragraphs.

Classmate's comments:

1. First sentence can change to " Summer vacation is my favorite vacation."
2. And "I ride motorcycle go to everywhere." You can change to " I rode motorcycle to everywhere."

The second article of student A

The most important person in my life

In our lives we meet many people and some of they important in one way or another. However, the person who has most important me is my mother.

In my childhood, my mother taught me to choose good friends and avoid choosing bad friends. She also stressed the importance of morality and encouraged me to be a good person. For this reason my conduct had not too bad.

I hope I can reward my mother by doing well on the society.

Comments from the first teacher

The most important person in my life

In our lives we meet many people and some of they *important in one way or*

(In our life, we meet many people and some of them are)

another. However, the person who has most important me *is my mother.*

(the person who is the most important to me)

In my childhood, my mother taught me to choose good friends and avoid choosing bad friends. She also stressed the importance of morality *and encouraged me to be a*

(what do you mean in this sentence)

good person. For this reason my conduct had not too bad.

(Because of this, I have good behavior.)

I hope I can reward my mother by doing well on *the society.*

(in)

Comments from the second teacher:

1. You write a well-organized article.
2. Try to pay attention on the grammatical error; for example, some of them, not some of they.
3. Pay attention on what you express because some sentence we cannot understand ; such as "She also stressed the importance of morality"

Comments from the classmate:

1. In our lives we meet many people and some of they (them)…
2. I hope I can reward my mother by doing well on(in) the society.

Data Analysis of Student A

According to these two articles from the student A, he/she doesn't improve much comparing the in the class which the teacher uses the web 2.0 concept inside the class.

The student A still makes a lot of grammatical error, and he/she may not express his/her opinions well. From the point of view of vocabulary, student A seems not improve a lot. From the viewpoint of content, the student also cannot write more than the students who are in the previous class. From the viewpoint of organization, student A seems can divide into three paragraphs. From punctuation of viewpoint, it seems the same as the previous class.

Finding and Discussion

Comparing these two articles from the second class, we can see the student didn't improve much in their writings. The student has still made much grammatical error and they still cannot express clearly on what they would like to write. The reason may be that they do not read enough articles; therefore, they have less "input", then they cannot have the well "output". It seems that they may improve less than the first class which the teacher uses the concept of web 2.0 in the class.

In these two classes, students seem to be less improving in the viewpoint of punctuation. However, from the point of view of content, grammar and vocabulary, the first class that utilizes the concept of web 2.0 seems to be improved more than the later class. Consequently, the English writing teachers may utilize this new method in their writing class because students have more time to study themselves and they have time to cooperate with other classmates. In addition, they also can learn a lot from other classmates' comments and read more articles.

Research Remarks

In this research, the teacher has just used one semester to do this research, so for some students may not see much difference from the beginning of the writing essay to the end of writing essay. In addition, the writing course is only two hours in a week, there are only 18 weeks in one semester, therefore, the students may not get enough "input" in their writing. Furthermore, since the teacher sets the blog, so sometimes, students may feel less interested in it. That is also a problem my let students feel less fun.

CONCLUSION

Recommendations to the Writing Teachers

Combining web2.0 to the English writing course may be a good method for the future writing course, particularly for college writing course. Because most writing course is two to four hours a week in Taiwan, the teacher can use the class blog to motivate students to write the article. In addition, from learning other classmates' writing, students can write better according to read more articles. Students also can imitate other classmates' writing to improve their own writing skills.

Suggestions for the Further Research

Due to the restriction of time, financial constraints and regional consideration, the investigation realm of this study was limited. Consequently, there are several suggestions for the further research. First, this study only two schools were evaluated and only one class was evaluated in each school. In addition, the both colleges are in urban areas. Therefore, we suggest that a further study choosing several colleges in both urban and rural areas in Taiwan. Second, the samples are limited to only evaluated by two teachers. Therefore, further research can select more samples and select more classes and teachers to join this research. Finally, this study has had to speculate on the students' point of view—students' interview would contribute an important aspect to a more complete case study of writing learning among students in college level in Taiwan or all around the world.

REFERENCES

Anderson, P. (2007). *What is Web 2.0? Ideas, technologies and implications for education.* JISC Technology and Standards Watch.

Azmitia, M. (2002). Self, self-esteem, conflicts, and best friendships in early adolescence. In Brinthaupt, T. M. (Ed.), *Understanding early adolescent self and identity: Applications and interventions* (pp. 167–192). Albany, NY: State University of New York Press.

Bandura, A. (1977). *Social learning theory.* New York: General Learning Press.

Brown, B. B., & Lohr, M. J. (1987). Peer-group affiliation and adolescent self-esteem: An integration of ego-identity and symbolic-interaction theories. *Journal of Personality and Social Psychology, 52*, 47–55. doi:10.1037/0022-3514.52.1.47

Dillenbourg, P. (1999). What do you mean by collaborative learning? In Dillenbourg, P. (Ed.), *Collaborative learning: Cognitive and computational approaches* (pp. 1–19). Oxford: Elsevier.

Festinger, L. (1954). A theory of social comparison processes. *Human Relations, 7*, 117–140. doi:10.1177/001872675400700202

Freeman, S. W. (Ed.). (1985). *The acquisition of written language: revision and response.* Norwood, NJ: Ablex.

Glogoff, S. (2006). The LTC wiki: experiences with integrating a wiki in instruction. In Mader, S. L. (Ed.), *Using Wiki in education.*

Hillocks, G. (1982). The interaction of instruction, teacher comment, and revision in teaching the composing process. *Research in the Teaching of English, 16*, 261–278.

Hwang, Y., & Li, T. (2009). Conquer Web 2.0 motivational challenges from social context evolution. *Proceedings of the 2009 5th International Joint Conference on INC, IMS and IDC.* (pp.1836-1841).

Jones, J. F. (2001). Call and responsibilities of teachers and administrations. *ELT Journal, 55*(4). doi:10.1093/elt/55.4.360

Miller, N. E., & Dollard, J. (1941). *Social learning and imitation.* New Haven, CT: Yale University Press.

Nystand, M. (1990). Sharing word: The effects of readers on developing writers. *Written Communication, 7*(1), 3–24. doi:10.1177/0741088390007001001

Reid, J. (1993). *Teaching ESL writing.* Englewood Cliffs, NJ: Regents Prentice Hall.

Richard-Amato, P. (1988). *Making it happened: Interaction in the second language classroom.* New York: Longman.

Savin-Williams, R. C., & Berndt, T. J. (1990). Friendship and peer relations. In G.R. Elliott. & S. Feldman (Eds.), *At the threshold: The developing adolescent.* Cambridge, MA: Harvard University Press.

Wikipedia. (2009). Retrieved on September 20, 2009, from http://en.wikipedia.org/wiki/Web_2.0

Zemach, D. E., & Rumisek, L. A. (2003). *College writing: From paragraph to essay.* Oxford: Macmillian Education.

ADDITIONAL READING

Ala-Mutka, K., Punie, Y., & Ferrari, A. (2009). Review of Learning in Online Networks and Communities. *Lecture Notes in Computer Science, 5794*, 350–364. doi:10.1007/978-3-642-04636-0_34

Blaye, A., Light, P., & Rubtsov, V. (1992). Collaborative learning at the computer; How social processes 'interface' with human-computer interaction. *European Journal of Psychology of Education, 7*(4), 257–267. doi:10.1007/BF03172892

Boyd, E. M., & Fales, A. W. (1983). Reflective learning: Key to learning from experience. *Journal of Humanistic Psychology, 23*(2), 99–117. doi:10.1177/0022167883232011

Capuano, N., Miranda, S., & Orciuoli, F. (2009). E-Learning at Work in the Knowledge Virtual Enterprise. *Studies in Computational Intelligence, Intelligent Collaborative e-Learning Systems and Applications,* 246, pp. 53-63.

Cress, U., & Kimmerle, J. (2008). A systemic and cognitive view on collaborative knowledge building with wikis. *Computer-Supported Collaborative Learning, 3*, 105–122. doi:10.1007/s11412-007-9035-z

Davoli, P., Monari, M., & Severinson Eklundh, K. (2009). Peer activities on Web-learning platforms—Impact on collaborative writing and usability issues. *Education and Information Technologies, 14*(3), 229–254. doi:10.1007/s10639-008-9080-x

de Abreu, G., & Elbers, E. (2005). The social mediation of learning in multiethnic schools: Introduction. *European Journal of Psychology of Education, 20*(1), 3–11. doi:10.1007/BF03173207

Deiglmayr, A., & Spada, H. (2010). Developing Adaptive Collaboration Support: The Example of an Effective Training for Collaborative Inferences. *Educational Psychology Review, 22*(1), 103–113. doi:10.1007/s10648-010-9119-6

Fernandez, C., Cannon, J., & Chokshi, S. (2003). A US-Japan study collaboration reveals critical lenses for examining practice. *Teaching and Teacher Education, 19*, 71–185. doi:10.1016/S0742-051X(02)00102-6

Hawryszkiewycz, I. T. (2009). Identifying and Supporting Collaborative Architectures. *Lecture Notes in Computer Science, 5914*, 442–449. doi:10.1007/978-3-642-10488-6_42

Hwang, Y.-C., & Yuan, S.-T. (2009). Ubiquitous collaborative iTrust service: Exploring proximity collective wisdom. *Information Systems Frontiers, 11*(1), 43–60. doi:10.1007/s10796-008-9148-6

Kirschner, P., Strijbos, J.-W., Kreijns, K., & Beers, P. J. (2004). Designing electronic collaborative learning environments. *Educational Technology Research and Development, 52*(3), 47–66. doi:10.1007/BF02504675

Konstantinidis, A., Tsiatsos, & Pomportsis, A. (2009). Collaborative virtual learning environments: design and evaluation. *Multimedia Tools and Applications, 44*(2), 279–304. doi:10.1007/s11042-009-0289-5

Larusson, J. A., & Alterman, R. (2009). Wikis to support the "collaborative" part of collaborative learning. *Computer-Supported Collaborative Learning, 4*(4), 371–402. doi:10.1007/s11412-009-9076-6

Lonchamp, J. (2009). A three-level analysis of collaborative learning in dual-interaction spaces. *Computer-Supported Collaborative Learning, 4*, 289–317. doi:10.1007/s11412-009-9068-6

McCotter, S. S. (2001). Collaborative groups as professional development. *Teaching and Teacher Education, 17*(6), 685–704. doi:10.1016/S0742-051X(01)00024-5

Notari, M. (2006). How to use a wiki in education: Wiki based effective constructive learning. *Proceedings of the 2006 International Symposium on* Wikis (pp. 131–132). New York: ACM.

Pea, R. D. (2004). The social and technological dimensions of scaffolding and related theoretical concepts for learning, education, and human activity. *Journal of the Learning Sciences*, *13*(3), 423–451. doi:10.1207/s15327809jls1303_6

Puchner, L. D., & Taylor, A. R. (2006). Lesson study, collaboration and teacher efficacy: Stories from two school based math lesson study groups. *Teaching and Teacher Education*, *22*, 922–934. doi:10.1016/j.tate.2006.04.011

Ramirez, A., Hine, M. J., Ji, S., Ulbrich, F., & Riordan, R. (2009). Learning to succeed in a flat world: Information and communication technologies for a new generation of business students. *Learning Inquiry*, *3*(3), 157–175. doi:10.1007/s11519-009-0043-y

Rogers, Y., Connelly, K., Hazlewood, W., & Tedesco, L. (2010). Enhancing learning: A study of how mobile devices can facilitate sensemaking. *Personal and Ubiquitous Computing*, *14*(2), 111–124. doi:10.1007/s00779-009-0250-7

Roschelle, J., & Teasley, S. D. (1995). Construction of shared knowledge in collaborative problem solving. In O'Malley, C. (Ed.), *Computer-supported collaborative learning* (pp. 69–197).

Velásquez, J. D., & Nof, S. Y. (2009). *Collaborative e-Work, e-Business, and e-Service* (pp. 1549–1576). Springer Handbook of Automation.

Vescio, V., Ross, D., & Adams, A. (2008). A review of research on the impact of professional learning communities on teaching practice and student learning. *Teaching and Teacher Education*, *24*(1), 80–91. doi:10.1016/j.tate.2007.01.004

Wagner, C. L., & Fernandez-Gimenez, M. E. (2009). Effects of Community-Based Collaborative Group Characteristics on Social Capital. *Environmental Management*, *44*(4), 632–645. doi:10.1007/s00267-009-9347-z

Walker, E., Rummel, N., & Koedinger, K. R. (2009). CTRL: A research framework for providing adaptive collaborative learning support. *User Modeling and User-Adapted Interaction*, *19*(5), 387–431. doi:10.1007/s11257-009-9069-1

KEY TERMS AND DEFINITIONS

Collaborative Learning: A situation that two or more people learn something together and interact by sharing experiences.

E-Learning: The use of ICT-based technologies in learning opportunities.

English Writing Course: A course that provide students with a range of strategies for developing both academic writing and communication skills.

Network Effect: The phenomenon whereby a service becomes more valuable as more people use it, thereby encouraging ever-increasing numbers of adopters.

Online Interaction: The interaction takes place that individuals interact with one another via the network or ICT-based infrastructure.

Peer Editing: A useful way to improve writing skill by showing student's work to another student to provide compliments, suggestions, and corrections.

Web 2.0: A concept that facilitate interactive information sharing, interoperability, user-centered design and collaboration on the World Wide Web.

Chapter 8
A Case Study of Integrated Innovation Model in the Cultural Innovation Industry in Taiwan

Te Fu Chen
Lunghwa University of Science and Technology, Taiwan

ABSTRACT

Taiwan's diverse cultural background should bolster innovation and development. The cultural innovation industry (cultural and creative industry) in particular constitutes an emerging sector in Taiwan, and a vehicle for many countries today to show off their unique cultural characteristics. Taiwan's rich and diverse cultural foundation has garnered international attention in recent years in many areas including visual and performing arts, film and literature, setting the standard for others to follow. The development of the cultural innovation industry encompasses culture, art, technology and local traditions. This chapter describes the procedures of promotions formulated for the development of the cultural and creative industry, including definition, scope, development, strategies and government assistance. The chapter is intended to give the general public an idea of the chain effects expected to bring for the society by the development of the cultural and creative industry.

First of all, the study goes through literature review and content analysis to develop a research framework into an integrated innovation model. Secondly, the chapter details a case study to develop a more complete and practical integrated model and researches propositions for practitioners in cultural innovation organizations and future researchers. Additional research is needed to provide managers and consultants with important perspectives to consider when implementing cultural innovation programs and practices in their organizations. The results from such research could also benefit academics by providing select factors to focus on in future studies. This research will give more in-depth proposition

DOI: 10.4018/978-1-60960-129-4.ch008

to practitioners in cultural innovation to achieve implementation of innovation programs. Likewise, it will provide a framework in understanding why certain innovation initiatives fail and how that can be improved. This will benefit both academics and practitioners.

This research was focused on case study based on qualitative analysis, literature review and depth interview, discussing inner management and external relations in Liuli Gongfang, in order to offer the concrete suggestion of development in the future. In accordance with this case, Council for Cultural Affairs pursues its ideal in the scope of the capability, communicating with each other could obtain the trust and cooperation. From the development and strategy of Liuli Gongfang, it continues to move towards the road of Culture Creative Industries continuously, however, it will be no definite answer in the future. Thus, it will remind the front office to examine both relations carefully, and must consider the actual condition in the future.

INTRODUCTION

Background

Taiwan's manufacturing sector has found itself in a difficult situation owing to the cost of production factors rising and developing nations catching up fast. It's no longer enjoy competitive advantage in Taiwan for large-scale manufacturing operations; in order to create new sources of competitive advantage Taiwanese industry needs to adopt the new concepts of the knowledge economy, developing new areas of production where innovative design is the core element. Only then will it be possible for Taiwanese companies to differentiate themselves from their overseas competitors and create more value added.

The cultural and creative industry are emerging businesses in Taiwan. Culture and creation has come to refer to a wide range of economic activities that draw from a country's culture and creative talent to generate prosperity and employment. Such cultural and creative centers act as channels between industry and government by building paradigms to guide small creative and cultural businesses to work with the government and possibly embark on international business projects. Not only do local businesses obtain business opportunities, but also help spread the knowledge of Taiwan culture abroad. If the cultural innovation industry (Cultural and Creative Industry) can strengthen their creativity and design capabilities and adopt effective business management methods, then they should have great potential. Their development will stimulate the growth of related peripheral industry, thereby boosting overall domestic demand and contributing to export growth. Meanwhile, if fair, reasonable pricing and licensing methods can be adopted in the cultural industry and the art world, and if they can be integrated effectively with consumer goods industry (for example through the laser printing of famous paintings onto scarves and cups), applying digital content technology to culture and creativity, then not only will this be a shot in the arm to the competitiveness of Taiwanese industry, but the resulting growth in exports will stimulate the ongoing development of the Taiwanese economy as a whole. While helping traditional industry to upgrade and transform themselves, the adoption of new information technology will also facilitate the development of new industry and the creation of new employment opportunities, breathing new life into Taiwanese industry.

In 1995, the Council for Cultural Affairs proposed the concept of "Developing Cultural Industry, and Bringing Culture into Industry" in the Conference on the Cultural Industry. This "Cultural Industry" concept later became the core idea of "Community Development" in the nation.

Under the impetuses of globalization and technological advancement, a new economical model that centers on "Creativeness" has been formed, which we call the "K-Economy" (Knowledge-based Economy), and the idea of "Think Globally, Act Locally" has become the mainstream concept in the twenty-first century. To get closer to the source of this vibe, the government officially listed the "Culture Software" – the "Cultural and Creative Industry" – into the "Challenge 2008 National Development Plan" in 2002.

The rehabilitation and reuse of culture assets were exerted a tremendous influence by the government. Since Executive Yuan started to promote the policy of "Challenging 2008: The Focal Point of National Development" in 2002, the "Culture" and "Industry" has been combined in the thinking of Culture Creative Industries as its target. However, the government will have its difficulties while promoting some aspirations, and it will need an intermediary to go for management and carry on planning, then Non-profit Organizations can become the media of combining the government and Culture Creative Industries. Cultural Creative Industries are plural, complicated commercial specialties. As Culture Creative Industries are operated by Nonprofit Organizations, will they stand for the mission, or follow the market? How can they pursue the wave on the market, but don't betray their soul, then strengthen sustainable development.

Motivations

With the Development Plan for the Cultural and Creative Industry, products with local cultural characteristics are expected to be developed through a combination of art creativeness and commercial operations, which will not only deepen people's cultural identities toward their own cultures but also increase the added value for these industry.

Taiwan's economy has entered a new phase of industrialization, and the existing production model of large-scale manufacturing has gradually lost its competitive advantage. In addition to high-tech development, Taiwan must build a more flexible productive organization system to increase the competitiveness of the knowledge-based economy. In fact, the value-added model of the knowledge-based economy should be the core of innovative design in production, especially artistic and esthetic creation, which has been ignored during the past. Most industry that are labor-intensive and science and technology intensive, are very easily imitated, and unable to maintain their competitive advantage for long.

Enduring competitive advantage can only be created within an economic system that is founded upon a rich culture. But such a system requires innovativeness as its core skill in order to lend momentum and value to economic development. There are numerous examples of social, cultural and economic innovations (Drucker, 1994). Innovation is a proposed theory or design concept that synthesises extant knowledge and techniques to provide a theoretical basis for a new concept (Sundbo, 1998; Bright, 1969). Hence, innovation has many facets and is multidimensional. This is why the cultural innovation industry has become an important indicator of national competitiveness all over the world. Latest predictions (from KPMG) are that the creative industry could grow by 46% in employment and 136% in output in the two decades to 2015 (DCMS, 2006). Taiwan needs a spectrum of international experiences for better understanding of culture projects to develop cultural innovation industry.

In the 21st century, the era of globalization, culture innovation industry has become the key of enhancing a country's competitiveness. The cultural innovation strategy featured by both culture and economy is considered the core strategy for each country's economic development. For this reason, the culture innovation industry has become an important tendency for international development. In cooperation with the central government's mechanism of cultural policy, Taiwan

Government has encouraged the development of local cultural innovation industry, thus boosting its development and reactivating the overall economy. Based upon the features of the culture innovation industry's development in Taiwan and from the viewpoint of non-profit organizations in respect of culture innovation industry's development, the study discusses the core strategy and function model that the local culture industries apply and the effectiveness and influence that emerge under the coordination mechanism with both the public and private institutions. The chosen local culture industries include Liuli Gongfang and LIULI CHINA Museum.

The function of museums has extended from traditional exhibitions, research, collection, and education to more innovative communications, information, empiricism, leisure and more. Museums are like media, history, church, and school combined. They are the sources for the innovative industry or representative offices for culture and art. More and more scholars and experts take museums as a goldmine for culture or industries. Especially in the non-profit business, museums have more energy to express and are more inspiring to new thoughts in the new world.

Based on the above-mentioned reasons, research on the cultural industry has been embarked upon in the international community, whose foundation is knowledge and economy. This subject is being studied and carried to redefine cultural work with new thoughts and contribute to the prosperity of the cultural industry and innovative ideas of similar types.

Research Problems

According to abovementioned, the study assumed there are five research problems as follows:

1. What is the industry's current state of development for cultural innovation industry.
2. Which sources of innovation is the most important for cultural innovation industry to cultivate innovation capacity?
3. Which enablers of internal and external innovation are necessary to enhance innovation in the cultural innovation industry?
4. How to integrate sources of innovation and the internal and external innovation to add value and raise competitiveness for cultural innovation industry?
5. How to identify key successful factors (KSF) of cultural innovation for Taiwanese cultural innovation industry?

Research Objectives

According to backgrounds, motivations and problems of this paper, the study proposed the objectives of this study as follows:

1. Provide an overview of the industry's current state of development for cultural innovation industry.
2. Provide a complete and practical integrated innovation model for cultural innovation industry to be an easy-to-follow framework when they implement innovation initiatives, and to link corporate innovation capacity and then to support continue innovation for adding value and raising competitiveness.
3. Present a case study of successful enterprises in the cultural innovation industry so that their experience in terms of products and commercialization strategies can be of benefit to other industry, in the hope that this will lead to the creation of new business opportunities and new jobs.
4. Provide some policy recommendations to government for the promotion of the cultural innovation industry are put forward.
5. Study how Taiwanese cultural innovation industry to identifying KSF of cultural innovation and how they to integrate source of innovation, internal and external innovation

to create industrial survival space in competitive markets in knowledge economy.

BACKGROUND (LITERATURE REVIEW)

The Current State of Taiwan's Cultural and Creative Industry

What is meant by the term "cultural and creative industry"? Put simply, it is those industry that have their origins in innovation or cultural accretion, and which have the potential to create wealth or create jobs through the production and utilization of intellectual property, and which can help to enhance the living environment for society as a whole. Just how large is Taiwan's cultural and creative industry? According to data produced by the Ministry of Finance Tax Data Center, in 2002 the total operating revenue of the cultural and creative industry came to approximately NT$523.24 billion. If one subtracts the value of intermediates, overall production value came to around NT$302.62 billion; the industry included just over 47,800 enterprises, employing more than 325,500 people. On-site interviews would be needed to determine the production value of the designer brand and fashion industry; the innovative lifestyle industry is a "compound industry" which extends over the food, clothing, accommodation, travel, sport and entertainment sectors. By assuming that 5% of the total production value of these sectors displays a high level of creativity, a rough estimate of production value can be made. The four industry with the highest production value are the construction design industry, broadcasting industry, publishing industry and handicrafts industry. The industry employing the largest number of people are the design industry, digital leisure industry, advertising industry and publishing industry (Moeasmea, 2004).

The UK has the most highly developed cultural and creative industry of any country in the world. In 2000 the cultural and creative industry accounted for around 7.9% of Britain's GDP. With total exports of £8.7 billion, the industry held a 3.3% share of Britain's total exports, while accounting for 4.1% of the employed population. In Hong Kong, the cultural and creative industry accounts for 2.0% of GDP, and 3.7% of the employed population; in Australia it accounts for 3.3% of GDP; in New Zealand the industry accounts for around 3.1% of GDP and 3.6% of the employed population. In Taiwan, the cultural and creative industry has total production value of NT$302.62 billion; it accounts for approximately 2.9% of GDP, and employs about 325,500 people, 3.47% of the employed population (Moeasmea, 2004).

It can thus be seen that the share of GDP held by the cultural and creative industry in Taiwan is slightly higher than in Hong Kong, but lower than in Australia and New Zealand, and much lower than in the UK. Clearly, Taiwan still has considerable room for growth in the development of thecultural and creative industry. Regarding the percentage of the total employed population who are working in the cultural and creative industry, the figure for Taiwan is slightly lower than those for Hong Kong, Australia and New Zealand, and much ower than the figure for the UK. In Britain, the cultural and creative industry has created around 1.32 million jobs, a testimony to the important role that this industry can play in stimulating the appearance of new employment opportunities and in reducing income disparities within society (Moeasmea, 2004).

Definition and Scope of the Cultural Innovation (Cultural and Creative) Industry

Definition of the Cultural Innovation (Cultural and Creative) Industry

In March and July 2003, resolutions passed in the 2nd and 3rd "Cultural and Creative Industry Promotion Team" meetings, formed jointly by the Ministry of Economic Affairs, Ministry of Education, Government Information Office, and the Council for Cultural Affairs, established the definition and scope of the Cultural and Creative Industry in Taiwan. The following characteristics are considered when identifications are to be made:

1. Whether there are more employments or participants
2. Whether the production value is bigger or the associated effects are higher
3. Whether there is a large growth potential
4. Whether the originality or the Creativeness is higher
5. Whether there will be a high added value

Cultural innovation (Cultural and creative) industry are defined as "Industry originated from creativeness and accumulation of culture and formed and utilized through intellectual properties that have the potential to create wealth and employment opportunities and prospects to promote upgrading of the overall living environment". This definition is coined with references to Britain and UN's definitions of cultural and creative industry. Currently, the British government's creative industry policies are the most comprehensive in internationally. They is defined as "creative industry originated from personal creativity, skills, and talents that have potentials to create wealth and employment opportunities after produced and developed through intellectual property rights". And, the UNESCO defines them as "industry combined with innovation, production, and commercial contents and at the same time the nature of the contents have the qualities as intangible assets and cultural concepts that are protected under intellectual property rights and presented in forms of products or services".

There are diverse names in the different countries and areas, and it is called as "Cultural and Creative Industry (CCI) in the UNESCO. Taiwan chose to merge them into the Cultural & Creative Industry (CCI). The definition of Cultural & Creative Industry includes original creativity, skill and ability, or any formulation of intelligent properties and the development of the potential wealth (HKDTC, 2002). In comparison with the conventional industry, which pay more attention to their economic values, the accumulation and application of cultural and creative type of industry have their special meanings and values. UK, Denmark, Singapore, Hong Kong, Canada and New Zealand all have significantly developed Cultural & Creative Industry. The total output production assets is about 3.04 trillion dollars and is expected to reach 6.1 trillion dollars by the year of 2020 (DSDTI, 2005).

According to UNESCO's definition, Cultural Industry are those based on tangible or intangible cultures going through conceptual formulation, production and manufacturing processes and at the end present themselves as commercial products or services in the market. They usually have patent or copy right protections (UNESCO, 2000). In Taiwan, Cultural & Creative Industry products are considered to be activities originating from creativity, culture, art and design, going through intelligent property operations and having the potential to generate fortune and employment opportunities (Cultural and Creative Industry Promotion Organization 2005a). They have multiple meanings and functions when examined from their cultural contents, creativity, economics, jobs and future potential viewpoints. According to UNESCO's definition, there are printing, publishing, carving, design, architecture, visual and performing arts, music instrumentation, movie production, cultural recreations, etc. in the CCI and these all have cultural and economical meanings. CCI definitions from various countries are mostly similar, while Taiwan's definition of Cultural & Creative Industry includes visual arts, music and performing arts, cultural exhibition and performance facilities, industrial craft, motion pictures, radio broadcasting and TV, publishing, advertising, design, brand and fashion design, architectural design, creative living, digital Gaming

& entertainment, etc. In general, these categories are similar to those of the UK, New Zealand and Hong Kong, except that Cultural Exhibition and Creative Living are uniquely included in Taiwan's definition of Cultural & Creative Industry (see Table 1).

Scope of the Cultural Innovation (Cultural and Creative) Industry

According to Luna Liu (2003), "The concept "innovative cultural enterprises" basically involves two aspects: artistic creativity and economic activity. Broadly speaking, "cultural enterprises" have existed in human society since time immemorial, comprising both traditional and modern-day artistic work in such fields as literature, music, architecture, drama, dance, photography and cinematography. Also included within the scope of cultural enterprises, and providing new directions of development for traditional cultural enterprises, are such economic activities as publishing, art galleries, international art trade, radio and television broadcasting, movie theatres, clothes design, furniture design, and industrial design.

The scope of the Cultural and Creative Industry in Taiwan covers a range of thirteen categories including visual arts, music and performing arts, crafts, cultural display facilities, the design industry, publishing, TV and broadcast, movie,

Table 1. Cultural and creative industry definitions by major developed countries

	Taiwan	UK	Australia	New Zealand	Korea	Hong Kong
1	Visual Arts	Arts and Antiques Market	Visual Arts	Visual Arts	Fine Arts	Arts & Antiques
2	Music and Performing Arts	Music and Performing Arts	Music Composition / Performing Arts	Music and Performing Arts	Music and Performing Arts	Music and Performing Arts
3	Cultural Exhibition and Performance Facilities					
4	Industrial Craft	Crafts	Industrial Design	Crafts	Crafts	
5	Motion Pictures	Film and Video	Film and Video	Film and Video Production	Film and Video	Film and Comics
6	Radio Broadcasting & TV	TV & Radio	TV & Radio	TV & Radio	Broadcasting	TV
7	Publishing	Publishing	Writing / Publishing and Print Media	Publishing	Publishing and Printing	Publishing
8	Advertising	Advertising	Advertising	Advertising	Advertising	Advertising
9	Design	Design	Design	Design	Design	Design
10	Brand and Fashion Design	Designer Fashion		Designer Fashion		Designer Fashion
11	Architectural Design	Architecture	Architecture	Architecture		Architecture
12	Creative Living					
13	Digital Gaming & Entertainment	Interactive Leisure Software / Software & Computer Services	Entertainment Software - Cartoon and Computer Games	Software and Computer Services	Digital Contents / Games	Game Software / Software and IT Services
14	Others		Graphic Design and Marketing		Character	

Sources: British DCMS (2005), Australia NOIE(2005)/DSDTI(2005), New Zealand NZIER(2002), Korea KOCCA(2005), Hong Kong HKTDC(2002), Council for Economic Planning and Development, Executive Yuan, Taiwan, etc.

advertising, digital recreation and entertainment, the designer fashion industry, the architectural design industry, and the lifestyle industry. The Council for Cultural Affairs manages the first four categories. For administrative bodies assigned to the rest of the categories see Table 2.

The content of a cultural industry must include the following ten items: Artistic artifacts; a place for learning knowledge; creativity; the production of a thing within a thing; repetitive application and social value; community service and education; derivative aesthetics not fully stake-holding; artifacts that can be combined, publicly exhibited, or privately owned for non-profit business purpose; center for tourism and media between individuals and communities and for national development; symbols of the times and characteristics of environments as well as civic consciousness; and public property, including historical, social, and religious beliefs, media for realistic views, totems symbolizing a nation's advancement, or social values.

The above-mentioned are some important elements, with more to be covered because the cultural industry is extensive. Cultural institutions such as museums, memorials, theaters and galleries as well as people-oriented services, such as education, religion, and customs, and positions such as handicraft learners, planners, researchers and implementers are all included in the scope of the cultural industry.

Definition of Museum

According to Huang Kuang-Nan (2008), "A lot of the scope of the cultural industry involves the definition of museums because establishment of museums and the exercise of their functions are the key presentations of culture. As a result, museums can carry the functions of schools, churches, divine arenas, studios, research labs, temples, storage rooms, leisure places, tourist sites or sightseeing spots. They are organizational, non-profit, and permanent institutions. They are public places. Based on these ideas, museums must be equipped with definite purposes, either research, educational, recreational, or entertaining purposes. Also, museums must have buildings, collections, researchers, and educators, as well as security guards, and must possess long-term objectives and missions. The reason that museums have become important places to pursue knowledge or even for people to pursue high quality lives is because they are non-profit and public institutions. Public or private museums are established with certain requirements".

Backgrounder of Cultural Innovation (Cultural & Creative) Industry

"Creative Industries": The Promising Future—An Inevitable Trend

According to an article "Cultural & Creative Industry Backgrounder" on CreativeTaiwan.net, noted futurist Alvin Toffler once predicted that creative and cultural industries would become the dominant sector in the world economy, that whoever takes the high ground of creativity can take the world, as creativity will be the force controlling the 21st century economic lifeline. These "chimneyless" industries that turn experience into pleasurable memories, and creativity into fortune as well as career opportunities are indeed the hottest and most environment-conscious sector which thrive the knowledge-based economy!"Creative economy" has been taken as one of the major projects each country works on to strengthen its competitiveness, which indicates that "Cultural innovation (Cultural & Creative) Industries" will become the trend in the future. These "industries without smokestacks", or "knowledge-based industries", turn experiences into great memories, and ideas into fortune and job opportunities.

According to "Copyright Industry in the U.S. Economy: The 2006 Report", published by the International Intellectual Property Alliance in January 2007, the value of U.S.'s copyright

Table 2. Scope of the cultural and creative industry in Taiwan and the administrative agencies

No.	Name of Industry	Admin.	Summary of Industry
1	Visual arts	C. for Cultural Affairs	Businesses involving in painting, sculpture, and other art creation, auction and retail of arts, gallery operations, art brokerage, art valuation, and art restoration.
2	Music and performing arts	C. for Cultural Affairs	Businesses operating drama (original scripts, acting training, and performance), musical plays and operas) original music, music performance training, and performance), performance facility management (theater, music hall, and open-air stages), performing art brokerage, performing art hardware services (prop production/management, stage construction, lighting and audio equipments), and art festival operations.
3	Cultural display facilities	C. for Cultural Affairs	Businesses involving in operations of fine art museums, museums, artists' villages.
4	Crafts	C. for Cultural Affairs	Businesses involving in craft creation, craft design, craft retail, and craft valuations.
5	Movie	Gov. Info Office	Businesses involving in movie production, publishing and showing, and other peripheral services.
6	TV and broadcast	Gov. Info Office	Businesses operating wireless TV, cable TV, satellite broadcasting, TV station management, and program production and supply.
7	Publishing	Gov. Info Office	Businesses involving in publishing of news, magazines (periodicals), books, records, cassettes, and computer software. However, those involving in movie publishing should be categorized into category 8520 (movie publishing industry) and those operating TV program broadcasting and publishing of recorded programs should be categorized into category 8630 (Broadcast Program Suppliers).
8	Advertising	M. of Economic Affairs	Businesses involving in operations of various media including design, graphic production, photographing, model making, production, and installation. Independent advertisement distribution and solicitation are also included in this category.
9	Design industry	M. of Economic Affairs	Businesses involving in product design/planning, product exterior design, mechanism design, prototype and model production, fashion design, patent logo design, brand visual design, graphic design, packaging design, webpage/multimedia design, and design consultancy.
10	Designer fashion	M. of Economic Affairs	Businesses conducting fashion design, consultancy, manufacturing, and distribution related matters for designer brands.
11	Architectural design	M. of Interiors	Businesses involving in architectural design, interior/space design, exhibition design, commercial space design, signboard design, garden design, landscape design, and scenery design.
12	Lifestyle industry	M. of Economic Affairs	All businesses match the following definitions: 1. Businesses originated from creativity or cultural accumulation and operated with innovative ways to provide products or services for food, clothing, accommodation, transportation, education, and recreation. 2. Businesses utilizing combo operations that are creative and regenerative and provides learning experience activities.
13	Digital recreation and entertainment	M. of Economic Affairs	Businesses involving in operations of digital recreation/entertainment facilities, environmental/ecological recreation services, and social/life recreation services. 1. Digital recreation/entertainment facilities – 3DVR facilities, sports machines, combat competition machines, guiding systems, electronic vending machines, motion movie facilities. 2. Environmental/ecological recreation services – digital/multimedia theme parks, motion picture theme parks, museum theme parks. 3. Social/life recreation services – commercial digital entertainment centers, community digital entertainment centers, Internet cafes, family entertainment/learning centers, and after-school classes/schools

Source: Cultural and Creative Industry Promotion Team, Ministry of Economic Affairs, February 2004. Taiwan Cultural and Creative Industry – Guide to the Development Plan

industry in 2005 has increased to USD1 trillion 388.1 billion. This value is equivalent of 11.12% of the US GDP, contributing as much as 23.78% of overall economic growth. Cultural industry outperformed traditional industry to create more than 11 million job opportunities for the country, as Hollywood films, television programs produced by the three major networks, and popular music under the Time Warner group spread throughout the world to lead global fashion and style trends with an influence comparable to Wall Street's financial power (TAITRA, 2008).

According to Table 3, data on Taiwan is estimated by the Chung-Hua Institution for Economic Research, where the production value and workforce size are calculated using figures from only 12 and 8 out of the 13 creative and cultural industry, respectively; as a result, the percentage of production value in GDP and workforce percentage are likely to have been underestimated. Some fine-tuning was done to ensure a better match between the industry categories of different countries: Taiwan's production value includes figures from the online game, computer animation and audio-visual application industry. The software and computer service industry is excluded from the figures for the U.K., Australia and New Zealand. The U.S. figure incorporated the core copyright industry only. With respect to Hong Kong, the workforce figure excludes those in the software and computer service industry. The production value of individual industry in the creative and cultural sector in Hong Kong and China is unavailable; hence no adjustment is made to the industry categories to the percentage of production value in GDP respectively. The character/icon industry value is excluded from the figure of South Korea (TAITRA, 2008).

Table 4 shows the advantages of Taiwan in cultural innovation industry

About TAITRA

Founded in 1970 to help promote foreign trade, the Taiwan External Trade Development Council (TAITRA) is the foremost non-profit trade promotion organization in Taiwan. Jointly sponsored by the government, industry associations, and several commercial organizations, TAITRA assists Taiwan businesses and manufacturers with reinforcing their international competitiveness and in coping with the challenges they face in foreign markets (TAITRA, 2008).

Government to Continue Supporting Cultural Industry

According to Ma, the cultural innovation sector is one of the nation's most competitive industry, with great potential for future development in the global arena. (Central News Agency, 2009)

Table 3. Index of the development of cultural & creative industry in leading countries

Country	Production Value in GDP (%)		Workforce Percentage (%)	
	Before Adjustment	After Adjustment	Before Adjustment	After Adjustment
Taiwan (2006)	2.59	3.16	2.06	2.06
U.S. (2005)	11.12	6.56	8.49	4.03
U.K. (2005)	8.10	4.53	2.54	1.27
South Korea (2004)	6.37	5.83	2.03	2.00
Australia (2000)	3.30	2.93	3.80	3.80
New Zealand (2001)	3.10	1.69	3.60	2.34
Hong Kong (2005)	4.00	4.00	4.89	3.9
China (2006)	2.45	2.45	1.48	1.48

Source: Office for the Promotion of Cultural and Creative Industries, Ministry of Economic Affairs

Cabinet Approves Plan to Boost Cultural and Creative Industry

The government also plans to achieve an industry cluster effect through the establishment of creative culture parks in Taipei, Taichung, Chiayi, Tainan and Hualien. It also aims to make the National Palace Museum a promotion center for the country's cultural and creative industry. The plan was approved at a weekly Cabinet meeting chaired by Premier Liu Chao-shiuan. Liu said he hopes the proposal will soon clear the legislative floor, and he instructed the relevant authorities to solicit suggestions and opinions from industry representatives on the development of the sector. He said one of the major goals is to consolidate and integrate the different aspects of Taiwanese culture, which he described as a rich and special blend that has evolved out of various cultural influences over the centuries (Department of Economic Development Taipei City Government, 2008).

Under the plan, the different influences, such as the aboriginal culture, the immigrant cultures of different periods in Taiwan's history and the

Table 4. The advantages of Taiwan in cultural innovation industry

Advantages	Contents
Taiwan: the world's no. 2 innovative ability & no.1 patent productivity	According to the Switzerland-based Institute for Management Development's World Competitiveness Report 2006, Taiwan's competitive strength comes from its outstanding Hi-Tech infrastructure, business management, and labor force. The astonishing number of patented technologies developed by Hi-Tech sector makes Taiwan a world leader in patent productivity. Taiwan's economy is made up mainly of small and medium-sized enterprises, which are known for their mobility and creativity. This has made Taiwan's companies relatively strong in the ability to adjust themselves to the needs of the market.
Taiwan: springboard to Chinese-speaking markets	Taiwan's design industry is ahead of Hong Kong and China, acquiring a total of 133 awards in the world's four major design competitions: iF, Reddot, G-Mark and IDEA in 2007. Taiwan shares many similar characteristics in culture and language with other Chinese-speaking areas, giving it a competitive advantage in these markets. Its background puts it in a perfect position to tap into China's rising market. It provides freedom for capital flow and information exchanges, allowing it to link up with world trends, pushing Taiwan's cultural and creative industry to the top.
Outstanding human resources and innovative marketing	Abundant talents: Taiwanese workers are famous for being industrious, pragmatic, careful, and passionate to their work, sticking to professional ethics, and enjoying innovation. These characteristics are the niche for Taiwan to develop cultural and creative industry. Cultural and creative industry in Taiwan are mainly small and medium sized solely-owned or joint-venture enterprises, which have the strengths of flexible creativity, fast mobility, and efficient executive ability. They show their creativity in continuously developing new products, their mobility in rapidly responding to market demands, and executive ability in putting ideas into actions and products as soon as possible. These are the advantages for Taiwan's cultural and creative industry to actively develop in both the country and the rest of the world. Cultural innovation requires creative people, and so Taipei City has revamped its school curriculum to place a higher emphasis on creative thinking. Today's graduates are ideally-suited to work in innovative industry; Taipei's quality of human resources is unmatched. The city has also assembled advisory teams to gradually steer creative teams toward productization and branding, and established incubation and sales platforms to assist start-ups. Moreover, the city also helps firms boost the visibility of innovative products. A city's attitude toward its culture industry reflects that city's vitality and thinking. Taipei continually strives to open new doors and create new opportunities by learning from it sown past. Thus the city gene rates the maximum energy possible for local culture.
Cultural Innovation and High value	Taiwan is the world's center of Chinese culture, and as such, it boasts copious cultural resources. The National Palace Museum, located in Taipei City, has the most significant collection of Chinese cultural artifacts in the world. And situated downtown, Huashan Cultural Park has been set aside exclusively for the development of art and culture. These irreplaceable facilities and prevailing conditions serve as the ideal platform for developing the cultural innovation industry in Taipei City. To focus its energies on that development, the Taipei City Government established the Cultural Industry Promotional Committee. In 2006, Taipei City's cultural innovation industry boasted productivity in excess of NT$300 billion, illustrating both its impressive production thus far and its potential for further growth.

Source: TAITRA (2008) and Central News Agency (2009)

traditional Chinese culture, will be highlighted, the premier said. The cultural innovation industry, one of six flagship industry selected by the government for intensive development, is closely related to the information technology industry, as digitization is an inevitable trend, Liu said. The other five industry selected for major development are tourism and leisure, medical care, biotechnology, green energy, and refined agriculture (Central News Agency, 2009).

Government Promotes Cultural Innovation Plan

According to the China Post news staff (2009), to integrate resources quickly and efficiently in order to promote the cultural and creative industry, the government has a total of 13 projects to promote the cultural and creative industry — five by the Ministry of Economic Affairs (MOEA), four by the CCA, three by the Government Information Office, and one by the Ministry of the Interior. The Executive Yuan (Cabinet) approved a project May 14 for accelerated development of the cultural and creative industry with an aim to make Taiwan a regional hub and generate NT$1 trillion (US$30.3 billion) in production value by 2012. The plan, drafted mainly by the Council for Cultural Affairs (CCA), was approved at a weekly Cabinet meeting chaired by Premier Liu Chao-shiuan. Liu said the government would invest NT$27.5 billion in the sector over a four-year period in television, film, pop music, digital content and handicraft industry. The National Development Fund will provide NT$20 billion to establish a venture capital fund to help nurture more companies in the field. According to the Council for Cultural Affairs (CCA), the initiator and chief organizer of the plan. The project is intended to generate more than 20 percent growth in media production value, create 200,000 jobs, triple overseas sales of media products and stimulate the local consumption rate for cultural and creative products and services for an increase to 15 percent from the current 13 percent. Under the plan, the different influences, such as the aboriginal culture, the immigrant cultures of different periods in Taiwan's history and the traditional Chinese culture, will be highlighted, the premier said. The cultural innovation industry is closely related to the information technology industry, as digitization is an inevitable trend, Liu said. The six flagship industry selected by the government for intensive development will cover television contents, films, pop music, digital contents, designing, and handicraft and industrial artworks (The China Post news staff, 2009).

In addition, the China Post news staff (2009) indicated, cultural innovation is the sixth and last emerging industry spearheaded by the administration led by President Ma Ying-jeou for major development. Premier Liu said one of the major goals is to consolidate and integrate the different aspects of Taiwanese culture, which he described as a rich and special blend that has evolved out of various cultural influences over the centuries. The government also plans to achieve an industry cluster effect through the establishment of creative culture parks in Taipei, Taichung, Chiayi, Tainan and Hualien. It also aims to make the National Palace Museum a promotion center for the country's cultural and creative industry. In addition to offering investment and tax incentives to attract more capital to the sector, the government will also establish a cultural and creative affairs foundation to provide assistance to companies. The huge Mainland Chinese market will be cultivated through closer cooperation by companies of the two sides to beef up competitive edge by combining their resources and sharing the common cultural background, Liu said. The premier instructed the relevant authorities to solicit suggestions and opinions from industry representatives on the development of the sector. He also expressed the hope that lawmakers are able to ratify the draft cultural creativity law governing the development of cultural and creative affairs proposed by the Cabinet during the current legislative session (The China Post news staff, 2009).

In September 2003, the "Council for Cultural Affairs Creative Industry Project Center" was officially set up, which formed a single-window administrative service counter and an internet platform to provide an information channel for art workers or businesses interested in joining the Cultural and Creative Industry. Up to the end of December 2003, the Center has provided consultation services to fifty-six cases. The Council for Cultural Affairs Creative Industry Project Center is composed of five teams set up for different types of services (Table 5):

Taiwan's CCI development plan mentioned six indices to measure the effects on the promotion of the Cultural & Creative Industry: (1) Increase the total CCI's net assets by 200%, (2) Increase the ratio of CCI employees with college degrees to 50%, (3) Increase CCI employment opportunities by 200%, (4) Increase International competition awards for CCI products by 200%, (5) Increase Culture expenses per family to 15% of total family expense and (6) Increase CCI related intelligent property registrations by 10% annually (Cultural & Creative Industry Promotion Organization, 2005b, see Figure 1).

The Council for Economic Planning and Development, Executive Yuan, Taiwan, ROC also passed the "Service Industry Development Guidelines and Action Plan" in late 2004. This plan also mentioned the following goals to be achieved by 2008: (1) Increase CCI's production assets by 150%, (2) Increase CCI's employment by 150%, (3) Increase the cultural related expenses per family from 12.9% to 15%, (4) Increase college degreed employment for CCI from 30% to 50%, (5) Increase international awards on CCI products by 300% and (6) Increase intelligent property registration by 10% (CEPD, 2004a). Both plans mentioned the same goals, although the percentages of increases differed from one another. Among the six indices, college or above college education resource is the most important key in building up the net asset and its competitive strength for the Cultural & Creative Industry (Cultural & Creative Industry Promotion Organization, 2005b).

Table 5. Five teams set up for different types of services of the Council for Cultural Affairs Creative Industry Project Center

Team Categories	Services
1. Legal Research and Services	1. Research on relevant legal systems. 2. Provide art workers legal consultations. 3. Provide legal knowledge forums and courses.
2. Management Consultation	1. Assist in upgrading management abilities. 2. Provide financial, taxation, and management consultations. Promote Cultural and Creative Industry Incubation programs. 3. Administer tax discounts and financing services. 4. Promote incubator plans for the development of the Cultural and Creative Industries.
3. Promotion and Enducation	1. Provide human resource development services, promote policies relevant to the plan, and promote the cultural and creative industries. 2. Set up entrepreneur club to match interested investors. 3. Conduct various forums and policy conferences.
4. Industrial Marketing	1. Provide information on industrial development, market intelligence and government purchasing. 2. Assist in setting up of distribution channels and expansions into the international market. 3. Set and maintain the project center website
5. Administrative coordination	Provide a single-window service counter to coordinate internally of the project center as well as relevant administrative affairs.

Source: http://english.cca.gov.tw/public/Attachment/411317374171.pdf

Figure 1. Indices to measure the Growth Effects on Cultural & Creative Industry. Source: Cultural and Creative Industry Promotion Organization (2005b)

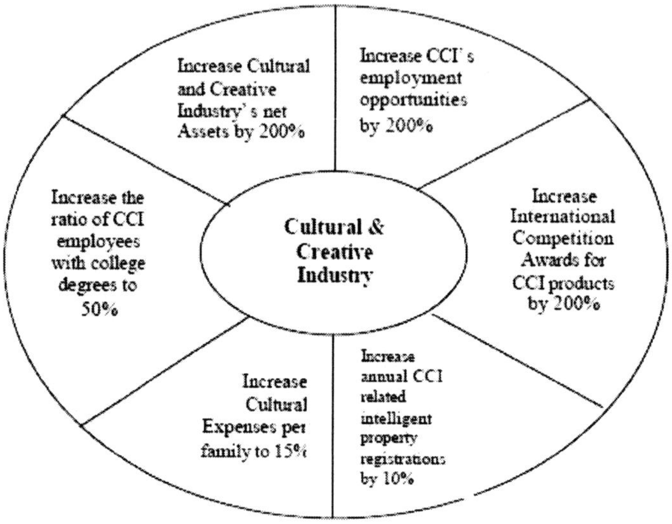

EU Views Cultural Enterprises as Playing Key Role in Balancing Europe's Social Development

In 1996 members of the European Commission signed a policy communiqué regarding cultural cooperation, regional development and promotion of employment opportunities. In the view of troubles stemming from structural transformations in traditional industry and employment, the characteristic types of employment to which cultural enterprises and regional ecological / ecology-friendly development have given rise have, in Europe's major countries, become important as avenues for new business and job opportunities. Through an synergistic mix of traditional cultural and innovative elements, the joint efforts of Europe's public and private sectors — most notably including the EU government's allocation of resources — have resulted in public policies relating to cultural and innovation enterprises becoming more long-term and integrated in nature (European Commission, 1996). The content of such policies may indeed serve as important references for Taiwan's policy making regarding the development of cultural and innovative enterprises. (Luna Liu, 2003)

Study Notes Importance on Non-Profit Creative Industry

John Stark (2007) indicated Non-Profit Arts Yields Annual $77.6 Million. Americans for the Arts announced at its National Conference in Las Vegas last week that the non-profit arts and cultures industry creates $166 billion in economic activity and 5.7 million jobs annually. In Santa Barbara alone the non-profit arts and culture industry creates $77.6 million in local spending, $41.4 million of those dollars coming from event-related spending by the audiences and the remaining $36.2 million from event organizers. In addition, the non-profit arts and culture industry creates generates 2,288 fulltime jobs in the Santa Barbara area which adds up to $41.57 million in income and 7.62 million in local and State tax revenue. After attending the Las Vegas conference, County Arts Commission Executive Director Ginny Brush noted the importance of this sector of Santa Barbara life. "These figures will do much to shift the perception of the arts viewed 'as frills' to acknowledge the vital economic role of the creative class plays in communities," Brush said in a prepared statement. Nationwide the non-profit arts and culture industry creates $104.2 billion in residential income which leads to $7.9 billion in local tax revenue, $9.1 billion in State tax revenue and $12.6 billion in Federal tax revenue. The figures are the results of the most in-depth study of the arts and culture industry and its economic impact of the United States ever conducted. The study was conducted in 156 communities that reflect all 50 states and the District of Columbia in areas both urban and rural. Researchers gathered comprehensive attendance and expenditure data from 6,080 non-profit art and culture organizations.

Keys to Multi-Culturalism and a Sustainable Taiwan Economy

Luna Liu (2003) indicated, "The impact of economic globalization in particular has provided us with the opportunity to understand the role which innovative cultural enterprises can play, as well as the importance of redefining and further developing our native culture". Furthermore, she pointed out "In consideration of practical realities, cultural innovation can directly and indirectly create many new employment opportunities: It can encourage the creation of new small and middle-size enterprises and stimulate technical innovation, in addition to stimulating the development of related, peripheral industry. Thereby, cultural innovation can significantly stabilize domestic employment opportunities. In this connection, it is worth noting that new, integrated ways of thinking about policies relating to ecological protection and economic activity — particularly regarding the redefinition of regional and environmental interests and the renovation of smaller municipalities — serve as indices for the development of innovative cultural enterprises. Under the mounting competitive pressures accompanying globalization, the rich diversity of cultural elements with which Taiwan is blessed can be incorporated into marketing and strategy-making mechanisms, thereby injecting a new vitality into our society and economic system, and creating new opportunities for the development of our cultural enterprises and small-town regional economies. Moreover, inasmuch as cultural enterprises are typically dependent upon elements of local culture and local talent, because they are oriented toward both domestic and foreign consumption, and because they involve effective, long-term cooperation among local resource providers, they are broadly beneficial to the enhancement of regional development and the quality of regional tourism". (Luna Liu, 2003)

Integrated Thinking and Resources on Innovative Cultural Enterprises

According to Luna Liu (2003), "While culture is founded most fundamentally on creative activity, cultural enterprises must take into consideration practical, economic factors in conjunction with artistic creativity. It is only through doing so that such cultural enterprises as product design, radio and television broadcasting, and the music recording industry can have sustainable, stable operations. Development of public support for the fine arts and design arts is regarded as an indispensable requisite for the cultivation of cultural enterprises". She further indicated, "Given that cultural enterprises do indeed present opportunities for economic development, there is a great need for new funding as well as for professional training. The study suggests Taiwan's official policy directions include: the promotion of social integration, regional development, cultural development and educational development; the establishment of a center for developing cultural enterprises; investment of resources in reinforcing the spirit of entrepreneurship and innovative concepts; and nurturing the development of new types of cultural-industry techniques. Such goals first require adequate funding arrangements. Public funding, together with coordination of presently available private financial services and cultural demands, can serve as the initial step in developing cultural industry. Beyond this, it is also necessary to encourage private funding of cultural activities, as for example, through company sponsorships. Further, we should erect a framework for cooperation between business, government and researchers which can provide guidance for policy-making, and help all sectors of Taiwan society to come to a new realization of our present strengths and weaknesses so that we may make solid progress in cultural development."

In addition, she indicated, "A penetrating study of the effectiveness of promoting innovative cultural enterprises must take into consideration not only the matters of carrying forward the structural transformation of our country's economic activity and the diversification of employment opportunities and new businesses; further, it must give thought to transformation of the limitations of the one-sided process of government-initiated public policy-making. This entails the integration of efforts by the various government agencies and the close-knit coordination of the public and private sectors. Because the promoting the development of innovative cultural enterprises presents a great number of opportunities as well as challenges, in addition to depending upon the vitality and innovative input of the private sector, its promotion is further in need of related government agencies' pooling of resources and financial investment" (Luna Liu, 2003).

Moeasmea (2004) indicated, the cultural and creative industry could be divided into the handicraft industry, where commercialization is relatively easy to implement, and the "cultural economy" where this is less true. The following section examines ways in which the government and private-sector companies can work together to promote the development of the cultural and creative industry.

Commercialization in the Handicrafts Industry

According to moeasmea (2004), if a maker of handicrafts wishes to transform their business from a small-scale workshop into a fully-fledged company, first of all they need to start thinking about costs and profits. If the gross profit margin is less than 50%, then the company may find that it is unable to bear the cost of R&D and distribution channel development. One also needs to consider whether the company's products are sufficiently innovative and distinctive for brand development to be successful, or whether the company possesses some particular edge in terms of technology, or has a niche market that it can develop. The transformation from workshop into company is bound to involve major upheavals in terms of personnel and management, and if external funding sources are tapped then the company will find itself under heavy pressure with respect to profitability and market development. If a company feels that establishing its own brand right away is too risky, then an alternative strategy would be that adopted by Seagull – undertaking ODM/OEM work for leading vendors, or licensing one's products to other companies while insisting that they continue to bear your trademark. In this way, companies can maintain a steady flow of profits while slowly building up brand recognition and waiting until the time is ripe to move into branded manufacturing.

The "Industrialization of Culture"

According to moeasmea (2004), the process whereby culture becomes industrialized can be divided into several stages: The "original idea stage," the "innovation formation stage," the "start-up stage," and the final "industrialization stage." The requirements imposed by these stages, and the restrictions relating to the provision of assistance by the government result in a situation where the "industrialization of culture" is best suited to those companies that possess innovation, originality, their own brands, and the capabilities needed for successful commercialization.

METHODOLOGY

Research Design

This research is qualitative in orientation, exploratory in approach and interpretative in nature. An interpretative study is suggested for more subjective, organizational and managerial research questions, particularly where concerned with industry practice (Galliers, 1991; Lee, 1991; Walsham, 1995). The research method is mainly based on the quantitative research and will be divided into two parts. The first part is the secondary data from literature review about KM and cultural innovation. The second part is to carry out the primary data by doing the interview. This paper describes a piece of qualitative research involving one case study, which have been developed from a series of questionnaires of interview and in-depth interviews.

Data Collection

The study collects data by consisting of documents and corporate website of the case study companies, analysis of secondary data, questionnaires of interview and in-depth interviews. The interview questionnaires will be sent out about 20. Individual in-depth interviews are chosen as the main method for the collection of data as they allow the respondent to remain anonymous and provide the opportunity to probe and clarify points arising. It is also the most practical way of getting participation from busy executives and managers. Written notes are used in this phase. A two-page interview questionnaire will be developed, typically the subjects represented in the interviews covered directors or managers of the case company. The present study builds on five in-depth interviews with cultural innovation related directors or managers in the fields of CEO office, IT, HRM, Marketing, R&D. The interviews are semi-structured and informal with a topic guide to provide some structure and consistency to the interviews. The topic guide is used to give a direction to the interview, but it is not used as a straitjacket and respondents are encouraged to talk at length within and around the topic areas. In addition follow-up questions are used in the course of the interviews, where necessary, to get respondents to clarify or develop their responses. All interviews undertaken are recorded and transcribed. The transcripts are then coded with concepts and transformed and simplified in order to facilitate display, analysis and comparison along the lines recommended by Miles and Huberman (1994). The coding is revised and developed as the research progressed. Displays are developed for the different concepts, summarizing the response of each respondent.

Sample

According to international organizations such as United Nations Educational, Scientific and Cultural Organization (UNESCO) and the General Agreement on Tariffs and Trade (GATT), cultural industry (creative industry) combine the creation, production, and distribution of goods and services that are cultural in nature and usually protected by intellectual property rights. Cultural industry worldwide have adapted to the new digital technologies and to the arrival of national, regional and international (de) regulatory policies. According to above, the study defines cultural innovation industry as "develops new insights into situations and applies innovative solutions to make organizational improvements; creates a work environment that encourages creative thinking and innovation; designs and implements new or cutting-edge programs/processes." The cultural innovation industry for the case study was selected based on the above definitions. Twenty (20) cultural innovation industry from the following broad categories –textual, music, art, museum, television, film production and publishing, as well as crafts and design were considered. The initial questionnaire guide was sent to those twenty firms.

Figure 2. An integrated innovation model in the cultural innovation industry

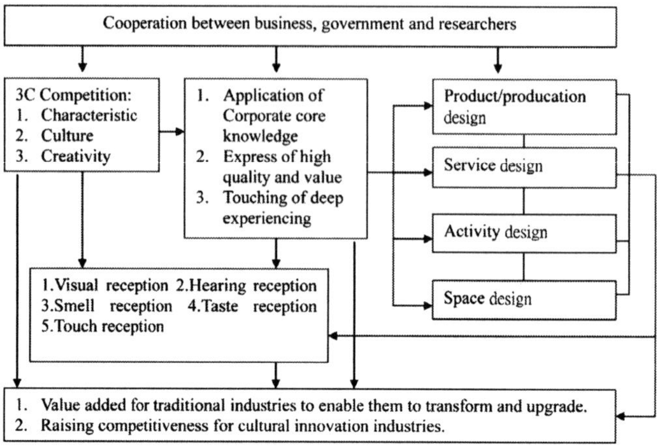

Based on the responses one firm was selected. One larger cultural innovation companies (70–200 employees) was selected. This diversity amongst the organisation should help to map the basic innovation phases, activities and routines carried out by cultural innovation organisation in practice. The contact details of the above companies will be taken from public sources.

An Integrated Innovation Model in the Cultural Innovation Industry in Taiwan

According to comprehensive literature review, the study proposed an integrated innovation model in the cultural innovation industry as Figure 2:

The theoretical framework developed in this paper needs to be compared to practitioners' perspectives. The following section will adopt a case study to examine the framework.

CASE STUDIES ANALYSIS

The case study analyzes a successful enterprise in the cultural innovation and creative industry. The following sections examine the case firm: Liuli Gongfang due to above integrated innovation model in the cultural innovation industry, explore how it grew from a small workshop into one of the world's leading glassware makers.

Development of Liuli Gongfang

Liuli Gongfang was established in Tamsui in Taiwan in 1987. The founders Yang Huei-Shan and Chang Yi once were a famous actress and a famous director in the movies. On the basis of love to folk art culture and the insistence of life faith, Yang Huei-Shan and Chang Yi resolutely retired at the height of their movie career, threw themselves into modern lazurite art which was not popular then in Taiwan and established the first lazurite art studio- Liuli Gongfang. "Liuli" was the name of glass in ancient China. The reason why the studio is named "Liuli" is that the founders want to convey craft beauty and emphasize the belonging and existence to history and art through the process of lazurite study and creation. The ideal of Liuli Gongfang is to create exquisite virtu by using "Pate-de-verre" as a basic skill and have place in lazurite art that is flourishing in the world except for in Taiwan. During the past twenty years, Liuli Gongfang's works have been invited to display in many countries such as Japan, America, England, Italy, France, German, South

Figure 3. Liuli Gongfang museum in china. Source: http://www.liulichinamuseum.com/

Africa etc. The style and idea of Liuli Gongfang's works make them become the representative of lazurite art in Taiwan, and receive the recognition of being collected in the most important museum in the world.

As of 2008, Liuli Gongfang employed 900 employees in 67 locations around the world, including 3 locations in United States: Los Angeles, San Francisco, and New York. Their successes have earned them the moniker of "founders of contemporary Chinese glass art" and "the Georg Jensen of the glassware world" (Freundl, Diana, 2005). Works created by Liuli Gongfang have become part of the permanent collection of London's Victoria and Albert Museum as well as the Palace Museum in Beijing's Forbidden City (Xu, Wei, 2006). People First Party chairman James Soong, during his visit to Mainland China (the second of a major Republic of China politician figure, after that of Lien Chan), presented People's Republic of China President Hu Jintao with a Liuli Gongfang sculpture; Hu gave him Jingde porcelain in return (Eastern Television News, 2005).

LIULI CHINA Museum

According to liulichinamuseum.com (2006), "We do not treat this place as a museum. It does not have that cold and solemn feel people come to expect from such an establishment. We wish for it to be filled with light, with music, with moving images – we want it to tell a story. As we look upon the commanding display of international Liuli art, as the various incarnations of Liuli appear before our eyes, the feeling we feel deep in our hearts is pure joy".

What is culture? Liuli is our tool, urging us to see clearer and to dig deeper. For Chang Yi, Loretta Hui-shan Yang and the twenty years of Liuligongfang, it has all been about the hopes, the courage and the dreams that came true. Located in Xintiandi, Shanghai, LIULI CHINA Museum is a striking and relevant meeting point of the world. With one wall constructed entirely of 12,000 Liuli tiles, LIULI CHINA Museum has accomplished its goal, loud enough to shake the very earth! The realization of a 20-year dream – welcome to LIULI CHINA MUSEUM. (Chang YI Founders LIULI CHINA Museum)

April 29th, 2006 marked the birth of LIULI CHINA, China's first Liuli art museum. The museum is formed in tripartition: ancient Chinese Liuli, contemporary Liuli art by Loretta Hui-shan Yang, and international Liuli art. Every piece represented at LIULI CHINA is a splendor in its own right. Liuligongfang's Chang Yi and Loretta Hui-shan Yang founded LIULI CHINA with the vision to enhance the place of Liuli in Chinese art and culture. The distinguishing image of the museum is the Liuli wall comprised of 12,000 unique pieces of Liuli bricks that evoke an image of a "Inscription tablet" - symbolic of Liuligongfang's 20 year history. Each Liuli is handmade, no two are alike; as a whole they illustrate the dedication of perpetual creation as upheld by LIULI CHINA and Liuligongfang. LIULI CHINA surpasses the scope of Liuligongfang. Not only does it pay homage to the history of Chinese Liuli, it acknowledges the contributions and eminence of Liuli as a contemporary art medium throughout the world (liulichinamuseum.com, 2006).

LIULI CHINA has become a "station" where each work serves as an imprint of an artist's creative journey. The station becomes a space to rethink, adjust, and gear up for the next expedition of excellence. It is also a "salon" for intellectual discussion, inspiring dialogue between artists, spectators, and professionals alike. LIULI CHINA is a "window" for learning ; both Chinese and international, historical and contemporary, visitors are exposed to a vast variety of Liuli art. Within the first exhibition hall is a replica of the oldest known Liuli artifact, an ear cup from Chinese Western Han Dynasty (4 B.C.). Originally cited as the oldest Pate-de-verre glass artifact, it is to Liuligongfang and LIULI CHINA the representation of the extensive history of Chinese Liuli. It is also what inspired the "LIULI CHINA" theme of the Liuligongfang Museum. LIULI CHINA - an international standard. (Tang Si-fu Director LIULI CHINA Museum)

The company began life as a small workshop located in Tanshui, Taipei County. Initially, Chang and Yang had just seven employees, and they had to develop their production technology more or less from scratch. Glassware manufacturing is an R&D-intensive industry, but one involving small-volume production of a large number of different products, and it was difficult to find experts who were interested in, or had the capabilities needed for, working in this industry. Liuli Gongfang had to feel its way by trial and error, and, spending a large amount of money on R&D, the company found itself heavily in debt. However, through sheer perseverance and constant willingness to learn, the Liuli Gongfang gradually found its feet. The company had played a leading role in the development of modern Chinese glassware making, and had succeeded in developing its own distinctive brand image (moeasmea, 2004).

In considering the factors behind Liuli Gongfang's success, it is necessary to focus on the following areas: Space design, Application of Corporate core knowledge, Production design, Touching of deep experiencing, Product design, Characteristic, Culture and Creativity, Express of high quality and value, Service design, Activity design strategy. The study will discuss and analyze in the following sections.

Space Design

According to the website of liuli.com and 104info.com, Liuli Gongfang strives to promote its creation space of Pate-de-verre to a scope and a level which have not been reached in the world, and it is generally acknowledged as the best Pate-de-verre studio in the world. Yang Huei-Shan and Chang Yi are regarded as the founders and pioneers of modern Chinese lazurite art. Liuli Gongfang is engaged in building a new culture creation image of China lazurite art. On the basis of "creating works which are good for human heart without end", with ethical, educational and wholesome works and through the process of lazurite study and creation, Liuli Gongfang expects to awake the precious value of Chinese national tradition in modern society to an extent, to provide constructive direction of Chinese culture regeneration in the future, and to bring Chinese lazurite craft into a broader stage. In late 1990, Liuli Gongfang held its first exhibition in the Eslite art gallery. This exhibition marked the first step in the company's efforts to promote the art of glass-making in Taiwan and develop a local market for its products; at around the same time, Liuli Gongfang also began to market its glassware overseas. After more than a decade of effort, in 2001 Liuli Gongfang had combined domestic and overseas sales of more than NT$700 million. By the end of 2002, the company had over 50 outlets and two factories, its capitalization exceeded NT$150 million, and it had more than 800 employees, including 12–14 R&D personnel. Liuli Gongfang had been invited to exhibit its products in Japan, the US, the UK, Italy, Germany and South Africa, and several of its pieces had been acquired by leading international museums to form part of their permanent collections (moeasmea, 2004).

Furthermore, LIULI CHINA Museum welcomes everyone to fulfill their revolutionary Virtual travel fantasy from May 12, 2008. Embark on a new dimension in the Virtual LIULI CHINA Museum-- A new interactive and explorative art space. Virtual LIULI CHINA Museum quests in pertaining their passion of LIULI Glass by simulating virtual experience; providing the best learning environment from the technological domain's three-dimensional space. The visual discoveries are a breakthrough experience in cyber-communication. Virtual LIULI CHINA Museum, will lead the audience through a narrated multimedia presentation with interaction – to new experiences far beyond expectations! (liulichinamuseum.com, 2006).

Application of Corporate Core Knowledge

According to moeasmea (2004), "The key factor was the lead that Liuli Gongfang established over its competitors in the area of technology. The Core Technology – Lost-wax Casting Due to the restrictions imposed by the equipment available to them, in the early days Liuli Gongfang had to rely on glass-blowing technology. However, using this technology they found it very difficult to increase their production capacity. Another consideration was that glass-blowing technology had been in existence for several hundred years in many countries around the world, and as a late entrant, it seemed unlikely that Liuli Gongfang would be able to achieve any real success in this area. Furthermore, glass-blowing techniques were not suited to the uniquely Chinese style that Yi Chang was trying to develop. Liuli Gongfang therefore began to look for new ways of making glass. The method the company ultimately adopted – "patte-de-verre" lost-wax casting – provided maximum malleability and made it possible to achieve a high level of precision in replication and mass production. Using this new method, the company was able to produce glassware of exquisite beauty that conformed to the Liuli Gongfang ideal of reviving the art of Chinese glass making" (moeasmea, 2004).

Production Design

Yang and Chang developed a comprehensive production process based on methods that they had developed themselves. The key factor was the lower production costs that resulted from locating production in Mainland China. Reducing Production Costs by Establishing a Factory in Mainland China In 1995, Liuli Gongfang established its second factory, located in the Qibao Industrial Park in the Minxing District of Shanghai. The lower production costs of this new production facility had a significant positive impact on the company's operational performance (moeasmea, 2004).

Touching of Deep Experiencing

Hui-Shan Yang shoots in 123 movie's processes, was almost equal to that has attempted 123 individual life experiences, she felt very sincerely actually has one kind of heaviness. 20 years' glass artistic creation, when the technical question no longer is one kind puzzles, she starts to ask herself, what wants to say? Movie's experience and artistic creation's experience, turns an overall experience suddenly, she studies slowly, originally the very major part of life, is not joyful. Drama's ingredient of Movie hopes to make those unhappy life shift and sublimation by another kind of model. Buddhism's idea and goal is the same, it hoped that you have the wisdom, understood the phenomenon in life, lives, old, gets sick, dies, the resentful hatred meeting, the love to leave depart, to ask not to, the five human attributes be prosperous, is actually very natural. If possible, art is also hope that through a medium, lets each person feel the different appearance of life. Hope to make oneself happy and joyfully and enables everybody happy as well. She does greatest effort to share her learning experience with everybody.

According to moeasmea (2004), "The main focus in Liuli Gongfang's marketing strategy has been on building up name recognition and overall brand image via touching of deep experiencing. The company's products, which are distinctively "Chinese," are produced in limited editions; in addition, Liuli Gongfang has worked hard to develop international distribution channels. The fame that both Hui-Shan Yang and Yi Chang enjoyed in Taiwan helped Liuli Gongfang to secure media exposure when the company was first getting off the ground. The media and the general public rapidly became familiar with the concept of "artistic glassware"; this was an important factor in the company's early development. Liuli Gongfang was well aware of the importance of overall brand image; its marketing concepts, strategies and implementation displayed a high level of consistency. At both the company's own direct outlets and department store outlets, Liuli Gongfang personnel handle the sales operations themselves. Detailed rules govern everything from store layout and product packaging through to customer reception and product presentation" (moeasmea, 2004).

Product Design, Characteristic, Culture and Creativity

Liuli Gongfang took an ancient technique and has turned it into a refined scientific process. The main objective of Liuli Gongfang's research and development department is to go abroad to study at international glass art schools, and to research and develop superior techniques. After only thirteen years of development, Liuli Gongfang is already one of the best pate-de-verre glass studios in the world. Products with a distinctly "Chinese culture" character: Liuli Gongfang's ultimate objective has always been to create glassware with a unique "ethnic" style. With Chinese cultural coordinates as the foundation, Liuli Gongfang has developed its own modern artistic vocabulary to express the essence of Chinese culture, and their products thus have a distinct "cultural" aspect to them that has proved extremely attractive on both domestic and international markets. In positioning the products, Yi Chang has tried to focus on the philosophy and the emotions they evoke, rather than on the objects themselves. With this in mind, he developed Liuli Gongfang's "product explanations." The idea is to express what inspired each piece in a few succinct sentences. For glassware enthusiasts from a different cultural background, these explanations help to give the pieces a whole new level of meaning (moeasmea, 2004).

Express of High Quality and Value

In line with the emphasis that Liuli Gongfang's corporate culture places on "integrity," the company has never gone in for large-volume production or efforts to maximize profits. Instead, its products are all issued in limited editions. Before production begins, each step in the production process is rated for difficulty; these scores are then added together to provide a basis for calculating the unit price, and the total amount being invested in that particular piece is divided by the unit price to determine the number of pieces that will be produced. Once the agreed number of pieces has been made, production is terminated and the molds are destroyed. Each piece has engraved on its base the serial number of that particular piece and the total number that were produced. This limited edition strategy helps to maintain the value of Liuli Gongfang glassware, creating the potential for pieces to increase in value after purchase; it also encourages constant innovation by the Liuli Gongfang team (moeasmea, 2004).

Service Design

For servicing global customer, Liuli Gongfang develops international distribution channels. Liuli Gongfang held its first overseas exhibition in 1992, at the Mitsukoshi Art Gallery in the Ginza district of Tokyo. Since then, the company has held exhibitions in Italy, the US, Germany, Singapore, Switzerland, South Africa, the Czech Republic and the UK. Today, besides the company's 20 outlets in Taiwan, Liuli Gongfang has a distribution network that covers Mainland China, Singapore, Europe and the US. In Mainland China, there are now more than 20 Liuli Gongfang galleries in Shanghai, Beijing, Hangzhou, Dalian and Harbin. These Mainland China outlets now account for more than 50% of total sales revenues, and sales are continuing to grow rapidly (moeasmea, 2004).

Moreover, Luili Gongfang attaches great importance to the cultivation of human talent. In order to boost the capabilities of its employees for giving the best service to its customers, Liuli Gongfang employs experts to collect and collate the latest information on new glassware-making developments from all over the world and to study the latest pieces by leading designers. Liuli Gongfang spent a considerable sum of money to establish a library (open to the general public) on the third floor of its Tanshui production facility, containing several hundred books relating to the arts, culture and philosophy. In order to give company employees the opportunity to learn new skills and to achieve a higher level of interaction with the international glass-making community, Liuli Gongfang also sends employees to study overseas on a regular basis (moeasmea, 2004).

Activity Design Strategy

In order to integrate the art of glassware into people's everyday lives, Liuli Gongfang has begun to expand into architecture, interior design and lifestyle products (such as sets of glasses and light fittings). Towards the end of 2001, Liuli Gongfang opened the TMSK restaurant, the first restaurant of its kind in Shanghai, in Xin Tiandi luxury shopping center. Later, Liuli Gongfang opened the TMSK restaurant in Hong Kong (Figure 4). TMSK uses glassware for all of its interior furnishings, and features a glass lotus pond, glass lamps and a glass-embellished dome, etc. With its unique atmosphere, TMSK has become a favorite meeting place for Shanghai and HK trendsetters, particularly foreigners. By making glassware part of the lives of Shanghai's and HK's elite, Liuli Gongfang has succeeded in raising the visibility of its products, and has created a new source of revenue (moeasmea, 2004).

IMPLICATIONS OF THE CASE STUDY

The study examines the case firm: Liuli Gongfang due to above integrated innovation model in the cultural innovation industry, explore how it grew from a small workshop into one of the world's leading glassware makers. Development of Liuli Gongfang: through sheer perseverance and constant willingness to learn, the Liuli Gongfang gradually found its feet. The company had played a leading role in the development of modern Chinese glassware making, and had succeeded in developing its own distinctive brand image. In considering

Figure 4. TMSK restaurant in Hong Kong. Source: http://www.tmsk.com/

the factors behind Liuli Gongfang's success, it is necessary to focus on the following areas:

1. **Space design:** This exhibition marked the first step in the company's efforts to promote the art of glass-making in Taiwan and develop a local market for its products; at around the same time, Liuli Gongfang also began to market its glassware overseas.
2. **Application of Corporate core knowledge:** The Core Technology – Lost-wax Casting Due to the restrictions imposed by the equipment available to them. The method the company ultimately adopted – "patte-de-verre" lost-wax casting – provided maximum malleability and made it possible to achieve a high level of precision in replication and mass production.
3. **Production design:** Yang and Chang developed a comprehensive production process based on methods that they had developed themselves. The key factor was the lower production costs that resulted from locating production in Mainland China.
4. **Touching of deep experiencing:** The main focus in Liuli Gongfang's marketing strategy has been on building up name recognition and overall brand image via touching of deep experiencing.Liuli Gongfang was well aware of the importance of overall brand image; its marketing concepts, strategies and implementation displayed a high level of consistency.
5. **Product design, Characteristic, Culture and Creativity:** Liuli Gongfang's ultimate objective has always been to create glassware with a unique "ethnic" style. With Chinese cultural coordinates as the foundation, Liuli Gongfang has developed its own modern artistic vocabulary to express the essence of Chinese culture, and their products thus have a distinct "cultural" aspect to them that has proved extremely attractive on both domestic and international markets.
6. **Express of high quality and value:** its products are all issued in limited editions. Before production begins, each step in the production process is rated for difficulty; these scores are then added together to provide a basis for calculating the unit price, and the total amount being invested in that particular piece is divided by the unit price to determine the number of pieces that will be produced. Once the agreed number of pieces has been made, production is terminated and the molds are destroyed. This limited edition strategy helps to maintain the value of Liuli Gongfang glassware, creating the potential for pieces to increase in value after purchase; it also encourages constant innovation by the Liuli Gongfang team.
7. **Service design:** For servicing global customer, Liuli Gongfang develops international distribution channels. Moreover, Liuli Gongfang attaches great importance to the cultivation of human talent. In order to boost the capabilities of its employees for giving the best service to its customers.
8. **Activity design strategy:** In order to integrate the art of glassware into people's everyday lives, Liuli Gongfang has begun to expand into architecture, interior design and lifestyle products. By making glassware part of the lives of Shanghai's and HK's elite, Liuli Gongfang has succeeded in raising the visibility of its products, and has created a new source of revenue.

FUTURE RESEARCH DIRECTION

The research limitations are that to generalize the usefulness of the proposed model, more cases need to be analyzed. Although the model presented in this paper has made integrated perspectives on culture innovation implementation in one case company, it has to be pointed out that this paper has serious limitations in that it is basically a case study of one organization. The arguments of this paper, before they can be generalized, must be corroborated further with other cultural innovation organizations with various strategies and other specificities.

In the near future, the study will develop more complete and practical integrated innovation model for various cultural innovation industries and future researchers via more case studies. Additional research is needed to provide managers and consultants with important perspectives to consider when implementing cultural innovation programs and practices in their organizations. The results from such research could also benefit academics by providing select factors to focus on in future studies. This research will give more in-depth proposition to practitioners in cultural innovation to achieve successfully implementation of innovation programs, and will provide a framework in understanding why certain innovation initiatives fail and how that can be improved. This will benefit both academics and practitioners.

CONCLUSION

This chapter describes the procedures of promotions formulated for the development of the Cultural and Creative Industry, including definition, scope, development, strategies and government assistance. The paper is intended to give the general public an idea of the chain effects expected to bring for the society by the development of the Cultural and Creative Industry.

First of all, the study through literature review and content analysis to develop a research framework: integrated innovation model. Secondly, the study through a case study to develop a more complete and practical integrated model and researches propositions for practitioners in cultural innovation organizations and future researchers, the study provides managers and consultants with important perspectives to consider when implementing cultural innovation programs and practices in their organizations. The results from such research could also benefit academics by providing select factors to focus on in future studies. The study gives some in-depth propositions to practitioners in cultural innovation to achieve successfully implementation of innovation projects. It provides a framework in understanding why certain innovation initiatives fail and how that can be improved. This benefits both academics and practitioners.

This research was focused on case study based on qualitative analysis, literature review and depth interview, discussing inner management and external relations in Liuli Gongfang, in order to offer the concrete suggestion of development in the future. In accordance with this case, Council for Cultural Affairs pursues its ideal in the scope of the capability, communicating with each other could obtain the trust and cooperation.

Government's role as active integrator to promote culture innovation industry: A key topic of concern regarding culture innovation industry is how to help them advance into new domestic and international markets and effectively operate and manage their businesses. One objective of this study is to explore what role governments should play and how they may intervene in an appropriate, timely manner. Examine the various elements in "cultural enterprise systems," how governments take the initiative in playing a bridging, facilitating role — bringing together potential workers, local organizers and "know-how" providers to build a sound environment for development, how governments facilitate the commercial systemization of culturally oriented activity with respect to marketing, operations and management.

Governments have to bear a heavy burden of responsibility for pressing forward systematization of their commercial operations in developing cooperative partnerships with cultural enterprises. This study indicated, how governments bring together and organize their various administrative agencies in an effort to assure the effectiveness of cultural innovation enterprise operations.

Definitely, government coordination with cultural enterprises poses a number of difficult challenges such as, regarding to the passage of new intellectual property rights laws and the many practical details relating to the development of small and middle-size enterprises, each of which must be dealt with in a thorough manner.

REFERENCES

action service industry). Retrieved August 5, 2005, from http://www.amcham.com.tw/dl/service_industry _english.doc

Bright, J. R. (1969). Some management lessons from technological innovation research. *Long Range Planning*, *2*(1), 36–41. doi:10.1016/0024-6301(69)90022-3

Central News Agency. (February 14, 2009). *Government to continue supporting cultural industry.*

CEPD. (2004a). *Service industry development guidelines and action plan (guidelines and*

CEPD. (2004b). *Cultural and creative service industry development guidelines and action*

Council for Cultural Affairs (CCA). (May 15, 2009). *Government OKs cultural innovation plan.* The China Post. Taipei.

Council for Cultural Affairs Creative Industry Project Center. (2005). *CCACIPC.* Retrieved from http://english.cca.gov.tw

Council of Cultural Affairs. (2003). *International Symposium on Creative industry-a global thought and future action,* Taiwan.

Cultural and Creative Industry Promotion Organization. (2005a). *What is cultural & creative industry?* Retrieved August 5, 2005, from http://www.cci.org.tw/portal/plan/what.asp/

Cultural and Creative Industry Promotion Organization. (2005b). *Introduction of the cultural and creative industry plan.* Retrieved August 5, 2005, from http://www.cci.org.tw/portal/plan /what.asp/

Cultural and Creative Industry Promotion Team. (2004). *Scope of the cultural and creative industry in Taiwan and the administrative Agencies.* Ministry of Economic Affairs.

DCMS. (2005). *Creative industry.* Department for Culture, Media and Sport. Retrieved September 5, 2005, from http://www.culture.gov.uk/creative_industry/

Department of Economic Development, Taipei City Government. (May 14, 2008). Cabinet approves plan to boost cultural and creative industry. Central News Agency.

Drucker, P. F. (1994). *Innovation and entrepreneurship: Practice and principles.* Oxford: Butterworth Heinemann.

DSDTI. (August 5, 2005). Development of creativity is big business-a framework for the future. Queensland government, Department of State Development, Trade and Innovation. Retrieved on November 11, 2005, from http://www.sdi.qld.gov.au/dsdweb/v3/guis/templates/content/gui_cue_cntnhtml.cfm?id=2253

Eastern Television News. (August 1, 2005). Hu Jintao gives Soong Jingde porcelain; Soong gives Liuli Gongfang creation in return. Retrieved from http://www.ettoday.com/2005/05/12/11345-1789683.htm.

European Commission. (1996). *A policy communiqué: EU views cultural enterprises as playing key role in balancing Europe's social development.* European Commission.

EUSA-Taiwan. (2003). *EUSA.* Retrieved from http//: eusa-taiwan.org

Freundl, D. (2005). *The way of Liuli.* Retrieved on January 11, 2008, from http://www.taipeitimes.com/News/feat/archives/2005/06/02/2003257650

Galliers, R. D. (1991). Information Systems strategic planning, myths, reality, and guidelines for successful implementation systems planning. *European Journal of Information Systems*, *1*(1), 55–64. doi:10.1057/ejis.1991.7

Gongfang, L. (2009). *Liuliu.* Retrieved from http://www.liuli.com/E_index01.htm

Government Information Office. (2002). *Challenge 2008 National Development Plan.* Retrieved from http://www.gio.gov.tw/taiwan-website/4-oa/20020521/2002052101.html

HKTDC. (2002). *Creative industry in Hong Kong.* Hong Kong Trade Development Council.

Huang, K.-N. (2008). *Museum, tourism and the culture industry in Taiwan.* National Taiwan University of Art, 2008 International Museum management commission: NZ annual meeting report.

International Intellectual Property Alliance. (2007). *Copyright industry in the U.S. economy: The 2006 Report.* International Intellectual Property Alliance.

KOCCA. (2005). *White Paper on Korean culture industry.* Ministry of Culture and Tourism.

LCM. (2006). *Liuli China Museum.* Retrieved from www.liulichinamuseum.com

Lee Allen, S. (1991). Integrating positivist and interpretive approaches to organizational research. *Organization Science*, *2*(4), 342–365. doi:10.1287/orsc.2.4.342

Liu, L. (2003). *Challenges and opportunities presented by globalization—development of new cultural enterprises in Taiwan and lessons to be learned from Europe.* Member, European Union study association-Taiwan.

Miles, M. B., & Hubeman, A. M. (1994). *Qualitative data analysis: An expanded source book.* Sage Publishing.

Moeasmea. (2004). *White Paper on SMEs in Taiwan: The development of the cultural and creative industry in Taiwan and its significance for SMEs.* Retrieved from http://www.moeasmea.gov.tw/public/Attachment/65161430571.pdf

NOIE. (2005). *The National Office for the Information Economy.* Australia. Retrieved September 5, 2005, from http://www.noie.gov.au/

NZIER. (2002). *Creative industry in New Zealand economic contribution.* NZ Institute for Economic Research (Inc.).

Office for the Promotion of Cultural and Creative Industry. (2007). *Index of the development of cultural and creative industry in leading countries.* Ministry of Economic Affairs.

plan. Retrieved August 5, 2005, from http://www.cepd.gov.tw/upload/SECT/Industry/008@537202.744030078@.doc

Stark, J. (2007). *Study notes importance on non-profit creative industry: Non-profit arts yields annual $77.6 million.* Retrieved from http://www.independent.com/news/2007/jun/14/non-profit-arts-yields-annual-776-million/

Sundbo, J. (1998). *The organization of innovations in services.* Frediksberg, Denmark: Roskilide University Press.

Switzerland-based Institute. (2006). *Taiwan's competitive strength comes from its outstanding hi-tech infrastructure, business management, and labor force.* Management Development world competitiveness report.

TAITRA. (2008). Creative *Taiwan 2008: Cultural and creative background.* Taiwan External Trade Development Council. Retrieved from http://www.taipeitradeshows.com.tw/creativetaiwan/visitor/backgrounder.shtml

TMSK. (2010). *TMSK*. Retrieved from http://www.tmsk.com/

UHK. (2004). *A study on Hong Kong creativity index interim report*. Centre for Cultural Policy Research, the University of Hong Kong.

UNESCO. (2000). *What do we understand by culture industry?* Retrieved March 1, 2005, from http://www.unesco.org/culture/industry/trade/html_eng/question1.shtml

Walsham, G. (1995). Interpretive case studies in IS research: Nature and method. *European Journal of Information Systems*, *4*, 74–81. doi:10.1057/ejis.1995.9

Wei, X. (2006). *Transparently animated*. Retrieved on January 11, 2008, from http://english.eastday.com/eastday/englishedition/features/userobject1ai1806146.html

104Workforce Bank. (2000). *Effective manpower-department distribution chart*. Retrieved September 5, 2005, from http://www.104.com.tw/cfdocs/2000/analysis/graph/man_user4.gif/

Executive Yuan. (2004). *Major social indicators of selected countries*.

ADDITIONAL READING

Beyers, W. B. (2002). Culture, Services and Regional Development. *The Service Industry Journal, 22*(1).

Caves, R. E. (2000). *Creative Industries: Contracts Between Art and Commerce*. Cambridge, Mass. London: Harvard University Press.

DCMS. (2006). DCMS Creative Economy Programme Regional Development Agencies' draft Working Paper, 7 June 2006 at http://www.cep.culture.gov.uk/index.cfm?fuseaction=main.viewBlogEntry &intMTEntryID=2977

Drake, G. (2003). This Place Gives me Space: Place and creativity in the creative industry. *Geoforum*, *34*, 511–524. doi:10.1016/S0016-7185(03)00029-0

Florida R., Gates G., Knudsen B., & Stolarick K. (2006). The University and The Creative Economy, 1-3.

Hui, D. (2003). *Baseline Study on Hong Kong's Creative Industry, Centre for Cultural Policy Research*. The University of Hong Kong.

Kelly, A. (2001). The Media and Cultural Industry Development in Bristrol – 1993 - 2001. *Journal of Media Practice*, *2*(1), 48–57. doi:10.1386/jmpr.2.1.48

Mercer, C. (2003). *From Indicators to Governance to the Mainstream: Tools for Cultural Policy and Citizenship*. Cultural Policy and Planning Research Unit Nottingham Trent University.

Muir, J. (2002). Creative Industry Cluster Reporter 2002.

Ray, L., & Sayer, A. (1999). *Culture and economy after the cultural turn*. Sage, Landon.

Scott, A. J. (1996). The Craft, Fashion and Cultural-Products Industry of Los Angeles: Competitive Dynamics and Policy Dulemmas in a Multisectoral Image-producing Complex. *Annals of the Association of American Geographers. Association of American Geographers*, *86*(2), 306–325. doi:10.1111/j.1467-8306.1996.tb01755.x

Sintas, J. L., & Alvarez, E. G. (2002). The Consumption of Cultural Products: An Analysis of the Spanish Social Space. *Journal of Cultural Economics*,(26): 115–140. doi:10.1023/A:1014473618476

UNESCO. (2009), Creative Industry, http://portal.unesco.org/culture/en/ev.php-URL_ID=35024&URL_DO=DO_TOPIC&URL_SECTION=201.html

Yang, C. (2010). CCIC nurtures talents for the cultural and creative industry, http://www.culture.tw/index.php?option=com_content&task=rdmap&id=1673&Itemid=262

Zukin, S. (1995). *The Culture of Cities*. London: Blackwell.

KEY TERMS AND DEFINITIONS

Cultural and Creative Industry: It is those industry that have their origins in innovation or cultural accretion, and which have the potential to create wealth or create jobs through the production and utilization of intellectual property, and which can help to enhance the living environment for society as a whole.

Cultural Innovation Industry: UNESCO defines them as "industry combined with innovation, production, and commercial contents and at the same time the nature of the contents have the qualities as intangible assets and cultural concepts that are protected under intellectual property rights and presented in forms of products or services".

Creative Economy: It has been taken as one of the major projects each country works on to strengthen its competitiveness, which indicates that "Cultural innovation (Cultural & Creative) Industry" will become the trend in the future. These "industry without smokestacks", or "knowledge-based industry", turn experiences into great memories, and ideas into fortune and job opportunities.

Innovative Cultural Enterprises: Basically involves two aspects: artistic creativity and economic activity. Broadly speaking, "cultural enterprises" have existed in human society since time immemorial, comprising both traditional and modern-day artistic work in such fields as literature, music, architecture, drama, dance, photography and cinematography. Also included within the scope of cultural enterprises, and providing new directions of development for traditional cultural enterprises, are such economic activities as publishing, art galleries, international art trade, radio and television broadcasting, movie theatres, clothes design, furniture design, and industrial design.

3C Competition: (1) Characteristic; (2) Culture; (3) Creativity

Lost-Wax Casting: According to Wikipedia, Lost-wax casting sometimes called by the French name of cire perdue (from the Latin cera perduta) is the process by which a bronze or brass is cast from an artist's sculpture; in industrial uses, the modern process is called investment casting. An ancient practice, the process today varies from foundry to foundry, but the steps which are usually used in casting small bronze sculptures in a modern bronze foundry are generally quite standardized. Other names for the process include "lost mould," which recognizes that other materials besides wax can be used, including tallow, resin, tar, and textile; and "waste wax process" or "waste mould casting", because the mould is destroyed to unveil the cast item. Other methods of casting include open casting, bivalve mould, and piece mould. Lost-wax casting was widespread in Europe until 18th century, when a piece-mold process came to predominate.

Liuli: It means ancient Chinese glass/crystal. It has a lineage stretching back thousands of years, first making its appearance in the 11th century BC. The art of Liuli left an indelible trail throughout Chinese history until the 19th century when China opened its door to imported goods, and effectively stifled traditional artisan skills. The discovery in 1968 of the tomb of Liu Shun, a nobleman from Man-Chung County in Hopei Province, unearthed the earliest recorded example of pate-de-verre. A glass ear cup was found behind the renowned "jade suit with gold thread." Archaeologists confirmed the glass material was of Chinese origin, indicating the pate-de-verre technique was indeed indigenous to China. This revelation was astounding and engendered in the group of artists a profound sense of mission to revive the artistry embedded in their own ancestry.

Chapter 9
An Innovative Business Model in NPOs:
From Venture Philanthropy 1.0 to 2.0

Te Fu Chen
Lunghwa University of Science and Technology, Taiwan

ABSTRACT

This chapter reviews Venture Philanthropy (high engagement Philanthropy), social Venture Philanthropy (SVP) model, Philanthropy 1.0 and Philanthropy 2.0: Leveraging the venture capital model. In addition, the chapter explores e-Philanthropy (1.0) business models and a new framework for e-Philanthropy, building a new business model for the philanthropy 2.0 advisory industry. Furthermore, the work analyzes some case studies of new business models from Philanthropy 1.0 to 2.0. The question is which new philanthropy business model or combination of models will come out on top?

Therefore, first of all, this chapter introduces the new model of e-philanthropy can provide value added content, resources, and tools that will allow both users and charities to leverage the potential power of the Internet. People are given the ability to act immediately; it is their satisfaction with the process that will dictate the speed at which this industry moves forward. The facilitation of donations to NPOs and charities is an old market with new possibilities, e-philanthropy is a disruptive strategic innovation that has fundamentally changed the competition in the traditional philanthropic industry. This innovation will eventually overtake the traditional gift-giving market.

Secondly, donors have always gathered in various communities, but today there are more and more people thinking about co-funding, funder collaboratives and other ways that they can leverage their giving through interacting with other donors. As nonprofits move from fundraising (philanthropy 1.0)

DOI: 10.4018/978-1-60960-129-4.ch009

to friend raising (philanthropy 2.0), they are recognizing the power of building a web 2.0 community of supporters and donors are beginning to see the value of this community as well.

Thirdly, nonprofits and charities have a strong opportunity to engage in meaningful conversations (that may lead to contributions) with the social media savvy–especially those who are uncultivated. This indicates a growing market for distribution of information via social networks. Trust in social media is significant among social media savvy, would-be donors. They trust social networks and blogs to provide important information. Social media use is also very high with users participating in social networks, participating in blogs, and participating in message boards. Social Networks: it's about the relationship and trust.

Finally, this chapter integrates different new business model of venture philanthropists from different theories of worldwide scholars, practitioners, undeveloped, developing and developed countries to construct an innovative business model: philanthropy 2.0. It integrates web 2.0 technology with trust and relationships to build a network platform of Philanthropy 2.0 is the key to successfully connect VP with donors, charities and funders. It hopes to help NPOs to connect supporters, donors with other donors and supporters and with charities, NPOs, and organizations to share knowledge and experiences, finally to help the people who are really need help. Meanwhile, charities, NPOs, and organizations all are able to achieve self-growth and sustainable operation to reach triple win.

INTRODUCTION

According to International Venture Philanthropy Forum (2001), just as the "new economy" is revolutionizing the global capital market of the for-profit sector, the emerging field of "venture philanthropy" is poised to have a significant impact on the face of philanthropy around the world. Venture philanthropy is an emerging field of philanthropic "double bottom-line investment" that combines the practices of long-term investment and venture capital models of the for-profit sector with the mission-driven principles of the nonprofit sector.

NPOs (Non-Profit Organizations)

The International Center for Not-For-Profit Law defined a non-profit organization (NPO) is an organization that does not distribute its surplus funds to owners or shareholders, but instead uses them to help pursue its goals (Gary M. Grobman, 2008). Examples of NPOs include charities (i.e. charitable organizations), philanthropy, trade unions, and public arts organizations. Most governments and government agencies meet this definition, but in most countries they are considered a separate type of organization and not counted as NPOs. They are in most countries exempt from income and property taxation.

Contexts, Definitions and Characteristics of Venture Philanthropy

In the mid-1990s, modern forms of VP emerged in the USA, and spread to Europe about five years ago. However, the very first modern VP organisation is arguably the Phyllis Trust (now known as Andrews Charitable Trust), set up in 1965 by Briton Cecil Jackson-Cole. The Trust played an important role in the creation and growth of a number of charities, including Oxfam, ActionAid and Help the Aged. UK and other European venture philanthropists have adapted and evolved the American model to reflect differing socio-political and funding environments. For example, most American venture philanthropy is grant-based, whereas in Europe there is a broader spectrum of financing, such as loans and surplus sharing mechanisms, often used in combination with grants. Europeans also typically are more open to investing in initiatives that are not registered charities – such as social enterprises, social businesses or individuals – in part stemming from the varying legal forms of organisation and charitable tax relief in different countries. European VPs also are more likely to actively seek to work in partnership with other funders or government to advance their mission (Jamkit and Philanthropy UK, 2009).

VP still remains a small percentage of total grant-making regardless of its rapid growth over the last 10 years, even in the USA. In 2001, there were only 42 "high-engagement" VP organisations, together making grants of about $50m, less than 0.2% of total foundation grant-making. However, Venture Philanthropy Partners found that compared to the 50,200 charitable foundations in the USA making a total of $27.6 billion in grants in 2000 Foundation Center. Yet whilst VP remains limited in size, its influence continues to grow as larger, traditional grant-makers adopt some of its key principles(Jamkit and Philanthropy UK, 2009).

Jamkit and Philanthropy UK (2009) defined Venture philanthropy (VP) is an approach to charitable giving that applies venture capital investment principles – such as long-term investment and capacity-building support – to the voluntary and community sector. According to Wikipedia, Venture Philanthropy, also known as philanthrocapitalism, takes concepts and techniques from venture capital finance and high technology business management and applies them to achieving philanthropic goals (Tierwriting.com, 2010). VP is a form of 'engaged' philanthropy.

According to the European Venture Philanthropy Association, the key characteristics of European venture philanthropy are (Jamkit and Philanthropy UK, 2009):

1. High engagement
2. Tailored financing
3. Multi-year support
4. Non-financial support
5. Organisational capacity-building
6. Performance measurement

Moreover, due to Tierwriting.com (2010), Venture philanthropy is characterized by:

1. Willingness to experiment and try new approaches.
2. Focus on measurable results: donors and grantees assess progress based on mutually determined benchmarks.
3. Readiness to shift funds between organizations and goals based on tracking those measurable results.
4. Giving financial, intellectual, and human capital.
5. Funding on a multi-year basis - typically a minimum of 3 years, on average 5-7 years.
6. Focus on capacity building, instead of programs or general operating expenses.
7. High involvement by donors with their grantees. For example, some donors will take positions on the boards of the non-profits they fund.

E-Philanthropy

Chung-Shing Lee and Eli Berniker (2006) adopted the term "e-philanthropy" to include e-giving, online charity or gift-giving, intranet workplace giving, or online donations; terms that are all more or less synonymous with each other. Austin (2001) describes e-philanthropy as the use of the Internet to raise money and recruit volunteers. The concept allows individuals the ability to setup donation pledges and facilitates the electronic transfer of funds to the charity or organization of one's choosing. E-philanthropy services have the potential to reduce the fund raising costs of philanthropic fund raising to Non-Profit Organizations (NPOs) and to disrupt the business models of commercial fund raising organizations that utilize direct mail or telephone marketing (Chung-Shing Lee and Eli Berniker, 2006).

It is necessary to classify the various types of participants in the industry to understand philanthropy as an industry. NPOs are a large variety of organizations that receive donations and funding to provide goods and services to clients. Donors are individuals who make philanthropic donations. Some fund raising organizations (i.e. United Way in the US) who raise money from the community and dispense that money to a variety of NPOs. Moreover, some commercial fund raising organizations whose business is to raise funds for NPOs. Finally, some foundations that grant money to NPOs. e-philanthropy innovations and disruptions will impact and disrupt the traditional relationships between all of these participants. It is in this context that we will identify business models and value propositions (Chung-Shing Lee and Eli Berniker, 2006).

Problems and Objectives of this Research

The problems of this research is:

1. Which new philanthropy business model or combination of models will come out on top?
2. What is the Venture Philanthropy model?
3. What is the Social Venture Philanthropy (SVP) model
4. What is the Philanthropy 1.0 model?
5. What is the Philanthropy 2.0 model? How it leverages the venture capital model?
6. What is the approach to successfully connect VP with donors, charities and funders?

The objectives of this research is:

1. Explores e-Philanthropy (1.0) business models and its new framework for e-Philanthropy
2. Builds a new business model for the philanthropy 2.0 industry.
3. Analyzes some case studies of new business models from Philanthropy 1.0 to 2.0.
4. Integrates different new business model of venture philanthropists from different theories of worldwide scholars, practitioners, to construct an innovative business model: philanthropy 2.0.
5. Integrates web 2.0 technology with trust and relationships to build a network platform of Philanthropy 2.0 to successfully connect VP with donors, charities and funders.

BACKGROUND (LITERATURE REVIEW)

There are three models for engaging in venture philanthropy. The first is traditional foundations practicing high-engagement grantmaking. The second is organizations which are funded by individuals, but all engagement is done by professional staff. Good examples of this type of venture philanthropy are the Robin Hood Foundation in New York City and Tipping Point Community in the San Francisco Bay Area. The third is the partnership model, in which partner investors both donate the financial capital and engage with the grantees. Most of these are pass-through funds (i.e. they do not have an endowment, but rather grant out all the money they are given annually). An example of this model is the Silicon Valley Social Venture Fund in San Jose, California. Some other examples of venture philanthropy foundations include Social Venture Partners, The Children's Investment Fund Foundation (CIFF), NewSchools Venture Fund, Acumen Fund, and New Profit Inc. The following sections will review the new model: Venture Philanthropy (High Engagement Philanthropy), Social Venture Philanthropy model, Philanthropy 1.0 and Philanthropy 2.0: Leveraging the venture capital model.

The New Model: Venture Philanthropy (High Engagement Philanthropy)

What is "venture philanthropy" and does it actually differ from charitable giving, as we've known it? Is it simply a new generation of individuals who are engaged in philanthropic efforts? And what is meant by "social entrepreneurship," and what is its attraction to current philanthropists? "Venture Philanthropy," "social venture philanthropy," "the new philanthropy," "social venturing," and other terms abound in today's discussions, particularly among professionals involved in the high-tech, venture capital and foundation worlds. Kirschfoundation (2009) indicated Venture Philanthropy Partners, together with Community Wealth Ventures, published a report in 2004 called "High-Engagement Philanthropy: A Bridge to a More Effective Social Sector," profiling the relationships between funders and organizations they support. "So much of the discussion over the years about high-engagement philanthropy, also called venture philanthropy, has focused on dollar investments, who is involved, and their broad approaches. This report provides a rare look at how this kind of philanthropy gets put into practice, its risks and rewards and benefits and pitfalls." Rob John (2006) indicated in its modern form, venture philanthropy developed significantly in the US in the mid 1990s, took hold in the UK from 2002 and is now expanding into continental Europe. Venture philanthropy in Europe has strong links to the private equity and venture capital community, giving it opportunities to influence the corporate social responsibility of a set of major players in Europe's financial services industry.

Venture philanthropy has the potential to contribute to developing a more responsive and diverse capital market for the social sector. Its focus on building organisational capacity in entrepreneurial social purpose organisations, matching appropriate finance with strategic business-like advice, makes it a distinctive provider of capital. Venture philanthropy provides a blend of performance-based development finance and professional services to social purpose organisations in helping them expand their social impact. This is a high-engagement, partnership approach analogous to the practices of venture capital in building the commercial value of companies. As a relatively young industry, venture philanthropy faces many challenges in communicating and marketing what it does; developing a menu of financial instruments and advisory services; measuring performance and social impact; collaborating with complementary capital providers such as foundations (Rob John, 2006).

Porter & Kramer (2002) suggest a four-point model to increase impact through leveraging influence:

1. Selecting the best organisations
2. Signaling to others to co-invest
3. Building the capacity of these orgs
4. Advancing the knowledge and practice of the field thus influencing bigger players, policy etc

The VP funders studied were implementing 1-3 but there was still a distinct lack of stories and communication between funders and indeed between charities. This remains ever elusive. Hartnell (2006) reports that although capacity building has been very successful, ongoing funding remains a problem. Most funders were reinvesting._The main form of gradual exit was through co-investments. The development of local investor circles so that charities can develop relationships with a variety of funders from an early stage has worked in some places._Whether successful exit is possible is still a big question as perhaps the nature of the sector is such that there will always be a need for support.

Moreover, a 2007 Stanford Social Innovation Review article takes the conversation deeper. In "Social Entrepreneurship: The Case for Definition," the authors argue that it is now time to distinguish among social entrepreneurs, social activists and social service providers in order to clarify the value proposition. This distinction should also enable the philanthropic community to accurately determine and support the different funding needs of entrepreneurs, activists and providers. The explosive growth of the Internet and the rapid spread of information technologies in the second half of the 1990s infused the economy of the United States with an exuberance and creativity not seen since the "go-go years" of the 1960s. Suddenly, new economic models and talk of "the long boom" were all the rage, as industry after industry scrambled to reinvent itself. In the nonprofit sector, the leaders of established philanthropies were challenged by a new generation of high-tech millionaires to "think different." Charitable gift funds, giving circles, and venture philanthropy funds, which promised to marry the business discipline and hands-on engagement of venture capitalists with social-benefit causes, popped up like daffodils on the first day of spring. Then the dot-com boom went bust. Euphoria gave way to concern and, after the terrorist attacks of September 11, fear and anxiety. As millions and then billions of dollars in wealth evaporated, venture philanthropists struggled to adjust to the changed environment and, in many cases, took steps to distance themselves from the negative connotations that had attached to the venture philanthropy label (Kirschfoundation, 2009).

Social Venture Philanthropy: A Business Model for Non-Profits

Smile Foundation (2008) indicated a national level development organisation is based on the unique concept of 'Social Venture Philanthropy' (SVP). This model is a replica of very successful and innovative business concept called "Venture Capital". Smile Foundation for the first time in the development sector adopted the unique concept of 'Social Venture Philanthropy' (SVP). The model is inspired from a successful business concept, 'Venture Capital', where networks of accomplished individuals combine financial contributions and professional skills with a passion for philanthropy. The reason to choose SVP model was to leverage the collective expertise and resources of business managers to create the maximum community impact. Motivated from the achievements of the corporate world in spreading consumerism, Smile Foundation thought to apply the concept for the development of the underprivileged.

The SVP model has a multiplier effect, particularly in the optimum distribution of resources. In other terms, the strategy involves providing seed money for the project, expansion, professional guidance, training support, capacity building and even counselling on productivity and efficiency enhancement. Under its SVP model, SMILE identifies and nurture grass root efforts in order to achieve four key aspects; substantially, accountability, credibility and leadership in the development sector. The SVP model seeks consciously to broad-base investment in the belief that this will maximise reach and optimise returns. Instead of confining attention to a single project and a limited number of beneficiaries, the model helps reach out to and strengthen a large number of like minded individuals and organisations countrywide. The methodology has helped Smile Foundation reach out to an exceptionally large number of beneficiaries, primarily children, than it would have done with any conventional model prevalent in the sector so far. The most important gain of SMILE's delivery model is reaching to the un-reached without wasting a fraction of the resources (Smile Foundation, 2008).

SMILE through this model had been successful to make intervention at national level and experience delightful results from across 21 states. In a nutshell, Smile Foundation has been successful in replicating SVP model in a decentralized and vast scale. The social entrepreneurs from Smile Foundation include a barely literate woman working for empowering children and women, a retired head master dedicating his life to teach rural children in rural Rajasthan, a group of educated and employed youth making a movement and transforming lives of thousands of orphan and street children in remote Orissa, two young MBA graduates in Chennai working hard to make hundreds of underprivileged girls employable in retails chains and many more (Smile Foundation, 2008).

Philanthropy 1.0

E-philanthropy is an innovation in the Digital Economy, i.e., the use of new knowledge (both technological and market) to offer products or services that customers want. E-philanthropy is not a radical innovation but it is disruptive in that the traditional organizations (e.g., NPOs) lack the necessary models of competitive architecture and organizational capabilities, and is therefore unable in critical ways to do what must be done (Miller and Morris, 1999). E-philanthropy provides a new architecture to an existing service. It emphasizes different product or service attributes. With the increase in options for both organizations and users, along with the flexibility, speed, and fee alternatives, it also brings to market very different value propositions than had been available (Christensen, 1997). As would be expected, e-philanthropy started out as small and low-margin "businesses." Generally, disruptive strategic innovations under perform established mainstream products or services. Only one percent of charitable giving was done through the Internet in 2001. Over time, e-philanthropy business models and technology will improve to the extent that it is able to deliver performance considered good enough in the old attributes, that established competitors require, while offering new attributes that produce superior potential, attracting a large share of the established market. (Chung-Shing Lee and Eli Berniker, 2006).

Chung-Shing Lee and Eli Berniker (2006) compare key performance attributes of the traditional approach of contributing to charity and the disruptive attributes of e-philanthropy. Some of the most prominent disruptive attributes are:

1. **Pricing or fee structure:** ultimately costing less per transaction, meaning more of the donation will make it to the supported cause or program.
2. **Personalization of the process:** Through the use of individual accounts, many options can be used to mold the process to the donors personal preferences.
3. **Increased transparency:** Up-to-date news information, financials, and ratings. Along with streamlining the process, moving it online creates the need for fundraisers, charities and NPOs to make public any and all information about how donations are used, the standing of the organization(s) managing it, and fees taken out of the original donation.
4. **Virtually paperless:** Funds are transferred electronically, occasionally a service provider may issue a check to a recipient but the majority of the process is electronic, even the donation receipts.
5. **Customization:** Fundraising campaigns, events and personal accounts are all viable options when a service of this type is implemented. Original setups can allow fundraisers and NPOs to easily create customizations needed for specific needs. If not setup originally, new services can be put in place that should take care of needs at little extra cost.
6. **Increased efficiency:** ETF is common, safe and fast, requiring little human input once a system is in place. Organizations could save on resources by implementing such a system or outsourcing it to a service provider.

7. **Ability for smaller organizations to compete for donations:** Smaller charities and NPOs can utilize this process and the Internet to inform and educate those interested and compete head to head with larger more recognizable organizations.
8. Knowledge base possibilities allowing NPOs the ability to perform campaigns customized for and targeted at specific markets.

Even though the technologies underlying the advancement of e-philanthropy are not radical – both computing and communication technologies have been improved incrementally over the past decades, e-philanthropy is disruptive to the traditional fundraising businesses and NPOs. E-philanthropy is transforming the rules of competition and inventing new value propositions and business models (Chung-Shing Lee and Eli Berniker, 2006). Austin (2001) argues that the benefits of adopting e-philanthropy will depend on how vigorously the philanthropy industry embraces the new approach. The e-philanthropy industry has a list of unique performance attributes that have the potential to attract more users. The effectiveness of recent political fundraising suggests that the mainstream may be amenable to rapid change. Such fundraising taps into the same population groups that are NPO donors. Although the industry can count on three very important factors to increase mainstream users – tragedy, trust, and time, it does not have any control over them (Chung-Shing Lee and Eli Berniker, 2006).

Philanthropy 2.0: Leveraging the Venture Capital Model

According to Sean Foote (2007), rather than threatening the world, the venture capital-entrepreneurial complex is creating business models to save the world. This incredibly long presidential election cycle will eventually end with one president's farewell address and another's Oath of Office. This brings to mind the famous farewell address of Dwight Eisenhower, where he warned of the "military-industrial complex," saying "we must never let the weight of this combination endanger our liberties or democracy." Eisenhower never anticipated the latest industrial complex-the "venture capital-entrepreneurial complex." But this complex is different. It could be called as Philanthropy 2.0. In the world of Philanthropy 2.0, it's not just about giving back. It's about maximizing that impact in whatever innovative way possible. Take advantage of Silicon Valley's social networks and business acumen.

One challenge of philanthropy is reaching scale. Traditional philanthropic models start small and work hard to become large, just like traditional companies like Ford or GM in the 1920s. But today's startups sidestep one part of that by outsourcing their work, leveraging the skill sets and assets of other companies to achieve their objectives. Investing in new technologies, funding entrepreneurs and taking gambles on exciting ideas are commonplace for venture capitalists. Now, this successful model and hard-learned experience is being replicated to address philanthropic goals. Enter "venture philanthropy" funds, the Philanthropy 2.0 way of allocating capital to social causes. (Sean Foote, 2007).

People-powered capital: "Venture philanthropy funds seek startup ideas that could grow to the next CARE or UNICEF-the next Google of social improvement." The Internet has revolutionized many businesses, and now Philanthropy 2.0 is starting to harness the medium to solve many startup problems. One big problem of socially focused organizations is money. Most organizations must raise large sums of money to run their infrastructure and fund their social efforts. Yet Internet companies such as YouTube or LinkedIn have proven the Web's ability to bring people together and aggregate audiences. Socially focused companies are learning from these Valley startups, using the Internet to generate dollars and partnerships (Sean Foote, 2007).

BUILDING INNOVATIVE BUSINESS MODELS IN VENTURE PHILANTHROPY INDUSTRY

E-Philanthropy (1.0) Business Model

Rappa (2003) defined a business model is the method of doing business by which a company can generate revenue to sustain itself. It describes the basic framework of a business. It also tells what market segment is being served (who), the service that is being provided (what), and the means by which the service is produced (how) (Chaudhury and Kuilboer, 2002), as well as how the business plans to make money long term using the Internet (Afuah and Tucci, 2003). Lee and Vonortas (2004) argue that a viable business model in the Digital Economy must follow the fundamental economic principles (i.e., the underlying economic logic that explains how organization can deliver value to customers at an appropriate cost), and also capitalize on the "disruptive attributes" of the Internet and e-commerce. Customization in the online gift-giving market can be broadly broken down into seven different business models presently utilized by various NPOs and for-profit companies. Regardless of status, most garner a fee in some form or another for the processing of the funds transfer. Table II compares the value propositions and revenue models for each e-philanthropy business model. We identify each of these models with the three business roles defined earlier: fundraising, transaction processing, and philanthropy search engines. (Chung-Shing Lee and Eli Berniker, 2006).

Chung-Shing Lee and Eli Berniker (2006) suggest that fundraising NPO's have not found effective models to prevent their disintermediation. They are able to make employee giving more efficient for employers. They have not converted their representation of community fundraising into portals. Many models take advantage of the transaction processing economies of e-philanthropy. A few are portals that could evolve into philanthropy search engine models. Another business model is emerging that treats e-philanthropy as a secondary service adjunct to commercial business. As this models grows, it threatens to disrupt traditional thrift stores.

Chung-Shing Lee and Eli Berniker (2006) proposed a new framework for e-Philanthropy as follows:

1. **New Philanthropist**

The philanthropists of today are younger and more involved. They are not waiting until their death to take on a cause or make that big donation. By giving now, rather than transferring their wealth to foundations after death, the new philanthropists can make sure their gifts fund the causes they have chosen in the most efficient way possible (Conlin and Hempel, 2003). The Michael and Susan Dell Foundation is not looking at supporting established programs but instead wants to create their own, where they can measure the results (McWilliams, 2003). As larger foundations, such as the Dell's or the Bill and Melinda Gates Foundation, are moving toward this direct appeal for accountability and results, smaller more specialized charities need to offer this type of transparency to compete for donations. We can expect e-philanthropy to become the vehicle of choice for smaller and specialized NPOs. (Chung-Shing Lee and Eli Berniker, 2006).

The new philanthropists follow venture capitalist criteria when it comes to the distribution of funds. This means the organizations that will utilize the charitable funds will have to "produce" before they receive, i.e., they must go through extensive planning and the setting of objectives and goals. They must also be open to input during the project because philanthropists may want direct involvement and even more importantly, they may be able to significantly contribute through knowledge and non-monetary resources. Fund receiving organizations must also allow the new philanthropist continued involvement after project completion (e.g., a role as consultant). Today's philanthropy is about being involved and insuring a difference is made. It is for this reason that a framework that defines the new roles and relationships among e-philanthropy industry players is needed. (Chung-Shing Lee and Eli Berniker, 2006).

2. New Relationships

Olsen, et al. (2001) developed a methodology for comprehensive online donor cultivation and fundraising through building and maintaining one-to-one e-mail relationships with donors and friends of an organization. However, to fully exploit the Internet as an enabler of innovation, companies need to complement their direct channels of customer interaction with indirect, or mediated, interactions. Sawhney, et al. (2003) contend that those points of contact can be carried out by third parties that function as knowledge brokers, helping companies overcome the gaps in knowledge about customers that impede innovation. Innomediaries utilize the concept and practice of the virtual value chain (Rayport and Sviokla, 1995) by aggregating and disseminating customer-generated knowledge, in ways that would help companies improve their innovation processes (Sawhney, Prandelli, and Verona, 2003). By applying this concept to the e-philanthropy industry an innomediary could have access to endless relationships and opportunities. If innomediaries operate more like search engines, they will not seek to control either donors or NPOs. Given the transparency that the web offers, innomediaries should be careful in choosing business models that might put them in conflict with the intentions of donors. Blau (2001b) notes that in 1999, individual donors contributed $144 billion compared to $20 billion by foundations. Thus, it will be individual donors whose actions will determine successful business models in e-philanthropy. (Chung-Shing Lee and Eli Berniker, 2006).

Kintera Inc., a provider of software as a service that enables NPOs to use the Internet for marketing and revenue generation, currently offers abilities that parallel concepts discussed in this paper. Recently, Kintera purchased a company that possesses a powerful screening tool used by NPOs to find, profile, and rank the "wealth" in their databases. This is a knowledge creation tool. From the outside looking in, Kintera has the ability to be an innomediary or at the very least supply the necessary tools NPOs can utilized to become innomediaries themselves. GreaterGood.com, the United Way and corporate foundations could all utilize an innomediary based relationship structure, capitalizing on the one item that is the cornerstone of e-philanthropy, knowledge. (Chung-Shing Lee and Eli Berniker, 2006).

3. Internet Utilization

Internet technology has brought into the home countless new tools and information options. The use of Internet technology on issues of philanthropy is no different. Any individual or group, looking for a cause to support, or in need of supporters, now has a tool for collaboration. The role of an innomediary, whether as a fundraiser or philanthropy search engine, would be to support, legitimize and increase the functionality of the Internet as a tool, providing aid such as facilitation and virtual workspace. To give parties involved a sense of security through the screening of users and most importantly providing those interested with a place to exchange ideas, information, and expertise, to reach common goals. This will overcome the gaps in knowledge about customers that impede innovation. Philanthropists could "follow the money", giving them an additional sense of security. Ultimately an innomediary structure could be used to build an information and knowledge base that will spawn new innovative business and operations possibilities in philanthropy. A note of caution is in order. The innomediary role may be a candidate for an open source attack. Communities of donors may prefer an innomediary structure that empowers NPOs and donors rather than for-profit businesses. (Chung-Shing Lee and Eli Berniker, 2006).

Chung-Shing Lee and Eli Berniker (2006) identified three core business roles for e-philanthropy innovations. These are to act as the fund raising organization, to act as a transaction processor for NPOs, or become philanthropy search engines (PSEs) serving donors and processing transactions. The business models of each of these roles will be associated with the benefits of e-philanthropy to suggest their value propositions.

Building a New Business Model: Philanthropy 2.0 for the Philanthropy Advisory Industry

Philanthropy 2.0 generates all the advantages of a traditional VP structure, plus it provides a unique, one-to-one connection between people with very disparate backgrounds and experiences. Its model is sustainable and is operating at break-even. Web 2.0 is working with VP to help reduce its operating costs as well as promote the organization. The venture capital-entrepreneurial complex is doing something vastly different than the military-industrial complex-innovating not just in business, but also in philanthropy. Already, firms are developing new ways of extending their reach through leverage, using VC capital acquisition models and the Internet. The Philanthropy 2.0 is as big, and as varied, as Web 2.0 (Sean Foote, 2007).

According to Karim Harji (2009), Sean Stannard-Stockton's blog - Tactical Philanthropy - has long been a credible and updated reference point on the current state of philanthropy and where it is headed. His insight and analysis has spawned critical commentary and responses from some of the leading thinkers in this space, and has demonstrated the tremendous latent demand for a clear and reasoned voice on issues related to social investing. Many other blogs, including this one, continue to be inspired by the breadth and depth of the issues that Sean weaves into his blog on a regular basis. What's even more exciting, however, is where Sean is headed next. He's just launched Tactical Philanthropy Advisors to build a new business model for the philanthropy advisory industry. The new firm - a for-profit company preparing to file for B Corp status - will be working on bringing the language and tools of social finance to high net worth donors. The firm has already established working arrangements with Schwab Charitable, Fidelity Charitable Gift Fund, Calvert Giving Fund and Foundation Source to provide administrative back office services, as well as advisory services, for clients with $1 million to $50 million or more in philanthropic assets.

There's a number of other pieces that make Sean's new venture unique. The firm is making a commitment to support the work of the Philanthropic Ventures Foundation, a public charity that that helps donors of all levels of wealth to engage in creative philanthropy. TPA will also be working with Jed Emerson and IDEO to build a Tactical Philanthropy Knowledge Network that will launch later this year. And it will also be working with Exponent Partners – the firm that developed the PULSE social investment tracking system for Acumen Fund and a Salesforce powered grant management system for Google.org – to build a grantmaking and impact reporting platform geared to the needs of individual donors. Given how much impact the Tactical Philanthropy blog has had on the industry in a relatively short period of time, it will be interesting to track how this model will evolve to address multiple needs in the social investment marketplace, and how the philanthropic advisory industry needs to evolve, as well as the corresponding shifts around notions of risk, return and (social) impact (Karim Harji, 2009).

A CASE STUDY OF NEW BUSINESS MODELS FROM PHILANTHROPY 1.0 TO 2.0

Philanthropy 1.0 Case Study: UniversalGiving

Kristin Ladd (2009) indicated for social entrepreneur Pamela Hawley, the "season of giving" is about nine months too short. Hawley has been a philanthropist since she was 12, when she got her first startling look at poverty and hunger during a family trip to Mexico. Since then, she has been a volunteer around the world—from soup kitchens and crisis hotlines in the United States to poor neighborhoods in Guatemala. Now she has turned her lifelong passion for giving into a virtual business, UniversalGiving. Though the holiday season is one of the most wonderful times of the year as people share, give and thank one another, opportunities for such actions are accessible year-round. However, searching online for philanthropic opportunities can take hours—and can quickly turn you into a misanthrope. And that's exactly why Hawley started her business. As she says, "A lot of people have good intentions, but they don't know how to find [the right place for them]. We needed a mechanism for everyone to be able to do this. I wanted to run an efficient, principled endeavor. So I started my business." Hawley had previously worked in sales and marketing in the for-profit world. Later, she co-founded VolunteerMatch.com, so she knew she had the business experience and personal motivation to start UniversalGiving.

Hawley launched UniversalGiving.org in 2002, with a platform that provides giving and volunteering opportunities in more than 70 countries. First, she chose people inspired by the same vision she had; that is, a vision of pure, nonprofit services. The 20 team members are an amalgamation of philanthropists with specific skills in everything from web development to marketing. Then the team began to develop UniversalGiving's mission. Team members wanted site visitors to trust the organization. So they went completely nonprofit. One hundred percent of donations go to charities, with no cut for UniversalGiving. As well, these charities must be trustworthy. "[We are] social entrepreneurs who are really dedicated to the community. Anyone looking for a charitable opportunity can search by country or by issues, and the site will return a list of possible projects," Hawley says. Easily navigable, the site's home page has two main categories: Donate and Volunteer. There, you can search for different opportunities according to region, country or issue (such as hunger, housing or human rights). The site also provides a list of Top Volunteer Opportunities and Top Gift Packages for those who would like to help but are unsure where to begin. Visitors can register for an account with UniversalGiving that allows them to track their donations, search histories and build their philanthropic interests. Since its launch, "we have passed $1.5 million through our site and matched nearly 10,000 volunteers," Hawley says (Kristin Ladd, 2009)

UniversalGiving chooses projects and charities based on a rigorous format rooted firmly in business values. "The quality model is a 10-stage process, and we view it like a venture capitalist would," Hawley says. "We look at the business idea behind the project. Then we say, 'OK, great idea, who is the management team?' We get to know the leaders of it and have personal relationships with them. It is a management-relationship perspective," which allows Hawley and her team to produce objective and subjective requirements for the charities they select. Of course, to keep the business going, Hawley had to figure out a way to gain revenue. Deciding to tap into the corporate social responsibility market, she came up with the model for UniversalGiving Corporate. Now, she says, "We help Fortune 500 companies with their CSR strategies and hook them up with reliable NGOs [non-governmental organizations]." In return for those services, corporations provide the finances UniversalGiving needs to adhere to its nonprofit principles. These principles not only allow the site to continue to grow and gain rapport with its visitors, but Hawley says they also give her "a strong anchor on a value-based and spiritual level." (Kristin Ladd, 2009).

As most social entrepreneurs would agree, a company is not simply an entity to make money. Hawley says, "It's important to tie your own life back to something greater. Like any entrepreneurship endeavor, perseverance and sticking to your vision are so essential. It's like a marathon. You put on your running shoes and you're going to hit some milestones, but it's still going to be difficult. So find something you're going to be willing to run the marathon for. With UniversalGiving, it's so important that their vision stay very active. Their vision is to create a world in which giving and volunteering are a natural part of everyday life." Hawley believes that everyone should find his or her own place in service. "That doesn't necessarily mean that you're a social entrepreneur; you could be a dentist or a banker. Everyone has a call to service and living in kindness every day." Hawley, herself, says she's wired purely for business; she's just taking some new circuits to change how that business functions and what it can produce to make a more humanitarian world. And if you're a social entrepreneur, what is her advice for you? "Have a sense of balance. Keep your values and family close to you--especially those that keep you inspired. Yes, your business can inspire you, but it is not the end all, be all. Keeping the other parts [of your life] meaningful, joyful and balanced is what will keep you going." (Kristin Ladd, 2009).

Philanthropy 2.0 Case Study: Entrepreneurs Foundation, Acumen Fund, Case Foundation and Kiva

(1) A Case Study of Entrepreneurs Foundation

Entrepreneurs Foundation (EF) is an example of utilizing leverage for maximizing impact. EF's goal is simple-to increase individual and corporate commitment to community involvement. The innovation? Leverage hundreds of companies and thousands of their employees to impact communities. The community cause celebre? Whatever the company wants it to be. EF, started nine years ago by Gib Myers of Mayfield Fund, works with companies of all sizes (particularly emerging companies) to design, create and manage corporate foundations and community programs. Recognizing cash is not readily available at these young companies, EF uses another currency to help these companies become active citizens in their community-stock options. Pre-IPO stock is set aside in a company foundation. A small part of this stock is used to pay Entrepreneurs Foundation. Then, EF acts as an outsourced director of community relations, helping companies create and execute strategic community programs that match their businesses and employee interests while also serving community needs. "It's the best bargain I've negotiated since becoming CEO," says Ashley Stirrup, CEO of Ultriva. Ashley and Ultriva became one of EF's 500 member companies, joining companies from Aruba Networks to Yahoo. "We're doing something for society while building a business, and it's not a distraction." (Sean Foote, 2007).

Indeed, it's this combination of business and societal good that is the key to EF's success. "Our companies report that hiring and team-building are easier when the firm has a community service program," reports EF Executive Director Diane Solinger. When surveyed in the Cone Corporate Citizenship Study, 81% of Americans say a company's commitment to a social issue is important when they decide where to work. EF also leverages relationships with venture capitalists, who act as a sales force to their portfolio companies. Venture capitalists from Austin Ventures, Charles River Ventures, Focus Ventures, Kleiner Perkins Caufield & Byers, Mayfield Fund, New Enterprise Associates, Sequoia Capital and Trinity Ventures encourage their portfolio companies to set aside equity for the community through EF. Leveraging Silicon Valley's startup companies has allowed Entrepreneurs Foundation to do far more than a traditional philanthropic model. EF now works with 500 companies, 200 venture capitalists and 15,000 employees distributing $8 million and countless volunteer hours to 200 community service organizations. "In the world of Philanthropy 2.0, it's not just about giving back. It's about maximizing that impact in whatever innovative way possible." (Sean Foote, 2007).

(2) Acumen Fund: Entrepreneurial Approaches

Venture philanthropy funds seek startup ideas that could grow to the next CARE or UNICEF-the next Google of social improvement. An early leader of this approach is the Acumen Fund, a non-profit global venture fund investing in entrepreneurial approaches to solving the problems of global poverty. The organization seeks to prove that small amounts of philanthropic capital, combined with business acumen, can build thriving enterprises that target the 4 billion people living on less than $4 a day. Stuart Davidson, one of the partners at Labrador Ventures, sits on the Acumen board. "We are organized and operate just like any other venture capital firm," he says. "We have focus areas and a disciplined process in selecting and managing philanthropic investments and measuring social and financial returns." The investment approach of the Acumen fund even sounds quite similar to a typical venture fund: "Acumen focuses on design, pricing, distribution and marketing of critical goods and services," with just one difference, "to the poor." At the same time, the fund intends to be sustainable, the latest buzzword for not requiring additional grants to fund operations. Its risk management team aims to generate positive returns where possible and recover a substantial portion of capital to reinvest in new philanthropic ventures (Sean Foote, 2007).

The impact of the organization since its founding in 2001 is remarkable. In this short time, it has improved the lives of over 1 million people through its investments, mostly in the form of loans and equity. Because of Acumen's investments, more than 500,000 people have been protected from malaria, 12,000 women have received microfinance loans, 5,000 farmers have increased their income by purchasing drip irrigation systems, and 11,000 families have been able to buy life-saving de-fluoridation water filters. The venture model of philanthropy is an extremely efficient method of capital allocation, sidestepping much of the overhead of traditional methods. Through Acumen, as little as $50 can protect 12 individuals from the risks of malaria for five years, while $100 allows three Pakistani women to create sustainable livelihoods to support themselves and their children. (Sean Foote, 2007).

(3) Philanthropy 2.0: Case Foundation

Catherine Curan (2008) indicated the way we've been doing things, the way we talk about what we do, it's all really out-of-date with how young people think today, says Jean, the CEO of the Washington, D.C.based Case Foundation. "We really need some new branding here." This realization inspired the Cases to rethink both how they define giving and how they promote it. When Steve and Jean (also a former AOL executive) founded their charitable organization in 1997, they believed they had to set aside the consumer-marketing skills they had honed during the Internet revolution and adopt only the nonprofit arena's methods. Now, however, the Cases have realized the value of applying consumer-marketing principles to further their foundation's mission of helping underserved families and fostering economic development. They had been at the forefront of popularizing personal Internet use through the spread of AOL. Technology has since transformed personal communications and shopping habits, but philanthropy has consistently lagged behind this trend. The Cases want to help it catch up. Instead of a closed circle of insiders, the Cases-along with Napster co-founder Sean Parker and a handful of major foundations-are defining charity as something that everyone should make part of their daily lives. To further that new ideal, they are hosting online competitions that help donors choose grant recipients. They are also tapping online social networks such as Facebook and Second Life to foster new ways for philanthropic groups to coalesce and to find new solutions for persistent social ills. In keeping with the consumer-business model, philanthropists are also seeking ways to use technology to reach out to those who want to give, rather than relying on traffic to a particular website. That might mean, for example, allowing people to use their cell phones to make donations after attending a film or event highlighting a cause (Catherine Curan, 2008).

Causes on Facebook

Parker, who at age 28 has already spearheaded two large-scale online communities-the music site Napster and the address-book site Plaxo-and been part of Facebook's executive team in its early phase, launched a new venture last year called Causes on Facebook. The project is designed to replicate online the networks that support grass-roots social and political movements. Causes allows Facebook's more than 61 million active users to create a cause complete with a real-world nonprofit beneficiary. Users then invite friends on the site to join, and members can even donate to the cause directly through Facebook. From its May 2007 launch through mid-January, Causes had 10.2 million users who donated hundreds of thousands of dollars to 52,391 recipients. Parker is the chairman of Causes, which he cofounded with Joe Green, a veteran of John Kerry's presidential campaign. He is also an investor via the Founders Fund, a venture capital firm in which he is a partner. The Founders Fund invested $2.35 million in Causes. Right now you've got to be a large nonprofit or a huge PAC to have an impact socially or politically, Parker says. We are putting tools in the hands of individual activists to change the world on a large scale (Catherine Curan, 2008).

A Wider Net

With the broadening of philanthropy's reach, wealthy individuals gain greater access to innovative projects in need of funds. They also have unprecedented opportunities to market their causes and generate far more funding via numerous small donations than traditionally they would have made by writing a few large checks. What's more, the collaborative spirit found in social-networking websites and in the contests with public feedback is starting to find its way into the giving side.

Jean Case, for example, recently teamed up with an old corporate rival to back a new social-networking site affiliated with MTV. In December, the Case Foundation announced plans to give $750,000 to charity in partnership with Parade magazine, Network for Good, GlobalGiving and Causes on Facebook. Marketed as a giving challenge, this effort will award funds to the charities that are able to drum up the most donations online. "A lot of times, the nonprofit sector has been criticized for not collaborating enough or for being too competitive. But really, funders haven't been very collaborative, either, Case says. I think that there's a huge potential for folks to co-invest and collaborate around big ideas and achieve more outcome as a result. Despite all the enthusiasm and some hugely successful online contests-American Idol: Idol Gives Back, for example, raised more than $75 million last year for poor children in the U.S. and Africa-these strategies are still new tools being tested mainly in small ways. The Robert Wood Johnson Foundation awarded about $400 million in grants in 2006; the $750,000 it gave to Changemakers.net, which hosts collaborative online competitions to help foster social change, was merely a fraction of that budget. And as high-net-worth individuals and foundations explore new ideas, they must strive to match modern technologies with appropriate projects, rather than simply racing to adopt the latest online fad. The challenge is to figure out how the Internet fits their mission, says Steve Gunderson, the president of the Council on Foundations in Washington, D.C. (Catherine Curan, 2008).

Mass Philanthropy

Testing these innovations also reveals new hurdles, specifically in the matter of website security. Lapses can be embarrassing, as the New York charity City Harvest discovered last year. The organization sent out warning letters in the summer to 12,500 donors, informing them that their credit card data might have been stolen by hackers. Foundations accustomed to receiving grant proposals via mail are also finding it difficult to manage the vast amounts of diverse information that the online competitions generate. Case received 4,641 applications for the Case Foundation's Make It Your Own contest. She also received hundreds of responses to a call for potential judges, and chose about 70. Similarly, after the Rockefeller Foundation's Ideas Portal-a section of its website for submitting ideas that will help further the organization's philanthropic mission-launched in November 2006, it drew nearly 35,000 visitors and yielded 3,700 ideas within a year. The ability to absorb that, and absorb that well, has been a challenge, says Nadya Shmavonian, the vice president of foundation initiatives at the Rockefeller Foundation, based in New York (Catherine Curan, 2008).

While working on ways to maximize new technologies, philanthropists are already seeing clear benefits from these innovations. Contests and online calls for ideas have yielded access to hundreds of ideas and individuals that otherwise would not have been discovered. Posting ideas online offers exposure to a broad audience and fosters collaboration among participants. That breaks with the usual winner-takes-all outcome, in which many good ideas end up discarded. Because Make It Your Own was designed to bring in people who are traditionally shut out of the grant process, Case and her team at the foundation determined that they would focus on ideas rather than sterling grammar and spelling skills. This approach yielded an unprecedentedly diverse group of entrants across age, racial, ethnic and geographic lines. Another huge benefit of this kind of process is that ideas solicited online arrive far more quickly than through traditional means. In the past, the Robert Wood Johnson Foundation has spent up to two years researching a new field and developing a program. Now that time frame can collapse to just two-and-a-half months. This gives a very fast, very broad environmental scan that provides a framework that is extremely valuable. While the grants awarded so far have been relatively small, wealthy funders are enthusiastic about new technology's unprecedented power to leverage funds. When Sean Parker left Facebook, he considered setting up a foundation. He says he believes in personal donations, but saw greater potential in applying the skills he acquired from his Internet businesses toward an online forum for spreading ideas. Parker says "I thought I could have a much bigger impact by investing my time and money in a platform to bring about systemic change" (Catherine Curan, 2008).

Community Service

Case has used Facebook to share her interest in PlayPumps, which provides merry-go-rounds that double as water pumps in Africa. Though the charity is not something she would normally promote to her friends, by posting it on her Facebook profile she has brought attention to the cause in a low-key way. Both Case and her husband are listed among the 65 friends of PlayPumps, which has also attracted a group of 695 members. It allows more of an always-on relationship than email. Case also has teamed up with the Bill and Melinda Gates Foundation, the Goldhirsh Foundation and the MCJ Amelior Foundation to back Think MTV (think.mtv.com), a social-networking site. She declined to disclose the investment, but noted that the Case Foundation typically spends $8 million to $10 million a year. Case says her children did not influence the MTV deal-it was a high-profile way to reach young people. We're using that co-investment with our partners to try to make sure that visibility is given and there's some promotion of doing good as part of what you're doing when you're online as a young person, she says. Judging success in this arena can mean applying a different set of standards than for traditional philanthropy. Case notes that with PlayPumps there are clear ways to measure and evaluate the results: Progress includes solving the basic problem of disease and helping more girls go to school instead of spending their time fetching water. When judging Make It Your Own, however, Case is interested in expanding the pool of givers and promoting greater civic engagement. She hopes new approaches like online contests and Causes on Facebook will allow many more young people to make giving a regular part of their lives-even if they aren't familiar with that old-fashioned word philanthropy. We think it's healthier if a million people give $10 than if one person gives $10 million, Case says. We just think it makes a healthier society (Catherine Curan, 2008).

(4) Philanthropy 2.0: Kiva

A great example of Internet philanthropy is San Francisco-based Kiva.org, the brainchild of husband and wife team Matt and Jessica Flannery. Jessica was working with microfinance organizations in Africa, which loan small amounts of money to entrepreneurs in third-world countries. Matt had extensive technical skills. Rather than attempt to raise money to fund a traditional microfinance institution of their own, they built a website to connect individuals in the United States who were willing to make loans to entrepreneurs in other countries. Lenders select a business to sponsor using Kiva's website, then offer a six- to 12-month loan. Lenders receive periodic journal updates from the entrepreneurs and, at the end of the loan period, are repaid in full. To maximize Kiva's impact on emerging businesses, the firm leverages in-country microfinance lending agencies to identify qualified entrepreneurs throughout the developing world. "We generate all the advantages of a traditional microfinance structure, plus we provide a unique, one-to-one connection between people with very disparate backgrounds and experiences," says Premal Shah, president of Kiva. "Plus it scales at Internet speed." Kiva has grown in just one year to be one of the largest microfinance organizations in the country, lending over $2 million per month. Its model is sustainable-Kiva is operating at break-even. Both PayPal and Google are working with Kiva to help reduce its operating costs as well as promote the company. Kiva has also been featured on "The Oprah Winfrey Show" and in Bill Clinton's latest book on social giving. (Sean Foote, 2007).

Richard MacManus (2007) indicated a non-profit site called kiva.org - calling it "web 2.0 meets the 2006 Nobel Peace Prize". Kiva.org lets you loan money to an entrepreneur in the developing world. On the homepage there is a list of relatively small loan requests (usually $2000 or less), from people in developing countries. Incidentally, Kiva is a Swahili word meaning "agreement" or "unity". Kiva.org even addresses the question of "Will I get repaid", with a little popup box that states: "So far, Kiva has experienced a 100% repayment rate on all businesses with completed loan terms." In terms of utilizing the Web for non-profit purposes, Kiva.org is a shining example. It has the usual 'web 2.0' things like RSS feeds, journals with comments (like blogs), facewall that links to user profiles, badges for websites, easy Web payments (using credit card, Paypal, etc), recommendations, and more.

As Kiva.org explains on its About page, they facilitate connections using the Web: "Kiva is using the power of the internet to facilitate one-to-one connections that were previously prohibitively expensive. Child sponsorship has always been a high overhead business. Kiva creates a similar interpersonal connection at much lower costs due to the instant, inexpensive nature of internet delivery. The individuals featured on our website are real people who need a loan and waiting for socially-minded individuals like you to lend them money." Interestingly, Kiva.org seems to have good support from Silicon Valley - in the FAQ it states that "Kiva.org currently has financial support from a number of angel investors, including Silicon Valley donors, and corporate sponsors including Microsoft Research." Also Kiva.org has received good press coverage. The Seattle Times called it "Philanthropy 2.0" and noted: "The power of the Internet not only makes it possible for donors to find organizations and causes they support around the world, but it means that even small amounts by individuals can make a big difference because of the sheer volume of givers." Overall Kiva.org is an impressive use of the Web and shows there's much more to web 2.0 than just Flickr, del.icio.us, YouTube and MySpace. Read/WriteWeb will be profiling more of these web-empowered non-profits in future posts - they literally give new meaning to 'world wide web'! (Richard MacManus, 2007)

Study Results of Community Philanthropy 2.0

According to Philanthropy 2.0 Study Results Published on Mashable, Beth Kanter (2009) indicated a common critic of online giving through social media is that the dollar amounts are too low per donor and donations tend to be transactional, not relationship-based or one-time donors. This has been found in a number of surveys over the past few years. If we look back a year ago at donation trends on Facebook Causes, we also see the same complaint.

- Causes reports o is first year - $2.5 Million For 20,000 Charities and non-profits by Michael Arrington, TechCrunch.Com, Washington Post, May 29, 2008;
- $2.5 Million and Counting, The Agitator, May 29, 2008.
- Social Networks: It's About the Relationship by Stephen MacLaughlin, BlackBaud Blog, May 29, 2008
- The Long Tail of Facebook Causes. Frogloop Blog. James O'Malley and Justin Perkins. July 24, 2007

The demographics of social networks are aging and we are beginning to observe that the social web is becoming more of a place for fundraising for causes as well as philanthropic discussions. While the social web has been a fantastic place for nonprofits to harness the long tail of giving with movements like Twestival and the Case Foundation's Giving Challenge, high dollar donor cultivation has not been prevalent. The goal of our Community Philanthropy 2.0 survey one month ago was to determine whether there is potential for nonprofits to cultivate significant donors online (defined as someone who gives $1,000 or more), and how that can be accomplished. There were a number of good points made about the challenge of transitioning to social media infused fundraising. While there may be tremendous opportunity, your organization won't be able to reap the benefits if it is stuck in doing the same strategy year after year (Beth Kanter, 2009).

Social Media for Social Causes Study: The Results

Qui Diaz, Beth Kanter and Geoff Livingston (2009), who are working on a special project, dubbed "Philanthropy 2.0" to provide non-profits the information they need to best serve donors and advocates. While the social web has been a fantastic place for nonprofits to harness the long tail of giving with movements like Twestival and the Case Foundation's Giving Challenge, high dollar donor cultivation has not been prevalent. The goal of Community Philanthropy 2.0 survey one month ago was to determine whether there is potential for nonprofits to cultivate significant donors online (defined as someone who gives $1,000 or more), and how that can be accomplished.

Table 1. The difference between Philanthropy 1.0 and Philanthropy 2.0 (Source: Lucy Bernholz 2009)

Philanthropy 1.0 Vs. Philanthropy 2.0	The difference
Altruism vs. Enlightened self-interest	It might be replaced "altruism" by "sacrifice" or "obligation". But either way it gets to the idea that donors have begun to shift to thinking about philanthropy as a non-zero sum game. Giving to a nonprofit does not benefit the nonprofit and hurt the donor, if done right it can enhance the well being of everyone involved.
Problems vs Solutions	Philanthropists have always looked for great solutions, but there is a way in which solutions have gotten more attention recently. For instance, microfinance has captured so much attention due to the solution itself. It is not the plight of poor women in India that so many donors are focusing on, it is the solution of microfinance.
Services vs. Impact	Focusing on delivering impact is probably Philanthropy 3.0. But donors today are focused more on results or "outcomes". They are getting more interested in the difference a nonprofit's programs are achieving rather than the activity the nonprofit is engaging in.
Single donors vs. Community of believers	Donors have always gathered in various communities, but today there are more and more people thinking about co-funding, funder collaboratives and other ways that they can leverage their giving through interacting with other donors. In addition, as nonprofits move from fundraising to "friend raising", they are recognizing the power of building a community of supporters and donors are beginning to see the value of this community as well.
Donations vs "Sustainable Revenue Streams"	Authors of the report meant earned income when they wrote sustainable revenue. There is more of a focus on earned income, but sometimes that elevating earned income as somehow superior to donations forces nonprofits to shift their attention away from their mission. Donations are sustainable. In fact, the volatility of donations is lower than GDP and so on a national level donations are more sustainable and predictable than income. But there is a push for a more sophisticated approach of understanding how a nonprofit can create a sustainable business instead of hoping to close the budget each year.
Top-down vs. Bottom-up	This is the big one. This is the core of my original definition of the second great wave of philanthropy: "While the traditional top-down hierarchical system describes the way Rockefeller's foundation distributed grants to charities, which then provided services for the public, a flat structure is the model of the Second Great Wave. This shift acknowledges that no one person or entity has all the answers and instead leads to a virtuous cycle of information feedback. The philanthropists of the 21st century will be smaller in size, but much larger in numbers than the philanthropists of the last century."
Few vs Many	The point is captured in top-down vs bottom-up. The "democratization of philanthropy" is in full swing. In 1980 about 6% of Americans were invested in the stock market. By 2000, it was more than 50%. The baby boomers that fueled that move during their retirement planning years are now retiring and hitting peak giving years. Today something like 6% of Americans are engaged in proactive, intentional philanthropy, but that within 20 years we might push that number north of 50%. While the exact numbers are up for debate, directionally the trend is clear.

Tremendous Opportunity for Nonprofits

What we found was a tremendous opportunity for nonprofits to participate as trusted providers of credible information and ultimately cultivate the next generation of major donors through the social web. Between blog posts on MashableMashable, Social Media Club and the Society of New Communications Research, 426 people responded to our 30-question survey (commissioned by The Columbus Foundation, The Saint Paul Foundation and The San Francisco Foundation). Our analysis of these social media power users revealed the group was younger than the traditional composition of donors one would find in a charity's database. The rest of this analysis focuses on the 30-49 and over 50 age brackets as they represent the greatest opportunity for online cultivation of high dollar donors. Social media power users of both the new 30-49 age brackets and the over 50 bracket have used social media to discuss philanthropy. In fact, 84 percent of the social media savvy aged 30-49 and 55 percent of those older than 50 used conversational media for these purposes. This confirms social media is a potential growth area through which major donors can be cultivated. The social media savvy stated clearly that email is their preferred method of contact from charitable organizations. Additionally, some prefer social networks and also use social networks. This indicates a growing market for distribution of information via social networks. Trust in social media is significant among social media savvy would-be donors. They trust social networks and blogs to provide important information. Social media use is also very high with users participating in social networks, participating in blogs, participating in message boards (Qui Diaz, Beth Kanter and Geoff Livingston, 2009).

Group Social Media Preferred Over Personal Efforts

Of all the forms of social media used by 30-49-year-olds, only social networks and blogs received greater than 40 percent rankings for "trust." Perhaps one of the most interesting points that arose from this data was that both social media savvy groups prefer group social media, with the exception of blogs. Whether for personal use or trust in third party sites, blogs represent the second most viable source of information next to social networks (among both the digital rich and the traditional brackets). After blogs, message boards, forums, wikis and review sites were all deemed more credible than videos or podcasts (the terrain of traditional "personal" social media). Social media savvy respondents demonstrate a significant opportunity for foundations to provide social media. Privacy was not much of a concern for the 30-49 year olds who said they look for in philanthropic social media. The numbers were very similar among the 50 and older bracket (Qui Diaz, Beth Kanter and Geoff Livingston, 2009).

In summary, nonprofits and charities have a strong opportunity to engage in meaningful conversations (that may lead to contributions) with the social media savvy (30-49 and >50) – especially those who are uncultivated. Clear indicators reveal types of conversations the social media savvy are seeking (Qui Diaz, Beth Kanter and Geoff Livingston, 2009).

Philanthropy 1.0 vs. Philanthropy 2.0

Lucy Bernholz (2009) indicated lots of people have used the terms "Philanthropy 2.0", "New Donors" or other phrases that suggest that something has fundamentally changed about the field of philanthropy. The subtitle of this blog is "chronicling the second great wave of philanthropy," which also implies that something new is replacing an older approach. Lucy Bernholz (2009) discussed the Table 1, which lays out one take on the difference between Philanthropy 1.0 and Philanthropy 2.0. This table comes from a new report from BBMG a branding and marketing firm. The report is titled From Legacy to Leadership: Is Philanthropy Ready for the New Consumer?

Lucy Bernholz (2009) indicated plenty of people told venture philanthropists in the 90's that they weren't doing anything that the Ford Foundation wasn't doing in the 1950's. Philanthropy does have a tendency like most fields to always believe that "this time is different" and that everything has changed. The new donors exist in the Philanthropy 1.0 toward Philanthropy 2.0 framework.

FUTURE RESEARCH DIRECTIONS

In the world of Philanthropy 2.0, it's not just about giving back. It's about maximizing that impact in whatever innovative way possible. One challenge of philanthropy is reaching scale. Traditional philanthropic models start small and work hard to become large, but today's startups sidestep one part of that by outsourcing their work, leveraging the skill sets and assets of other companies to achieve their objectives. Investing in new technologies, funding entrepreneurs and taking gambles on exciting ideas are commonplace for venture capitalists. Now, this successful model and hard-learned experience is being replicated to address philanthropic goals. Enter "venture philanthropy" funds, the Philanthropy 2.0 way of allocating capital to social causes. The future research will study how to transform this successful model and hard-learned experience of Philanthropy 2.0 to VP structure.

The Internet has revolutionized many businesses, and now Philanthropy 2.0 is starting to harness the medium to solve many startup problems. Socially focused companies are learning from these Valley startups, using the Internet to generate dollars and partnerships. Philanthropy 2.0 generates all the advantages of a traditional VP structure, plus it provides a unique, one-to-one connection between people with very disparate backgrounds and experiences. Its model is sustainable and is operating at break-even. The future research will focus on how to balance the perspectives between a business and NPOs.

The future for VP does not lie with processing online donations or with pursuing a single model of giving but it must be able to design various innovative business models that capitalize on the disruptive performance attributes and value propositions to provide real solutions to meet or exceed a customer's expectations. Focusing on delivering impact is probably Philanthropy 2.0. But donors today are focused more on results or "outcomes". They are getting more interested in the difference a nonprofit's programs are achieving rather than the activity the nonprofit is engaging in. Hence, the future research will focus on the process design of activity and measurement of outcome performance for VP.

CONCLUSION AND RECOMMENDATIONS

Conclusion

(1) Bring Greater Value to Venture Philanthropists (VP)

Venture philanthropists are people with a very strong sense of how to do things. The people in Venture philanthropists (VP) are not always familiar with the non-profit world, how it works or the values that vitalize people in the sector. It is too pushy for VP to run non-profits like businesses, too quick to offer solutions to non-profits without understanding the complexity of the sector and too concerned for fast results. Business models were being forced on a sector that had different sensitivities. VP is not about making charities more business like, it is important that models are adapted and are not prescriptive. We must see beyond the business models and realize they are just a means to an end.

The main thing is to bring greater value to the organization. The importance of a balanced perspective so that a focus remained on values was emphasized. Some consultants sent by the funder were mismatched and had a poor understanding of the charity sector. Matching consultants that were familiar with the sector and that suited the organisations well was reported as being important._Emphasis on more two-way learning, especially what funders could learn from charities. Still felt there was an artificial divide between the charity and business sector.

(2) Leverage the Potential Power of the Internet: E-Philanthropy (1.0)

This new model of e-philanthropy (1.0) can provide value added content, resources, and tools that will allow both users and charities to leverage the potential power of the Internet. People are given the ability to act immediately; it is their satisfaction with the process that will dictate the speed at which this industry moves forward. It seems that nonprofits and charities alike may not be maximizing the possibilities of online services and the Internet to stimulate giving. There may be a low awareness of the possibilities that are currently available from service providers and software. Charities and NPOs may also assume they could not safely and securely manage this type of transaction and the handling of information. Donors share this concern. Getting the information out and educating the public as to how the system and organizations run are steps all industries moving onto the Internet should take. Sharing personal or financial information online is safe; it is the newness and unfamiliarity that puts potential users on edge.

Online, Internet, intranet, donations or gift giving allows quick and simplified processing of designated funds. With this online process comes the ability to investigate and gather information so the individual user can make a well-informed decision when allocating gifts to charity. The Internet is an important medium for the education of the public on how nonprofits and charities work and what they do. Use of the Internet to compare, contrast and find information on charities is growing. An organization or NPO with a presence on the World Wide Web will enable donors to find, judge and make decisions on where their money goes. Also, charities and NPOs are able to monitor what others are doing, allowing them to keep up to date on campaign strategies and techniques as well as new marketing possibilities. The Internet gives people the option to research nonprofits and their financial activities, therefore making the organizations more accountable to those who finance their operations.

The e-philanthropy revolution is here to stay, and it will transform charitable giving in as profound a way as technology is changing the commercial world (Austin, 2001). The facilitation of donations to NPOs and charities is an old market with new possibilities, e-philanthropy is a disruptive strategic innovation that has fundamentally changed the competition in the traditional philanthropic industry. This innovation will eventually overtake the traditional gift-giving market. The question is which new e-philanthropy business model or combination of models will come out on top. E-philanthropy comes in a variety of customizable tools that can be used individually or pooled with other innovative and traditional methods to fulfill specific needs. It allows a cost effective process to conveniently move money to a desired recipient, allowing more money to go to programs where it can do the most good. The benefits to the gift recipients should be larger portions of donations retained for the specified use, as well as an inexpensive route for them to solicit and receive money directly from individuals. (Chung-Shing Lee and Eli Berniker, 2006).

Charities and NPOs will still need to continue marketing and campaign promotions as they always have. They now have new approaches (e.g. new business models) and tools (e.g. intranet and online communities) to use in soliciting funds from the public. Various e-philanthropy models can be implemented to sustain their business models without the need to rely on major tragedies to raise large amounts of donations. (Chung-Shing Lee and Eli Berniker, 2006). However, with the broadening of philanthropy's reach, wealthy individuals gain greater access to innovative projects in need of funds. They also have unprecedented opportunities to market their causes and generate far more funding via numerous small donations than traditionally they would have made by writing a few large checks. What's more, the collaborative spirit found in social-networking websites and in the contests with public feedback is starting to find its way into the giving side. New approaches like online contests and Causes on Facebook will allow many more young people to make giving a regular part of their lives-even if they aren't familiar with that old-fashioned word philanthropy, it's called philanthropy 2.0. It's healthier if a million people give $10 than if one person gives $10 million, it makes a healthier society.

There is a need for charities, NPOs, and organizations to look at new types of relationships with benefactors. The new philanthropist wants to be involved and emerge with self-gratification on a job well done. These relationships need to be cultivated and built into long-term partnerships, not just one offs satisfying someone's individual desire to do well. Finally, to operationalize the concept of disruptive innovation, this paper proposes a new method that can be applied to assist innovation managers and entrepreneurs in identifying the unique attributes and designing an innovation business model in order to capture the full benefits of a disruptive innovation. In addition, this paper also proposes a new system that utilizes the concept of the virtual value chain and innomediation to produce new knowledge, services or outlets for users to advance their needs. (Chung-Shing Lee and Eli Berniker, 2006).

(3) Nonprofits Move from Fundraising (Philanthropy 1.0) to Friend Raising (Philanthropy 2.0)

Donors have always gathered in various communities, but today there are more and more people thinking about co-funding, funder collaboratives and other ways that they can leverage their giving through interacting with other donors. In addition, as nonprofits move from fundraising (philanthropy 1.0) to friend raising (philanthropy 2.0), they are recognizing the power of building a web 2.0 community of supporters and donors are beginning to see the value of this community as well.

In terms of utilizing the Web for non-profit purposes, Kiva.org is a shining example. It has the usual 'web 2.0' things like RSS feeds, journals with comments (like blogs), facewall that links to user profiles, badges for websites, easy Web payments (using credit card, Paypal, etc), recommendations, and more. Kiva creates a similar interpersonal connection at much lower costs due to the instant, inexpensive nature of internet. The Seattle Times called it "Philanthropy 2.0" and noted: "The power of the Internet not only makes it possible for donors to find organizations and causes they support around the world, but it means that even small amounts by individuals can make a big difference because of the sheer volume of givers." Overall Kiva.org is an impressive use of the Web and shows there's much more to web 2.0 than just Flickr, del.icio.us, YouTube and MySpace. Read/WriteWeb will be profiling more of these web-empowered non-profits in future posts - they literally give new meaning to 'world wide web'!

Technology has since transformed personal communications and shopping habits, but philanthropy has consistently lagged behind this trend. The Cases want to help it catch up. foundations- are defining charity as something that everyone should make part of their daily lives. To further that new ideal, they are hosting online competitions that help donors choose grant recipients. They are also tapping online social networks such as Facebook and Second Life to foster new ways for philanthropic groups to coalesce and to find new solutions for persistent social ills. In keeping with the consumer-business model, philanthropists are also seeking ways to use technology to reach out to those who want to give, rather than relying on traffic to a particular website. The project is designed to replicate online the networks that support grassroots social and political movements.

Causes allows Facebook's more than 61 million active users to create a cause complete with a real-world nonprofit beneficiary. Users then invite friends on the site to join, and members can even donate to the cause directly through Facebook. We are putting tools in the hands of individual activists to change the world on a large scale. Which hosts collaborative online competitions to help foster social change, was merely a fraction of that budget. And as high-net-worth individuals and foundations explore new ideas, they must strive to match modern technologies with appropriate projects, rather than simply racing to adopt the latest online fad.

The challenge is to figure out how the Internet fits their mission. While working on ways to maximize new technologies, philanthropists are already seeing clear benefits from these innovations. The collaborative spirit found in social-networking websites and in the contests with public feedback is starting to find its way into the giving side. Contests and online calls for ideas have yielded access to hundreds of ideas and individuals that otherwise would not have been discovered. Posting ideas online offers exposure to a broad audience and fosters collaboration among participants. That breaks with the usual winner-takes-all outcome, in which many good ideas end up discarded. Because Make It Your Own was designed to bring in people who are traditionally shut out of the grant process. Focus on ideas yielded an unprecedentedly diverse group of entrants across age, racial, ethnic and geographic lines. This confirms social media is a potential growth area through which major donors can be cultivated.

Nonprofits and charities have a strong opportunity to engage in meaningful conversations (that may lead to contributions) with the social media savvy – especially those who are uncultivated. This indicates a growing market for distribution of information via social networks. Trust in social media is significant among social media savvy would-be donors. They trust social networks and blogs to provide important information. Social media use is also very high with users participating in social networks, participating in blogs, participating in message boards. Social Networks: It's About the Relationship and trust.

In summary, this chapter integrates different new business model of venture philanthropists from different theories of worldwide scholars, practitioners, undeveloped, developing and developed countries to construct an innovative business model: philanthropy 2.0, it integrates web 2.0 technology with trust and relationships to build a network platform of Philanthropy 2.0 is the key to successfully connect VP with donors, charities and funders. It hopes to help NPOs to connect supporters, donors with other donors and supporters and with charities, NPOs, and organizations to share knowledge and experiences, finally to help the people who are really need help. Meanwhile, charities, NPOs, and organizations all are able to achieve self-growth and sustainable operation to reach triple win.

Recommendations

(1) Recommendations for Academics

Currently, it seems that nonprofits and charities alike may not be maximizing the possibilities of online services and the Internet to stimulate giving. There may be a low awareness of the possibilities that are currently available from service providers and software. Charities and NPOs may also assume they could not safely and securely manage this type of transaction and the handling of information.

Philanthropy 1.0 comes in a variety of customizable tools that can be used individually or pooled with other innovative and traditional methods to fulfill specific needs. It allows a cost effective process to conveniently move money to a desired recipient, allowing more money to go to programs where it can do the most good. The benefits to the gift recipients should be larger portions of donations retained for the specified use, as well as an inexpensive route for them to solicit and receive money directly from individuals. However, the model lacks of "trust" and "relationships" among the participators for VP, hence, the future researcher could address how to integrate web 2.0 even web 3.0 technology with trust and relationships to build a network platform of Philanthropy 2.0 or 3.0 to successfully construct an innovative business model for VP to connect donors, charities and funders. Moreover, the future researcher could study how to move forward with a Philanthropy

2.0 strategy for charity or fundraising: What are best small learning pilots to get started to attract bigger dollar donors through Philanthropy 2.0? How is your organization planning to incorporate a Philanthropy 2.0 strategy in your fundraising efforts to attract larger dollar donors? What are the challenges? What works? How to attract and employ right people to design and implement Philanthropy 2.0 business model?

(2) Recommendations for Charities and Funders

Charities should very clear know about your organisation's mission and what it is you want to achieve, when research venture philanthropy, Charities have to thoroughly and carefully consider if it is suitable for your organization, and carefully research the venture philanthropy funders and try to identify a suitable match against their selection criteria. Use your organisations networks and try to make a connection, you will need a champion from within the organisation who believes in the approach to push through the process. It is important to make your presentation business like, using investment language and setting out clear expectations from the outset. Manage the expectations of your staff and plan ahead. Make sure to build regular time into the process for reflection. Funders should be clear on your definition of VP, your area of focus and your reasons for this. Endeavour to have greater communication and co-ordination between organizations involved in the VP and social investment marketplace so that there might be clearer segmentation in the field. Set out the expectations of commitment very clearly from the start. Consider providing a full time management assistant to the CEO as part of the model. Be open to learning from the charity sector and demonstrate adaptability of business models to suit the needs of the sector. Bigger is not always better. Develop methods of demonstrating impact that do not always involve scaling up. Look to develop local funding relationships for charities supported from the outset as a means of working towards exit.

Nonprofits such as charities and funders have a strong opportunity to engage in meaningful conversations (that may lead to contributions) with the social media (web 2.0) savvy – especially those who are uncultivated. This indicates a growing market for distribution of information via social networks. Trust in social media is significant among social media savvy would-be donors.

REFERENCES

Afuah, A., & Tucci, C. L. (2003). *Internet business models and strategies: Text and cases (2nd ed)*. New York: McGraw-Hill/Irwin. Austin, J.E. (2001). The e-philanthropy revolution is here to stay. *Chronicle of Philanthropy, 13*(10), 72-73.

Bernholz, L. (2009). *Philanthropy 1.0 vs. Philanthropy 2.0*. Retrieved from http://www.tacticalphilanthropy.com/2009/10/philanthropy-2-0

Blau, A. (2001b) *More than bit players: How information technology will change the ways nonprofits and foundations work and thrive in the information age.* A report to the Surdna Foundation. Retrieved from http://www.surdna.org/documents/morefinal.pdf

Chambers, R. (2008). *Social Venture Philanthropy–a business concept for non-profits, Venture Philanthropy.* Paper presented at 'The Social Investment Seminar' series. South Bank University, London.

Chaudhury, A., & Kuilboer, J. (2002). *E-business and e-commerce infrastructure: Technologies supporting the e-business initiative*. NY: McGraw-Hill/Irwin.

Christensen, C. M. (1997). *Innovator's dilemma: When technologies cause great firms to fail*. Boston: Harvard Business School Press.

Conlin, M., & Hempel, J. (2003). The top givers: Today's philanthropists aren't leaving the good works to future generations–they're making their mark now. *BusinessWeek*, 78-84.

Curan, C. (May 1, 2008). Philanthropy 2.0. *Worth Magazine*. Retrieved from http://www.atlanticphilanthropies.org/news/philanthropy-20

Diaz, Q., Kanter, B., & Livingston, G. (2009). *Social media for social causes study: The results*. Retrieved from http://mashable.com/2009/03/26/social-media-nonprofit-study/

Foote, S. (2007). *Philanthropy 2.0: Leveraging the venture capital model*. Venture Capital Journal.

Grobman, G. M. (2008). *The nonprofit handbook: Everything you need to know to start and run your nonprofit organization*. White Hat Communications.

Harji, K. (2009). *Building a new business model for the philanthropy advisory industry*. Retrieved from http://www.socialfinance.ca/blog/post/building_a_new_business_model_for_the_philanthropy_advisory_industry/

International Venture Philanthropy Forum. (2001). *Venture philanthropy*. Retrieved from http://forum.nesst.org/.

Jamkit & Philanthropy UK. (2009). *Venture philanthropy*. Retrieved from http://www.philanthropyuk.org/Resources/Venturephilanthropy

John, R. (2006). *The evolution of high engagement philanthropy in Europe*. Skoll Centre for Social Entrepreneurship, Saïd Business School.

Kanter, B. (2009). *Philanthropy 2.0 study results published on Mashable*. Retrieved from http://beth.typepad.com/beths_blog/2009/03/philanthropy-20-study-results-published-on-mashable.html

Kirschfoundation. (2009). *Venture philanthropy: The new model*. Retrieved from http://www.kirschfoundation.org/why/venture.html

Ladd, K. (2009). *Philanthropy with a business model*. Retrieved from http://www.foxbusiness.com/story/personal-finance/women-in-business/philanthropy-business-model/

Lee, C. S., & Berniker, E. (2006). *E-philanthropy: Disruptive innovations in non-profit fund raising*. ePLU E-Commerce & Technology Management Center, Pacific Lutheran University, IAMOT Conference Archive.

Lee, C. S., & Vonortas, N. S. (2004). Business model innovation in the digital economy. In Doukidis, G., Mylonopoulos, N., & Pouloudi, N. (Eds.), *Social and economic transformation in the digital era* (pp. 164–181). Hershey, PA: Idea Group Publishing.

MacManus, R. (2007). *Kiva: Philanthropy 2.0*. Retrieved from http://www.readwriteweb.com/archives/kiva_philanthropy20.php

McWilliams, G. (October 2, 2003). Dells plan hands-on approach to charity donations, programs. *The Wall Street Journal*, p. B10.

Miller, W. L., & Morris, L. (1999). *Fourth generation R&D: Managing knowledge, technology, and innovation*. New York: John Wiley & Sons, Inc.

O'Malley, J., & Perkins, J. (2007). *The long tail of Facebook causes*. Frogloop Blog.

Olsen, M., Keevers, M. L., Paul, J., & Covington, S. (2001). E-relationship development strategy for the nonprofit fundraising professional. *International Journal of Nonprofit and Voluntary Sector Marketing*, *6*(4), 364–373. doi:10.1002/nvsm.161

Porter, M. E. (2002). The competitive advantage of corporate philanthropy. *Harvard Business Review*, *80*(12), 57–68.

Rappa, M. (2003). *Business models on the Web: Managing the digital enterprise*. Retrieved from http://digitalenterprise.org/models/models.html.

Rayport, J. F., & Sviokla, J. J. (1995). Exploiting the virtual value chain. *Harvard Business Review*, *73*(6), 75–85.

Sawhney, M., Prandelli, E., & Verona, G. (2003). The power of innomediation. *Sloan Management Review*, *44*(2), 77–82.

Shoemaker, P. (2002). *Social venture partners: Venture Philanthropy in a changed world*. Retrieved from http://foundationcenter.org/pnd/newsmakers/nwsmkr.jhtml?id=13200025

Smile Foundation. (2008). *Social Venture Philanthropy–a business concept for non-profits*. Retrieved from http://www.1888pressrelease.com/social-venture-philanthropy-a-business-concept-for-non-pro-pr-81751.html

The International Center for Not-For-Profit Law. (2010). *FAQ: What is the difference between non-profit and not-for-profit?* Retrieved from http://www.icnl.org/contact/faq.htm#difference

Tierwriting.com. (2010). About Venture Philanthropy. Retrieved from http://tierwriting.com/2010/03/about-venture-philanthropy/

Wallace, N. (2002). Outlook for online donations is cloudy, experts say. *Chronicle of Philanthropy*, *14*(11), 27.

ADDITIONAL READING

Amabile, T. M. (1988). A model of creativity and innovation in organization." Edited by Behavior, 10: p.123-167.

Amabile, T. M. (1997). Entrepreneurial creativity through motivational synergy. *The Journal of Creative Behavior*, *31*(1), 18–26.

Awazu, Y., & Desouza, K. C. (2004). Open knowledge management: Lessons from the open source revolution. *Journal of the American Society for Information Science and Technology*, *55*(11), 1016–1019. doi:10.1002/asi.20050

Baldridge, J., & Burnham, R. (1975). Organizational innovation: Industrial, organizational, and environmental impact. *Administrative Science Quarterly*, 165–176. doi:10.2307/2391692

Brown, J. S., & Duguid, P. (2002). Local knowledge - Innovation in the networked age. *Management Learning*, *33*(4), 427–437. doi:10.1177/1350507602334002

Buffett, G., Weiss, T., & Clark Forbes, H. (2006). 'Venture philanthropy' is new buzz in business, http://www.msnbc.msn.com/id/13556127/

Cavallo, D. (2004). Models of growth — towards fundamental change in learning environments. *BT Technology Journal*, *22*(4). doi:10.1023/B:BTTJ.0000047588.81509.4c

Chou, S. W., & Tsai, Y. H. (2004). Knowledge creation: individual and organizational perspectives. *Journal of Information Science*, *30*(3), 205–218. doi:10.1177/0165551504042803

CNET News.com (2004). Does venture philanthropy work? http://news.cnet.com/2030-1030_3-5206330.html

Cooper, R. G., & Kleinschmidt, E. J. (1987). Success factors in product innovation. *Industrial Marketing Management*, (16): 215–223. doi:10.1016/0019-8501(87)90029-0

Daft, R. L. (1978). A dual-core model of organization innovation. *Academy of Management Journal*, (21): 193–210. doi:10.2307/255754

Damanpour, F. & Fariborz. (1996). Organizational complexity and innovation: Developing and testing multiple contingency models. *Management Science*, *4*(2), 693–716. doi:10.1287/mnsc.42.5.693

Delbridge, R. (2003). Knowledge, innovation and institutional change. *Work, Employment and Society*, *17*(1), 187–196. doi:10.1177/0950017003017001279

Gilmour, D. (2003). How to fix knowledge management - Companies should stop trying to capture knowledge and instead help employees truly connect. *Harvard Business Review*, *81*(10), 16.

Helmig, B., Jegers, M., & Lapsley, I. (2004). Challenges in Managing Nonprofit Organizations: A Research Overview. *Voluntas*, *15*(2), 107–116. doi:10.1023/B:VOLU.0000033176.34018.75

Hemmings Kahn, E. (2007). *2007 Philanthropy Development Report*, Social Venture Partners International Demonstrating, www.svpi.org

Higgins & James M. (1995). Innovation: The core competence. *Planning Review*, (23), 32-36.

Hull, C. E., & Lio, B. H. (2006). Innovation in Non-profit and For-profit Organizations: Visionary, Strategic, and Financial Considerations. *Journal of Change Management*, *6*(1), 53–65. doi:10.1080/14697010500523418

Hussey & David E. (1997). *Creativity, innovation and strategy: The innovation challenge*. London: John Wiley & Sons Ltd.

Jaskyte, K., & de Riob, M. S. R. M. (2004). Characteristics of Innovative Nonprofit Organizations in Argentina. *Voluntas*, *15*(1), 71–79. doi:10.1023/B:VOLU.0000023634.07861.70

Johnson, L. D., Neave, E. H., & Pazderka, B. (2002). Knowledge, innovation and share value. *International Journal of Management Reviews*, *4*(2), 101–134. doi:10.1111/1468-2370.00080

Kim, L. (1980). Organizational innovation and structure. *Journal of Business Research*, (8): 225–245. doi:10.1016/0148-2963(80)90012-0

Kusunoki, K., Nonaka, I., & Nagata, A. (1998). Organizational capabilities in product development of Japanese firms: A conceptual framework and empirical findings. *Organization Science*, *9*(6), 699–718. doi:10.1287/orsc.9.6.699

Lemon, M., & Sahota, P. S. (2004). Organizational culture as a knowledge repository for increased innovative capacity. *Technovation*, *24*(6), 483–498. doi:10.1016/S0166-4972(02)00102-5

Light, D. A. (2004). Knowledge management - When learning stops. *MIT Sloan Management Review*, *45*(4), 10–11.

Majchrzak, A., Cooper, L. P., & Neece, O. E. (2004). Knowledge reuse for innovation. *Management Science*, *50*(2), 174–188. doi:10.1287/mnsc.1030.0116

Mason, D. D. M. (2004). Knowledge management: Current issues and challenges. *The Electronic Library*, *22*(2), 193.

Mercier (2003). Lectures on knowledge management: Paradigms, challenges and opportunities. *Knowledge Organization, 30*(1), 42-44.

Meyer, A. D., & Goes, J. B. (1988). Organizational assimilation of innovations: A multilevel contextual analysis. *Academy of Management Journal*, (31): 897–923. doi:10.2307/256344

Miller, D., & Friesen, P. H. (1982). Innovation in conservative and entrepreneurial firms: Two models of strategic momentum. *Strategic Management Journal*, (3): 1–25. doi:10.1002/smj.4250030102

Moch, Michael K., Edward V., & Morse. (1977). Size, centralization and organizational adoption of innovations. *American Sociological Review*, (42): 716–725. doi:10.2307/2094861

Nicholson, N. (1990). Organizational innovation in context: Culture, interpretation and application. In West, M. A., & Farr, J. L. (Eds.), *Innovation and creativity at work* (pp. 179–20). New York: Wiley.

Nonaka, I. (1991). The knowledge creating company. *Harvard Business*, *69*(6), 96–104.

Nonaka, I., Takeuchi, H., & Umemoto, K. (1996). A theory of organizational knowledge creation. *International Journal of Technology Management*, *11*(7-8), 833–845.

Nonaka, I., Umemoto, K., & Senoo, D. (1996). From information processing to knowledge creation: A paradigm shift in business management. *Technology in Society*, *18*(2), 203–218. doi:10.1016/0160-791X(96)00001-2

Normann, R. (1971). Organizational innovativeness: Product variation and reorientation. *Administrative Science Quarterly*, (16): 203–215. doi:10.2307/2391830

Oates & Keith. (1997). Innovation is everybody's business. *Management Services*, *41*(5), 8–13.

Osborne, S. P. (1998). Naming the beast: Defining and classifying service innovations in social policy. *Human Relations*, *51*(9), 1133–1155. doi:10.1177/001872679805100902

Papert, S. (1980). *Mindstorms: children, computers, and powerful ideas*. New York: Basic Books.

Papert, S. (1991). Situating constructionism. In Harel, I., & Papert, S. (Eds.), *Constructionism*. Ablex Publishing Corporation.

Perri (1993). Innovation by nonprofit organizations: Policy and research issues. *Nonprofit Management and Leadership* *3*(4), 397–414.

Sveiby (2003). How (and why) did the field of knowledge management come into being? *Ekonomiska Samfundets Tidskrift, 56*(3), 185-188.

Tushman, N. L., & Nadler, D. A. (1986). Organizing for innovation. *California Management Review*, *28*, 74–92.

Van de Ven, Andrew H., & Rogers, E.M. (1988). Innovation and organizations-critical perspectives. *Communication Research*, (15): 632–651.

Wolfe, R. A. (1994). Organizational innovation: Review, critique and suggested research directions. *Journal of Management Studies*, *31*(3), 405–430. doi:10.1111/j.1467-6486.1994.tb00624.x

KEY TERMS AND DEFINITIONS

E-Philanthropy: Austin (2001) describes e-philanthropy as the use of the Internet to raise money and recruit volunteers. The concept allows individuals the ability to setup donation pledges and facilitates the electronic transfer of funds to the charity or organization of one's choosing. E-philanthropy services have the potential to reduce the fund raising costs of philanthropic fund raising to Non-Profit Organizations (NPOs) and to disrupt the business models of commercial fund raising organizations that utilize direct mail or telephone marketing.

NPOs: Non-Profit Organizations, A non-profit organization (abbreviated as NPO, also known as a not-for-profit organization (The International Center for Not-For-Profit Law) is an organization that does not distribute its surplus funds to owners or shareholders, but instead uses them to help pursue its goals (Gary M. Grobman, White Hat Communications, 2008). Examples of NPOs include charities (i.e. charitable organizations), trade unions, and public arts organizations. Most governments and government agencies meet this definition, but in most countries they are considered a separate type of organization and not counted as NPOs. They are in most countries exempt from income and property taxation.

Philanthropy 2.0: In the world of Philanthropy 2.0, it's not just about giving back. It's about maximizing that impact in whatever innovative way possible. Take advantage of Silicon Valley's social networks and business acumen. Investing in new technologies, funding entrepreneurs and taking gambles on exciting ideas are commonplace for venture capitalists. Now, this successful model and hard-learned experience is being replicated to address philanthropic goals. Enter "venture philanthropy" funds, the Philanthropy 2.0 way of allocating capital to social causes. The Internet has revolutionized many businesses, and now Philanthropy 2.0 is starting to harness the medium to solve many startup problems. One big problem of socially focused organizations is money. Most organizations must raise large sums of money to run their infrastructure and fund their social efforts. The future of Philanthropy 2.0 is as big, and as varied, as Web 2.0. (Sean Foote, 2007).

Social Venture Philanthropy' (SVP): This model is a replica of very successful and innovative business concept called "Venture Capital". Smile Foundation for the first time in the development sector adopted the unique concept of 'Social Venture Philanthropy' (SVP). The model is inspired from a successful business concept, 'Venture Capital', where networks of accomplished individuals combine financial contributions and professional skills with a passion for philanthropy.

Venture Philanthropy (VP): Jamkit and Philanthropy UK (2009) defined Venture philanthropy (VP) is an approach to charitable giving that applies venture capital investment principles – such as long-term investment and capacity-building support – to the voluntary and community sector. According to Wikipedia, Venture philanthropy, also known as philanthrocapitalism, takes concepts and techniques from venture capital finance and high technology business management and applies them to achieving philanthropic goals (Tierwriting.com, 2010).

Section 3
Implementing New Business Models:
Technology and Applications

Chapter 10
Rethinking Business Process Reengineering:
The Empirical Modelling Approach

Yih-Chang Chen
Chang Jung Christian University, Taiwan

ABSTRACT

The purpose of this chapter is to introduce a new approach–Empirical Modelling–to computing and business modelling. Today most business processes rely on informal knowledge and social behaviour but these are areas which have not, so far, been well suited for modelling with computer-based techniques. For this, Empirical Modelling is introduced to modelling with computers, which has natural application to business process modelling. This chapter will suggest a way of applying this approach to integrated system development with BPR. A framework using this approach, SPORE (situated process of requirements engineering), is extended to encompass applications to participative BPR (i.e. supporting many users in a distributed environment). An outline of an application of our methods to a warehouse management system is included.

INTRODUCTION

The core of this chapter is aimed at introducing an innovative approach to business process reengineering (BPR) and the development of associated information systems. This first section starts with the aims and motivation for the research, and gives the primary overview of the challenges and potential problems faced in these subjects. At the end of this section, the outline of this chapter is presented.

Today most corporations are faced with a highly competitive market environment changing at an accelerating rate. In the early 1990s several

DOI: 10.4018/978-1-60960-129-4.ch010

analysts were suggesting that the conventional incremental style of organisational change was inadequate for this challenge. To gain competitive advantage or even maintain market position, it was argued, would require so-called 'radical' change. It had become common to use the metaphor of 'engineering' to describe change that is planned or designed (cf. 'software engineering'). So it was natural for describing this new order of change that 'Business Process Reengineering', or 'Business Process Re-design' (BPR), became the preferred terms. From this perspective it was crucial that business processes should be re-designed in a cross-functional process 'vision' guided by overall objectives and new resources, particularly the resources of information technology (IT). There was an optimism for IT reminiscent of the early days of artificial intelligence: "IT capabilities .... can work miracles by the standards of previous generations. How else but through this technology can we manage our processes globally, instantly, efficiently, and correctly? It is clear that no other tools are comparable." (Davenport, 1993, p. 66). However, it was not to be long before disillusion with the BPR vision appeared. In 1996 Davenport himself published an article entitled *Why Re-engineering Failed: The Fad that Forgot People* in which he admits:

To most business people in the United States, re-engineering has become a word that stands for restructuring, lay-offs, and too often, failed change programmes...companies that embraced [re-engineering] as the silver bullet are now looking for ways to re-build the organisation's torn fabric. (Davenport, 1996, p. 70)

Thus far only around 30% of BPR projects are regarded as a success. The earlier promise of BPR had not been fulfilled. One reaction to this outcome was to retain faith in IT as a dominant support and just admit that since it could not adapt – or at least not at acceptable levels of cost – then business activities must adapt to IT. For example:

The pendulum has swung from 'continuous reengineering and re-inventing' to 'pick an application package and force our business processes to comply with the package'. (Riemer, 1998, p. 69)

Another response was to be more relaxed over the likely role of IT in business:

IT can often be a catalyst in this process [of change] and IT opportunities for new or enhanced products and services should certainly not be overlooked. (Galliers, 1998, p. 226)

There are, no doubt, many reasons for the limited success of the BPR programme. It was surely over-hyped in the first place. There is only a certain amount, and rate, of change that people and organisations can accommodate while maintaining their basic business objectives. Most business processes depend crucially at every point upon people and their informal knowledge and social behaviour. But these are areas for which conventional computer-based techniques are not well suited and there was, and still remains today, a substantial gap between the need to model business process innovations and the capabilities and mechanisms available from IT to support the task.

In so far as IT is itself the problem here – as opposed to the solution it was intended to be – the problem lies more with software than with hardware. Hardware developments – multimedia functions, networks, storage and processor performance, screen display – have been impressive over recent years. But although object-oriented methods have made an important contribution, the 'software crisis' has still not been solved. Taking proper account of human factors is well known to be a major challenge for all interactive software. And the first human factor to be considered is the requirement of the software system. The most sensitive and difficult area of software development lies in requirements engineering. Should this be a phase with an end-point – as the programmer would prefer? Or should it be a continuous evolution – as the customer would prefer? There are notorious difficulties for conventional development methods in having to define, and make a commitment to, a hard system boundary in advance of any system development work. For example, a requirement specification is often referred to as the basis for a contract between the developer and the customer. That specification, and contract, represents the documentation of such a boundary. At the design level the concept of a rigid boundary re-appears in making decisions about the objects or components to be used in an application program. The difficulties that affect object-oriented methods in analysis and design are discussed in (Kaindl, 1999) with reference to the movement from the problem domain (real world application) to the solution domain (world of programs and systems).

In this paper, we introduce a novel, human-centred approach to modelling and system development. It is human-centred in taking seriously the subjective experience of the modeller – both as a starting point for model construction and as a guiding principle throughout development. The central role in our approach given to observation and experiment has led to it being called 'Empirical Modelling' (EM). It is not so much a methodology as a broad outlook on computing which has far-reaching consequences. Indeed it can be thought of as a reengineering of the computing process itself. We describe it in greater detail in section 3. Then in section 4 we explain how EM can be applied to BPR. The main idea here is that it is essential within EM to take account of the wider context of a desired 'system' in terms of the purposes, people and other resources which will form the environment of the system. A problem-oriented framework SPORE (situated process of requirements engineering) is described. By applying SPORE to the software requirements of a business, possible solutions to problems in the business domain can be explored in an open-ended and situated manner. We propose that the SPORE concept can be extended to support effective and efficient participative BPR. Within this framework, people participating in the business process can create and use the models as a powerful means of supporting their collaborative interaction for 'growing' solutions, or reengineering processes, in a distributed environment.

In section 5 a case study applying this framework to a warehouse distribution system is discussed. A 'use case driven' version of this case study appears in (Jacobson et al., 1992). In contrast to the Jacobson version we model some of the processes as they might have been prior to the proposed computer system. They are modelled as a series of interactions between agents (both human and non-human agents). The resulting environment is suited to reengineering the processes through negotiation between the existing (problem) situation and possible solutions defined by requirements for system components (including software).

BUSINESS PROCESS REENGINEERING

We sketch here an outline of some of the issues and problems involved in BPR. Although this discussion is brief, we hope it will be sufficient to show the relevance and potential of the approach (EM) that we describe in later sections.

The Key Concepts

In 1990s two key publications (one by Hammer and Champy, another by Davenport) brought widespread attention to the emerging field of BPR. The very concept of 'business process' required a re-orientation of managers' thinking about their business activities. It is defined by Hammer and Champy (2003) as a set of activities which produces an output valuable to the customer. This concept cut across traditional boundaries in the structure of a business (e.g. departments, sections, functions). For example, the process of new product development cut across departments for R&D, for manufacturing and for marketing. Then 'reengineering' meant discovering how a process currently operates, re-designing that process to improve efficiency and remove wastage, and finally implementing the new process using whatever enabling technology was appropriate. The force of the new terminology was to draw attention to a perceived need for 'radical change', not mere 'improvement'. The scale of change envisaged by the term 'reengineering', or 'innovation' as preferred by Davenport, is described as follows:

Objectives of 5% or 10% improvement in all business processes each year must give way to efforts to achieve 50%, 100%, or even higher improvement levels in a few key processes. (Davenport, 1993, p. 1)

The lesson we take from this is that when the business context and resources are changing rapidly, radical change may need to take place regularly. In order to model such changes effectively with computers we require environments with the greatest flexibility.

Participative BPR

BPR seeks to devise new ways of organising tasks, organising people and making use of IT systems so that the resulting processes will better support the goals of the organisation. Vidgen et al. (1994) define the central tenets of BPR as:

- Radical change and assumption challenge;
- Process and goal orientation;
- Organisational re-structuring;
- The exploitation of enabling technologies, particularly information technology.

Thus, BPR has more of an organisational focus than a technical one. The effort is directed at changing people's thinking and must therefore take into account expectations and viewpoints. The process view of the business activities involved in new product development, for example, reflects the customer's viewpoint more than the producer's viewpoint.

While the thought of the scale of change mentioned above by Davenport might be intoxicating for managers to consider, it is likely to be a less exciting prospect for those employees who are directly driving such order of magnitude changes in performance. Thus Sherwood-Smith (1994) advocates a less strident form of BPR which is people-centred and driven by needs, rather than by IT.

Administrative systems involving people should not be reengineered, they should be participatively re-designed. (Sherwood-Smith, 1994, p. 536)

Such a participative approach respects the culture and social context of an organisation. This demands a high degree of communication and evaluation. In reference to CASE tools supporting BPR, Sherwood-Smith continues (in the same paper):

Because we believe Business Process Re-Design is essentially a group activity and should be participative, one key aspect of the tool set is that it must run in a collaborative environment. (Sherwood-Smith, 1994, p. 543)

This sentiment is an exception to what seems to be the more usual undemanding and uncritical attitude to IT from authors on BPR. Available software resources are often accepted as given and their limitations go uncommented although it is, we suspect, precisely their profound limitations that are a significant factor in the 'failure' of some BPR efforts. Many current applications are designed in a 'take it or leave it' fashion which is inappropriate to a rapidly changing business environment. With frequent mergers and outsourcing of activities businesses need computing environments which support unforeseen changes in needs and can exploit opportunities as they arise. The EM approach creates such environments and they support collaborative working.

Modelling Business Processes

Organisations and their business processes are complex. Understanding anything involves making some kind of model of the thing in our heads. Thus a fundamental motive for modelling business processes is to help understand them. It is controversial in the BPR literature exactly how much understanding of a process is necessary or desirable prior to its re-design. Hammer and Champy (2003) argue that a very detailed analysis of process is not needed because the goal of the reengineering effort is not to improve the existing process but to design a 'totally new and superior design'. As both Hammer and van Meel et al. have observed most business structures have not been designed at all, but have simply 'emerged'. But such evolution has occurred in a social and technical context that is not arbitrary. There are usually reasons for the way things emerge and sometimes they turn out to be very important reasons (that are only discovered after a disastrous re-design!). So we take the view that in the case of processes of any complexity it is important to have as thorough an understanding of the process as possible. It is only then one can dare responsibly to propose a really new design. Since this is a controversial issue we note that (Jacobson et al., 1995) supports our view. In a chapter devoted to this theme ('Reversing the Existing Business') they write:

... we do believe that you need a good picture of your current organization before you can finally decide on the best way to change it. If the reengineers understand the business as it is today, they will be able to avoid making unfeasible change proposals. (p.153)

Modelling a business process helps us to understand it and so to re-design it. In a comprehensive, Germanic style the modelling task has been described as follows:

Modelling business processes first means to express the flow and the dependencies of steps in the respective processes in order to make the dynamic behaviour explicit, to be able to communicate it, to analyse it with respect to possibilities of improvement, and to use it for simulations as well as for controlling automated workflow. (Schader & Korthaus, 1998, p. 57)

This statement effectively summarises the four 'requirements' of a modelling method for BPR given by Gerrits (1994). Gerrits emphasises the role of simulation both for assessing the quality of the models of the current situation on the one hand, and the performance of the re-designed processes, on the other hand.

According to van Meel et al. (1994), the methods for achieving business engineering given in the literature 'roughly follow the pattern of general problem solving'. To offer more support for BPR these authors suggest a model-based problem solving approach summarised in Figure 1 (amended from Keen & Sol, 2008). The term 'empirical model' used by these authors means something very different from our usage in EM as described in section 3. For example, the Keen and Sol's empirical model is a text-based version of a

Figure 1. The process of problem solving

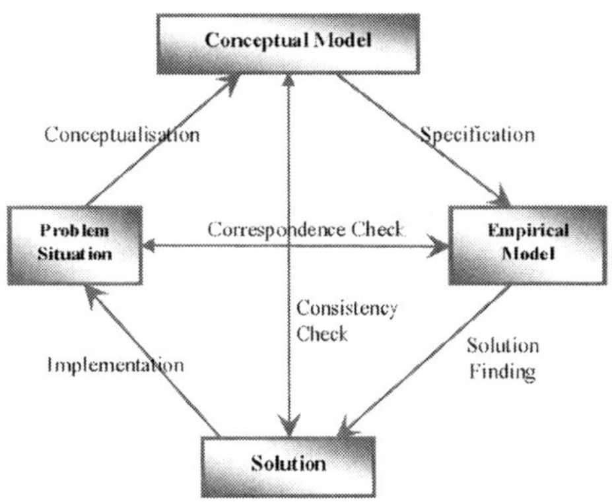

conceptual model; an EM model is a computer-based version of an experiential model.

To sum up, for Keen and Sol's model, the process starts with a problem perceived by a problem owner. Next a conceptual model of the problem situation, a data void representation of the problem solver's mental model of the problem situation, is constructed. This model acts as the basis for the specification activity, i.e. the problem situation is specified in more detail, resulting in an empirical model. Then a correspondence check is performed to assess whether the empirical model is a valid representation of the problem situation. From the empirical model, solutions are identified and analysed, and solutions are also checked to see whether they are consistent with the conceptual model.

Nevertheless there are striking structural similarities between the Keen and Sol's approach and ours, for example in the notion of an experimental, correspondence check between the model and the problem situation. We mention this approach also because the framework here of *problem situation and solution [space]* is a recurring and unifying theme of our approach. It is one that has recently been used in EM work on requirements, and we apply it in this paper for the application of EM to BPR.

Object-Orientation and Use Cases

The emergence of BPR in the early 1990s coincided with a dramatic rise in claims and interest in object-oriented (OO) methods of software development. There was unprecedented investment in OO by industry and huge co-operation between industries to establish standards and tools for OO (e.g. the formation of the powerful Object Management Group). The was a mushrooming of textbooks and obligatory courses on OO academia. Since BPR laid emphasis on exploiting the resources of IT, it was natural that those in charge of reengineering projects should turn to OO methods. Among many others the series of well-known works by Jacobson and his co-authors (e.g. Jacobson et al., 1992; Jacobson et al., 1995; Jacobson et al., 1997; Jacobson & Ng, 2004; Jacobson, 2009) no doubt helped to forge these links between BPR and OO approaches to system development. The 'use case driven' development method for software was the subject of the first work, then it was applied in (Jacobson et al., 1995) to the modelling of business processes. A use case is literally a 'case of use' of a proposed or existing system and refers to some specific use by an 'actor' (a role of a potential user of the system). It is a sequence of events corresponding to some function of the system useful to the user. At one level such a sequence or 'course' of events corresponds closely to a (business) process. At a lower level of abstraction it may, in some cases, also correspond to a functional requirement for a software system. The collection of all use cases constitutes the use case model which is a major part of the requirements model in Jacobson's software development method.

Schader and Korthaus (1998) draw attention to the range of attributes (e.g. 'iterative', 'use case driven', 'incremental') which can apply equally to both software development and business modelling. As Warboys et al. (1999) state:

Both the business process practitioner and the software process modeller have much in common ..... One has to design dynamically changeable and efficient processes, and the other the process knowledgeable software to support them. (p. 12)

Another link between BPR and software development lies in the common pattern of negotiation between a problem situation and a solution space. In BPR, this is reflected in the optimum level of goal satisfaction in the light of resources available, and in software, in the ongoing evolution of a requirement. In a way similar to the work of Jacobson et al. (1995), Nurcan et al. (1998) also try to identify and describe business processes by use cases and scenarios. They describe the relationship between the business process and a use case as:

A use case specification comprises a description of the context of the BP, the interactions between the agents involved in the BP, the interactions of these agents with an automated system supporting the BP and attached system internal requirements. (p. 1)

It is now widely recognised that the concept of use cases is independent of object-orientation. But both ideas, highly influential as they have been over the past decade, have also not been without their critics. We have already mentioned (Kaindl, 1999) for drawing attention to the deep problems, for long generally unacknowledged, that arise when representing informal objects in an application domain by formal objects in the programming domain. Among others, the series of papers by Simons (e.g. Simons, 1999; Simons & Graham, 1998; Simons & Graham, 1999) describe some of the serious semantic confusions surrounding use cases and object modelling.

We share with conventional methods for system development the aim of harnessing computer power to solve problems and do useful tasks. But we are doubtful that there are universal 'methods' for doing this and doubtful that the required behaviour of a complex 'system' can successfully be prescribed in use cases in advance of the construction and use of the system. This seems to us particularly true of volatile contexts with a high dependency on human factors – such as many business processes. This radical, and perhaps immodest, scepticism is one motivation for building models in the way we do in EM. Our ultimate aim is, indeed, to develop useful systems, but to do so we suggest the need in general to take a more roundabout, indirect route. We need first to understand what will be useful and how this might change. For this we need to model a wider context than that of the future system itself and EM offers the possibility to do this.

EMPIRICAL MODELLING: AN OVERVIEW

Empirical Modelling (EM) is an approach to computer-based modelling that has been developed at the University of Warwick since 1983. In this section we will give an overview of EM and summarise how our approach differs from conventional modelling methods.

Principles

The EM principles are based on the concepts of observation, agency and dependency. The initial analysis of a domain to be modelled is made by identifying *observables* considered relevant by the modeller. Then these observables are grouped around the *agents* regarded as 'centres', or sources, of change in those observables. The other source of change in the observables is where there are *dependencies* holding between them expressed by definitions. These are 'law-like' dependencies like Newton's law, the physical constraints of rigidity in a solid material, or the conventions of when a game has been won. All these identifications (of observables, dependencies, and agents) are provisional and subjective: they represent the viewpoint of the modeller. The dependencies between observables are expressed in *definitions*. A set of definitions – a *definitive script* – corresponds to a single state of the model. Any particular state of the model should directly correspond to a possible state of its external *referent*. EM is an agent-oriented approach. That is, a key idea is to attribute the state-changing activities that do not arise from dependency maintenance to agents which are associated with certain observables. Here an agent can be a human actor or any other state-changing component or device. The identification of agency and dependency is based on previous knowledge and experience, and supplemented by new observation and experiment.

There is therefore a primary emphasis in EM on state, not in a public sense but *state-as-*

perceived-by-agent, or *state-as-experienced.* It is for this reason that we describe our approach as 'experience-based'. This distinguishes EM from many conventional approaches to modelling in which concepts of state are taken for granted and more attention is given to reproducing desired behaviours. The use case driven method mentioned in section 2.4 is an example of this emphasis on behaviour.

Techniques

The main technical focus of our modelling approach is the so-called *interactive situation model* (ISM). An ISM is open to experiment in much the same way that its real world referent is open to experiment. That is, we can devise changes in the ISM, introduce new factors, and have direct experience of the results in any way we choose at the time. This leads to patterns of interaction, and a quality of close human engagement in the interaction which is unusual in computer-based models with the major exception of spreadsheet models. The concept of an ISM in fact generalises the spreadsheet in several radical ways (Rasmequan et al., 2000). The word 'situation' in ISM refers to the fact that the model is rooted in a concrete context that affects the modeller's expectation and interpretation. The model is partial, but not disconnected from the physical world (cf. Figure 2).

All EM models, and conventional spreadsheet models, are examples of ISMs. These models incorporate the agency and dependency revealed during the analysis and construction processes. At the same time they maintain the correspondence between the values of variables in a definitive script and the values of observables perceived by the modeller in both the model and its referent. So each state of the computer model may be directly perceived alongside the corresponding state of its referent. There is no preconceived systematic process to be followed in analysing a domain and constructing the ISM. That is, the modelling activity is genuinely open-ended, observations may agree or disagree with expectations and thereby affect further construction. An ISM always presents only a partial and provisional artefact to the modeller.

Notations

The roles of agents are documented using a notation that classifies observables as follows: those whose values act as stimuli for action (*oracles*), those that can be conditionally redefined (*handles*), ones whose existence depends on that of the agent itself (*states*), the relationships between observables representing the interaction between the agent and its environment (*derivates*), and the privileges of agents for state-changing action (*protocols*). We record these observations in an informal but structured notation known as LSD. Such an LSD account reflects the internal perspective of each agent in the account together with the external perspective of the modeller. Such an account is not essential but can be useful throughout the construction process. It can be maintained and refined while the main scripts are being developed.

Figure 2. Structure of the model

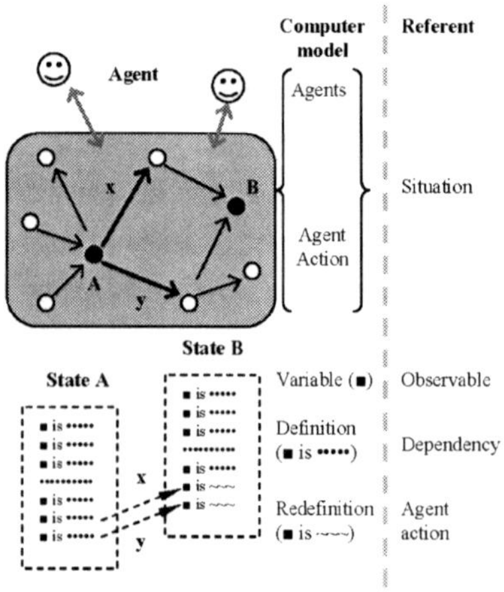

The definitions, representing dependencies, play a central technical role in EM. A typical definition takes the form of

x **is** f (*a,b,c*)

where *x, a, b*, and *c* are associated with observables in the referent. The variables *a, b* and *c* are defined elsewhere in the script and f is some operation which reflects the perceived dependency of *x* on *a, b* and *c*. The operation f will usually be some user-defined function. Such a definition is a one-way dependency rather than a constraint. It expresses the fact that changes in *a, b* and *c* will result in indivisible change in *x*; the '**is**' in the definition is a keyword indicating that this dependency will be maintained automatically. The values of variables represent the observed state from the point of view of the modeller. Changes of state occur either through re-definitions or the addition of new definitions. A script containing many definitions may have hundreds of automatic updates arising from a single re-definition. A simple event or action will typically be represented as a collection of several re-definitions grouped together. The notations providing all these facilities are known collectively as EDEN. They comprise a general purpose definitive notation together with other notations for line drawing and window management. These three notations can be used freely together in the construction of models. There is some limited assistance to users for the management and debugging of scripts but EDEN is primarily a research tool – it supports the principles of EM but lacks the robustness, efficiency and consistency needed for general end-user development.

The EM Modelling Process

There is a fundamental difference between EM and conventional modelling in the way the modeller interacts with the state of the model. In a procedural, or object-oriented, language a door object, for example, would be defined with attributes and methods carefully planned in advance of being programmed. These attributes (e.g. dimensions and manner of opening) and methods (e.g. for changing position and for display) form the door *data* for manipulation in the computer model. That data determines in advance the complete state space of the door and all possible interactions with the door. The program can, of course, be edited and re-compiled. But it remains an inherent feature of the paradigm that the program forms a boundary within which state and interaction must be preconceived. The interpretation of program state (even in the presence of visualisation) must take place across this boundary. That is, interpretation involves an association between real-world observations and program abstractions. The validity of this association – which depends on such factors as context and purpose – generally requires human judgement. The computer's manipulation of data is oblivious to such matters and when exceptions and errors arise to render an interpretation invalid, major problems are likely.

Within EM the language for the description of state is the language of *observables*. The state of the model is presented to the user by a perceptual process that is of the same kind as that by which we apprehend state in the real world. There is, then, a comparability and connectedness between observations of the model and observations of its referent. This comparability is lacking in conventional computer modelling because there the 'observation' of the model is the reading of an abstracted value, or the preconceived interpretation of a preprogrammed display. The real-world observation is a subjective, situated experience. The association required for interpreting the model is therefore an association between two things of quite different kinds.

There are three features of an EM model that give the comparability referred to above a special leverage. The link between the observable and a variable in a definition is direct and simple. This contrasts with the situation in many procedural programs where the interpretation of variables and their states can become highly problematic. We acknowledge that the variables in a definitive script must have the 'abstracted' quality we referred to above in connection with conventional programs. But this is a 'limited abstraction' in which the connection between the concrete and the abstract is deliberate and familiar – like that in the use of natural language for description of the world. As described in (Beynon et al., 2002):

There is a fundamental mismatch between abstract data that is interpreted by the human in direct association with its counterpart in the real-world referent and situation, and abstract data that is manipulated according to computational rules that can only take account of prespecified and preprogrammed features of this association. (p. 130)

The second feature is that the observation of the model is through a visualisation which is indivisibly linked to the script of the model. The very definition of a line in the line-drawing notation in EDEN is accompanied by its display, just as the existence of a physical edge in the field of vision of a person with normal faculties is automatically accompanied by its perception. The combination of the directness of these two features make for the third feature – the quality of interaction offered in an EM model. There is no preconceived limitation in the revisions the modeller may make at any time in the model and there is a built-in coherence and integrity to all interactions which invoke dependencies. There are some kinds of interaction where there are automated actions from which the human user is excluded. This is appropriate where there are specific and clearly prescribed functions – for example, when using a canned drink dispenser or a washing machine. In such interactions we do *not* wish for more flexibility or more scope for human intervention. But it is when there is no such function to be prescribed – for example, in conversation or driving a vehicle – when the 'purpose' of the interaction is to explore or experiment, that we need a different kind of interaction: one in which the participants can have a close and continuous engagement with each other. It is this latter kind of interaction which – in principle, if not yet always in practice – is offered in an EM model.

Closely allied with the difference just described concerning interaction with state is another fundamental difference between EM and conventional modelling. This is the way change of state takes place. In a conventional program change methods must be planned and preconceived as described above. The control of change is 'handed over' to actions within the program boundary. When these actions are complex and the context alters, or error conditions occur, it may be very hard to make the appropriate changes. In an EM model change either occurs as a dependency update which should always have clear and simple real-world semantics – maintaining the integrity of state – or the change occurs as a direct action of an agent. Initially, except in very simple predictable circumstances, this will be a human agent. Only when certain patterns of change have been experimented with and are known to be operating with reliability over a wide range of local states can those patterns be delegated to an 'automated' agent action.

The agency concept is a much more primitive one than that of control structures in conventional programming. But it is a very general and powerful notion that allows EM to encompass many conventional paradigms for programming and state change. Furthermore, the notion of dependency is a natural way to preserve the integrity of state change, and the real-world semantics of interaction, in a direct and comprehensible fashion.

While observations of the computer model in EM have a qualitative similarity to observations of the world, they are inevitably limited by properties of the interface (e.g. size of pixels on display) and typically require the use of visual metaphor to supplement direct observation. For the sake of understanding a domain, the faithfulness of experimental interaction matters more than the faithfulness of the representation. For example, in understanding electrical circuits the iconic representation of components, together with selected measurements is preferable to photographic images of components and comprehensive measurements.

Finally in this section we mention three further differences between EM and conventional modelling. Firstly, there is really no counterpart in EM to the 'planning' phase mentioned at the beginning of this section with regard to the example of a door object. This is because such early conceptual modelling in EM can conveniently be directly put into a script with a visualisation and experimented with on the computer. Secondly, the experimentation referred to here, and in relation to the establishment of reliable components mentioned above, corresponds in some measure to the testing of conventional models or programs, but it is significant that this testing occurs here *in advance of any commitment* to a particular form of program. And thirdly a further symptom of the difference in approach of EM is the stage at which we consider an interface to a desired system. It is typical of rapid prototyping approaches to offer a 'mock-up' of an interface to a future system at an early stage. We see an example of this in the use case description given on p.351 of (Jacobson et al., 1992). In an EM development it is typical that the interface is left until an advanced stage of the development – when the purpose and requirement has been clarified through extensive use of the very open-ended phase of model construction and exploration.

APPLYING EM TO BPR

The Wider Context

Having surveyed some of the issues and problems presented by BPR (section 2), and reviewed the broad approach to computation and modelling that is EM (section 3) we now turn to showing how the principles and tools of EM are well suited for application to BPR. Business engineering calls for technical support at two levels that we shall call the *cognitive* and the *operational*. The cognitive level corresponds with the essential processes of understanding the business as a whole, its place in the wider world, and the place of existing processes within the whole. Such understanding is pre-requisite to any reengineering of processes. The operational level refers to the provision of systems which workers can use to perform business activities effectively and efficiently. We envisage that such systems will typically comprise people as well as software components and other kinds of device. Object-oriented business engineering seeks (as EM does) to provide a common framework for both the cognitive and operational levels of support.

There has been a multitude of approaches to implementing BPR and even within the OO approaches Jacobson's is one among many. We used the terminology and concepts of Jacobson's work in section 2.4 above because it is well known and illustrates many of the issues surrounding the use of technology for BPR. In that section use cases are described as corresponding at one level to business processes, and at another level to the functional requirement of software systems. How we understand the relation of business processes to software systems is crucial for understanding the potential contribution of EM to BPR. Part of Jacobson's viewpoint is (Jacobson et al., 1997):

The object-oriented business engineering models are similar in spirit to those of Object-Oriented Software Engineering (OOSE). The biggest difference is that the 'system' being modelled is now a business organization instead of a software system. (p. 23)

Adopting the viewpoint of EM we would claim that modelling a business organisation and modelling a software system are not so very different.

But we are approaching the difference that does exist from the opposite direction to that of an OO approach. Our principles and tools very directly support the modelling of a collection of agents performing structured activities in an open environment where unforeseen changes may occur at any time. This is a description which maps onto a business environment more naturally than that of a software system. It is also plausible that many software systems can be viewed as circumscribed special cases of business processes. Thus when approaching the application of EM to BPR we are not immediately confronted with the usual mismatch that arises when the informal problem world (of business) meets the formal solution world (of programming).

In OOSE, the collection of all use cases, each associated with an actor, forms the use case model. Such modelling is the major technique used in the early stages of Jacobson's approach to offer cognitive support to business engineering. It relies on extensive textual description and the use of the wide range of diagramming methods offered in the Unified Modelling Language (UML). These documents and diagrams record the understanding and imaginative work of participants in the business and of system analysts. When bringing EM methods to bear upon problems of BPR an important difference in comparison with a UML approach is that these early conceptual visions and insights can be directly supported and embodied in the building of our computer artefact. Documents and diagrams may, of course, still be important for contractual, auditing and explanatory reasons and these can be developed in parallel with the artefact construction. But the benefits of having an evolving and shareable computer model from the outset of conceiving a system – for the sake of communication, for monitoring and validating requirements, for smooth system development, and so on – are obvious and substantial.

The use case model is a major part of the requirements model in OOSE. The elaboration and maintenance of the requirements for a system is central for any further development. It plays a key role at both the cognitive and operational levels. We have always seen the issue and challenges of requirements for modern systems as an area of natural application for EM to conventional software. We now turn in the next section to an EM perspective on the evolution of requirements.

The SPORE Framework

A major theme of this paper is the need to consider the larger context of the processes we are interested in and are modelling. In a business application, this means including the objectives of an organisation, the viewpoints of the people concerned in any particular process, and the motives, knowledge and expectations of users of systems being considered. The application of EM requires us to widen our focus from an intended computer system to include the entire business processes (the environment) and the people involved (the human factors). It also means shifting our first attention from software requirements to business requirements. The former should be a result of the latter.

The framework that is described in more detail in this section is primarily directed towards requirements. But by 'requirements' we do not mean the elicitation and formulation of required behaviour. Instead we have in mind the *embodiment* of the requirement. That is, a computer model which exhibits, through visualisation and interaction, the behaviour and features of the system or solution required. We are not primarily concerned here with textual specification of the requirement (although this would not be difficult to produce on the basis of such a model). It is a feature of EM that the conventional phases of system development (specification, design, implementation, testing etc) tend to be conflated and are continuously elaborated during the evolution of our models. It is for this reason that we sometimes speak of 'cultivating requirements' in the same breath as 'building an ISM'; they are the same process viewed from different perspectives. So the building of an ISM is somewhat like building a prototype – although not one that is thrown away – but one that is elaborated and can be refined and optimised into a final useful system.

SPORE is a problem-oriented framework in which requirements – viewed as solutions to the problems identified in the application domain – are developed in an open-ended and situated manner. Within this framework, people participating in the requirements engineering process are able to cultivate requirements through collaborative interaction with each other aimed at solving the identified problems, rather than searching for requirements from the 'jungle' of user's needs (Chen, 2001). For a given application, a family of artefacts or interactive situation models (ISMs) are developed which form the medium for the problem-solving process of requirements cultivation.

The SPORE framework for building situated models for the requirements engineering process is depicted in Figure 3. The inputs of the SPORE model are:

- *Central problems* of the domain which are identified by the participants with reference to their concern for the functional and non-functional requirements of the developing system. The identification of problems can occur at any time during the process and is rarely regarded as completed.
- *Relevant contexts*, such as the organisation's goals and policy and the relationships between participants, act as motives and constraints for the participants in creating the outputs.
- *Available resources*, such as documents, technology and past experiences of participants, are used to facilitate the creation of the SPORE model's outputs.

The four kinds of outputs from the SPORE model are: *provisional solutions* which are developed by participants on the basis of the available resources and the relevant contexts. The other outputs, including *new contexts*, *new resources* and *new problems*, combine with their earlier versions and form new inputs for creating the next output. That is, all these contexts, resources and problems, even during the development of solutions, always remain modifiable and extensible. In view of this, participants can develop requirements

Figure 3. The SPORE framework

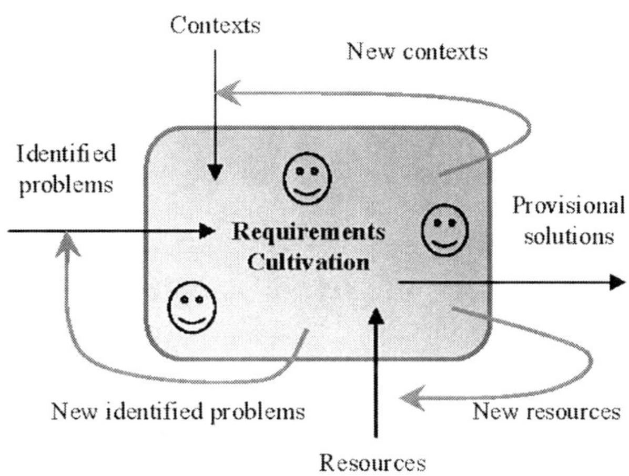

in a situated manner to respond to the change in the contexts, resources and even the problems themselves. Thus this framework addresses the fact that requirements may be changing all the time and can rarely be regarded as complete.

The nature of the SPORE framework is iterative and incremental which means that the ISMs are built in a sequence of structured development cycles, each of which is adding a new portion to the whole model. The delivery of small increments allows continuous feedback and evaluation of the progress achieved.

This experimental interaction is particularly powerful because the participants can interact with each other as well as with the model. Using network facilities the interaction of a participant can be propagated to the artefacts of other participants and consequently affect their insights. Within SPORE all computer models of participants can be connected together. When definitions are propagated they first change the visualisation of other participants' artefacts (given suitable authorisation) and subsequently may alter their insights as well. So participants can collaboratively interact with each other through their artefacts.

In such a collaborative environment, a working understanding of the key problems and their solutions, i.e. requirements, can be established. This working understanding can then be cultivated, i.e. grown incrementally, through the successive interaction between participants for exploring and integrating individual insights. On the whole, greater consistency between the individual insights indicates improved mutual understanding. For this reason, participants will continually refine their interaction with a view to achieving greater coherence and consistency.

Using SPORE for Participative BPR

We have emphasised in the previous section the importance of gaining a shared understanding of problems – or at least a working understanding of them – in order to negotiate towards consensus and agreement on their solutions. No doubt people and organisations have always sought to do this, but predominantly by using natural language, diagrams and, possibly, physical artefacts. We suggest that computers, when viewed in the broad perspective described in section 3, are now allowing us a new means for sharing understanding and knowledge. What we are aspiring to do in EM, and with the SPORE framework, is to introduce a powerful electronic modelling medium for the shared construction of artefacts that can faithfully and flexibly embody existing, and planned, real world systems. This embodiment, which exploits the physical aspects of computers, has far-reaching consequences. There is a continuous evolution possible from an original conception of a system to a useful developed form. It also means this evolution is at all times open to revision and interaction, with immediate feedback. The feedback may be in the form of direct experiential knowledge as well as more conventional propositional and mathematical representations. Any EM model with visualisation is such an embodied artefact, or an ISM as we have described it in earlier sections (3.2 and 4.2).

A family of ISMs built in the SPORE framework can be regarded, according to the patterns of interaction invoked, as a *requirement* (when we interact in the roles of particular users), or a *system* (when we interact in the 'roles' of key components, or agents in the EM sense, and so are exploring the internal structure of the model), or a *business process* (when we interact in the roles of workers, markets, suppliers etc). It is such flexibility of interpretation – according to style of interaction – that allows the SPORE framework to be naturally applied to BPR.

At the end of each subsection of section 2, we gave some hints as to how EM might contribute to BPR. We now gather those together in the light of the above. For 2.1 we have already indicated the unusual flexibility of ISMs to accommodate unforeseen and arbitrary changes in an environment. In 2.2 we stressed the importance of the key problem that many have diagnosed with conventional BPR: namely the difficulties, and yet necessity, of truly involving all relevant people in a reengineering process. EM is a human-centred approach which now has tools supporting distributed working with sophisticated modes of communication. The same benefits of working participatively on requirements that we mentioned in 4.2 naturally carry over to any BPR application. Many of the features of business process modelling that are highlighted in 2.3, for example, making dynamic behaviour explicit, being able to communicate it and analyse it, have been addressed already, albeit briefly. The use of modelling for simulation and control of automated workflow can be seen in our case study example in section 5.3. The framework of problem situation and solution space also described in 2.3 as appropriate to BPR is adopted in SPORE. Finally, the need to implement reengineered processes by means of building systems, and the way this has been done using OO methods are sketched in 2.4. The reservations expressed there about OO methods and the need for a wider context have now been amplified. We believe we can derive useful systems directly from our artefacts although we have only limited experience so far of doing so, and only with small scale examples. Some indications of how this can be achieved are given in (Beynon et al., 2000).

We now proceed to a more detailed consideration of a practical example of using EM methods for the analysis of a problem and construction of an ISM. This could be the basis of establishing part of a requirement for a system, for the reengineering of existing processes in a business, and for the development of an associated useful system.

EM FOR A WAREHOUSE SYSTEM: A CASE STUDY

EM offers an open-ended environment that provides an alternative approach both to business modelling and to system development. It also promotes the participation of users (stakeholders) in the business modelling activity. Since the stakeholders share a common interest in the success of the business, it is important that our framework supports sharing and distribution of information and knowledge, as well as the learning and experimentation that contribute to the continuous evolution in its organisation.

A warehouse management system is taken as a case study to illustrate the potential for applying the SPORE framework in BPR. This case study was adopted by Jacobson et al. in their text *Object-Oriented Software Engineering* (1992). At that time, their main concern was to identify the requirements of proposed computer systems by use case analysis and modelling. The idea behind the use case approach is that if we understand the roles of the users who need access to the system, then we shall identify some of the essentials from which requirements are elicited. For Jacobson, each use case is associated with a particular kind of interaction between human agents (actors) and the system, such as might be directed towards one of the required functions of the warehouse (e.g. manual redistribution between warehouses). In a subsequent book, *The Object Advantage*, Jacobson et al. (1995) extend the use case approach to modelling business processes by introducing the concept of a 'business use case', and propose a method for object-oriented business engineering. There the use case model serves as a process model of the existing business (the outside view of the company), which is used as the basis for prioritising the processes to be reengineered.

In this paper, we also regard it as important to address BPR in the broader context of developing a business process model. This means widening our focus to include the 'real world' (the environment and human factors) rather than the computer system alone. When we adopt this perspective, the role of EM is to develop a computer-based model that can be used to explore all the characteristic transactions of the warehouse.

To this end, the character of our framework is through-and-through agent-oriented, so that the warehouse activity is conceived with reference to state-changing protocols for human and automated components with the system. In as much as human actions are constrained by the business process and follow some reliable patterns, it is possible to regard their co-operative activity as a form of computation (in the same way that we might say "the users are programmed"). The human users and computer-based components can then be viewed as computational agents in a complex system. This agency is mediated through the user-computer interface: the input of the user influences the state of the computer, and the output of the computer changes the environment of the user (Beynon & Russ, 1994).

Introduction to the Warehouse Example

This case study involves applying the SPORE framework to a warehouse management system to achieve BPR. Our goal is to illustrate the use of the EM concepts discussed earlier, but it is not possible to give a complete overview or fully illustrate the entire study.

The proposed system is to support warehouse management. The main function of a warehouse is to provide its customers with warehouse space. The operations of the warehouse also include storing different kinds of items and using trucks to redistribute the items. The aim of introducing computer systems into the warehouse is to offer automatic support to the storage and redistribution services. This involves keeping track of the locations and status of items, differentiating between kinds of items (those that are perishable or flammable), maintaining security and integrity checks, and managing storage, retrieval and relocation. (The possibility that some of the functions of the warehouse associated with the physical storage and retrieval of items might also be automated using robots is not beyond the scope of our approach, but this is not directly addressed here.) The people in the warehouse who will use this system may include: the *foreman* responsible for the warehouse; the *warehouse worker* who is responsible for loading and unloading; the *forklift operator* who drives a forklift in the warehouse; the *truck driver* who drives a truck between different warehouses; the *office personnel* who receive orders and requests from customers, arrange the truck routine, and keep records of all warehouses.

Business Process Model for Warehouse

In applying the traditional use case approach, the first step is to create a simple picture of a system that describes the system boundaries and the actors (users) of the system (cf. Figure 4 (amended from Jacobson et al., 1992)). The EM approach differs in a significant respect – the boundary of the system is not preconceived but grows with the understanding of the modeller. In conventional system development, because the boundary is defined in advance, the modeller focuses on those interactions that respect the functionality that is imposed on the system. In an EM approach, the warehouse operation is conceived in terms of each agent's perception of states and state changes. For this reason, our initial concern in developing the business process model is with studying

Figure 4. Diagram of the initial warehouse system with actors identified

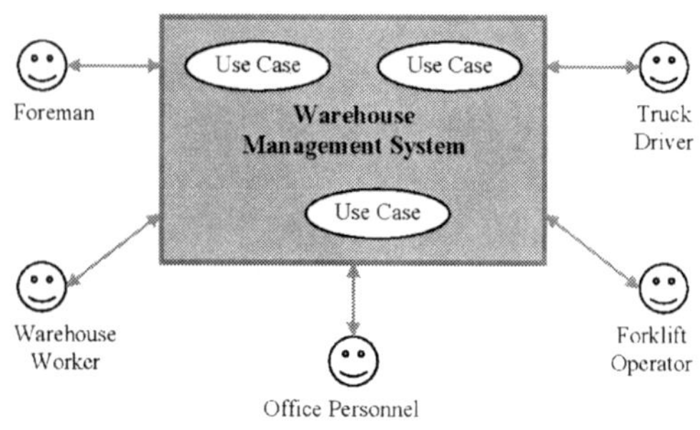

the capabilities of the agents that are intended to operate, and examining the possibilities for their unconstrained interaction in an experimental manner. This is the basis for subsequently exploring the protocols these agents can realistically follow in order to carry out the preconceived characteristic transactions of the warehouse.

In traditional modelling approaches for business, the issue of how agents apprehend the current state of a business process is not explicitly addressed. Of course, there are some key observables that are recognised from the outset to be strongly related both to the daily work of personnel within the warehouse and to the phases in preconceived transactions. For instance, in the warehouse case study, these include the items stored in the warehouse and their locations. The EM approach pays much more serious attention to the true character of real-world observation. As a result, the role of observables in the business process differs in three important respects. Firstly, the precise way in which states and events are observed by an agent is considered to be crucially important. It is not simply the fact that an item is at a location, or that a truck has arrived at the warehouse that is deemed significant; it also matters how and by whom the presence of an item or the arrival of a truck is or can be observed. Secondly, the fact that agents are aware of the abstract stage that has been reached in the business process is taken into account in identifying their observables. For instance, the office personnel will distinguish the abstract status of a redistribution process according to whether a group of items is still at the warehouse, in transit or has now been successfully relocated. Thirdly, there has to be a means by which agents interpret physical observation of real world state as disclosing the status of abstract business transactions. For instance, there must be some concrete indication that is now timely to register that an item has now officially left the warehouse, and that a new phase in the redistribution process has begun.

Our EM business model is framed with reference to the state change of an abstract nature that is associated with observation of a process. For this purpose, the relevant observables relate to the current status in communicating information about characteristic warehouse operations between warehouse personnel. The corresponding state changes are concerned with the systematic execution of protocols and the associated transition from one phase to the next. By using such state changes as a representation for business processes, we will easily identify the existing processes, and (from potential problems or dissatisfaction from customers or employees) can also find those that are candidates for BPR activity. An important aspect of the observables in our business model is that they should not only serve to determine the current state, but must also supply a transaction history appropriate for auditing.

In order to understand the existing business processes properly, the ISM we develop to represent the business process model is modelled on the practices that would have been used in the operation of the warehouse prior to the introduction of computers. (This is consistent with Jacobson's emphasis on the benefits of modelling existing practice (Jacobson et al., 1995).) In this context, forms and paper delivery serve as records of the operation of the model. This kind of manual data entry following systematic processes of form delivery can represent both the current status of all transactions (such as which items were in transit) and the history of transactions. The objective of BPR is to automate these transactions by introducing computer systems, and to try to find alternatives that will, for example, reduce the work-hours of personnel and achieve a more efficient process for business.

From our perspective, the forms can be interpreted as a *paper-based* ISM for the business process. In carrying out a particular transaction, specified procedures are to be followed in filling forms and transferring them between personnel. For instance, as depicted in Figure 5, when a manual redistribution between warehouses is initiated, four copies of redistribution forms (RFs) are transferred from the foreman to the warehouse worker. The manual activities of processing forms effectively identify which agents have roles in the transaction, which are currently active in any phase, and how their interaction is synchronised (cf. Figures 5 and 6). The current status of any transaction is determined by what sections of forms are currently completed and who currently holds the forms.

The modifications that agents make to forms, and the movement of the forms themselves, can be construed as tracing a path through the business process. To elaborate this in more detail we must refer to the observational and interactional context for each agent: the observables it can refer to (its *oracles*), those it can conditionally change (its *handles*) and the protocol that connects these. Note that the relevant observables in this context may refer to the state of the warehouse itself (e.g. an item can be signed off only if it is presently to

Figure 5. A collaborative working environment for manual redistribution between warehouses

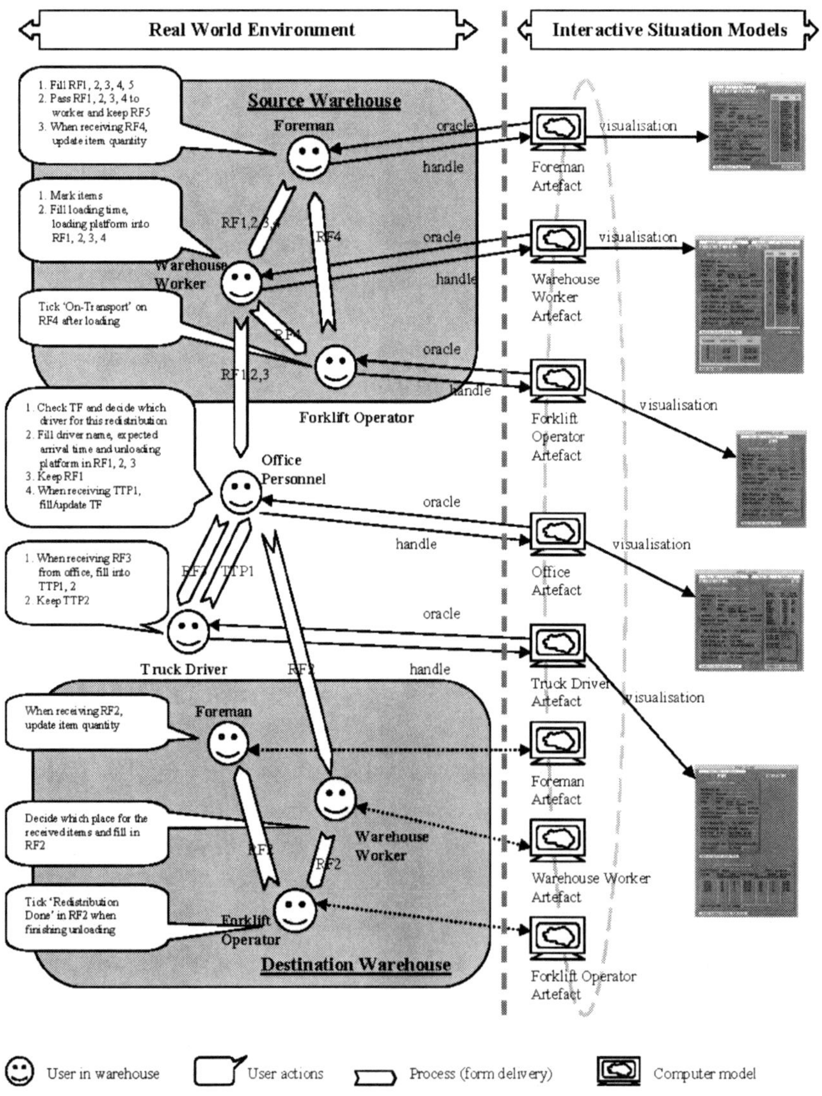

hand), and relate to the high-level context for interpretation (e.g. issues of legality, safety etc.). The persistence of the record that the forms supply is also significant for auditing and traceability.

Our account of the observational and interactional context makes use of the agent-oriented modelling notation LSD, as illustrated in Figure 7. In this account, the interpretation of agent actions may vary according to the current status

*Figure 6. (A) Detailed view of the forms used in the warehouse artefacts; (B) Detail of panels representing observables (**handles** or **oracles**) for some warehouse agents*

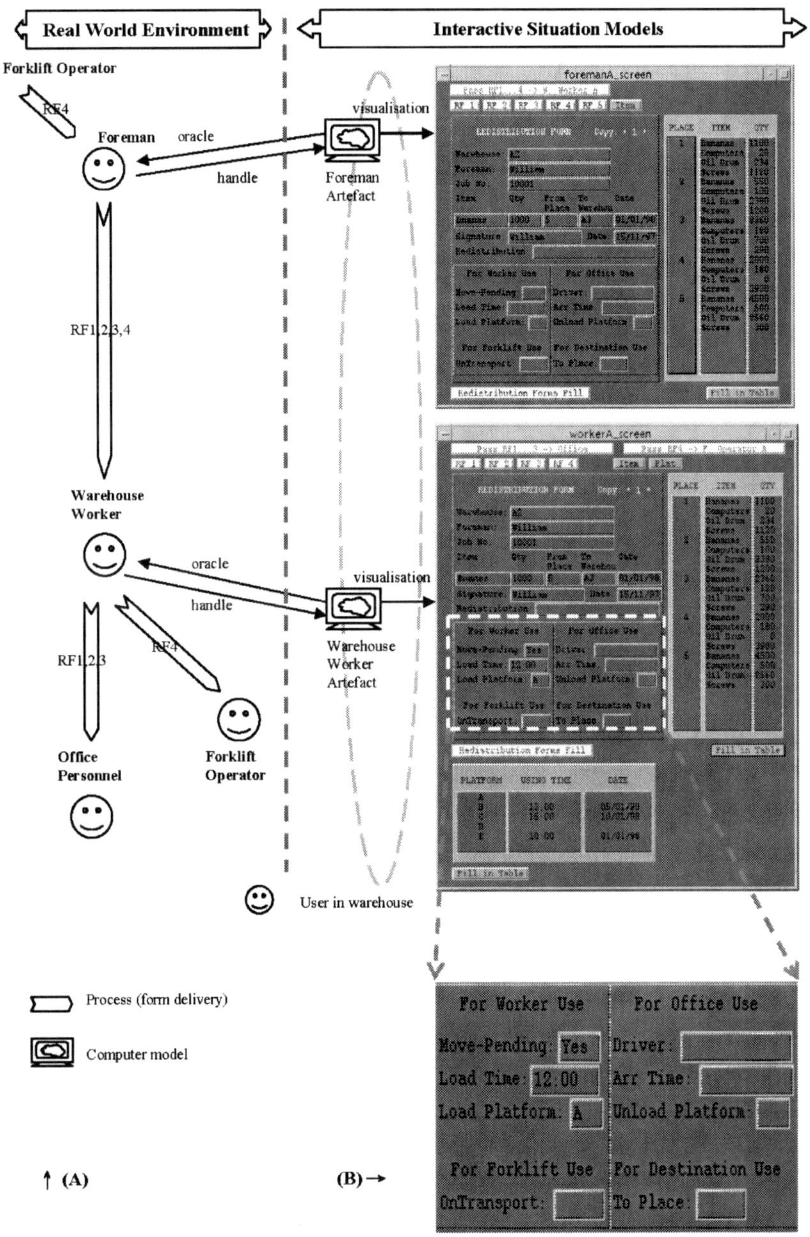

Figure 7. Part of the outline LSD specification for the warehouse management system

```
AGENT warehouseWorker(w) {
   STATE
   ORACLE
      rf_item[1...4],
      rf_quantity[1...4],
      rf_from_place[1...4],
      rf_date[1...4],
      rf_item[2],
      rf_quantity[2],
      rf_date[2]
   HANDLE
      rf_moving_pending[1...4]  ,
      rf_loading_time[1...4],
      rf_loading_platform[1...4],
      rf_redistribution_confirm[1...4],
      rf_to_place[2],
      rf_redistribution_confirm[2]
   DERIVATE
   PROTOCOL
      *** Receiving RF1...4 from foreman ***
            --> read rf _item[1...4]; read rf_quantity[1...4];
                read rf_from_place[1...4]; read rf_date[1...4];
                write rf_moving_pending[1...4];
            --> write rf_loading_time[1...4];
                write rf_loading_platform[1...4];
            --> *** Pass RF1,2,3 to office and RF4 to forklift operator; ***
                                          // For loading
      *** Item not enough ***
            --> write rf_redistribution_confirm[1...4]
                   ==('Error'&&'Item  not enough');
            --> *** Pass RF1...4 back to foreman; ***
      *** Receiving RF2 from office ***
            --> read rf_item[2]; read rf_quantity[2]; read rf_date[2];
            --> write rf_to_place[2];
            --> Pass RF2 to forkli ft operator; ***
                                          // For unloading
      *** All places full ***
            --> write rf_redistribution_confirm[2]
                   ==('Error'&&'All places full');
            --> *** Pass RF2 back to forem  an; ***
}

AGENT rf(n=1...5) {                         // Redistribution Form
   STATE
      rf_warehouse[n]=@,                    // Information in RF1,2,3,4,5
      tf_foreman_name[n]=@,                 // Information in RF1,2,3,4,5
      rf_job_number[n ]=@,                   // Information in RF1,2,3,4,5
      rf_item[n]=@,                         // Information in RF1,2,3,4,5
      rf_quantity[n]=@,                     // Information in RF1,2,3,4,5
      rf_from_place[n]=@,                   // Informat   ion in RF1,2,3,4,5
      rf_to_warehouse[n]=@,                 // Information in RF1,2,3,4,5
      rf_date[n]=@,                         // Information in RF1,2,3,4,5
      rf_moving_pending[n]=@,               // Information in RF1,2,3,4
      rf_loading_ time[n]=@,                 // Information in RF1,2,3,4
      rf_loading_platform[n]=@,             // Information in RF1,2,3,4
      rf_driver[n]=@,                       // Information in RF1,2,3
      rf_arrival_time[n]=@,                 // Information    in RF1,2,3
      rf_unloading_platform[n]=@,           // Information in RF1,2,3
      rf_on_transport[n]=@,                 // Information in RF4
      rf_to_place[n]=@,                     // Information in RF2
      rf_redistribution_confirm[n]=@          // May appear in RF1,2,3,4
   ORACLE
   HANDLE
   DERIVATE
   PROTOCOL
}
```

of the business process being investigated, and the modeller's current understanding of it. For instance, Beynon (1997) and Ness (1997) identify three views of agents, each appropriate to a different context. In the early stages of familiarisation with an environment or putative system, an agent has unexplored potential to affect system state (view 1). (The 'system' in our warehouse case study is regarded as the whole organisation, not only the computer system itself.) At a later stage, an agent may be construed as reliably following some particular patterns of stimulus-response within the system (view 2). When an appropriate business process has been successfully identified and implemented, each agent enacts a pattern of stimulus-response interaction that can be entirely circumscribed and predicted (view 3). In view 1 our concern is whether an entity has any influence over its environment and in view 3 our concern is whether the exact nature of the influence is known. The term 'agent-oriented' is commonly used to refer to activities that are being interpreted from the view 3 perspective (Shoham, 1993), but EM promotes the idea that the concept of agency is only meaningful in relation to the development of understanding from view 1 to view 3 perspectives.

In our warehouse case study, there are contexts in which all the human agents can be viewed in each of these various ways. Whilst the modeller is initially unfamiliar with the environment and the processes of the business, the personnel will represent examples of view 1 agents whose interaction with the warehouse environment and the operation of its business is as yet unexplored. When the roles of a particular employee, such as foreman, have been more clearly identified, they can be regarded as view 2 agents whose pattern of stimulus-response can be in some respects clearly identified. The aim of our modelling process is to fully understand the whole business process and attribute automatic agency to view 3 agents whose pattern of stimulus-response is entirely predictable. This accords with our thesis that the business model is a form of generalized program, and that business process reengineering closely resembles program requirements capture.

The LSD account can be viewed as identifying and classifying the observables that capture the modeller's current understanding of the warehouse operation. If experimental interaction with the model in due course justifies the transition from a view 1 to a view 3 perspective, the LSD account can be regarded as specifying the observables that describe the stimulus-response patterns in the organisation. In an LSD account, observables that are attached to an agent are referred to as *states*. In general, these observables can be directly manipulated by another agent. For example, the agent warehouseWorker can change the status of an item to 'moving pending' by manipulating the rf_moving_pending observable which is a state for the agent rf. The *oracles* are the observables to which an agent responds. For example, rf_item and rf_quantity in the agent warehouseWorker are examples of oracles for the warehouse worker, who has to know the identity and quantity of items to be redistributed before changing their status (cf. Figure 6 and Figure 7). The *handles* for an agent are those observables that are conditionally under its control. The observable rf_moving_pending is an example of a *handle* for the agent warehouseWorker.

The stimulus-response patterns for an LSD agent are modelled in two ways. The *derivates* are used to represent stimulus-response relationships that are indivisibly coupled. For example the observable transportationError, which indicates whether there is truck available for the specific time at which the foreman intends to make redistribution, is a *state* for the agent environment but also a *derivate* for the agent foreman. That is to say, any change in the status of truck availability will be deemed to simultaneously change this observable. Looser coupling of stimulus and response is modelled in *protocols*, which consist of a set of guarded actions, each of which takes the form of an enabling condition and an associated sequence of redefinitions of observables. Each guarded action can be regarded as a privilege to act. That is, if an enabling condition pertains, a particular action may be performed. As an example of this principle, the agent warehouseWorker receives redistribution forms from the foreman (the enabling condition), then decides the loading time and platform, and passes the forms to both the office and forklift operator (the guarded action).

The ISMs for the Warehouse State

In interpreting the business process model, and ensuring that its abstract phases are or can be appropriately embodied in agent perception and action, it is essential to take account of the physically explicit observables associated with the warehouse. In keeping with the situated nature of SPORE framework, the ISM is used to incorporate the matter-of-fact observations of the current state of the warehouse. As mentioned earlier, typical observables that are significant in this view are the items and locations in the warehouse, and the inventory that connects items with locations. An ISM to represent these observables will supply visual representations for items and locations, and display the status of the inventory. Such a representation of the current warehouse state is complemented by informal actions, such as represent the relocation of items, item look-up in the inventory or receipt of a new item for storage. In some contexts, this will motivate visualisations to represent intermediate states in the operation of the warehouse, associated with items in transit, or items located via the inventory but yet to be retrieved from the warehouse.

A model of the warehouse has to incorporate such aspects of state and state change in order to be faithful to its referent. It must also provide the setting in which to consider behaviours that are undesirable or outside the scope of normal operation. Relevant observables required for this purpose might address issues such as the loss of items or warehouse locations, the concept of items being mislaid, or of items being perishable.

There is no single ISM that can represent all the aspects of the warehouse state. The state of the warehouse will typically be represented by different ISMs according to what problems are being addressed in the SPORE framework. The scale of an ISM is limited by the number of definitions that can be conveniently stored, rapidly accessed and efficiently processed, but in these respects it is well-suited to those concerns that lie within the modeller's conceptual grasp. The ISM we construct here incorporates the 'seed' ISMs for the warehouse: the form-based abstractions that capture the state of the business process model and the activities of the agents; the storage, retrieval and distribution of items; and additional observations such as are associated with the wider significance of the warehouse operation (e.g. concerned with the legality and the integrity of the business process). The potential framework for BPR established by applying SPORE is illustrated by the transformation from a paper-based to a computer-based ISM.

The distributed version of EDEN enables us to separate the viewpoints of the agents in the model, and to complement these with an external observer's interpretation. Figure 6 illustrates how computer-based forms are used to represent the environment for each agent's interaction. In this way, the distributed ISM can serve as a medium in which to identify and enact appropriate transactions, and to debug and refine these through collaborative interaction between the various participants. Many possible issues in requirements can be addressed by SPORE in this way:

- Through experimentation at different workstations, we can identify issues that are problematic from the perspective of particular agents: for instance, "how does the office know which drivers are available?", "how does the office determine whether a transaction is completed?".
- Through the elaboration of different seed ISMs, we can address additional issues, such as transportation costs, perishable goods, security and trust concerns.
- Through modifying dependencies and communication strategies, we can consider the effects of different technologies, such as are associated with the use of mobile communications, the Internet, optical bar code readers, or electronic locking agents.
- Through collaboration and synthesis of views, we can distinguish between subjective and objective perceptions of state e.g. to contrast "I remember doing X" with "I have some record of doing X" with "There is an official record of X", or to model misconceptions on the part of an agent.
- Through intervention in the role of super-agent, it is possible to examine the consequences of singular conditions that arise from opportunistic interaction or Acts-of-God, and to assess activities outside the scope of normal operation such as are associated with fraud, or manual back-up to automated procedures.

CONCLUSION

We have introduced a novel approach to modelling that is based on a view of computation and programming that is significantly broader than conventional views. Empirical Modelling (EM) is a new and radically different approach to complex systems design and business modelling. The primary focus of EM is on the comprehension and on the use of computer-based interactive situation models (ISMs) that represent the way in which the aspects of systems behaviour are constructed in terms of agencies, observables and dependencies. On this EM view, computer-based models of business processes can be built in a way similar to that in which human beings make conceptual models of such processes. We can then specialise and circumscribe our models to derive software systems. In this way EM can offer both cognitive and operational support to BPR from the very early, conceptual stages of modelling.

To sum up, EM serves as an open development approach with the following two characteristics:

- **Situatedness:** A model built using EM is situated because it is the model of the relationship between a situation and the observer. The modeller can directly experience the results from his introduction of changes to the model. Thus the ISM can reflect a change in the real-world situation or new knowledge gained by the modeller. The roles of ISMs in four main fields most relevant to BPR: for HCI, the ISMs can be used for interface construction; for the development of processes from the ISMs, an observation-oriented analysis and an associated simulation of behaviour can be done along the construction of the model; for requirements engineering, the ISMs serve as a prototype which help to understanding the current problems and visualise the reality of the future system; for decision making the ISMs can be used to explore a set of alternatives for the problems.
- **Computer-Based Artefacts:** In EM the computer is used as an interactive and open-ended artefact for facilitating knowledge construction by situated modelling. This is different to the conventional use of the computer as just an application tool for knowledge representation. In EM the computer is used to generate the metaphorical representation of particular states. It helps not only knowledge representation, but also knowledge construction, to enrich the modeller's knowledge. With the aid of networked communication, all the participants in the modelling process can interact with each other in a visible and communicable manner through the synchronisation between the evolution of computer models and individual participant's insights.

We have emphasised that BPR will not be successful without the support and active participation of its people, and concluded that BPR should be people-centred. In section 2 we proposed the concepts to emphasise the importance of people participation in the modelling process: participative BPR. The SPORE framework and the EM approach to system development and BPR are centred around this 'tenet'. Through the user participation in the modelling process, we can take the holistic view of the cross-functional interactions and processes in the real-world context rather than the piecemeal engineering of isolated parts of a system (either computer system or business system). The main potential advantage of EM is that it provides an ideal environment for participants to interact with each other in a flexible and open-ended manner. This character and flexibility of ISMs encourage a different kind of relationship between human modellers and the automated business activity. And the potential benefits of introducing the SPORE framework here are its flexibility, openness and the richness of interaction possible between many participants in the modelling environment. This interpersonal interaction within the distributed EM environment can model the agencies in two levels: (1) the modeller as an *external* observer can shape the agency in the context of his role in the task, such as developers or users; or (2) the modeller as an *internal* observer can act as an agent to carry out the interaction between agents through pretend play. This being-participant-observer approach under the EM framework enables the participants to shape the agency within the system in their customary context rather than the modeller's context. And participants' interaction with, as well as the construction of, ISMs enable a mode of operation which is loosely tied to a routine process, and encourages a creative, opportunistic, situated (re-) thinking and problem-solving activity. Our case study shows the potential for modelling current practice in a business. There is clearly much future work to be done on exploring the scalability of our approach and the derivation of practical systems from our models.

FUTURE RESEARCH DIRECTIONS

There is clearly future work to be done on exploring the scalability of the EM approach and the derivation of other applications from the models. The research represented in this chapter has addressed some of the fundamental problems with system development and BPR, and these give the direction for the further work in these areas. This section provides an overview of some areas of future interest.

The first is the possible applications of EM in software system development. The work in this research was to investigate the development of software systems for the support of BPR. However for software system development itself (or software engineering), EM is potentially applicable to this research area and the relevant research connecting EM with software development is ongoing. For example, the support by EM for situated problem-solving activity in requirements engineering, and reengineering the user interfaces through exploring statecharts (Chen, 2001). Further work may include the detailed investigation of the difference between EM and other development methods (such as OO or Harel's statecharts), especially in their different modelling philosophy. The evaluation of computer-mediated interaction among participants through the distributed nature of EM models, instead of traditional face-to-face interaction, is another direction for investigation of EM in software development, especially to identify how participative process modelling can contribute in this area.

The second is the investigation of the linkage of different spheres relevant to BPR in which EM may make a contribution. For example, EM's emphasis on the process of model construction can address many of the significant issues raised by Warboys et al. (1999) such as the modelling of software and organisational processes or evolutionary design of software systems. Applied to human-computer interaction (HCI), EM has the potential for applications in scenario-based design which include system development, object-orientation and process modelling. EM may also have potential in decision support systems which can provide an environment for the learning of modellers through the modelling process, rather than merely providing several alternatives. EM can contribute in this area because decision-making in an organisation is always influenced by the context, which involves people with different perceptions and interests. One clue for investigating how the EM approach will be applied to these areas is through the concept of 'participative' modelling which was the core of this chapter.

In addition, the systems thinking and the evolutionary paradigm for system development are also reference points for further work of EM. Apart from system development or BPR, the further development of EM should be emphasised in taking the holistic view to include the environment of the applications developed. In this perspective, the open-ended and situated characteristics of EM show its potential for application in many different disciplines.

REFERENCES

Beynon, W. M. (1997). Empirical Modelling for educational technology. In *Proceedings of the Second International Conference on Cognitive Technology*. 54-68. University of Aizu, Japan.

Beynon, W. M., Rasmequan, S., & Russ, S. B. (2002). A new paradigm for computer-based decision support. *Decision Support Systems: The International Journal*, *33*(2), 127–142. doi:10.1016/S0167-9236(01)00140-3

Beynon, W. M., Rungrattanaubol, J., & Sinclair, J. (2000). Formal specification from an observation-oriented perspective. *Journal of Universal Computer Science*, *6*(4), 407–421.

Beynon, W. M., & Russ, S. B. (1994). *Empirical Modelling of Requirements.* Research Report No. 277, Department of Computer Science, University of Warwick, UK.

Chen, Y. C. (2001). *Empirical Modelling for participative business process reengineering*, Unpublished doctoral thesis, Department of Computer Science, University of Warwick, UK.

Davenport, T. H. (1993). *Process innovation: Re-engineering work through Information Technology*. Boston: Harvard Business School Press.

Davenport, T. H. (1996). Why re-engineering failed: The fad that forgot people. *Fast Company*, *1*(1), 70–74.

Davenport, T. H. (2009). How to design smart business experiments. *Harvard Business Review*, (February): 68–77.

Ellis, T. I., Dooner, M., & Swift, K. G. (1997). Better the devil you know–the role of pragmatic modelling. In *First International Conference: Managing Enterprises–Stakeholders, Engineering, Logistics, and Achievement (ME-SELA'97)*, 151-156. Loughborough University, United Kingdom.

Galliers, B. (1998). Reflections on BPR, IT and organisational change. In Galliers, R. D., & Baets, W. R. J. (Eds.), *Information Technology and organisational transformation* (pp. 225–243). London: John Wiley and Sons, Ltd.

Galliers, R. D., & Leidner, D. E. (2003). *Strategic information management: challenges and strategies in managing Information Systems* (3rd ed.). Oxford: Butterworth-Heinemann.

Gerrits, H. (1994). *Business modelling based on logistics to support business process re-engineering* (pp. 279–288).

Glasson, B. C., Hawryszkiewycz, I. T., Underwood, B. A., & Weber, R. A. (Eds.). (1994). *Business process re-engineering: Information Systems opportunities and challenges*. Elsevier Science.

Hammer, M., & Champy, J. (2003). *Reengineering the corporation: A manifesto for business revolution*. Harper Business.

Hutchison, A. (1994). *CSCW as opportunity for business process re-engineering* (pp. 309–318).

Jacobson, I. (2009). *Object-oriented software engineering: A use case driven approach*. Addison-Wesley.

Jacobson, I., Christerson, M., Jonsson, P., & Overgaard, G. (1992). *Object-oriented software engineering: A use case driven approach*. Addison-Wesley.

Jacobson, I., Ericsson, M., & Jacobson, A. (1995). *The object advantage: Business process re-engineering with object technology*. Addison-Wesley.

Jacobson, I., Griss, M., & Jonsson, P. (1997). *Software reuse–architecture, process and organisation for business success*. Addison-Wesley.

Jacobson, I., & Ng, P. W. (2004). *Aspect-oriented software development with use cases*. Addison-Wesley.

Kaindl, H. (1999). Difficulties in the transition from OO analysis to design. *IEEE Software*, (September/October): 94–102. doi:10.1109/52.795107

Keen, P. G. W., & Sol, H. G. (2008). *Decision enhancement services: Rehearsing the future for decisions that matter*. IOS Press.

Ness, P. E. (1997). *Creative software development: An Empirical Modelling Framework*, Unpublished doctoral thesis, Department of Computer Science, University of Warwick, UK.

Nurcan, S., Grosz, G., & Souveyet, C. (1998). Describing business processes with a guided use case approach. In *Proceedings of the 10th International Conference (CaiSE'98),* June 1998, Pisa, Italy.

Rasmequan, S., Roe, C., & Russ, S. B. (2000). Strategic decision support systems: An experience-based approach. In *Proceedings of the 18th IASTED Conference on Applied Informatics*, February 2000, Innsbruck, Austria.

Riemer, K. (1998). A process-driven, event-based business object model. In *Proceedings of Second International Workshop in Enterprise Distributed Object Computing (EDOC'98)*, (pp. 68-74). La Jolla, CA.

Schader, M., & Korthaus, A. (1998). Modelling business processes as part of the BOOSTER approach to business object-oriented system development based on UML. In *Proceedings of the Second International Enterprise Distributed Object Computing (EDOC '98) Workshop*, (pp. 56-67). La Jolla, CA.

Sherwood-Smith, M. (1994). *People centred process re-engineering: An evaluation perspective to office system re-design.* (pp.535-544).

Shoham, Y. (1993). Agent-oriented programming. *Artificial Intelligence*, *60*(1), 51–92. doi:10.1016/0004-3702(93)90034-9

Simons, A. J. H. (1999). Use cases considered harmful. In R. Mitchell, A.C. Wills, J. Bosch, & B. Meyer (Eds.), *Proceedings of the 29th Conference Tech. Object-Oriented Programming Language and Systems (TOOLS-29 Europe)*, (pp. 194-203) Los Alamitos: IEEE Computer Society

Simons, A. J. H., & Graham, I. (1998). 37 things that don't work in Object Modelling with UML. In S. Kent & R. Mitchell (Eds.), *British Computer Society Object-Oriented Programming Systems Newsletter, 35*.

Simons, A. J. H., & Graham, I. (1999). 30 things that go wrong in Object Modelling with UML 1.3. In Kilov, H., Rumpe, B., & Simmonds, I. (Eds.), *Behavioral Specifications of Businesses and Systems* (pp. 221–242). Kluwer Academic Publishers.

van Meel, J. W., Bots, P. W. G., & Sol, H. G. (1994). *Towards a research framework for business engineering*. (pp.581-592).

Vidgen, R., Rose, J., Wood, B., & Wood-Harper, T. (1994). *Business process re-engineering: The need for a methodology to revision the organisation.* (pp.603-612).

Vogel, D. (1994). *Re-engineering towards the meeting of the future* (pp. 35–45).

Warboys, B., Kawalek, P., Robertson, I., & Greenwood, M. (1999). *Business Information Systems: A process approach*. McGraw-Hill Publishing.

ADDITIONAL READING

Adigun, M. O., & Biyela, D. P. (2003). Modelling an Enterprise for Re-engineering: A Case Study. In *Proceedings of the 2003 Annual Research Conference of the South African Institute of Computer Scientists and Information Technologists on Enablement through Technology*, 153-164.

Beynon, W. M. (2005). Radical Empiricism, Empirical Modelling and the Nature of Kknowing. In I. E. Dror (Ed.) *Cognitive Technologies and the Pragmatics of Cognition: Special Issue of Pragmatics and Cognition*, 13(3), 615-646.

Beynon, W. M. (2007). Computing Technology for Learning – In Need of a Radical New Conception. *Journal of Educational Technology & Society*, *10*(1), 94–106.

Beynon, W. M. (2009). Constructivist Computer Science Education Reconstructed. *HEA-ICS ITALICS e-Journal*, 8(2), June 2009, 73-90.

Beynon, W. M., Boyatt, R. C., & Chan, Z. N. (2008). Intuition in Software Development Revisited. In *Proceedings of 20th Annual Psychology of Programming Interest Group Conference*, Lancaster University, United Kingdom, September 2008.

Beynon, W. M., & Chan, Z. N. (2006). A Conception of Computing Technology Better Suited to Distributed Participatory Design. In *NordiCHI Workshop on Distributed Participatory Design*, Oslo, Norway, October 2006.

Beynon, W. M., Chen, Y. C., Hseu, H. W., Maad, S., Rasmequan, S., & Roe, C. (2001). The Computer as Instrument. [Springer-Verlag.]. *Lecture Note in Artificial Intelligence*, *2117*, 476–489.

Beynon, W. M., & Harfield, A. (2007, May). Lifelong Learning, Empirical Modelling and the Promises of Constructivism. *Journal of Computers*, *2*(3), 43–55. doi:10.4304/jcp.2.3.43-55

Beynon, W. M., Rasmequan, S., & Russ, S. B. (2002). A New Paradigm for Computer-Based Decision Support. *Decision Support Systems: The International Journal*, *33*(2), 127–142. doi:10.1016/S0167-9236(01)00140-3

Beynon, W. M., & Roe, C. (2006). Enriching Computer Support for Constructionism. In Alkhalifa, E. (Ed.), *Cognitively Informed Systems: Utilizing Practical Approaches to Enrich Information Presentation and Transfer* (pp. 209–233). Idea Group Publishing.

Beynon, W. M., Roe, C., Ward, A., & Wong, A. (2001). Interactive Situation Models for Cognitive Aspects of User-Artefact Interaction. [Springer-Verlag.]. *Lecture Note in Artificial Intelligence*, *2117*, 356–372.

Beynon, W. M., & Russ, S. B. (2008). Experimenting with Computing. *Journal of Applied Logic*, *6*, 476–489. doi:10.1016/j.jal.2008.09.008

Beynon, W. M., Russ, S. B., & McCarty, W. (2006). Human Computing: Modelling with Meaning. *Literary and Linguistic Computing*, *21*(2), 141–157. doi:10.1093/llc/fql015

Beynon, W. M., Boyatt, R. C., & Russ. S. B. (2006). Rethinking Programming. In *Proceedings IEEE Third International Conference on Information Technology: New Generations (ITNG 2006)*, April 2006, Las Vegas, Nevada, USA, 149-154.

Chen, Y. C. (2001). *Empirical Modelling for Participative Business Process Reengineering*, Unpublished PhD Thesis, Department of Computer Science, University of Warwick, United Kingdom.

Davenport, T. H. (1993). *Process Innovation: Re-engineering Work through Information Technology*. Harvard Business School Press.

Davenport, T. H. (2009). How to Design Smart Business Experiments. *Harvard Business Review*, (February): 68–77.

Delen, D., Dalal, N. P., & Benjamin, P. C. (2005). Integrated Modeling: the Key to Holistic Understanding of the Enterprise. *Communications of the ACM*, *48*(4), 107–112. doi:10.1145/1053291.1053296

Evans, M., Beynon, W. M., & Fischer, C. N. (2001). Empirical Modelling for the Logistics of Rework in the Manufacturing Process. In *Proceedings of the 16th Brazilian Congress of Mechanical Engineering*, November 2001, 226-234.

Fernandes, K., Raja, V., Keast, J., Beynon, W. M., Chan, P. S., & Joy, M. (2002). Business and IT Perspectives on AMORE: A Methodology for Object-Orientation in Re-engineering Enterprises. In P. Henderson (Ed.) *Systems Engineering for Business Process Change: New Directions* (pp. 274-297). Springer-Verlag.

Hammer, M., & Champy, J. (2003). *Reengineering the Corporation: A Manifesto for Business Revolution*. Harper Business.

Harmon, P. (2007). *Business Process Change, Second Edition: A Guide for Business Managers and BPM and Six Sigma Professionals*. Elsevier.

Jacobson, I. (2009). *Object-Oriented Software Engineering: A Use Case Driven Approach*. Addison-Wesley.

Jacobson, I., Ericsson, M., & Jacobson, A. (1995). *The Object Advantage: Business Process Reengineering with Object Technology*. Addison-Wesley.

Khosrow-Pour, M. (2006). *Cases on Information Technology And Business Process Reengineering*. Idea Group Publishing.

Kock, N. F. (2006). *Systems Analysis & Design Fundamentals: A Business Process Redesign Approach*. Sage Publications, Inc.

Kohli, R., & Hoadley, E. (2006). Towards Developing a Framework for Measuring Organizational Impact of IT- Enabled BPR: Case Studies of Three Firms. *ACM SIGMIS Database*, *37*(1), 40–58. doi:10.1145/1120501.1120505

Paul, R. J., & Serrano, A. (2003). The Process of Process Reengineering: Simulation for Business Processes and Information Systems Design. In *Proceedings of the 35th Conference on Winter Simulation: Driving Innovation*, New Orleans, Louisiana, USA, 1787-1796.

Ren, C., Wang, W., Dong, J., Ding, H., Shao, B., & Wang, Q. (2008). Towards a Flexible Business Process Modeling and Simulation Environment. In *Proceedings of the 40th Conference on Winter Simulation*, Miami, Florida, 1694-1701.

Shapiro, D. (2005). Participatory Design: The Will to Succeed. In *Proceedings of the 4th Decennial Conference on Critical Computing: Between Sense and Sensibility*, Aarhus, Denmark, 29-38.

Tsai, H. L. (2003). *Information Technology and Business Process Reengineering: New Perspectives and Strategies*. Praeger.

van Leijen, H., & Baets, W. R. J. (2003). A Cognitive Framework for Reengineering Knowledge-Intensive Processes. *HICSS (Proceeding of the 36th Annual Hawaii International Conference on System Sciences)*, Track 3, pp. 97a.

Warboys, B., Kawalek, P., Robertson, I., & Greenwood, M. (1999). *Business Information Systems: A Process Approach*. McGraw-Hill Publishing.

Z, D. (2008). Business Process-Reengineering: 7 Critical Success Factors for a Smooth Transformation of Your Organization Processes. *Wordclay.*

KEY TERMS AND DEFINITIONS

Empirical Modelling (EM): The term 'Empirical Modelling' supplanted the term 'Agent-oriented modelling' in 1992. The epithet 'empirical' was adopted in part because our modelling principles are based on observation and experiment, and in part to avoid confusion with the concept of 'agent-orientation' that became mainstream over the period 1987-92. The term 'modelling' is more appropriate than 'programming', since EM involves the construction of artefacts, and an accompanying identification of primitive patterns of interaction with artefacts, that may or may not lead to the type of functionally determined behaviour that is characteristic of a classical computer program. Such artefacts are not models of a theory, but have the characteristics of a model in that they serve as a source of experiences for the modeller that are significant only in relation to other independent experiences to which they refer. An EM artefact differs from a program in much the same way that the private artefacts developed by an experimental scientist to record a first tentative interpretation of a phenomenon differs from a engineering product based on a subsequent more comprehensive understanding of an underlying scientific theory. By way of example, contrast the simple artefacts that Faraday first constructed when investigating what could be deemed to be the primitive notions of electromagnetism with the electric motor he later developed.

Business Process Reengineering (BPR): Business Process Reengineering is the analysis and redesign of workflow within and between enterprises. BPR reached its heyday in the early 1990's when Michael Hammer and James Champy published their best-selling book "Reengineering the Corporation". The authors promoted the idea that sometimes radical redesign and reorganization of an enterprise (i.e. wiping the slate clean) was necessary to lower costs and increase quality of service and that information technology was the key enabler for that radical change. The authors felt that the design of workflow in most large corporations was based on assumptions about technology, people and organisational goals that were no longer valid. They suggested seven principles of reengineering to streamline the work process and thereby achieve significant levels of improvement in quality, time management and cost: (1) Organize around outcomes, not tasks; (2) Identify all the processes in an organization and prioritize them in order of redesign urgency; (3) Integrate information processing work into the real work that produces the information; (4) Treat geographically dispersed resources as though they were centralized; (5) Link parallel activities in the workflow instead of just integrating their results; (6) Put the decision point where the work is performed, and build control into the process; (7) Capture information once and at the source.

Use Case: A use case is a methodology used in system analysis to identify, clarify and organise system requirements. The use case is made up of a set of possible sequences of interactions between systems and users in a particular environment and related to a particular goal. It consists of a group of elements (for example, classes and interfaces) that can be used together in a way that will have an effect larger than the sum of the separate elements combined. The use case should contain all system activities that have significance to the users. A use case can be thought of as a collection of possible scenarios related to a particular goal, indeed, the use case and goal are sometimes considered to be synonymous. A use case (or set of use cases) has these characteristics: (1) organizes functional requirements; (2) models the goals of system/actor (user) interactions; (3) records paths (called scenarios) from trigger events to goals; (4) describes one main flow of events, and possibly other ones, called exceptional flows of events; (5) is multi-level, so that one use case can use the functionality of another one. Use cases can be employed during several stages of software development, such as planning system requirements, validating design, testing software, and creating an outline for online help and user manuals.

Spreadsheets: There are strong connections between EM models and spreadsheets. Spreadsheet cells typically represent observables, and their defining formulae capture dependencies amongst observables. EM principles have been described as a 'radical generalisation of the principles underlying the spreadsheet', but this can be misleading. EM certainly subsumes activities that are associated with spreadsheet creation and use, and operates with sets of definitions similar to those that lie behind a spreadsheet grid. Spreadsheets do however have sophisticated forms of dependency based on the geometric organisation of cells that are not easy to express in definitive scripts. They also have qualities as software applications that are not shared by simple EM construals.

State-as-Experienced: The term 'state-as-experienced' is used to emphasise the fact that the state of a construal cannot in general be viewed and described in the way that the state of a computer program is described. Classical computer science specialises in characterising the states of a program with reference to its behaviour, as formally modelled by an abstract machine, such as a Turing machine. In the preliminary experimental investigation of a scientific phenomenon, the experimenter in general has inadequate knowledge of how to interact in such a way as to generate reliable stable patterns of observation, and cannot possibly characterise state solely with reference to a program-like automatic behaviour. The association between a construal and its referent is in contrast far more subjective and personal – it takes the form of a directly perceived relationship between experience of the construal and experience of the referent. The perceived *indivisibility of change to different observables* that is characteristic of dependencies has a crucial significance in this context. In considering state-as-experienced there is no role for semantic connections that are not immediately apparent through some interaction.

Observation-Oriented Modelling: The application of modelling with definitive scripts to represent state encompasses modelling the perspective of a putative external observer on the concurrent interaction of agents within a system. Such an observer is in general 'putative' on the basis that every experience of concurrent interaction is that of an individual agent who must construe the actions of other agents by indirect observation informed by projection from personal experience. In a concurrent design scenario, the concept and status of an extenal observer is particularly problematic, since the visions of different designers may be incoherent and inconsistent. In the context of programming a concurrent system, there is a presumption that there is an objective external perspective within which the interactions of the constituent agents can be rendered coherent and consistent. Observation-oriented modelling applies to EM of concurrent systems whatever their nature. Both human participants and inanimate components are represented as agents. A systematic empirical analysis of the observables through which stimulus and response are deemed to be mediated is accompanied by their metaphorical representation using modelling with definitive scripts.

LSD Notation: LSD is a special-purpose notation that can be used to classify the observables deemed to inform agent interaction in a concurrent system. Giving an LSD account of such agent interaction involves identifying the state-changing *agents* of the system – the perceived and relevant 'sources of change' – and the observables that mediate their interaction. The observables are then classified according to the way in which they are related to the agents as follows. Those (1) that are owned by the agent (i.e. that would not exist without the agent) are its state *observables*; (2) to which the agent may be able to respond are its *oracles*; (3) that the agent may be able to change are its *handles*. The same observable can be classified in more than one way (e.g. an observable may be a handle to one agent and an oracle to the same or another agent). Dependencies amongst observables that are deemed to hold in the view of the agent are *derivates*. Where the agent is deemed to be conditionally able to make changes to observables these privileges are expressed as a set of guarded sequences that make up its *protocol*. An LSD account can be developed prior to the construction of an EM artefact, typically in an initial domain analysis that is provisional, subjective and personal. It may also be developed in conjunction with an artefact, when it may serve the purpose of documenting the modeller's significant interactions with the construal. An LSD account does not have a formal operational semantics, but serves to describe aspects of interactions amongst agents that, in the appropriate context, may be sufficient to identify automatic behaviours.

Chapter 11
Modeling Multi-Criteria Promotional Strategy Based on Fuzzy Goal Programming

B. K. Mangaraj
Xavier Labour Relations Institute, India

ABSTRACT

Promotional strategy is one of the four major facets of marketing; informative on how to advertise and sell products. This can be divided into two broad categories: personal selling strategy (selling the product door-to-door) and mass marketing strategy (announcing the product to the customers). The very first and most important step in choosing the right promotional strategy requires understanding of the target customers. Knowing how the target customer likes a thing can greatly influence the type of promotional item that one considers and how well the promotion performs in the marketing domain. Apart from designing advertising messages, the problem lies with selecting suitable advertising media vehicles which would communicate the message to the right segment at the right time. At the same time, it should have specific and measurable marketing objectives. This paper presents a multi-criteria promotional model for a rural product of a co-operative society in TV channels through popular programmes. An interactive fuzzy goal programming model has been developed for the purpose to handle this problem for selection of TV programmes in some networks for communicating the message of the product. A case study in Indian context has been considered for highlighting the promotion of handloom products by the Bottom of Pyramid producers of the Indian economy to be marketed in all segments through an optimal media selection process.

DOI: 10.4018/978-1-60960-129-4.ch011

INTRODUCTION

A successful product means nothing unless the benefit of such product can be communicated to the target market. Promotion is a communication tool of marketing strategy. Its objective is to convince the target market of the product's differential advantage. It needs to be guided by a promotional strategy - a plan for the optimal use of a promotional mix. An organization's promotional strategies can consist of advertising, public relations, sales promotion, personal selling etc. Advertising is a non-personal paid form of communication using any form of mass media. It influences market share, the consumer behaviour, brand loyalty, perception of attributes etc. Media strategy refers to how the organization is going to deliver its message regarding the product. What type of promotional mix will the organization use to deliver its message strategy? Where it will promote? Clearly, the company must take into account the viewers as well as the general behaviour of its target audience before selecting its media strategy. What newspaper does its target market read? What TV programme do they watch? Which places do they often go? Effective targeting of its media campaign could help the organization in meeting the marketing targets even in the presence of its competitors. This requires selection of appropriate media vehicles for different segments of the target market in order to arouse latent needs of the consumers to become potential buyers of its products.

In this paper, media selection for the promotional strategy of handloom products of Orissa state has been considered those are produced by a particular class of people of Indian economy. This sector which was well-known in India and foreign countries for its cotton and silk fabrics is currently facing tremendous competition due to the effects of globalization. Lack of innovation for new product development as well as suitable marketing strategies have led to the weakening of this industry. The traditional and indigenous knowledge of this area which provided livelihood to thousands of weavers can't sustain the pressure from the modern textile industries. However, the movements of cooperatives and self help groups are trying to revive this sector by creating new markets through product innovations and advertising. This requires studying and analyzing consumer behaviour which stimulates buying of ethnic items in the presence of modern products and also looks attractive in terms of price and quality. At the same time, there is a necessity for a well structured promotional strategy with the help of suitable media vehicles aiming at different market segments in order to reach the consumers within a permissible budget. In other words, care should be taken to achieve competing objectives like cost and exposure within various marketing, cultural and geographical constraints. With the dramatic changes in the overall structure of the television business environment coupled with the continuing fragmentation of the television advertising economy and the sophistication of the technology, local TV channels have greater role than ever before in promotional activities.

In this context, a business model for preservation and promotion of an intangible cultural heritage (ICH) of India has been presented for creating an exposure of handloom products for better marketing activities. This model is in the form of a "multi-criteria marketing decision-system" involving various programmes in TV channels as decision variables which has been handled by a soft computing methodology. An interactive fuzzy goal programming (FGP) algorithm with additive aggregation operator has been utilized to provide the solution in 0-1 format for selecting specific media vehicles targeted towards consumer segments in order to generate maximum promotional effectiveness. A handloom co-operative society has been taken as a case study to demonstrate the business model. It needed an efficient solution procedure for getting a business decision which should be highly competitive in terms of consumer requirements at one end and benefit of rural artisans at the other who are instrumental in preserving the ICH of the region. The solution obtained for such a model in a participatory framework has the potentiality for improving the market share of the co-operative as well as the handloom sector of Orissa in a broader perspective.

BACKGROUND

Handloom is one of the oldest cottage industries in India. Despite the onslaught of modern technology based industrialization which led proliferation of power looms and composite textile mills in independent India, handloom continues to occupy a prominent place in the country's economy. In a labour surplus economy like India, this traditional cottage industry has remained a major source of employment and livelihood next only to agriculture. Goods manufactured in the handloom sector have also a high export potentiality. Certain products of handloom such as sarees, loin clothes and room decorative materials are highly popular in foreign countries. The silk and cotton sarees of various states of India, viz., Orissa, West-Bengal, Andhra Pradesh, Tamil Nadu and Uttar Pradesh have a wider market inside the country besides their good export potentiality. And above all, the industry meets a large portion of clothing requirements of the Bottom of Pyramid (BOP) sector of India, who constitutes the major percentage of Indian population.

Weaving in the handloom, especially cloths of artistic design is an intricate process. The weaver acquires the technique of weaving including various types of preparatory work as a member of the weaver household since his childhood. The adult members of the household teach their children, both males and females and make them acquainted with the various stages of weaving work by utilizing their services at various stages of operations. As a result, handloom weaving in the country has remained more or less a traditional caste and family based occupation. Very few members of other non-traditional weaving castes are found engaged in the handloom sector despite high rate of unemployment in the economy and scope of earning a minimum level of livelihood in this industry with a little sum capital of investment.

The production system of handloom industry in India is carried under three different patterns, i.e, independent weavers, master weavers and cooperative weavers. The independent weavers purchase yarns and other essential raw materials on his own money, weaves cloth and sells the produce on his own either in the open market or to the traders and middlemen. His sale and output of clothes are always determined by the local marketing conditions. But, due to increasing consumerism culture, the tastes and preferences of clothes among consumers are changing very frequently. As a result the independent weaver has to always depend on traders and middlemen for the marketability of his goods. On account of this type of dependency relationship, the weavers are getting exploited by the traders and middlemen and lead a hand to mouth existence. The master weavers advance yarn and raw materials to the weavers and pay wages to them on receipt of woven cloth. Although the marketability aspect of their goods are taken care of by them, they provide employment to weavers whenever the market conditions are favourable. As a result, the weavers working under master weavers lead a very precarious life. Due to unorganized nature of the industry and weak bargaining power of the weavers, the wage rate is also very low. On the other hand, in order to give protection to the handloom industry in the face of competition from the power looms and composite textile mills as well as to reduce the high level of exploitation of the weavers by the private master weavers and middlemen, the Government of India has intensified the promotion of weavers' cooperative societies. These societies in their operational areas try to bring all weavers to their fold by opening membership to them at a very nominal share with subsidy from the government. They provide yarns and essential raw materials to weaver members for producing cloth as per the given specification, receive the finished goods on payment of wages/ conversion charges and above all arrange for the sale of their finished goods. The members are entitled to share the profit of the society and get bonus in proportion to their output of cloth.

Handlooms are part of Indian cultural heritage; they exemplify the richness and diversity of Indian culture and the artistry of weavers. The background of the study is based on the assumption that handloom products of any region with all its traditional inherent quality and design represent the culture of that region as cultural manifestations get reflected on the traditional products and their designs. Simultaneously, the products can also be cross-cultural with a distinct design pattern of one region getting imprinted upon the cloths of some others. Hence, cross-cultural products can be aimed at the consumption culture of the target segments. As design of these products are planned for better market appeal, diversified target markets are to be studied more scientifically to know the consumption cultures, their preferences and priorities. Also, an innovative product line with accurate market survey to know the characteristics of specific target market is not sufficient to succeed effectively in the market. A well planned promotional strategy with the help of various media vehicles is a must for communicating the differential advantage of the products to the right segment in right time.

The present study is based on the "Weavers' Co-operative Society of Nuapatna" where the weavers are highly attached to their caste-based traditional occupation. It has been observed that very few from this caste work as agricultural labourers, construction workers or other informal sector workers. On the other hand, few people from traditionally non-weaving castes have started weaving tie and dye sarees of both fine cotton and silk varieties in the recent years. They have the expertise of weaving cotton and silk sarees with various design patterns already known to them since long as well as some new ones compatible with their knowledge-base as per the requirement of customers. These skills are unique to this area only and are a part of the local culture. As majority of the villagers are dependent upon this activity for their socio-economic development, weaving becomes the key activity for an endogenous development (UNESCO, 1995) which can be linked to the changing requirement of the outside world for the overall development of this area and can also be sustainable. This clearly shows that handloom weaving is still a viable occupation for many people in rural India who do not derive their livelihood from other informal sector occupations such as agriculture, construction and the like. Besides, this ancient and traditional occupation in rural India demonstrates a varied and rich cultural heritage being reflected in various design patterns and these unique skills of weavers should be preserved as a part of UNESCO's mission on safeguarding ICH and, at the same, time availing to these BOP producers a competitive advantage in the era of globalization.

Prahalad & Hammond (2002) and Prahalad, & Hart (2002) propounded the theory that BOP consumers with income less than $2 per day can be a viable and profitable segment to market. They placed the onus of these activities on MNC's who have ignored this market till date. Prahalad (2005) said that serving BOP could become a win-win situation for the consumers as well as the companies who also find it as a source of innovation. On the contrary, Karnani (2007, 2009) argues that the BOP approach looks at the low income consumers as alternative markets and, with the current low levels of income, this seems to be a difficult proposition to accept. He emphasizes that rather than looking at BOP consumers as buyers of products produced by big companies, they should be seen as producers. This is the only way in which the real income of the consumers would increase and there would be poverty alleviation. This paper considers the approach of both the schools of thought where poor people in the rural as well as in urban areas are the consumers. Besides, many weavers in the BOP segment who are in the verge of quitting their traditional profession and acquired skills have been treated as producers BOP segment and outside world. A suitable promotional strategy through various media vehicles to increase the marketing potentiality of rural products would be able to serve the purpose.

PROMOTIONAL MODEL

The primary objective of developing a promotional model is to select a business plan for promotion of handloom products through awareness programme as these items are confined to their respective geographical boundaries only. Hence, this model aims at maximizing the consumer reach through a promotional campaign which conflicts with a minimum investment for this activity. An ethnographic survey has been carried out to find out the effectiveness of various promotional media in the region. It has been found out that TV programmes attract maximum viewers and at the same time consumers' buying behaviour is mostly influenced by televisions than other media. But, the cost of advertisement and its effectiveness largely depend upon the type of network as well as the TV programmes where the product is advertised. Hence, the presence of conflicting decision criteria along with various marketing constraints creates a dilemma for selecting the media vehicles which were the most suited slots for which the impact factor of the advertisements can be optimum. The cooperative society decided to have a promotional campaign in TV channels in the evening programmes on each day as these programmes have more number of viewers as has been observed in the survey. The strategy is to identify suitable programmes which would satisfy competing promotional criteria at one end, and marketing constrains at the other, which can stimulate consumers to take favorable actions towards buying decision.

Gench (1970, 1973) observed that the media selection problem was challenging because of the multiplicity of reasonable alternatives, complexity of the advertising phenomena and the economic importance of this decision to a firm. Aaker (1975) presented a model ADMOD which was an advertising decision model designed to address simultaneously the budget decision, the copy decision, and the media allocation decision. Arthur and Calvin (2009) proposed an integer goal programming model that handled conflicting management goals that realistically reflected the complexity of the media decision environment. Looking at these works, a modeling approach was conceptualized using fuzzy logic and multi-objective modeling framework for selection of an optimal media-mix in the promotional strategy. A fuzzy goal programming (FGP) algorithm has been utilized to select TV programmes for effectively communicating the message of the products to the consumers.

FGP: An Information Management Tool for Business Strategy

FGP is a major step to handle a class of decision problems involving multiple, conflicting, non-commensurable and imprecise criteria in the decision environment. The fuzzy goal version of a multi-criteria decision-making (MCDM) model can be stated as:

Determine $x \in \{0, 1\}$

$$\text{S.t. } G_i(x) \gtrsim g_i : i = 1, 2......m \qquad (1)$$

$$A_j(x) \le b_j : j = 1, 2......k$$

where '~' signifies the fuzzification of the i-th goal. The model (1) whose crisp substitute can be obtained by identifying i–th fuzzy goal as a fuzzy set $\tilde{G}_i$ defined over the set of feasible solutions and then aggregating all these fuzzy sets $\tilde{G}_i$

to get a single fuzzy decision set $\tilde{D}$. The membership function of this set serves the purpose of an overall objective function and the solution which maximizes it is the satisfying decision. The crux of the decision process lies in defining the decision function by aggregating the fuzzy sets $\tilde{G}_i$ using a suitable operator. The membership function of $\tilde{G}_i$ may be defined linearly (Zimmermann 1976, 1978, 1983) as follows:

$$\mu_{\tilde{G}_i}(x) = \begin{cases} 1 & : for \\ (G_i(x) - p_i)/(g_i - p_i) & : for \\ 0 & : for \end{cases}$$

$$G_i(x) \geq g_i$$
$$G_i(x) \in [p_i, b_i] \quad \ldots\ldots\ldots\ldots\ldots\ldots \quad (2)$$
$$G_i(x) \leq p_i$$

Quite a few FGP algorithms have already been developed and also have their applications in different fields of knowledge. Some of the algorithms are due to Hannan (1981(a), 1981(b)), Llena (1985), Narasimhan (1980, 1981), Rubin & Narasimhan (1985), Sinha et.al (1988, 1989), Tiwari et.al (1986), Lin (2004), Yaghoobi et al (2008), Arora and Gupta (2009) etc. Kim et al (1998) have investigated the application of tolerance concepts to goal programming in a fuzzy environment. L-Husan and Feng-Chou (2001) formulated FGP incorporating different importance and pre-emptive priorities using an additive model to maximize the sum of achievement degree of all fuzzy goals. Jiménez et al (2005) showed how non-linear membership function could be approximated to piecewise linear membership function. Ching-Ter ((2007) proposed a new idea of how to program the binary FGP model which could then be solved using the integer programming method. Application of such type of algorithms can very well be observed from Sinha et al (1988, 1989), Mangaraj and Das (2008) in agricultural planning; Pickens et al (1991) in Forestry; Rao et. al. (1992) in situational optimization; Shankar et. al (1999) in cellular manufacturing; Mangaraj (1999) and Mangaraj et al (2001) in capital budgeting; Mangaraj et al (2000, 2002, 2008), and Mishra et. al. (2003) in Marketing; Manoj Kumar et al (2004), in supply chain; etc. Pandian (2004) established the usefulness of modified S-curve membership function in limited supply production planning problem with continuous variables where the optimal solution was obtained by incorporating fuzziness in a linear programming model through the objective functions and constraints. It was observed that a better level of satisfactory solution was obtained compared to non-fuzzy linear programming problem. FGP approach for water quality management in a river basin has been done by Lee and Wen (1997). Parra et al (2001) have discussed a FGP approach to portfolio selection. Roy and Maiti (1998) have discussed multi-objective inventory models of deteriorating items with some constraints in fuzzy environment. Irfan and Mustafa (2007) discussed application of FGP in production process. Liang (2007) presented a FGP approach for solving the integrated production transportation planning decision (PTPD) problems with fuzzy multiple goals in uncertain environments. The proposed model aimed at simultaneously minimizing the total distribution and production costs, total number of rejected items, and the total delivery time with reference to available capacity, labor level and quota flexibility constraints at each source, as well as forecasting demand and warehouse space at each destination. The algorithm adopted piecewise linear memberships functions to represent the fuzzy goals of the decision maker(DM) for the integrated PTPD problems in a supply chain, and achieved more flexible doctrines via an interactive decision-making process. Sharma et al (2007) presented a FGP approach for optimal allocation of land under cultivation and proposed an annual agricultural plan for different crops. A tolerance based FGP technique was used to quantify fuzziness of different goals for the problem. As a measure of sensitivity, the problem was solved using different weighting structures specified by the DM. Tsai et al (2008) presented a FGP based model to address a steel supplier's channel allocation problem that included a decision of channel-mix and capacity allocation for each distribution channel. The problem was formulated as a fuzzy mixed integer multiple goal programming problem that included business competitive advantages such as maximizing net profits, minimizing the rate of end user claims, and minimizing the rate of late lading, and was subject to constraints regarding manufacturing capacity, customer's demand, channel capacity, channel quota flexibility, budget limitations, and so on. Realistic data from Taiwan's largest steel company was implemented for the effectiveness of the model. Tsai and Hung (2009) proposed a FGP approach that integrated activity-based costing and performance evaluation in a value-chain structure for optimal GSC supplier selection and flow allocation. Sharma et al (2009) presented how FGP techniques can be efficiently applied in developing sophisticated investment decision making models to provide feasible solutions for credit union portfolio management problems for constructing efficient portfolios. They have formulated additive and weighted additive models for investment decisions using fuzzy goals Giannikos and Polychroniou(2009) in their paper presented a FGP model for allocating tasks to employees in teamwork. Each task as well as each employee was represented in a multidimensional ability space on a team basis. The model also considered the possibility of improving employees' abilities through training and of using subcontracting or overtime, if necessary. Reddy et al (2007) in their work discussed distributor selection and quota allocation, which was an important part of the supply chain of many firms using fuzzy goals and an additive aggregation operator. Belmokaddem et al (2009) presented an application of FGP with different importance and priorities (FGPIP) developed by L-Husan, and Feng-Choui (2001) to aggregate production planning for the state-run enterprise of iron manufactures.

In this paper an interactive FGP model with an additive operator has been developed in a 0-1 solution format to solve the MCDM problem whose steps are as follows:

- Solve the MCDM model (1) as a set of single objective 0 – 1 linear programming problems taking one objective at a time. These solutions obtained for the m objectives are termed as ideal solutions.
- Determine the corresponding values for each objective at the ideal solutions and a pay-off matrix can be constructed as follows:

$G_1(x)$ $G_2(x)$ . . . G_m (x)

$$\begin{array}{c} x^1 \\ x^2 \\ . \\ . \\ x^m \end{array} \begin{bmatrix} G_1^*(x^1) & G_2(x^1) & . & . & . & G_m(x^1) \\ G_1(x^2) & G_2^*(x^2) & . & . & . & G_m(x^2) \\ . & . & & & & . \\ . & . & & & & . \\ G_1(x^m) & G_2(x^m) & . & . & . & G_m^*(x^m) \end{bmatrix}$$

Here x^1, x^2, ……, x^m are the ideal solution of the objectives $G_1(x)$, $G_2(x)$….$G_m(x)$ respectively.

Convert all the objectives $G_i(x)$ to their equivalent fuzzy goals and combine them using an "additive" operator. Formulate the MCDM model (1) into a linear programming problem as:

$$\text{Max} \sum_{i=1}^{m} \mu_{Gi}(x)$$

$$\text{St. } \mu_{Gi} \leq \frac{G_i(x) - G_i(x)^{Min}}{G_i^*(x) - G_i(x)^{Min}} : i = 1,2 \ldots m \ .. \qquad (3)$$

$A_j(x) \leq b_j : j = 1,2\ldots l$

$x, \mu_{ik} \in \{0,1\} : k = 1, 2, 3, 4, 5$, where

$$\mu_{Gi} = \frac{\mu_{i1}}{10} + \frac{\lambda_{i2}}{10^2} + \frac{\lambda_{i3}}{10^3} + \frac{\lambda_{i4}}{10^4} + \frac{\lambda_{i5}}{10^5}$$

Solve the model (3) which yields $\mu_{Gi}(x) = \mu_i$. If the decision results satisfactorily for all objectives, then go to Step 6.

The DM is asked as to whether he can make some concession in the level of any membership function, whose attainment in his opinion is more satisfactory to improve those that are less satisfactory. Suppose the DM is not satisfied with the solution $x = x'$ and he can concede an amount $\Delta\lambda_h$ from the membership value of hth objective. Then transform

$$G_i(x)^{Min} \longrightarrow G_i(x') \text{ and}$$
$$G_i^*(x) \longrightarrow G_i^*(x) \text{ for all } i \neq h$$

and construct modified membership function $\theta_{Gi}(x)$ for all i.

Solve the equivalent model as:

$$\text{Max} \sum_{i=1}^{m} \theta_{Gi}(x) = \theta \quad : i \neq h$$

$$\text{s. t. } \theta_{Gi} \leq \frac{G_i(x) - G_i(x')}{G_i^*(x) - G_i(x')} : i \neq h$$

$$G_h(x) \geq G_h(x') - \Delta\lambda_h(G_h^*(x) - G_h) \quad \ldots\ldots\ldots \tag{4}$$

$A_j(x) \leq b_j$: j = 1,2….l

$x, \theta_{ik} \in \{0,1\}$: k = 1,2….5

Where, $\theta_{Gi} = \frac{\theta_{i1}}{10} + \frac{\theta_{i2}}{10^2} + \frac{\theta_{i3}}{10^3} + \frac{\theta_{i4}}{10^4} + \frac{\theta_{i5}}{10^5}$

- If the solution is satisfactory to the DM, then the associated solution is the final solution, otherwise go to step 4 and repeat the procedure until the DM becomes satisfied with the attainment levels of all the membership functions.

Problem Formulations

The decision variables, constants and symbols for the problem are as follows:

i: 1, 2, 3 and 4 for TV channels viz., OTV(General), ETV(Oriya), Dooradarshan (DD, Oriya) and OTV(Taranga) respectively

j: 1, 2, ….8 for promotion time of 30 seconds during 7-7.30, 7.30- 8.00,………, 10.30-11.00 pm. respectively.

k: 1,2,..,7 for different days in a week, viz., Monday,…., Sunday respectively

l: 1,2 for normal and festival time respectively.

X_{ij}^{kl}: Market promotion in i-th TV at j-th period on k-th day during l-th time.

C_{ij}^{kl}: Cost of promotion in the i-th TV at j-th period on k-th day during l-th time.

V_{ij}^{kl}: Viewers of . i-th TV at j-th period on k-th day during l-th time.

Y_{ij}^{ki}: Market promotion of a competitor in the i-th TV at j-th period on k-th day during l-th time.

C^{Min}, C^{Max}: Min/Max value of investment permissible for promotion.

V^{Min}, V^{Max}: Min/ Max number of targeted viewer ship.

The formulation of the system constraints and goals is given as:

i) Non-Overlapping

The programmes during the evening hours in various channels have been considered and it has been observed that regional news time in all the TV channels is the same, i.e. 7-7.30 except OTV (Taranga) which is an entertainment channel of OTV. In these programmes, important news of Orissa state is generally broadcasted and most of the news items presented in these channels have the same contents. The viewers who watch this programme normally see one of these channels even if commercial networks have the provision of all the channels. As a result, the entire viewers of news programme are divided into three groups. In this context, promotion can be restricted to a maximum one channel only during this time. Hence,

$$\sum_{i=1}^{3} X_{i1}^{kl} \leq 1 \text{ for all k and l}$$

ii) Preferential

Some programmes are preferred in specified channels depending upon consumer culture. Amongst the rural viewers "Dasi" a popular serial in DD at 9.30 during Thursday to Saturday has the maximum number of viewers whereas in urban areas maximum people watch OTV channel for "News Fuse" at 10.00 on Monday and Wednesday which is most popular. Similarly, the other popular programmes are Oriya movie and serial Jai Jagannath in ETV and OTV (Taranga) respectively. Mathematically, the media preference can be defined as:

$X_{ij}^{kl} \geq 1$ for all i and l and some j & k . .

iii) Differential Advantage

A competitor can neither be overlooked nor accepted fully. So, a careful analysis needs to be done and certain programmes used by the competitors should be considered. When there is a promotion of a competitor in a TV programme, it is advisable to have the promotion of the proposed products in the same channel and to show the differential advantage of the product over the other. This is necessary to put the consumer in a competitive platform and to minimize the effect of the competing product in the consumer's mind. Some of the programmes taken for the purpose are Police file, Shopping time, Box office and Great political circus where some of the well known synthetic manufactures advertise for their similar products. Mathematically, it can be put as:

$X_{ij}^{kl} \geq Y_{ij}^{kl}$ for all i,j, k and l

when, $Y_{ij}^{ki} \geq 1$

iv) Regional

Each segment should be able to view the promotion in TV channels. As people in the upper income group take connection through OTV and ETV to view multiple channels, it was felt to cover this group of consumers at least once and twice per day during normal and festival time respectively. This can be made to attract consumers in the higher economic stratum towards these products with ethnic designs having a flavor of modernity and giving a social message that purchase of each item would help in poverty alleviation apart from preservation of local cultural heritage which is in the agenda of UNESCO in the World Decade for Cultural Development as well as mission for the safeguarding of ICH. Mathematically, it can be put as:

$$\sum_{i=1}^{4} \sum_{j=1}^{8} X_{ij}^{k1} \geq 1 \text{ for all k and i} \neq 3 \text{ (Normal time)}$$

$$\sum_{i=1}^{4} \sum_{j=1}^{8} X_{ij}^{k2} \geq 2 \text{ for all k and i} \neq 3 \text{ (Festival time)}$$

v) Minimum Selectivity

Dooradarsahn (DD) is a Government television network and is available to all viewers at free of cost by erecting a low cost TV antenna. Two channels, one for the National and the other for the state (oriya) can be viewed by all unlike paid channels of commercial networks like Ortel Communications (OTV), Ennadu TV (ETV), Tata-sky, Reliance TV etc. People in both urban and rural segments having paying capacity subscribe to these networks in order to view a number of paid channels apart from channels provided by Dooradarshan. Since the number of viewers of DD is comparatively higher than other channels and covers all from lower income group, it has been felt that advertisement of the product should be made in DD at least once and twice per day during normal and festival time respectively to cover the consumers in BOP segment which is also available to other category of viewers. Mathematically, it can be put as:

$$\sum_{j=1}^{8} X_{3j}^{k1} \geq 1 \text{ for all k (Normal time)}$$

$$\sum_{j=1}^{8} X_{3j}^{k2} \geq 3 \text{ for all k (Festival time)}$$

vi) Limiting Frequency

Management of the cooperative took a decision to show the advertisement visuals at the most twice/day in each of the TV channels during normal season. Similarly, it can go up to four times a day in festival seasons as traditionally people buy new clothes during this period for wearing as well as gifting to friends and relatives as per the practice in the local culture. Mathematically, it can be put as:

$$\sum_{j=1}^{8} X_{ij}^{k1} \leq 2 \text{ for all i and k (Normal time)}$$

$$\sum_{j=1}^{8} X_{ij}^{k1} \leq 4 \text{ for all i and k(Festival time)}$$

The competing decision criteria in this decision system in terms of fuzzy goals can be stated as:

i) Exposure

The effective utility of any media vehicle for any specific promotional programme is measured through exposure. Maximization of exposure is highly necessary in any promotional campaign as it enables bringing more and more consumers into the marketing domain of the product. It is nothing but the total number of people effectively reached by any media vehicle in any specific period of time. A person being exposed to any message through a media vehicle retains it in his long term memory if he is exposed to the same a number of times. This influences his decision-making process in buying behaviour and a positive response fulfils the promotional objective. It can be achieved first by maximizing the total coverage through the selected media vehicles or on the other hand, getting more satisfied with a targeted goal. Mathematically, it can be put in a fuzzy goal form as:

$$\textbf{Satisfy} \sum_{i=1}^{4}\sum_{j=1}^{8}\sum_{k=1}^{7}\sum_{l=1}^{2} V_{ij}^{kl} X_{ij}^{kl} \in \left[V^{MIn}, V^{Max}\right]$$

ii) Cost of Promotion

Cost is an important criterion in promotional decision-making as it has to be made looking at the budget consideration of the organization. Sometimes, it may be viewed as minimization of advertising expenditure or on the other hand it may be considered within permissible limits.

This includes the amount to be spent for the preparation of TV clippings, administrative cost as well as cost of transmitting the clippings in the TV programmes. Since the cost of broadcasting depends upon the selection of TV network as well as the programme, it becomes highly necessary to do so in such a manner that the cost of such an operation is linked with the optimum satisfaction of the organization. Also, cost of advertisement varies depending upon the selling season i.e. whether it is done during normal time and festival time. Looking at all these, the fuzzy goal form of cost of promotion, particularly for broadcasting can be mathematically written as:

$$\text{Satisfy } \sum_{i=1}^{4}\sum_{j=1}^{8}\sum_{k=1}^{7}\sum_{l=1}^{2} C_{ij}^{kl} X_{ij}^{kl} \in \left[C^{MIn}, C^{Max}\right]$$

(0,1) Restriction

Each decision variable has to take 0 or 1 as its solution in the rejection-acceptance format. Mathematically, it can be represented as:

$X_{ij}^{kl} \in \{0,1\}$ for each i, j, k and l.

DISCUSSION AND CONCLUSION

The media selection problem for promotion of handloom products has been conceptualized as a MCDM problem with its FGP equivalent for selection of an optimum media vehicle-mix. The multiple numbers of criteria in the model have been formulated as fuzzy goals along with the necessary restrictions. The basic purpose of implementing FGP in this problem is due the fact that decision criterion is more meaningful through a fuzzy goal than an objective function. The fuzzy goal gives a scope for translating the aspiration of the DM for each criterion in terms of an interval target and a graded level of satisfaction. Linear membership functions have been considered for translating these decision criteria into fuzzy sets in this research work. The decision matrix presented in step-2 of the algorithm has given an insight for constructing interval targets and membership functions for such goals representing the satisfaction of the DM or organization in terms of [0,1] interval so that higher value of a criterion in the interval target signifies higher level of satisfaction. Also, multiple numbers of competing and non-commensurable criteria have been translated into a single attribute in the decision environment, i.e. the satisfaction level. The crux of this approach is to maximize the overall satisfaction in the decision system so that each criterion can be achieved to a compromise level obtained in a competitive manner. In this paper, an additive operator has been used to aggregate the criteria in terms of fuzzy sets. But, the compromise solution which can be obtained in this manner might not satisfy the DM /organization as far as all the criteria are concerned. Hence, an interactive procedure for obtaining such a solution becomes necessary making some trade-offs amongst the competing criteria. Hence, the multi-criteria problem can be converted into a set of linear programming problems which has standard algorithms and computer software for getting optimum solution. In the present work, the proposed algorithm has reduced the multi-criteria media-selection problem to a 0-1 linear programming form for selection of the media vehicles in the decision process.

The problem has been considered assuming that the buying behaviour of the consumer largely depends upon his knowledge on various attributes of the product as well as the need arousing capacity of the advertising campaign. Also, various studies on promotional planning reveal that the frequency of an advertisement has a dominant role in this aspect of human behaviour. However, considering competitions in the same media, message delivery capacity of the promotional materials has been carefully analysed and planned properly to show the product's differential advantage over the competitors. The data regarding consumer viewer- ship were taken from 1000 viewers both from urban and rural areas. The number of respondents from both the groups was decided based on the population proportion in both the areas. The study was done for a cooperative society having 214 weavers for marketing of their products at the society level. To promote the production of the local products, the cooperative society has planned for adoption of a business strategy availing loan from Indian Bank and State bank of India and aiming at a serious promotional drive to increase the number of consumers through promotional programme as well as innovating new products depending upon the consumers' requirements. In rural sector, it has more number of people having less buying power and in urban sector, it is just the reverse. The society targeted at promoting its products in both the sectors as clothing is an important requirement and in a growing economy, fashion has become a symbol of modernity. With more and more number of people preferring cotton and silk fabrics with ethnic designs, the traditional handloom market is gaining popularity and becoming an important sector in the Indian economy which was dominated by synthetic markets.

The ethnographic survey that was carried out to observe the viewing habit of the people in both the segments also determined the exposure of each programme in consumer segments. The cost of advertising during the programmes in the channels was obtained from their respective offices in their current rate. The budget allocation for the same during normal as well as festival season was collected from the society management. The interval goals for the viewer-ship and cost of broadcasting were decided through a participatory discussion method along with the inputs generated from the model. The planning horizon has considered one week each in normal as well as festival time for the promotional campaign. Some of the most popular programmes and possible competitors were also considered for selecting the programmes. The viewer-ship and cost of promotion goals which were competing amongst themselves with respect to various restrictions were compromised to a satisfactory level for the selection suitable media vehicles.

The optimum numbers of programmes chosen for the promotional strategies, viz., exposure maximization, cost minimization have been presented in Table 1. These represent the number of programmes in different TV networks during normal and festival times which would have maximum viewer ship or with a minimum investment. But, looking at a permissible investment and desired viewers within these limits, the compromise strategy involving these two conflicting criteria has been obtained by using the FGP algorithm stated above for a satisfactory solution in an interactive manner. The various programmes selected for the purpose have been presented in Tables 2 and 3 for normal as well as festival time. It has been observed that, the programmes which were identified for the purpose have satisfied all the constraints and the competing goals. The compromise solution obtained in the first iteration was modified by increasing the investment level by another 10% to select those programmes through which the exposure level was expected to increase by another 19%. Hence, the final solution represented a compromise strategy (Table 1)

Table-1.

No. of Promotions	DD(N)	DD(F)	ETV(N)	ETV(F)	OTV(N)	OTV(F)	OTV-T(N)	OTV-T(F)
EXP. MAX	22	32	22	32	23	28	24	28
COST-MIN	7	12	8	12	7	14	10	12
COMP-Strategy	11	22	10	15	8	16	11	17

Table 2.

	DD(Oriya) (Normal	DD(Oriya) (Festival)	ETV (Normal)	ETV (Festival
MON	News (7 .00-7.30)	News (7.00-7.30) Serial-1(8.00-8.30) Serial-2(9.30-10.00)	Serial-1(8.30-9.00	Serial-1(8.30-9.00) Serial-2(9.30-10.00)
TUE	News (7.00-7.30)	News (7.00-7.30) Serial-1(8.00-8.30) Serial-2(9.30-10.00)	Serial-1(8.30-9.00)	Serial-1(8.30-9.00) Serial-(9.30-10.00)
WED	News (7.00-7.30)	News (7.00-7.30) Serial-1(8.00-8.30) Serial-2(9.30-10.00)	Serial-1(8.30-900) Serial -2(9.30-10.00)	Serial-1(8.30-900) Serial-2(9.30-10.00)
THU	News (7.00-7.30), Dasi(9.30-10.00)	News (7.00-7.30), Dasi(9.30-10.00) Serial-1(10.00-10.30)	Serial-1(8.30-9.00)	Serial-1(8.30-9.00) Serial-2(9.30-10.00)
FRI	News (7.00-7.30), Serial-1(9.30-10.00)	News (7.00-7.30) Serial-1(9.30-10.00) Serial-2(10-10.30)	Serial-1(8.30-9.00)	Serial-1(8.30-9.00) Serial-2(9.30-10.00)
SAT	News (7.00-7.30), Dasi(9.30-10.00)	News (7.00-7.30) Dasi(9.30-10.00) Serial-1(10-10.30)	Oriya-Movie (7.30-9.00)	Oriya-Movie (7.30-8.30) & (9.00-10.00)
SUN	News (7.00-7.30), Serial-2(8.30 9.00)	News (7.00-7.30), Opera(9.00-10 30)	Serial-1(8.30-9.00)	Serial-1(8.30-9.00) Serial-2(9.30-10.00)

having competing goals at one end and marketing constraints at the other obtained through human satisfaction variable.

SUGGESTED FUTURE RESEARCH

FGP is a soft computing approach to MCDM in an imprecise environment. The central idea behind this approach is that imprecise decision-making problem can not be handled with the help of precise analytical tools and when modeled via fuzzy logic to fuzzy sets can be reduced to precise mathematical structures for possible solution. There can be several situations for MCDM problems with pre-emptive priority structures for various competing criteria; imprecise parameters due to unavailability of precise data; unequal importance of the objectives/goals in the same priority level etc., which can also be handled by FGP approach. Also, in many situations the satisfaction function need not be linear which require non-linear approximation of the same. This leads to numerous possible methodological developments in the field of FGP along with software tools to assist decision-making process making it an important area in the field of soft computing.

As has been observed from the literature, several applications of this approach in the design of business models, viz., product planning, product design, marketing-mix, portfolio-selection, capital budgeting, resource allocation, etc. are possible when such systems are modeled in MCDM format. When probability theory can handle imprecision due to randomness, fuzzy logic is an alternative to tackle problems with imprecision due to fuzziness. Business models for profit and non-profit sectors due to their socio-economic contexts can never be stated precisely and for that reason precise computational tools have limitations in handling them. However, some of these can be nicely captured and sorted out when the problems are viewed in a soft computing framework which can not only give a valid and reliable result but also

Table 3.

	OTV (Normal	OTV (Festival)	OTV(Taranga) (Normal)	OTV(Taranga) (Festival
MON	News Fuse (10.00-10.30)	Serial-1((9.00-9.30) News Fuse (10.00-10.30)	Serial-1(7.30-8.00) Jai Jagannath (8.00-8.30)	Serial-1(7.30-8.00) Jai Jagannath (8.00-8.30)
TUE	Police File (10.00-10.30)	Serial-1(9.00-9.30) Police File (10.00-10.30)	Serial-1(7.30-8.00)	Serial-1(7.30-8.00) Serial-2(8.00-8.30)
WED	News Fuse (10.00-10.30)	Serial-1(9.00-9.30) News Fuse (10.00-10.30)	Serial-1(7.30-8.00) Jai Jagannath (8.00-8.30)	Serial-1(7.30-8.00) Jai Jagannath (8.00-8.30)
THU	Shopping Time (7.30-8.00)	Shopping Time 7.30-8.00 National News-9.00-10.00	Serial-1(7.30-8.00)	Serial-1(7.30-8.00) Serial-2(8.00-8.30)
FRI	Serial-1(10.00-10.30)	Serial-1(9.00-9.30) Serial-2(10.00-10.30)	Serial-1(7.30-8.00) Jai Jagannath (8.00-8.30)	Serial-1(7.30-8.00) Jai Jagannath (8.00-8.30)
SAT	Box-Office (7.30-8.00)	Box-Office (7.30-8.00) Serial-1(8.00-8.30) Serial-2(9.00-9.30)	Serial-1(7.30-8.00)	Serial-1(7.30-8.00) Serial-2(8.00-8.30) Sercial-3(9.30-10.00)
SUN	Great Orissa Political Circus (10.00-11.00)	Serial-1(9.00-9.30) Great Orissa Political Circus (10.00-11.00)	Serial-1(7.30-8.00) Jai Jagannath (8.00-8.30)	Jai Jagannath (8.00-8.30) Serial-2(9.00-9.30) Serial-3(9.30-10.00)

with a meaning in socio-economic perspective. This empowers FGP with the ability for designing as well as solving complex business situations for meaningful decisions (Table 2, Table 3).

REFERENCES

Aaker, D. (1975). ADMOD: An advertising decision model. *JMR, Journal of Marketing Research*, *12*(1), 37–45. doi:10.2307/3150656

Arora, S. R., & Gupta, R. (2009). Interactive fuzzy goal programming approach for bi-level programming problem. *European Journal of Operational Research*, *194*(2), 368–376. doi:10.1016/j.ejor.2007.12.019

Arthur, J. K., & Calvin, P. D. (2009). Integer goal programming in advertising media selection. *Decision Sciences*, *10*(4), 577–592.

Belmokaddem, M., Mekidiche, M., & Sahed, A. (2009). Application of fuzzy goal programming approach with different importance and priority to aggregate production planning. *Journal of Applied Quantitative Methods*, *4*(3), 317–331.

Ching-Ter, C. (2007). Binary fuzzy goal programming. *European Journal of Operational Research*, *180*(1), 29–37. doi:10.1016/j.ejor.2006.03.030

Gensch, D. H. (1970). Media factors: A review article. *JMR, Journal of Marketing Research*, *7*(2), 216–225. doi:10.2307/3150112

Gensch, D. H. (1973). *Advertising planning: Mathematical models in advertising media planning*. Amsterdam: Elsevier Scientific Publishing Company.

Giannikos, I., & Polychroniou, P. (2009). Fuzzy goal programming model for task allocation in teamwork. *International Journal of Human Resources Development and Management*, *9*(1), 97–115. doi:10.1504/IJHRDM.2009.021557

Hannan, E. L. (1981a). On Fuzzy goal programming. *Decision Sciences*, *12*, 522–531. doi:10.1111/j.1540-5915.1981.tb00102.x

Hannan, E. L. (1981b). Linear programming with multiple fuzzy goals. *Fuzzy Sets and Systems*, *6*, 235–248. doi:10.1016/0165-0114(81)90002-6

Irfan, E., & Mustafa, G. (2007). Fuzzy goal programming and an application in production process. In P. Melin, W. Pedrycz, J. Kacprzyk, E. Ramirez & O. Castillo (Eds.), *Analysis and design of intelligent systems using soft computing techniques*. (pp. 649-659). Berlin/Heidelburg: Springer-Verlag

Jiménez, M., Arenas, M., Bilbao, A., & Rodríguez-Uría, M. V. (2005). Approximate resolution of an imprecise goal programming model with nonlinear membership functions. *Fuzzy Sets and Systems*, *150*, 129–145. doi:10.1016/j.fss.2004.05.001

Karnani, A. (2007). The mirage of marketing to the bottom of the pyramid. *California Management Review*, *49*(4), 90–111.

Karnani, A. (2009). The bottom of the pyramid strategy for reducing poverty: A failed promise. *DESA Working Paper*, No.80, ST/ESA/2009/DWP/80.

Kim, J.-S., & Whang, K.-S. (1998). The tolerance approach to the fuzzy goal programming problems with unbalanced triangular membership function. *European Journal of Operational Research*, *107*, 614–624. doi:10.1016/S0377-2217(96)00363-3

L-Husan, C, and Feng-Chou, T. (2001). Fuzzy goal programming with different importance and priorities. *European Journal of Operational Research*, *133*, 548–556. doi:10.1016/S0377-2217(00)00201-0

Lee, C.-S., & Wen, C.-G. (1997). Fuzzy goal programming approach for water quality management in a river basin. *Fuzzy Sets and Systems*, *89*, 181–192. doi:10.1016/S0165-0114(96)00089-9

Liang, T. F. (2007). Applying fuzzy goal programming to product/transportation planning decision in supply chain. *International Journal of Systems Science*, *38*(4), 293–304. doi:10.1080/00207720601159381

Lin, C. C. (2004). A weighted max-min model for fuzzy goal programming. *Fuzzy Sets and Systems*, *142*(3), 407–420. doi:10.1016/S0165-0114(03)00092-7

Llena, J. (1985). On fuzzy linear programming. *European Journal of Operational Research*, *22*(2), 216–223. doi:10.1016/0377-2217(85)90229-2

Mangaraj, B. K. (1999). Fuzzy multi-objective programming in capital budgeting decision system. *Finance India*, *8*(44), 1161–1172.

Mangaraj, B. K., Aparajita, U., & Mishra, A. (2000). Fuzzy set in product planning decision. *Journal of Discrete Mathematical Science and Cryptography*, *3*(1-3), 57–81.

Mangaraj, B. K., & Das, D. (2008). *Interactive fuzzy multi-objective programming in land re-organisational planning for sustainable rural development* (pp. 721–730). Paris: Proceedings of World Academy of Science, Engineering and Technology.

Mangaraj, B. K., Mishra, A., & Aparajita, U. (2008). Fuzzy goal programming in marketing-mix selection. J*ournal of Science . Technology and Management*, *1*(1), 61–68.

Mangaraj, B. K., Nayak, M., & Mangaraj, T. (2001). Fuzzy multi-objective zero-one programming for capital budgeting. *Finance India*, *15*(1), 475–486.

Manoj, K., Vrat, P., & Shankar, R. (2004). A fuzzy goal programming approach for vendor selection problem in a supply chain. *Computers & Industrial Engineering*, *46*, 69–85. doi:10.1016/j.cie.2003.09.010

Mishra, A., Mangaraj, B. K., & Aparajita, U. (2003). Media selection decision in social system: A fuzzy goal programming approach. *Journal of Academy of Business and Economics*, *1*(2), 191–208.

Narasimhan, R. (1980). Goal programming in a fuzzy environment. *Decision Sciences*, *11*, 525–538. doi:10.1111/j.1540-5915.1980.tb01142.x

Narasimhan, R. (1981). On fuzzy goal programming-some comments. *Decision Sciences*, *121*, 532–538. doi:10.1111/j.1540-5915.1981.tb00103.x

Pandian, M.V. (2004). Application of multi-objective fuzzy linear programming to supply production planning problem. *Journal of Technology, 40*(D), 37-48.

Parra, M. A., Terol, A. B., & Uria, M. V. R. (2001). A fuzzy goal programming approach to portfolio selection. *European Journal of Operational Research*, *133*, 287–297. doi:10.1016/S0377-2217(00)00298-8

Pickens, J. B., & Hof, J. G. (1991). Fuzzy goal programming in forestry: An application with special solution problems. *Fuzzy Sets and Systems*, *39*(3), 239–246. doi:10.1016/0165-0114(91)90095-8

Prahalad, C. K. (2005). *The fortune at the bottom of the pyramid: Eradicating poverty through profits*. USA: Pearson Education/Wharton School Publishing.

Prahalad, C. K., & Hammond, A. (2002). Serving the world's poor, profitability. *Harvard Business Review*, (September): 4–11.

Prahalad, C.K. & Hart, S.L. (2002). The fortune at the bottom of the pyramid, *Strategy + Business, 26*, 1-14.

Rao, S. S., Sundaraju, K., Prakasah, B. G., & Balakrishnan, C. (1992). Fuzzy goal programming approach for situational optimizations. *Fuzzy Sets and Systems*, *39*(3), 239–246.

Reddy, C.B., Rajgopal, Z.K. & Reddy, H. (2007). Fuzzy goal and additive fuzzy goal programming: Application to distributor selection in supply chain, *Journal of Engineering and applied Sciences. 2*(10), 1533, 1538.

Roy, T. K., & Maiti, M. (1998). Multi-objective inventory models of deteriorating items with some constraints in a fuzzy environment. *Computers & Operations Research*, *25*(12), 1085–1095. doi:10.1016/S0305-0548(98)00029-X

Rubin, P. A., & Narasimhan, R. (1985). Fuzzy goal programming with nested priorities. *Fuzzy Sets and Systems*, *14*, 115–129. doi:10.1016/0165-0114(84)90095-2

Shankar, R., & Vrat, P. (1999). Some design issues in cellular manufacturing using fuzzy programming approach. *International Journal of Production Research*, *37*(11), 2345–2363.

Sharma, D. K., Jana, R. K., & Gaur, A. (2007). Fuzzy goal programming for land allocation problems. *Yugoslav Journal of Operations Research*, *17*(1), 31–42. doi:10.2298/YJOR0701031S

Sharma, H.P., Sharma, D.K. & Jana, R.K. (2009). Credit union portfolio management: An additive fuzzy goal programming approach. *International Research Journal of Finance and Economics, 30.*

Sinha, S. B., Rao, K. A., & Mangaraj, B. K. (1988). Fuzzy goal programming in multi-criteria decision system: A case study in agricultural planning. *Socio-Economic Planning Sciences*, *22*(2), 93–102. doi:10.1016/0038-0121(88)90021-3

Sinha, S. B., Rao, K. A., Mangaraj, B. K., & Tripathy, P. K. (1982). Fuzzy technique to agricultural planning. *Journal of Information and Optimization Science*, *10*, 257–274.

Tsai, K. M., Shinu-Yuan, L., Yu-Hsin, Y., & Tsai, C. H. (2008). A fuzzy goal programming approach for channel allocation problems in steel industry. *Expert Systems with Applications: An International Journal*, *34*(3), 1870–1876. doi:10.1016/j.eswa.2007.02.034

Tsai, W. H., & Hung, S. J. (2009). A fuzzy goal programming approach for green supply chain optimisation under activity-based costing and performance evaluation with a value chain structure. *International Journal of Production Research*, *47*(18), 4991–5017. doi:10.1080/00207540801932498

UNESCO. (1995). *The cultural dimension of development: towards a practical approach*. Paris: UNESCO.

Yaghoobi, M. A., Jones, D. F., & Tamiz, M. (2008). Weighted additive model for solving fuzzy goal programming problem. *Asia-Pacific Journal of Operational Research*, *28*(5), 715–733. doi:10.1142/S0217595908001973

Zimmermann, H. J. (1976). Description and optimization of fuzzy sets. *International Journal of General Systems*, *2*, 209–215. doi:10.1080/03081077608547470

Zimmermann, H. J. (1978). Fuzzy programming and linear programming with several objective functions. *Fuzzy Sets and Systems*, *1*, 45–55. doi:10.1016/0165-0114(78)90031-3

Zimmermann, H. J. (1983). Using Fuzzy Sets in Operational Research. *European Journal of Operational Research*, *13*(3), 201–216. doi:10.1016/0377-2217(83)90048-6

ADDITIONAL READING

Aaker, D. (1992). The CPM rule: An integrative approach to media planning . *Canadian Journal of Marketing Research*, *11*, 47–54.

Barnard, N., & Gillow, J. (2002). *Traditional Indian textiles*. London: Thames & Hudson.

Bell, S. S., & Carpenter, G. S. (1992). Optimal multi-objective marketing strategies . *Marketing Letters*, *3*(4), 383–393. doi:10.1007/BF00993922

Bellman, R. E., & Zadeh, L. A. (1970). Decision-making in a fuzzy environment . *Management Science*, *17*, 141–164. doi:10.1287/mnsc.17.4.B141

Benayuon, R., Dc Montagolfier, J., Tergny, J., & Lorithechev, O. (1971). Linear programming with multiple objective functions: STEP method(STEM) . *Mathematical Programming*, *1*, 366–375. doi:10.1007/BF01584098

Biswas, A., & Pal, B. B. (2005). Application of fuzzy goal programming technique to land use planning in agricultural system . *Omega*, *33*, 391–398. doi:10.1016/j.omega.2004.07.003

Cable, V., Weston, A., & Jain, L. C. (1986). *The commerce of culture*. New Delhi: Lancer International.

Chen, Y.-W., & Tzeng, G. H. (2001). Fuzzy multi-objective approach to the supply chain model . *International Journal of Fuzzy Systems*, *2*(3), 220–226.

Deckro, R. F., & Murdock, G. W. (1987). Media selection via multiple objective integer programming . *Omega*, *15*(5), 419–427. doi:10.1016/0305-0483(87)90043-0

Dhamija, J.(2002). *Handicrafts of India: Our living cultural Traditions*, New-Delhi: National Book Trust.

El-Wahed, W. F. A., & Lee, S. M. (2006). Interactive fuzzy goal programming for multi-objective transportation problems . *Omega*, *34*, 158–166. doi:10.1016/j.omega.2004.08.006

Gurevitch, M., & Hass, H. (1973). On the use of mass media for important things . *American Sociological Review*, *38*(2), 164–181. doi:10.2307/2094393

Ignizio, J. P. (1982(a)). *Linear programming in single and multiple objective systems*, NJ: Englewood Cliffs.

Ignizio, J. P. (1982). (b)). on the re(discovery) of fuzzy goal programming . *Decision Sciences*, *13*, 331–336. doi:10.1111/j.1540-5915.1982.tb00152.x

Kreshel, P., Lancaster, K. M., & Toomay, M. A. (1985). How leading advertising agencies perceive effective reach and frequency . *Journal of Advertising*, *14*(3), 32–38.

Liang, T. F. (2006). Distribution planning decisions using interactive fuzzy multi-objective linear programming . *Fuzzy Sets and Systems*, *157*, 1303–1316. doi:10.1016/j.fss.2006.01.014

Liang, T. F. (2008). (a)). Interactive multi-objective transportation planning decisions using fuzzy linear programming . *Asia-Pacific Journal of Operational Research*, *25*, 11–31. doi:10.1142/S0217595908001602

Liang, T. F. (2008). (b)).Integrating production-transportation planning decision with fuzzy multiple goals in supply chains . *International Journal of Production Research*, *46*, 1477–1494. doi:10.1080/00207540600597211

Ozcan, U., & Tokulu, B. (2009). Multi-criteria decision-making in two sided assembly line balancing: A goal programming and fuzzy goal programming models . *Computers & Operations Research*, *36*, 1955–1965. doi:10.1016/j.cor.2008.06.009

Pandian, V., Nagarajan, R., & Yaacob, S. (2004). Decision making in industrial production planning using fuzzy linear programming . *IMA Journal of Management Mathematics*, *15*(1), 53–65. doi:10.1093/imaman/15.1.53

Ramik, J. (2000). Fuzzy foals and fuzzy alternatives in goal programming problems . *Fuzzy Sets and Systems*, *111*, 81–86. doi:10.1016/S0165-0114(98)00454-0

Rommelfanger, H. (1996). Fuzzy linear programming and application . *European Journal of Operational Research*, *92*, 512–527. doi:10.1016/0377-2217(95)00008-9

Sahidul, I. (2008). Multi-objective marketing planning inventory model: A geometric programming approach . *Applied Mathematics and Computation*, *205*(1), 238–246. doi:10.1016/j.amc.2008.07.037

Singh, G. (1994). *Non-Farm rural products: Marketing & financing, New Delhi*. Oxford: IBH.

Sissors, J. Z., & Lincon, B. (1971). Matching media with markets . *Journal of Advertising Research*, *11*(5), 39–43.

Stasch, S. F. (1967). Linear programming and media selection: A comment . *JMR, Journal of Marketing Research*, *4*(2), 205–207. doi:10.2307/3149369

Tiwari, R. N., Dharmar, S., & Rao, J. R. (1987). Fuzzy goal programming-An additive model . *Fuzzy Sets and Systems*, *19*, 251–259. doi:10.1016/0165-0114(86)90054-0

UNESCO. (1987). *A practical guide for world decade for cultural development*. Paris: UNESCO.

Wang, R. C., & Liang, T. F. (2004). Application of fuzzy multi-objective linear programming to aggregate production planning . *Computers & Industrial Engineering*, *46*, 17–41. doi:10.1016/j.cie.2003.09.009

Wiedey, G., & Zimmermann, H. J. (1978). Media selection and fuzzy linear programming . *The Journal of the Operational Research Society*, *29*, 1071–1084.

Winter, F. W. (1980). Matching target markets to media audience . *Journal of Advertising Research*, *20*(1), 61–66.

Yager, R. R., & Basson, D. (1975). Decision-making with fuzzy sets . *Decision Sciences*, *17*, 560–600.

Zadeh, L. A. (1965). Fuzzy sets . *Information and Control*, *8*, 129–153. doi:10.1016/S0019-9958(65)90241-X

Zeki Aya gcaron, Rıfat Gürcan Özdemir (2007). A combined fuzzy AHP-goal programming approach to assembly line selection, *Journal of Intelligent and Fuzzy systems*, 18(4), 345-362.

Zeleny, M. (1974). A concept of compromise solution and the methods of displaced ideal . *Computers & Operations Research*, *1*, 209–215.

Zeleny, M. (1982). *Multiple criteria decision making, New-York*. McGraw-Hill Book Company.

Zimmermann, H. J. (1978). *Fuzzy sets and systems, Amsterdam: North Holland Publishing Company, Zimmermann, H.J. (1996). Fuzzy set theory and its applications*. Boston: Kluwer.

KEY TERMS AND DEFINITIONS

Bottom of Pyramid (BOP) Producers: The Indian pyramid has too large a bottom consisting of the poorest socio-economic group. Majority of the Indian population live in the primary sector engaged in production related activities. To help alleviate poverty, business models need to be designed looking at the core competencies of the BOP producers at one end and emerging markets of their produces at the other.

Fuzzy Goal Programming (FGP): It is a goal programming approach to handle MCDM problems in a fuzzy decision environment. FGP utilizes the concept of fuzzy goals which can be conceptualized as fuzzy sets. Fuzzy logic enables combining these fuzzy sets to obtain a fuzzy decision set. This technique makes it possible for the decision-maker to explicitly identify a graded satisfaction level for each criterion as the significance of fuzzy goal. In this perspective, this methodology has wide applications in various decision situations involving imprecision due to fuzziness.

Fuzzy Sets: Classical set theory is governed by a logic that permits a proposition to possess one of only two values: true or false. This logic does not accord well with the need to represent vague concepts. We see things in shades of grey: not only in black and white. The key idea of fuzzy set theory is that an element has a degree of membership in a fuzzy set. Then a proposition need not be simply true or false, but may be partially true to any degree. We usually assume that this degree is a real number in the interval [0,1]. The concept of fuzzy sets was formalized by L.A. Zadeh at the University of California in 1965. From a strictly mathematical point of view this concept is a brilliant generalization of the classical notion of a set. Fuzzy logic, the logic of fuzzy sets more closely found to be useful for dealing with real world phenomena and has established itself as an important and practical construct of modeling.

Handlooms: Hand woven fabrics of India have been known since time immemorial. Handlooms are an important craft produced and comprise the largest cottage industry of the country. Millions of looms across the country are engaged in weaving cotton, silk and other natural fibers. There is hardly any state of the country where weavers do not exist, each weaving out the traditional beauty of India's own precious heritage. Given the wide and exciting range of handlooms, it is not surprising that the rich and beautiful products of the weavers of India have been called, “exquisite poetry in colorful fabrics”.

Intangible Cultural Heritage (ICH): Several years of research done by UNESCO on the functions and values of cultural expressions as well as their practices has lead to the new way of understanding, protection and respect for cultural heritage of humanity. Intangible Cultural Heritage(ICH) as per UNESCO means the practices, representations, expressions, knowledge, skills – as well as the instruments, objects, artifacts and cultural spaces associated therewith – that communities, groups and, in some cases, individuals recognize as part of their cultural heritage. This ICH, transmitted from generation to generation, is constantly recreated by communities and groups in response to their environment, their interaction with nature and their history, and provides them with a sense of identity and continuity, thus promoting respect for cultural diversity and human creativity.

Media Vehicle: It is a specific example of media type that one chooses to advertise. In a promotional plan it has a significant role to play. Media plan establishes the combination of media vehicles to be used for promotion, the time the advertisement will appear in media such as television, radio, newspapers, magazines etc. Having a right mix of media vehicles ensures meeting the objectives of the promotional campaign.

Multi-Criteria Decision-Making (MCDM): Classical optimisation approaches evaluate an action with its performance on a single criterion, viz., maximisation of the benefit function or minimisation of the risk function. Though a single criterion model is usually the simplified form of decision-making, most of the times, it does not lead to a satisfactory solution due to multi-dimensionality of the reality. In a complex system, a good decision is possible only when multiplicity of criteria is taken into account and such criteria are often conflicting and non-commensurable. Hence, there does not exist a single solution which can maximise (minimise) all the criteria. The existence of a set of alternatives out of which a “good action” also termed, as “compromise solution” necessitates the evolution of a decision process known as multiple-criteria decision-making.

Saree: It is a versatile piece of fabric. Handloom sarees are woven in cotton as well as in silk. In multifaceted diversity of Indian society, it embraced different communities and cultures together in its fold as common form of apparel. As a product the traditional saree is recognized by the way it is designed and woven. Its surface is clearly divided into three distinct parts – the body, the boarder and the pallav or the end piece. It is usually 1.2 to 1.4 meter wide and could be 5.5 to 6 meter long. The price of a piece of saree usually depends upon the quality of cotton/silk, its make as well as the design.

Soft Computing: Conventional computing approaches could model and precisely analyze only relatively simpler systems. However, real life complex systems could not use such tools in a meaningful way. In this context, soft computing techniques resemble biological processes and form a group of tools that imitate human intelligence with an objective of faming methods having some human-like capabilities such as learning, reasoning and decision-making which are based on fuzzy logic, neural networks, genetic algorithms etc.

Chapter 12
Implementing an Electronic Infrastructure:
Developments in Banking in Germany and Finland

Reima Suomi
University of Turku, Finland

ABSTRACT

The Internet has already now revolutionised many industries. The biggest changes are yet maybe to come in many industries, but the banking field can be seen as a pioneer in the application of modern information technology in general and of the Internet in particular. For example, in banking hardly anyone speaks about e-Banking: e-activity is banking as normal, no especial "e" is needed. This chapter discusses the banking industry as a user of the Internet and other modern information and communication technology (ICT). Germany and Finland are used as case examples and make comparisons between them. The banking industry has utilized several technologies of computer networking over several decades, and also got a "flying start" to the Internet technologies, that nowadays are a backbone of the banking industry. As stated, this chapter compares some of the related developments in Germany and in Finland.

INTRODUCTION

On January 1, 1999, the European Economic and Monetary Union and the Euro were introduced. In year 2002, we got the Euro as a bar money into circulation. This laid a solid ground for harmonization of many payment-related issues in the European Union. Still, however, national differences in the European Union are big as it comes to payment systems and customer's habits.

DOI: 10.4018/978-1-60960-129-4.ch012

For historical reasons and on account of differences in the legal, regulatory and institutional framework, the variety and structure or payment and securities settlement systems differs from country to country. (March 25-26 2002 Workshop Participants and the 3 ECSAs, 2002). In this article we study the extent of these differences between Germany and Finland.

"One single payment area" is the vision forwarded clearly by the European banking industry (March 25-26 2002 Workshop Participants and the 3 ECSAs, 2002). The report "Euroland – our single payment area" describes the current state of art of banking payment systems as follows (March 25-26 2002 Workshop Participants and the 3 ECSAs, 2002):

- Five main instruments fulfilling customer needs today
- Efficient national infrastructures, but very different from each other
- High straight-through-processing (STP)-rates for each country, which are again very different from each other
- Standards and infrastructures for cards in place for seamless domestic and cross-border processing, but significant price differences between domestic and cross-border transactions.

The same report summarizes the key trends in payment systems as follows (March 25-26 2002 Workshop Participants and the 3 ECSAs, 2002):

- Customers need to have convenient access to payment services, with transparent pricing and minimum service levels (quality, security and execution time) equal for domestic and cross-border transactions
- Banks should be able to decrease the overall cost of payments and have room to offer value-added services at a premium
- The optimal components of payment schemes should be developed in a concerted way within the Eurozone.

Payment systems are a major business and affect the daily life of both private citizens and companies. For Europe and for year 2001 it was estimated that there are 207 million electronic payment transactions (also not including cash payments) daily, also summing up to 138 transactions per each citizen yearly. (Hegarty, Verheul, Steupaert, & Skouma, 2003) The importance of payment and securities settlement systems in modern economies has been growing considerably over the past decades. Central banks not only face the task of steering the monetary conditions in the economy, but also have a direct interest in the prudent design and operation of the payment and settlement systems processing their currency. Payment systems play a pivotal role in a modern economy. (European Central Bank, 2002a)

The Internet provides a good platform for electronic banking. Not only does it save costs, but studies also document that Internet customers usually are better customers to banks as traditional customers not using the Internet. (Hitt & Frei, 2002) National differences in the adoption of Internet in general and in its use in banking in particular are big. Many banking institutions have not yet found the potential of Internet. (Colgate, 2000) Ignoring the power of Internet can lead to the erosion of the whole industry feasibility. (Holland, Lockett, & Blackman, 1997) In this article we tackle this phenomenon taking Germany and Finland as case examples. Our focus is on private banking.

Adaptation of modern ICT technology including Internet banking is dependent on many variables that account for national differences and differences between different customer groups. Expectations of accuracy, security, network speed, user-friendliness, user involvement and convenience were the most important quality attributes underlying perceived usefulness (Liao &

Cheung, 2002). A European study found there are wide divergences between countries and between e-commerce and e-banking sites. Across the EU, 83% of e-banking sites analysed provided clear information with 100% scores for Denmark, Greece, Spain, Ireland, Luxembourg, the Netherlands, Finland and Sweden. But only 55% of e-commerce sites were clear with their security information with French (77%), British (76%) and Spanish (71%) sites scoring highest. In terms of clarity, e-commerce consumers in Sweden (15% of sites clear), the Netherlands (16%) and Luxembourg (17%) seem to be the least well-served. (Hegarty et al., 2003)

For banks, investments in electronic banking are huge. In the U.S.S, the Total non-branch activity is growing at 15% a year. (McChesney, 1997)

Technical innovations are not enough, if people do not trust electronic payment systems for some reason. An European e-payment trust study provided the following trust indexes for different EU-15 countries, scale 0-10 (Hegarty et al., 2003):

- Finland: 8,41
- The Netherlands: 7,91
- Sweden: 7,79
- Luxemburg: 7,58
- England: 7,50
- Denmark: 7,46
- Germany: 7,34
- Belgium: 7,12
- France: 6,96
- Ireland: 6,91
- Austria: 6,66
- Italy: 6,62
- Spain: 6,46
- Portugal: 5,51
- Creece: 5,25
- EU-15 average: 7,08

Our research question in this article is: How do banking industry market structures and customer preferences and orientations affect Internet usage in private banking.

Figure 1. Topics structure of the comparison Finland-Germany

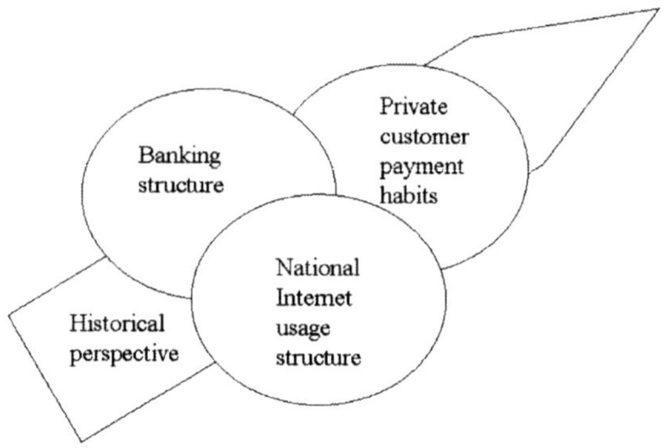

Our analysis discusses three interrelated topics: the banking industry structures, private customer payment habits and Internet usage structure in both of the countries. In addition, we try to put these current structures into a historical perspective. The topic structure is documented in Figure 1.

Methodologically our paper relies on secondary sources, the article is not based on own empirical studies. However it gains from our other research initiatives even with the banking industry in the area of Internet usage.

COMPARISON GERMANY-FINLAND

Basic Data about the Countries

To give background to the banking industry comparison, first some basic data about the countries is given in Table 1.

Banking History

Some key milestones in the development of the Finnish banking environment are summarized in Table 2, and some milestones in the German banking industry in Table 3.

In Finland, banking is already very much performed on-line, the big structural changes of banks took place already in the 1990s and, and

Table 1. Some basic data about Germany and Finland, adapted from (Internet World Stats, 2005)

		Germany	Finland
1	Population	82,726,188	5,246,920
2	Country area km^2	357,021	338,145
3	Capital	Berlin	Helsinki
4	GNI per capita US$	25,250	27,020

Table 2. Some key milestones in Finnish banking technology (adapted from (Suomen Pankkiyhdistys, 2004))

1939	Introduction of post giro transfer
1942	Introduction of bank transfer
1962	Salaries first time paid to banks
1970	On-line systems to bank branches
1971	Introduction of automatic cash dispenser machines
1978	Finland joins the SWIFT-network
1980	Introduction of the Bank Debit Card
1984	Introduction of home terminal services
1990	Nationwide network for automatic banking teller machines
2000	Introduction of the International IBAN account number

the industry is quite concentrated. Germany is quite opposite in many aspects: the bigger market is served by a plentitude of banks, and customers stick more to traditional payment methods. Even though the industry is also in a flux in Germany, the big structural changes are maybe yet to come. Finland has gone through a very severe banking crisis at the beginning of 1990s, that led to a new market structure; the market with already few players lost many participants. On the longer run, this might have been a blessing, as the market structure for Finnish banks is now considered to be quite healthy.

From Tables 2 and 3 we can infer that for a long time Finland was some two to four years behind in development of Germany in banking

Table 3. Some key milestones in German banking technology (adapted from (Karasu, 2005))

1918	German Central Giro Association founded
1960	Salaries first time paid to banks
1968	Introduction of the eurocheque-system (ec-Karte)
1973	Germany joins the SWIFT-network
1977	Introduction of automatic cash dispenser machines
1977	Introduction of ec-Karte as a debit card
1980	Introduction of home terminal services
1999	Nationwide network for automatic banking teller machines
1990	Electronic cash Point-of-Sale (POS) system introduced
2000	Introduction of the International IBAN account number

technology. However, Finland was very fast to establish a nation-wide network for automatic teller machines and could establish that already in 1990, whereas this was accomplished in Germany first 1999.

Current Banking Structure

Currently Finland and Germany have the banking industry structure as summarized in Table 4.

As can be seen in Table 4, the number of banks per population is twice as big in Finland as in Germany. The Finnish banking industry is also more fragmented than the German one. This might however be a misleading conclusion, as according to the German Banking association (Association of the German Banks, 2005): "*The four big banks have a combined market share of just over 16% (measured in terms of total assets). Despite the falling number of banks, there is evidently still very little concentration in the German banking sector. No other country in the European Union has such a fragmented banking market.*" In Finland, the three biggest banks (two of them with Headquarter in Finland) have a total market share of over 80 percent (Suomen Pankkiyhdistys, 2005). In Finland also the biggest banks are more dominant than in Germany but in total the market is more fragmented than in Germany.

Because of the size differences of the countries (Germany 82.5 million inhabitants, Finland 5.3 million inhabitants), Finland is totally lacking banks in the biggest category (100 Mrd Euro balance sheet or more).

The German banking system is quite complicated one and its participants are depicted in Figure 2.

In Finland, it is customary to define between the following banking institutions as in Table 5.

National Internet Usage Structure

In a recent study by the journal "The Economis" the e-readiness of 65 leading countries in Europe were studied (The Economist Intelligence Unit, 2005). Germany landed at a shared 12th place with Canada, with a total score of 8.03 (7.83 in 2004). Finland took the shared sixth place with Hong Kong, with a total score of 8.32 (8.08 in 2004). In the report, Germany is not analyzed in greater detail, but Finland in mentioned in connection with the innovations in mobile communication products.

Criminality in general and corruption in particular can be harmful to e-business. Corruption

Table 4. Key banking structure figures in Germany and Finland (year 2001), rows 6-12 from (Bundesverband deutscher Banken, 2002) and rows 1-4 from (Suomen Pankkiyhdistys, 2004) for Finland and (Bundesverband deutscher Banken, 2002) for Germany

		Germany	Finland
1	Total number of banking institutions[1]	2575	344
2	Banking institutions per 1 million people	31	64
3	Bank branch offices	56627	1585
4	Bank branch offices per 1 million people	686	299
5	Financial institutions with a balance sheet of 10-100 Mrd Euro	60	2
6	Financial institutions with a balance sheet of over 100 Mrd Euro	10	0
7	Bank balance sheets as a percentage of the balance sheets in the Euro area (%)	34,6	0,9
8	Total number of workers in the banking industry	751050	24870
9	Total number of workers per banking branch	13	13

Figure 2. The German Banking system (Engelbrecht, 2005)

Universal Banks			**Specialist Banks**		
Private Commercial banks	**Cooperative banks**	**Public-sector banks**		**Private banks**	**Public-sector banks**
Big branch banks	Credit cooperatives (Volksbanken and Raiffeisenbanken)	Savings banks Central giro institutions		Private mortgage banks Ship mortgage banks	Public mortgage banks Banks with special functions
Regional banks and other commercial banks	Cooperative central institutions		Guarantee banks (including cooperative credit Guarantee associations)	Banks with special functions Investment companies Private building and loan associations	Public building and loan associations Postal giro and postal savings bankoffices
Private bankers Branches of foreign banks			Housing associations with savings facilities	Central securities depositories	

amount in different countries has long been studied by Transparency International. According to the newest index from year 2009 (Transparency International, 2010) Finland was the sixth least corrupted country in the world, as documented in Table 6. Germany also performed well and landed at place 14.

Table 7 contains summary data of certain information society indicators for Germany and Finland.

Table 5. Groups and number of banks in Finland, Data for 2003 adopted from (Kallonen, 2002). Data for 2004 adopted from (Suomen Pankkiyhdistys, 2005)

	2002	2004
Commercial banks	8	0
Savings banks	40	40
Cooperative banks	256	284
Branches of foreign banks	6	11
Total	320	344

Table 6. Top 10 countries in the Transparency International Corruption Perceptions Index 2009 (Transparency International, 2010)

Rank 6	**Country/Territory**	**CPI 2009 Score**	**Surveys Used**	**Confidence Range**
1	New Zealand	9.4	6	9.1 - 9.5
2	Denmark	9.3	6	9.1 - 9.5
3	Singapore	9.2	9	9.0 - 9.4
3	Sweden	9.2	6	9.0 - 9.3
5	Switzerland	9.0	6	8.9 - 9.1
6	Finland	8.9	6	8.4 - 9.4
6	Netherlands	8.9	6	8.7 - 9.0
8	Australia	8.7	8	8.3 - 9.0
8	Canada	8.7	6	8.5 - 9.0
8	Iceland	8.7	4	7.5 - 9.4

Table 7. Key information society indicators for Finland and Germany, adapted from (EITO, 2004)

Indicator	Germany	Finland
Change in ICT investments as % of GFGP	2,8	10,5
Change in MFP growth from 1980-1990 to 1990-2000	-0,6	0,8
Internet users as % of population 2003	51	40,8*
Internet users as % of population 2007, forecast	71,8	83*
Mobile subscriptions as % of population 2003	76	89
Mobile subscriptions as % of population 2006, forecast	87	101
ADSL lines as % of population 2003	5,3	4
ADSL lines as % of population 2006, forecast	10	7,4

* Nordic average

The Internet World Stats (Internet World Stats, 2005) reports that 47,182,628 Internet users as of Oct/2004, 57.1% of the population, according to Nielsen//NetRatings. The same figures for Finland from the same source are: 3,260,000 Internet users as of March/05, 62.1% penetration. According to a recent study, 68 percent of Finns aged 15 or more use the Internet (Suomen Pankkiyhdistys, 2004).

The data available shows that in International rankings, Finland seems to perform better than Germany. In mobile communication, too, Finland is having a lead over Germany However, when looking at the Internet adoption, the data available gives a little inconsistent result. To take a total assessment, however, there are no big differences between the two countries as it comes to the application of modern information and communication technology, and the lack of basic infrastructure or skills should be no obstacle for developing electronic banking.

Payment Habit Structure

Data on the payment habit structures and money transfer systems in Germany and Finland is collected to Table 8.

The most eye-catching difference between the two countries is the amount of liquid money circulating in the economy. In Germany there are about three times as much coins per inhabitant in circulation as in Finland. As it comes to transferable deposits per inhabitant, the value is some 20% bigger in Germany as compared to Finland. In Germany cash money is partly substituted by electronic money cards, that are there some 61 millions, also penetration rate of 74% In Finland the figures are just 0,6 million and 3,1%.

Finns have more Point of Sale debit terminals than Germans with a marginal of some 40%. The average number of transactions per citizen and year is almost fourfold as compared to Gemany, 12,6 and 49,3 respectively. On the other hand, Germans have bigger transactions in Point of Sale debiting, averaging 95,2 Euros, whereas Finns come along with an average value of 60,9 Euros.

As it comes to public banking infrastructure, Germany is about 40% better equipped with ATM's than Finland. This might be a reason to the fact that the number of ATM transactions is per inhabitant is 2,4 times bigger in Finland than in Germany. To this might lead also to the fact that the average transaction value in Germany is 146 Euros, whereas in Finland it is just 70 Euros.

Finnish customers have 2,8 million agreements with their banks about electronic payment services (Suomen Pankkiyhdistys, 2004). With a population of 5,3 million inhabitants this means a penetration rate of 54 percent.

Table 8. Key banking payment structure data for Germany and Finland for year 2000, data from (European Central Bank, 2002b), expect rows 6-7 from (Suomen Pankkiyhdistys, 2004) for Finland and (Bundesverband deutscher Banken, 2005) for Germany

1	Coins in circulation outside credit institutions, value per inhabitant	1522	556
2	Transferable deposits held by non-banks, value per inhabitant	7172	5461
3	Number of accounts from which payments can be made per inhabitant	1,05	2,1
4	Total number of branches offering payment services per 1 00 0000 inhabitants	683	366
5	**ATM's**		
6	Number of ATM's (Germany 2003, Finland 2004)	51460	2110
7	Number of ATM's per 1 000 000 inhabitants (Germany 2003, Finland 2004)	624	398
8	Number of ATM's per 1 000 000 inhabitants	580	412
9	Number of ATM transactions per inhabitant	20	47
10	Average value per transaction	146	70
11	**POS with debit functions**		
12	Number of POS terminals with debit functions per 1 000 000 inhabitants	7196	11978
13	Number of debit card transactions per inhabitant	12,6	49,3
14	Average value per transaction	73,4	38
15	Number of credit card transactions per inhabitant	4,3	22,2
16	Average value per transaction	95,2	60,9
17	Electronic money cards, millions	61	0,6
18	**Cards per 1000 inhabitant**		
19	Cards with a cash function	1294	1137
20	Cards with a debit function	1207	493
21	Cards with a credit function	216	786
22	Cards with an e-money function	739	120
23	**Use of cards**		
24	Payments per card with a credit function	19,8	21,7
25	Payments per card with a debit function	10,5	99,9
26	Usage of cheques, million transactions	437	1
27	Usage of cheques per inhabitant	5	0,2
28	Payments per credit/debit cards per inhabitant	15	71
29	Direct debits per inhabitants	67	8

The Finnish very current data (October 2003) about population payment habits is as follows (The Finnish Banker's Association, 2003). The question was: Which is the most usual way through which you pay your bills?:

- Through Internet: 53%
- Through payment teller machines: 19%
- Through direct debit: 10%
- In the bank's service desk, cash or bank transfer: 8%
- As bank payment service, through sending the bills to the bank: 6%
- Through telephone: 1%

From Table 8 we can also see that both Germans and Finns use credit cards about 20 times yearly, whereas Finns are more eager to use debit cards such as bank cards. Cheques are still being used in Germany to some extent, but in Finland they have practically vanished. Germans organize their permanent bills to be handled by direct debits from their accounts, whereas this service is very much less used in Finland (Germany 67 per inhabitant and year, Finland 8).

CONCLUSION

Electronic banking has a good soil to grow in both in Germany and Finland. Though differences can be found in many aspects through a detailed scanning of statistics, both countries are well off to prepare themselves for the electronic banking business.

The biggest differences according to our analysis are discussed more in detail below.

Germany seems to be still more dependent on cash than Finland. Amount of cash in circulation is three times as big per inhabitant than in Finland. Almost each citizen has an electronic money card, whereas in Finland they are not a real working part of the card infrastructure. As it comes to liquidity, Germans also seem to hold bigger bank accounts than the Finns.

This cashless nature of Finland is confirmed by the fact that the number of debit card transactions per person is over triple in Finland as compared with Germany. In credit cards, there is no such huge difference. Point of sale terminals with debit functions per inhabitant are 40 percent more in Finland than in Germany, and they are applied four times more often in Finland than in Germany. On the other hand, the average transaction is almost double as compared to the Finnish one.

The physical network of banks in Germany is almost double as compared with Finland. Bank branches are over 80 percent more in Germany than in Finland per inhabitant, and ATM's some 60 percent more. As a result, Finns use ATM's much more, but withdraw very much smaller sums at a time.

Data about electronic banking at home is very difficult to find, and data about mobile payments about nonexistent. As it comes to daily household payments, Germany is a society of direct debits from accounts, whereas the Finns use this possibility very much less.

Our analysis of the banking history should confirm the idea that the banking industry had prepared itself to the Internet time over decades. Innovations such as bank giro transfers and the SWIFT network paved the banks' way to the Internet world. However, much remains still to be done for example in the field of international harmonization, for example before we can really talk about a Single European Payment Area.

REFERENCES

Association of the German Banks. (2005). *Association of the German Banks market shares of the commercial banks*. Retrieved from http://www.germanbanks.org/

Bundesverband deutscher Banken. (2002). *Übersicht über das Bankgewerbe im Euro-Währunggebiet*.

Bundesverband deutscher Banken. (2005). *Bundesverband deutscher Banken*. Retrieved from http://www.bankenverband.de/

Colgate, M. (2000). Marketing and marketing information system sophistication in retail banking. *The Service Industries Journal*, *20*(1), 139–152. doi:10.1080/02642060000000008

EITO. (2004). *European Information Technology Observatory 2004*. Frankfurt/Main: European Economic Interest Grouping (EEIG).

Engelbrecht, H. (2005). *The German banking system*. Retrieved May 15, 2005, from http://hans.engelbrecht.com/banksys/banksys1.htm

EPC. (2002). *Euroland: Our Single Payment Area*. March 25-26 2002 Workshop Participants and the 3 ECSAs

European Central Bank. (2002a). *Payment and securities settlement systems in accession countries. Blue book*. Frankfurt am Main: European Central Bank.

European Central Bank. (2002b). *Payment and securities settlement systems in the European Union. Blue Book*. Frankfurt am Main: European Central Bank.

Hegarty, T., Verheul, E., Steupaert, D., & Skouma, G. (2003). *Study on the security of payment, products, and systems in the 15 member states*. European Commission. Internal Market DG.

Hitt, L. M., & Frei, F. X. (2002). Do better customers utilize electronic distribution channels? The case of PC banking. *Management Science*, *48*(6), 732–748. doi:10.1287/mnsc.48.6.732.188

Holland, C. P., Lockett, G. A., & Blackman, I. D. (Eds.). (1997). The impact of globalisation and Information Technology on the strategy and profitability of the banking industry. *Proceedings of HICSS-30 Conference*. Hawaii.

Internet World Stats. (2005). *Internet world stats, usage, and population statistics*. Retrieved May 17, 2005, from http://www.internetworldstats.com/

Kallonen, T. (2002). *Pankit muutoksessa*: Suomen pankkiyhdistys.

Karasu, I. (2005). Privatkundengeschäft und Banktechnologie: Meilensteine auf dem Weg ins Online-Zeitalter. *Die Bank, 44*(6).

Liao, Z., & Cheung, M. T. (2002). Internet-based e-banking and consumer attitudes: An empirical study. *Information & Management*, *39*(4), 283–295. doi:10.1016/S0378-7206(01)00097-0

McChesney, M. C. (1997). Banking in cyberspace: An investment in itself. *IEEE Spectrum*, *34*(2), 54–59. doi:10.1109/6.570831

Suomen Pankkiyhdistys. (2004). *Pankkitekniikka Suomessa*. Helsinki: Suomen Pankkiyhdistys.

Suomen Pankkiyhdistys. (2005). *Pankit 31.12.2004*. Helsinki: Suomen Pankkiyhdistys.

The Economist Intelligence Unit. (2005). *The 2005 e-readiness rankings*. London: The Economist Intelligence Unit Limited The Finnish Banker's Association. (2003). *Statistical data on the bank's payment systems in Finland 1993-2002*. The Finnish Banker's Association.

Transparency International. (2010). *Corruption Perceptions Index 2009*. Retrieved from http://www.transparency.org/policy_research/surveys_indices/cpi/2009/cpi_2009_table

ADDITIONAL READING

Buhl, H. U., Kundisch, D., et al. (2000). IT-Enabled Sophistication Banking. *Proceedings of the Eighth European Conference on Information Systems, Vienna*.

Chau, P. Y. K., & Lai, V. S. K. (2003). An Empirical Investigation of the Determinants of User Acceptance of Internet Banking. *Journal of Organizational Computing and Electronic Commerce*, *13*(2), 123–145. doi:10.1207/S15327744JOCE1302_3

Damsgaard, J., & Farhoomand, A. F. (1999). Building Electronic Commerce Infrastructure: Hong Kong Consumer Goods Distribution. *Proceedings of the Seventh European Conference on Information Systems*, Copenhagen, Copenhagen Business School.

Gillett, S. E. (2000). Universal service: Defining the policy goal in the age of the Internet. *The Information Society*, *16*(2), 147–149. doi:10.1080/01972240050032906

Hitt, L. M., & Frei, F. X. (2002). Do better customers utilize electronic distribution channels? The case of PC banking. *Management Science*, *48*(6), 732–748. doi:10.1287/mnsc.48.6.732.188

Hyppönen, H., Salmivalli, L., et al. (2005). Organizing for a National Infrastructure Project: *The Case of the Finnish Electronic Prescription. Hawaii International conference on Systems Sciences 2005* (HICSS-38), Big Island, Hawaii.

Karjaluoto, H., & Mattila, M. (2002). Electronic banking in Finland: Consumer beliefs and reactions to a new delivery channel. *Journal of Financial Services Marketing*, *6*(4), 346–361. doi:10.1057/palgrave.fsm.4770064

Karjaluoto, H., & Mattila, M. (2002). Factors underlying attitude formation towards online banking in Finland. *International Journal of Bank Marketing*, *20*(6), 261–272. doi:10.1108/02652320210446724

Liao, Z., & Cheung, M. T. (2002). Internet-based e-banking and consumer attitudes: An empirical study. *Information & Management*, *39*(4), 283–295. doi:10.1016/S0378-7206(01)00097-0

Pollard, C. (2003). E-service adoption and use in small farms in Australia: Lessons learned from a government-sponsored programme. *Journal of Global Information Technology Management*, *6*(2), 45–63.

Sääksjärvi, M. (2000). The Roles of Corporate IT Infrastructure and Their Impact on IS Effectiveness. *Proceedings of the Eighth European Conference on Information Systems*, Vienna.

Stylianou, A. C., & Robbins, S. S. (2003). Perceptions and attitudes about eCommerce development in China: An exploratory study. *Journal of Global Information Management*, *11*(2), 31–47.

Suomi, R. (2005). Management of infrastructures: What can the internet developers learn from the history of railways? *Journal of Management History*, *43*(6), 896–905.

Wang, Y.-S., & Wang, Y.-M. (2003). Determinants of user acceptance of Internet banking: An empirical study. *International Journal of Service Industry Management*, *14*(5), 501–519. doi:10.1108/09564230310500192

KEY TERMS AND DEFINITIONS

Automatic Teller Machine (ATM): An automat from which cash can be withdrawn or through which other financial transactions can happen.

ec-Karte (ec-card): An European debit card, used mainly in German-speaking countries.

International Bank Account Number (IBAN): Identifier of a bank account. A key component in the European Single payment area.

Payment System: A system for delivering financial transactions between different bank accounts.

Point-of-Sale System: A system to take care of financial transactions at a cashier or service counter, where the customer interaction takes place.

Single Payment Area: In the European connection, refers to the EU-internal regulation and infrastructure, within which bank transfers between different countries can be made with the same terms as within countries.

SWIFT: (1) The Society for Worldwide Interbank Financial Telecommunication; (2) A financial transaction network operated by the above Society

ENDNOTE

[1] Rows 1-4 Finnish data for year 2004

Chapter 13
Employee Attitudes towards Business-to-Employee (B2E) Portals Use:
Analysing the Role of Demographic Characteristics

Md Mahbubur Rahim
Monash University, Australia

Mohini Singh
RMIT University, Australia

Mohammad Quaddus
Curtin University, Australia

ABSTRACT

B2E portals represent a state of the art technology for organisations (businesses) to deal with employees using electronic communication, access and data management. B2E portals enable reduced operation costs for organisations and satisfied employees by offering them convenience, flexibility and agility. However, adoption, continued use, and eventual success of portals depend to a large extent on employees' attitudes towards portal use, which generally impinges on demographic characteristics of employees. To establish the influence of demographic characteristics on employee attitudes towards portal use, this chapter reports a study on B2E portal use and employee attitudes from a large Australian university. This chapter highlights that employees' attitudes towards portal use is only somewhat positive, and not

DOI: 10.4018/978-1-60960-129-4.ch013

overwhelmingly favourable. Although not statistically significant, attitudes of employee varied based on age and educational background. Senior management of organisations should thus formulate strategies to develop positive attitudes for portal use to accelerate its diffusion among employee communities. Such strategies should take into consideration of the possible effect of employees' age and educational characteristics. E-commerce researchers could undertake further research to find out whether demographic characteristics become more significant once the portals are in use for sometime.

INTRODUCTION

In the current climate of global economic crisis, many organisations are aspiring for a lean organisational structure and a more productive workforce. Adoption of innovative web-based B2E portals can be regarded as an important mechanism to help organisations maintain committed and satisfied employee community. B2E portals, by providing customised services and information tailored to employees' roles and needs, can help improve their decision making abilities (Singh, 2005; Turban et al, 2008). They also streamline the way employees handle information and execute business processes (Mootheril and Singh, 2009; Urbach et al, 2009), and reduce expenses related to employee travel and improve corporate communication (Singh and Waddell, 2008; Tojib et al, 2008). With improved business processes, enhanced learning, electronic communications, and knowledge management (Singh and Waddell, 2008), it is possible for B2E portals to help organisations in outperforming competitors. However, it would be inappropriate to assume that employees would happily embrace B2E portals once senior management of their organisations decides to introduce these technologies. This is because employee acceptance and subsequent usage of technologies is quite often influenced by their attitudes. Our view is in line with the arguments expressed in several theoretical frameworks (elaborated in Section 2) reported in the existing IS/IT literature. We also believe that the formation of employee attitudes towards use of portals is often influenced by their demographic characteristics. This is rooted in the cumulative empirical evidence and theoretical arguments [e.g. Zmud's (1979) MIS success model] reported in the literature. Examining the influence of demographic orientations on employees' attitudes is important because negative attitudes can form a barrier for successful adoption and subsequent use of B2E portals by employees. In addition, knowledge of demographic characteristics is also insightful because management could identify those segments of their workforce which are more likely to offer resistance and demonstrate a lack of cooperation for the acceptance of portals. Appropriate policies can then be formulated by management to help those segments of employees develop more positive attitudes towards portal use.

As B2E portals represent a new type of technology, little has been published about how employees feel about the use of portals and whether there exists a significant difference in employee attitudes based on their demographic characteristics. The lack of research in this area is not surprising given the fact that academic research literature tends to lag behind practice (Kim and Han, 2001). We acknowledge that although some studies are reported in the existing literature on users' attitudes and use of various types of Internet-based applications (e.g. Nachmias et al, 2000; Zhang, 2005; Konradt et al, 2006), their findings are not directly applicable to the B2E portal context because of the existence of differences in characteristics and purposes of use.

In this chapter, we thus report the findings of a survey among 161 employees of a large Australian university which has introduced an employee portal in recent years. Empirical evidence suggests that employees have somewhat positive (but not overwhelmingly favourable) attitudes towards their use of portals. Although, employees' attitudes vary based on their age and educational background such variations are not statistically significant. Furthermore, no significant relationships are observed between employees' attitudes and their gender, job role and job types. We also find that attitudes are strongly related to employees' use of portals, this is consistent with the predictions of the relevant theoretical models discussed in Section 2. These findings are useful to practitioners and research community alike.

This chapter has been organised as follows. The next section presents a critical review of the relevant streams of literature on attitudes and demographic characteristics of users of technology. This is followed by a set of research hypotheses developed from the review. The research approach is then described. The survey data collected from 161 responding employees from a leading Australian university are then analysed and discussed. Finally, the contributions and some limitations of this study are indicated, and future research directions are proposed.

BACKGROUND LITERATURE

B2E Portal Literature

Existing B2E portal literature is limited. Those few studies that are reported in the literature did not examine employees' attitudes towards the use of portals, rather they have addressed such concerns as *organisational adoption decisions of B2E portals, benefits arising from the adoption of B2E portals, and employee satisfaction with B2E portals*. Typical examples representing the first concern include studies undertaken by Rahim et al. (2005), Sugianto et al. (2005) and Rahim (2007a). In their study, Sugianto et al. (2005) looked at some factors affecting the adoption of B2E portal but they did not provide any empirical validation. In another study, Rahim et al. (2005) examined a particular stance of B2E portal adoption in a large university but their work lacks a rigorous validation. This weakness was later addressed by Rahim (2007a) in a subsequent study in which he reported on the employee portal adoption experience of two large Australian universities and identified the key factors affecting their adoption decisions.

Another group of scholars investigated the benefits of B2E portals. For instance, Rahim (2006) and Rahim and Singh (2006) have reported the benefits of intranet-based employee portals for both employees and their organisations. In their study, Scornvacca et al. (2006) examined the organisational impact of a mobile B2E application in a New Zealand restaurant. In another study, Rangone (2006) looked at the characteristics and benefits offered by mobile B2E portal like applications among some Italian companies.

Finally, several authors have measured success of B2E solutions in terms of employee satisfaction. For example, Huang et al. (2004) analysed satisfaction of employees with a B2E benefit system at a Taiwanese company and found that such factors as convenience, interface, accuracy, price and security affected employee satisfaction with that application. In another study, Sugianto and Tojib (2006) proposed a conceptual model to measure user satisfaction with employee portal and identified nine factors that could affect employee satisfaction with portals. In a subsequent study, Tojib and Sugianto (2007) empirically tested that model in a large Australian university setting and found that five factors including usefulness, ease of use, portal design, confidentiality and convenience affected user satisfaction with employee portals.

Related Literature on Attitudes and Demographic Factors

As the existing literature on B2E portals does not focus on employee attitudes towards their use of portals at work life settings, we have consulted three relevant streams of literature (i.e. social psychology, IS/IT implementation, and e-commerce) in which attitudes towards technology acceptance has been widely discussed. In the following subsections, we provide a brief but insightful review of the theoretical foundations and empirical evidence reported in these literature streams about attitudes towards technology use and the role of demographic characteristics on attitudes.

Theoretical Foundations on Attitudes

Social Psychology Literature: This stream of literature suggests two influential models: Theory of Reasoned Action (TRA) of Fishbein and Ajzen (1975) and Theory of Planned behaviour (TPB) of Ajzen (1991). These two models help explain how a person's attitude relates to his/her behaviour in a given situation. According to TRA (shown in Figure 1), attitude refers to the affect that one feels for or against some object or behaviour. Fishbein and Ajzen distinguish two different kinds of attitudes: attitudes towards objects (e.g. portal, computer, Internet) and attitudes concerning behaviours (e.g. portal use). Using this distinction, an individual's attitude toward an IT system would be considered an attitude toward an object. On the other hand, an attitude concerning system use would be considered an attitude concerning a behaviour. According to TRA, an individual's attitude and subjective norms together influence that person's intention to perform a behaviour (e.g. IT system use). Subjective norm is the influence of behavioural expectations of people who are important to an individual weighted by the individual's motivation to comply with them, on the individual's behavioural intention. In other words, *subjective norm* can be defined as an individual's perception of the significant others' expectations about whether the behaviour should be performed.

TPB (as shown is Figure 2) is an extension of the TRA. It includes perceived behavioural control (PBC) which is considered to be another determinant of behaviour. PBC refers to an individual's perception of ease or difficulty of performing a given behaviour of interest (Ajzen, 1991). Attitudes and subjective norms still remain the mediating variables affecting behavioural intention in this model. However, unlike TRA, PBC is believed to affect both intention and actual behaviour. Moreover, intention has a higher chance of being transformed into actual behaviour if the behaviour itself is voluntary.

IS/IT Implementation Literature: This stream of literature provides a range of models to help explain acceptance and usage of IT applications by users. Among them, three models in particular have received considerable attention: Technology Adoption Model (TAM) introduced by Davis et

Figure 1. Theory of reasoned action

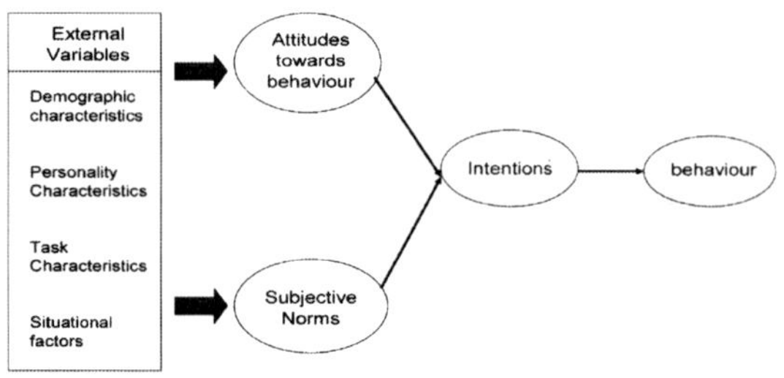

Figure 2. Theory of planned behaviour

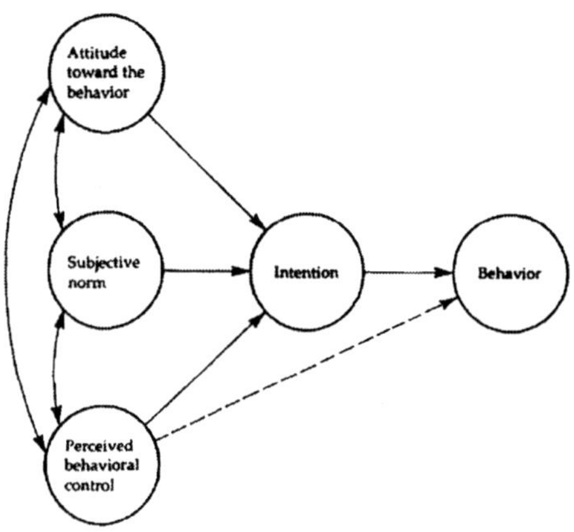

Figure 3. Technology acceptance model

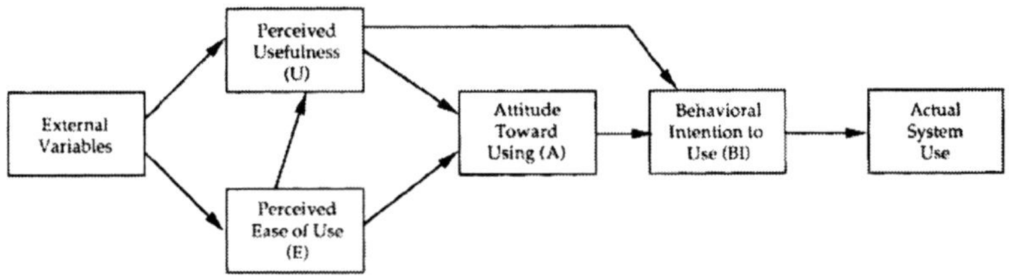

al. (1989), Interactional Model (Nelson, 1992) and Zmud's (1979) MIS success model.

TAM is an adaptation of TRA, specifically modified to suit the information systems context. The core concept of TAM is that a person's attitude toward using an IT system is jointly determined by perceived ease of use and perceived usefulness. Attitude in turn affects a person's behavioural intention to use a system. Perceived usefulness is defined as "the prospective user's subjective probability that using a specific application system will increase his or her job performance within an organizational context". Perceived ease of use refers to "the degree to which a person believes that using a particular system would be free of effort". However, TAM does not include TRA's subjective norms construct as it was found to be insignificant. Many authors have applied TAM model in explaining use of various types of business IT applications. However, analysis of the empirical research with TAM is not totally conclusive.

Nelson (1990), in his well cited article published in MIS Quarterly, suggested an Interactional Model to help explain the need for individual adjustment necessary to use information-driven technologies. The central tenet of his model (shown in Figure 4) is the notion that organisational context and differences of individuals affect their attitudes and behaviour. More specifically, individuals may vary in terms of their demographic characteristics and cognitive styles which in turn affect their attitudes for using innovative technologies.

Zmud (1979) developed a model (shown in Figure 5) that portrays the manner in which individual differences influence MIS success. Two distinct paths are conceptualised. An upper path finds individual differences amplifying or dampening limitations in human information processing and decision behavior, which in turn impose or suggest MIS design alternatives directed toward motivating or facilitating MIS usage. A lower path

Figure 4. Interaction model of technology acceptance

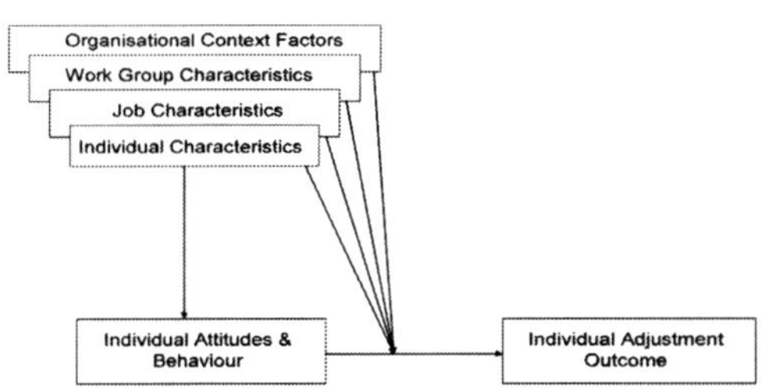

Figure 5. Zmud's MIS success model

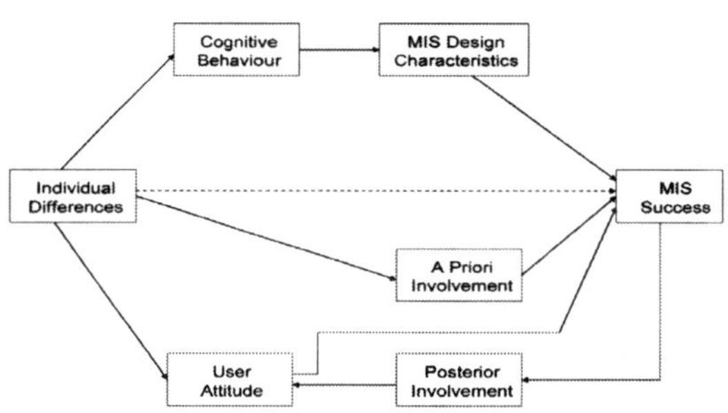

reflects the impact of individual differences upon the attitudes held by potential MIS users and upon the tendencies for MIS users to involve themselves in the MIS development effort. These paths can thus be characterized as representing the cognitive and attitudinal influences of individual differences upon MIS success.

Demographic Factors and Attitudes: Theoretical Foundations

The potential influence of demographic characteristics on a person's attitudes towards performing a given behaviour has been acknowledged in the above mentioned three streams of literature. In the following sub-sections, we now summarise our observations:

While Fishbein and Ajzen (1975) claim that attitude (toward the behavior), subjective norm, and intention are the prime determinants of behavior, they do not deny the possibility that other factors will also have a relationship with behavior. However, they claim that all such factors, labelled external variables (shown in the left side of Figure 1), influence behavior indirectly through their influence on attitude concerning the behaviour. Examples of external variables include demographic variables and personality characteristics. Likewise, as TPB is derived from TRA, it can be argued that external variables may also have an effect on the components of TPB. Thus, both TRA and TPB can act as a useful framework for explaining the effects of demographic characteristics on user attitudes and their system use.

In TAM, several external variables (shown in the left hand side of Figure 3) were incorporated which may influence user belief structure towards perceived ease of use and usefulness. Some of these variables include user characteristics (including demographic variables) and situational context. Davis et al. (1989) however recommended the need for further research to closely examine the role of these variables. In his interactional model, Nelson (1990) explicitly acknowledges the influence of individual differences on the formation of attitudes towards accepting an innovation. Likewise, in Zmud's (1979) model on MIS success, the role of individual differences is explicitly recogonised. The individual differences are grouped into three groups: cognitive style, personality, and demographic/situational variables. The demographic/situational variables cover a broad spectrum of personal characteristics. Both general intellectual abilities and knowledge of specific content areas are believed to influence MIS usage, as have attributes such as gender, age, experience, education, professional orientation, and organisational level.

Demographic Factors and Attitudes: Empirical Evidence

The relationship between demographic characteristics and a person's attitudes as indicated by various theoretical models outlined in the previous section have been empirically evaluated in various streams of literature. In the following sections, we provide an indicative evidence from four literature sources related to B2E portals:

The IS/IT literature contains many empirical evidence to suggest that demographic factors affect users attitudes towards using computer technologies. In addition, several variables like age, gender, education also have been examined for their relationship with computer attitudes. For example, Rafaeli (1986) found that women have more positive attitudes towards computer use than men. The effect of age of workers' attitudes towards computer use was investigated by Zoltan and Chapanis (1982) who reported that older workers possess less favourable attitudes than younger workers for computer use. Likewise, Lucas (1976) and Mumford and Bank (1967) found that older individuals exhibited less positive attitudes towards MIS. Lucas (1978) further reported that less educated individuals exhibited less positive attitudes towards MIS use.

E-commerce literature acknowledges the importance of examining the role of demographic factors of employees because such factors may impact and constrain the usage of the Internet by affecting their attitudes. For example, Schofield and Davidson (1997) emphasised the need to address demographic factors and employee attitudes in order to achieve the full potential of the Internet use. Nachmias et al (2000) attempted to identify whether gender and age might affect the use of the Internet. They found more boys than girls used the Internet due to their positive attitudinal perceptions. On the other hand, Anandarajan et al. (2000) did not find age and gender to be significantly correlated with their belief towards the Internet usage in workplace. Mahatanankoon (2002) suggested that employees in their workplaces should be encouraged to increase their productivity by using the Internet via changing employees' attitudes. In a more recent study, Zhang (2005) reported that employees' attitudes towards internet use (expressed in terms of their anxiety) vary significantly in terms of their educational levels, gender and age groups.

In the sales automation literature, some scholars have attempted to evaluate sales person's attitudes and use of technology. For example, Keillor et al. (1997) measured salespersons' attitudes toward the use of technology applications and reported that attitudes affect how the technologies were implemented within the sales process. In another study, Speier and Venkatesh (2002) found that age and gender of sales employees to have influenced their perceptions on how sales force automation technologies could be used.

The influence of demographic factors on attitudes towards IT-enabled HR information systems used by human resources professionals is widely highlighted. For example, a group of HR scholars (e.g. Teo et al., 2007; Stone et al., 2006) have focused on the acceptance and usage of HR information systems from the perspective of individual employees. They found individual characteristics of employees and their attitudes to be the determinants of employees' acceptance and subsequent usage of HR related information systems. In another study, Konradt et al. (2006) found significant negative relationship between age of employees and their perceptions of online ESS usage.

Gaps in the Existing Literature

It is our observation that current research on B2E portals implicitly assume that adoption decisions (owing to enormous benefits that can be potentially delivered by B2E portals) made by senior management could possibly lead to wide spread diffusion of portal technologies among workforce. As a result, e-commerce researchers were perhaps reluctant to make a specific call to investigate the attitudinal beliefs that may potentially motivate employees to embrace and use portals at their work settings. In addition, drawing on the critical analysis of those streams of literature which are loosely related to B2E portals (e.g. Zhang, 2005; Teo et al., 2007; Stone et al., 2006) we suggest that demographic characteristics of employees are likely to influence their attitudes towards using portals. However, no empirical evaluation has yet been reported to assess the association between employees' attitudes and their demographic characteristics. Hence, there is a clear need to further investigate this concern.

RESEARCH HYPOTHESES

Drawing on the literature review, we have identified five demographic characteristics that may influence attitudes of employees towards portal use. These include: gender, age, educational background, job role and job type. Detail explanations justifying the selection of these characteristics are given below:

Gender: The role of gender on the formation of employees' attitudes towards use of B2E portals can be appreciated by reviewing the following arguments expressed in the IS/IT literature. First, some scholars (e.g. Heinseen et al, 1987) indicated that female employees are more likely to be anxious about using IT systems than their male counterparts. We argue that this is true for portals context as well. As portals involve complex technology, anxiety could be reflected in terms of attitudinal dispositions towards portal use. Second, based on the observations of Venkatesh and Morris (2000), it can be argued that attitudes of male employees are more dominated by their perceptions of portal's usefulness. In contrast, attitudes of female employees are often guided by their attitudinal perceptions towards portal's ease of use. Third, male employees tend to be more confident with the execution of complex tasks using IT systems than their female counterparts (Vallerand, 1997). For the portal context, this means that male employees would form more favourable attitudes when they are convinced that their use of portals would assist them perform complex tasks with greater confidence. This may not be the case for female employees. Therefore, the following hypothesis is derived:

H1: *There is a significant difference in attitudes towards B2E portal use between male and female employees*

Age: Existing IS/IT literature suggests that an individual employee's attitudes towards an IT system use can be affected by his/her age. One reason is that older employees are more likely to form an attitude for using an application based on their perceptions of the degree of effortlessness in using that particular application (Morris and Venkatesh, 2000). In other words, older employees tend to form positive attitudes towards an IT system when usage of those applications does not demand considerable effort on their part. In the context of the B2E portal usage, the role of age in influencing employee attitudes is based on the fact that older individuals tend to be more rigid in changing their work style because habits and beliefs which they have formed over the years are much stronger among them than for younger individuals. Thus, perceptions about compatibility of the B2E portal with their past experience and work practices would play a vital role in determining their attitudes towards portal use. This may not be the case for younger employees. According to Vallerand (1997), motivation plays a different role based on an employee's age such that younger employees would pay more emphasis on using an application based on the positive job related values associated with using it. Thus, perceived job related performance improvement through B2E portal usage helps forming a more positive attitude among younger employees more (due to potential career progression as a result of better performance) than older ones. As such, the following hypothesis is derived:

H2: *There is a significant difference in attitudes towards B2E portals use between young and more mature employees*

Education: Attitudes of employee are likely to vary significantly based on the level of their educational orientations. This is because several studies have found a negative relationship between education and people's attitudinal dispositions towards anxiety for using computer-based applications (Gutek and Bikson, 1985; Igbaria and Parasuraman, 1989). This may also apply to employees wanting to use portals at their work settings. Furthermore, according to Evanschitzky and Wunderlich (2006), people with higher levels of education are better able to perform more comprehensive information gathering and processing than less educated people. As portals enable employees to draw on information from multiple sources and help superior information processing and interpretation, employees with higher research degree are more likely to establish greater positive attitudes towards portal use than those who have less education. In addition, for B2E portal context, we thus argue that greater years of formal education of an employee would influence his/her ability to recognise business values by being able to identify ways to use portals innovatively in support of their work. As such, the following hypothesis is proposed:

H3: *There is a significant difference in attitudes towards B2E portals use between employees 'with higher research degree as opposed to those having undergraduate degree*

Job Role: Job roles held by employees may also influence their attitudes towards portal use. This is primarily due to the differences in perceived information needs between managerial and operational staff (Hjelt, 2006). For example, an operations manager may depend heavily on information drawn from several detailed reports while a strategic manager may require only high level information from various sources. Based on the information needs, employees' interaction with a particular IT application differs such that the higher up the person is in the organisational hierarchy, the lesser will be the usage because that person's attitudinal beliefs towards perceived usefulness of the application to address his/her information needs would be low. For B2E portal, we argue that a senior manager's needs are so diverse that portals alone may not be adequate to satisfy all his/her needs. Hence, employees with managerial responsibilities are more likely to demonstrate less favourable attitudes towards portal use as opposed to operational employees. Thus, the following hypothesis is developed:

H4: *There is a significant difference in attitudes towards B2E portal use between managerial and operational employees.*

Job Type: In academic settings, we argue that the attitudes of academic staff towards portal use are likely to differ from those of administrative staff. This is because of the presence of clear and distinct difference in their duties and activities. According to Fisher (1994), academic staff are generally required to act as teacher, researcher, organiser, and administrator. Moreover, the activities performed by academic staff often involve ambiguity On the other hand, functional roles and activities of general staff tend to be well structured. This view is supported by Winefield et al. (2003) who found that considerable differences exist between Australian academics and general staff in terms of their functional roles, work load and work ambiguity. We thus conjecture that academic staff are required to draw on information from various sources and may require services which may not be readily provided through portals. Hence, they are likely to establish less favourable attitudes as opposed to administrative staff towards portal use. Moreover, due to the nature of job, information gathering and processing strategies used by academic staff are likely to differ from those of administrative staff. In contrast, administrative employees are generally expected to carry out repeated structured tasks for which information requirements can be well supported by portals. Hence, the following hypothesis is offered:

H5: *There is a significant difference in attitudes towards B2E portal use between academic and administrative employees*

RESEARCH APPROACH

Justification of Exploratory Approach

Our research is exploratory and theory building (Yin, 2003) in nature because we wanted to discover the existence of possible influence of employees' demographic characteristics on their attitudes towards B2E portals usage. We have thus adopted an exploratory survey approach. However, one important characteristic of our approach is that we have relied on several qualitative interviews from two senior managers from the case organisation in which the survey was conducted. This was done in order to better interpret the survey results.

Choice of the Case Organisation

The participating case organisation is a large Australian university. It was selected for the following four reasons: (a) it has implemented a campus wide web-enabled employee portal which can be accessed by all staff from both home and at their workplaces, (b) the authors had access to the case site, and (c) the university agreed to participate in both survey and subsequent interviews, and (d) it has several campuses (including overseas) and thus maintain dispersed workforce for which portal is quite suitable.

Sample Size

In keeping with the exploratory nature of this study, a convenience sampling approach was considered appropriate. A survey questionnaire was distributed among 500 staff of Business and IT faculties of the participating university. These two faculties were selected because the portal was rolled out among them first, at a later stage the portal was made available to the remaining faculties and administrative units of the university. A total of 161 responses were received yielding a response rate of 32.2%.

Operationalisation of the Research Variables

A survey instrument was developed that included 35 items which operationalise employee attitudes towards portal use, self reported portal usage of employees, various factors affecting portal use (e.g. perceived ease of use, perceived usefulness) and demographic characteristics of employees. In this chapter, we restrict our attention to employees' attitudes and their demographic characteristics only. A summary of the research variables pertaining to our research concern is summarised in Table 1.

Three demographic characteristics such as gender, job role and job type were measured on a dichotomous scale. However, according to the suggestions of MacCallum et al. (2002), the remaining two characteristics (i.e. age and educational background) were measured on a ratio scale. Based on the work of Hartwick and Barki (1994), attitude was measured using three items (as shown

Table 1. Research variables and their operatioanlisations

Research variables	Measurement	Literature Sources
Employee attitudes towards portal use	Five-point differential scales. 3 items were used which were later averaged to create a score for user attitude. Item 1: My use of the portal is: Good: 5 4 3 2 1 Bad Item 2: My use of the portal is: Terrific: 5 4 3 2 1 Terrible Item 3: My use of the portal is: Valuable: 5 4 3 2 1 Worthless	Hartwick and Barki (1994)
Gender	Dichotomous scale	
Age	Ratio scale	MacCallum et al. (2002)
Educational background	Ratio scale	MacCallum et al. (2002)
Job role	Dichotomous scale	
Job type	Dichotomous scale	

in the second column of Table 1). Each item was measured on a five-point interval scale.

Refinement of the Survey Instrument and Research Variables

The survey instrument was initially reviewed by 3 domain experts who were selected following the guidelines of Kitchenham and Pfleeger (2002). Two of them have experience in implementing B2E portals and one is a senior academic who has about 10 years teaching and research experience in the areas of e-commerce. Several changes were incorporated based on their feedback which greatly improved the clarity of the survey instrument.

Instrument Reliability and Validity

As the employees' attitudes towards B2E portal use were measured using multiple items, we have determined their reliability using Cronbach alpha (Nunnaly, 1978) which were found to be quite satisfactory (Alpha =.859). Furthermore, to address validity of these variables, exploratory factor analysis was carried out which produced one factor solution; thus confirming the unidimensionality of the portal attitude factor. The attitude factor loadings are quite high and are shown in the second column of Table 2. In factor analysis, it is generally desirable to have larger number of respondents than items. The ratio of sample size to items was (53:1), which is well over (10:1) ratio suggested by Nunnally (1978) for exploratory type of research.

EMPIRICAL FINDINGS

Profile of the Participating Employees

A profile of the surveyed employees is provided in Table 3. A number of observations can be deduced: (a) a slight majority of female employees is observed; (b) although, employees of all age groups are well represented in the sample, a vast majority of the respondents are over 29 years old, (c) likewise, employees from all educational backgrounds also participated. However, one third of the participating employees have PhD as their highest academic qualification, (d) employees representing managerial roles (11.81%) is limited. This makes sense because not all staff have high level of managerial responsibilities, and (e) finally academic and administrative staff both were equally represented.

Table 2. Results of exploratory factor analysis

Attitude items	Factor Loadings	Eigen Values	% of Variance	Reliability
Indicate your feelings concerning the use of the portal on the scales shown below. My use of the portal is: Good: 5 4 3 2 1 Bad	.890	2.340	77.99	.859
My use of the portal is: Terrific: 5 4 3 2 1 Terrible	.855	1.393	13.11	
My use of the portal is: Valuable: 5 4 3 2 1 Worthless	.903	1.267	8.88	
Kaiser-Meyer-Olkin Measure of Sampling Adequacy:.724 Bartlett's Test of Sphericity: Approx. Chi-Square = 222.16, df= 3, Sig =.000 Total variance explained: 77.9%				

Extraction Method: Principal Component Analysis.

Table 3. A summary of employee profile

Characteristics of employees	Frequency	Percent
Gender		
Male	76	47.2
Female	85	52.8
Age		
18 – 29 years	20	12.4
30 – 39 years	41	25.5
40 – 49 years	42	26.1
49 years and above	58	36.0
Education		
Undergraduate degree	27	16.1
Postgraduate degree	48	29.8
PhD or equivalent	57	34.8
Others	29	18.0
Job Role		
Managerial	19	11.8
Non-managerial	142	88.2
Job Type		
Academic staff Administrative staff	80 81	49.3 50.7

Intercorrelation Matrix between Demographic Characteristics

The intercorrelation matrix for the demographic variables is shown in Table 4. Age and gender are negatively correlated (r = -.07), with male employees generally being older than their female counterparts. Age also appears to be positively related with educational level (r =.156), thereby implying that older employees tend to be highly educated than younger ones. Job type is highly related to gender (r =.333) indicating that most female employees are of administration type.

Attitudes of the Participating Employees towards B2E Portal Use

The average score of employees for each attitude item is given in Table 5. Overall, employees have slightly positive feelings towards the use of employee portals (as the mean score is over the neutral score of 3 but vary between 3.2 and 3.5).

In order to better understand employees' attitudinal perceptions, the histograms representing frequency distribution of employee responses to each attitude item are shown in Figures 6 to 8. The following observations can be deduced from these diagrams: (a) very few (about 15%) of employees have negative attitudes towards portal use (as they selected a rating of either 1 or 2 on

Table 4. Correlation matrix

		Age	Gender	Edu	Job Role	Job Type
Age	Pearson Correlation	1	-.070	.156(*)	-.087	-.045
	Sig. (2-tailed)		.379	.049	.273	.568
Gender	Pearson Correlation	-.070	1	-.063	.001	.333(**)
	Sig. (2-tailed)	.379		.426	.988	.000
Edu	Pearson Correlation	.156(*)	-.063	1	-.015	-.032
	Sig. (2-tailed)	.049	.426		.855	.686
Job Role	Pearson Correlation	-.087	.001	-.015	1	.041
	Sig. (2-tailed)	.273	.988	.855		.609
Job Type	Pearson Correlation	-.045	.333(**)	-.032	.041	1
	Sig. (2-tailed)	.568	.000	.686	.609	

* Correlation is significant at the 0.05 level (2-tailed).
** Correlation is significant at the 0.01 level (2-tailed).

Table 5. Statistics about attitude items

Attitude item	Mean Attitude	Standard deviation
Item 1: My use of the portal is: Good: 5 4 3 2 1 Bad	3.49	.963
Item 2: My use of the portal is: Terrific: 5 4 3 2 1 Terrible	3.27	.880
Item 3: My use of the portal is: Valuable: 5 4 3 2 1 Worthless	3.50	.963

Figure 6. Frequency distribution of employees' responses for attitude item 1

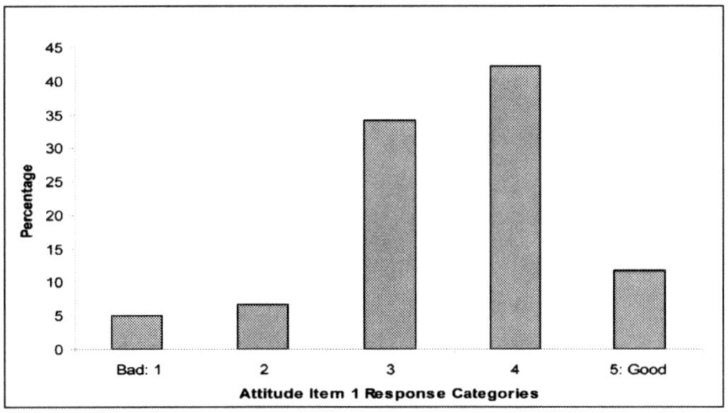

Figure 7. Frequency distribution of employees' responses for attitude item 2

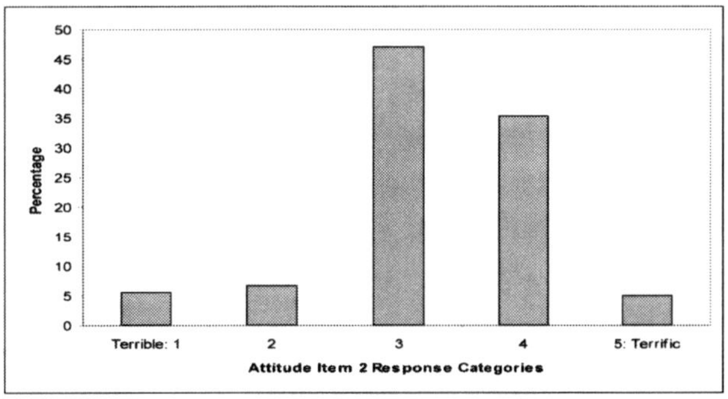

a scale of 1 to 5), (b) most employees have either neutral or somewhat positive attitudes towards portal use (this is reflected by the majority of employees selecting either rating 3 or 4), and (c) only about 20% of employees have very positive attitudes (as they selected a rating of 5) towards portal use. These observations are a surprise given the fact that the portal was introduced in the university for over 5 years.

Testing Hypotheses

We have performed student t-tests (shown in Table 6) to find out whether a significant difference in employees' attitudes towards B2E portal use can

Figure 8. Frequency distribution of employees' responses for attitude item 3

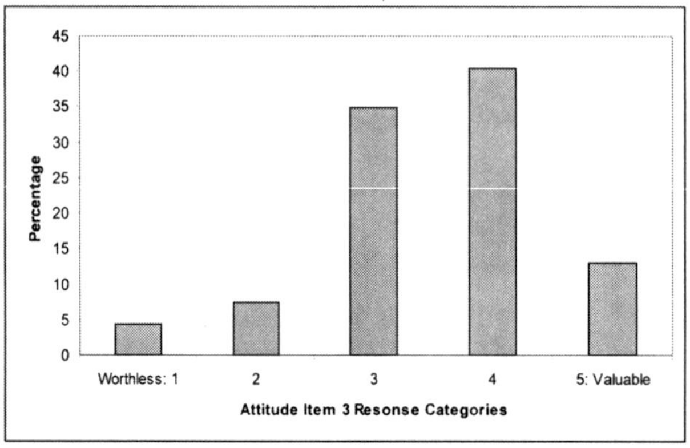

be observed based on their gender, job role and job type. In general, female employees demonstrated slightly more positive attitudes (means attitudes: 3.43) towards portal use than their male counterparts (mean attitudes: 3.40). However, the difference is not statistically significant. Hence, hypothesis H1 is not supported. Likewise, employees with non-managerial roles exhibited more positive attitudes (mean attitudes: 3.43) than those employees who have managerial roles (mean attitudes: 3.29). However, the difference is not statistically significant. Hence, hypothesis H4 is not supported. Finally, administrative employees were found to have more positive attitudes (mean attitudes: 3.43) towards portal use than their academic counterparts (mean attitudes: 3.40), but the difference is not statistically significant. Hence, hypothesis H5 is rejected.

Two separate one-way ANOVA analyses were carried out to determine if employees' attitudes towards portal use differ significantly based on their age and educational background. The results (summarised in Table 7) clearly indicate the absence of a significant difference in employee attitudes. Hence, hypotheses H2 and H3 are both rejected.

To gain more insight about the influence of age on employee attitudes, the mean employee attitude towards portal use for each age group is

Table 6. Student t-test results

Research variables	Attitudes		
	Mean	t-value	p-value
Gender Male Female	3.40 3.43	-.209	.834
Job Role Managerial Non-managerial	3.29 3.43	-.696	.487
Job Type Academic Administration	3.40 3.43	-.260	.795

Note: df = 159

Table 7. Results of ANOVA analysis

Research Variables	Attitude		
	Mean	F-value	p-value
Age			
18 – 29 years	3.65	.647	.586
30 – 39 years	3.43		
40 – 49 years	3.35		
50 years and above	3.37		
Education			
Undergraduate	3.54	.454	.715
Postgraduate	3.40		
PhD or equivalent	3.33		
Others	3.49		

NB: df = 3

shown in Figure 9. It appears that employees' attitudes decline with age with the most positive attitudes are found for employees belonging to 18 to 29 years category. Attitudes however improve slightly for employees representing age group of over 50 years. These differences however are not statistically significant; but still they form an interesting observation.

Likewise, mean attitudes for portal use decline as employees gain higher degree. Employees with PhD degree have the lowest attitudes in contrast to employees who have a Bachelor degree. However, such a difference is not statistically significant.

DISCUSSION

We were puzzled to find that the mean attitude of employees towards portal use was slightly over the neutral rating (i.e. 3 on a scale of 1 to 5) given the fact that the portal is in use for about 5 years. One would expect a more favourable attitude. Interestingly, portal use was also found to be not high. The mean score of portal use is 3.29 (on a scale of 1 to 5 where 1 means almost never, 2 means monthly, 3 means fortnightly, 4 means weekly, and 5 means daily). The low value of employees attitudes may help explain limited usage of portals (r =.40, p =.000). The low value of employee attitudes and portal use both are indicative of the existence of some deficiencies within the portal. In order to interpret this finding, we have conducted two interviews with members of the portal committee responsible for the introduction of the portal in the case organisation. Their viewpoints help shed insight into why employee attitudes are not favourable. According to them, the absence of very favourable attitudes of employees and their limited use of the portal can be broadly attributed to employees' perceptions of low value offered by portals. The functionalities offered through the portal provide limited assistance to the employees who require contents that are not fully supported by the portal. The employees in general find the portal to be inadequate with regard to the contents and services that the portal provides to them. In other words, the portal does not contain many attractive killer applications to help staff develop positive attitudes towards portal use. According to the head of the IT function: "*I must admit that our staff are not too big in the portal usage, they do not consider it to be very useful.*"

Drawing on the collective empirical findings presented in the previous section, we now suggest that the demographic characteristics of employees, in broad sense, are not related to their attitudes towards B2E portal use. This finding was not expected given the sound theoretical arguments

Figure 9. Distribution of mean attitude based on employee age

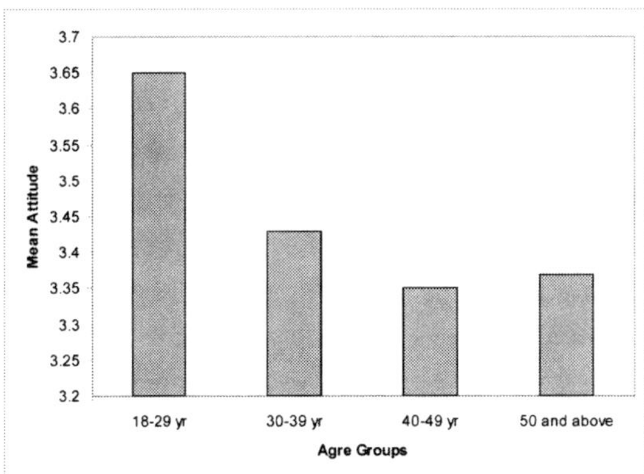

Figure 10. Distribution of mean attitude based on employees' educational background

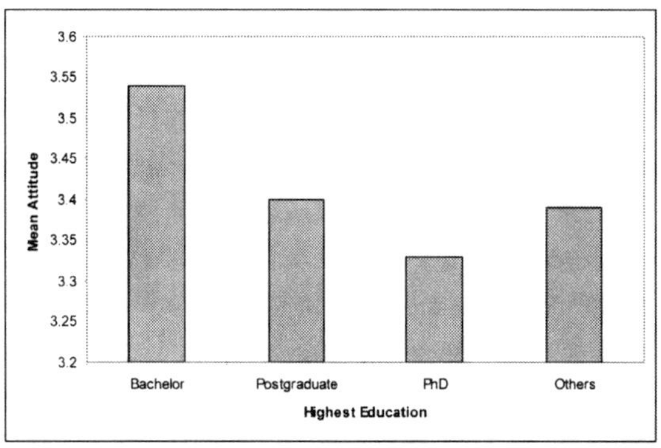

and rich body of empirical evidence (discussed in Section 2) advocating the existence of a possible relationship. We offer two plausible explanations for this. First, our choice of convenience sample and narrow focus on two faculties may have created a distortion in data. Second, contrary to the views expressed in the relevant literature streams, it is possible that for the B2E portal context – employee attitudes may not be influenced directly by the demographic profile of employees. Rather, perceived usefulness (via availability of killer applications) as acknowledged by the Head of the IT function may have mediated the variations in employees' attitudes towards their portal use. This line of interpretation is more in line with TAM (Davis et al., 1989) rather than Zmud's success model (1979).

Despite this, our findings can still be considered interesting. For example, although not statistically significant, there is a clear pattern in the variations of employees' attitudes based on their age and educational background. However, contrary to our predictions about employees with higher research degree to have more positive attitudes towards portal use, we found the opposite. Another interesting observation is that attitudes appear to be most favourable among young employees (age group 18 to 29 years) and employees attitudes decline as their age increase. However, an exception is the attitude of employees who are 50 years or older. We believe that two reasons may help explain why attitudes of 50 plus employees again rise.: (a) many employees over 50 years of age tend to work from home as they do not work full-time and voluntarily accept a reduction in their work load arrangement such as from 100% (meaning 5 days a week) to 60% to 80% (3 or 4 days a week) due to financial incentives for tax purpose and hence they need to use portal more frequently to stay in touch with their peers and the university authority, (b) most senior managers represent an age group of over 50 years and hence, they are more likely to be mobile as they travel more frequently to various campuses and, therefore, they tend to find portal more useful and hence demonstrate a more positive attitude.

CONCLUSION

In current global financial turmoil, organisations are keen to maintain a lean structure and highly productive workforce. Many organisations are introducing web-based portals (which have the potential to offer services and information customised to employee roles and preferences) to maintain an efficient and satisfied employee community. However, without evaluating employee attitudes towards portal use, it would be inappropriate to assume that employees would readily accept portal technology and would continue to use it when adoption decisions are made by senior management. Attitudes of employees need to be made favourable to facilitate portal acceptance and their continued use. Moreover, demographic characteristics of employees may affect their attitudes for portal use. As no prior investigations have been done to evaluate employees' attitudes towards portal use, we initiated this study in which 161 employees from a large Australian university participated. Overall, the results indicate that employees demonstrated somewhat positive attitudes towards portal use. In addition, some interesting observations were made indicating the existence of a possible relationship between age and educational background of employees with their attitudes towards portal use. However, these observations were not statistically significant. We also found a strong relationship between employees' attitudes and their self-reported portal usage behaviour. Moreover, attitudes of employee did not vary significantly based on their gender, job role and job types. The lack of a clear relationship between demographic characteristics and employee attitudes was not expected, and it contradicts the existing views expressed in the related literature. We thus advise to treat this finding with caution. This is perhaps because our research sample is not representative of the employees from all discipline areas of the participating university.

Drawing on our findings, we however advise that management of organisations should formulate strategies to develop positive attitudes for portal use to accelerate its diffusion among employee community. Such strategies should take into consideration of the possible effect of employees' age and educational characteristics. E-commerce researchers should further examine ways to improve the attitudes of employees for portal use by addressing the requirements unique to various employee groups who may vary based on their age and academic orientations. This study even contributes to theory construction by developing an empirical foundation based on which operationalisation and analysis of employee attitudes towards B2E portal can be further extended.

Our research findings could be improved in several ways. First, the use of staff selected from only two faculties of the participating university may have restricted our analytical ability to interpret these results in light of the existing literature. Future studies thus should involve a larger sample size chosen from all the faculties. This may produce more meaningful findings. Second, there may be some other demographic characteristics of employees (e.g. length of service, status of job – part-time or full-time) that were not considered in this study. Future studies should examine the influence of these characteristics on employees' attitudes towards portal use. Third, further studies are needed to collect attitudinal views of participants chosen from both academic and commercial institutions. This may help improve generalisability of our findings. Fourth, it would also be important to conduct longitudinal research to find out whether changes in employee attitudes occur as a result of continued use of portals and whether demographic characteristics become dominant at a later stage. Finally, the findings are limited to the Australian context. A cross-cultural study is thus recommended to further examine the role of demographic characteristics.

REFERENCES

Ajzen, I. (1991). The theory of planned behavior. *Organizational Behavior and Human Decision Processes*, 179–211. doi:10.1016/0749-5978(91)90020-T

Anandarajan, M., Simmers, C., & Igbaria, M. (2000). An exploratory investigation of the antecedents and impact of internet usage: An individual perspective. *Behaviour & Information Technology*, *19*(1), 69–85. doi:10.1080/014492900118803

Cox, T. (1993). *Stress research and stress management: putting theory to work. Health and safety Executive (HSE) Contract research report No. 61/1993*. London, UK: HMSO.

Davis, F. D. (1989). Perceived usefulness, perceived ease of use, and user acceptance of information technology. *Management Information Systems Quarterly*, *13*, 319–340. doi:10.2307/249008

Evanschitzky, H., & Wunderlich, M. (2006). An examination of moderator effects in the four-stage loyalty model. *Journal of Service Research*, *8*(4), 330–345. doi:10.1177/1094670506286325

Fishbein, M., & Ajzen, I. (1975). *Belief, attitude, intention and behaviour: An introduction to theory and research*. Reading, MA: Addison-Wesley.

Fisher, S. (1994). *Stress in academic life: The mental assembly line*. Buckingham, UK: Society for Research into Higher Education and Open University Press.

Gutek, B. A., & Bikson, T. K. (1985). Differential experiences of men and women in computerized offices. *Sex Roles*, *13*(3), 123. doi:10.1007/BF00287905

Hansen, M., & Deimler, M. (2001). Cutting costs while improving morale with B2E management. *MIT Sloan Management Review.*, *43*(1), 96–100.

Hartwick, J. & Barki, H. (1994). Explaining the role of user participation in information system use. *Management Science*.

Heinssen, R. K., Glass, C. R., & Knight, L. A. (1987). Assessing computer anxiety: Development and validation of the computer anxiety rating scale. *Computers in Human Behavior*, *3*, 49–59. doi:10.1016/0747-5632(87)90010-0

Hjelt, M. (2006). *End-user attitudes towards EDM use in project work: A case study of the Kamppi Center project.* Unpublished Master of Science Thesis, Swedish School of Economics and Business Administration.

Huang, J. H., Jin, B. H., & Yang, C. (2004). Satisfaction with business-to-employee benefit systems and organizational citizenship behaviour - an examination of gender differences. *International Journal of Manpower*, *25*(2), 195–210. doi:10.1108/01437720410535990

Igbaria, M., & Parasuraman, S. (1989). A path analytic study of individual characteristics, computer anxiety and attitudes toward microcomputers. *Journal of Management*, *15*(3), 373–383. doi:10.1177/014920638901500302

Keillor, B. D., Bashaw, E. R., Edward, R., & Pettijohn, C. E. (1997). Sales force automation issues prior to implementation: The relationship between attitudes toward technology experience and productivity. *Journal of Business and Industrial Marketing*, *12*(3/4), 209–219. doi:10.1108/08858629710188045

Kim, B., & Han, H. (2001). The strategic planning of B2B ehub. In *Proceedings of the Pacific Asia Conference on Information Systems (PACIS'01)*, Seoul.

Kitchenham, B., & Pfleeger, S. L. (2002). Principles of survey research questionnaire evaluation. *Software Engineering Notes*, *27*(3), 20–23. doi:10.1145/638574.638580

Konradt, U., Christophersen, T., & Schaeffer-Kuelz, U. (2006). Predicting user satisfaction, strain and system usage of employee self-services. *International Journal of Human-Computer Studies*, 1141–1153. doi:10.1016/j.ijhcs.2006.07.001

Lucas, H. C. Jr. (1976). *The implementation of computer based models*. New York: National Association of Accountants.

Lucas, H. C. Jr. (1978). Empirical evidence for a descriptive model of implementation. *Management Information Systems Quarterly*, *2*(2), 27–52. doi:10.2307/248939

MacCallum, R. C., Zhang, S., Preacher, K. J., & Rucker, R. D. (2002). On the practice of dichotomization of quantitative variables. *Psychological Methods*, *7*(1), 9–40. doi:10.1037/1082-989X.7.1.19

MacFarlane, A. (1994, May 13). Time to get teaching on board. []. London.]. *Times Higher Education Supplement*, 14.

Mahatanankoon, P. (2002). Explaining production deviant use of the Internet technology in the workplace: An integrated model. *Dissertation Abstract International, 63*, 03A.

Mann, F. C., & Williams, L. K. (1960). Observations on the dynamics of a change to electronic data processing equipment. *Administrative Science Quarterly*, *5*, 217–256. doi:10.2307/2390779

Mootheril, F., & Singh, M. (2009). Achieving organisational effectiveness from B2E e-Business. In the *Proceedings of the Pacific Asia Conference on Information Systems* (PACIS), India.

Morris, M.G., & Venkatesh, V. (2000). Age differences in technology adoption decisions: Implications for a changing workforce. *Personnel Psychology*.

Mumford, E., & Banks, O. (1967). *The computer and the clerk*. London: Routledge and Kegan Paul.

Nachmias, R., Mioduser, D., & Shemla, A. (2000). Internet usage by students in an Israeli high school. *Journal of Educational Computing Research*, *22*(1), 55–73. doi:10.2190/2XLG-FQQJ-1Y65-9K2E

Nelson, D. L. (1990). Individual adjustment to information-driven technologies: A critical review. *Management Information Systems Quarterly*, (March): 79–98. doi:10.2307/249311

Nunnally, J. C. (1978). *Psychometric theory*. New York: McGraw-Hill.

Rafaeli, A., & Sutton, R. (1986). Word processing technology and perceptions of control among clerical workers. *Behaviour & Information Technology*, *5*(5), 31–37. doi:10.1080/01449298608914496

Rahim, M. M. (2006). Understanding adoption and impact of B2E e-business systems: Lessons learned from the experience of an Australian university. *Proceedings of the Collaborative Electronic Commerce Research Conference (CollECTeR)*, Adelaide, Australia.

Rahim, M. M. (2007a). Factors affecting adoption of B2E e-Business systems: A case of the Australian Higher Education Industry. Proceedings of the *Pacific Asia Conference on Information Systems (PACIS2007)*, New Zealand.

Rahim, M. M. (2007b). Identifying barriers to using Business-to-Employee (B2E) Portals: Some lessons learned from an Australian University. *Proceedings of the Hawaii Int. Conference on Systems Science*, Hawaii.

Rahim, M. M., & Singh, M. (2007). Understanding benefits and impediments of B2E e-business systems adoption: Experiences of two large Australian universities. *Journal of Internet Commerce*, *6*(2), 3–17. doi:10.1300/J179v06n02_02

Rahim, M. M., Sugianto, L., & Shameem, N. (2005). Understanding the adoption of business-to-employee portals: An experience of a large Australian university. *Proceedings of the 5th International Conference on Electronic Business*, (pp.316-322). Hong Kong.

Rangone, A. (2006). B2E mobile internet: An exploratory study of Italian companies. *Business Process Management Journal*, *12*(3), 330–333. doi:10.1108/14637150610667999

Robey, D. (1979). User attitudes and management information system use. *Academy of Management Journal*, *22*(3), 527–538. doi:10.2307/255742

Schofield, J. W., & Davidson, A. L. (1997). The Internet in school: The shaping of use by organizational, structural, and cultural factors. *Proceedings from the WebNet 97 World Conference of the WWW, Internet & Intranet*. Toronto.

Scornavacca, E., Prashad, M., & Lehmann, H. (2006). Exploring the organisational impact and perceived benefits of wireless personal digital assistants in restaurants. *International Journal of Mobile Communications*, *4*(5), 558–567.

Singh, M. (2002). *Evolving e-Business models: A process of technology, in e-Business in Australia, concepts and cases* (pp. 8–22). Australia: Pearson Education.

Singh, M. (2005). (B2E): e-Management. In *Proceedings from the Sixth International Working for e-Business Conference*. Melbourne, Australia: Business to Employee.

Singh, M., Waddell, D., & Rahim, M. M. (2008). B2E e-business model: service to employees or organisational management? *WSEAS Transactions on Business and Economics*, *5*(5), 270–279.

Speier, C., & Venkatesh, V. (2002). The hidden minefields in the adoption of sales force automation technologies. *Journal of Marketing*, *66*(July), 98–111. doi:10.1509/jmkg.66.3.98.18510

Stone, D. L., Stone-Romero, E. F., & Lukaszewski, K. (2006). Factors affecting the acceptance and effectiveness of electronic human resources systems. *Human Resource Management Review*, *16*, 229–244. doi:10.1016/j.hrmr.2006.03.010

Sugianto, L., & Rahim, M. M & Alahakoon, D. (2005). B2E portal adoption: A conceptual model. *Proceedings of the International Conference on Information and Automation (ICIA2005)*, Colombo, Sri Lanka.

Sugianto, L., & Tojib, D. (2006). Modeling user satisfaction with an employee portal. *International Journal of Business and Information*, *1*(2), 239–255.

Swanson, E. B. (1982). Measuring user attitudes in MIS research: A review. *Omega*, *10*(2), 157–165. doi:10.1016/0305-0483(82)90050-0

Teo, T. S. H., Lim, G. S., & Fedric, A. A. (2007). The adoption and diffusion of human resources information systems in Singapore. *Asia Pacific Journal of Human Resources*, *45*(91), 44–62. doi:10.1177/1038411107075402

Tojib, D., & Sugianto, L. (2007). The development and empirical validation of the B2E portal user satisfaction (B2EPUS) scale. *Journal of Organizational and End User Computing*, *19*(3), 1–18.

Tojib, D., Sugianto, L., & Sendjaya, S. (2008). User satisfaction with business-to-*employee* portals: Conceptualisation and scale development. *European Journal of Information Systems*, *17*(6), 649–667. doi:10.1057/ejis.2008.55

Turban, E. (2008). *Electronic commerce: A managerial perspective*. New Jersey: Prentice Hall.

Urbach, N., Smolnik, S., & Riempp, G. (2009). A conceptual model for measuring the effectiveness of employee portals. In *proceedings of the 15th Americas Conference on Information Systems*, San Francisco, California.

Vallerand, R. J. (1997). Toward a hierarchical model of intrinsic and extrinsic motivation. *Advances in Experimental Social Psychology*, 271–360. doi:10.1016/S0065-2601(08)60019-2

Venkatash, V., & Morris, M. (2000). Why don't men ever stop to ask for directions? Gender, social influence, and their role in technology acceptance and usage. *Management Information Systems Quarterly*, *24*, 115–139. doi:10.2307/3250981

Winefield, A. H., Gillespie, N. A., & Boyd, C. (2003). Occupational stress in university staff. *International Journal of Stress Management*, *8*(4), 51–63. doi:10.1037/1072-5245.10.1.51

Zhang, Y. (2005). Age, gender, and Internet attitudes among employees in the business world. *Computers in Human Behavior*, *21*, 1–10. doi:10.1016/j.chb.2004.02.006

Zikmund, W. G. (1997). *Business Research Methods* (5th ed.). Orlando: Dryden Press.

Zmud, R. W. (1979). Individual differences and MIS success: A review of the empirical literature. *Management Science*, *25*(10), 966–979. doi:10.1287/mnsc.25.10.966

Zoltman, E., & Chapanis, A. (1982). What do professional persons think about computers? *Behaviour & Information Technology*, *1*(1), 55–68. doi:10.1080/01449298208914436

KEY TERMS AND DEFINITIONS

Business-to-Employee (B2E): It represents an employee centric e-business initiative. Typical examples include various types of innovative web-based B2E products including employee portals, e-HR systems and ESS.

Portal: It is defined as a web site or service that offers a broad array of resources and services (e.g. e-mails, search engines, online shopping malls) to individuals. The first web portals were online services, such as AOL, that provided access to the Web.

Chapter 14
Assessing Empirical Relations of Music Piracy Behaviors with Lifestyle and Internet Self-Efficacy of Taiwan's Web Users

Ti Hsu
Chinese Culture University, Taiwan

Weng Wong
Chinese Culture University, Taiwan

Chien-Chih Wang
Chinese Culture University, Taiwan

Yeen Ni Li
Chinese Culture University, Taiwan

Pu Chuan Li
Chinese Culture University, Taiwan

Min Chi Tsai
Chinese Culture University, Taiwan

Yu Kai Tsai
Chinese Culture University, Taiwan

Sheng Hong Su
Chinese Culture University, Taiwan

ABSTRACT

Unlike past research on online music piracy with a focus on the economic or the legal perspective, the present study was designed to evaluate Web users' behaviors related to the music piracy empirically. In light of the newly ratified Copyright Law in Taiwan, the behavioral intentions of Web users towards the music downloading and/or P2P file sharing were studied using a sample of 317 Taiwan's Internet users. Results indicated that Web users were likely to reduce or modify their behaviors in order not to be in conflict with the new law. Results also showed that methods of music piracy used by respondents had nothing to do with lifestyle, but were more correlated to the Internet self-efficacy. Findings and their implications are discussed and suggestions for future work are offered in this chapter.

INTRODUCTION

The opening up of the Internet to the general public in 1995 and the passage of the Telecommunications Act of 1996 in the U. S. have had substantial impacts on the life of everyone, male or female, young or old, from how we live at home to how we learn in schools and/or how and what we do in the workplaces. While the availability of the Internet has certainly improved the lives of many, it has

DOI: 10.4018/978-1-60960-129-4.ch014

brought in a few potential problems as well. One of the problems would be what is referred to as the "social divide," or "digital divide" (Compaine, 2001; Young, 2001). Another area of concerns to the general public as well as the legislative body is the Internet privacy. A third area of potential problems is associated with the protection of the "intellectual property," including the copyright laws and the pattern laws.

Today, P2P (peer to peer) is considered by many to be a disruptive technology that may have changed the content ecosystem (Hietanen et al., 2008). One reason is because Internet users are increasingly paying less and less attentions to intellectual rights and copyrights. Copyright owners believe that their business, especially in the recording business, the movie industry, and the software industry, are hurting because of illegal downloading and file sharing freely among Internet users.

The recording business was booming in the 1990s and their album sales, according to the International Federation of the Phonographic Industry, IFPI, had a healthy 60% growth during the decade from US$24.1 billion to US$38.6 billion dollars. Digital music revenues were also increased from US$0.4 billion dollars in 2004 to US$2.9 billion dollars in 2007 and digital music as the percent of the total industry went from 2% in 2004 to 5% in 2005 to 11% in 2006 and to 15% in 2007 (IFPI, 2008). The healthy growth of the digital music might be partially attributed to the following reason: "Digital technology has shifted power to consumers, and music marketing must evolve from 'push' to 'pull'." according to Mark Hodgkinson, Executive Vice President of Global Marketing, EMI Music, "Our focus is to embrace this power and become completely consumer focused. By listening to and responding to our consumers and to our artists we aim to unlock the incredible potential for music in the digital environment" (IFPI, 2008, p.8).

However, the good days of the 1990s were over thanks to music piracy in general and to a new company named Napster in particular, which was created in June 1999. Sales worldwide on recorded music went down to US $32 billion dollars in 2002, which was a loss of 7% comparing to 2001, according to a news released by IFPI (2003), while sales of CD albums also suffered a 6% loss. This was the third consecutive loss in a row following a 5% loss in 2000 and a 8.8% loss in 2001. In other words, tens of billions of illegal music files, according to IFPI's estimates, were exchanged each year globally at an estimated ratio of 19 illegal downloads from digital platforms per track sold (IFPI, 2009). This could translate roughly into US$14.06 billion dollars globally (digital platforms in 2008, according to IFPI music report 2009, accounted for 20% of recorded music sales, 95% of online downloads were unauthorized, and total sales were estimated to be US$3.7 billion dollars).

On the other hand, researchers had a somewhat different perspective toward the amount of lost sales due to the music piracy. According to Zentner's study (2006), an average of 30% would have been lost due to the P2P file sharing. Another study conducted by Lee (2004) on the effect of bootlegging, which is entirely different type of sound recording infringement. His findings included "(1) the music released on bootlegs is music which has had no official release from a legitimate record label; (2) bootlegging is a relatively small-scale activity; (3) the people who buy bootlegs are extremely committed fans who use bootlegs as a way of maintaining an ongoing, meaningful relationship with their favoured artists or bands" (p. 167). This is not to mention the study done by Boorstin (2002), whose conclusion indicated that Internet access definitely had a positive and statistically significant effect on CD sales.

Despite the huge difference in perspectives viewed by the music industry and researchers, they both seem to agree that the music piracy has massively damaged potential investments in music and its creators, the artists. That probably explained why the Recording Industry Association of America (RIAA) in June 2003 took close to 600 people to court for the first time and sued them for music piracy. Today, more than 35,000 persons have been sued for infringing the copyright law over P2P networks.

Past research tends to focus on either the legal or the economic viewpoint, very little attention has been paid to the behavioral aspect (Kwong & Lee, 2002; LaRose et al., 2005). The present study intends to fill the gap by searching answers to the following four research questions. First, what were the media consumption behavior and habits of those who were engaged in online music downloading and/or file sharing in Taiwan? Second, what were the lifetstyles of those who downloaded music and/or shared music files online in Taiwan? Third, did the Internet self-efficacy play a role in affecting those who were involved in the music downloading/or file sharing? The fourth question was: what would the potential impact of the newly ratified Copyright Law in Taiwan be on the Internet users' behavior with regard to violations of intellectual rights and copyrights online? The fourth question was added into the study during the execution of the study. It's because the Legislative Yuan in Taiwan ratified the new addition to the Copyright Law on April 21, 2009, which was coincided with our work on the development of the survey questionnaire for the study. Under the new version of the Law, Internet service providers (ISP) are empowered to "strike out" any Internet users who would violate other people's copyrights and/or post unauthorized contents online.

BACKGROUND

Internet Self-Efficacy

The theory of self-efficacy was first conceptualized and brought to life by Bandura (1977). It is an important concept to help individuals understand how quickly they are capable of adopting new tools so that they may use the tools to help develop new skills. Self-efficacy relates to one's own perception or belief about his capability to perform a certain task (Bandura, 1977). How much an effort an individual is willing to make in order to deal with a given situation depending, to a large extent, on the strength of her belief. Self-efficacy, according to Gist and Mitchell (1992), is expected to affect not only one's effort, but also one's commitment and persistence. Oliver and Shapiro (1993) asserted that anyone with a high self-efficacy is more likely to be successful in a given task. "Self-efficacy belief," according to Choi et al., (2003), "is a significant predicator of behavioral choices in terms of goal settings, the amount of effort devoted to a particular task, and actual performance" (p. 357). Studies have shown that individuals with high self-efficacy tend to perform better than those with low self-efficacy because the perceived capabilities can significantly affect their willingness to engage in higher challenging tasks and their performance when everything else is being equal (Bandura, 1982).

Bandura (1977, 1986) suggests that expectations of personal efficacy can come from a variety of sources, including performance accomplishments, vicarious experience, verbal persuasion, and emotional arousal. Individuals often like to conduct a self-evaluation about their capabilities in line with the above sources before making their choices and committing their efforts, on the one hand, and may also compare their own capabilities against others, on the other. Self-efficacy is normally consisted of three components, namely, magnitude, strength, and generality. The magnitude portion is connected to the levels of task difficulty that individuals perceive they can achieve. The strength aspect of the self-efficacy is associated with a conviction regarding magnitude. As for the generality, it is the degree to which the expectation may be generalized across situations. Assessing the three components is intended to help explain and predict the dispositions, intentions, and actions of a person. Self-efficacy is a dynamic construct that can change across time pending on whether a person has expanded his information or experience.

Since self-efficacy is specific in terms of the context and domain, many variations of the self-efficacy scales, including the Internet self-efficacy, have been advanced for different disciplines and/or applications. Based primarily on Compeau and Higgin's computer self-efficacy scale (1995), Eastin and LaRose (2000) developed the first Internet self-efficacy scale, which was comprised of eight (8) items to measure a single factor, the basic knowledge of Internet, both the hardware and the software. It is not surprising to note that empirical studies (Mbengue & Hsu, 2006; Hsu & Huang, 2006) have shown the existence of a strongly positive correlation between the computer self-efficacy and the Internet self-efficacy, suggesting they might be interchangeable.

The Internet self-efficacy scale developed by Torkzadeh and Van Dyke (2001) was to measure three factors, namely browsing, encryption/decryption, and system manipulation and Tsai's Internet self-efficacy scale (2004) consisted of two factors: exploration and communication. Previous research has found significant correlations between the Internet self-efficacy and work/task performance (Joo et al., 2000; Tsai & Tsai, 2003; Hsu & Wang, 2003), the time spent online (Tsai, 2004), and the academic performance (Lynch & Dembo, 2004).

Since the early Internet self-efficacy scales developed by Eastin and LaRose (2000), Torkzadeh and Van Dyke (2001), Hinson et al., (2003), and Tsai (2004) were all pre-date the rise in the importance of Internet-related skills and all those skills covered in the early Internet self-efficacy scales could be considered as common or basic skills among today's users of the Internet, but today's Internet applications based upon Web 2.0 are much more advanced and sophisticated in terms of the skills needed to take advantage of their usage. This may simply suggest that the earlier Internet self-efficacy scales may have become obsolete and developments of new scales to assess the competence of today's Internet users are urgently needed. That may also help explain why recent empirical studies have uncovered no relationships between the Internet self-efficacy and Internet users' intentions to seek disaster-related information on the Internet (Lu et al., 2005), the instructors' decision not to adopt e-learning (Mbengue & Hsu, 2006), or students' willingness to participate in an online collaborative learning (Hsu, 2009).

Hypothesis 1: *A Web user's Internet self-efficacy was hypothesized to have a positive correlation with his/her downloading and/or file sharing behavior and habits.*

Lifestyle

An Austrian psychologist, Alfred Adler coined the term of "lifestyle" back in 1929 (Wiki, 2009). Since the 60s, the meaning of "lifestyle" has been broadened substantially. The simplest definition of lifestyle came from the sociological viewpoint, which characterized lifestyle to be the way a person lives. It might also reflect the attitudes, values, and viewpoints of someone. In marketing, "lifestyle", however, has been used as the foundation to segment individuals, a large crowd, in terms of their purchasing behavior in order to come up with what is called "market segmentations."

The concept of lifestyle, unlike the personality, may be utilized to evaluate a person's life in terms of his/her economic resources, i. e., time and money (Anderson & Golden, 1984). Two of the most widely used lifestyle measurements have been activities, interests, and opinions (AIO) rating statements and SRI's VALS (Moven & Minor, 2001).

Using a sample of 294 Web users, Kim et al., (2002) employed 27 lifestyle items to measure their Internet lifestyle. They were able to extract six factors, including fashion leader/innovator, imitator/flatter, considerable purchaser, social person, conservative/polite person, and family-oriented person. Based upon the factors, they uncovered a strong relationship of the Internet consumers' lifestyle with their attitudes towards Internet advertising and eventually product purchase intentions.

Another study by Yang (2004) also examined the impacts of Internet users' lifestyle on their views towards Internet advertisements. He concluded that segmentation based on lifestyle could indeed be used to discriminate users into different groups, so that innovative ads might be used to target those segmented audience effectively.

Hypothesis 2: *Lifestyle was hypothesized to have a significant relationship with methods of music downloading used by Web users.*

RESEARCH METHODOLOGY

Instruments

Two well developed instruments were adopted and used in the present study: lifestyle and the Internet self-efficacy.

In view of the lack of any reliable and valid Internet lifestyle instrument, the SRI's VALS-2 was used to measure the lifestyle of Internet downloaders and/or file sharers. The VALS-2 instrument had 35 items with a 4-point Likert scale (1=disagreeable and 4= agreeable). The reason for adopting the VALS-2 instrument is because "Perhaps the most frequent used psychological inventory of consumers is the VALS lifestyle classification scheme. Developed by the Stanford Research Institute (SRI), VALS has been widely used…to segment the market and provide guidance for developing advertising and product strategy" (Mowen & Minor, 2001, p. 114). The second version of VALS is called VALS-2, which was specifically designed to measure consumer buying patterns (Mowen & Minor, 2001). The VALS-2 instrument is also popular among researchers on consumers in Taiwan.

The Internet self-efficacy scale that was adopted here was developed by Hsu and Huang (2006). We decided to use the 36 items that survived the pilot test in that study as the starting point. A 7-point Likert scale was used where 1 indicates "strongly disagree" and "7" indicates "strongly agree." The Cronbach's alpha of the original scale was found to be 0.935.

Pilot Test

Hair et al., (1998) suggested the use of the following three criteria to test the reliability of an instrument: (1) the corrected item-to-total correlation must be >0.5; (2) squared multiple correlations exceed 0.3; and (3) the lower limit of Cronbach's alpha needs to be >0.6 for the exploratory research. The results based on a sample of 175 useful returns showed that the Cronbach's alpha for the 33-item VALS-2 (two items failed to satisfy the above mentioned criteria and were therefore deleted) to be 0.935; and for the 36-item Internet self-efficacy scale to be 0.963.

Procedure & Participants

The Website, www.my3q.com, was used to post the final version of the questionnaire. Www.my3q.com is based in Hong Kong and offers researchers to post their survey forms on it free of charge for two weeks. Currently, it is the most popular website among Web users who are interested in conducting Internet-related studies in Taiwan. For the present study, it was posted on www.my3q.com for a period of two weeks in April, 2009. At the end of two weeks, a total of 317 (145 males) useful returns were received.

Table 1. Music downloading preference of participants

Type of music	Number	percentage	Language of Music	Number	Percentage
Pop	104	13.28%	Mandarin	130	41.01%
Rock	34	10.73%	English	77	24.29%
Classic	31	9.78%	Japanese	64	20.19%
R & B	42	13.25%	Cantonese	24	7.57%
Jazz	21	6.62%	Taiwanese	4	1.26%
Others	85	26.81%	Others	18	5.68%
Total	317	100%		317	100%

RESEARCH FINDINGS

Profile of Participants

Nine different information items are included in the profile of participants: sex, age, educational attainment, monthly disposable income, daily usage and weekly usage of Internet by hours and days, respectively, favorite music, language of the preferred music, and methods of music downloading. The age distribution was from a low of 14 years old to a high of 30 years old with a mean of 21.35 years old, meaning respondents as a whole were a group of very young Internet users.

The majority of the respondents had at least college degrees (277 with bachelor's degrees and another 16 with Master's degrees), indicating that participants were a bunch of highly educated Web users. Only 14 of them were in senior high schools and five were in junior high school.

16.4% or 52 participants had less than two thousand dollars to spend as their monthly disposable income. Over one-third (116) of the respondents had a disposable income per month between NT$2k and NT$5K. Another 108 respondents (34.07%) had a monthly free spending money between NT$5k and NT$10k. The remaining 41 (12.93%) participants had more than NT$10k to spend as they please each month.

252 (118 males) respondents were using the Internet seven days a week. Only 65 (38 females) respondents used Internet less than daily. Of the 65 participants, 22 logged onto the Internet less than five days a week. When they were online, 28 (20 males) users stayed on 1 or 2 hours a day; 117 (58 females) consumed 3 or 4 hours a day; 103 (36 males) surfed 5 or 6 hours a day; and 69 (39 females) sit in front of the computer more than 6 hours daily.

When it came to the type of music they liked, pop music was on top of the list with 102 (41 males) followers. They were followed by R&B music (42 persons), Rock music (38 respondents) and classic music (31 fans). Chinese (Mandarin) music understandably was the most favored music with respondents (130 fans). English was the second most popular music among 77 persons. Japanese music was ranked the third in term of its preference with 74 followers.

Participants were also asked their preferred means of downloading music. Seven different methods were offered and participants were allowed to check more than one method. In other words, multiple choices were permitted in this question. 183 participants, as Table 2 shows, relied on the Web music sites to download their favorite music. The second most popular means of music downloading was to use special software such as foxy.bt and there were 157 respondents doing so. Music transferred from CD to PCs was picked as the third most popular means with 145 Internet users preferring it. Another 120 individuals indicated that they also liked to download music from Web forums making it the fourth preferred means of music downloading. Since there were 317 participants and 709 choices, it means that each participant used on average 2.23 methods, or

Table 2. Music downloading methods

Downloading methods (multiple choices)	Frequency	Percentage
Transfer music from CDs to PCs	145	20.5%
Downloading music with cell phones	16	2.3%
Using software, e.g., foxy.bt to download music	157	22.1%
Downloading from music Web sites	183	25.8%
P2P file sharing	60	8.5%
Downloading directly from music artist's Web sites	28	3.9%
Downloading from Web forums	120	16.9%
Total	709	100%

between two and three different methods to download their favorite music online.

Factor Analysis

A principal components analysis based upon the varimax rotation method was performed. In the process, the following criteria were utilized: (1) the assessment of the factorability of the correlation matrix; (2) the measure of sampling adequacy (MSA) to be 0.5 or higher; and (3) the communality that exceeds 0.6. Moreover, to determine how many factors to be retained, two other criteria including (1) eigenvalue that exceeds 1.0; and (2) the factor loading that exceeds 0.4 (for a sample size of 200 or higher) were employed (Hair et al., 1998).

Only 19 items of the VALS-2 survived the test of the first three criteria and were then used to help extract five factors labeled as follows: challenge, DIY, Confidence, Science & Engineering, and Fashion. The eigenvalue and percent of variance explained by each factor were: 6.519, 34.308%; 1.865, 9.77%; 1.57, 8.265%; 1.339, 7.049%; and 1.1012, 5.325%, respectively. Collectively, those five factors were able to explain 64.719% of the total variance. In comparison to Lin's (2000) findings with the VALS-2 instrument, the present study is different from Lin's in terms of two areas while both samples were drawn from Taiwan's Internet users. First, this study merely revealed five factors rather than seven factors that were uncovered by Lin. Here, the factors of "Learning" and "Narrowness" were excluded. Second, the present study relied on 19 items to explain 64.719% of the variance whereas Lin's study used 28 items to have a 63.74% of accumulated variance explained. The differences might be attributed to the difference in year, i.e., 2000 vs. 2009. Profile of Internet users in 2009 was drastically different from the profile of Internet users in 2000 in terms of demographic variables involved. This is because the number of Internet users has increased three or four times since the year of 2000. Back then, the vast majority of the Web users aged between 18 and 26 years old and were either college or graduate students. The age distribution of the present study was from a low of 14 years old to a high of 30 years old. As such, all the other socio-economic variables have been different as well.

Out of the 36 items of the Internet self-efficacy scale, one item did not meet the minimum criterion for the communality, which was 0.6, and was deleted as a result. The remaining 35 items that passed the test of the three criteria described above helped generate six factors, which are labeled as follows: instant messengers (F1), blogs (F2), online shopping information (F3), video functions (F4), photo albums (F5), and video sharing (F6). The eigenvalue and percent of the variance explained by each factor were: 12.554, 18.838% (F1); 3.631, 17.186% (F2); 2.462, 14.378% (F3); 1.999, 12.214% (F4); 1.422, 10.013% (F5); and 1.151, 7.435% (F6). Those six factors together explained 80.664% of the variance.

The differences between the present study and the earlier study conducted by Hsu and Huang (2006) might be attributed to two reasons. First, it has something to do with the difference in time. Data for the earlier study were collected in 2006 as opposed to the data collection efforts made in 2009 for the present study. Second, the sample

Table 3. Results of factor analysis on lifestyle & Internet self-efficacy

Lifestyle	Items	Internet self-efficacy	Items
Challenge	2,3,8,15,21,26, 29,30	Instant messengers	9,10,11,12,13,14
DIY	6, 12,14,19	Blogs	1,2,3,4,5,6,7
Confidence	5,17,24	Shop information	15,16,17,18,19
Science & Engineering	16,31	Video Functions	29,30,31,32
Fashion	4,28	Photo Albums	20,21,22,23
		Video sharing	33,34,35

of Hsu and Huang's (2006) study was composed of 100 percent college students using a snowball technique and whether they were Internet users or not was not a concern. The sample of the present study consisted exclusively Internet users and college students were accounted for 87% of the sample leaving the other 13% to be high school students, graduate students, or younger workers.

Correlation Analysis

Two correlation analyses were carried out, one for methods of music downloading with lifestyles and the other for methods of music downloading with the Internet self-efficacy. The results are presented in Tables 4 and 5, respectively.

Basically, not a single method of music downloading, as Table 4 above reveals, had a strongly, either positive or negative, correlation statistically with any of the five different lifestyles except one. The lone exception was the one between method number one, transferring music from CDs to PCs, and DIY ($r=0.116$, $p<0.05$). Technically speaking, transferring music from CDs to PCS may not be considered as downloading, but rather uploading.

A quick review of Table 5, one can see that only three Internet self-efficacy skills (factors), "video functions", "photo albums," and "video sharing," were significantly correlated to three methods of music downloading, including Method 3, Method 4, and Method 7. Specifically, Method 3 using software to downloading music online was positively correlated with photo albums ($r=0.135$, $p<0.05$). Method 4 (Downloading from music Web sites) was negatively correlated with video functions ($r=-0.151$, $p<0.05$). Method 7, downloading from Web forums, had a positive correlation with video sharing ($r=0.174$, $p<0.01$).

Potential Effects of New Copyright Law

On April 21, 2009, the Legislative Yuan of Taiwan ratified a new version of the so-called "Copyright Law (the China Post, 2009)." Under the new law, Internet service providers (ISPs) are empowered to strike out Web users who violate the copyrights

Table 4. Correlation results between methods of music downloading and lifestyles

	Meth 1	Meth 2	Meth 3	Meth 4	Meth 5	Meth 6	Meth 7
Challenge	.053	.069	.009	-.001	.096	-.077	-.025
confidence	.080	-.017	.046	-.043	.065	-.074	-.077
Fashion	.029	.040	.053	.109	.099	-.036	-.057
Science	.016	-.070	-.100	.010	.083	-.025	.072
DIY	.116*	.039	.027	.027	.076	.037	-.045

Note: see Table 2 for details of the downloading methods

Table 5. Correlation results between methods of music downloading and Internet self-efficacy

	Meth 1	Meth 2	Meth 3	Meth 4	Meth 5	Meth 6	Meth 7
Ins messag	.022	-.066	.082	-.098	.069	.028	.026
Blog	.032	.007	.057	.004	.107	.066	-.030
Shop info	.047	.043	.106	-.006	.040	.060	.078
Video Func	.109	.151	.114	-.151*	.066	.036	.052
Photo Alb Video	.052	.049	.135*	-.014	-.014	.054	.001
Shar	.048	-.019	.077	-.070	.074	.009	.174**

Note: see Table 2 for details of the downloading methods

of others or post unauthorized contents on the Internet. The new version of the law added five new articles into the existing Copyright Law, which were also referred to as the "four Nos and one Without." Specifically, there were: 1) NO Web downloading of music, videos, or software is allowed (article 1); 2) NO P2P file sharing on copyrighted articles, music, videos, or software is allowed (article 2); 3) NO post of other people's pictures or copyrighted articles without prior approval is allowed (article 3); 4) NO copyrighted music can be used in your own blog (article 4); and 5) WITHOUT prior authorization, other people's copyrighted materials cannot be sold online (article 5) (United Daily Newspaper, April 22, 2009).

We intended to examine Web users' responses toward the new law in terms of the following three new articles, namely article 1, article 2, and article 4. Table 6 below showed the results of the T-test on effects of new copyright law in terms of the three articles. The t-value was -11.104 for article one, which was significant at the 99% level; was -4.364 for article 2, which was also significant at the 99% level; and was 1.664 for article 4, which was only significant at the 90% level.

DISCUSSION AND CONCLUSION

Based on the statistical results discussed above, we may have uncovered a number of interesting points. First, profile of those who were actively involved in music piracy via either the music downloading on the Web or the P2P file sharing on music begin to surface. They tend to be college students, regardless of gender, whose ages are between 19 and 23 years old; whose disposable incomes fall between NT$2k and NT$10k per month; who are online seven days a week and spend at least 5 hours on the Web each day; who prefer Mandarin or English pop or R& B music; who generally download their music directly from music Web sites or used special music downloading software, such as Foxy.bt to get their preferred music; and who can perform a variety of Internet functions, including most of the seven Internet self-efficacy skills (factors).

Second, the statistical findings seem to flatly reject the first hypothesis regarding the lifestyle. The correlation between lifestyle and music downloading methods essentially does not exist at all except for a low positive correlation

Table 6. Results of T-test on effects of new copyright law

	t-value	Df	Sig (2-tailed)
Arti 1 (post-prio)	-11.104	316	0.000
Arti 2 (post-prio)	-4.364	316	0.000
Arti 4 (post-prio)	1.664	316	0.097

Article 1: I do download music or software online

Article 2: I do share music or other people's copyrighted articles with online friends

Article 4: I do use other people's music in my blog

($r=.116$, $p<.05$) between DIY and method one, which was the transfer of music from CDs to PCs. Strictly speaking, transferring music from legally purchased CDs to PCs may not be considered as downloading because it is more of uploading. If and when the uploading is not totally legitimate, how high a priority will this be in comparison to other illegal downloading activities? Moreover, what and how will the law enforcement people do to enforce the law in this regard?

Can the lack of any correlations between lifestyles of Web users in Taiwan and methods of music downloading be attributable to the fact that there was actually no correlations what-so-ever between the two variables, or that an inappropriate survey instrument, VALS-2 in this case, which, as we are fully aware, was designed to measure the offline, not online, behavior of individuals, was used? We don't know the answer to this question. A number of studies have been devoted to the development of an online lifestyle scale (Kim et al, 2001; Swinyard & Smith, 2003). Unfortunately, the validity of those instruments is still in question. In fact, the Swinyard & Smith's (2003) Internet shopper lifestyle measurement was tested initially in the present study, but failed drastically. As a result, we opted to go back to the VALS-2 instead.

In rejecting the first hypothesis due to the absence of any correlations between methods of music downloading and lifestyles of Taiwan's Internet users, we may conclude that the findings concerning lifestyle are inconsistent with many earlier studies (Kucukemiroglu, 1997; Kim et al, 2001; Swinyard & Smith, 2003; Lass & Hart, 2004; Yang, 2004; Brengman et al, 2005), which found lifestyle to be an important variable explaining consumers' behaviors.

Third, the correlation between music downloading methods and the Internet self-efficacy is somewhat a different story. Three skills (factors) of the Internet self-efficacy were found statistically to be correlated to three methods of music downloading, thus upholding the second hypothesis regarding the Internet self-efficacy. The three skills were "video functions," "photo albums", and "video sharing." However, the three correlations, two positive and one negative, were all low, meaning while the correlations were statistically significant, their relationships were all weak.

Since the P2P file sharing has a lot to do with the use of the instant messenger, the identification of the instant messenger skill in this case is justifiable and understandable. The existence of the correlation between the video sharing and the method of using Web forums to download and/or share music files does make sense. The skill of the file sharing is a necessary, though not a sufficient, skill to do the video sharing on the Web. Therefore, a person who is equipped with the skill of the video sharing online, he/she definitely will be able to carry out file sharing activities.

Web privacy is the only variable that was found to carry a negative correlation with methods of downloading music. The negative sign between Web privacy and music downloading methods in theory may be interpreted as follows: The more concern a Web user has toward the privacy, the less likely he/she will be involved in the music downloading activities, whether they use the special downloading software or the Web forums to do the downloading.

Finally, the ratification of the new Copyright Law in April 2009 in Taiwan may have strong impacts on Web users, who were used to downloading music online and doing P2P file sharing of music. For example, participants indicated that they intended to decrease ($t=-11.104$, $P<0.000$) the use of the Internet as a platform to download their music because it might violate the first "NO" article, i. e. NO Web downloading of music, videos, or software is allowed, and it could be a serious offense. They further revealed that their P2P file sharing activities involving the unauthorized distribution of copyrighted music track(s) to third parties online would also be reduced ($t=-4.364$, $p<0.000$) because it would be in a direct conflict with the newly added second article of the new Copyright Law, i. e., NO P2P file sharing on copyrighted articles, music, videos, or software is allowed. The behavioral intentions of participants in the study towards the first two articles of the Copyright Law are certainly in line with Fishbein and Ajzen's (1975) Theory of Reasoned Actions.

However, the finding regarding the post of unauthorized music on blogs may be in conflict with the Theory of Planned Behavior (Ajzen, 1985). Participants contended that they intended to step up its use ($t=1.164, p<0.097$) despite of the newly ratified Copyright Law. Why this would be the case is unknown. Could it be that they considered this "WITHOUT" clause in the new Copyright Law to be a less offensive act comparing to the other four "NO"? Or, were they inclined to believe that transferring music from their legally purchased CDs onto their blogs would be justified the use? In fact, they were not alone in this line of thinking. A Finnish study earlier discovered the same results and went even further to state that "...participants knew what amounted to copyright infringement, they had difficulties in recognising the legal uses of works that copyright laws permit (Hietanen et al, 2008, p. 31)." Whatever the thinking behind their responses on this one is certainly worthwhile looking into it in the future.

SUGGESTED FUTURE RESEARCH

In addition to the suggestion for further study cited above, there are a number of other areas that future researchers may be interested in exploring. First, the present study did not include the motivation of music piracy in its scope. For instance, do Web users pirate music online because their favorite music is not available in stores? Or is it because they prefer to sample the music online prior to making a purchase? Or is it because they don't like to buy the entire album just for one or two songs in that album? Those and other questions would be worth exploring in future research on music piracy.

Second, the number of Web users using file-sharing services for music, according to IFPI (2008), has been flat due to newer governmental laws and regulations and industrial efforts to crack down on the illegal use of music downloading and file sharing, does it mean that the number of music files downloaded or exchanged per user will be kept flat or constant as well? Or is it possible that those who intend to continue the use of music piracy will increase their practices in the number or frequency of music file sharing or downloading?

Third, as the mobile technology advances rapidly, newer forms of digital music piracy including the use of blogs, instant messengers, local network sharing, Bluetooth mobile sharing, etc. have emerged. What role or effects will flat rate 3G like in Japan play in or have on the future illegal music piracy?

Fourth, a recent study has indicated the potential dangers of newer forms of illegal downloading, which may lead to the installation of Trojan downloaders without the awareness of the Internet user. When and if Web users become aware of the potential dangers of those newer forms of illegal downloading, will they continue to practice the music piracy?

Finally, another potential area for future study would be to expose piracy behavior in the workplace. Nearly 10% of the British workers, according to a report submitted by ipsos-MORI to IFPI in 2007, took advantage of the workplace facilities to download music. Needless to say, British employees were not alone in this regard. The problem was even more serious in the U. S. with 15% of its workers downloading music illegally. We can only assume that piracy in the workplace may be equally bad in other parts of Europe, in Asia, including Taiwan, and the rest of the world. But how serious it is, we don't know. It certainly would be an interesting area to look into in the future.

REFERENCES

Ajzen, I. (1985). From intentions to actins: A theory of planned behavior. In Kuhl, J., & Bechmann, J. (Eds.), *Action-control: From cognition to behavior* (pp. 11–39). NY: Springer, Heidelberg.

Anderson, W.-T., & Golden, L. (1984). Lifestyle and psychographics: A critical review and recommendation. *Advances in Consumer Research. Association for Consumer Research (U. S.), 11*(1), 405–411.

Boorstin, E.-S. (2002). Music sales in the age of file sharing, Unpublished Bachelor's Thesis, Princeton University, Princeton, N. J.

Brengman, M., Geuens, M., Weijters, B., Smith, S.-M., & Swinyard, W.-R. (2005). Segmenting Internet shoppers based on their Web-usage-related lifestyle: A cross-culture validation. *Journal of Business Research, 58*, 79–88. doi:10.1016/S0148-2963(02)00476-9

Choi, J.-N., Price, R.-H., & Vinokur, A.-D. (2003). Self-efficacy changes in groups: Effects of diversity, leadership, and group climate. *Journal of Organizational Behavior, 24*(4), 357–372. doi:10.1002/job.195

Compaine, B.-M. (Ed.). (2001). *The digital divide: Facing a crisis or creating a myth?*Cambridge, MA: MIT Press.

Eastin, M.-S., & Larose, R. (2000). Internet self-efficacy and the psychology of the digital divide. *Journal of Computer-Mediated Communication*, 6(1). Retrieved on April 20, 2006 from http://jcmc.indiana.edu/vol6/issue1/eastin.html.

Fishbein, M., & Ajzen, I. (1975). *Belief, attitude, intention, and behavior: An introduction to theory and research*. Reading, MA: Addison-Wesley.

Gist, M.-E., & Mitchell, T.-R. (1992). Self-efficacy: A theoretical analysis of its determinants and malleability. *Academy of Management Review, 17*(2), 183–211. doi:10.2307/258770

Hair, J.-F., Anderson, R.-E., Tatham, R.-L., & Black, W.-C. (1998). *Multivariate data analysis* (5th ed.). Upper Saddle River, NJ: Prentice Hall.

Hietanen, H., Huttunen, A., & Kokkinen, H. (2008). Criminal friends of entertainment: analysing results from recent peer-to-peer surveys. *SCRIPTed, 5*(1), 31–49. doi:10.2966/scrip.050108.31

Hsu, T. (2009). Effects of Internet self-efficacy, emergent leaders, and personality on online discussion participation. In C. Fulford & G. Siemens (Eds.), *Proceedings of the ED-MEDIA 2009—World Conference on Educational Multimedia, Hypermedia, & Telecommunications*. (pp. 1730-1735). Chesapeake, VA: AACE.

Hsu, T., & Huang, L.-C. (2006). Developing an Internet self-efficacy scale of 2006. In T. Reeves and S. Yamashita (Eds.), *Proceedings of the 2006 World Conference on E-Learning in Corporate, Government, Healthcare & Higher Education*. (pp. 2000-2008). Chesapeake, VA: AACE.

Hsu, T., & Wang, H. F. (2003). Gender effects on collaborative learning behavior in CSCL. In A. Rossett (Ed.), *Proceedings of the 2003 World Conference on E-Learning in Corporate, Government, Healthcare & Higher Education*. (pp. 1919-1926). Chesapeake, VA: AACE.

International Federation of the Phonographic Industry. (2003). *Global sales of recorded music down 7% in 2002*. Retrieved on August 15, 2009 from http://www.ifpi.org/content/section_news/20030409.html

International Federation of the Phonographic Industry, (2008). *IFPI digital music report 2008: Revolution, innovation and responsibility*. Retrieved on August 15, 2009 from http://www.ifpi.org/content/section_news/20030409.html

International Federation of the Phonographic Industry (2009). *IFPI digital music report 2009: New business models for a changing environment*. Retrieved on August 15, 2009 from http://www.ifpi.org/content/section_news/20030409.html

Joo, Y.-J., Bong, M., & Choi, H.-J., (2000). Self-efficacy for self-regulated learning, academic self-efficacy, and Internet self-efficacy in Web-based Instruction. *Educational Technology, Research and Development*, 48(2), 5-17.

Kucukemiroglu, O. (1997). Consumer lifestyle dimensions and ethnocentrism: An empirical study. *European Journal of Marketing, 33*(5/6), 470–487. doi:10.1108/03090569910262053

Kwong, T.-C.-H., & Lee, M.-K.-O. (2002). Behavioral intention model for the exchange mode Internet music piracy. In R.-H. Sprague, Jr. (Ed.), *Proceedings of the 35th Hawaii International Conference on System Sciences*. (pp. 1-10). Big Island, HI: University of Hawaii.

LaRose, R., & Kim, J.-G. (2007). Share, steal, or buy? A social cognitive perspective of music downloading. *Cyberpsychology & Behavior, 10*(2), 267–277. doi:10.1089/cpb.2006.9959

LaRose, R., Lai, R.-J., Lange, R., Love, B., & Wu, Y.-H. (2005). Sharing or piracy? An exploration of downloading behavior. *Journal of Computer-Mediated Communication*, 11(1), Retrieved on August 10, 2006 from http://jcmc.indiana.edu/vol11/issue1/larose.html

Lass, P., & Hart, P. (2004). National cultures, values and lifestyles influencing consumers' perception towards sexual imagery in alcohol advertising: An exploratory study in the UK, Germany and Italy. *Journal of Marketing Management, 20*, 607–623. doi:10.1362/0267257041323936

Lee, M. (2004). The effects of piracy upon the music industry: A case study of bootlegging. *Media Culture & Society, 26*(2), 163–181. doi:10.1177/0163443704039497

Liao, C.-H., Tsou, C.-W., & Kao, Y.-C. (2007). Explaining consumer acceptance of online digital music. In R. Lee (Ed.), *Proceedings of the 13th Asia Pacific Management Conference*. (pp. 829-842). Melbourne University.

Lin, C.-Y. (2000). A study of the e-mail users' involvement in the viral marketing in Taiwan, Unpublished Master's Thesis, Da-Yeh University, Taiwan.

Lu, H.-Y., Case, D.-O., Lustria, M.-L. A., Kwon, N., Andrews, J.-E., & Cavendish, S. (2005). Predictors of online information seeking by international students when disaster strikes their countries. *Cyberpsychology & Behavior, 10*(5), 709–712. doi:10.1089/cpb.2007.9965

Lynch, R., & Dembo, M. (2004). The relationship between self-regulation and online learning in a blended learning context. *International Review of Research in Open and Distance Learning, 5*(2), 1–16.

Mbengue, I., & Hsu, T. (2006). To adopt a Web-based instruction: Is authority exercise an issue? In T. Reeves and S. Yamashita (Eds.), *Proceedings of the 2006 World Conference on E-Learning in Corporate, Government, Healthcare & Higher Education*. (pp. 2209-2216). Honolulu, HI: AACE.

Mowev, J.-C., & Minor, M.-S. (2001). *Consumer behavior: A framework*. Upper Saddle River, NJ: Prentice Hall.

Oliver, T.-A., & Shapiro, F. (1993). Self-efficacy and computers. *Journal of Computer-based Interactions, 20*, 81–85.

Swinyard, W.-R., & Smith, S.-M. (2003). Why people (don't) shop online: A lifestyle study of the Internet consumer. *Psychology and Marketing, 20*(7), 567–597. doi:10.1002/mar.10087

The China Post, (April 22, 2009). Piraters, Beware, p. 1.

Tsai, M. (2004). Developing the Internet self-efficacy scale (ISES). In L.Cantoni & C. McLoughline, (Eds.), *Proceedings of World Conference on Educational Multimedia, Hypermedia and Telecommunications*. (pp. 4406-4408). Chesapeake, VA: AACE.

Tsai, M.-J., & Tsai, C.-C. (2003). Information searching strategies in Web-based science learning: The role of Internet self-efficacy. *Innovations in Education and Teaching International*, *40*, 43–50. doi:10.1080/1355800032000038822

United Daily Newspaper. (April 22, 2009). Four nos and one without. P. 4.

Wikipedia (2009). *Lifestyle*. Retrieved on July 29, 2009 from http://en.wikipedia.org/wiki/Lifestyle.

Yang, K.-C.-C. (2004). A comparison of attitudes towards Internet advertising among lifestyle segments in Taiwan. *Journal of Marketing Communications*, *10*, 195–212. doi:10.1080/1352726042000181657

Young, J.-R. (2001, Nov. 9). Does "digital divide" rhetoric do more harm than good? *The Chronicle of Higher Education*, *48*, 1–5.

Zentner, A. (2006). Measuring the effect of online music piracy on music sales. *The Journal of Law & Economics*, *49*, 63–90. doi:10.1086/501082

ADDITIONAL READING

Arthur, C. (2003). Music download system Napster is back—but this time it's totally legal. *Independent*. Retrieved on Oct. 10, 2009 from http://news.independent.co.uk/digital/news/story.jsp?story=451710.

Bangeman, E. (2007). RIAA anti-P2P campaign a real money pit. Retrieved on Aug. 20, 2009 from http://arstechnica.com/news.ars/post/20071002-music-industry-exec-p2plitigation-is-a-money-pit.html.

Bhattacharjee, S., Copal, R.-D., & Sanders, G.-L. (2003). Digital music and online sharing: Software piracy2.0? *Communications of the ACM*, *46*(7), 107–111. doi:10.1145/792704.792707

Boston, W. (Nov. 2, 2000). Bertelsmann is betting that users, content rule with Napster deal. *The Wall Street Journal*.

Chen, A.-C. (2007). Copy locally, share globally: A survey of P2P litigation around the world and the effect on the technology behind unauthorized file sharing. *Intellectual Property & Technology Law Journal*, *19*(9), 1–4.

Chen, Y.-N., & Peng, I.-P.-L. (2003). Information goods pricing and copyright enforcement: Welfare analysis. *Information Systems Research*, *14*(1), 107–123. doi:10.1287/isre.14.1.107.14762

Clark, D. (Dec. 9, 1999). Recording industry group sues Napster, Alleging copyright infringement on Net. *The Wall Street Journal*, B18.

Giesler, M., & Pohlmann, M. (2003). The social form of Napster: Cultivating the paradox of consumer emancipation. *Advances in Consumer Research. Association for Consumer Research (U. S.)*, *30*(1), 94–100.

Giesler, M., & Pohlmann, M. (2003). The anthropology of file sharing: Consuming Napster as a gift. *Advances in Consumer Research. Association for Consumer Research (U. S.)*, *30*(1), 273–279.

Goodenough, O.-R., & Decker, G. (2006). Why do good people steal intellectual property? *The Gruter Institute Working Papers on Law, Economics, and Evolutionary Biology*, 4(1), Article 3. Retrieved on Oct. 30, 2009 from http://www.bepress.com/cgi/viewcontent.cgi?article=1017&context=giwp.

Gopal, R.-D., Sanders, G.-L., Sudip, B., Agrawal, M., & Wagner, S.-C. (2004). A behavioral model of digital music piracy. *Journal of Organizational Computing and Electronic Commerce*, *12*(4), 89–105. doi:10.1207/s15327744joce1402_01

Howe, J. (2003). Big champagne is watching you. *Wired Issue* 11.10, Retrieved Oct. 30, 2009 from http://www.wired.com/wired/archive/11.10/fileshare.html

Huang, C.-Y. (2006). File sharing as a form of music consumption. *International Journal of Electronic Commerce*, *9*(4), 37–55.

Hui, K.-L., & Peng, I.-P.-L. (2003). Piracy and the legitimate demand for recorded music. *Economic Analysis and Policy*, *2*(1), 1160–1166.

Jaisingh, J. (2007). Piracy on file-sharing networks: Strategies for recording companies. *Journal of Organizational Computing and Electronic Commerce*, *17*(4), 329–348.

Liebowitz, S. J. (2006). File-sharing: Creative destruction or just plain destruction? *The Journal of Law & Economics*, *49*(April), 1–28. doi:10.1086/503518

Petridis, A. (July 5, 2003). Let the playground pirates rule: The music industry's anti-download scare tactics just won't wash. *Guardian*. Retrieved on Oct. 30, 2009 from www.guardian.co.uk/online/comment/story/0,12449,992006,00.html.

Sudip, B., Gopal R. D., Kaveepan, L., Marsden, & James R. (2006). Impact of legal threats on music sharing activity: An analysis of music industry legal actions. *Journal of Law and Economics*, 49:1 91-114.

Wechsler, A., & Schink, G. (May 21, 2002). CDs: A better value than ever, *LECG*. Retrieved on Oct. 30, 2009 from http://web.archive.org/web/20040621120548/http://www.riaa.com/news/newsletter/pdf/CDValueStudy2002.pdf

KEY TERMS AND DEFINITIONS

Web Users: Those are the Internet users who are surfing on the World Wide Web to search for information, to communicate with other users, or conduct business activities.

Telecommunication Act of 1996: The Act that was approved by the 104th Congress on Jan. 3, 1966 and subsequently signed into law by President Clinton on Feb. 8, 1966, was the first major overhaul of the telecommunications law in the U. S. in 62 years ever since the enactment of the Communications Act of 1934. The primary consideration of the Act was to get rid of the regulatory barriers to entry in order to increase the "intramodal" competition among competitors relying on the same underlying technology to provide service. The Act however failed to foresee the "intermodal competition" and as such, the current statutory and regulatory framework may be inconsistent with, or unresponsive to, current market conditions (www.wikipedia.com, retrieved on Jan. 6, 2010).

Social Divide: It is also referred to as the digital divide, which is the gap between those who have and those who have not in terms of the knowledge and resources needed to effectively access to the Internet.

Internet Privacy: Internet privacy is the concern of personal privacy/information on the Internet. It includes a person's ability to control what information he/she reveals about oneself over the Internet and to control who gets to access that information.

Lifestyle: In its simplest way, lifestyle is defined by sociologists as the way a person lives. It might also reflect someone's attitudes, values, and viewpoints. In marketing, "lifestyle", however, has been used in connection with the concept of "market segmentations" meaning it serves as the foundation to segment consumers in terms of their purchasing behavior.

Internet Self-Efficacy: The theory of self-efficacy was first conceptualized and brought to life by Bandura (1977). It is an important concept to help individuals understand how quickly they are capable of adopting new tools so that they may use the tools to help develop new skills. Internet self-efficacy may be related to one's own perception or belief about his/her capability to perform a certain task on the Internet (Bandura, 1977).

Uploading and Downloading: In the information technology area, downloading is referred to the process of transferring data or files to a local system from a remote system, whereas uploading, which is an inverse operation, can be regarded as the process of sending data or files from a local system to a remote system.

Music Piracy: In the Internet age, any activities or behavior connected to the unauthorized or illegal reproduction and distribution of music online is considered as music piracy. The word "piracy" is used because copyright violation or copyright infringement may have been involved.

Peer-to-Peer File Sharing: File sharing, according to www.wikipedia.com, is "the practice of distributing or providing access to digitally stored information, such as computer programs, multi-media (audio, video), documents, or electronic books." File sharing may be conducted through various storage, transmission, and distribution models. The most popular way to do the file sharing nowadays is the use of peer-to-peer networking. While file sharing per se is not illegal, but the sharing of copyright protected music files without proper authorization is illegal. And there has been an increasing P2P file sharing of illegal music since 1990s with the aids of mp3.com, Napster.com, and other file sharing software and networks.

Chapter 15
Validity and Reliability Evidence of a New Version of the Internet Self-Efficacy Scale

Ti Hsu
Chinese Culture University, Taiwan

Liang Cheng Huang
National Taiwan University, Taiwan

ABSTRACT

The introduction of the theory of self-efficacy has had a profound impact on people in the academic arena. Its applications are like a wild-fire that has spread from one disciplinary area to the other. As such, various self-efficacy instruments have been developed and applied to various domain areas. Like all other disciplinary fields, the information technology field was affected as well. First, there was the computer self-efficacy scale developed by Murphy, Coover, and Owen (1989) and then the internet self-efficacy scale proposed by Eastin and LaRose (2000).

Applying the Internet self-efficacy scale, many studies have found significantly positive relationships between the Internet self-efficacy and behaviors under various settings. However, some late empirical research has failed to support the strongly positive correlations involving the Internet self-efficacy (Mbengue & Hsu, 2006; Hsu, 2009). This might be attributed to two factors: self-efficacy is, as Bandura (2006) indicated, a context-specific and/or domain specific, and the out-of-date of the earlier Internet self-efficacy scales due to a drastic advancement of the Internet technology.

DOI: 10.4018/978-1-60960-129-4.ch015

The purpose of the research was designed to bridge the gap and to update the Internet self-efficacy scale. Based on a sample of 1123 college students with 10 different majors in the northern, central, and southern portions of Taiwan, a new Internet self-efficacy scale based on 26 items was developed and validated statistically. The new version of the Internet self- efficacy scale was composed of five domains including blogs, auction, video sharing, photo albums, and wiki. Detailed evidence of the reliability and factorial analytic work were presented and suggestions for the future research were also discussed.

INTRODUCTION

The theory of self-efficacy was originally introduced and conceptualized by Bandura (1977). It is an important concept to help individuals understand how quickly they are capable of adopting new tools to help develop skills required by work that might previously be off limit to them earlier. Self-efficacy relates to one's own perception about his/her capability to perform a certain task (Bandura, 1977). An individual who will make an effort to deal with a given situation depends, to a large extent, on the strength of his/her beliefs. Self-efficacy, according to Gist and Mitchell (1992), is expected to affect one's effort, commitment, and persistence. The higher the self-efficacy a person has, according to Oliver and Shapiro (1993), the better chance that person will have to succeed in a given task. Conversely, the lower the self-efficacy he/she has, the better chance that person will fail. Studies have shown that individuals with a high self-efficacy tend to perform better than those with a low self-efficacy because the perceived capabilities can significantly affect their willingness to engage in higher challenging tasks and their performance when everything else is being equal (Bandura, 1982; Mentro et al., 1980).

Bandura (1977, 1986) suggests that expectations of personal efficacy can come from four different sources of information: namely, performance accomplishments, vicarious experience, verbal persuasion, and emotional arousal. Individuals often evaluate their capabilities in terms of those four sources of information before determining what choices to make and how much effort to put in. Individuals may also compare their own capabilities against others. Self-efficacy is normally composed of three components including magnitude, strength, and generality. The magnitude portion is related to the levels of task difficulty perceived by them in order to perform such a task. The strength aspect of the self-efficacy is associated with a conviction connecting to the magnitude. As far as the generality is concerned, it is the degree to which the expectation is generalized across situations. The purpose of the assessment of the three components is intended to help explain and predict the dispositions, intentions, and actions of a person. Self-efficacy is a dynamic construct that can change from time to time depending upon whether a person has acquired new information, experience, or skills.

Ever since the introduction of the concept, it has continuously gained its popularity and its practice had been rapidly proliferated. Actual applications of the concept of self-efficacy have been extended from the general self-efficacy (Schwarzer, 1992) to a wide variety of domains, including, but not limited to, career decision-making self-efficacy (Taylor & Betz, 1983), computer self-efficacy (Murphy, Coover, & Owen, 1989; Compeau & Higgins, 1995; Marakas et al., 1998), condom self-efficacy (Lawrence et al., 1990), creative self-efficacy (Tierney & Farmer,2002; Beghetto, 2006), COPD self-efficacy (Wigal et al., 1991), diabetics management self-efficacy (van der Bijl, 1999), drug avoidance self-efficacy (Martin, 1992), exercise self-efficacy (Benisovich, et al.,

1998), family business self-efficacy (DeNoble et al., 2007), HIV self-efficacy (Prochaska, 1992), mathematics self-efficacy (Betz & Hackett, 1983), occupational self-efficacy (Betz & Hackett, 1981), physical self-efficacy (McAuley & Gill,1983), science teaching self-efficacy (deLaat & Watters, 1995), and Web-based learning self-efficacy (Nahm & Resnick, 2008). The concept of self-efficacy has even be expanded beyond individuals into groups or communities, such as collective teachers self-efficacy (Schwarzer, Schmitz, & Daytner, 1999), community collective efficacy (Carrol et al., 2005), group self-efficacy (Gobson et al., 2000), team efficacy (Pease et al., 2001), and efficacy in technology-mediated distributed teams (Fuller et al., 2006-7).

Needless to say, Internet self-efficacy was also derived from the general self-efficacy concept and has been a very hot topic among practitioners of IT applications ever since the Internet became available to the general public. There has been a number of Internet Self-efficacy scales that were developed over time by various researchers (Eastin & LaRose, 2000; Torkzader & Van Dyke, 2001; Hinson, DiStefano, & Daniel, 2003; Tsai, 2004). Using those scales, past research discovered that the Internet self-efficacy had significant impacts on the use of IT-based system, on the time spent online (Tsai, 2004), on the preference toward constructivist web-based learning (Liang & Tsai, 2008), on the academic performance (Lynch & Dembo, 2004), on the high task perseverance (Hong, 2006), on the work/task performance (Barsnan, 1998; Joo, Bong, & Choi, 2000; Tsai & Tsai, 2003; Hsu & Wang, 2003), to name just a few.

Since self-efficacy is a context-specific and/or domain-specific (Bandura, 2006) and the rapid advancement of the Internet technology, the previously published Internet self-efficacy scales (Eastin & LaRose, 2000; Torkzader & Van Dyke, 2001; Hinson, DiStefano, & Daniel, 2003; Tsai, 2004) may no longer accurately assess the competence of individuals to perform a wide range of activities or tasks based upon or derived from Web 2.0 tools. For example, the Eastin and LaRose's Internet self-efficacy scale, which relied heavily on Compeau and Higgins' computer self-efficacy (1995) to develop its 8-item instrument, was to measure a single factor, the basic knowledge of Internet, both the hardware and the software. The development of Torkzadeh and Van Dyke's Internet self-efficacy scale (2001) was to measure three factors, namely browsing, encryption/decryption, and system manipulation. Tsai's (2004) Internet self-efficacy scale was proposed for measuring two subscales: exploration and communication.

In other words, both the computer self-efficacy and the previously proposed Internet self-efficacy scales might have been out of date in measuring today's users' self-efficacy online. It is because they were pre-date the rise in the importance of Internet-related skills and all those skills covered in the early Internet self-efficacy scales may be considered as common or basic skills among today's users of the Internet. That may help explain why recent empirical studies have uncovered no relationships between the Internet self-efficacy and Internet users' intentions to seek disaster-related information on the Internet (Lu et al., 2005), the instructors' decision not to adopt e-learning (Mbengue & Hsu, 2006), or students' participation in online discussions (Hsu, 2009).

Clearly, there is an urgent need for researchers and/or IT practitioners to propose new Internet self-efficacy scales in order to accept challenges brought up by the rapid advancement of the information technology in both the hardware and the software areas as well as its applications, such as Web 2.0, wikis, YouTube, Facebook, twitters, etc. The present study had two purposes in mind. First, it was intended to develop a new version of the Internet self-efficacy scale based on the most popular applications online today. Second, it was to verify that the previously published Internet self-efficacy scales were indeed all out of date.

METHODOLOGY

Instrument

The present study was primarily designed to develop a reliable, valid, and up-to-date version of an Internet self-efficacy construct to measure an user's belief of his/her capability to achieve independently the required task on the Internet. The development of a new version of the Internet self-efficacy scale was based on a review of the previously published self-efficacy scales (Eastin & LaRose, 2000; Torkzader & Van Dyke, 2001; Hinson, DiStefano, & Daniel, 2003; Tsai, 2004) and the relevant research work on the Internet self-efficacy along with authors' personal experiences with the Internet. Eventually, an instrument consisting of 125 items in 15 domains was initially proposed. This instrument used a seven-point Likert scale (Maurer & Piece, 1998) with one being the least agreeable and seven being the most agreeable, which was different from the scale adopted by Compeau and Higgins' computer self-efficacy (1995) and the Eastin and LaRose's (2000) Internet Self-efficacy scale. In addition, Bandura's guides for constructing self-efficacy scales (2006) were also consulted when the new Chapter became available. For the validity purpose, several MIS faculty members were also consulted for the contents of the instrument.

Pilot Test

Two classes of undergraduate students were used to serve as the sample of the pilot test. They were 113 students majoring in business from the largest private university in Taiwan. Three criteria (which would be discussed in more details in the reliability analysis section below) suggested by Hair, et al., (1998) were adopted in conducting the reliability analysis of the pilot test. As a result, 108 items in 15 domains (see Appendix) passed the initial test. The 15 domains were: browsing (9 items), searching (6 items), email (12 items), instant messenger (15 items), P2P (2 items) FTP (3 items), blogs (14 items), homepage (2 items), wiki (4 items), photo albums (7 items), photo sharing (5 items), online shipping (4 items), bbs (4 items), auction (11 items), and video sharing (10 items). The revised form of the instrument that contained 108 items in 15 domains was used in the study. Table 1 presents the mean, the standard deviation, and the size of the sample for each of the 108 items that survived the pilot test.

Participants

The sample employed in the research consisted of 1123 participants who answered the final version of the questionnaire, which would be discussed in the "instrument" section below. They were all traditional college students with majors in ten different fields, including but not limited to, business, liberal arts, medical sciences, performing arts, sciences and technology, and social sciences from various universities located in three parts of Taiwan: north, central and south.

The decision to use traditional college students as the sample was simple and straightforward. College kids were not only the first Internet generation kids, who would not be afraid of the new challenges brought up by the new technology, but also the segment of the population that used and still use the Internet most often and the most skillfully. Using today's college students as the sample to develop a new Internet self-efficacy sale, the new version of the scale hopefully would last longer than previous ones and than a version whose sample would base upon the general population rather than the college kids.

Since the participants of the study were all traditional college undergraduates, the range of their ages were mainly between 18 years old and 23 years old. Of the total participants, 22 percents or 247 participants were male students and 52 percents or 584 participants were female students. That leaves 26 percent or 292 participants who opted not to disclose their sex. It should be noted,

Table 1. Descriptive statistics of the 108 items

No.	Valid N	Mean	Std.D.	No.	Valid N	Mean	Std.D.	No.	Valid N	Mean	Std.D.
v1	1121	2.79	1.004	v37	1118	3.58	0.911	v73	1104	3.2	1.31
v2	1123	3.46	0.902	v38	1118	3.53	0.993	v74	1104	2.97	1.419
v3	1123	2.73	1.137	v39	1118	3.05	1.358	v75	1104	2.58	1.58
v4	1123	2.32	1.256	v40	1118	3.12	1.282	v76	1104	2.85	1.461
v5	1123	2.68	1.264	v41	1118	2.98	1.393	v77	1104	3.63	0.735
v6	1123	1.63	1.359	v42	1116	3.15	1.272	v78	1104	3.5	0.977
v7	1123	3.53	0.736	v43	1120	2.14	1.605	v79	1104	3.44	1.094
v8	1121	3.51	0.736	v44	1120	1.9	1.583	v80	1104	3.66	0.776
v9	1121	3.48	0.771	v45	1118	2.13	1.494	v81	1104	3.38	1.062
v10	1121	3.57	0.8	v46	1118	1.67	1.472	v82	1104	3.36	1.077
v11	1119	0.95	1.34	v47	1118	1.95	1.485	v83	1104	3.31	1.105
v12	1121	3.52	0.79	v48	1118	2.69	1.513	v84	1102	2.64	1.541
v13	1119	3.54	0.737	v49	1118	3.37	1.118	v85	1104	0.87	1.328
v14	1120	2.92	1.158	v50	1118	3.38	1.09	v86	1104	0.86	1.305
v15	1121	2.71	1.268	v51	1118	3.26	1.218	v87	1104	1.06	1.404
v16	1119	1.95	1.496	v52	1120	3.23	1.221	v88	1104	3.58	0.923
v17	1119	1.83	1.497	v53	1120	2.47	1.544	v89	1104	3.52	0.933
v18	1121	3.56	0.783	v54	1116	2.54	1.563	v90	1102	3.43	1.007
v19	1119	3.62	0.734	v55	1118	2.27	1.547	v91	1102	3.2	1.196
v20	1121	3.72	0.649	v56	1118	2.21	1.589	v92	1102	2.88	1.427
v21	1121	3.49	0.89	v57	1118	2.8	1.555	v93	1102	2.82	1.527
v22	1121	3.31	1.019	v58	1118	2.64	1.582	v94	1102	2.37	1.74
v23	1121	3.63	0.698	v59	1118	2.27	1.569	v95	1102	2.14	1.705
v24	1121	3.5	0.896	v60	1118	2.29	1.517	v96	1102	2.2	1.753
v25	1119	3.65	0.758	v61	1118	2.14	1.542	v97	1102	2.32	1.744
v26	1121	2.29	1.437	v62	1118	2.47	1.405	v98	1102	2.31	1.747
v27	1121	2.09	1.48	v63	1112	3.22	1.172	v99	1102	3.51	0.929
v28	1121	3.65	0.745	v64	1114	1.02	1.329	v100	1102	3.34	1.079
v29	1121	3.64	0.786	v65	1114	1.04	1.34	v101	1102	3.1	1.35
v30	1119	3.65	0.747	v66	1114	0.99	1.297	v102	1099	2.71	1.53
v31	1117	3.72	1.877	v67	1114	1.07	1.345	v103	1103	2.31	1.625
v32	1118	3.65	0.749	v68	1104	3.7	0.734	v104	1103	1.96	1.631
v33	1118	3.6	0.829	v69	1104	3.6	0.822	v105	1103	1.89	1.606
v34	1118	3.38	1.077	v70	1104	3.23	1.289	v106	1103	1.39	1.514
v35	1120	3.68	0.752	v71	1104	3.03	1.41	v107	1103	1.69	1.611
v36	1120	3.61	0.873	v72	1104	3.24	1.309	v108	1103	1.55	1.543

however, that female Internet users for the first time in 2005 surpassed the male users in Taiwan. In other words, starting 2005, there were slightly more females Internet surfers than the male counterparts in Taiwan. Hence, the majority of those who did not identify their gender were more likely to be male students in this case. Why they chose not to reveal their sex is unknown.

Procedure

Basically, the sampling method adopted in the present study was the snowball technique. More specifically, the initial approach was to contact three different college faculty members who were friends of the authors in three different universities with different disciplines and were asked if they were willing to use one class of their students to participate in the study. Once agreed, sufficient copies of the instrument were handed over in person or mailed to them to distribute among their students in classes. Students in those classes were briefed initially and then asked to participate voluntarily. If a student who was unwilling to do so was excused from answering the survey form.

Each of those instructors was further requested to recommend a friend who also was a college faculty member in different field at a different school in a different location. That person was subsequently contacted to ask his/her permission to participate in the study. This same process continued until a big enough sample was obtained. The data collection effort took more than a month in April and May of 2006. It should be noted, however, that a small percentage of participants did not complete the entire survey form because some of the questions might not applicable to them or they elected not to answer some of the questions in the survey form for one reason or another.

Statistical Analysis

The process of developing and validating a new Internet Self-efficacy instrument took place in two phases from the statistical viewpoint. A reliability analysis was first conducted in order to flush out those items that could not meet the three basic criteria, which are stated below in the reliability analysis section. It was then followed by a factor analysis to see how many factors the instrument could generate. The SPSS software was employed for the purposes of the statistical analysis.

RESULTS

Reliability Analysis

To conduct the reliability analysis, three criteria as suggested by Hair, et al., (1998) were adopted. First, an item was eliminated in performing the reliability analysis if the corrected item-to-total correlation (the correlation of the item to the summated scale score) was less than 0.40. The domain-sampling model provides a rational for this procedure. The key assumption of the domain sampling model is that all items, if they belong to the domain of the concept, have an equal amount of common core. If all the items in a measure are drawn from the domain of a single construct, responses to those items should be highly intercorrelated. The item-to-total correlation provides a measure of this. The second criterion used to delete an item was the multiple squared correlations, if the value of that item was below 0.30.

Finally, we examined the internal consistency (reliability) of an item using Cronbach's alpha to determine if additional item should be deleted without substantially lowering the reliability. The cutoff point for this criterion was less than 0.90 in the value of its Cronbach's alpha.

As a result of the reliability analysis, 72 of 108 items were eliminated from the further analysis. Another word, 36 remaining items were included in the second phase of the statistical analysis, i. e., the factor analysis, which will be discussed below. Table 2 presents only the 26 items that survived the reliability analysis, whose Cronbach's alpha

Table 2. Results of the reliability analysis, communality, and MSA

Item #	Corrected Item-Total Correlation	Squared Multiple Correlation	Cronbach's Alpha if Item Deleted	Extraction Communalities	MSA
v48	0.581476	0.624947	0.948501	0.606949	0.978
v53	0.685123	0.83115	0.947386	0.826804	0.937
v54	0.683888	0.84426	0.947392	0.848132	0.939
v55	0.725893	0.851529	0.946939	0.820658	0.931
v56	0.73866	0.815059	0.946766	0.770515	0.945
v57	0.630371	0.844468	0.947982	0.773965	0.912
v58	0.678478	0.816462	0.947448	0.753063	0.932
v59	0.661206	0.601092	0.947642	0.581237	0.982
v64	0.536252	0.834412	0.948922	0.867462	0.901
v65	0.529307	0.871592	0.948988	0.932259	0.858
v66	0.532045	0.828539	0.948961	0.847989	0.895
v70	0.61157	0.786984	0.948242	0.752991	0.93
v71	0.665205	0.736077	0.947659	0.653142	0.935
v72	0.605132	0.856369	0.94829	0.89877	0.894
v73	0.632654	0.851729	0.948035	0.887603	0.905
v74	0.668829	0.686511	0.947614	0.673953	0.967
v94	0.645052	0.750097	0.947872	0.756812	0.969
v95	0.635287	0.824809	0.94797	0.839417	0.952
v96	0.679838	0.807706	0.947447	0.818112	0.962
v97	0.681945	0.898058	0.947418	0.931931	0.916
v98	0.659336	0.870906	0.947699	0.89613	0.929
v104	0.606657	0.651985	0.948269	0.625508	0.939
v105	0.611261	0.648109	0.948207	0.622459	0.939
v106	0.574041	0.675035	0.948581	0.685582	0.949
v107	0.613004	0.777737	0.948189	0.811749	0.900
v108	0.586969	0.773409	0.948452	0.82165	0.899

was 0.95, and the tests of the Kaiser's measure of sampling adequacy (MSA) and the final communality estimates.

Factor Analysis

The 36 items that survived the reliability analysis were included in the factor analysis. In performing the exploratory factor analysis, two other criteria were added in the process in order to determine if further cuts were needed. They were the Kaiser's measure of sampling adequacy (MSA) and the communality estimates (Hair, et al., 1998). MSA quantifies the degree of inter-correlations among the variables and the appropriateness in the factor analysis. This index ranges from 0 to 1, reaching 1 when each variable is perfectly predicted without error by the other variables. The cutoff point for the measure of sampling adequacy was below 0.50. The final test for an item to remain in the factor analysis was the communality, whose criterion was 0.60 or above. In other words, an item had to exceed 0.60 in communality in order to be included in the maximum likelihood analysis. All the 36 items passed the test of the Kaiser's measure of sampling adequacy. However, 10 items failed to meet the test of the final communality estimates and were subsequently eliminated. Consequently, only 26 items were left for the inclusion of the maximum likelihood analysis.

An exploratory factor analysis was in line to be carried out using the Maximum Likelihood as the means of extraction and the Promax with Kaiser Normalization technique as the method of rotation. Without specifying the number of factors, the factor analysis was conducted utilizing an eigenvalue of 1.0 or higher, or the screen, and a factor loading of 0.40 or above. It eventually came up with five different factors derived from 26 items. Table 3 displays the five factors derived from the 26 items along with their eigenvalues, the variance explained by each factor and the cumulative variance explained collectively by the five factors.

The factor structure was easy to interpret corresponding to blogs, auction, video sharing, photo albums, and wiki. As can be seen from Table 3, factor 1, blogs, with eight items and an eigenvalue of 11.12873, was able to explain 42.80282% of the variance all by itself. The second factor, auction, which had five items and an eigenvalue of 4.055477, explained another 15.59799% of the variance. The third factor was video sharing, which was also a five-item factor with an eigenvalue of 2.0847423 and explained another 8.0182395% of the variance. Photo albums, another five-item factor, had an eigenvalue of 1.613102 and explained 6.204237% of the variance. Finally, it was the wiki, which was a three-item factor and had an eigenvalue of 1.422789. The wiki factor was able to explain 5.472266 of the variance. Collectively, those five factors helped explain 78.09555 of the total variance.

Table 4 presents the Pearson correlation matrix among the five factors derived from the factor analysis. The correlation matrix clearly indicates that all correlations were positive and were statistically significant at the 99%. Specifically, blogs had a positive correlation with auction ($r=0.378$, $p<0.01$); with video sharing ($r=0.377$, $p<0.01$); with video sharing ($r=0.625$, $p<0.01$); and with wiki ($r=0.339$, $p<0.01$). Auction also had a positive correlation with video sharing ($r=0.553$, $p<0.01$); with photo albums ($r=0.384$, $p<0.01$); and with wiki ($r=0.418$, $p<0.01$). The correlation between video sharing and photo albums was a positive and medium one ($r=0.365$, $p<0.01$) and the correlation between video sharing and wiki was also a positive one ($r=0.547$, $p<0.01$). Finally, there was a positive correlation between photo albums and wiki ($r=0.183$, $p<0.01$).

DISCUSSION AND SUMMARY

Findings

The statistical findings of the present study revealed two facts, which basically offer answers to the two underlying research questions. First, it uncovered that there were five domains that today's Internet users would consider to be competent in terms of its current applications. Second, none of the domains that were included in the previously published Internet self-efficacy scales survived either the reliability test or the factor analysis.

The findings of the five domains are not surprised at all, they were simply a reflection of the reality, a reality that we as researchers have to face because today's users are much too complex than the Internet users of a few years ago in terms of the applications and their preferences. For example, Firefox browser usage globally, according to OneStat.com's survey conducted in Nov. 2005 (Computerworld, July 12, 2006), was up 2.82% from April 2005 at 11.51%. Microsoft's IE went down by 1.18% from April 2005 to 85.45%. The other popular browsers globally were Apple Inc.'s Safari which had 1.84% usage; Opera whose

Table 3. Factor analysis results of the Internet self-efficacy measure

	Factors				
Item number	**Blogs**	**Auction**	**Video**	**Photo Albums**	**Wiki**
v53	0.944				
v54	0.94				
v55	0.919				
v56	0.851				
v58	0.849				
v57	0.843				
v48	0.707				
v59	0.696				
v97		0.974			
v98		0.969			
v95		0.927			
v96		0.859			
v94		0.855			
v108			0.951		
v107			0.926		
v106			0.773		
v105			0.749		
v104			0.744		
v72				0.986	
v73				0.959	
v70				0.827	
v74				0.699	
v71				0.66	
v65					0.972
v64					0.927
v66					0.902
Eigenvalue	11.12873	4.055477	2.0847423	1.613102	1.422789
percent of Variance explained	42.80282	15.59799	8.0182395	6.204237	5.472266
Cumulative percent of variance explained	42.80282	58.40081	66.419046	72.62328	78.09555
Extraction Method: Maximum Likelihood. Rotation Method: Promax with Kaiser Normalization. Rotation converged in 6 iterations.					

global usage was 1%; and Netscape which had 0.16% usage.

Phishing, according to the new Anti-Phishing Act of 2005 in California (McMillian, 2005), was made illegal. This new law was designed to protect Internet users from tricking into revealing their own personal information, including personal ID, social security number, banking account numbers,

Table 4. The Pearson correlation matrix

Factor	1. blogs	2. auction	3. Video sharing	4. Photo albums	5. Wiki
1	1.000	.378**	.373**	.625**	.339**
2	.378**	1.000	.553**	.384**	.418**
3	.373**	.553**	1.000	.365**	.547**
4	.625**	.384**	.365**	1.000	.183**
5	.339**	.418**	.547**	.183**	1.000

** Correlation is significant at the 0.01 level (2 tailed)

date of birth, password, etc. Without the law, how many Internet users would know how to identify phishing when they see one? The above examples just show how different current users' preferences or behavior may have been altered as a result of the change of their applications.

In a study to test if the exercise of authority was an issue for college faculty members to consider the adoption of the Web-based instruction, Mbengue and Hsu (2006) found that the Internet self-efficacy was not a factor at all. Hsu (2009) studied the effects of Internet self-efficacy, leadership emergence, and personality on online group interactions among EMBA Students and uncovered that Internet self-efficacy also was unimportant. In either case, the author(s) included a previously published Internet self-efficacy scale as part of the questionnaire. The exclusion of the items associated with the previously published Internet self-efficacy scales in the present study seem to be consistent with the results of Mbengue and Hsu (2006).

LIMITATIONS AND SUGGESTIONS FOR FUTURE RESEARCH

In the process of developing the new version of the Internet self-efficacy scale, we were encountered or made realize a number of problems and/or limitations that are worth noting and that may serve as the new directions for future studies.

First and foremost, the life cycle of an Internet self-efficacy scale seems to get shorter and shorter because new applications of Internet technologies are popping up so fast and so sudden. For example, between the time we first initiated the project in late 2005 and the time when we completed the draft of the instrument in April, 2006, we witnessed the emergence and the rapid gaining popularity of a few new applications, such as podcast, widget/gadget/dashboard and AJAX, etc. This is not to mention the term of iLife (abbreviation of "Internet Life"), which, according to wikipedia (www.wikipedia.com), is a collection of software products created by Apple and designed for Mac OS X, for the use of creating, organizing, viewing and manipulating digital contents. As of iLife '06, iLife consisted of six components: iTunes, iPhoto, iMovie, iDVD, GarageBand, and iWeb. The application suite is included with all Macintoshes bought from Apple.

We were debating constantly as to which one, if any, of the newer applications should be included in the instrument that was being developed. We finally ended up with a new instrument containing 15 domains of applications with 125 items to be tested and validated. As such, we had to leave regretfully many of the newer applications, such as the ones cited above, out. It is doubtless in our mind that these and other new applications will gain their momentum soon, thus making the need for a new scale an inevitable task in the not too distant future.

Second, to develop a list of possible Internet technologies for the inclusion of the new instrument turned out to be a much tougher job than either of us had anticipated. Take the purchasing behavior for example. Should we combine the buying behavior of the tangible goods, such as books, CDs, with intangible goods, such as data, files, pictures, logos, etc. into one category or should we separate them as two different categories? Moreover, should we distinguish purchases of goods from dot.com only from purchases of goods from click-and-mortars? If so, how? Another case in point is the web browser. After reviewing many relevant literatures and discussing with various experts and professionals in the information technology area, we were still not sure if there were major differences between surfing on the Internet and the web browser from the viewpoints of end-users, who after all would be the ones to answer the instrument.

Next, the sample was drawn entirely from traditional college students in Taiwan and not in a random fashion. There are actually two issues involved here. The first was the college sample. There was in fact a debate whether the population should be the general public or should it be limited to the college students. Eventually two factors dictated the final decision. One consideration had something to do with the life cycle of the instrument. We thought using college students, who basically nowadays are Internet generation kids, would give us an instrument that could last somewhat longer than the general public might have given us. The other thinking was that given the large number of subjects required, normally a ratio of 10:1 (10 subjects per one item) to conduct the needed statistical analyses and the financial constraint faced by us, it would be easier to rely on the college kids to serve as the population.

The second issue was the randomness of the sample. The decision to go with the snowball technique in the sampling method was purely a financial one, especially to gather such a large sample in a relatively short time period. Therefore, the representativeness of the sample could probable be an issue given that there are vast differences among college students in terms of public vs. private universities, majors or disciplines, and the location of the school drawn, such as urban, suburban, or even rural areas.

The generalization of the present research is limited by the geographic scope of the sample. The sample contained disproportionately small representations of young people and females. As a one-shot survey study, the direction of causation cannot be established. Indeed, within SCT reciprocal causation is recognized. For example, self-efficacy may serve as the necessary, though not the sufficient, condition for achieving a task successfully, which may in turn help increase one's self-efficacy.

Moreover, the potential problem rests on the instrument itself. Despite the fact that we narrowed down the total items from more than two hundreds to 108 items after the pilot test, the total number of items included in the final instrument remained, as we believed, too big. As a result, the quality of the results we received from the respondents might have suffered due to a lack of patience or negligence of respondents.

Finally, the present research presents a signal which is loud and clear. That signal is that the Internet self-efficacy instrument needs periodically update because self-efficacy is after all a context- and/or domain-specific and because the Internet usage applications evolve so rapidly, so drastically, and so fundamentally. As such, it may be a good idea to revise the instrument once every few years. In addition, mobile technology including 3G and 3.5G is gaining a lot attention lately. It may explain why Wang and Wang's work (2008) on the development of a mobile computer self-efficacy scale is not a surprise at all and may be a new trend for future research as well.

REFERENCES

Bandura, A. (1977). Self-efficacy: Toward a unifying theory of behavioral change. *Psychological Review*, *84*, 191–215. doi:10.1037/0033-295X.84.2.191

Bandura, A. (1982). Self-efficacy mechanisms in human agency. *The American Psychologist*, *37*, 122–147. doi:10.1037/0003-066X.37.2.122

Bandura, A. (1997). *Self-efficacy: The exercise of control*. New York: W.H. Freeman.

Bandura, A. (2006). Guides for constructing self-efficacy scales. In Pajares, F., & Urdan, T. (Eds.), *Self-efficacy beliefs of adolescents*. Greenwich, Conn: IAP – Information Age Publication, Inc.

Beghetto, R.-A. (2006). Creative self-efficacy: Correlates in middle and secondary students. *Creativity Research Journal*, *18*(4), 447–457. doi:10.1207/s15326934crj1804_4

Benisovich, S.-V., Rossi, J.-S., Norman, G.-J., & Nigg, C.-R. (1998). *Development of a Multidimensional Measure of exercise Self-efficacy*. Poster presented at the Society of Behavioral Medicine (SBM). New Orleans.

Betz, N.-E., & Hackett, G. (1998). *Manual for the occupational self-efficacy scale*. Retreived on Aug. 24, 2009 fromhttp://seamonkey.ed.asu.edu/-gail/occsel.htm.

Carroll, J.-M., Rosson, M.-B., & Zhou, J.-Y. (2005). Collective efficacy as a measure of community, computers and human interface, Portland.

Compeau, D.-R., & Higgins, C.-A. (1995). Computer self-efficacy: Development of a measure and initial test. *Management Information Systems Quarterly*, *19*(2), 189–211. doi:10.2307/249688

Computerworld, (July 12, 2006). *Firefox use growing around the world.*

deLatrt, J., & Watters, J. (1995). Science teaching self-efficacy in a primary school: A case study. *Research in Science Education*, *25*(4), 453–464. doi:10.1007/BF02357387

DeNoble, A., Ehrlich, S., & Singh, G. (2007). Toward the development of a family business self-efficacy scale: A resource-based perspective. *Family Business Review*, *20*(2), 127–240. doi:10.1111/j.1741-6248.2007.00091.x

Dinev, T., & Koufteros, X. (2002). *Self-efficacy and Internet usage: Measurement and factorial validity*. Paper presented at the Decision Science Institute Conference, San Diego, CA.

Eastin, M.-S., & Larose, R. (2000). Internet self-efficacy and the psychology of the digital device. *Journal of Computer-Mediated Communication*, 6(1). Retrieved on April 20, 2006 from http://jcmc.indiana.edu/vol6/issue1/eastin.html.

Ertnet, P.-A., Evenbeck, E., Cennamo, K.-S., & Lehman, J.-D. (1994). Enhancing self-efficacy for computer technologies through the use of positive classroom experience. *Educational Technology Research and Development*, *42*(3), 45–62. doi:10.1007/BF02298094

Fuller, M.-A., Hardin, A.-M., & Davison, R.-M. (n.d.). (2006-7). Efficacy in technology-mediated distributed teams. *Journal of Management Information Systems*, *23*(3), 209–235. doi:10.2753/MIS0742-1222230308

Gist, M.-E., & Mitchell, T.-R. (1992). Self-efficacy: A theoretical analysis of its determinants and malleability. *Academy of Management Review*, *17*(2), 183–211. doi:10.2307/258770

Gobson, C.-B., Randel, A.-E., & Earley, P.-C. (2000). An empirical test of multiple assessment methods. *Group & Organization Management*, *25*(1), 67–97. doi:10.1177/1059601100251005

Gorsuch, R.-L. (1983). *Factor analysis*. Hillsdale, N.J.: Lawrence Erlbaum Associates.

Hinson, J., DiStefano, C., & Daniel, C. (2003). The Internet self-perception scale: measuring elementary students' level of self-efficacy regarding Internet use. *Journal of Educational Computing Research*, *29*(2), 209–228. doi:10.2190/BWGN-84AE-9AR6-16DY

Hong, T. (2006). The Internet and tobacco cessation: The roles of Internet self-efficacy and search task on the information-seeking process. *Journal of Computer-Mediatated Communication*, 11(2), Retrieved on July 5, 2008 from http://jcmc.indiana.edu/vol11/issue2/hong.html.

Hsu, M.-H., & Chiu, C.-M. (2004). Internet self-efficacy and electronic service acceptance. *Decision Support Systems*, *38*, 369–381. doi:10.1016/j.dss.2003.08.001

Hsu, T. (2009). Effects of Internet self-efficacy, emergent leaders, and personality on online discussion participation. In C. Fulford and G. Siemens (Eds.), *Proceedings of the ED-MEDIA 2009—World Conference on Educational Multimedia, Hypermedia, & Telecommunications*. (pp. 1730-1735). Chesapeake, VA: AACE.

Hsu, T., & Wang, H.-F. (2003). Gender effects on collaborative learning behavior in CSCL, In A Rosset (Ed.), *Proceedings of the 2003 - World Conference on E-Learning in Corporate, Government, Healthcare & Higher Education*. (pp. 1919-1926). Chesapeake, VA: AACE.

Joo, Y.-J., Bong, M., & Choi, H.-J. (2000). Self-efficacy for self-regulated learning, academic self-efficacy, and Internet self-efficacy in Web-based instruction. *Educational Technology Research and Development*, *48*(2), 5–17. doi:10.1007/BF02313398

Kaiser, H.-F. (1970). A second-generation little jiffy. *Psychometrika*, *35*, 401–415. doi:10.1007/BF02291817

Kaiser, H.-F. (1974). Little jiffy, mark IV. *Educational and Psychological Measurement*, *34*, 111–117. doi:10.1177/001316447403400115

Lawrence, L., Levy, S., & Rubinson, L. (1990). Self-efficacy and AIDS prevention for pregnant teens. *The Journal of School Health*, *60*, 19–24. doi:10.1111/j.1746-1561.1990.tb04771.x

Liang, J.-C., & Tsai, C.-C. (2008). Internet self-efficacy and preferences toward constructivist Internet-based learning environments: A study of pre-school teachers in Taiwan. *Journal of Educational Technology & Society*, *11*(1), 226–237.

Lynch, R., & Dembo, M. (2004). The relationship between self-regulation and online learning in a blended learning context. *International Review of Research in Open and Distance Learning*, *5*(2), 1–16.

Ma, Q.-X., & Liu, L.-P. (2005). The role of Internet self-efficacy in the acceptance of Web-based electronic medical records. *Journal of Organizational and End User Computing*, *17*(1), 38–57.

Marakas, G.-M., Yi, M.-Y., & Johnson, R.-D. (1998). The multilevel and multifacted character of computer self-efficacy: Toward clarification of the construct and an integrated framework for research. *Information Systems Research*, *9*, 126–163. doi:10.1287/isre.9.2.126

Maurer, T.-J., & Piece, H.-R. (1998). A comparison of Likert scale and traditional measures of self-efficacy. *The Journal of Applied Psychology*, *83*(2), 324–329. doi:10.1037/0021-9010.83.2.324

Mbengue, I., & Hsu, T. (2006). To adopt a Web-based instruction: Is authority exercise an issue? In T.C. Reeves & S.F. Yamashita (Eds.), *Proceedings of the 2006 World Conference on E-Learning in Corporate, Government, Healthcare & Higher Education*, (pp. 2209-2216). Chesapeake, VA: AACE.

McAuley, E., & Gill, D. (1983). Reliability and validity of the physical self-efficacy scale in a competitive sport setting. *Journal of Sport & Exercise Psychology*, *5*(4), 410–418.

McMillian, R. (Dec. 12, 2006). Rock band "Phish" blamed for surge in phishing. *Infoworld.* Retrieved on June 10, 2009 from http://www.infoworld.com/article/06/12/12/HNrockphish_1.html.

Murphy, C.-A., Coover, D., & Owen, S.-V. (1989). Development and validation of the computer self-efficacy scale. *Educational and Psychological Measurement*, *49*, 893–899. doi:10.1177/001316448904900412

Nahm, E.-S., & Resnick, B. (2008). Development and testing of the Web-based learning self-efficacy scale (WBLSES) for older adults. *Ageing International*, *32*(1), 3–14. doi:10.1007/s12126-008-9003-6

Oliver, T.-A., & Shapiro, F. (1993). Self-efficacy and computers. *Journal of Computer-Based Interactions*, *20*, 81–85.

Pease, D.-G., Zhang, J.-J., & Barkouras, A.-K. (2001). Relations of game role and team success to team efficacy in boys' varsity high school basketball teams. *Research Quarterly for Exercise and Sport*, *72*(1), A90.

Prochaska, J., DiClemente, C., & Norcross, J. (1992). In search of how people change: applications to addictive behaviors. *The American Psychologist*, *47*, 1102–1114. doi:10.1037/0003-066X.47.9.1102

Robinson, J.-P., Shaver, P.-R., & Wrightsman, L.-S. (1991). Criteria for scale selection and evaluation. In Robinson, J.-P., Shaver, P.-R., & Wrightsman, L.-S. (Eds.), *Measurement of personality and social psychological attitude*. San Diego, CA: Academic Press.

Schwarzer, R., Schmitz, G.-S., & Daytner, G.-T. (1999). Collective teachers self-efficacy. Retrieved on Aug. 24, 2009 from http://web.fu-berlin.de/gesund/skalen/Language_Selection/Turkish/Collective_Teacher_Self-Effica/collective_teacher_self-effica.htm.

Tierney, P., & Farmer, S.-M. (2002). Creative self-efficacy: Its potential antecedents and relationship to creative performance. *Academy of Management Journal*, *45*, 1137–1148. doi:10.2307/3069429

Torkzadeh, G., & Van Dyke, T.-P. (2001). Development and validation of an Internet self-efficacy scale. *Behaviour & Information Technology*, *20*(4), 275–280. doi:10.1080/01449290110050293

Tsai, M. (2004). Developing the Internet self-efficacy scale (ISES). In L. Cantoni & C. McLoughlin (Eds.), *Proceedings of World Conference on Educational Multimedia, Hypermedia and Telecommunications*, (pp. 4406-4408). Chesapeake, VA: AACE.

Tsai, M.-J., & Tsai, C.-C. (2003). Information searching strategies in Web-based science learning: The role of Internet self-efficacy. *Innovations in Education and Teaching International*, *40*, 43–50. doi:10.1080/1355800032000038822

van der Bijl, J., van Poelgeest-Eeltink, A., & Shortridge-Baggett, L. (1999). The psychometric properties of the diabetes management self-efficacy scale for patients with Type 2 diabetes mellitus. *Journal of Advanced Nursing*, *30*(2), 352–359. doi:10.1046/j.1365-2648.1999.01077.x

Wang, Y.-S., & Wang, H.-Y. (2008). Development of validating an instrument for measuring mobile computing self-efficacy. *Cyberpsychology & Behavior*, *11*(4), 405–413. doi:10.1089/cpb.2007.0061

Wigal, J.-K., Greer, T.-L., & Kotses, H. (1991). *The COPD self-efficacy scale. CHEST Online*, 99, 1193-1196. Retrieved on June 20, 2009 from http://chestjournal.chestpubs.org/content/99/5/1193.

ADDITIONAL READING

Chen, G., Gully, S.-M., & Eden, D. (2001). Validation of a new general self-efficacy scale. *Organizational Research Methods*, *4*(1), 62–83. doi:10.1177/109442810141004

Lai, M.-L. (2008). Technology readiness, Internet self-efficacy and computer experience of professional accounting students. *Campus-Wide Information Systems*, *25*(1), 18–29. doi:10.1108/10650740810849061

Lam, J., & Lee, M. (2005). Bridging the digital divide——-The role of Internet self-efficacy towards learning computer and the Internet among elderly in Hong Kong, China. *Proceedings of the 38th Annual Hawaii International Conference on System Sciences*, Hawaii: University of HaiwiiHawaii.

Lee, B., & Tamborini, R. (2005). Third-person effect and Internet pornography: The influence of collectivism and Internet self-efficacy. *The Journal of Communication*, *55*(2), 292–310. doi:10.1111/j.1460-2466.2005.tb02673.x

Lee, H.-Y. (2008*). The study of the relationships among the self-directed learning, family support, and the Internet self-efficacy of middle-aged and senior adults*. Unpublished Master's Thesis, National Taiwan University of Science and Technology, Taiwan.

Linnenbrink, E.-A., & Pintrich, P.-R. (2003). The role of self-efficacy beliefs in student engagement and learning in the classroom. *Journal of Reading and Writing Quarterly*, *19*(2), 119–137. doi:10.1080/10573560308223

Mento, A.-J., Cartledge, N.-D., & Lock, E.-A. (1980). Maryland vs. Michigan vs. Minnesota: Another look at the relationship of expectancy and goal difficulty to task performance. *Organizational Behavior and Human Performance*, *25*, 419–440. doi:10.1016/0030-5073(80)90038-0

Monoi, S., O'Hanlon, N., & Diaz, K.-R. (2005). Online search skills: Development of an inventory to assess self-efficacy. *Journal of Academic Librarianship*, *31*(2), 98–105. doi:10.1016/j.acalib.2004.12.005

Partridge, H.-L. (2007). *Redefining the digital divide: attitudes do matter!* Proceedings 70th American Society for Information Science and Technology (ASIS&T) Annual Meeting, Joining Research and Practice: Social Computing and Information Science 44, Milwaukee, Wisconsin, USA.

Ren, P.-A. (1999). Self-efficacy and the search for government information. *Reference and User Services QyarterlyQuarterly*, *38*(3), 283–291.

Sung, S.-J. (2008). Psychometric properties of the Internet self-efficacy scale: An application of item response theory. *Communication Methods and Measure*, *2*(4), 294–312. doi:10.1080/19312450802310490

Thompson, L.-F., Meriac, J.-P., & Cope, J.-G. (2002). Motivating online performance: the influences of goal setting and Internet self-efficacy. *Social Science Computer Review*, *20*(2), 149–159. doi:10.1177/089443930202000205

Torkzadeh, G., Chang, J. C.-J., & Demirhan, D. (2006). A contingency model of computer and Internet self-efficacy. *Information & Management*, *43*, 541–550. doi:10.1016/j.im.2006.02.001

Torkzadeh, G., & Van Dyke, T.-P. (2002). Effects of training on Internet self-efficacy and computer user attitudes. *Computers in Human Behavior*, *18*, 479–494. doi:10.1016/S0747-5632(02)00010-9

Torres, J.-B., & Solberg, V.-S. (2001). Role of self-efficacy, stress, social integration, and family support in Latino college student persistence and health. *Journal of Vocational Behavior*, *59*, 53–63. doi:10.1006/jvbe.2000.1785

Tsai, C.-C., & Lin, C.-C. (2004). Taiwanese adolescents' perceptions and attitudes regarding the Internet: Exploring gender differences. *Adolescence*, *39*(156), 725–734.

Whitty, M.-T., & McLaughlin, D. (2007). Online recreation: the relationship between loneliness, Internet self-efficacy and the use of computers in human behaviors, 23,1435-1446.

Wu, Y.-T., & Tsai, C.-C. (2006). University students' Internet attitudes and Internet self-efficacy: A study at three universities in Taiwan. *Cyberpsychology & Behavior*, *9*(4), 441–450. doi:10.1089/cpb.2006.9.441

KEY TERMS AND DEFINITIONS

Computer Self-Efficacy: This is an extension of the theory of self-efficacy into the computer technology area. More specifically, it is referred to one's own perception about his/her capability to accept, understand, and use the computer technology.

Internet Self-Efficacy Scale: This is a measurement tool designed to evaluate a person's capability to accept, understand, and use the Internet. To be considered as a good measurement tool, it has to meet the three major criteria: validity, reliability, and practicality, discussed above.

Internet Self-Efficacy: Like computer self-efficacy, Internet self-efficacy is also part of the information technology and is referred specifically to individual's own perception about self's capability to accept, understand, and use the Internet technology.

Practicality: Unlike validity and reliability which are scientific requirements for the measurement process, practicality is the operational requirements. It normally takes three factors into consideration, namely, economy (cost), convenience, and interpretability.

Reliability: It is referred to the accuracy and precision of a measurement procedure adopted. This is a necessary condition to, but is not a sufficient condition for validity.

Self-Efficacy: Self-efficacy, according to Bandura (1977), is referred to one's own perception about his/her capability to perform a certain task.

Theory of Self-Efficacy: The theory of Self-efficacy originally introduced by Bandura (1977) is an important concept to help individuals understand how quickly they are capable of adopting new tools to help develop skills required by work that might previously be off limit to them earlier.

Validity: It is one of the three major criteria utilized to evaluate a measurement tool. The others are reliability and practicality. Validity may have many different forms in research settings, including external validity and internal validity. The former is referred to the ability of the data used to generalize the research findings across subjects, settings, and time frame, whereas the latter is associated with the ability of a research instrument to measure what it is intended to measure.

APPENDIX

Table 5. I'm confident to...

No.	Item	Valid N	Mean	Std.D.
v1	overcome obstacles encountered during browsing	1121	2.79	1.004
v2	reorganize my own Web	1123	3.46	.902
v3	browse various Websites programmed using different architectures	1123	2.73	1.137
v4	set proxy to browse the Web	1123	2.32	1.256
v5	use anonymity on the Web	1123	2.68	1.264
v6	hide my IP on the Web	1123	1.63	1.359
v7	surf on the Web	1123	3.53	.736
v8	browse information on the Web	1121	3.51	.736
v9	search for information on the Web	1121	3.48	.771
v10	use Web searching engine to look for text information	1121	3.57	.800
v11	use Boolean expressions	1119	.95	1.340
v12	use Web searching engine to look for product information	1121	3.52	.790
v13	use Web searching engine to look for pictures	1119	3.54	.737
v14	use online databases	1120	2.93	1.158
v15	use a directory portal	1121	2.71	1.268
v16	receive email via pop3 protocol	1119	1.95	1.496
v17	send email via smtp protocol	1119	1.83	1.497
v18	use Webmail services	1121	3.56	.783
v19	receive emails via Webmail services	1119	3.62	.734
v20	send others email via Webmail services	1121	3.72	.649
v21	use the address book function of Webmail services	1121	3.49	.890
v22	group my contact list in Webmail services	1121	3.31	1.019
v23	forward email I received	1121	3.63	.698
v24	forward files I gathered	1121	3.50	.896
v25	receive emails forwarded by others	1119	3.65	.758
v26	encrypt the email to be sent	1121	2.29	1.437
v27	decrypt the email I received	1121	2.09	1.480
v28	use the instant messenger	1121	3.65	.745
v29	use the instant messenger to send messages	1121	3.64	.786
v30	send messages to others via the instant messenger	1119	3.65	.747
v31	send files to others via the instant messenger	1117	3.72	1.877
v32	receive files from others via the instant messenger	1118	3.65	.749
v33	use emoticons to express my feelings and emotions in the instant messenger	1118	3.60	.829
v34	use two or more instant messaging software simultaneously	1118	3.38	1.077
v35	add contacts in the instant messenger	1120	3.68	.752
v36	classify contacts into different categroies in the instant messenger	1120	3.61	.873

continued on following page

Table 5. Continued

v37	delete contacts in the instant messenger	1118	3.58	.911
v38	block contacts in the instant messenger	1118	3.53	.993
v39	send audio messages via the instant messenger	1118	3.05	1.358
v40	receive audio messages via the instant messenger	1118	3.12	1.282
v41	send video messages via the instant messenger	1118	2.98	1.393
v42	receive video messages via the instant messenger	1116	3.15	1.272
v43	download files by p2p (peer to peer) software	1120	2.14	1.605
v44	upload files via the P2P software	1120	1.90	1.583
v45	download files from others' FTP sites around me	1118	2.13	1.494
v46	set up a home FTP server	1118	1.67	1.472
v47	download files from others' FTP sites not around me	1118	1.95	1.485
v48	edit a part of my blog (weblog)	1118	2.69	1.513
v49	visit blogs owned by people around me	1118	3.37	1.118
v50	visit blogs recommended by people around me	1118	3.38	1.090
v51	visit blogs owned by people not around me	1118	3.26	1.218
v52	visit blogs recommended by people not around me	1120	3.23	1.221
v53	attract people around me to visit my blogs	1120	2.47	1.544
v54	invite people around me to visit my blogs	1116	2.54	1.563
v55	attract people not around me to visit my blogs	1118	2.27	1.547
v56	invite people not around me to visit my blogs	1118	2.21	1.589
v57	accept messages left on my blogs by people around me	1118	2.80	1.555
v58	accept messages left on my blogs by people anot around me	1118	2.64	1.582
v59	leave my contact information on my own blogs	1118	2.27	1.569
v60	disclose information about my work in my blog article	1118	2.29	1.517
v61	disclose my private information in my blog article	1118	2.14	1.542
v62	edit a part of my site/page	1118	2.47	1.405
v63	visit Websites owned by people around me	1112	3.22	1.172
v64	edit my own wiki	1114	1.02	1.329
v65	browse a wiki owned by me	1114	1.04	1.340
v66	edit a wiki not owned by me	1114	.99	1.297
v67	browse a wiki not owned by me	1114	1.07	1.345
v68	enjoy Web albums owned by people around me	1104	3.70	.734
v69	enjoy Web albums owned by people not around me	1104	3.60	.822
v70	share my own Web albums with people around me	1104	3.23	1.289
v71	share my own Web albums with people not around me	1104	3.03	1.410
v72	upload my photos to my own Web albums	1104	3.24	1.309
v73	upload photos with myself in them to my own Web albums	1104	3.20	1.310
v74	upload photos owned by others to my own Web albums	1104	2.97	1.419
v75	upload pictures to the anonymous space on the Web	1104	2.58	1.580

continued on following page

Table 5. Continued

v76	scan pictures to the computer	1104	2.85	1.461
v77	download pictures from a Website	1104	3.63	.735
v78	download pictures from Web albums photos	1104	3.50	.977
v79	move photos from my digital camera to my computer	1104	3.44	1.094
v80	browse shopping Websites	1104	3.66	.776
v81	compare prices of same products on different Web shopping sites	1104	3.38	1.062
v82	compare prices of similar products on different Web shopping sites	1104	3.36	1.077
v83	compare features of same products on different Web shopping sites	1104	3.31	1.105
v84	browse a bbs	1102	2.64	1.541
v85	set up a bbs	1104	.87	1.328
v86	manage a bbs	1104	.86	1.305
v87	manage the discussion forum of a bbs	1104	1.06	1.404
v88	surf an auction Website	1104	3.58	.923
v89	search a product information on an auction Website	1104	3.52	.933
v90	compare products on an auction Website	1102	3.43	1.007
v91	inquire about a product on an auction Website	1102	3.20	1.196
v92	send my bid in to an auction Website	1102	2.88	1.427
v93	win a bid in an auction Website	1102	2.82	1.527
v94	auction my merchases in an auction Website	1102	2.37	1.740
v95	post pictures of a product in an auction Website	1102	2.14	1.705
v96	post pictures of a product obtained online in an auction Website	1102	2.20	1.753
v97	offer detailed information about a product in an auction Website	1102	2.32	1.744
v98	answer questions regarding a product to be auctioned in an auction Website	1102	2.31	1.747
V99	enjoy video files owned by people around me	1102	3.51	.929
v100	enjoy video files owned by people not around me	1102	3.34	1.079
v101	share my video files with people around me	1102	3.10	1.350
v102	share my video files with people not around me	1099	2.71	1.530
v103	upload my video files to a Website of which I am a member	1103	2.31	1.625
v104	upload video files not owned by me to a Website of which I am a member	1103	1.96	1.631
v105	upload video files of which I am part to a Website	1103	1.89	1.606
v106	upload controversial video files onto a Website	1103	1.39	1.514
v107	upload my video files to an anonymous virtual space of a Website	1103	1.69	1.611
v108	upload video files not owned by me to an anonymous virtual space of a Website	1103	1.55	1.543

Compilation of References

Aaker, D. (1975). ADMOD: An advertising decision model. *JMR, Journal of Marketing Research, 12*(1), 37–45. doi:10.2307/3150656

Afuah, A., & Tucci, C. L. (2003). *Internet business models and strategies: Text and cases (2nd ed)*. New York: McGraw-Hill/Irwin. Austin, J.E. (2001). The e-philanthropy revolution is here to stay. *Chronicle of Philanthropy, 13*(10), 72-73.

Ajzen, I. (1991). The theory of planned behavior. *Organizational Behavior and Human Decision Processes*, 179–211. doi:10.1016/0749-5978(91)90020-T

Ajzen, I. (1985). From intentions to actins: A theory of planned behavior. In Kuhl, J., & Bechmann, J. (Eds.), *Action-control: From cognition to behavior* (pp. 11–39). NY: Springer, Heidelberg.

al Banna, S. (2000). *Knowledge Management and strategies for development in a rapidly changing global environment.* (p. 12)

Alavi, M., & Leidner, D. E. (2001). Review: Knowledge Management and Knowledge Management systems: Conceptual foundations and research issues. *Management Information Systems Quarterly, 25*(1), 107–136. doi:10.2307/3250961

Alvesson, M. (1995). *Management of knowledge-intensive companies*. Berlin: Walter de Gruyter.

Anahotu, N. D. (1998). Empowerment and production workers: a knowledge-based perspective. *Empowerment in Organisations, 6*(7), 177–186. doi:10.1108/14634449810242611

Anandarajan, M., Simmers, C., & Igbaria, M. (2000). An exploratory investigation of the antecedents and impact of internet usage: An individual perspective. *Behaviour & Information Technology, 19*(1), 69–85. doi:10.1080/014492900118803

Anderson, R. I., Fok, R., & Scott, J. (2000). Hotel industry efficiency: An advanced linear programming examination. *American Business Review, 18*(1), 40–48.

Anderson, P. (2007). *What is Web 2.0? Ideas, technologies and implications for education.* JISC Technology and Standards Watch.

Anderson, W.-T., & Golden, L. (1984). Lifestyle and psychographics: A critical review and recommendation. *Advances in Consumer Research. Association for Consumer Research (U. S.), 11*(1), 405–411.

Andreu, R., & Sieber, S. (1999). *Knowledge and problem solving: A proposal for a model of individual and collective learning*. Barcelona: IESE Publishing.

Angeles, R., & Nath, R. (2003). Electronic supply chain partnerships: Reconsidering relationship attributes in customer-supplier dyads. *Information Resources Management Journal, 16*(3), 59.

Arora, S. R., & Gupta, R. (2009). Interactive fuzzy goal programming approach for bi-level programming problem. *European Journal of Operational Research, 194*(2), 368–376. doi:10.1016/j.ejor.2007.12.019

Arthur, J. K., & Calvin, P. D. (2009). Integer goal programming in advertising media selection. *Decision Sciences, 10*(4), 577–592.

Association of the German Banks. (2005). *Association of the German Banks market shares of the commercial banks*. Retrieved from http://www.germanbanks.org/

Atkinson, H., & Brown, J. B. (2001). Rethinking performance measures: assessing progress in UK hotels. *International Journal of Contemporary Hospitality Management, 13*(3), 128–135. doi:10.1108/09596110110388918

Azmitia, M. (2002). Self, self-esteem, conflicts, and best friendships in early adolescence. In Brinthaupt, T. M. (Ed.), *Understanding early adolescent self and identity: Applications and interventions* (pp. 167–192). Albany, NY: State University of New York Press.

Bandura, A. (1977). *Social learning theory*. New York: General Learning Press.

Bandura, A. (1977). Self-efficacy: Toward a unifying theory of behavioral change. *Psychological Review, 84*, 191–215. doi:10.1037/0033-295X.84.2.191

Bandura, A. (1982). Self-efficacy mechanisms in human agency. *The American Psychologist, 37*, 122–147. doi:10.1037/0003-066X.37.2.122

Bandura, A. (1997). *Self-efficacy: The exercise of control*. New York: W.H. Freeman.

Bandura, A. (2006). Guides for constructing self-efficacy scales. In Pajares, F., & Urdan, T. (Eds.), *Self-efficacy beliefs of adolescents*. Greenwich, Conn: IAP – Information Age Publication, Inc.

Barros, C. P. (2004). Productivity in the tourism industry. *International Advances in Economic Research, 10*(3), 215–226. doi:10.1007/BF02296216

Barros, C. P. (2005). Evaluating the efficiency of a small hotel chain with a Malmquist productivity index. *International Journal of Tourism Research, 7*(3), 173–184. doi:10.1002/jtr.529

Beghetto, R.-A. (2006). Creative self-efficacy: Correlates in middle and secondary students. *Creativity Research Journal, 18*(4), 447–457. doi:10.1207/s15326934crj1804_4

Belmokaddem, M., Mekidiche, M., & Sahed, A. (2009). Application of fuzzy goal programming approach with different importance and priority to aggregate production planning. *Journal of Applied Quantitative Methods, 4*(3), 317–331.

Bender, S., & Fish, A. (2000). The transfer of knowledge and the retention of expertise: The continuing need for global assignments. *Journal of Knowledge Management, 4*(2), 125–137. doi:10.1108/13673270010372251

Benisovich, S.-V., Rossi, J.-S., Norman, G.-J., & Nigg, C.-R. (1998). *Development of a Multidimensional Measure of exercise Self-efficacy*. Poster presented at the Society of Behavioral Medicine (SBM). New Orleans.

Benkler, Y. (2002). *The wealth of networks: How social production transforms markets and freedom*. Yale University Press. Retrieved from http://www.benkler.org/Benkler_Wealth_Of_Networks.pdf

Bentham, J. (1987). *The theory of legislation*. Littleton, CO: Fred B. Rothman & Co.

Benus, B. (1993). *Organizational modeling and Knowledge Management*. Department of Social Science Informatics, University of Amsterdam.

Berg, B. L. (1995). *Qualitative Research Methods for the Social Sciences*. Boston: Allyn and Bacon.

Bernholz, L. (2009). *Philanthropy 1.0 vs. Philanthropy 2.0*. Retrieved from http://www.tacticalphilanthropy.com/2009/10/philanthropy-2-0

Betz, N.-E., & Hackett, G. (1998). *Manual for the occupational self-efficacy scale*. Retreived on Aug. 24, 2009 fromhttp://seamonkey.ed.asu.edu/-gail/occsel.htm.

Beynon, W. M., Rasmequan, S., & Russ, S. B. (2002). A new paradigm for computer-based decision support. *Decision Support Systems: The International Journal, 33*(2), 127–142. doi:10.1016/S0167-9236(01)00140-3

Beynon, W. M., Rungrattanaubol, J., & Sinclair, J. (2000). Formal specification from an observation-oriented perspective. *Journal of Universal Computer Science, 6*(4), 407–421.

Beynon, W. M. (1997). Empirical Modelling for educational technology. In *Proceedings of the Second International Conference on Cognitive Technology*. 54-68. University of Aizu, Japan.

Beynon, W. M., & Russ, S. B. (1994). *Empirical Modelling of Requirements*. Research Report No. 277, Department of Computer Science, University of Warwick, UK.

Bhatt, G. (2001). Knowledge Management in organisations: Examining the interaction between technologies, techniques, and people. *Journal of Knowledge Management, 5*(1), 68–75. doi:10.1108/13673270110384419

Bhatt, G. D. (2000). Organising knowledge in the knowledge development cycle. *Journal of Knowledge Management, 4*(1), 15–26. doi:10.1108/13673270010315371

Bhatt, G. D. (2002). Management strategies for individual knowledge and organisational knowledge. *Journal of Knowledge Management, 6*(1), 31–39. doi:10.1108/13673270210417673

Binwal, J. C. (2001). Knowledge Management. *IASLIC Bulletin, 46*(2), 65–78.

Blau, A. (2001b) *More than bit players: How information technology will change the ways nonprofits and foundations work and thrive in the information age.* A report to the Surdna Foundation. Retrieved from http://www.surdna.org/documents/morefinal.pdf

BlogSpot. (2009). *Value drivers in Web 2.0.* Retrieved from ValueWeb2.BlogSpot.com

Boorstin, E.-S. (2002). Music sales in the age of file sharing, Unpublished Bachelor's Thesis, Princeton University, Princeton, N. J.

Bowen, D. E., & Lawler, E. E. (1992). The empowerment of service workers: What, why, how and when. *Sloan Management Review*, (Spring): 31–39.

Boyd, B. K. (1995). CEO duality and firm performance: A contingency model. *Strategic Management Journal, 16*(4), 301–312. doi:10.1002/smj.4250160404

Brengman, M., Geuens, M., Weijters, B., Smith, S.-M., & Swinyard, W.-R. (2005). Segmenting Internet shoppers based on their Web-usage-related lifestyle: A cross-culture validation. *Journal of Business Research, 58*, 79–88. doi:10.1016/S0148-2963(02)00476-9

Bright, J. R. (1969). Some management lessons from technological innovation research. *Long Range Planning, 2*(1), 36–41. doi:10.1016/0024-6301(69)90022-3

Brown, B. B., & Lohr, M. J. (1987). Peer-group affiliation and adolescent self-esteem: An integration of ego-identity and symbolic-interaction theories. *Journal of Personality and Social Psychology, 52*, 47–55. doi:10.1037/0022-3514.52.1.47

Bundesverband deutscher Banken. (2002). *Übersicht über das Bankgewerbe im Euro-Währunggebiet.*

Bundesverband deutscher Banken. (2005). *Bundesverband deutscher Banken.* Retrieved from http://www.bankenverband.de/

Burgess, R. (1998). Avoiding supply chain management failure: lessons from business process re-engineering. *International Journal of Logistics Management, 9*, 15–23. doi:10.1108/09574099810805717

Butlergroup. (2008). *Enterprise Web 2.0: Building the next generation workplace.* Retrieved from http://www.butlergroup.com/research/reportHomepages/EntWeb.asp.

Carneiro, A. (2001). The role of intelligent resources in Knowledge Management. *Journal of Knowledge Management, 5*(4), 358–367. doi:10.1108/EUM0000000006533

Carroll, A. B., & Buchholtz, A. K. (2006). *Business and society: Ethics and stakeholder Management.* (pp 19-20, 612-22). Ohio: South-Western.

Carroll, J.-M., Rosson, M.-B., & Zhou, J.-Y. (2005). Collective efficacy as a measure of community, computers and human interface, Portland.

Central News Agency. (February 14, 2009). *Government to continue supporting cultural industry.*

CEPD. (2004a). *Service industry development guidelines and action plan (guidelines and*

CEPD. (2004b). *Cultural and creative service industry development guidelines and action*

Chambers, R. (2008). *Social Venture Philanthropy–a business concept for non-profits, Venture Philanthropy.* Paper presented at 'The Social Investment Seminar' series. South Bank University, London.

Chandra, C., Grabis, A., & Tumanyan, A. (2007). Problem taxonomy: a step towards effective information sharing in supply chain management. *International Journal of Production Research*, *45*(11), 2507–2544. doi:10.1080/00207540601020486

Charnes, A., Cooper, W. W., & Rhodes, E. (1978). Measuring the efficiency of decision making units. *European Journal of Operational Research*, *2*(6), 429–444. doi:10.1016/0377-2217(78)90138-8

Charron, F. (2006a). *Social computing: How networks erode institutional power, and what to do about it.* Forrester Research.

Charron, C., Favier, J., & Li, C. Joseph, J., Neurauter, M., Cohen, S.M., et al. (2006). *D. Richard Dance, a book review: CPA and principal of Soft Resources LLC.* Retrieved from http://www.forrester.com/Research/Document/Excerpt/0,7211,38772,00.html

Chaudhury, A., & Kuilboer, J. (2002). *E-business and e-commerce infrastructure: Technologies supporting the e-business initiative.* NY: McGraw-Hill/Irwin.

Chen, C. (2004). *Corporate governance law and prospect of its actual practice* (p. 20). Taipei: Sharing Culture Enterprise.

Chen, Y. C. (2001). *Empirical Modelling for participative business process reengineering*, Unpublished doctoral thesis, Department of Computer Science, University of Warwick, UK.

Chiang, T., Cheng, B., Wu, T., & Cheng, C. (2006). Organizational loyalty. In Cheng, B. & Chiang, T., et al. (Eds.), *Chinese organizational behaviors–topics, methods, and publication.* (p. 152). Taipei: Hua-tai.

Ching-Ter, C. (2007). Binary fuzzy goal programming. *European Journal of Operational Research*, *180*(1), 29–37. doi:10.1016/j.ejor.2006.03.030

Choi, J.-N., Price, R.-H., & Vinokur, A.-D. (2003). Self-efficacy changes in groups: Effects of diversity, leadership, and group climate. *Journal of Organizational Behavior*, *24*(4), 357–372. doi:10.1002/job.195

Choi, Y. S. (2000). *An empirical study of factors affecting successful implementation of knowledge management.* Unpublished academic dissertation, University of Nebraska.

Christensen, C. M. (1997). *Innovator's dilemma: When technologies cause great firms to fail.* Boston: Harvard Business School Press.

Civi, E. (2000). Knowledge management as a competitive asset: A review marketing intelligence and planning. *Journal of Knowledge Management*, *18*(4), 166–174.

Colgate, M. (2000). Marketing and marketing information system sophistication in retail banking. *The Service Industries Journal*, *20*(1), 139–152. doi:10.1080/02642060000000008

Colley, J. L. Jr, Doyle, J. L., Logan, G. W., & Stettinius, W. (2003). *Corporate governance* (pp. x, 6, 230). New York: McGraw- Hill.

Collins, J. C., & Porras, J. I. (1994). *Built to Last: Successful habits of visionary companies.* NY: HarperCollins Publishing Inc.

Collins English Dictionary. (2004).

Coltman, M. M. (1978). *Hospitality management accounting.* Boston: CBI Publishing Co., Inc.

Compaine, B.-M. (Ed.). (2001). *The digital divide: Facing a crisis or creating a myth?* Cambridge, MA: MIT Press.

Compeau, D.-R., & Higgins, C.-A. (1995). Computer self-efficacy: Development of a measure and initial test. *Management Information Systems Quarterly*, *19*(2), 189–211. doi:10.2307/249688

Computerworld, (July 12, 2006). *Firefox use growing around the world.*

Conlin, M., & Hempel, J. (2003). The top givers: Today's philanthropists aren't leaving the good works to future generations–they're making their mark now. *Business-Week*, 78-84.

Cope, M. (1998). Developing a working definition. *Knowledge Management Review*, *1*(1), 26–31.

Council for Cultural Affairs (CCA). (May 15, 2009). *Government OKs cultural innovation plan*. The China Post. Taipei.

Council for Cultural Affairs Creative Industry Project Center. (2005). *CCACIPC*. Retrieved from http://english.cca.gov.tw

Council of Cultural Affairs. (2003). *International Symposium on Creative industry-a global thought and future action,* Taiwan.

Cox, T. (1993). *Stress research and stress management: putting theory to work. Health and safety Executive (HSE) Contract research report No. 61/1993*. London, UK: HMSO.

Creswell, J. W. (2003). *Research design: Qualitative, quantitative, and mixed method approaches* (2nd ed.). Thousand Oaks, CA: Sage.

Cultural and Creative Industry Promotion Organization. (2005a). *What is cultural & creative industry?* Retrieved August 5, 2005, from http://www.cci.org.tw/portal/plan/what.asp/

Cultural and Creative Industry Promotion Organization. (2005b). *Introduction of the cultural and creative industry plan*. Retrieved August 5, 2005, from http://www.cci.org.tw/portal/plan /what.asp/

Cultural and Creative Industry Promotion Team. (2004). *Scope of the cultural and creative industry in Taiwan and the administrative Agencies*. Ministry of Economic Affairs.

Curan, C. (May 1, 2008). Philanthropy 2.0. *Worth Magazine*. Retrieved from http://www.atlanticphilanthropies.org/news/philanthropy-20

Davenport, T. H. (2005). *Thinking for a living: How to get better performance and results from knowledge workers*. Boston: Harvard Business School Press.

Davenport, T. H., & Harris, J. G. (2007). *Competing on analytics: The new science of winning*. Boston: Harvard Business School Press.

Davenport, T., & Prusak, L. (1998). *Working knowledge: How organizations manage what they know* (p. 5). Cambridge, MA: Harvard University Press.

Davenport, T. H., & Prusak, L. (1998). *Working knowledge: Managing what your organization knows*. Boston: Harvard Business School Press.

Davenport, T. H. (1993). *Process innovation: Re-engineering work through Information Technology*. Boston: Harvard Business School Press.

Davenport, T. H. (1996). Why re-engineering failed: The fad that forgot people. *Fast Company*, *1*(1), 70–74.

Davenport, T. H. (2009). How to design smart business experiments. *Harvard Business Review*, (February): 68–77.

Davies, A. (1999). *A strategic approach to corporate governance* (pp. 14–17). Hampshire, UK: Gower House.

Davila, T., Epstein, M. J., & Shelton, R. (2006). *Making innovation work: How to manage it, measure it, and profit from it*. Pearson Education Ltd.

Davis, E. W., & Spekman, R. E. (2004). *The extended enterprise: gaining competitive advantage through collaborative supply chains*. Upper Saddle River, NJ: Prentice Hall.

Davis, F. D. (1989). Perceived usefulness, perceived ease of use, and user acceptance of information technology. *Management Information Systems Quarterly*, *13*, 319–340. doi:10.2307/249008

DCMS. (2005). *Creative industry*. Department for Culture, Media and Sport. Retrieved September 5, 2005, from http://www.culture.gov.uk/creative_ industry/

de la Mar, V. (2007). *Value drivers in e-Business 2.0: How Web 2.0 is changing the landscape of e-Business.* Retrieved from http://valueweb2.blogspot.com/2007_03_01_archive.html

deLatrt, J., & Watters, J. (1995). Science teaching self-efficacy in a primary school: A case study. *Research in Science Education, 25*(4), 453–464. doi:10.1007/BF02357387

Delong, D. W. (2004). *Lost knowledge: Confronting the treat of an aging workforce.* New York: Oxford University Press.

Denning, S. (2000). *The springboard: How storytelling ignites action in knowledge-era organizations.* Boston: Butterworth Heinemann.

DeNoble, A., Ehrlich, S., & Singh, G. (2007). Toward the development of a family business self-efficacy scale: A resource-based perspective. *Family Business Review, 20*(2), 127–240. doi:10.1111/j.1741-6248.2007.00091.x

Department of Economic Development, Taipei City Government. (May 14, 2008). Cabinet approves plan to boost cultural and creative industry. Central News Agency.

Derksen. (2007a). *Update Web 2.0.* Retrieved from http://www.upstream.nl/comments.php?id=496_0_1_0_C.

Desouza, K., & Awazu, Y. (2003, November). Knowledge Management. *HRMagazine*, 107–112.

Diaz, Q., Kanter, B., & Livingston, G. (2009). *Social media for social causes study: The results.* Retrieved from http://mashable.com/2009/03/26/social-media-nonprofit-study/

Dillenbourg, P. (1999). What do you mean by collaborative learning? In Dillenbourg, P. (Ed.), *Collaborative learning: Cognitive and computational approaches* (pp. 1–19). Oxford: Elsevier.

Dinev, T., & Koufteros, X. (2002). *Self-efficacy and Internet usage: Measurement and factorial validity.* Paper presented at the Decision Science Institute Conference, San Diego, CA.

Donaldson, T., & Dunfee, T. (1994). Toward a unified conception of business ethics: Integrative social contract theory. *Academy of Management Review, 19*(2), 262. doi:10.2307/258705

Donaldson, T., & Dunfee, T. (1999). *Ties that bind-a social contract approach to business ethics.* (pp. 34-38, 69). Cambridge, MA: Harvard Business School Press.

Drucker, P. F. (1954). *The practice of management.* New York: Harper & Row, Publishers Inc.

Drucker, P. F. (1957). *The landmarks of tomorrow.* New York: Harper & Row, Publishers Inc.

Drucker, P. F. (1999). *Management challenges for the 21st century.* New York: HarperCollins Publishers, Inc.

Drucker, P. F. (1994). *Innovation and entrepreneurship: Practice and principles.* Oxford: Butterworth Heinemann.

DSDTI. (August 5, 2005). Development of creativity is big business-a framework for the future. Queensland government, Department of State Development, Trade and Innovation. Retrieved on November 11, 2005, from http://www.sdi.qld.gov.au/dsdweb/v3/guis/templates/content/gui_cue_cntnhtml.cfm?id=2253

Dumas, J. (2008). IFC Global Logistics: Our successful story. *International Journal of e-Business Management, 2*(2), 47-51.

Dychtwald, K., Erickson, T. J., & Morison, R. (2006). *Workforce crisis: How to beat the coming shortage of skills and talent.* Self-published.

Earlystage. (2009). *Enterprise 2.0: Myths.* Retrieved from http://www.earlystage.be/enterprise20/myths.php

Eastern Television News. (August 1, 2005). Hu Jintao gives Soong Jingde porcelain; Soong gives Liuli Gongfang creation in return. Retrieved from http://www.ettoday.com/2005/05/12/11345-1789683.htm.

Eastin, M.-S., & Larose, R. (2000). Internet self-efficacy and the psychology of the digital divide. *Journal of Computer-Mediated Communication, 6*(1). Retrieved on April 20, 2006 from http://jcmc.indiana.edu/vol6/issue1/eastin.html.

Eastin, M.-S., & Larose, R. (2000). Internet self-efficacy and the psychology of the digital device. *Journal of Computer-Mediated Communication*, 6(1). Retrieved on April 20, 2006 from http://jcmc.indiana.edu/vol6/issue1/eastin.html.

Egan, M. (2003). Creating a knowledge bank. *Strategic Human Resource Review*, *2*(2), 30–34.

Eisenhardt, K. M. (1989). Agency theory: An assessment and review. *Academy of Management Review*, *14*(1), 57–74. doi:10.2307/258191

EITO. (2004). *European Information Technology Observatory 2004*. Frankfurt/Main: European Economic Interest Grouping (EEIG).

Ellis, T. I., Dooner, M., & Swift, K. G. (1997). Better the devil you know–the role of pragmatic modelling. In *First International Conference: Managing Enterprises–Stakeholders, Engineering, Logistics, and Achievement (ME-SELA'97)*, 151-156. Loughborough University, United Kingdom.

Engelbrecht, H. (2005). *The German banking system*. Retrieved May 15, 2005, from http://hans.engelbrecht.com/banksys/banksys1.htm

EPC. (2002). *Euroland: Our Single Payment Area*. March 25-26 2002 Workshop Participants and the 3 ECSAs

Ertnet, P.-A., Evenbeck, E., Cennamo, K.-S., & Lehman, J.-D. (1994). Enhancing self-efficacy for computer technologies through the use of positive classroom experience. *Educational Technology Research and Development*, *42*(3), 45–62. doi:10.1007/BF02298094

European Central Bank. (2002a). *Payment and securities settlement systems in accession countries. Blue book.* Frankfurt am Main: European Central Bank.

European Central Bank. (2002b). *Payment and securities settlement systems in the European Union. Blue Book.* Frankfurt am Main: European Central Bank.

European Commission. (1996). *A policy communiqué: EU views cultural enterprises as playing key role in balancing Europe's social development*. European Commission.

EUSA-Taiwan. (2003). *EUSA*. Retrieved from http//: eusa-taiwan.org

Evanschitzky, H., & Wunderlich, M. (2006). An examination of moderator effects in the four-stage loyalty model. *Journal of Service Research*, *8*(4), 330–345. doi:10.1177/1094670506286325

Executive Yuan. (2004). *Major social indicators of selected countries.*

Fama, E. F. (1980). Agency problems and theory of the firm. *The Journal of Political Economy*, *88*(2), 288–307. doi:10.1086/260866

Fama, E. F., & Jensen, M. C. (1983). The separation of ownership and control. *The Journal of Law & Economics*, *26*, 301–325. doi:10.1086/467037

Fawcett, S. E., Osterhaus, P., Magnan, G. M., Brau, J. C., & McCarter, M. W. (2007). Information sharing and supply chain performance: The role of connectivity and willingness. *Supply Chain Management*, *12*(5), 358. doi:10.1108/13598540710776935

Fay, C. T., Rhoads, R. C., & Rosenblatt, R. L. (1971). *Managerial accounting for hospitality service industries. Dubuque, IO: William C.* Brown Publishers.

Fernandes, J., & Usher, J. M. (1999). An object-oriented application of tool selection in dynamic process planning. *International Journal of Production Research*, *37*(13), 2879–2894. doi:10.1080/002075499190329

Ferrell, O. C., Fraedrich, J., & Ferrell, L. (2005). *Business ethics: Ethical decision making and cases* (pp. 9–14). Boston: Houghton Mifflin.

Festinger, L. (1954). A theory of social comparison processes. *Human Relations*, *7*, 117–140. doi:10.1177/001872675400700202

Fishbein, M., & Ajzen, I. (1975). *Belief, attitude, intention and behaviour: An introduction to theory and research.* Reading, MA: Addison-Wesley.

Fisher, S. (1994). *Stress in academic life: The mental assembly line*. Buckingham, UK: Society for Research into Higher Education and Open University Press.

Fishler, O. (2008). *Leveraging Enterprise Web 2.0 for competitive advantage*. Edgewater Technology Weblog. Retrieved May 1, 2008, from http://edgewatertech.wordpress.com

Fitzgerald, L., Johnston, R., Brignall, T. J., Silvestro, R., & Voss, C. (1991). *Performance measurement in service businesses*. London: The Chartered Institute of Management Accountants.

Foote, S. (2007). *Philanthropy 2.0: Leveraging the venture capital model*. Venture Capital Journal.

Freeman, S. W. (Ed.). (1985). *The acquisition of written language: revision and response*. Norwood, NJ: Ablex.

Freundl, D. (2005). *The way of Liuli*. Retrieved on January 11, 2008, from http://www.taipeitimes.com/News/feat/archives/2005/06/02/2003257650

Fuller, M.-A., Hardin, A.-M., & Davison, R.-M. (n.d.). (2006-7). Efficacy in technology-mediated distributed teams. *Journal of Management Information Systems*, *23*(3), 209–235. doi:10.2753/MIS0742-1222230308

Galliers, R. D. (1991). Information Systems strategic planning, myths, reality, and guidelines for successful implementation systems planning. *European Journal of Information Systems*, *1*(1), 55–64. doi:10.1057/ejis.1991.7

Galliers, R. D., & Leidner, D. E. (2003). *Strategic information management: challenges and strategies in managing Information Systems* (3rd ed.). Oxford: Butterworth-Heinemann.

Galliers, B. (1998). Reflections on BPR, IT and organisational change. In Galliers, R. D., & Baets, W. R. J. (Eds.), *Information Technology and organisational transformation* (pp. 225–243). London: John Wiley and Sons, Ltd.

Gelinas, R., & Bigras, Y. (2004). The characteristics and features of SMEs: Favorable or unfavorable to logistics integration? *Journal of Small Business Management*, *42*(3), 263–278. doi:10.1111/j.1540-627X.2004.00111.x

Gensch, D. H. (1970). Media factors: A review article. *JMR, Journal of Marketing Research*, *7*(2), 216–225. doi:10.2307/3150112

Gensch, D. H. (1973). *Advertising planning: Mathematical models in advertising media planning*. Amsterdam: Elsevier Scientific Publishing Company.

Geraint, J. (1998). Share strength. *People Management*, *4*(16), 44–47.

Gerrits, H. (1994). *Business modelling based on logistics to support business process re-engineering* (pp. 279–288).

Giannikos, I., & Polychroniou, P. (2009). Fuzzy goal programming model for task allocation in teamwork. *International Journal of Human Resources Development and Management*, *9*(1), 97–115. doi:10.1504/IJHRDM.2009.021557

Gist, M.-E., & Mitchell, T.-R. (1992). Self-efficacy: A theoretical analysis of its determinants and malleability. *Academy of Management Review*, *17*(2), 183–211. doi:10.2307/258770

Glasson, B. C., Hawryszkiewycz, I. T., Underwood, B. A., & Weber, R. A. (Eds.). (1994). *Business process re-engineering: Information Systems opportunities and challenges*. Elsevier Science.

Global Logistics, I. F. C. (2008). *About us–IGC Global Logistics*. Retrieved on March 7, 2007, from http://www.ifc.com.au/about_us.html

Glogoff, S. (2006). The LTC wiki: experiences with integrating a wiki in instruction. In Mader, S. L. (Ed.), *Using Wiki in education*.

Gobson, C.-B., Randel, A.-E., & Earley, P.-C. (2000). An empirical test of multiple assessment methods. *Group & Organization Management*, *25*(1), 67–97. doi:10.1177/1059601100251005

Goleman, D. (1995). *Emotional intelligence*. New York: Bantam Books.

Goman, C. (2002). What leaders can do to foster knowledge sharing. *Knowledge Management Review*, *5*(4), 10–11.

Gongfang, L. (2009). *Liuliu*. Retrieved from http://www.liuli.com/E_index01.htm

Gorsuch, R.-L. (1983). *Factor analysis*. Hillsdale, N.J.: Lawrence Erlbaum Associates.

Government Information Office. (2002). *Challenge 2008 National Development Plan*. Retrieved from http://www.gio.gov.tw/taiwan-website/4-oa/20020521/2002052101.html

Greco, J. (1999). Knowledge is power. *The Journal of Business Strategy*, *20*(2), 18–22. doi:10.1108/eb039990

Greengard, S. (1998a). Will your culture support Knowledge Management? *Workforce*, *77*(10), 93–94.

Greengard, S. (1998b). Storing, shaping, and sharing collective wisdom. *Workforce*, *77*(10), 82–87.

Grobman, G. M. (2008). *The nonprofit handbook: Everything you need to know to start and run your nonprofit organization*. White Hat Communications.

Gunasekaran, A., & Ngai, E. W. T. (2003). The successful management of a small logistics company. *International Journal of Physical Distribution & Logistics Management*, *33*(9), 825–842. doi:10.1108/09600030310503352

Gurteen, D. (1998). Knowledge, creativity and innovation. *Journal of Knowledge Management*, *2*(1), 513–522. doi:10.1108/13673279810800744

Gutek, B. A., & Bikson, T. K. (1985). Differential experiences of men and women in computerized offices. *Sex Roles*, *13*(3), 123. doi:10.1007/BF00287905

Hair, J.-F., Anderson, R.-E., Tatham, R.-L., & Black, W.-C. (1998). *Multivariate data analysis* (5th ed.). Upper Saddle River, NJ: Prentice Hall.

Halley, A., & Guilhon, A. (1997). Logistics behaviour of small enterprises: Performance, strategy and definition. *International Journal of Physical Distribution & Logistics Management*, *27*(8), 475–495. doi:10.1108/09600039710182644

Hamel, G. (2007). *The future of management*. Self-published.

Hamel, G. (2009). Moon shots for management. *Harvard Business Review*, (February): 2009.

Hammer, M., & Champy, J. (2003). *Reengineering the corporation: A manifesto for business revolution*. Harper Business.

Hannan, E. L. (1981a). On Fuzzy goal programming. *Decision Sciences*, *12*, 522–531. doi:10.1111/j.1540-5915.1981.tb00102.x

Hannan, E. L. (1981b). Linear programming with multiple fuzzy goals. *Fuzzy Sets and Systems*, *6*, 235–248. doi:10.1016/0165-0114(81)90002-6

Hansen, M., & Deimler, M. (2001). Cutting costs while improving morale with B2E management. *MIT Sloan Management Review.*, *43*(1), 96–100.

Harji, K. (2009). *Building a new business model for the philanthropy advisory industry*. Retrieved from http://www.socialfinance.ca/blog/post/building_a_new_business_model_for_the_philanthropy_advisory_industry/

Harris, P. J. (1999). *Profit planning* (2nd ed.). Oxford: Butterworth-Heinemann.

Hartwick, J. & Barki, H. (1994). Explaining the role of user participation in information system use. *Management Science*.

Hedlund, G. (1994). A model of knowledge management and the n-form corporation. *Strategic Management Journal*, *15*(2), 73–90. doi:10.1002/smj.4250151006

Hegarty, T., Verheul, E., Steupaert, D., & Skouma, G. (2003). *Study on the security of payment, products, and systems in the 15 member states*. European Commission. Internal Market DG.

Heinssen, R. K., Glass, C. R., & Knight, L. A. (1987). Assessing computer anxiety: Development and validation of the computer anxiety rating scale. *Computers in Human Behavior*, *3*, 49–59. doi:10.1016/0747-5632(87)90010-0

Hennart, J. F. (1991). Control in multinational firms: The role of price and hierarchy. *Management International Review*, *31*, 71–96.

Hietanen, H., Huttunen, A., & Kokkinen, H. (2008). Criminal friends of entertainment: analysing results from recent peer-to-peer surveys. *SCRIPTed*, *5*(1), 31–49. doi:10.2966/scrip.050108.31

Hill, C. W. L., & Jones, G. R. (2007). *Strategic management theory* (pp. 385, 397–399, 403–406). New York: Houghton Mifflin.

Hillocks, G. (1982). The interaction of instruction, teacher comment, and revision in teaching the composing process. *Research in the Teaching of English, 16*, 261–278.

Hinchcliffe, D. (2006a). *Welcome to the Web 2.0 world of Flickr,*del.icio.us, *Writely, Basecamp, Digg, and many others*. Retrieved October 13, 2006, from http://www.web2journal.com/read/178008.htm

Hinchcliffe, D. (2007). *Social media goes mainstream*. Retrieved March 14, 2007, from http://web2.socialcomputingmagazine.com/social_media_goes_mainstream.htm

Hinson, J., DiStefano, C., & Daniel, C. (2003). The Internet self-perception scale: measuring elementary students' level of self-efficacy regarding Internet use. *Journal of Educational Computing Research, 29*(2), 209–228. doi:10.2190/BWGN-84AE-9AR6-16DY

Hislop, D. (2003). Linking human resource management and Knowledge Management via commitment. *Employee Relations, 25*(2), 182–202. doi:10.1108/01425450310456479

Hitt, M. A., Ireland, R. D., & Hoskisson, R. E. (2003). *Strategic management-competitiveness and globalization* (pp. 312, 332–333). Ohio: South- Western.

Hitt, L. M., & Frei, F. X. (2002). Do better customers utilize electronic distribution channels? The case of PC banking. *Management Science, 48*(6), 732–748. doi:10.1287/mnsc.48.6.732.188

Hjelt, M. (2006). *End-user attitudes towards EDM use in project work: A case study of the Kamppi Center project*. Unpublished Master of Science Thesis, Swedish School of Economics and Business Administration.

HKTDC. (2002). *Creative industry in Hong Kong*. Hong Kong Trade Development Council.

Holland, C. P., Lockett, G. A., & Blackman, I. D. (Eds.). (1997). The impact of globalisation and Information Technology on the strategy and profitability of the banking industry. *Proceedings of HICSS-30 Conference*. Hawaii.

Hong, P., & Jeong, J. (2006). Supply chain management practices of SMEs: From a business growth perspective. *Journal of Enterprise Information Management, 19*(3), 292–302. doi:10.1108/17410390610658478

Hong Kong Tourism Board, (2007). *Monthly operation report of hotel in December 2006*.

Hong, T. (2006). The Internet and tobacco cessation: The roles of Internet self-efficacy and search task on the information-seeking process. *Journal of Computer-Mediatated Communication*, 11(2), Retrieved on July 5, 2008 from http://jcmc.indiana.edu/vol11/issue2/hong.html.

Horvath, L. (2001). Collaboration: The key to value creation in supply chain management. *Supply Chain Management: An International Journal, 6*(5), 205–207. doi:10.1108/EUM0000000006039

Hsu, K. (2004). Virtue, intervention, and personal freedom. *Poultry Science Reviews, 20*, 9–16.

Hsu, M.-H., & Chiu, C.-M. (2004). Internet self-efficacy and electronic service acceptance. *Decision Support Systems, 38*, 369–381. doi:10.1016/j.dss.2003.08.001

Hsu, T. (2009). Effects of Internet self-efficacy, emergent leaders, and personality on online discussion participation. In C. Fulford & G. Siemens (Eds.), *Proceedings of the ED-MEDIA 2009—World Conference on Educational Multimedia, Hypermedia, & Telecommunications*. (pp. 1730-1735). Chesapeake, VA: AACE.

Hsu, T., & Huang, L.-C. (2006). Developing an Internet self-efficacy scale of 2006. In T. Reeves and S. Yamashita (Eds.), *Proceedings of the 2006 World Conference on E-Learning in Corporate, Government, Healthcare & Higher Education*. (pp. 2000-2008). Chesapeake, VA: AACE.

Hsu, T., & Wang, H. F. (2003). Gender effects on collaborative learning behavior in CSCL. In A. Rossett (Ed.), *Proceedings of the 2003 World Conference on E-Learning in Corporate, Government, Healthcare & Higher Education*. (pp. 1919-1926). Chesapeake, VA: AACE.

Huang, Z., & Gangopadhyay, A. (2004). A simulation study of supply chain management to measure the impact of information sharing. *Information Resources Management Journal, 17*(3), 20–32.

Huang, J. H., Jin, B. H., & Yang, C. (2004). Satisfaction with business-to-employee benefit systems and organizational citizenship behaviour - an examination of gender differences. *International Journal of Manpower, 25*(2), 195–210. doi:10.1108/01437720410535990

Huang, H. (2003). *A discussion on the accountant's role and regulations from the perspective of corporate governance*. (pp. 30-33). Unpublished Master's thesis, Department of Law, National Taipei University.

Huang, K.-N. (2008). *Museum, tourism and the culture industry in Taiwan.* National Taiwan University of Art, 2008 International Museum management commission: NZ annual meeting report.

Huang, M. (2001). *The law for publicly-traded corporations and corporate supervision.* (pp. 12-17, 24). Taipei: Angle Publication.

Hubard, D. W. (2007). *How to measure anything: Finding the value of intangibles in business*. Hoboken, NJ: John Wiley & Sons, Inc.

Hutchison, A. (1994). *CSCW as opportunity for business process re-engineering* (pp. 309–318).

Hwang, S., & Chang, T. (2003). Using data envelopment analysis to measure hotel managerial efficiency change in Taiwan. *Tourism Management, 24*(4), 357–369. doi:10.1016/S0261-5177(02)00112-7

Hwang, A. (2003). Training strategies in the management of knowledge. *Journal of Knowledge Management, 7*(3), 92–104. doi:10.1108/13673270310485659

Hwang, Y., & Li, T. (2009). Conquer Web 2.0 motivational challenges from social context evolution. *Proceedings of the 2009 5th International Joint Conference on INC, IMS and IDC.* (pp.1836-1841).

Igbaria, M., & Parasuraman, S. (1989). A path analytic study of individual characteristics, computer anxiety and attitudes toward microcomputers. *Journal of Management, 15*(3), 373–383. doi:10.1177/014920638901500302

International Federation of the Phonographic Industry. (2003). Global sales of recorded music down 7% in 2002. Retrieved on August 15, 2009 from http://www.ifpi.org/content/section_news/20030409.html, International Federation of the Phonographic Industry, (2008). IFPI digital music report 2008: Revolution, innovation and responsibility. Retrieved on August 15, 2009 from http://www.ifpi.org/content/section_news/20030409.html, International Federation of the Phonographic Industry (2009). IFPI digital music report 2009: New business models for a changing environment. Retrieved on August 15, 2009 from http://www.ifpi.org/content/section_news/20030409.html, Joo, Y.-J., Bong, M., & Choi, H.-J., (2000). Self-efficacy for self-regulated learning, academic self-efficacy, and Internet self-efficacy in Web-based Instruction. *Educational Technology, Research and Development*, 48(2), 5-17.

International Intellectual Property Alliance. (2007). *Copyright industry in the U.S. economy: The 2006 Report*. International Intellectual Property Alliance.

International Venture Philanthropy Forum. (2001). *Venture philanthropy*. Retrieved from http://forum.nesst.org/.

Internet World Stats. (2005). *Internet world stats, usage, and population statistics*. Retrieved May 17, 2005, from http://www.internetworldstats.com/

Interview data (2008). The data was collected by the author from her interviews with senior managers at IFC, Melbourne in 2008.

Irfan, E., & Mustafa, G. (2007). Fuzzy goal programming and an application in production process. In P. Melin, W. Pedrycz, J. Kacprzyk, E. Ramirez & O. Castillo (Eds.), *Analysis and design of intelligent systems using soft computing techniques.* (pp. 649-659). Berlin/Heidelburg: Springer-Verlag

Jacobson, I. (2009). *Object-oriented software engineering: A use case driven approach.* Addison-Wesley.

Jacobson, I., Christerson, M., Jonsson, P., & Overgaard, G. (1992). *Object-oriented software engineering: A use case driven approach*. Addison-Wesley.

Jacobson, I., Ericsson, M., & Jacobson, A. (1995). *The object advantage: Business process re-engineering with object technology*. Addison-Wesley.

Jacobson, I., Griss, M., & Jonsson, P. (1997). *Software reuse–architecture, process and organisation for business success*. Addison-Wesley.

Jacobson, I., & Ng, P. W. (2004). *Aspect-oriented software development with use cases*. Addison-Wesley.

Jamkit & Philanthropy UK. (2009). *Venture philanthropy*. Retrieved from http://www.philanthropyuk.org/Resources/Venturephilanthropy

Jaokar, A., & Fish, T. (2006). *Mobile Web 2.0 - The innovator's guide to developing and marketing the next generation wireless/mobile applications*. London: Futuretext Limited.

Jensen, M. C., & Meckling, W. H. (1976). Theory of the firm: Managerial behavior, agency costs and ownership structure. *Journal of Financial Economics*, *3*, 305–360. doi:10.1016/0304-405X(76)90026-X

Jensen, M. C., & Ruback, R. S. (1983). The market for corporate control: The scientific evidence. *Journal of Financial Economics*, (May): 5–50. doi:10.1016/0304-405X(83)90004-1

Jiménez, M., Arenas, M., Bilbao, A., & Rodríguez-Uría, M. V. (2005). Approximate resolution of an imprecise goal programming model with nonlinear membership functions. *Fuzzy Sets and Systems*, *150*, 129–145. doi:10.1016/j.fss.2004.05.001

John, R. (2006). *The evolution of high engagement philanthropy in Europe*. Skoll Centre for Social Entrepreneurship, Saïd Business School.

Johnson, M. E. (2006). Supply chain management: technology, globalization, and policy at a crossroads. *Interfaces*, *36*(3), 191–195. doi:10.1287/inte.1060.0214

Jones, G. R., & George, R. W. (2003). *Contemporary management* (3rd ed.). New York: McGraw-Hill Companies, Inc.

Jones, J. F. (2001). Call and responsibilities of teachers and administrations. *ELT Journal*, *55*(4). doi:10.1093/elt/55.4.360

Joo, Y.-J., Bong, M., & Choi, H.-J. (2000). Self-efficacy for self-regulated learning, academic self-efficacy, and Internet self-efficacy in Web-based instruction. *Educational Technology Research and Development*, *48*(2), 5–17. doi:10.1007/BF02313398

Kaindl, H. (1999). Difficulties in the transition from OO analysis to design. *IEEE Software*, (September/October): 94–102. doi:10.1109/52.795107

Kaiser, H.-F. (1970). A second-generation little jiffy. *Psychometrika*, *35*, 401–415. doi:10.1007/BF02291817

Kaiser, H.-F. (1974). Little jiffy, mark IV. *Educational and Psychological Measurement*, *34*, 111–117. doi:10.1177/001316447403400115

Kalakota, R., & Robinson, M. (2001). *e-Business 2.0: Roadmap for success (2nd ed.)*. Addison-Wesley Information Technology Series. Longman, Inc.

Kalakota, R., & Robinson, M. (2009). *e-Business 2.0: Emerging business models*. Indianapolis: Informit.

Kallonen, T. (2002). *Pankit muutoksessa*: Suomen pankkiyhdistys.

Kanter, B. (2009). *Philanthropy 2.0 study results published on Mashable*. Retrieved from http://beth.typepad.com/beths_blog/2009/03/philanthropy-20-study-results-published-on-mashable.html

Kaplan, R. S., & Norton, D. P. (1996). *Balanced scorecard: Translating strategy into action*. Boston: Harvard Business School Press.

Karasu, I. (2005). Privatkundengeschäft und Banktechnologie: Meilensteine auf dem Weg ins Online-Zeitalter. *Die Bank*, *44*(6).

Karnani, A. (2007). The mirage of marketing to the bottom of the pyramid. *California Management Review, 49*(4), 90–111.

Karnani, A. (2009). The bottom of the pyramid strategy for reducing poverty: A failed promise. *DESA Working Paper*, No.80, ST/ESA/2009/DWP/80.

Katz, D. (1964). The motivational basis of organizational behavior. *Behavioral Science, 9*, 131–146. doi:10.1002/bs.3830090206

Keen, P. G. W., & Sol, H. G. (2008). *Decision enhancement services: Rehearsing the future for decisions that matter*. IOS Press.

Keillor, B. D., Bashaw, E. R., Edward, R., & Pettijohn, C. E. (1997). Sales force automation issues prior to implementation: The relationship between attitudes toward technology experience and productivity. *Journal of Business and Industrial Marketing, 12*(3/4), 209–219. doi:10.1108/08858629710188045

Kidwell, J. J., Van der Linde, M. K., & Johnson, L. S. (2000). Applying corporate Knowledge Management practices in higher education. *EDUCAUSE Quarterly, 4*, 28–33.

Kim, J.-S., & Whang, K.-S. (1998). The tolerance approach to the fuzzy goal programming problems with unbalanced triangular membership function. *European Journal of Operational Research, 107*, 614–624. doi:10.1016/S0377-2217(96)00363-3

Kim, B., & Han, H. (2001). The strategic planning of B2B ehub. In *Proceedings of the Pacific Asia Conference on Information Systems (PACIS'01)*, Seoul.

Kimes, S. E. (1989). The basics of yield management. *The Cornell Hotel and Restaurant Administration Quarterly, 30*(3), 14–19. doi:10.1177/001088048903000309

Kirschfoundation. (2009). *Venture philanthropy: The new model*. Retrieved from http://www.kirschfoundation.org/why/venture.html

Kitchenham, B., & Pfleeger, S. L. (2002). Principles of survey research questionnaire evaluation. *Software Engineering Notes, 27*(3), 20–23. doi:10.1145/638574.638580

KOCCA. (2005). *White Paper on Korean culture industry*. Ministry of Culture and Tourism.

Kock, N. (2007). Global funding of e-collaboration research: Challenges and opportunities. *International Journal of e-Collaboration, 3*(2), 1–5.

Kock, N., Lynn, G. S., Dow, K. E., & Akgun, A. E. (2006). Team adaptation to electronic media: Evidence of compensatory adaptation in new product development teams. *European Journal of Information Systems, 15*(3), 331. doi:10.1057/palgrave.ejis.3000612

Konradt, U., Christophersen, T., & Schaeffer-Kuelz, U. (2006). Predicting user satisfaction, strain and system usage of employee self-services. *International Journal of Human-Computer Studies*, 1141–1153. doi:10.1016/j.ijhcs.2006.07.001

Koplowitz & Young. (2007). *What is Web 2.0? And how are businesses making use Of Web 2.0 tools and techniques?* Retrieved from http://www.forrester.com/rb/teleconference/what_is_web_20_and_how_are/q/id/1846/t/1

Kotas, R. (1975). *Market orientation in the hotel and catering industry*. Guildford, UK: Surrey University Press.

Kotzab, H., Skjoldager, N., & Vinum, T. (2003). The development and empirical validation of an e-based supply chain strategy optimization model. *Industrial Management & Data Systems, 103*(5), 347–360. doi:10.1108/02635570310477406

Kreitner, R., & Kinicki, A. (2004). *Organizational behavior* (pp. 76–78). New York: McGraw- Hill.

Kucukemiroglu, O. (1997). Consumer lifestyle dimensions and ethnocentrism: An empirical study. *European Journal of Marketing, 33*(5/6), 470–487. doi:10.1108/03090569910262053

Kuglin, F. A., & Rosenbaum, B. A. (2001). *The supply chain network at Internet speed: Preparing your company for the e-commerce revolution*. New York: Amacom.

Küng, H. (1998). *A global ethic for global politics and economics* (pp. 251–253, 274–275). New York: Oxford University Press.

Kwong, T.-C.-H., & Lee, M.-K.-O. (2002). Behavioral intention model for the exchange mode Internet music piracy. In R.-H. Sprague, Jr. (Ed.), *Proceedings of the 35th Hawaii International Conference on System Sciences*. (pp. 1-10). Big Island, HI: University of Hawaii.

Ladd, K. (2009). *Philanthropy with a business model*. Retrieved from http://www.foxbusiness.com/story/personal-finance/women-in-business/philanthropy-business-model/

Laforet, S., & Tann, J. (2006). Innovative characteristics of small manufacturing firms. *Journal of Small Business and Enterprise Development*, *13*(3), 363–380. doi:10.1108/14626000610680253

Lagrosen, S. (2005). Effects of the internet on the marketing communication of service companies. *Journal of Services Marketing*, *19*(2), 63–70. doi:10.1108/08876040510591376

LaRose, R., & Kim, J.-G. (2007). Share, steal, or buy? A social cognitive perspective of music downloading. *Cyberpsychology & Behavior*, *10*(2), 267–277. doi:10.1089/cpb.2006.9959

LaRose, R., Lai, R.-J., Lange, R., Love, B., & Wu, Y.-H. (2005). Sharing or piracy? An exploration of downloading behavior. *Journal of Computer-Mediated Communication*, 11(1), Retrieved on August 10, 2006 from http://jcmc.indiana.edu/vol11/issue1/larose.html

Lass, P., & Hart, P. (2004). National cultures, values and lifestyles influencing consumers' perception towards sexual imagery in alcohol advertising: An exploratory study in the UK, Germany and Italy. *Journal of Marketing Management*, *20*, 607–623. doi:10.1362/0267257041323936

Laurent. (2008). *Belgian government: e-gov 2.0 study*. Retrieved October 2, 2008, from http://www.earlystage.be/belgian-government-e-gov-20-study

Lawrence, L., Levy, S., & Rubinson, L. (1990). Self-efficacy and AIDS prevention for pregnant teens. *The Journal of School Health*, *60*, 19–24. doi:10.1111/j.1746-1561.1990.tb04771.x

LCM. (2006). *Liuli China Museum*. Retrieved from www.liulichinamuseum.com

Lee, C.-S., & Wen, C.-G. (1997). Fuzzy goal programming approach for water quality management in a river basin. *Fuzzy Sets and Systems*, *89*, 181–192. doi:10.1016/S0165-0114(96)00089-9

Lee, M. (2004). The effects of piracy upon the music industry: A case study of bootlegging. *Media Culture & Society*, *26*(2), 163–181. doi:10.1177/0163443704039497

Lee Allen, S. (1991). Integrating positivist and interpretive approaches to organizational research. *Organization Science*, *2*(4), 342–365. doi:10.1287/orsc.2.4.342

Lee, C. S., & Vonortas, N. S. (2004). Business model innovation in the digital economy. In Doukidis, G., Mylonopoulos, N., & Pouloudi, N. (Eds.), *Social and economic transformation in the digital era* (pp. 164–181). Hershey, PA: Idea Group Publishing.

Lee, H. L., & Whang, S. (2002). Supply chain integration over the Internet. In Genunes, J. (Eds.), *Supply chain management: Models, applications, and research directions* (pp. 3–18). Bordrecht, The Netherlands: Kluwer Academic Publishers.

Lee, C. S., & Berniker, E. (2006). *E-philanthropy: Disruptive innovations in non-profit fund raising*. ePLU E-Commerce & Technology Management Center, Pacific Lutheran University, IAMOT Conference Archive.

Lefebvre, E., Cassivi, L., Lefebvre, L. A., & Loger, P. (2003). E-collaboration within one supply chain and its impact on firms' innovativeness and performance. *Information Systems and E-business Management, 173*(2).

Leiner, B. M., Cerf, V. G., Clark, D. D., Kahn, R. E., Kleinrock, L., & Lynch, D. C. (2003). *A brief history of the Internet, version 3.32*. Internet Society.

Leonard, D., & Swap, W. C. (2005). *Deep smarts: How to cultivate and transfer enduring business wisdom*. Boston: Harvard Business School Publishing Corporation.

Levy, M. (2009). WEB2.0 Implications on Knowledge Management. *Journal of Knowledge Management*, *13*(1), 120–134. doi:10.1108/13673270910931215

L-Husan, C, and Feng-Chou, T. (2001). Fuzzy goal programming with different importance and priorities. *European Journal of Operational Research, 133*, 548–556. doi:10.1016/S0377-2217(00)00201-0

Li, G., Yan, H., Wang, S., & Xia, Y. (2005). Comparative analysis on value of information sharing in supply chains. *Supply Chain Management, 10*(1), 34. doi:10.1108/13598540510578360

Liang, T. F. (2007). Applying fuzzy goal programming to product/transportation planning decision in supply chain. *International Journal of Systems Science, 38*(4), 293–304. doi:10.1080/00207720601159381

Liang, J.-C., & Tsai, C.-C. (2008). Internet self-efficacy and preferences toward constructivist Internet-based learning environments: A study of pre-school teachers in Taiwan. *Journal of Educational Technology & Society, 11*(1), 226–237.

Liao, Z., & Cheung, M. T. (2002). Internet-based e-banking and consumer attitudes: An empirical study. *Information & Management, 39*(4), 283–295. doi:10.1016/S0378-7206(01)00097-0

Liao, C.-H., Tsou, C.-W., & Kao, Y.-C. (2007). Explaining consumer acceptance of online digital music. In R. Lee (Ed.), *Proceedings of the 13th Asia Pacific Management Conference*. (pp. 829-842). Melbourne University.

Lin, H.-Y. (2007a). Business ethics under the framework of Hans Küng's global ethic theory. *The Journal of Global Business Management, 3*(1), 38–45.

Lin, H.-Y. (2009a). Correlation between universal ethic and business ethics–explorations from the perspective of Hans Küng's global ethic. *Journal of International Management Studies, 4*(1), 182–188.

Lin, H.-Y. (2009b). Universal ethic factors and Hans Küng's global ethic in contemporary capitalist values. *The Journal of Global Business Management, 5*(1), 12–19.

Lin, H.-Y. (2009c). From Hans Küng's global ethic to value community–re-thinking the construction of business ethics theory. *The Journal of Human Resource and Adult Learning, 5*(1), 10–18.

Lin, C. C. (2004). A weighted max-min model for fuzzy goal programming. *Fuzzy Sets and Systems, 142*(3), 407–420. doi:10.1016/S0165-0114(03)00092-7

Lin, C.-Y. (2000). A study of the e-mail users' involvement in the viral marketing in Taiwan, Unpublished Master's Thesis, Da-Yeh University, Taiwan.

Lin, H. (2004). *A study of corporate features, entrepreneurship, organizational performance, and capacity of the board of directors*. Unpublished doctoral thesis, Department of Technology Management, Chung Hua University.

Lin, H.-Y. (2007b). *Using Hans Küng's global ethic to construct a set of business ethics to research the agency problems within corporate governance.* Unpublished doctoral thesis, Graduate Institute of European Studies, Tamkang University.

Lin, S. (2004). A *study of corporate features, entrepreneurship, organizational performance, and capacity of directors.* Unpublished doctoral thesis, Department of Technology Management, Chung Hua University.

Liu, S. (2002). *From Chuang-zi to Enron-A+ corporate governance* (pp. 70–85). Taipei: Common Wealth.

Liu, L. (2003). *Challenges and opportunities presented by globalization—development of new cultural enterprises in Taiwan and lessons to be learned from Europe.* Member, European Union study association-Taiwan.

Llena, J. (1985). On fuzzy linear programming. *European Journal of Operational Research, 22*(2), 216–223. doi:10.1016/0377-2217(85)90229-2

Lu, H.-Y., Case, D.-O., Lustria, M.-L. A., Kwon, N., Andrews, J.-E., & Cavendish, S. (2005). Predictors of online information seeking by international students when disaster strikes their countries. *Cyberpsychology & Behavior, 10*(5), 709–712. doi:10.1089/cpb.2007.9965

Lucas, H. C. Jr. (1976). *The implementation of computer based models.* New York: National Association of Accountants.

Lucas, H. C. Jr. (1978). Empirical evidence for a descriptive model of implementation. *Management Information Systems Quarterly, 2*(2), 27–52. doi:10.2307/248939

Lynch, R., & Dembo, M. (2004). The relationship between self-regulation and online learning in a blended learning context. *International Review of Research in Open and Distance Learning*, *5*(2), 1–16.

Ma, Q.-X., & Liu, L.-P. (2005). The role of Internet self-efficacy in the acceptance of Web-based electronic medical records. *Journal of Organizational and End User Computing*, *17*(1), 38–57.

MacCallum, R. C., Zhang, S., Preacher, K. J., & Rucker, R. D. (2002). On the practice of dichotomization of quantitative variables. *Psychological Methods*, *7*(1), 9–40. doi:10.1037/1082-989X.7.1.19

MacFarlane, A. (1994, May 13). Time to get teaching on board. []. London.]. *Times Higher Education Supplement*, 14.

MacManus, R., & Porter, J. (2005). *Web 2.0 for designers*. Digital Web Magazine.

MacManus, R. (2007). *Kiva: Philanthropy 2.0*. Retrieved from http://www.readwriteweb.com/archives/kiva_philanthropy20.php

Mahatanankoon, P. (2002). Explaining production deviant use of the Internet technology in the workplace: An integrated model. *Dissertation Abstract International*, *63*, 03A.

Mangaraj, B. K. (1999). Fuzzy multi-objective programming in capital budgeting decision system. *Finance India*, *8*(44), 1161–1172.

Mangaraj, B. K., Aparajita, U., & Mishra, A. (2000). Fuzzy set in product planning decision. *Journal of Discrete Mathematical Science and Cryptography*, *3*(1-3), 57–81.

Mangaraj, B. K., & Das, D. (2008). *Interactive fuzzy multi-objective programming in land re-organisational planning for sustainable rural development* (pp. 721–730). Paris: Proceedings of World Academy of Science, Engineering and Technology.

Mangaraj, B. K., Mishra, A., & Aparajita, U. (2008). Fuzzy goal programming in marketing-mix selection. *Journal of Science. Technology and Management*, *1*(1), 61–68.

Mangaraj, B. K., Nayak, M., & Mangaraj, T. (2001). Fuzzy multi-objective zero-one programming for capital budgeting. *Finance India*, *15*(1), 475–486.

Mann, F. C., & Williams, L. K. (1960). Observations on the dynamics of a change to electronic data processing equipment. *Administrative Science Quarterly*, *5*, 217–256. doi:10.2307/2390779

Manoj, K., Vrat, P., & Shankar, R. (2004). A fuzzy goal programming approach for vendor selection problem in a supply chain. *Computers & Industrial Engineering*, *46*, 69–85. doi:10.1016/j.cie.2003.09.010

Marakas, G.-M., Yi, M.-Y., & Johnson, R.-D. (1998). The multilevel and multifacted character of computer self-efficacy: Toward clarification of the construct and an integrated framework for research. *Information Systems Research*, *9*, 126–163. doi:10.1287/isre.9.2.126

Maslow, A. H. (1943). A theory of human motivation. *Psychological Review*, *50*(4), 370–396. doi:10.1037/h0054346

Mathew, V. (2008). K-C Management: Building knowledge culture in the business organization for managing change. [Special KM edition]. *Effective Executive*, *6*(6), 68–78.

Mathew, V. (2008). Knowledge Management progression, issues, and approaches for organizational effectiveness in manufacturing industry: An implementation agenda. *ICFAI Journal of Knowledge Management*, *6*(1), 20–45.

Mathew, V., & Kavitha, M. (2008). Critical knowledge transfer in an organization: approaches. *ICFAI Journal of Knowledge Management*, *6*(4), 25–40.

Mathew, V. (2009). Virtual knowledge sharing and collaborative learning in organization. Paper accepted for First Virtual Conference on Business Management 2009 (VCOBAM 2009) conference.

Mattsson, L. (2003). Reorganization of distribution in globalization of markets: The dynamic context of supply chain management. *Supply Chain Management*, *8*(5), 416–427. doi:10.1108/13598540310500259

Maurer, T.-J., & Piece, H.-R. (1998). A comparison of Likert scale and traditional measures of self-efficacy. *The Journal of Applied Psychology*, *83*(2), 324–329. doi:10.1037/0021-9010.83.2.324

Mayer, R., Cullinane, T., De Witte, P., Knappernberger, W., Perakath, B., & Wells, S. (1992). *ICCE IDEF3 process description capture method report (al/tr-1992-0057). Technical report.* Air Force Systems Command.

Mbengue, I., & Hsu, T. (2006). To adopt a Web-based instruction: Is authority exercise an issue? In T. Reeves and S. Yamashita (Eds.), *Proceedings of the 2006 World Conference on E-Learning in Corporate, Government, Healthcare & Higher Education.* (pp. 2209-2216). Honolulu, HI: AACE.

McAfee, A. P. (2006). *Enterprise 2.0: The dawn of emergent collaboration.* MIT Sloan Management Review.

McAfee, A. P. (2006a). *I can quote them.* The Business Impact of IT.

McAfee, A. (Spring 2007). The future of the Web. *MIT Sloan Management Review*, 49-64.

McAuley, E., & Gill, D. (1983). Reliability and validity of the physical self-efficacy scale in a competitive sport setting. *Journal of Sport & Exercise Psychology*, *5*(4), 410–418.

McChesney, M. C. (1997). Banking in cyberspace: An investment in itself. *IEEE Spectrum*, *34*(2), 54–59. doi:10.1109/6.570831

McCormack, K. P., Johnson, W. C., & Walker, W. (2003). *Supply chain networks and business process orientation: Advanced strategies and best practices.* New York: St. Lucie Press.

McMillian, R. (Dec. 12, 2006). Rock band "Phish" blamed for surge in phishing. *Infoworld.* Retrieved on June 10, 2009 from http://www.infoworld.com/article/06/12/12/HNrockphish_1.html.

McWilliams, G. (October 2, 2003). Dells plan hands-on approach to charity donations, programs. *The Wall Street Journal,* p. B10.

Micklethwait, J., & Wooldridge, A. (2003). *The company.* (pp. 155-58, 198-92). New York: Random House.

Miles, M. B., & Hubeman, A. M. (1994). *Qualitative data analysis: An expanded source book.* Sage Publishing.

Miller, N. E., & Dollard, J. (1941). *Social learning and imitation.* New Haven, CT: Yale University Press.

Miller, W. L., & Morris, L. (1999). *Fourth generation R&D: Managing knowledge, technology, and innovation.* New York: John Wiley & Sons, Inc.

Mishra, A., Mangaraj, B. K., & Aparajita, U. (2003). Media selection decision in social system: A fuzzy goal programming approach. *Journal of Academy of Business and Economics*, *1*(2), 191–208.

Moeasmea. (2004). *White Paper on SMEs in Taiwan: The development of the cultural and creative industry in Taiwan and its significance for SMEs.* Retrieved from http://www.moeasmea.gov.tw/public/Attachment/65161430571.pdf

Moffett, S., McAdam, R., & Parkinson, S. (2003). An empirical analysis of Knowledge Management applications. *Journal of Knowledge Management*, *7*(3), 6–26. doi:10.1108/13673270310485596

Mohrman, S. A., Cohen, S. G., & Mohrman, A. M. Jr. (1995). *Designing team-based organizations: New forms for knowledge work.* San Francisco: Jossey-Bass Publishers.

Mondy, R. W., & Noe, R. M. (2005). *Human resource management* (p. 27). New Jersey: Prentice Hall.

Mootheril, F., & Singh, M. (2009). Achieving organisational effectiveness from B2E e-Business. In the *Proceedings of the Pacific Asia Conference on Information Systems* (PACIS), India.

Morey, R. C., & Dittman, D. A. (1995). Evaluating a hotel GM's performance. *The Cornell Hotel and Restaurant Administration Quarterly*, *36*(2), 18–32.

Morey, R. C., & Dittman, D. A. (2003). Update and extension to 'Evaluating a hotel GM's performance'. *The Cornell Hotel and Restaurant Administration Quarterly*, *44*(5), 60–68. doi:10.1016/S0010-8804(03)90108-X

Morris, M.G., & Venkatesh, V. (2000). Age differences in technology adoption decisions: Implications for a changing workforce. *Personnel Psychology*.

Mowev, J.-C., & Minor, M.-S. (2001). *Consumer behavior: A framework*. Upper Saddle River, NJ: Prentice Hall.

Mumford, E., & Banks, O. (1967). *The computer and the clerk*. London: Routledge and Kegan Paul.

Murphy, C.-A., Coover, D., & Owen, S.-V. (1989). Development and validation of the computer self-efficacy scale. *Educational and Psychological Measurement*, *49*, 893–899. doi:10.1177/001316448904900412

Nachmias, R., Mioduser, D., & Shemla, A. (2000). Internet usage by students in an Israeli high school. *Journal of Educational Computing Research*, *22*(1), 55–73. doi:10.2190/2XLG-FQQJ-1Y65-9K2E

Nahm, E.-S., & Resnick, B. (2008). Development and testing of the Web-based learning self-efficacy scale (WBLSES) for older adults. *Ageing International*, *32*(1), 3–14. doi:10.1007/s12126-008-9003-6

Narasimhan, R. (1980). Goal programming in a fuzzy environment. *Decision Sciences*, *11*, 525–538. doi:10.1111/j.1540-5915.1980.tb01142.x

Narasimhan, R. (1981). On fuzzy goal programming-some comments. *Decision Sciences*, *121*, 532–538. doi:10.1111/j.1540-5915.1981.tb00103.x

Nelson, D. L. (1990). Individual adjustment to information-driven technologies: A critical review. *Management Information Systems Quarterly*, (March): 79–98. doi:10.2307/249311

Ness, P. E. (1997). *Creative software development: An Empirical Modelling Framework*, Unpublished doctoral thesis, Department of Computer Science, University of Warwick, UK.

Nguyen, H. M., & Harrison, N. J. (2004). Electronic supply chain orientation and its competitive dimensions. *Production Planning and Control*, *15*(6), 596–607. doi:10.1080/09537280412331283946

NOIE. (2005). *The National Office for the Information Economy*. Australia. Retrieved September 5, 2005, from http://www.noie.gov.au/

Nonaka, I., & Takeuchi, M. (1995). *The knowledge creating company – How Japanese companies create the dynamics of innovation*. Oxford: The Oxford University Press.

Nunnally, J. C. (1978). *Psychometric theory*. New York: McGraw-Hill.

Nurcan, S., Grosz, G., & Souveyet, C. (1998). Describing business processes with a guided use case approach. In *Proceedings of the 10th International Conference (CaiSE'98),* June 1998, Pisa, Italy.

Nystand, M. (1990). Sharing word: The effects of readers on developing writers. *Written Communication*, *7*(1), 3–24. doi:10.1177/0741088390007001001

NZIER. (2002). *Creative industry in New Zealand economic contribution*. NZ Institute for Economic Research (Inc.).

O'Malley, J., & Perkins, J. (2007). *The long tail of Facebook causes*. Frogloop Blog.

O'reilly, T. (2005). *What is WEB2.0- design patterns and business models for the next generation of software*. Retrieved August 12, 2009, from http://oreilly.com/web2/archive/what-is-web-20.html

Office for the Promotion of Cultural and Creative Industry. (2007). *Index of the development of cultural and creative industry in leading countries*. Ministry of Economic Affairs.

Oliver, T.-A., & Shapiro, F. (1993). Self-efficacy and computers. *Journal of Computer-based Interactions*, *20*, 81–85.

Olsen, M., Keevers, M. L., Paul, J., & Covington, S. (2001). E-relationship development strategy for the non-profit fundraising professional. *International Journal of Nonprofit and Voluntary Sector Marketing*, *6*(4), 364–373. doi:10.1002/nvsm.161

O'Reilly, T. (2005). *What is Web 2.0: Design patterns and business models for the next generation of software*. Retrieved September 12, 2006, from http://www.oreillynet.com/pub/a/oreilly/tim/news/2005/09/30/what-is-web-20.html

Ould, M. (1993). Strim/rads. *Iopener, 1*(5), *2*(1&3).

OXFAM. Scarborough, H., & J. Swan. (2003). Discourses of Knowledge Management and organizational learning, their production and consumption. In M.E. Smith & M. Lyles (Eds.), *The Blackwell handbook of organizational learning and Knowledge Management.* Oxford: Blackwell Publishing.

Pan, S. L., & Scarbrough, H. (1999). Knowledge Management in practice: An exploratory case study of Buckman Labs. *Technology Analysis and Strategic Management, 11*(3), 359–374. doi:10.1080/095373299107401

Pandian, M.V. (2004). Application of multi-objective fuzzy linear programming to supply production planning problem. *Journal of Technology, 40*(D), 37-48.

Parra, M. A., Terol, A. B., & Uria, M. V. R. (2001). A fuzzy goal programming approach to portfolio selection. *European Journal of Operational Research, 133*, 287–297. doi:10.1016/S0377-2217(00)00298-8

Pearce, J. A., II, & Robinson, R. B. (2007). *Formulation, implementation, and control of competitive strategy*. (pp. 37-38, 64-66). New York: McGraw- Hill.

Pease, D.-G., Zhang, J.-J., & Barkouras, A.-K. (2001). Relations of game role and team success to team efficacy in boys' varsity high school basketball teams. *Research Quarterly for Exercise and Sport, 72*(1), A90.

Perez, C. (2002). *Technological revolutions and financial capital: The dynamics of bubbles and golden ages*. Cheltenham, UK: Edward Elgar.

Phillips, P. A. (1999). Performance measurement systems and hotels: A new conceptual framework. *International Journal of Hospitality Management, 18*(2), 171–182. doi:10.1016/S0278-4319(99)00016-X

Pickens, J. B., & Hof, J. G. (1991). Fuzzy goal programming in forestry: An application with special solution problems. *Fuzzy Sets and Systems, 39*(3), 239–246. doi:10.1016/0165-0114(91)90095-8

Pink, D. H. (2005). *A whole new mind: Why right-brainers will rule the future*. New York: Riverhead Books.

plan. Retrieved August 5, 2005, from http://www.cepd.gov.tw/upload/SECT/Industry/008@537202.744030078@.doc

Porter, M. E. (2002). The competitive advantage of corporate philanthropy. *Harvard Business Review, 80*(12), 57–68.

Prahalad, C. K. (2005). *The fortune at the bottom of the pyramid: Eradicating poverty through profits*. USA: Pearson Education/Wharton School Publishing.

Prahalad, C. K., & Hammond, A. (2002). Serving the world's poor, profitability. *Harvard Business Review*, (September): 4–11.

Prahalad, C.K. & Hart, S.L. (2002). The fortune at the bottom of the pyramid, *Strategy + Business, 26*, 1-14.

Prochaska, J., DiClemente, C., & Norcross, J. (1992). In search of how people change: applications to addictive behaviors. *The American Psychologist, 47*, 1102–1114. doi:10.1037/0003-066X.47.9.1102

Quinn, J., Anderson, P., & Finkelstein, S. (1996). Managing professional intellect. In *Harvard Business Review on Knowledge Management*. Boston: Harvard Business School Publishing.

Radjou, N. (2004). The Internet invigorates supply chains. *Industrial Management (Des Plaines), 46*(1), 13–18.

Rafaeli, A., & Sutton, R. (1986). Word processing technology and perceptions of control among clerical workers. *Behaviour & Information Technology, 5*(5), 31–37. doi:10.1080/01449298608914496

Rahim, M. M., & Singh, M. (2007). Understanding benefits and impediments of B2E e-business systems adoption: Experiences of two large Australian universities. *Journal of Internet Commerce*, *6*(2), 3–17. doi:10.1300/J179v06n02_02

Rahim, M. M. (2006). Understanding adoption and impact of B2E e-business systems: Lessons learned from the experience of an Australian university. *Proceedings of the Collaborative Electronic Commerce Research Conference (CollECTeR)*, Adelaide, Australia.

Rahim, M. M. (2007a). Factors affecting adoption of B2E e-Business systems: A case of the Australian Higher Education Industry. Proceedings of the *Pacific Asia Conference on Information Systems (PACIS2007)*, New Zealand.

Rahim, M. M. (2007b). Identifying barriers to using Business-to-Employee (B2E) Portals: Some lessons learned from an Australian University. *Proceedings of the Hawaii Int. Conference on Systems Science*, Hawaii.

Rahim, M. M., Sugianto, L., & Shameem, N. (2005). Understanding the adoption of business-to-employee portals: An experience of a large Australian university. *Proceedings of the 5th International Conference on Electronic Business*, (pp.316-322). Hong Kong.

Rangone, A. (2006). B2E mobile internet: An exploratory study of Italian companies. *Business Process Management Journal*, *12*(3), 330–333. doi:10.1108/14637150610667999

Rao, S. S., Sundaraju, K., Prakasah, B. G., & Balakrishnan, C. (1992). Fuzzy goal programming approach for situational optimizations. *Fuzzy Sets and Systems*, *39*(3), 239–246.

Rappa, M. (2003). *Business models on the Web: Managing the digital enterprise*. Retrieved from http://digitalenterprise.org/models/models.html.

Rasmequan, S., Roe, C., & Russ, S. B. (2000). Strategic decision support systems: An experience-based approach. In *Proceedings of the 18th IASTED Conference on Applied Informatics*, February 2000, Innsbruck, Austria.

Ray, R. (2000). *This is real e-Business*.

Rayport, J. F., & Sviokla, J. J. (1995). Exploiting the virtual value chain. *Harvard Business Review*, *73*(6), 75–85.

Reddy, C.B., Rajgopal, Z.K. & Reddy, H. (2007). Fuzzy goal and additive fuzzy goal programming: Application to distributor selection in supply chain, *Journal of Engineering and applied Sciences*. *2*(10), 1533, 1538.

Reid, J. (1993). *Teaching ESL writing*. Englewood Cliffs, NJ: Regents Prentice Hall.

Reynolds, D. (2003). Hospitality-productivity assessment using data-envelopment analysis. *The Cornell Hotel and Restaurant Administration Quarterly*, *44*(2), 130–137.

Reynolds, D., & Thompson, G. M. (2007). Multiunit restaurant productivity assessment using three-phase data envelopment analysis. *International Journal of Hospitality Management*, *26*(1), 20–32. doi:10.1016/j.ijhm.2005.08.004

Richard-Amato, P. (1988). *Making it happened: Interaction in the second language classroom*. New York: Longman.

Riemer, K. (1998). A process-driven, event-based business object model. In *Proceedings of Second International Workshop in Enterprise Distributed Object Computing (EDOC'98)*, (pp. 68-74). La Jolla, CA.

Ritchie, B., & Brindley, C. (2000). Disintermediation, disintegration and risk in the SME global supply chain. *Management Decision*, *38*(8), 575–583. doi:10.1108/00251740010378309

Robbins, S. P. (2005). *Organizational behavior*. New Jersey: Prentice Hall.

Robey, D. (1979). User attitudes and management information system use. *Academy of Management Journal*, *22*(3), 527–538. doi:10.2307/255742

Robinson, J.-P., Shaver, P.-R., & Wrightsman, L.-S. (1991). Criteria for scale selection and evaluation. In Robinson, J.-P., Shaver, P.-R., & Wrightsman, L.-S. (Eds.), *Measurement of personality and social psychological attitude*. San Diego, CA: Academic Press.

Robinson, M., Tapscott, D., et al. (1999). *e-Business 2.0: Roadmap for success*. Boston: Addison-Wesley Professional.

Rogers, E. M. (1995). *Diffusion of innovations* (5th ed.). NY: Free Press, Simon & Schuster.

Ross, D. F. (2003). *Introduction to e-supply chain management: Engaging technology to build market-winning business partnerships*. Boca Raton, FL: St. Lucie Press.

Roy, T. K., & Maiti, M. (1998). Multi-objective inventory models of deteriorating items with some constraints in a fuzzy environment. *Computers & Operations Research*, *25*(12), 1085–1095. doi:10.1016/S0305-0548(98)00029-X

Rubin, P. A., & Narasimhan, R. (1985). Fuzzy goal programming with nested priorities. *Fuzzy Sets and Systems*, *14*, 115–129. doi:10.1016/0165-0114(84)90095-2

Ruigrok NetPanel. (2007). *Web WHAT? - Web 2.0 research*. SlideShare Inc.

Salleh, Y., & Goh, W. K. (2002). Managing human resources toward achieving Knowledge Management. *Journal of Knowledge Management*, *6*(5), 457–468. doi:10.1108/13673270210450414

Sasser, W. E., Olsen, P. R., & Wyckoff, D. D. (1978). *Management of service operations*. Boston: Allyn and Bacon.

Sastry, T. (1999). Supply chain strategies for small firms facing high demand uncertainty and seasonality. *Vikalpa*, *24*(4), 7–15.

Savin-Williams, R. C., & Berndt, T. J. (1990). Friendship and peer relations. In G.R. Elliott. & S. Feldman (Eds.), *At the threshold: The developing adolescent*. Cambridge, MA: Harvard University Press.

Sawhney, M., Prandelli, E., & Verona, G. (2003). The power of innomediation. *Sloan Management Review*, *44*(2), 77–82.

Schader, M., & Korthaus, A. (1998). Modelling business processes as part of the BOOSTER approach to business object-oriented system development based on UML. In *Proceedings of the Second International Enterprise Distributed Object Computing (EDOC '98) Workshop*, (pp. 56-67). La Jolla, CA.

Schlenker, L., & Crocker, N. (2003). Building an e-business scenario for small business: The IBM SME Gateway project. *Qualitative Market Research: An International Journal*, *6*(1), 7–17. doi:10.1108/13522750310457339

Schofield, J. W., & Davidson, A. L. (1997). The Internet in school: The shaping of use by organizational, structural, and cultural factors. *Proceedings from the WebNet 97 World Conference of the WWW, Internet & Intranet*. Toronto.

Schreiber, A. T., Akkermans, J. M., Anjewierden, A. A., De Hoog, R., Van De Velde, W., & Wielinga, B. J. (1998). *Engineering of knowledge: The common KADS methodology*. University of Amsterdam.

Schwarzer, R., Schmitz, G.-S., & Daytner, G.-T. (1999). Collective teachers self-efficacy. Retrieved on Aug. 24, 2009 from http://web.fu-berlin.de/gesund/skalen/Language_Selection/Turkish/Collective_Teacher_Self-Effica/collective_teacher_self-effica.htm.

Scoble, R., & Israel, S. (2006). *Naked conversations: How bogs are changing the way businesses talk with customers*. Hoboken, NJ: John Wiley & Sons, Inc.

Scornavacca, E., Prashad, M., & Lehmann, H. (2006). Exploring the organisational impact and perceived benefits of wireless personal digital assistants in restaurants. *International Journal of Mobile Communications*, *4*(5), 558–567.

Senge, P. M. (1990). *The fifth discipline: The art & practice of the learning organization*. Doubleday, Random House, Inc.

Sexton, T. R. (1986). The methodology of data envelopment analysis. In Silkman, R. H. (Ed.), *Measuring efficiency: an assessment of Data Envelopment Analysis* (pp. 115–130). San Francisco: American Evaluation Association.

Shankar, R., & Vrat, P. (1999). Some design issues in cellular manufacturing using fuzzy programming approach. *International Journal of Production Research, 37*(11), 2345–2363.

Sharma, D. K., Jana, R. K., & Gaur, A. (2007). Fuzzy goal programming for land allocation problems. *Yugoslav Journal of Operations Research, 17*(1), 31–42. doi:10.2298/YJOR0701031S

Sharma, H.P., Sharma, D.K. & Jana, R.K. (2009). Credit union portfolio management: An additive fuzzy goal programming approach. *International Research Journal of Finance and Economics, 30.*

Sherwood-Smith, M. (1994). *People centred process re-engineering: An evaluation perspective to office system re-design.* (pp.535-544).

Shleifer, A., & Vishny, R. (1997). A survey of corporate governance. *The Journal of Finance, 52,* 737–783. doi:10.2307/2329497

Shoemaker, S., Lewis, R. C., & Yesawich, P. C. (2007). *Marketing leadership in hospitality and tourism: strategies and tactics for competitive advantage (4th ended.).* New Jersey: Pearson Prentice Hall.

Shoemaker, P. (2002). *Social venture partners: Venture Philanthropy in a changed world.* Retrieved from http://foundationcenter.org/pnd/newsmakers/nwsmkr.jhtml?id=13200025

Shoham, Y. (1993). Agent-oriented programming. *Artificial Intelligence, 60*(1), 51–92. doi:10.1016/0004-3702(93)90034-9

Sigala, M. (2004). Using data envelopment analysis for measuring and benchmarking productivity in the hotel sector. *Journal of Travel & Tourism Marketing, 16*(2/3), 39–60. doi:10.1300/J073v16n02_04

Simons, A. J. H., & Graham, I. (1999). 30 things that go wrong in Object Modelling with UML 1.3. In Kilov, H., Rumpe, B., & Simmonds, I. (Eds.), *Behavioral Specifications of Businesses and Systems* (pp. 221–242). Kluwer Academic Publishers.

Simons, A. J. H. (1999). Use cases considered harmful. In R. Mitchell, A.C. Wills, J. Bosch, & B. Meyer (Eds.), *Proceedings of the 29th Conference Tech. Object-Oriented Programming Language and Systems (TOOLS-29 Europe),* (pp. 194-203) Los Alamitos: IEEE Computer Society

Simons, A. J. H., & Graham, I. (1998). 37 things that don't work in Object Modelling with UML. In S. Kent & R. Mitchell (Eds.), *British Computer Society Object-Oriented Programming Systems Newsletter, 35.*

Singh, M. (2002). *Evolving e-Business models: A process of technology, in e-Business in Australia, concepts and cases* (pp. 8–22). Australia: Pearson Education.

Singh, M. (2005). (B2E): e-Management. In *Proceedings from the Sixth International Working for e-Business Conference.* Melbourne, Australia: Business to Employee.

Singh, M., Waddell, D., & Rahim, M. M. (2008). B2E e-business model: service to employees or organisational management? *WSEAS Transactions on Business and Economics, 5*(5), 270–279.

Sinha, S. B., Rao, K. A., & Mangaraj, B. K. (1988). Fuzzy goal programming in multi-criteria decision system: A case study in agricultural planning. *Socio-Economic Planning Sciences, 22*(2), 93–102. doi:10.1016/0038-0121(88)90021-3

Sinha, S. B., Rao, K. A., Mangaraj, B. K., & Tripathy, P. K. (1982). Fuzzy technique to agricultural planning. *Journal of Information and Optimization Science, 10,* 257–274.

Smile Foundation. (2008). *Social Venture Philanthropy–a business concept for non-profits.* Retrieved from http://www.1888pressrelease.com/social-venture-philanthropy-a-business-concept-for-non-pro-pr-81751.html

Smith, A. (1776). *The wealth of nations.* New York: Classic House Books.

Smith, H. (2003). Instilling a knowledge-sharing culture. (p. 1-17). Retrieved from www.business.queens.ca/kbe

Soliman, F. & Spooner, K. (2000). Strategies for implementing Knowledge Management: Role of human resource management. *Journal of Knowledge.*

Soo, C., Devinney, T. M., & Midgley, D. F. (2002). Knowledge creation in organizations: Exploring firm and context specific effects. *INSEAD*, 1-34. Retrieved May 19, 2005, from www.knoweldge.insead.edu

Speier, C., & Venkatesh, V. (2002). The hidden minefields in the adoption of sales force automation technologies. *Journal of Marketing*, *66*(July), 98–111. doi:10.1509/jmkg.66.3.98.18510

Stage, E. (2009a). *Enterprise 2.0 for IBA, a Belgian fast growing company*. Retrieved from http://www.earlystage.be/success-stories/

Stage, E. (2009b). *Challenges of the Enterprise 2.0: Ten facts*. Retrieved from http://www.earlystage.be/challenges/

Stark, J. (2007). *Study notes importance on non-profit creative industry: Non-profit arts yields annual $77.6 million*. Retrieved from http://www.independent.com/news/2007/jun/14/non-profit-arts-yields-annual-776-million/

Steinecke, C. (1993). *The federal total quality management handbook: Employee involvement and quality management in the federal government*. Washington, D.C.: U.S. Government Printing Office.

Stone, D. L., Stone-Romero, E. F., & Lukaszewski, K. (2006). Factors affecting the acceptance and effectiveness of electronic human resources systems. *Human Resource Management Review*, *16*, 229–244. doi:10.1016/j.hrmr.2006.03.010

Stone, C. (1993). Why the law can't do it. In Beauchamp, T. L., & Bowie, N. (Eds.), *Ethical theory and business* (3rd ed., pp. 162–166). New Jersey: Prentice Hall.

Stonehouse, G. H., & Pemberton, J. D. (1999). Learning and Knowledge Management in the intelligent organization. *Participation & Empowerment: An International Journal*, *7*(5), 131–144. doi:10.1108/14634449910287846

Sturgeon, W. (2006). *Cheat sheet: Web 2.0. What on earth is it and should you care?* Retrieved from http://networks.silicon.com/webwatch/0,39024667,39161662,00.htm

Sugianto, L., & Tojib, D. (2006). Modeling user satisfaction with an employee portal. *International Journal of Business and Information*, *1*(2), 239–255.

Sugianto, L., & Rahim, M. M & Alahakoon, D. (2005). B2E portal adoption: A conceptual model. *Proceedings of the International Conference on Information and Automation (ICIA2005)*, Colombo, Sri Lanka.

Sun, S., & Lu, W. M. (2005). Evaluating the performance of the Taiwanese hotel industry using a weight slacks-based measure. *Asia-Pacific Journal of Operational Research*, *22*(4), 487–512. doi:10.1142/S0217595905000595

Sun, C. (2000). *An exploration into problematic companies and financial organizations in Taiwan after the financial crisis*. (p. 4). Taipei: The Sun Yun-suan Academic Foundation.

Sundbo, J. (1998). *The organization of innovations in services*. Frediksberg, Denmark: Roskilide University Press.

Suomen Pankkiyhdistys. (2004). *Pankkitekniikka Suomessa*. Helsinki: Suomen Pankkiyhdistys.

Suomen Pankkiyhdistys. (2005). *Pankit 31.12.2004*. Helsinki: Suomen Pankkiyhdistys.

Surowiecki, J. (2004). *The wisdom of the crowds: Why the many Are smarter than the few and how collective wisdom shapes business, economies, societies and nations*. New York: Anchor Books, Random House.

Sveiby, K. E. (1997). *The new organizational wealth. Managing and measuring knowledge-based assets*. San Francisco: Berret-Koehler Publishers Inc.

Swanson, E. B. (1982). Measuring user attitudes in MIS research: A review. *Omega*, *10*(2), 157–165. doi:10.1016/0305-0483(82)90050-0

Swinyard, W.-R., & Smith, S.-M. (2003). Why people (don't) shop online: A lifestyle study of the Internet consumer. *Psychology and Marketing*, *20*(7), 567–597. doi:10.1002/mar.10087

Switzerland-based Institute. (2006). *Taiwan's competitive strength comes from its outstanding hi-tech infrastructure, business management, and labor force.* Management Development world competitiveness report.

Tai, T. (2006). Economic life and social obligations. Hu, G., et al. (Eds.), *Universal values and local care.* (p. 21). Taipei: KuanhChi Cultural Group.

TAITRA. (2008). Creative *Taiwan 2008: Cultural and creative background.* Taiwan External Trade Development Council. Retrieved from http://www.taipeitradeshows.com.tw/creativetaiwan/visitor/backgrounder.shtml

Taiwan Tourism Bureau. (2005). *Annual operation report of international tourist hotels, 2004.* Taipei: Republic of China Press.

Taiwan Tourism Bureau. (2007). *Monthly operation report of international tourist hotels, Dec. 2006.* Taipei: Republic of China Press.

Taiwan Tourism Bureau. (2007a). *Annual operation report of international tourist hotels, 2005.* Taipei: Taiwan Tourism Bureau Press.

Taylor, F. W. (1911). *The principles of scientific management.* New York: W.W. Norton & Company.

Temperley, N. C., & Galloway, J. (2004). *SMEs in Australia's high-technology sector: Challenges and opportunities.* AEEMA.

Teo, T. S. H., Lim, G. S., & Fedric, A. A. (2007). The adoption and diffusion of human resources information systems in Singapore. *Asia Pacific Journal of Human Resources*, *45*(91), 44–62. doi:10.1177/1038411107075402

Thakkar, J., Kanda, A., & Deshmukh, S. G. (2009). Supply chain management for SMEs: A research introduction. *Management Research News*, *32*(10), 970–993. doi:10.1108/01409170910994178

The China Post, (April 22, 2009). Piraters, Beware, p. 1.

The Economist Intelligence Unit. (2005). *The 2005 e-readiness rankings.* London: The Economist Intelligence Unit Limited The Finnish Banker's Association. (2003). *Statistical data on the bank's payment systems in Finland 1993-2002.* The Finnish Banker's Association.

The International Center for Not-For-Profit Law. (2010). *FAQ: What is the difference between non-profit and not-for-profit?* Retrieved from http://www.icnl.org/contact/faq.htm#difference

Tierney, P., & Farmer, S.-M. (2002). Creative self-efficacy: Its potential antecedents and relationship to creative performance. *Academy of Management Journal*, *45*, 1137–1148. doi:10.2307/3069429

Tierwriting.com. (2010). About Venture Philanthropy. Retrieved from http://tierwriting.com/2010/03/about-venture-philanthropy/

TMSK. (2010). *TMSK.* Retrieved from http://www.tmsk.com/

Tojib, D., & Sugianto, L. (2007). The development and empirical validation of the B2E portal user satisfaction (B2EPUS) scale. *Journal of Organizational and End User Computing*, *19*(3), 1–18.

Tojib, D., Sugianto, L., & Sendjaya, S. (2008). User satisfaction with business-to-*employee* portals: Conceptualisation and scale development. *European Journal of Information Systems*, *17*(6), 649–667. doi:10.1057/ejis.2008.55

Torkzadeh, G., & Van Dyke, T.-P. (2001). Development and validation of an Internet self-efficacy scale. *Behaviour & Information Technology*, *20*(4), 275–280. doi:10.1080/01449290110050293

Transparency International. (2010). *Corruption Perceptions Index 2009.* Retrieved from http://www.transparency.org/policy_research/surveys_indices/cpi/2009/cpi_2009_table

Tsai, K. M., Shinu-Yuan, L., Yu-Hsin, Y., & Tsai, C. H. (2008). A fuzzy goal programming approach for channel allocation problems in steel industry. *Expert Systems with Applications: An International Journal*, *34*(3), 1870–1876. doi:10.1016/j.eswa.2007.02.034

Tsai, W. H., & Hung, S. J. (2009). A fuzzy goal programming approach for green supply chain optimisation under activity-based costing and performance evaluation with a value chain structure. *International Journal of Production Research*, *47*(18), 4991–5017. doi:10.1080/00207540801932498

Tsai, M.-J., & Tsai, C.-C. (2003). Information searching strategies in Web-based science learning: The role of Internet self-efficacy. *Innovations in Education and Teaching International*, *40*, 43–50. doi:10.1080/1355800032000038822

Tsai, M. (2004). Developing the Internet self-efficacy scale (ISES). In L.Cantoni & C. McLoughline, (Eds.), *Proceedings of World Conference on Educational Multimedia, Hypermedia and Telecommunications*. (pp. 4406-4408). Chesapeake, VA: AACE.

Turban, E. (2008). *Electronic commerce: A managerial perspective*. New Jersey: Prentice Hall.

Tversky, A., & Kahneman, D. (1981). The framing of decisions and the psychology of choice, *Science. New Series*, *211*(4481), 453–458.

UHK. (2004). *A study on Hong Kong creativity index interim report*. Centre for Cultural Policy Research, the University of Hong Kong.

UNESCO. (1995). *The cultural dimension of development: towards a practical approach*. Paris: UNESCO.

UNESCO. (2000). *What do we understand by culture industry?* Retrieved March 1, 2005, from http://www.unesco.org/culture/industry/trade/html_eng/question1.shtml

United Daily Newspaper. (April 22, 2009). Four nos and one without. P. 4.

Urbach, N., Smolnik, S., & Riempp, G. (2009). A conceptual model for measuring the effectiveness of employee portals. In *proceedings of the 15th Americas Conference on Information Systems*, San Francisco, California.

Vallerand, R. J. (1997). Toward a hierarchical model of intrinsic and extrinsic motivation. *Advances in Experimental Social Psychology*, 271–360. doi:10.1016/S0065-2601(08)60019-2

van der Bijl, J., van Poelgeest-Eeltink, A., & Shortridge-Baggett, L. (1999). The psychometric properties of the diabetes management self-efficacy scale for patients with Type 2 diabetes mellitus. *Journal of Advanced Nursing*, *30*(2), 352–359. doi:10.1046/j.1365-2648.1999.01077.x

van der Sleen, G. (2007). *Nu alles 2.0! Web, e-Business, enterprise en meer?* Retrieved August 19, 2007, from http://the-efuture.blogspot.com/2007/03/nu-alles-20-web-e-business-enterprise.html

van der Vlist, E., & Vernet, A. (2007). *Professional Web 2.0 programming*. Indianapolis: Wiley Publishing, Inc.

Van Doren, C. S., & Gustke, L. D. (1982). Spatial analysis of the U.S. lodging industry. *Annals of Tourism Research*, *9*(4), 543–563. doi:10.1016/0160-7383(82)90072-X

van Hoek, R. (2001). E-supply chains–virtually non-existing. *Supply Chain Management: An International Journal*, *6*(1), 21–28. doi:10.1108/13598540110694653

van Meel, J. W., Bots, P. W. G., & Sol, H. G. (1994). *Towards a research framework for business engineering*. (pp.581-592).

Venkatash, V., & Morris, M. (2000). Why don't men ever stop to ask for directions? Gender, social influence, and their role in technology acceptance and usage. *Management Information Systems Quarterly*, *24*, 115–139. doi:10.2307/3250981

Vidgen, R., Rose, J., Wood, B., & Wood-Harper, T. (1994). *Business process re-engineering: The need for a methodology to revision the organisation*. (pp.603-612).

Vogel, D. (1994). *Re-engineering towards the meeting of the future* (pp. 35–45).

Wallace, N. (2002). Outlook for online donations is cloudy, experts say. *Chronicle of Philanthropy*, *14*(11), 27.

Walsh, B. (2006). *Content isn't King*. Retrieved August 12, 2009, from http://thepartycow.com/2006/10/content-isnt-king.html

Walsham, G. (1995). Interpretive case studies in IS research: Nature and method. *European Journal of Information Systems*, *4*, 74–81. doi:10.1057/ejis.1995.9

Waltz, G. (2003). *Knowledge Management in the intelligence enterprise*. Boston: Artech House Inc.

Wang, Y.-S., & Wang, H.-Y. (2008). Development of validating an instrument for measuring mobile computing self-efficacy. *Cyberpsychology & Behavior*, *11*(4), 405–413. doi:10.1089/cpb.2007.0061

Warboys, B., Kawalek, P., Robertson, I., & Greenwood, M. (1999). *Business Information Systems: A process approach*. McGraw-Hill Publishing.

Weatherford, L. R. (1995). Length of stay heuristics: do they really make a difference. *The Cornell Hotel and Restaurant Administration Quarterly*, *36*(6), 70–79.

Weatherford, L. R., & Bodily, S. E. (1992). A taxonomy and research overview of perishable-asset revenue management: yield management, overbooking and pricing. *Operations Research*, *40*(5), 831–844. doi:10.1287/opre.40.5.831

Wei, X. (2006). *Transparently animated.* Retrieved on January 11, 2008, from http://english.eastday.com/eastday/englishedition/features/userobject1ai1806146.html

Wigal, J.-K., Greer, T.-L., & Kotses, H. (1991). *The COPD self-efficacy scale. CHEST Online*, 99, 1193-1196. Retrieved on June 20, 2009 from http://chestjournal.chestpubs.org/content/99/5/1193.

Wijeysinghe, B. S. (1993). Breakeven occupancy for a hotel operation. *Management Accounting*, *71*(2), 32–33.

Wikipedia (2009). *Lifestyle*. Retrieved on July 29, 2009 from http://en.wikipedia.org/wiki/Lifestyle.

Wikipedia. (2009). Retrieved on September 20, 2009, from http://en.wikipedia.org/wiki/Web_2.0

Winefield, A. H., Gillespie, N. A., & Boyd, C. (2003). Occupational stress in university staff. *International Journal of Stress Management*, *8*(4), 51–63. doi:10.1037/1072-5245.10.1.51

Wing, K. (1999). What future knowledge management users may expect. *Journal of Knowledge Management*, *3*(2), 155–165. doi:10.1108/13673279910275611

Witt, C. A., & Witt, S. F. (1989). Why productivity in the hotel sector is low. *International Journal of Contemporary Hospitality Management*, *1*(2), 28–34. doi:10.1108/EUM0000000001669

Workforce Bank. (2000). *Effective manpower-department distribution chart.* Retrieved September 5, 2005, from http://www.104.com.tw/cfdocs/2000/analysis/graph/man_user4.gif/

Wu, C. F. (2002). *The practice of business ethics* (pp. 120–121). Taipei: Chien Cheng Publishing Co.

Wu, C. H. (2006). The key to a corporation's social responsibilities-corporate governance. *Gre-Tai Securities Market Monthly*, *116*, 22–28.

Wu, D. (2004). *Corporate governance-theories and practice.* (pp. 17-20, 26-27). Taipei: Securities & Futures Institute.

Yaghoobi, M. A., Jones, D. F., & Tamiz, M. (2008). Weighted additive model for solving fuzzy goal programming problem. *Asia-Pacific Journal of Operational Research*, *28*(5), 715–733. doi:10.1142/S0217595908001973

Yang, K.-C.-C. (2004). A comparison of attitudes towards Internet advertising among lifestyle segments in Taiwan. *Journal of Marketing Communications*, *10*, 195–212. doi:10.1080/1352726042000181657

Yang, C. (2007). *Strategic management-theories and practice.* (p. 428). Taipei: Hua-tai.

Yasin, M. M., Andrew, J. C., & Jeffrey, J. D. (1996). Breakeven occupancy for a hotel operation. *Management Accounting*, *7*(12), 32–33.

Ye, B. (2002). *Constructing businesses' social contracts* (pp. 70–72). Taipei: National Open University.

Ye, B. (2005). []. Taipei: Wu-Nan Book Inc.]. *Business Ethics (Oxford, England)*, 239.

Ye, Y. (2005). *Disappeared controlling shareholders-be the first to detect risks* (pp. 176, 178–196). Taipei: Business News Publishing Ltd.

Ye, Y., Li, T., & Ke, C. (2002). *Corporate governance and the evaluation system* (p. 23). Taipei: Business News Publishing Ltd.

Yee, S. T. (2005). Impact analysis of customized demand information sharing on supply chain performance. *International Journal of Production Research*, *43*(16), 3353–3373. doi:10.1080/00207540500095779

Yin, R. K. (2003). *Case study research: Design and methods* (3rd ed.). Thousand Oaks, CA: Sage.

Yin, V. (2009). New *Web: mainstream Web 2.0*. Verecom Web design blog. Retrieved from http://www.verecom.com.au/verecomblog/wordpress/new-web-mainstream-web-20-what-is-e-business-20/2009/02/

Young, J.-R. (2001, Nov. 9). Does "digital divide" rhetoric do more harm than good? *The Chronicle of Higher Education*, *48*, 1–5.

Zemach, D. E., & Rumisek, L. A. (2003). *College writing: From paragraph to essay*. Oxford: Macmillian Education.

Zentner, A. (2006). Measuring the effect of online music piracy on music sales. *The Journal of Law & Economics*, *49*, 63–90. doi:10.1086/501082

Zhang, Y. (2005). Age, gender, and Internet attitudes among employees in the business world. *Computers in Human Behavior*, *21*, 1–10. doi:10.1016/j.chb.2004.02.006

Zhao, F. (2006). *Maximize Business Profits through E-partnerships*. Hershey, PA: IDEA Group Publishing.

Zhao, F., McMurray, A. J., & Toomey, M. (2008). Effectiveness of Information Technology governance: Perceptions of board directors and senior managers. In Zhao, F. (Ed.), *Information Technology Entrepreneurship and Innovation*. Hershey, PA: IDEA Group Publishing. doi:10.4018/9781599049014.ch004

Zhao, F., & Dalrymple, J. (2002). E-partnerships in information era: Issues of information management. Organizational excellence: Managing information. *Proceedings of the 3rd Multinational Alliance for the Advancement of Organizational Excellence Conference,* Scotland.

Zhuang, Y. (2005). Does electronic business create value for firms? An organizational innovation perspective. *Journal of Electronic Commerce Research*, *6*(2), 146–156.

Zikmund, W. G. (1997). *Business Research Methods* (5th ed.). Orlando: Dryden Press.

Zimmermann, H. J. (1976). Description and optimization of fuzzy sets. *International Journal of General Systems*, *2*, 209–215. doi:10.1080/03081077608547470

Zimmermann, H. J. (1978). Fuzzy programming and linear programming with several objective functions. *Fuzzy Sets and Systems*, *1*, 45–55. doi:10.1016/0165-0114(78)90031-3

Zimmermann, H. J. (1983). Using Fuzzy Sets in Operational Research. *European Journal of Operational Research*, *13*(3), 201–216. doi:10.1016/0377-2217(83)90048-6

Zmud, R. W. (1979). Individual differences and MIS success: A review of the empirical literature. *Management Science*, *25*(10), 966–979. doi:10.1287/mnsc.25.10.966

Zoltman, E., & Chapanis, A. (1982). What do professional persons think about computers? *Behaviour & Information Technology*, *1*(1), 55–68. doi:10.1080/01449298208914436

About the Contributors

Te Fu Chen is an Assistant Professor in the Department of Business Administration at Lunghwa University of Science and Technology, Taiwan. He has taught in the Department of Information Management at Chang Jung Christian University. He has also taught in Department of International business at Ching Yun University and Cheng Shiu University, Taiwan. Dr Chen received his MBA degree in business and information management from MBA, Providence University Taiwan in 1999; and PhD degree in management from the University of Western Sydney, Australia in 2007. His research interests include business model innovation, knowledge-based innovation, knowledge management, e-commerce/e-business, CRM, SCM, international marketing and service innovation and management. Recently, he starts to research tourism and leisure management and cultural innovation and creative industry. Dr Chen has published over one hundred papers and books in international journals global publishers, such as Edward Elgar (EE) Publishing Ltd, IGI Global Publishing group in the UK and USA, Journal of Global Commerce and Management, Tamsui Oxford Journal of Management Sciences (International journal), Journal of Knowledge Management and Practice (Top 7 for KM among International journals), International Journal of e-business management (EI), International Journal of Central Asian Studies, Journal for SME Development, Journal of Entrepreneurship Research, Web Journal of Chinese management review (International journal), International Journal of Information Technology and Management (EI) etc. Currently, he is the book editor in IGI Global publishing group, USA and IBIMA Journal of Innovation Management in SMEs. Also, he has been the reviewer in Journal of Internet Technology (SCI-E), International Journal of Electronic Business (IJEB), a special issue for the quality papers presented in ICEB 2005, International Journal of Technology Management (SCI/SSCI) on the theme "Trade, Technology and Economic Development in China", reviewer and the member of Editor board, "Risk Assessment and Management in Pervasive Computing: Operational, Legal, Ethical and Financial Perspectives", IGI Global, USA., International conference on e-business 2005, Hong Kong, International conference on e-business 2007, Taiwan, 20th Australasian Conference on Information Systems 2009, Monash University: Caulfield Campus, Melbourne, The 44th Hawaiian International Conference on System Sciences (HICSS-44), 2010, one of the most reputable and influential conferences in the field of system sciences.

* * *

Yih-Chang Chen is an Assistant Professor in the Department of Information Management at Chang Jung Christian University, Tainan, Taiwan. Dr Chen received his BSc degree in Computer and Information Sciences from Tunghai University, Taiwan in 1992; MSc (Econ) degree in Information Systems Security from The London School of Economics and Political Science (LSE), University of London in 1996; and PhD degree in Computer Science from the University of Warwick, United Kingdom in 2002. His research interests include business process reengineering, empirical modelling, lean thinking and lean management, software engineering and requirements engineering, and the use-case approach to system development. Currently he is the deputy director of RFID Research Centre at Chang Jung Christian University, Taiwan.

Min-Ching Chen received her Master of Education from Education Department (TEFL) in University of Bristol, UK. Miss Chen is a lecture of Language Center in National Chiao Tung University. She is interested in English teaching approaches and methodology, material designing and evaluation.

Tsungting Chung (鍾從定) is a professor at the Department of Business Administration and Dean of International Affairs Office, National Yunlin University of Science and Technology, Yunlin, Taiwan, where he teaches International Management (MBA/EMBA, Ph.D. level), Cross-Culture Management, International Negotiation Theory and Practice (MBA/EMBA, Ph.D. level), and Cross Taiwan Strait Commercial Relations. He was the Chairman of Business Administration Department and Provost at Providence University, Taichung, Taiwan. Most of his research and publications are in the fields of negotiation and international management. Other than journal articles, he published two books, International Negotiation Theory and Practice and Research Methodology: Quantitative and Qualitative Approaches with co-author Chi-Shiun Lai. He is also a licensed mediator at Taichung District Court, and has served as Board member of Chamber of Commerce at Taichung City Government and Yunlin County Government, Taiwan, Republic of China. He received his Ph.D. from Graduate School of International Studies, University of Denver, USA and a certificate on Case Method and Participant-Centered Learning Program from Harvard Business School, Harvard University, USA.

Liang-Cheng Huang received his MBA Degree from Tamkang University, Taipei, Taiwan, Rep. of China in 2006. He is now a Ph. D. student with a major in Information Management at National Taiwan University. Currently, his research interests include collective actions, online behavior, and social networks. He is now also a research assistant with the Social Networks Group, Academia Sinica in Taiwan, Rep. of China.

Ti Hsu: Upon completing his Ph. D. at Syracuse University, Dr. Ti Hsu went to work for the Southeastern Michigan Transportation Authority as Manager of IS and Marketing Research and Project Manager of the Alternative Analysis Study, a 3-million plus dollars project of building a subway system in Detroit. He started his academic career in 1979 as a business professor at Rutgers University and has taught ever since. Currently, he is a business professor at the Chinese Culture University in Taiwan. Being an interdisciplinary person, he has conducted his research in a number of areas. But his primary research interests have always been evolved around information technology. Starting out with small group behavior initially, he then moved into GDSS, when PCs became available and later to virtual teams when the Internet emerged. From there, he got into CSCL/W and e-learning. Now, he is into virtual communities and social networking.

Yuan-Chu Hwang received his Ph.D. in Management of Information Systems from the College of Commerce of National Chengchi University. Dr. Hwang is an Assistant Professor of Information Management Department in National United University. His research interests include Collaborative e-Service Innovation, Ubiquitous Commerce and Privacy/Trust Issues for Social Mobile Applications.

Chieh-Heng Ko, Ph.D., is a lecturer in the Hospitality Department at the Chung Hua University in Taiwan. Ko got his Ph.D. at the University of Western Sydney in Australia. He also holds a BA in Political Science (Taiwan) and an MBA in Hotel Management at the University of Western Sydney. Before doing research, Ko worked as a front office manager at a Taiwanese hotel for seven years. His working experience in the hotel brought him interest in performance measurement in the hotel industry. In his research, he used data envelopment analysis to measure the relative operational efficiency of Taiwanese International Tourist Hotel and further explored the critical success factors that lead to hotels with good performance in Taiwan.

Moria Levy is the founder and CEO of ROM Knowledgeware, the largest Israeli firm specializing in Knowledge Management and Business Intelligence solutions (over 20 consultants). Moria has over 20 years of experience, and nearly 10 of them with expertise in Knowledge Management. Levy is now working on her PhD, focused on Knowledge Management Utilization in Organizations. She is the author of the book- "Management in the 21st Century: A personal blog". Levy also holds the position as the CEO of the Israeli Knowledge Management Forum, an association that consolidates all knowledge management practitioners in Israel.

Pu Chuan Li lives in Taipei, the capital city of Taiwan. Because the city is changing non-stop, and new technology and other modern things are being adopted, Li is very interested in surfing the web to understand the new technology and see information from all over the world. Of traveling, he said, "I need not spend money to go to other countries because I see them through the Internet's lens, but as an adage said 'Actions speak louder than words.' Hence, I plan to see the world, not by the mouse, but by my feet".

Yeen Ni Li: Being an Indian-born Chinese, I was more "Indian" than "Chinese" (Culturally) since I grew up in an Indian society. The economic boom, created by the rise of "Chindia", made me want to balance the Indian and the Chinese side in me. I chose Taiwan as a destination to pursue my Bachelor's degree in Business Administration for two reasons. I always had interest in the business world and felt that being in a foreign educational institution would be a good change, for one, and second, I could be more fluent in the Chinese language. Music has always played a significant part of people's life, including mine, and due to the development of computers and technologies; music can be downloaded very easily from the Internet. There is no doubt that the Internet is the "Big Thing" now, but we cannot be certain if it would be a Big Problem in the future.

Li Lin, born in Taipei in 1963, studied philosphy at the National Taiwan University from 1981 to 1985. Then he, after his military duty, continued his philosophical study in Germany and got a masters degree (1992) and the doctoral degree (1996) from University Trier. Since then he has taught at the Graduate Institute of European Studies of the Tamkang University located in Taipei County. Professor Li Lin is specialized in ethics and legal and political philosophy.

Nikita Hsiang-Yi Lin is affiliated with the Ching Yun University, Taiwan. He previously worked at the National Policy Foundation. He received his Ph.D. and M.A. from the Tamkang University in Taiwan. Having taught students of international business, business ethics, and management at both the undergraduate and graduate levels, Dr. Lin is a dedicated contributor to international business education. He previously held teaching or research appointments at the Moscow State University, Saint-Petersburg State University, Russian Academy of Sciences, and National Kaohsiung University of Applied Sciences at Kin Men. Dr. Lin specializes in global business ethics and corporate governance. He is also the author of more than 10 publications on various business ethics topics, including global business ethics and Catholic theology.

B. K. Mangaraj has been working as a Professor in Production & Operations Management Area at XLRI School of Business and Human Resources, Jamshedpur, India since 1st November, 2006. Prior to joining XLRI, he was a Professor and Head of the Department of Business Administration at Utkal University, Bhubaneswar, India. He did his M.Sc in Mathematics & Ph.D. in Operations Research, both from Indian Institute of Technology, Kharagpur, India. He also holds a D.Sc degree in Development Anthropology from Utkal University, India. His research interest includes Multi-Objective Decision-Making, Fuzzy Logic and their applications to organizational and societal development problems at one end and "Cultural Management" at the other. Several of his publications have already appeared in reputed journals and edited volumes, including IGI Global publication. He has also presented forty-two research papers in various conferences and has written management teaching cases for classroom discussion.

Viju Mathew's research involves wide subject area like Marketing, Strategy, Entrepreneurship, Knowledge Management, etc. The research profile of Dr. Viju Mathew involve more than 30 papers published in national and international journals and magazines showing a range of new models, theories, and quantitative and qualitative evidences added to the current knowledge. More recently, he focused on the Entrepreneurship and Marketing aspects in Middle East region considering various aspects and increasingly wide set of data sources, services, and entrepreneurial data analysis. Dr. Mathew is a Science graduate, and Management doctorate with wide experience working in different continents. He was also involved in financial industry developing and coordination Marketing strategy for the financial and non-financial product. Later joining the academics he was involved extensively in active teaching, research, consultancy, and developmental programs at various levels and capacities. Mathew's teaching interests include marketing management in Undergraduate and graduate level, as well as in higher active research. He was also involved in implementing multi-dollar DIF projects funded by International Development Agency (World Bank) and MoHE, FDRE. He is actively involved in conducting development programs, community service and development programs, and executive education from CEO grade and below. He is also part of advisory board for several educational projects and programs.

Sheng Hong Su was born in Kaohsiung, which is a lively and friendly city. The weather in Kaohsiung is suitable for working out. I usually play softball with my friends on weekends and watch MLB baseball games on TV, whenever possible. I have been watching baseball tournaments for more than 10 years and my favorite player is John Smoltz (Atlanta Braves). Other than watching baseball tournaments, I also like to listen to music on my free time. Music can soothe my soul and hence, it plays an important role in my life.

Reima Suomi is a professor of Information Systems Science at Turku School of Economics and Business Administration, Finland since 1994. He is a docent for the universities of Turku and Oulu, Finland. In 1992-93 he spent as a "Vollamtlicher Dozent" in the University of St. Gallen, Switzerland, where he led a research project on business process re-engineering. Currently he concentrates on topics around management of telecommunications, including issues such as management of networks, electronic and mobile commerce, virtual organizations, telework, and competitive advantage through telecommunication-based Information Systems. Different governance structures applied to the management of IS and enabled by IS belong, too, to his research agenda, as well as application of information systems in health care. Reima Suomi has worked on over 300 publications, and has published in journals such as Information & Management, Information Services & Use, Technology Analysis & Strategic Management, The Journal of Strategic Information Systems, Behaviour & Information Technology, Journal of Management History, and Information Resources Management Journal. For the academic year 2001-2002, he was a senior researcher "varttunut tutkija" for the academy of Finland. With Paul Jackson he has published the book "Virtual Organization and workplace development with Routledge, London.

Min Chi Tsai was born in Taichung, which is in the central part of Taiwan, and lived there till I completed High School. After that, I came to Taipei, the capital city of Taiwan, to pursue a college education with a major in Business Administration. Here, I can feel information being transmitted at a rapid speed as well as the convenience in obtaining it. The Internet has brought a lot of benefits to my life. For instance, I like to search for things that have interested me on the Web, like novels, magazines, music, books, and so on. At the same thing, I can make new friends with similar interests and chat with them online. Of late, I started blogging to exchange views and ideas with friends on the books I like reading and the music I enjoy hearing. Besides, I get to practice my writing skills in English. I would like to build up a career in the publishing industry in the future.

Yu Kai Tsai: Born in the busy city of Taipei, I like to relax myself by listening to music. Reading magazines about business and automobiles is also one of my hobbies in my leisure time. I also like to surf on the Internet to look for things that are of interest to me. For today's Internet-generation college kids, the Internet is an easy and convenient way to search for music and download the ones one likes, especially since file sharing on music is such a common practice. When I was exposed to the issues of the intellectual property, copyrights, Internet privacy, etc., in a business course, I began to appreciate the seriousness of music piracy and file sharing on movies, videos, and music. I participated in this research so that we could understand more about the problems associated with the music piracy.

Chien Chih Wang: My name is Mike and I was born in Ping Tung. I came from a small family and I am the only child in the house. My father is mainly engaged in sales of tea and my mother is a housewife. That is why they have a high expectation of me. As such, I am very serious about my education and learning. In general, I am an easygoing and ambitious person, but also very active. I like reading and listening to music. I also like going to the movies with my friends and taking part in outdoor activities. I decided to major in business management because I had, and still have, a generic interest in issues related to business management and leadership. I hope I can put the management knowledge that I learned in college into good use in the workplace in the future so that it could help me build my career as a professional manager.

Weng Wong: I was born, raised and bred in a populated island called Macau. As I grew older, I wanted to see the outside world. Hence, I came to Taiwan and met different people from different backgrounds. I have learned a lot about the culture here in Taiwan and gained more knowledge. I also picked up many interpersonal, communication, and leadership skills while I collaborated during execution of this project. I am sure this will help me a lot when I start to work.

Fang Zhao (PhD) is currently Associate Professor of Management in the American University of Sharjah (AUS), the UAE. She has authored/edited and published 3 peer-reviewed research books in the areas of e-business and IT management. She established the International Journal of e-Business Management in 2007 and has been the Editor-in-Chief ever since. She has also published over 65 research works in peer-reviewed journals, books and conferences internationally in the areas of entrepreneurship and innovation, research commercialization, knowledge management, TQM, etc. Her current research interests are in m-commerce and e-government practices in the Middle East and other regions. She was Senior Lecturer and Senior PhD Supervisor at the Royal Melbourne Institute of Technology University (RMIT) in Australia before joining AUS.

Index

D

E

O

P

R

S

Breinigsville, PA USA
20 March 2011
257931BV00002B/2/P

9 781609 601294